Country on
COMPACT
DISC

Country on COMPACT DISC

The Essential Guide to the Music

by the

Country Music Foundation
Paul Kingsbury, Editor

GROVE PRESS
New York

Grove Press
841 Broadway
New York, NY 10003

Library of Congress Cataloging-in-Publication Data

Published simultaneously in Canada.
Printed in the United States of America.

Country on compact disc: the essential guide to the music / by the
Country Music Foundation: Paul Kingsbury, editor.—1st ed.
ISBN 0-8021-3379-7

1. Country music—Discography. 2. Compact discs—Reviews.
I. Kingsbury, Paul. II. Country Music Foundation. ML156.4.C7C68
1993 016.781642'0266'—dc20   93-11887

FIRST EDITION 1993

Produced by Zenda, Inc.
Book design by Bruce Gore/Gore Studio, Inc.
Illustrations by Chris Ellis

10   9   8   7   6   5   4   3   2   1

CONTENTS

ACKNOWLEDGMENTS

BOOKS LIKE THIS require the cooperation and good will of many, many people. Thanks first to the reviewers who contributed insights with painstaking honesty and unstinting enthusiasm to every entry in this book; their lost sleep is our gain.

More than fifty record labels graciously donated free review copies of their entire CD catalogues for the purposes of this book. We could not have attempted this book without their generosity, and we gratefully acknowledge the contributions of the following helpful people: Ann Tangney and Mitch Cantor at Alcazar Records; Chris Strachwitz at Arhoolie Records; Vanessa Adair at Arista Records, Nashville; Bonita Allen at Asylum Records, Nashville; Jules Wortman and Greg Gosselin at Atlantic Records, Nashville; Heather McBee and Debbie Holley at BNA Entertainment; Robin Wilkes at Brentwood Music; Bill Doble at Cabin Fever Music; Wayne Watkins at Capitol Records, Hollywood; Mark Pucci and Marcia Flowers Sims at Capricorn Records, Kelley Sallee-Snead at Country Music Foundation Records; David Haerle at CMH Records; Sue Austin and Dennis Hannon at Curb Records, Nashville; Jennifer Leonard at Delta Music/LaserLight Records; Jerry Talmadge at DCC Compact Discs; Jeremy Tepper at Diesel Only Records; David Bither at Elektra Records, New York; Frances Pennington and Hillary Siskind at EMI Records, New York; Tor Elting at Flying Fish Records; Denise Roberts at the Gary Group; Susan Nadler at Evelyn Shriver Public Relations for Giant Records; Larry Sloven, Bruce Bromberg, and Darrel Anderson at HighTone Records; Tommy Hill and Mo Lyttle at Hollywood/IMG Records; Ed Keeley at Intersound International; Bill Hallquist at K-Tel International; Jeff Alexson at Kaleidoscope Records; Jon Howard, Susan Collier, and Kate Hagerty at Cathy Gurley Public Relations for Liberty Records; Susan Levy and Lorie Hoppers at MCA Records, Nashville; Sandy Neese and Kim Fowler at Mercury/PolyGram Records, Nashville; Pat Weaver at Mobile Fidelity Sound Lab; Paul Marotta at New World Records; Ginny Shea at North Star Records; Al Bunetta and Dan Einstein at Oh Boy Records/Blue Plate Music; Alan Nichols at Pair

Records; Greg McCarn at RCA Records, Nashville; Gary Reid and Chet Rhodes at Rebel Records; Chris Frymire at Red House Records; Liz Garrow at Restless Records; James Austin at Rhino Records; Ken Irwin at Rounder Records; Carrie Svingen at Rykodisc; John Delgatto at Sierra Records; Matt Walters at Smithsonian/Folkways Music; Holly Gleason, Wendy Shaffer, and Angie Mayes at Sony Music, Nashville; Sharon Pennington at Step One Records; Barry Poss and Beverly Paul at Sugar Hill Records; Charles McCardell at Time-Life Music; Spike Vail at the Vail Company; Jeff Ayeroff at Virgin Records; Susan Niles and Michael Harwood at Warner Bros. Records, Nashville; Darryl Burnett at Watermelon Records; and Michelle Anderson at Welk Music. Thanks also to Otto Kitsinger for generously providing valuable reference material and to Angela Corio at the Recording Industry Association of America, Inc., for providing complete information on gold and platinum certifications.

Heartfelt thanks to Morgan Entrekin and Anton Mueller of Grove/Atlantic and Charlie Phillips and Patricia Hogan of Zenda for their efforts, in matters of logistics and editorial guidance, to bring this book to the public.

This book is also a testament to the dedication of several CMF staffers. Many thanks to: Steve Betts and Alan Stoker for compiling vital reference tapes; Debbie Decker for researching gold and platinum certifications from the RIAA; Kelley Sallee-Snead for administrative support; Becky Bell for help in initially compiling our list of available country CDs and for providing reference CDs; Dean Crum for lending reference material; John Knowles, who designed the databases and translated the documents necessary to keep this complicated project running smoothly; Nicole Kauffman for compiling the indexes to #1 songs and 4 and 5 star CDs; Carolyn Tate for editoral advice; Patti Llovet Hughes for cheerfully handling a thousand and one administrative chores, including (but not limited to) compiling our CD wish lists for the record labels, researching our #1 song index, and word processing manuscripts typed by low-tech contributors; and the CMF's Research and Collections team—Bob Pinson, Ronnie Pugh, John Rumble, Chris Skinker, Linda Gross, and Alan Stoker—who patiently and enthusiastically fact-checked each of these reviews and offered hundreds of crucial suggestions for improving them. Special thanks to Kyle Young and Bill Ivey, without whose vision, guidance, and continuing support this book could never have been imaginable. And, of course, we all owe a debt of gratitude to the artists, without whom this world would be a quieter, lonelier place.

CONTRIBUTORS

Bob Allen, an Editor at Large for *Country Music* magazine, has written for *Esquire, Billboard, Rolling Stone,* and the *Journal of Country Music.* He is the author of *George Jones: Saga of an American Singer* (Doubleday, 1984).

Jack Bernhardt writes about country music for Raleigh, North Carolina's *News and Observer.* His writing has also appeared in *Bluegrass Unlimited, Music Row,* the *Journal of Country Music,* and other publications.

Patrick Carr is a columnist and Editor at Large for *Country Music* magazine. He edited the *Illustrated History of Country Music* (Doubleday, 1979), which he is currently updating for a revised edition.

Daniel Cooper has contributed many articles, essays, and reviews to the *Journal of Country Music,* the *Nashville Scene, Goldmine,* and various visual arts journals. He is currently writing a biography of Lefty Frizzell, to be published by Little, Brown in 1994.

Peter Cronin, formerly Developments Editor for *Musician,* is Associate Country Editor for *Billboard.*

Colin Escott has produced and annotated numerous record reissues since the late Seventies. As a journalist, he has written for *Goldmine,* the *Journal of Country Music,* and other publications. He is the author (with Martin Hawkins) of *Good Rockin' Tonight: Sun Records and the Birth of Rock & Roll* (St. Martin's, 1990) and is at work on a forthcoming biography of Hank Williams for Little, Brown.

Chet Flippo, former Senior Editor at *Rolling Stone,* is the author of *Your Cheatin' Heart, On the Road with the Rolling Stones,* and *Everybody Was Kung-Fu Dancing.* He is now working on a novel.

Ben Fong-Torres, former Senior Editor at *Rolling Stone,* has also been published in *Musician, Esquire, Playboy, GQ,* and many other magazines. He wrote *Hickory Wind: The Life and Times of Gram Parsons* (Pocket Books, 1991); his memoirs, *The Rice Room,* will be published by Hyperion in 1994.

Holly George-Warren is the coauthor of *Musicians in Tune: 75 Contemporary Musicians Discuss the Creative Process* (Fireside, 1992) and coeditor of *The Rolling Stone Album Guide* and the third edition of *The Rolling Stone Illustrated History of Rock & Roll* (both Random House, 1992). She has also written for a variety of magazines, including *Rolling Stone, Option,* and *Guitar World.*

Jimmy Guterman, formerly Editor in Chief of *CD Review,* is the author of *The Worst of Rock & Roll* (Citadel Press, 1991) and *Jerry Lee Lewis: Rockin' My Life Away* (Rutledge Hill, 1991) and has produced many reissue CDs.

Mark Humphrey's writing has appeared in *Esquire, Rolling Stone, Playboy, L.A. Weekly, Guitar Player,* the *Journal of Country Music,* and other publications. He contributed chapters to *Nothin' But the Blues: The Music and the Musicians* (Abbeville, 1993). He also teaches history and performance of American roots music through the state arts council of his native state, Oklahoma.

James Hunter writes about music for *Rolling Stone,* the *Village Voice,* the *New York Times, Musician,* and other publications.

Paul Kingsbury edits the *Journal of Country Music* for the Country Music Foundation. He edited the CMF's pictorial history *Country: The Music and the Musicians* (Abbeville, 1988), which won a Ralph Gleason Music Book Award. His writing has appeared in *Entertainment Weekly, CD Review, Music Row,* and other publications.

Michael McCall writes a weekly music column for the *Nashville Scene* and contributes regularly to *Country Music, Country America,* the *Los Angeles Times,* and *Tower Pulse.* His books include *The Superstars of Country Music, Garth Brooks: A Biography, The Best of 50s TV,* and *The Best of 60s TV,* among others.

Don McLeese covers popular music for the *Austin American-Statesman* and frequently contributes to *Rolling Stone* and *Request.* His work has also appeared in a variety of books and publications, including the third edition of *The Rolling Stone Illustrated History of Rock & Roll, Playboy, Creem, Spin,* the *New York Times Book Review,* and the *Chicago Sun-Times,* where he was the popular music critic for ten years before moving to Austin.

Bill C. Malone, Professor of History at Tulane University, is the author of *Country Music USA* (University of Texas Press, 1968, 1985), *Southern Music/American Music* (University of Kentucky Press, 1979), and *Singing Cowboys and Musical Moutaineers* (University of Georgia Press, 1993). He served as music editor for the *Encyclopedia of Southern Culture* (University of North Carolina, 1989) and as annotator and compiler for the *Smithsonian Collection of Classic Country Music.*

Edward Morris is Country Music Editor for *Billboard.* His books include the career histories *Alabama* (Contemporary, 1985) and *Garth Brooks* (St. Martin's, 1992).

Robert K. Oermann writes music features for the *Tennessean,* Nashville's morning newspaper, and is a nationally syndicated music writer with Gannett News Service. He hosts WSM-FM's "Music City's New Country" radio show and serves as a weekly commentator on the "Crook & Chase" cable TV show. He is the author of *Finding Her Voice: The Saga of Women in Country Music* (with Mary Bufwack) published by Crown in 1993.

Jay Orr, former Head of Technical Services for the Country Music Foundation, covers music for the *Nashville Banner.* His writing has also appeared in *Request, Billboard, BMI Music World, Music Row,* and the *Journal of Country Music.*

Neil V. Rosenberg, Professor of Folklore at Memorial University of Newfoundland, is author of *Bluegrass: A History* (University of Illinois, 1985). He recently edited *Transforming Tradition: Folk Music Revivals Examined,* a collection of essays published by the University of Illinois Press. Currently the sound recordings review editor of the *Journal of American Folklore,* he has published widely on aspects of bluegrass, country, and folk music.

Karen Schoemer covers popular music for the *New York Times, Rolling Stone, Mirabella,* and *Us* magazines.

Charles H. Seemann, former Deputy Director for Collections and Research at the Country Music Foundation, is a folklorist and western music expert now based in New Mexico. He co-edited *Folklife and Museums* (AASLH Press, 1987) and has written for the *Journal of Country Music, Journal of American Folklore, Western Folklore,* and other publications. He has contributed liner notes to more than thirty country reissues and compilations, including *Back in the Saddle Again,* which he produced and which was nominated for a Grammy award.

Rob Tannenbaum is the music columnist for *GQ* and a contributing editor for *Details.* He has also written for *Rolling Stone,* the *New York Times,* the *Village Voice, Musician,* and *New Musical Express.*

Nick Tosches is the author of *Country, Hellfire: The Jerry Lee Lewis Story, Unsung Heroes of Rock 'n' Roll, Power on Earth, Dino,* and the award-winning novel *Cut Numbers.* His work—fiction, nonfiction, and poetry—has appeared in a wide variety of publications, including *Rolling Stone, Vanity Fair,* and the *New Yorker.*

Ken Tucker is Critic at Large for *Entertainment Weekly.* He has written about country music for *Rolling Stone,* the *Village Voice,* the *Philadelphia Inquirer,* and *Vogue.* He is coauthor of *Rock of Ages: The Rolling Stone History of Rock & Roll* (Summit Books, 1986).

Charles K. Wolfe, Professor of English at Middle Tennessee State University, is author of more than a dozen books on American music, including *The Life and Legend of Leadbelly* (with Kip Lornell), published by HarperCollins in 1992. He has annotated over one hundred albums and has been nominated three times for Grammy awards.

INTRODUCTION

COUNTRY MUSIC NEVER stands still. More than any other form of popular music, country draws strength, indeed its very identity, from vocal and instrumental traditions of the past. Its roots go deep into the folk music of the Old World, fed from streams of music ranging from the British Isles to Africa. At its best, country music serves as a connection between the stories of today and the values of our forebears. But a tradition, by definition, can't exist without being handed down. It's got to grow.

As recently as 1985, country music seemed in danger of becoming an oldies backwater. Its biggest and most vital stars—Willie Nelson, Kenny Rogers, Waylon Jennings, Anne Murray, Conway Twitty—were pushing fifty. Not surprisingly, they appealed to a graying audience that wasn't getting any younger. Much of the music coming out of Nashville at the time had lost touch with country's roots and sounded more like pop music that was country in name only. Most alarming of all, new artists were no longer making headway on the charts. Country radio relied on playlists filled with hits five years old or more, leaving little room for newcomers to squeeze onto the air. When George Jones sang "Who's Gonna Fill Their Shoes" in early 1985, he was giving voice to a question a lot of people in country were asking.

Little did we know the answer was on its way. Since 1985—which was before Billy Ray Cyrus, before Garth Brooks, before even Randy Travis had a hit—there has been an 80 percent turnover in the rosters of the major record labels. That's right. Of the more than 200 country acts now on major-label rosters, less than forty of them were recording in 1985. And this in a business where artists like Hank Snow and Ernest Tubb used to stay with the same *label* for decades. Country hasn't seen a youthquake like it since the early 1950s and the glory days of Hank Williams, Lefty Frizzell, Kitty Wells, Webb Pierce, Faron Young, Carl Smith, Tennessee Ernie Ford, Marty Robbins, Hank Thompson, and Jim Reeves.

Here's something else to consider. As reported in *Billboard* magazine in May 1993, Randy Travis's debut album *Storms of*

Life, released in 1986 and now seen as a landmark for the new traditionalist revitalization of country, represents the oldest music heard in regular rotation on country radio stations today. That makes Travis, at age thirty-four, one of new country's grizzled veterans, along with twenty-nine-year-old Wynonna Judd, who first hit the charts nine years ago. With the landscape of contemporary music having changed so radically, we felt it was high time to compile a consumer guidebook that comprehensively surveys country—all of it, from pioneers like Roy Acuff, Kitty Wells, and Bill Monroe, to the hottest newcomers like Travis Tritt, Trisha Yearwood, and Garth Brooks. Even though country radio may not reach back beyond 1986, country's rich legacy of recordings goes all the way back to 1922. No matter how much it grows, country ceases to be country when it's cut off from its roots.

What is country anyway? And how did we decide what to include? Those are the kind of questions that music fans love to argue about. (And the staff of the Country Music Foundation is as argumentative on the question as anybody.) Some folks will tell you that the instruments define country. Fiddle and steel are country, the argument goes; electric keyboards and violin sections aren't. But then what do you do with Dwight Yoakam's "Two Doors Down," a barroom ballad that leans heavily on a Wurlitzer piano, or Patsy Cline's classic "Sweet Dreams," which is beautifully framed by a full string section? Is John Denver country? Is Olivia Newton-John? Don't forget: he won the Country Music Association's Entertainer of the Year award in 1975; she won the Female Vocalist award the previous year. What seems so simple at first turns out to be a pretty thorny issue, especially if you're trying to keep your country pure. So we approached country from a different angle.

To assemble our list of country artists, we began with the Country Music Foundation's own record and compact disc collection—which has been skillfully assembled for twenty years—as a benchmark. Then we included almost everyone who records for a Nashville branch of the major record labels. And we tried to include anyone currently played on country radio or on the Country Music Television video channel. That's why you'll find the Eagles' early albums reviewed here alongside the work of John Denver and Olivia Newton-John as well as folk-style newcomers like Nanci Griffith and John Gorka. We also included the occasional disc by a rock & roll artist who has shown a real affinity for country, such as Leon Russell and John Fogerty, reasoning that at its best country is more a state of mind than an exclusive club. Ultimately, of course, we relied on our own judgment. If we've erred, we hope that it's on the side of being more inclusive, rather than less.

Once we had decided which artists to include—and we ended up adding names as our reviewers and staff brought them to mind—we set about finding what they had in print on compact disc. Here we relied on the two bibles of record store clerks: *Phonolog* and *Schwann,* both comprehensive catalogues of music in print. Then with the help of more than fifty major and independent record labels, we double-checked our list of artists and available CDs, staying current through mid-1993.

We did not include bootleg albums, those gray-market products which are unofficially distributed. For one thing, these albums pay no royalties to artists or songwriters, but maybe even more importantly, they're hard for most country fans to find. For the same reason, we also didn't include import albums. Only in cases where imports are clearly far superior to anything available domestically do our reviewers mention them. These imports are not rated individually but noted within the text of the review. Invariably, it seems, the import albums that we do name have been issued by Bear Family Records of Germany, possibly the premier record reissue company in the world. Though Bear Family's work is unavailable in most record stores, department stores, and discount houses, don't abandon all hope: the bigger stores and specialty mail order houses do carry many of the label's lavish reissues.

Those who know *The Rolling Stone Album Guide* will find our format for reviews very familiar; we're certainly indebted to Dave Marsh and John Swenson, editors of that *Rolling Stone* volume, for blazing the trail.

Of course, we've added a few wrinkles to the now-standard album review format. To balance our reviewers' opinions, we enlisted the help of the Recording Industry Association of America (RIAA) to include an unusual feature for a book of this kind—gold and platinum certifications, which indicate the sales milestones of 500,000 and 1 million units, respectively. Keep in mind that the RIAA didn't begin awarding gold albums until 1958, platinum until 1976. Thus, many artists who had million-selling records before those awards were created aren't recognized. Also, RIAA certifications depend on the record label informing the RIAA of its sales figures. Most of the time, the record labels are very diligent about this, because these sales milestones have great promotional value. But sometimes artists slip through the cracks, and the label doesn't notice an act's album has quietly passed 500,000. This doesn't happen as much as it used to, but it has happened and is still happening here and there, particularly with older acts that are no longer on the label's active roster. Nevertheless, we still think that gold and platinum certifications are a useful addition to our evaluations. Because record companies rarely release detailed information on sales figures, RIAA certifications are all we have to judge long-term popularity.

Another unusual, but useful, feature of this guide is the index of #1 country songs at the back. Country music has traditionally been a singles format. (One could argue, in fact, that country albums didn't come into their own until Willie Nelson's master-piece, *Red Headed Stranger.*) So we have included an index to *Billboard*'s #1 songs, from 1944 through 1992, showing where they can be found on compact disc.

About our ratings format: Note that the CD listings preceding the reviews run in roughly chronological order based on original recording dates; the album year listed indicates the date that this particular collection of recordings was first issued (in some cases, that may be the original LP release date; a second date indicates reissue if the album changed substantially since its first issue). Here's how the listings look:

★★★★   **Best of the Best of Merle Haggard (Liberty C21Y-91254) 1972 ▲**

In this example, Merle Haggard's CD, titled *Best of the Best of Merle Haggard,* received a four-star rating. The record label and catalogue number are in parentheses, followed by the year that collection was first issued. The symbol at the end indicates that the album earned a platinum certification.

Almost all of the CDs listed here should be available through your local record store. In the event that they are not, here are a few mail-order outfits that can uncover that hard-to-find gem:

Country Music Hall of Fame Mail Order
4 Music Square East
Nashville, TN 37203
1-800-255-2357

County Sales
P.O. Box 191
Floyd, VA 24091
703-745-2001

Elderly Instruments
1100 North Washington
Lansing, MI 48901
517-372-7890

Rhino Mail Order
2225 Colorado Avenue
Santa Monica, CA 90404
1-800-432-0020

Roots & Rhythm
6921 Stockton Avneue
El Cerrito, CA 94530
415-525-1494

Roundup Records
P.O. Box 154
North Cambridge, MA 02140
1-800-443-4727

It's been only a decade since country music—or music of any kind, for that matter—was available on compact disc. When first introduced back in 1983, the technology—developed jointly by the Dutch and Japanese electronic giants Philips and Sony—was unfamiliar and expensive; players cost $800 to $1,000 (four or five times the price of a phonograph), while the discs themselves cost more than twice what LPs and cassettes were going for. Record companies, burned by the fad of quadraphonic sound in the mid-Seventies, approached the new playback medium warily. For the entire year, the labels released only ninety-nine popular music titles on CD. Of those, just five were country—Alabama's *The Closer You Get*, Ronnie Milsap's *Greatest Hits*, Willie Nelson's *Always on My Mind* and *Stardust*, Kenny Rogers's *Eyes That See in the Dark*, and Ricky Skaggs's *Highways and Heartaches*.

We've come a long way since then—as the more that 2,000 country CDs reviewed in the following pages attest. It will be exciting to see what the coming decade will bring. In the meantime, we hope this guide helps to give an accurate picture of where country has been and what country ought not to lose sight of as we move on.

—*Paul Kingsbury,* Editor
Country Music Foundation

LEGEND

★★★★★   **Classic.** Transcends the genre. Unreservedly recommended to anyone who likes country music.

★★★★   **Excellent.** No significant flaws. Highly recommended to most country music fans.

★★★   **Good.** More memorable music than filler. Recommended with minor reservations.

★★   **Fair.** Significantly flawed. Not recommended to most, though possibly of value to diehard fans of the style or the performer.

★   **Poor.** Incompetently performed or moronically conceived. The sort of recording that makes you angry at or embarrassed for those responsible.

●   gold record (sales of 500,000 units)

▲   platinum record (sales of 1,000,000 units)

CD listings run in roughly chronological order according to original recording dates. N. D. follows listings for which no release date is available. Multi-million sellers are indicated by a numeral following the platinum symbol.

A

ROY ACUFF

★★★ **Columbia Historic Edition (Columbia CK 39998) 1985**
▲▲▲ **The Essential Roy Acuff (Columbia Legacy CK 48956) 1992**
★★ **Best of Roy Acuff (Curb/CEMA D21K-77454) 1991**

When the "King of Country Music" died in 1992, embarrassed reporters noted that there were only a handful of his hundreds of records available. Although Acuff had been the centerpiece of the Grand Ole Opry for generations, he recorded little in later years, relying on a body of work done in the 1940s and 1950s to preserve his distinctive high, keening mountain singing style. Some of Acuff's earliest recordings, which preserve much of the old-time string band and gospel sound that characterized Acuff's work before he came to the Opry, are found on the *Columbia Historic Edition* set. These include the very first "Wabash Cannon Ball," in which Acuff does the fiddling and train whistle, but leaves the singing to fellow band member Dynamite Hatcher. More representative of Acuff's actual hits is *The Essential Roy Acuff, 1936-1949,* twenty beautifully remastered tracks that include original versions of "Great Speckled Bird," "The Precious Jewel," "Fireball Mail," "Night Train to Memphis," and others. Here is Acuff as he sounded at his peak, when he soared to national fame in the 1940s, riding the crest of network radio, B movies, and a fruitful music publishing partnership with songwriter Fred Rose. In later years, Acuff settled in comfortably as the grand ole man of the Opry, and his recording activity gradually tailed off. Confirmed fans may want to look for *Best of Roy Acuff* to get a ten-cut sampling of his later, less important work for Hickory Records. —C.K.W.

ALABAMA

★★½ **My Home's in Alabama (RCA 6912) 1980** ▲²
★★½ **Feels So Right (RCA 13930) 1981** ▲³
★★½ **Mountain Music (RCA 14229) 1982** ▲³
★★½ **The Closer You Get (RCA PCD1-4229) 1983** ▲²
★ **Roll On (RCA 14939) 1984** ▲³
★★★½ **40 Hour Week (RCA 5339) 1985** ▲²
★★★½ **Greatest Hits (RCA 7170) 1986** ▲³
★½ **The Touch (RCA 5649) 1986** ▲
★½ **Just Us (RCA 6495) 1987**●
★★ **Alabama Live (RCA 6825) 1988** ●
★★ **Southern Star (RCA 8597) 1989** ▲
★½ **Pass It on Down (RCA 2108) 1990** ▲
★★ **Greatest Hits II (RCA 61040) 1991** ●

★★½ **American Pride (RCA 66044) 1992 ▲**

During the first half of the 1980s, few commercially viable bridges to the great country sounds of the Fifties, Sixties, and Seventies seemed to exist. Artists like George Jones and Merle Haggard soldiered on, but after a decade dominated by rock, Nashville musicians struggled for a while before they arrived at much distinctive music, tradition-minded or otherwise. It was during this Reagan-era interregnum that four nondescript guys from Fort Payne, Alabama—lead singer-guitarist Randy Owen, singer-bassist Teddy Gentry, singer-lead guitarist Jeff Cook, and drummer Mark Herndon—named themselves after their home state and, for about six years, devised their own little world of contemporary country.

"Drinkin' was forbidden in my Christian country home/I learned to play the flat-top on them good old gospel songs/Then I heard about the barrooms across the Georgia line/Where a boy could make a livin' playin' guitar late at night." With these revealing lines from the band's first Top Twenty single, "My Home's in Alabama" (1980), Randy Owen set up six multiplatinum albums that owned the country charts in their day. Sentimental, designed and constructed with the premeditation and care of a shiny, state-of-the-art bowling alley, the singles from these albums appear on *Greatest Hits:* "Feels So Right," "Mountain Music," "Love in the First Degree," and seven others—all #1 hits. Very shrewdly, they combine Owen's unobtrusive, gruffly sincere lead singing with plush Nashville refittings of country-rock vocal harmonies, Southern rock guitar, traditional touches, and intense white-church sentiments. Sometimes, as on the imminently reasonable paean to regionalism "If It Ain't Dixie (It Won't Do)"—from *40 Hour Week,* Alabama's most compelling album—the group's approach pays real emotional dividends. Other times, Alabama sound like they're trying to be underachievers on purpose.

But being ordinary, for better or worse, was apparently essential to the Alabama style. "She and I," a bright Nashville adaptation of John Mellencamp-style rock, appeared on *Greatest Hits* and seemed to signal a fresh new direction for the band, but it turned out to be just a brief, pleasant detour. By 1986, Alabama's long run gave way, first to new traditionalism, then to Garthmusic. The group never seemed to grasp that both movements were about new ways to voice not well-done genericness but well-done distinctiveness. Recent singles like "I'm in a Hurry (And I Don't Know Why)" show some recognition of this current country value system. Yet whether Alabama, a decent act that lived large on refined mediocrity, will continue to reach the platinum level remains to be seen.—J.H.

PAT ALGER

★★★ **True Love and Other Short Stories (Sugar Hill SH-CD 1029) 1991**

Pat Alger, a one-time regular of the East Coast folk circuit, emerged in the 1990s as one of Nashville's most successful commercial songwriters, contributing hits to Garth Brooks, Trisha Yearwood, Kathy Mattea, Hal Ketchum, Don Williams, and others. As a singer, Alger's style has more in common with Williams's gentle warmth than Brooks's intense melodrama. His 1991 solo album features intimate interpretations of a few new songs and a sampling of those that others made famous, including "True Love," "Small Town Saturday Night," "Goin' Gone," "She Came from Fort Worth," and "Lone Star State of Mind."—M.M.

DEBORAH ALLEN

★★★½ **Delta Dreamland (Giant 9 24485-2) 1993**

In 1984, Allen had a Top Five hit with "Baby I Lied," but she found her subsequent success as a songwriter, frequently composing with her husband and partner, Rafe Van Hoy. Her songwriting talents are showcased on this thematically rich album, but it's her sensuous singing that glistens like gold, whether on steamy ballads such as "Chain Lightning" and "Into My Life," or the infectiously rhythmic "Rock Me (In the Cradle of Love)." A gifted stylist, Allen is to country music what Mary Lou Retton is to gymnastics: a creatively supple singer capable of vocally athletic leaps and twists that transform the most ordinary phrase into a work of art.—J.B.

DAVE ALVIN
★★★ **Romeo's Escape (Epic EK40921) 1987**
★★★½ **Blue Blvd (HighTone HCD-8029) 1991**

When Steve Earle and Dwight Yoakam attracted critical attention and radio airplay in 1986 as hip singer-songwriters on the edge of country, Alvin suddenly sounded like a contender himself, steeped as he was in the same roots traditions of rockabilly, blues, rock & roll, and hard country that inspired Earle and Yoakam.

Alvin came out of the Blasters, a Los Angeles-based roots rock band. Brother Phil did the singing while Dave wrote the songs and played lead guitar. In the late Seventies and early Eighties, on the heels of the stripped-down punk era, the Blasters and several other bands inspired a brief revival of interest in the elemental sound of rockabilly music.

Romeo's Escape reprises three Alvin songs from the Blasters era: "Border Radio," "Jubilee Train," and the Hank Williams-inspired "Long White Cadillac," which Dwight Yoakam later cut. Some songs, such as the title cut and "New Tatoo," are flat-out rock & roll numbers. Leaning more toward country, often with the help of Greg Leisz's steel guitar, are "Every Night About This Time," re-corded later by Joe Ely, "Fourth of July," cut by L.A. rock band X, "Border Radio," and "Far Away." "Brother on the Line" pits striker and scab against one another with quiet eloquence. It's a pity that Alvin's vocals, though expressive, aren't always equal to the material.

Alvin visited Nashville in the late Eighties, meeting writers and checking out the songwriting scene. He co-wrote the title track for *Blue Blvd*, a rock song, with Nashville-based writer Michael Woody. Though Leisz sometimes plays steel guitar, and Dwight Yoakam adds harmony vocals on "Haley's Comet," little about *Blue Blvd* is actually country. Alvin delivers a set of strong, sometimes turgid songs with touches of cool jazz, gospel, blues, rhythm & blues, and rock & roll. Arranged differently, "Why Did She Stay with Him" could be a country song. Alvin sings with more authority than on *Romeo's Escape,* and his outstanding guitar work is grounded in classic rock traditions.

Alvin produced and played on Sonny Burgess's 1992 album *Tennessee Border* (see Sonny Burgess), to which he contributed a fine rockabilly song, "Flattop Joint." Though he may work too far out on the edge to write a mainstream country hit, Alvin's work will continue to warrant serious attention from Nashville. —J.O.

BILL ANDERSON
★★ **Best of Bill Anderson (Curb D2-77436) 1991**

One of country music's most successful songwriters, "Whispering" Bill Anderson penned numerous hits for himself as well as for other artists (Ray Price, Connie Smith, and Roy Clark, to name a few). His breathy vocal delivery isn't very compelling, but it has not stopped him from hitting the top of the charts, as well as hosting popular TV game shows on TNN. Anderson is poorly served on CD, though, with only one brief collection of his songs presently available. *Best of* consists of hits from throughout Anderson's career, including his first #1, "Mama Sang a Song" (1962), in all its tear-jerkin' glory, and 1963's pop crossover blockbuster "Still." Anderson's *piece de resistance* "My Life (Throw It Away If I Want To)" sounds just as good today as it did in 1969, but his later singles don't fare as well. "I Wonder If God Likes Country Music," with the late Roy Acuff barely carrying a tune on the final verse, is embarrassing, as is the party-down "Southern Fried." "Thank You, Darling" is a twenty-years-later follow-up to "Still" and is as corny as they come. This collection definitely leans toward the schmaltzy; sorely missing are Anderson's duets with Jan Howard ("For Loving You") and his downhome classic "Po' Folks" from 1961.—H.G.-W.

JOHN ANDERSON
★★★★ **Greatest Hits (Warner Bros. 9 25169-2) 1984**
★★★ **Greatest Hits, Vol. 2 (Warner Bros. 9 26304-2) 1990**
★★★★ **Seminole Wind (BNA 61029-2) 1992 ▲**

Long undercredited as one of the prime movers of the early Eighties new traditionalist movement and long plagued by the vicissitudes of the music business,

John Anderson was well on his way into obscurity until "Straight Tequila Night" rehabilitated his career. That's good news, because this funky Floridian occupies a stylistic niche somewhere between George Jones and the Allman Brothers—hard-core country lyrics with a stiff dose of the blues and a whiff of outlaw attitude—much copied but never quite equaled by younger men (Travis Tritt, for instance). And there's more good news: *Seminole Wind,* the album which rendered the hit, is as good as (or better than) anything Anderson did the first time around.

The Warner Bros. *Greatest Hits* packages do a reasonable job with the first phase of his career, covering most of the significant bases from "I'm Just an Old Chunk of Coal" and "Wild and Blue" to "Swingin'" and "Black Sheep" (all on *Greatest Hits)* and even getting into stuff like "Tokyo, Oklahoma" and "Goin' Down Hill" (on the second volume). We ought to have CD reissues of all his work all the Warner Bros. albums in their entirety and all the MCA and Capitol tracks he cut between leaving Warners and arriving at *Seminole Wind*—but that's not how the business works, as Mr. Anderson knows all too well.—P.Ca.

LYNN ANDERSON
★★★ **Country Spotlight (Dominion 30032) 1991**
★★★ **Cowboy's Sweetheart (LaserLight 12 128) 1992**

One of the quintessential "girl singers" of the late Sixties and early Seventies, Lynn Anderson was a strong, supple singer, but she had neither the vocal identity nor the personal charisma of Tammy or Dolly or Loretta, and her time in the major leagues was relatively short. She's still around, though, and still in good voice, as the two volumes of her work available on CD attest. *Cowboy's Sweetheart,* which seems like her kind of project (she's an ardent equestrienne and Westerner), is clearly the more coherent work, featuring her takes on classy numbers like Ian Tyson's "Someday Soon" and Cole Porter's "Don't Fence Me In." The *Country Spotlight* disc, which looks like an anthology of her old material, isn't; everything old here, from "Rose Garden" (her biggie) to "Silver Threads and Golden Needles," is a new recording, and

not a great one at that. But the torch songs ("Keep Me in Mind," "Cry") work. In a perfect world she might have another whole career ahead of her.
—P.Ca.

EDDY ARNOLD
★★★½ **The Best of Eddy Arnold (RCA 3675) 1967** ●
★★ **Best of Eddy Arnold (Curb 77416) 1990**
★★½ **Hand-Holdin' Songs (RCA 9963) 1990**
★★ **You Don't Miss a Thing (RCA 3020) 1990**
★★★½ **Last of the Love Song Singers: Then and Now (RCA 66046) 1993**

In the Fifties and Sixties, Eddy Arnold's romantic tenor occupied country music's best-selling center, flanked by Don Gibson's dejected soul to the left and Webb Pierce's ebullient honky-tonk to the right. Audibly passionate yet overcome by his songs' losses and victories only at carefully chosen dramatic junctures, Arnold always seemed rooted in the pre-rock small-town values of his native Henderson, Tennessee. Yet he was also impressed by the Dean Martin-style Hollywood suaveness that compelled half of Elvis Presley. In 1967, when the CMA named Arnold its Entertainer of the Year, he'd long been the field's top commercial artist. He looked like a fullback, dressed like a Cadillac dealer, and, at his best, sounded like a classic Tennessee pop singer.

Arnold's many RCA hits from the mid-Forties through the Fifties are unavailable. They should be heard for historical reasons and, perhaps, by people who don't appreciate his mature style. In 1948, for example, Arnold went #1 with "Bouquet of Roses," a tune in which a woman receives roses, after the fact, "one for every time" she disappointed the singer. The song is very Arnold—patient, reasonable, gentlemanly—in that its narrator sees this call to his florist as the romantic high road, consistent with continuing love, not bitterness.

Since *The Best of Eddy Arnold* appeared in 1967, though, the standard "Bouquet of Roses" is a state-of-the-art Nashville Sound re-recording, with perfectly tinkling piano and silvery slide in lieu of fiddle. This better suits Arnold's definitive mid-career command.

Arnold may have been able to yodel up a fine "Cattle Call," but as a great record like "Anytime"— or a sterling take on a song as awesome as Hank Cochran's "Make the World Go Away" or Roger Miller's even better "The Last Word in Lonesome Is Me"—suggests, both his voice and his temperament were born for Sixties-style country-pop.

Accordingly, Arnold has stuck with this style, perhaps with a memory of even more lushness than was ever there, in his recent recordings with veteran producer Harold Bradley in the Nineties. (The 1990 Curb anthology collects indifferent Seventies recordings done for MGM.) *You Don't Miss a Thing* and the more nostalgic *Hand-Holdin' Songs* seek to emphasize the positive values of pre-rock country and pop songwriting that survive the decades. Arnold, in his early seventies, sings with the reserves of care and tone expected from his brand of professional. Yet both records suffer from indistinctness. Much more successful at making the case for pop and country traditionalism—and for Arnold—is *The Last of the Love Song Singers: Then and Now,* a two-CD box. On the *Now* disc, a cannier and more specific application of Arnold and Bradley's old/new sound, songs like "She Makes My Roses Grow" and "When the Wind Blows in Chicago," manage an even-handed town-and-country tug. *Then,* which duplicates the selections of *The Best of Eddy Arnold* a few times only, makes a worthy companion to the earlier Nashville Sound classic.—J.H.

ASLEEP AT THE WHEEL
★★★ Asleep at the Wheel (Epic EK33097) 1974
★★★½ Asleep at the Wheel (Dot MCAD-31281) 1988
★★★ Western Standard Time (Epic EK44213) 1988
★★★½ Live & Kickin': Greatest Hits (Arista 18698-2) 1992
★★★ The Swingin' Best of Asleep at the Wheel (Epic EK 53049) 1992

It's hard not to like Asleep at the Wheel. Committed to keeping the sound of vintage western swing alive—particularly the songs of Bob Wills—the band lovingly plays the oldies, occasionally sneaking in a few numbers of its own. Led by velveteen voiced guitarist Ray Benson, Asleep at the Wheel has managed to

survive more than sixty personnel changes since its inception in 1970. The band has jumped from label to label, but the CDs that exist are for the most part compilations, with many of the same songs (such as "Choo Choo Ch-Boogie" and "Chattanooga Choo Choo") appearing on various albums. Curiously, neither the Seventies Top Ten singles nor the Grammy-award-winning "One O'Clock Jump" appear on any of the CD anthologies. *Live and Kickin': Greatest Hits,* recorded at an Austin roadhouse in 1991, is a good overview, capturing the spirited band playing its favorites of the past twenty years. The Dot CD (compiled from two out-of-print recordings) mixes in some honky-tonk weepers and features guest vocalists Bonnie Raitt and Willie Nelson (who also appears on *The Swingin' Best of* and *Western Standard Time).*
—H.G.-W.

CHET ATKINS
★★★½ The RCA Years, 1947-1981 (RCA 2-07863-61095-2) 1992
★★★ Pickin' My Way/In Hollywood/ Alone (Mobile Fidelity 2-MFCD-10-20787) 1958/1971/1972
★★★ Chet Atkins Picks on the Hits (RCA Camden CAD1-2712) 1972
★★★ Guitar for All Seasons (RCA PDC2-1115) 1986
★★★★ Pickin' on Country (RCA Pair PDC2-1211) N. D.
★★★½ Tennessee Guitar Man (RCA Pair PDC2-1047) 1986
★★½ Stay Tuned (Columbia CK-39591) 1985
★★½ Street Dreams (Columbia CK-40256) 1986
★★½ Sails (Columbia CK-40593) 1987
★★½ Chet Atkins C.G.P. (Columbia CK-44323) 1989
★★★½ [with Mark Knopfler] Neck and Neck (Columbia CK-45307) 1990

For going on half a century, Chet Atkins has been one of the most influential people in Nashville. Heck, they even named a street after him. He's also earned his reputation as one of country music's biggest enigmas. But there can be no argument about his playing. Atkins came to Music City to stay in the early Fifties, and he was soon known and respected by all the best pickers in town. His impossibly pristine picking style and impeccable taste soon made his name synonymous with the guitar. Atkins, of course, went on to make at least as big a mark as a producer, and depending upon whom you ask, he's either the savior of country music or the chief architect of its dilution. Actually, there's a lot of truth in both of these arguments. As head of RCA studios during the Sixties, he developed a knack for capturing the raw talent of an artist while eliminating all the rough edges. Atkins the producer removed potentially "offensive "pedal steel and fiddle, substituting white-bread background vocals and very unfiddlelike strings. While he may have ticked off many a traditionalist, the masses loved it, and in what has been called the "Chet Atkins compromise," he succeeded in significantly expanding the boundaries of the country audience with hits by artists like Jim Reeves, Don Gibson, and Skeeter Davis.

Sanding the rough edges off of others' music all those years has left most of Atkins's later records in need of a little grit, the major exception being *Neck and Neck,* recorded with Dire Straits guitarist Mark Knopfler. Under the British rocker's influence, Atkins moves back toward the rootsier feel of his earliest recordings and away from the watered down lite jazz sound of Eighties releases like *C.G.P., Sails, Street Dreams,* and *Stay Tuned.* Although those records have their moments (*Street Dreams'* "Honolulu Blue," *C.G.P.'s* "I Still Can't Say Goodbye"), later Atkins recordings are filled with plucking strings and new age-y synthesizers, and you're better off sticking with the earlier stuff. Unfortunately, thanks to RCA's shoddy reissues, that's not as easy as it sounds. "Double Play" CDs like *Tennessee Guitar Man, Pickin' on Country, Guitar for All Seasons,* and *Picks on the Hits,* for all the great music they contain, claim to be equivalent to two albums. In actuality these packages, with their complete lack of track information, contain only around forty minutes of music, less than the typical single-album release. When you consider that the CD format is capable of storing over seventy minutes of music, this looks more like a ripoff than a deal.

One alternative to these flimsy collections is *The RCA Years, 1947-1981.* This two-CD set is a pretty good cross section of Atkins's work, with newer cuts like his wonderful take on Paul McCartney's "Junk" nicely complementing classics like "Chinatown, My Chinatown." The one drawback here is summed up in the liner notes with the phrase "chosen by Chet himself." Even more so than most artists, the self-effacing Atkins is not the best judge of his own work. As a result, for example, we get a Sousa-fied, with-the-Boston-Pops recording of "Country Gentleman" in place of the inspired 1953 original. But these are small complaints. It may take a little work to find Atkins's best stuff, but hearing this brilliant musician at his peak is worth a little extra effort. Let's hope RCA gets around to giving his early catalogue the objective and thorough treatment it deserves.—P.Cr.

MIKE AULDRIDGE
★★★★ Treasures Untold (Sugar Hill SH-CD-3780) 1990
★★★½ Eight String Swing (Sugar Hill SH-CD-3725) 1992

AULDRIDGE, REID & COLEMAN
★★★ High Time (Sugar Hill SH-CD-3776) 1989

Mike Auldridge's name is almost synonymous with the word dobro. His masterful playing brought the instrument to the forefront of contemporary bluegrass, first in New Shades of Grass (in the late Sixties) and then with the Seldom Scene (beginning in 1971). Auldridge's solo outings highlight his gorgeous bell-like tones in musical settings where he's joined by various Seldom Scene-sters (John Duffey, Tom Gray, Ben Eldridge, John Starling) and other bluegrass maestros (Doc Watson, Tony Rice). *Treasures Untold* is a delightful collection of mostly traditional old-time country songs, inspired by (and dedicated to) Auldridge's uncle, the steel guitarist Ellsworth T. Cozzens, who wrote the title track and played with Jimmie Rodgers. Rice, Watson, and Starling help out on vocals, and Auldridge himself takes a couple of leads, including that on *Treasures Untold.* On the instrumental *Eight-String Swing,* Auldridge plays eight-string dobro, because, as he writes in the liner notes, it enables him to "play things that I've had in my mind but could never quite get out of a conventional six-string dobro." *High Time* is a pleasant collection of contemporary country and newgrass numbers, featuring latterday Seldom Scene members T. Michael Coleman on bass and Lou Reid on vocals, mandolin, guitar, and fiddle. Of note are Coleman and Reid's originals, the plaintive "Wanting You" and the bluesy title track, featuring beautifully sung harmony vocals by Alison Krauss. —H.G.-W.

GENE AUTRY
★★★½ **Columbia Historic Edition (Columbia CK 37465E) 1982**
★★★★ **The Essential Gene Autry: 1933-1946 (Columbia/Legacy CK 48957) 1992**

Gene Autry is the quintessential singing cowboy of the movies. He began his singing career in 1929 as a Jimmie Rodgers imitator and recorded a number of Rodgers's songs for RCA Victor. He was so good at this that it is often difficult to distinguish him from Rodgers on some of those recordings. Autry soon developed his own style, though, becoming a mellow cowboy crooner with sophisticated but understated musical accompaniment, including sweet violins,

steel guitar, and sometimes a muted trumpet. Movies catapulted him into super-stardom, and he eventually appeared in almost 100 films. These two collections of Columbia recordings span his styles, from the early Jimmie Rodgers sound of "Yellow Rose of Texas" to the smooth version of the Carter Family's "I'm Thinking Tonight of My Blue Eyes," and include such well-known Autry favorites as "Deep in the Heart of Texas" and "Back in the Saddle Again." Of the two discs, *The Essential Gene Autry* has more to offer: eighteen cuts as opposed to only ten on the *Historic Edition,* and four of those ten are also included on the *Essential.* Still, both are well worth having. Now it would be great if someone would make his early RCA cuts from 1929-31 available on CD as well. (Note: a printing error resulted in one page of notes from the *Essential Roy Acuff* set being substituted for the first page of the Autry booklet in early pressings of the *Essential Gene Autry* CD. If you get one of these, contact the Sony Quality Control Hotline, 1-800-255-7514 for a replacement. The notes are excellent and worth the effort). C.H.S.

B

Gito 73

JOAN BAEZ

★★★½ **The Joan Baez Country Music Album (Vanguard VCD-105/6) 1979, 1987**

C'mon all you rockabilly ravers and redneck mothers—you can't hold it against her forever for having committed "Kumbaya" to vinyl. This sturdy compilation from Baez's Vanguard career is not only legitimate country, it's surprisingly contemporary to boot. If Kathy Mattea released the identical disc tomorrow, it would win CMA awards. Granted, Baez's high-pitched quaver can grate when her voice is too much of the show. But when backed by a full contingent of Nashville session pros, that same voice is a lovely instrument for handling what used to be called "progressive country" material by the likes of Mickey Newbury and Gram Parsons. Though Baez's "The Night They Drove Old Dixie Down" still pales before the Band's original, her soul-weary version of Parsons's "Hickory Wind" may be the best on record. The problems arise in the final quarter of the disc, which draws from Baez's pedantic early years when she sang folk tunes as if she had one foot in the coffeehouse and the other in the Library of Congress archives. Her take on traditional tunes like "Pal of Mine" can raise the horrid specter of peasant-skirted preppies holding hands around a campfire.—D.C.

BAILLIE & THE BOYS

★★ **Baillie & the Boys (RCA 6272-2-R) 1987**
★★½ **Turn the Tide (RCA 8454-2-R) 1988**
★★ **The Lights of Home (RCA 2114-2-R) 1990**
★★★½ **The Best of Baillie & the Boys (3118-2-R) 1991**

The closest Baillie & the Boys ever got to singing hard-country was when they supplied backing vocals for Randy Travis's first album. On their own releases, these transplants from the East Coast may credit an occasional fiddle and steel backup, but you'll have to strain to hear it. Nevertheless, lead singer Kathie Baillie's fluttery soprano does have that classic country quality of aching woundedness, which is well suited to the ballads of doubt and regret she's come to specialize in.

The first album showed Baillie & the Boys (husband Michael Bonagura on guitar and bassist Alan LeBoeuf) at its slickest and shallowest, epitomized by the high gloss of the group's first pop-country hit, "Oh, Heart." With *Turn the Tide,* the choice of material proved more judicious with the result that four singles hit the Top Ten—"Long Shot," "She Deserves You," "Heart of Stone," and the title track. *The Lights of Home* offered a little less of the same, with the exception of two nicely chosen covers. "Perfect," a

#1 in England for the British pop group Fairground Attraction, is a peppy slice of neo-rockabilly, while "Fool Such As I" masterfully retools the famous Hank Snow/Elvis Presley hit for contemporary country radio. The *Best of Baillie & the Boys* is truly that, featuring every hit single the act has released. It's a dependable collection for those who like their country light, with extra sweetening.—P.K.

KENNY BAKER
★★★ [with Josh Graves] The Puritan Sessions (Rebel/CD-1108) 1972, 1973, 1989
★★★★★ Master Fiddler (County Co-CD-2705) 1993

Kenny Baker established his reputation as the dean of bluegrass fiddlers playing for many years with the Father of Bluegrass, Bill Monroe. Baker is also a fine guitarist, and in 1972 and 1973 he teamed up with former Flatt & Scruggs dobroist Josh Graves to record two albums of guitar instrumentals, *Something Different* and *Bucktime,* which became underground classics among the bluegrass cognoscenti. All twenty-four cuts from those two LPs are included on the *The Puritan Sessions. Master Fiddler* showcases Baker's extraordinary fiddling prowess in twenty well-selected tunes recorded between 1968 and 1983 that provide a fine cross section of his repertoire. Baker's father and grandfather were also good fiddlers, and the disc includes family tunes he learned from them, like "Indian Killed a Woodcock" and "Brandywine," as well as traditional tunes he picked up from other fiddlers over the years, such as Arthur Smith's "Sugar Tree Stomp" and Tommy Magness's "Smoky Mountain Rag." Baker has also been a prolific composer, and this disc gives us a half-dozen Baker originals, including "Cross-Eyed Fiddler" and "Grassy Fiddle Blues." This is absolutely some of the finest bluegrass fiddle ever recorded. It's great to have these masterpieces all in one place and available on CD.—C.H.S.

DEWEY BALFA
★★★★★ The Balfa Brothers Play Traditional Cajun Music, Vols. 1 & 2 (Swallow SW-CD-6011) 1965, 1974, 1990
★★★★½ The Balfa Brothers: J'ai Vu Le Loup, Le Renard, et La Belette (Rounder CD 6007) 1975, 1989
★★★★ Dewey Balfa, Marc Savoy, and D. L. Menard: Under a Green Oak Tree (Arhoolie CD 312) 1976, 1989
★★★½ Cajun Legend: Dewey Balfa and Friends (Swallow CD-6063) 1991

Cajun fiddler Dewey Balfa, who died in 1992, and his brothers Will, Rodney, Harry, and Burke, were among the finest performers of traditional Cajun music ever to come out of Louisiana. They began playing together as a band in 1948 and made their first album, *The Balfa Brothers Play Traditional Cajun Music,* for Swallow in 1965. They recorded a second LP for Swallow in 1974, then entitled *The Balfa Brothers Play More Traditional Cajun Music.* Both of these classic albums are included in the two-volume Swallow CD reissue. The Rounder CD was originally released in France on the *Cezame* label in 1975. *Under a Green Oak Tree* features Dewey with two other legendary Cajun musicians with whom he did a landmark tour in 1976, accordionist (and noted accordion maker) Mark Savoy and D. L. Menard, "the Cajun Hank Williams." This historic album captures the first time the three recorded together in 1976. *Dewey Balfa and Friends* is a collection of mostly instrumental music recorded in 1986. All in all, this is some of the best contemporary traditional Cajun music on record. It's highly recommended.—C.H.S.

MOE BANDY
★★★★ Greatest Hits (Columbia CK 38315) 1982
★★ No Regrets (Curb CRBD-10600) 1988
★★ Many Mansions (Curb CRBD 10609) 1989
★★★ Greatest Hits (Curb D2-77259) 1990
★ Sings Great American Cowboy Songs (K-Tel 30232) 1991
★★ Live in Branson, MO, USA (LaserLight 12 134) 1993

In the 1970s, when the Ronnie Milsaps and John Denvers started taking charge of country radio, many saw Moe Bandy as the future of honky-tonk music as we knew it. It was tough not to root for a

singer whose debut album cover depicted
him at a tavern table, surrounded by the
wreckage from having busted a whiskey
bottle over the jukebox. Right on, Bubba.

Bandy has never had a knockout voice,
but in those days he made up for it with
good old boy charm. His preferred turf, at
the time, was the old-fashioned steel
guitar cheatin' song. Columbia's *Greatest
Hits* includes several, the best of which is
a duet with Janie Fricke called "It's a
Cheating Situation." "Barstool Mountain"
lives up to its promising title, while
"Hank Williams, You Wrote My Life" is
pretty self-explanatory. Even with his
pedestrian vocals, Bandy makes Ian
Tyson's "Someday Soon" work—though
it's such a beautifully written song
perhaps only a real clod could screw it up.
Curb's *Greatest Hits* derives from the
Reagan-Bush era and makes an interesting foil for the Columbia set. Ten to
fifteen years after raising hell in the
honky-tonks, Bandy invests "Till I'm Too
Old to Die Young" and "Back in My
Roarin' 20's" with real emotional
legitimacy. A duet with honky-tonk angel
Becky Hobbs, called "Pardon Me (Haven't
We Loved Somewhere Before)," sounds
like the couple from "It's a Cheating
Situation" meeting again on the far side
of broken homes. Whether you can
stomach "Americana" (also on *No
Regrets)* probably depends on how your
taste in country music lines up with
George Bush's.

As an A&R concept, the K-Tel disc
(Bandy singing the likes of "Cool Water"
and "Streets of Laredo") has its weird
surface appeal, but the results are
abysmal. And don't look for the *Live in
Branson* set to boost RV sales across
America.—D.C.

AARON BARKER
★ The Taste of Freedom (Atlantic 82354-
    2) 1992
Aaron Barker first made his mark as a
songwriter, writing "Baby Blue" and
"Love without End" for George Strait, but
he doesn't make much of an impression
on this first release. On the cover, the
Texas-based singer wraps himself in the
American flag à la Lee Greenwood and
serves up songs about Vietnam vets, '66
Chevys, lost dreams, and broken hearts.
If the themes sound a little tired, so does

the music. A pleasant baritone voice and
some pretty melodies can't save this
debut from being pretty mediocre.—P.Cr.

SHANE BARMBY
★½ Jukebox Symphony (Mercury 846
     976-2) 1991
Pre-fab, automated Nineties country.
Press "One Night" for Texas swing.
Punch "One and One and One" for soft-
shell honky-tonk. The whole production
sounds phoned in from the front office,
except for "A Cowboy Callin', " which
earns the half-star for its moody evoca-
tion of a lonely cowhand stranded
outside of Denver, at the end of his rope.
—D.C.

BEAUSOLEIL
★★★½ Deja Vu (Swallow CD-6080) 1990
★★★   Parlez-Nous à Boire and More
        (Arhoolie CD 322) 1981, 1984,
        1990
★★½   Bayou Boogie (Rounder CD 6015)
        1987
★★★★ Hot Chili Mama (Arhoolie 5040)
        1987
★★★★ Allons à Lafayette (Arhoolie C D
        308) 1989
★★★   Live! From the Left Coast
        (Rounder CD6035) 1989
★★★   Bayou Cadillac (Rounder CD
        6025) 1989
★★★   Cajun Conja (RNA R2 70525)
        1991
★★★★ Bayou Deluxe: The Best of Michael
        Doucet & Beausoleil (Rhino R2
        71169) 1993
Beausoleil, formed in the mid-1970s and
led by Cajun fiddler extraordinaire
Michael Doucet, is the country's hottest
and best known Cajun band. Long popular
regionally and on the folk festival circuit,
the band has achieved national attention
through appearances with mainstream
country artists such as Mary-Chapin
Carpenter and performances in the sound
tracks of motion pictures like *The Big
Easy* and *Belizaire the Cajun*. Firmly
rooted in traditional Cajun music, the
band also incorporates elements of other
contemporary forms of music.
Washington's *City Paper* perhaps said it
best: "They are to Southern Louisiana
music what Los Lobos are to Musica
Nortena and the Chieftains are to Irish
music: preservationists with a revisionist

freedom to experiment and modernize."
Deja Vu is a compilation of material from
various recordings done over the years for
Swallow and presents a good cross
section of cuts dating from 1976 to the
present. A better compilation is Rhino's
Bayou Deluxe, which presents a wider
selection of material from previous
Rounder, Arhoolie, and Rhino recordings
as well as from Swallow and includes an
informative booklet of notes. The other
discs date from the early 1980s to the
present, and all present good, solid
performances.
—C.H.S.

THE BELLAMY BROTHERS

★★★½   Greatest Hits (MCA/Curb MCAD-
        31012) 1982
★★★½   Greatest Hits, Vol. 2 (MCA/Curb
        MCAD-31013) 1986
★★★   Rebels without a Clue (MCA/Curb
        42224) 1988
★★½   Greatest Hits, Vol. 3 (MCA/Curb
        42298) 1989
★★★   Reality Check (MCA/Curb 42340)
        1990
★★★   Rollin' Thunder (Atlantic 82232)
        1991

Howard and David Bellamy are brother
harmonizers who don't sweat tradition
and who have never accepted a strict
definition of country. "Let Your Love
Flow," which crossed to the pop charts in
1976 and later was covered by Ray
Charles, defines one of the selling points
of everything to which the Bellamys ever
have lent their easygoing voices: a
distinct yet warmly familiar feel. *Greatest
Hits* also includes "If I Said You Have a
Beautiful Body Would You Hold It against
Me," which begins their career-long
appreciation of women, as well as "Sugar
Daddy" and "Get into Reggae Cowboy,"
which introduce both the Bellamys' often
cracked sense of humor, as well as their
natural affinity for rhythm, wherever it
originates.

   Rebels without a Clue, with a single
called "Big Love" (also on *Greatest Hits,
Vol. 3)* that rivals Fleetwood Mac's
record of the same name for harmonic
beauty, ably develops ideas, scenes, and
artifacts suggested by "Old Hippie," the
Bellamys' transitional 1987 country hit.
That record, on *Greatest Hits, Vol. 2,*
finds the duo trading in Seventies

hedonism for more sober reflections on
turning forty in the rock-'em-and-sock-
'em Eighties. It is a relief to hear the
Boomer Generation described by
songwriters who, unlike so many of their
rock peers, seem incapable of self-
congratulation. The second hits collection
also offers "Lie to You for Your Love,"
which delivers such brilliantly wry come-
ons ("I'm a doctor, I'm a lawyer, I'm a
movie star/I'm an astronaut, and I own
this bar") that it amounts to a comic
masterpiece. Both of the act's latest
albums retain the virtues of the Bellamys'
unique country. *Reality Check,* produced
by Emory Gordy Jr., emerges a little less
true to the Bellamys' atmospheric vibe
than does *Rollin' Thunder,* which they
produced themselves. The particular
biases of Nashville music men, though,
have never affected Bellamys' sessions
much. The duo's tuneful synthesis of the
carnal and the front-porch philosophical
is way too strong.—J.H.

MATRACA BERG

★★★★   Lying to the Moon (RCA 2056-2-R)
        1990

A clever songwriter (she wrote "That
Kind of Girl" for Patty Loveless) and an
explosive performer, Matraca Berg
debuted with a hard-headed yet open-
hearted recording that inexplicably
bombed. Berg's singing voice marries
Bonnie Raitt-style blues with conventional country; her songwriting voice, on
soaring country-rock excursions like "The
Things You Left Undone" and "Baby,
Walk On," puts her at the top of today's
Nashville writing pros.—J.G.

BYRON BERLINE

★★★½   Jumpin' the Strings (Sugar Hill SH-
        CD-3787) 1990
★★★   [Berline, Crary, Hickman] Now
        They Are Four (Sugar Hill SH-CD-
        3773) 1989
★★★   [California] Traveler (Sugar Hill
        SH-CD-3803) 1992

West Coast fiddler Byron Berline was
national old-time fiddle champion three
times before he stopped entering the
contest. He has always incorporated
western swing and Texas-style fiddling as
well as bluegrass into his playing. Berline
is also a fine composer of fiddle tunes,
and *Jumpin' the Strings* is a great

collection of twenty-one Berline originals, showcasing his fiddling at its best. Both of the other CDs feature Berline in the context of his latest superstar band (called California on the 1992 album *Traveler*), with flat-picking guitar wizard Dan Crary, John Hickman on banjo, John Moore on mandolin, and Steve Spurgin on bass, playing jazzy and progressive West Coast bluegrass.—C.H.S.

BILLY HILL

★★★½ **I Am Just a Rebel (Reprise 25915-2) 1989**

Maybe country music wasn't ready for a talented band that didn't take itself too seriously, or maybe the one-dimensional joke of the name simply sold the music short. Whatever the reason, Billy Hill only lasted through one album, which is unfortunate, for behind the silly moniker hid a solid country-rock band capable of breezy, good-time songs. "Nickel to My Name" and "Rollin' Dice" are rambunctious tunes ripe with sly wit, while "Drive on By" and "These Lonely Blues" were haunting ballads that anchored the album to solid emotional ground.

Billy Hill featured three worthy guitarists/vocalists—Dennis Robbins, John Scott Sherrill, Bob DiPiero—who had enjoyed success as songwriters. With capable rhythmic support from bassist Reno Kling and drummer Martin Parker, the band offered dynamic, good ol' boy country rock—sort of Hank Williams Jr. with less ego, better taste, and a sharper sense of humor. Robbins, who had issued a solo country album on MCA, revived his solo efforts on the Giant label after Billy Hill's demise.—M.M.

CLINT BLACK

★★★★★ **Killin' Time (RCA 9668-2-R) 1989** ▲²

★★★ **Put Yourself in My Shoes (RCA 2372-2-R) 1990** ▲²

★★★★ **The Hard Way (RCA 66003-2) 1992** ▲

★★★ **No Time to Kill (RCA 66239-2) 1993**

Though he'd been playing around his native Houston, Texas, for a few years, Clint Black seemed to come out of nowhere when his clean-cut brand of Texas country bulleted him to the top of the charts in the late Eighties. Of course,

like a lot of overnight sensations, Black had been at it for a while, gigging, writing, and home-recording demos with his guitarist/secret weapon Hayden Nicholas. After being discovered by ZZ Top manager Bill Ham, Black and band released *Killin' Time,* which yielded several #1 hits, including the title song. One of the first and best of a bumper crop of new country singers, Black admits influences that run from Ernest Tubb and Bob Wills to James Taylor and the Beatles, and his best songs (mostly co-written with Nicholas) contain equal parts Texas tradition and good old-fashioned pop hooks.

After the skyrocket success of his flawless debut, Black, perhaps understandably, sounds a little forced on *Put Yourself In My Shoes.* The title track and "One More Payment" are up to par, but songs like "Loving Blind" and "The Goodnight Loving" sound like filler. His insistence on using his own band in the studio, a cool idea the first time out, begins to hold him back on this sophomore effort. All that fame, a grueling schedule, management lawsuits, and a movie star-marriage didn't mar Black's creativity, however. His third release, *The Hard Way* (with session players onboard), is a refreshing return to form, and cuts like "When My Ship Comes In" and "A Woman Has Her Way" show that Black and Nicholas have survived all the hoopla and are still growing as songwriters.

That creative fire still burns, occasionally out of control, on Black's fourth release, *No Time to Kill.* The album's title cut almost drowns in its own cleverness, and "A Bad Goodbye," his vocal "event" with Wynonna Judd, is just a bad song. His knack for a hook remains undiminished, however, and melody and lyric come together beautifully on many of these tracks, including "Back to Back" and the ballad "Half the Man." Overall it sounds like Black might be thinking just a little too hard on some of these songs, and true to form, he describes his own dilemma perfectly on "Thinkin' Again."
—P.Cr.

NORMAN BLAKE

★★★★★ **The Norman and Nancy Blake Compact Disc (Rounder CD-11505) 1986**

★★★★½ **Slow Train through Georgia**
(Rounder CD-11526) 1987
★★★★ **[with Nancy Blake] Natasha's**
Waltz (Rounder CD-11530) 1987
★★★★½ **Blake and Rice** (Rounder CD-
0233) 1988
★★★ **[with Nancy Blake] Blind Dog**
(Rounder CD-0254) 1988
★★★★½ **Norman Blake and Tony Rice II**
(Rounder CD-0266) 1990
★★★★ **Fields of November/ Old & New**
(Flying Fish FF-004) 1992

This vastly talented flat-picker in the Doc
Watson tradition first gained attention as
a notable Nashville session pro for Bob
Dylan, Johnny Cash, Kris Kristofferson,
Joan Baez, and other country-folk stars of
the late 1960s and early 1970s. Since
embarking on his own recording career,
Blake has directed his own amazing
musical vision and dexterity toward
inspired revivalist explorations of
traditional rural American music. His
recorded repertoire is peppered with
songs by the Carter Family, Uncle Dave
Macon, Grandpa Jones, Scott Joplin, and
other down-home musical luminaries of
the past, and his original material is
composed with utter faithfulness to the
spirit of this traditional vein.

Blake's reedy voice and rustic but
meticulous flat-picking lend themselves
so naturally to the Appalachian and early
American music he favors that he's more
or less made the idiom his own. The
same can be said for his wife, Nancy (a
recording artist of stature herself), whose
mastery of the cello, fiddle, mandolin,
piccolo, mandola, and accordion has often
added vivid atmosphere and dimension to
her husband's music.

A purist and perfectionist, Blake has
seemingly never released an album before
its time. Though his accompanying
personnel often shift from one album to
the next, stylistically he never strays from
the narrow but rich musical path he
chooses to tread. *Slow Train through
Georgia* is an excellent twenty-two-track
CD collection drawn from his earliest
LPs. *Fields of November* is a no less
moving twenty-six-cut sampler that draws
from both older and newer recordings.
Norman and Nancy Blake in consort are
well represented by three Rounder CDs:
*The Norman and Nancy Blake Compact
Disc, Natasha's Waltz,* and *Blind Dog.*

These are so uniformly tasteful that it's
difficult to recommend one over the
other, though *The Norman and Nancy
Blake Compact Disc* contains the most
material—twenty-one cuts.

Blake has also recorded a couple of
fine duet albums with Tony Rice, the
celebrated newgrass guitarist: *Blake and
Rice* and *Norman Blake and Tony Rice II.*
—B.A

BLUE SKY BOYS
★★★★ **Radio Shows, Vol. 1** (Copper Creek
CCCD-0120) 1993
★★★★ **Radio Shows, Vol. 2** (Copper Creek
CCCD-0121) 1993
★★★★ **In Concert** (Rounder CD-11536)
1964

The Blue Sky Boys—Bill and Earl
Bolick—were a brother duet act from
Hickory, North Carolina, whose recordings from 1936 to 1951 included a wide
sampling of old-time country, pop, and
gospel music as well as some of the
closest and sweetest harmony singing
ever heard in American music. The Blue
Sky Boys' sparse prewar performances
consisted of only Earl's lead singing and
guitar rhythm accented by Bill's tenor
harmony and mandolin phrasing. That
mandolin—melodic, non-chorded, and
rich with tremolo—was Bill's unique
signature, and it was an indispensable
and easily recognized ingredient of their
sound. When the Bolicks resumed their
professional career in 1946 after military
service in World War II, they added a
fiddle to their performances and also
used a stand-up bass on their postwar
recordings. The essential Blue Sky Boys
sound never changed, however; the
brothers merely got better. Their early
retirement in 1951 was a tragedy for all of
those who love the sincere and unaffected
sound of parlor country music.

The Rounder CD is a remarkable
presentation of many of the songs
performed by the Bolicks at a comeback
concert at the University of Illinois on
October 17, 1964. The collection omits
Bill Bolick's spoken introductions, but it
gives us a good idea of how the brothers
sounded in live performances. Most
important, we learn that their repertoire
was broader than that preserved on
recordings. Old-time tragic and sentimental songs, such as "The Knoxville Girl,"

"In the Hills of Roane County," and "Midnight on the Stormy Deep," or gospel songs like "Whispering Hope" or "I'm Saved," prevailed, but such material was accompanied by tunes like "Quit That Tickling Me," modern country hits such as "The Last Letter," and humorous skits. The high point of the concert was Bill Bolick's resurrection of the full text of the 1890s pop standard "After the Ball."

Although their original RCA Victor and Bluebird recordings have been highly valued by fans, collectors, and students of old-time country music, the Bolicks reached their largest audiences through radio broadcasts on stations in the southeastern United States. The Copper Creek collections contain Blue Sky Boys material taken from radio transcriptions made for a couple of Jeep distributors in 1946 and 1947. The transcribed shows, complete with advertisements and comic skits, originally aired in fifteen-minute segments on radio stations in Atlanta, Macon, and Savannah, Georgia. Copper Creek has edited this material down to about forty complete songs and fiddle tunes, fragments of the group's theme song, "Are You from Dixie," a few advertisements, and some short chats between Bill Bolick and the comic character Uncle Josh, played by Earl Bolick. Except for the ads and Uncle Josh segments, the material heard here is very similar to that found on the Blue Sky Boys' Starday LP, *A Treasury of Rare Old Song Gems from the Past* (SLP 205), released several years ago. Of the forty complete songs, fully half are religious numbers like "Where We'll Never Grow Old" and "The Blood of Jesus," some of which the Bolicks sang trio style with Curly Parker. The remaining selections evenly divide between Parker's fiddle tunes and sentimental ballads like "Bury Me beneath the Willow" and "Goodbye Maggie." Such groupings are significantly different from the material found on the Blue Sky Boys' RCA and Bluebird recordings (available on CD compilations *Are You from Dixie* and *Something Got a Hold of Me*; see Various Artists), but, according to Bill Bolick, the radio songs were chosen almost exclusively from requests made by their listeners.

It is very satisfying to see this wonderful music made available again. These collections will be aesthetically pleasing to those who love the Blue Sky Boys or brother duet singing, and educational to those who want to know more about the powerful role played by radio in country music's development. —B.C.M.

JAMES BLUNDELL
★★★★ **Hand It Down (Capitol CDP 7 96247 2) 1991**

If a generation of Australian city kids could out-rock the Brits, why shouldn't a country boy from southeastern Queensland be able to teach American singer-songwriters a trick or two? Blundell sure can. *Hand It Down* suggests a blend of young Woody Guthrie and mature John Cougar Mellencamp: fine, muscular, thinking man's country-rock with lots of depth and a great, compassionate attitude. But of course it doesn't *sound* familiar at all; having never been processed in an American recording studio and having grown in the looking glass culture of Oz in the first place, this music is just a few fascinating hairs off any popular center. Blundell, too, evokes his country's presence (and its past) with a surer hand than do most singer-songwriters here, there, or anywhere. Perhaps that's because he's been closer to the land than most: he took up the music trade only because an angry bull put an end to his chosen career as a working cowboy.

His first album, *James Blundell*, went gold in Australia and attracted Capitol Nashville's interest in his second (*Hand It Down*), but not his third and best yet, *This Road*. But there's hope; word is that his fourth will be recorded and released over here, so retrospective U.S. release of the missing pieces is at least a possibility.—P.Ca.

SUZY BOGGUSS
★★★★★ **Somewhere Between (Liberty CDP 7 90237) 1989**
★★★ **Moment of Truth (Liberty CDP-7 92653-2) 1990**
★★★ **Aces (Liberty CDP 7 95847 2) 1991 ●**
★★★ **Voices in the Wind (Liberty CDP-7-98585-2) 1992**

Publicized as an educated, independent woman in control of her life and career, Suzy Bogguss has achieved commercial success with mature, only vaguely country ballads of the thoroughly modern Nashville-mainstream sort. Her kind of folkish material ("Outbound Plane," written by Nanci Griffith, is typical) fills the three albums she's recorded with Jimmy Bowen in the executive seat, and some of it is very nicely crafted. All of it shows off her wonderfully clear, capable contralto (as Chet Atkins has noted, "She is always in the tone center").

Those albums pale, however, in comparison with *Somewhere Between,* produced by singer-songwriter Wendy Waldman when Suzy was fresh in Nashville from her years working the West. Where the Bowen albums keep things cooking safely down the center of the radio friendly road, *Somewhere Between* soars off on all sorts of delightful tangents (Hank Williams's "My Sweet Love Ain't Around," several free-spirited Western songs like Patsy Montana's "I Want to Be a Cowboy's Sweetheart") while also driving a couple of stakes straight through the center of the heart. The Merle Haggard-penned title track in particular is one of the most powerful songs, and performances, to come out of Music Row in a long time. In fact, there's a creative thrill about *Somewhere Between* that's truly rare. Nashville in the Eighties didn't produce a better woman's album. Come to think of it, it still hasn't. —P.Ca.

JOHNNY BOND
★ **That Wild, Wicked, but Wonderful West (Starday SCD-147) 1987**
Western singer Johnny Bond was an important participant in the West Coast country music scene from the Forties through the Sixties. Along with performers like Tex Ritter, Merle Travis, and Wesley Tuttle, he was a regular on Southern California television shows such as "Town Hall Party." Unfortunately the sound on this Starday disc, which includes many of Bond's best-known songs, is so horribly screwed up that it's rendered virtually unlistenable; I don't know what happened in the reissue process here, but unless you are a die-hard Johnny Bond fan and can't live without this, I would pass it up. I hope

Starday will redo the CD and get it right.—C.H.S.

SIMON BONNEY
★★★★ **Forever (Mute/Elektra 9 61328-2) 1992**
Imagine a country record produced like an Ennio Morricone sound track for a Clint Eastwood western and sung by a somber rock poet like Leonard Cohen, and you'll have some idea of what to expect from Australian singer-songwriter Simon Bonney on his first stateside release. Windswept with plaintive fiddle and ghostly steel, *Forever* has an epic, *High Plains Drifter* atmosphere. But the very things that cohere so well here—the languorous, melancholy cadences; the big, echoing guitars; and the brooding over love gone hopelessly wrong—all but guarantee that you won't hear this record wafting out of pickup trucks or convenience markets. Does that mean it's no good? Well, Dwight Yoakam and "Twin Peaks" ' David Lynch would probably like it; Ricky Van Shelton and George Bush probably wouldn't. Is it country? I devoutly hope so.—P.K.

BOONE CREEK
★★★★ **One Way Track (Sugar Hill SH-CD-3701) 1977, 1991**
Ricky Skaggs put together Boone Creek in 1976. He was in his early twenties, and this was his first try at leading a bluegrass band after working for Ralph Stanley, the Country Gentlemen, and J. D. Crowe. They made two albums before Skaggs moved on to Emmylou Harris's Hot Band and began his rise to country stardom. *One Way Track* is a reissue of Boone Creek's second album, originally released after the group had disbanded. Three new cuts, taken from a television appearance, have been added to the original album; of these, two suffer from too much bass guitar in the mix. Generally, though, the album is a fine example of the bluegrass that Skaggs and his young contemporaries were playing in 1977, with tight vocal duets, trios, and quartets. Most of the songs come from the classic repertoire of bluegrass pioneers like Bill Monroe and Flatt & Scruggs. With Skaggs on mandolin and fiddle, Jerry Douglas on dobro, and Terry Baucom on banjo, Boone Creek turns the

old fiddle tune "Sally Gooden" into an instrumental tour de force.—N.V.R.

LARRY BOONE

★★   One Way to Go (Columbia CK 47050) 1991
★★★½   Get in Line (Columbia CK 48968) 1993

Larry Boone—who recorded three albums on Mercury, all now out of print, prior to his Columbia debut—has a pinched voice, curt delivery, and unadorned musical style that makes *One Way to Go* sound as though it was beamed in from another era. It would be nice to claim that his career woes demonstrate country radio's lack of interest in genuinely traditional music. More honestly, though, it demonstrates a less radical truth: purism is often boring. *Get in Line* is a few degrees rougher, as you'd guess from titles like "Her Only Bad Habit Is Me" and "Daddy's Honky Tonk Heart" (how did Hank Jr. miss this song?). Co-produced by Don Cook, who also works with Brooks & Dunn, the album recasts Boone in the manly blue-collar mode of that duo, and there is even a reference to "Boot Scootin' Boogie" on the title track, a shameless sop to the current vogue for line dancing. —R.T.

BOY HOWDY

★★   Welcome to Howdywood (Curb D2-77562) 1992

Anyone who questions the commercial viability of the country emanating from L.A. should look to Boy Howdy for evidence of a California band as polished, professional, and shallow as any dolloped out from Nashville. Fronted by bassist-singer-songwriter Jeffrey Steele, Boy Howdy's debut album kicks and croons with a calculated abandon sure to send shivers of excitement through the Sawyer Brown audience. As proof that they're wiggy cats, Boy Howdy offers the Kinks' "You Really Got Me" undone as cowpunk polka. Far out, dudes!—M.H.

JOHN BRANNEN

★½   John Brannen (Mercury 314-514 436-2) 1993

Occasionally Brannen's rocking attitude brings to mind Joe Ely, though his self-penned romantic material—strolling the gamut from A to B—is considerably more pedestrian. And too often his straining yelp recalls that of David Byrne, the singer for that arty rock band Talking Heads. Clearly, what's needed here is remedial instruction. Set 'em up, Joe, and play "Walkin' the Floor."—P.K.

BRANSON BROTHERS

★★   Heartmender (Warner Bros. 9 26979) 1992

These four harmonizing non-brothers (all hailing from Branson, Missouri) have a slick look and sound: matching black leather jackets and bola ties, an easy-stepping pop-twang blend, kind of like the Four Preps of contemporary country. But ultimately *Heartmender* is just another batch of undistinguished hard-workin', bad-lovin' songs, leading off with a drippy ode to the good little wife, "I Make the Livin' (She Makes the Livin' Worthwhile)."—K.S.

BROOKS & DUNN

★★★   Brand New Man (Arista 18658-2) 1991 ▲[3]
★★   Hard Workin' Man (Arista 18716-4) 1993 ▲

Singer-songwriters Kix Brooks and Ronnie Dunn's debut was an instant smash, yielding five hit singles and a 1992 Vocal Duo of the Year from the Country Music Association. They make pithy, macho-man country-rock that's surprisingly generous to the women in their lives ("I'm Still No Good," "Still in Love with You," "Lost and Found"). However, their sophomore effort, *Hard Workin' Man,* revealed a drop-off in the quality of the material, with an over-reliance on rock influences such as Creedence Clearwater Revival and the Eagles ("Mexican Minutes," "We'll Burn That Bridge," "Rock My World [Little Country Girl]").—K.T.

GARTH BROOKS

★★★★   Garth Brooks (Capitol 90897) 1989 ▲[4]
★★★★★ No Fences (Capitol 93866) 1990 ▲[10]
★★★★   Ropin' the Wind (Capitol Nashville 96330) 1991 ▲[9]
★★★   Beyond the Season (Liberty 98742) 1992 ▲[2]
★★★★   The Chase (Liberty 98743) 1992 ▲[5]

★★★★½ **In Pieces (Liberty 80857) 1993**
Garth Brooks was a historical inevitability: a country singer who grew up in the Seventies, an odd and uncertain decade when country radio played gentle pop-rock like Dan Fogelberg and rock stations played country-influenced bands like the Eagles. The barriers between country and rock briefly disappeared, which left a lasting impression on Brooks. Listen carefully to his records and you'll hear a textbook of Seventies pop: the confessional lyrics of Fogelberg and James Taylor, the mellow Colorado ease of Poco and Firefall, the fluid melodicism of Fleetwood Mac and Bread, and the thick guitar pomp of Kansas and Boston.

At times, his influences are obvious: Brooks's sweet, expansive tenor mimics George Strait on "Not Counting You," the swing number that opens his first album. There's a debt to George Jones on "I've Got a Good Thing Going," and Dan Fogelberg's delicately enunciated tremble stamps "The River" and "Unanswered Prayers." But the main components of Brooks's success—his warm singing, spacious and relaxed arrangements, and Allen Reynolds's sharply defined productions—are linked by an instinct for synthesis. Brooks sold more than 30 million records in his first four years, obliterating Nashville's standards of success, by unifying disparate musical elements and adding just enough Oklahoma twang to qualify as country without alienating pop fans.

Brooks seemed like one more hat act until the single releases of "If Tomorrow Never Comes" and "The Dance," two intensely anxious ballads that draw wisdom from heartache. After the latter song became Brooks's signature, he expanded his gift for epic metaphors on *No Fences.* Whether writing or choosing songs, Brooks takes familiar imagery— ships at sea, games of cards, burning bridges—and weaves subtle plot twists into his enraptured delivery. "The Thunder Rolls," a cheating song Brooks admitted was inspired by his own infidelity, ends uncertainly, with the moment of discovery, and "Unanswered Prayers" suggests that heartache is part of a divine plan. The first two records also balance solemnity with the witty small-town plaint "Nobody Gets Off in This

Town" ("Utility bill's the only thing that gets high/I'd go for a drink but this county is dry"), the sexy honky-tonk joy of Dennis Robbins's "Two of a Kind, Workin' on a Full House," and the besotted barroom singalong "Friends in Low Places."

After that, Brooks began to acknowledge the weight of superstardom. "Folks call me a maverick," he declares to start *Ropin' the Wind,* and the same self-consciousness results in extremes like "Papa Loved Mama," an outrageous honky-tonk murder yarn, and the Southern funk of "Rodeo." (Every album except *Beyond the Season,* a Christmas collection, includes a rodeo/cowboy song testifying to the addictiveness of roping and riding. The repetition is uncharacteristic and tiresome.) A cover of Billy Joel's "Shameless" furnishes an apt credo for Brooks's sense of grandiose drama and also clearly illustrates his musical technique: by transposing the opening melody from synthesizer to steel guitar and the middle solo to slide guitar, he transforms a pop ballad into contemporary country music.

The Chase, on the other hand, embraces responsibility in the form of social consciousness. "We Shall Be Free" is a radically progressive song which evokes a church setting (via organ and choir) to plead for racial and sexual tolerance; during a television interview, Brooks declared that his sister, the bassist in his road band, is a lesbian. And the album ends with Tony Arata's "Face to Face," which is as instructive and inspirational as a self-help pamphlet, and reveals an oracular impulse that also characterizes "The River" ("I'll never reach my destination if I never try/So I will sail my vessel 'til the river runs dry"). While his singing was always distinguished by a tenderness that risked effeminacy, *The Chase* expands his sensitivity to women via the implied date rape in "Face to Face," the lonely widow woman who seduces a virgin teenager in "That Summer," and the neglected wife in "Somewhere Other Than the Night" who greets her husband wearing only an apron. The commitment to adult themes also yields "Learning to Live Again," which details a divorcé (or maybe a widower) on a blind date, and refuses the comfort of a happy ending.

By pairing Patsy Cline's "Walking after Midnight" with Little Feat's "Dixie Chicken" in the middle of the album, Brooks formally declares the breadth of his ambition. At times, he's seemed overburdened by the responsibilities of fame. But to borrow one of his favorite metaphors, *The Chase* finds him still riding into unexplored territory—only "Night Rider's Lament," the requisite rodeo song, is predictable—and trying to expand his artistry to match the dimensions of his popularity.

The Chase sold more than five million copies, enough to make Sawyer Brown weep enviously. But compared to his previous albums, *The Chase* was still "a failure in the retail world," according to Brooks. He retooled on *In Pieces* by tilting the balance towards more raucous material. On the first single, "Ain't Going Down (Til the Sun Comes Up)," he drifts farther than ever from the boundaries of country. Chris Leuzinger's guitar introduction states a clear debt to Chuck Berry, while the lyrics about teenage defiance and lust, and Brooks's rollicking phrasing, tip the hat to "Maybelline." Except for Hank Jr., no country artist sings about the lure of sex as compulsively as Brooks, so it's no surprise to find backseat escapades recurring in "The Night Will Only Know." But what a puzzling song it is: one of five lyrics co-written by Brooks, it recasts the plot of "Long Black Veil" in the form of two married philanderers who succumb to "the fire down below" (a Bob Seger song title), witness a murder during their passion, but assume the burden of guilty silence to hide their unfaithfulness. With an awkward rhyme scheme and ominous descending guitar chords exacerbated by a halting martial beat, surpassing even the melodramatic overkill of "The Thunder Rolls," it invents a new genre: country-metal-artsong.

"Standing outside the Fire," a glorification of unrestrained emotionalism, will long stand as Brooks's most vibrant personal manifesto ("There's this love that is burning deep in my soul/ Constantly yearning to get out of control"). And elswhere, he incorporates new tricks, obviously borrowed from other sources, yet always given a personal twist.

A swinging tale of family, death, marriage, and romantic caprice, Tony Arata's "Kickin' and Screamin'" is Lyle Lovett without the detached narration, while "Callin' Baton Rouge" employs the New Grass Revival's string and harmony expertise. Brooks's singing reaches a new peak throughout the album, from the bluesy curls he inserts into "One Night a Day" to the breathless rhymes of "Ain't Going Down." The rhythmic twists of "American Honky-Tonk Bar Association" yield his most deft vocal since"Friends in Low Places," but on the heels of "We Shall Be Free," it's disappointing to hear Brooks celebrating blue-collar pride at the expense of "all of those standing in a welfare line," which is the kind of bluster best left to denim demagogues like Aaron Tippin. Still, with its expert pacing, distinctive arrangements, and consistent immersion in various forms of the blues, *In Pieces* shows how much Brooks and his recording team have learned about their craft —R.T.

KAREN BROOKS & RANDY SHARP
★★★ **That's Another Story (Mercury SACD 487) 1992**

These two have worked together many times, notably on Karen Brooks's solo efforts on Warner Bros. Records during the mid-1980s. Seek out her debut *Walk On* LP from 1982; it's one of the definitive female country-rock collections. In addition to showcasing the Orbison-like crescendos in Brooks's vocal style, it introduced the world to Sharp as the composer of the richly melodic "New Way Out" and "If That's What You're Thinking." He's also all over the album as a harmony singer deluxe.

After winning the Academy of Country Music's Best New Female Vocalist of 1983 prize, cowgirl Brooks had a bumpy ride that tossed her into the sawdust by the end of the decade. She reteamed with her former backup writer and singer on this comeback effort. Do not be misled by the billing: it is not a duet album. There are only two true duets. The rest are solo performances, split evenly between the two artists. Personality packed babbling Brooks steals the show with "Baby I'm the One"—the number includes country's first female rap. —R.K.O.

THE BROTHER BOYS
★★★　Plow (Sugar Hill CD-3805) 1992
Brother Boys Eugene Wolf and Eddie Lynn Snodderly call this "new hillbilly music," and it has overtones of the classic brother duets like the Delmores and the Louvins. Fine back-up and engaging original songs, produced by dobro ace Jerry Douglas.—C.K.W.

ALISON BROWN
★★★★　Simple Pleasures (Vanguard VHD 79459) 1990
★★★★　Twilight Motel (Vanguard VHD 79465) 1992
When Earl Scruggs first came to the attention of country audiences back in the mid-Forties, much was made of the fact that he was the first serious musician to reach stardom on the banjo, that before him, players on the instrument were comedians. Uncle Dave Macon praised Scruggs's musicianship but complained that he wasn't a damn bit funny. Likewise, until Alison Brown came along the best-known women banjo players in country music were comediennes. Like Scruggs, Brown is a serious picker who has been playing since childhood. An early partner was Nashville Bluegrass Band fiddler Stuart Duncan, who's heard on some cuts of *Twilight Motel*, her second album, and Brown was a member of Alison Krauss's band Union Station from 1989 to 1991. Interviews and promotional literature make much of her Harvard degree and her work as an investment banker, but that shouldn't obscure the fact that she has much to say musically. Her banjo chops are impressive, but disciplined; like Bela Fleck, who started in bluegrass and has now moved to jazz, she does some very sophisticated stuff on the ol' five.

On the newer of Brown's two albums, *Twilight Motel*, all of the tunes but one are her own. They range in style and sound from the jazzy "Blue Marlin," with its flute and piano; through "Saint Geneviève," a classical string quartet banjo based on a Buxtehude piece, "Gods of Brazil," a rhythmic number that includes steel pans; "Pelican Bay," a fast waltz with Tony Rice and producer Mike Marshall helping to give "new acoustic spin"; "Chicken Road," an old-time sounding duet with Mark Schatz's clawhammer banjo; and, to show that she can pick straight-ahead driving bluegrass, there's "Shoot the Dog." New acoustic music is at the center of her style; her first album, *Simple Pleasures,* was produced by the leading exponent of that style, David Grisman, and, with all of its contents composed by Brown, it has some of the same mix of textures as the newer album, although it tends to show the hand of the producer a bit more.

If you're looking for down-home versions of bluegrass standards from this banjoist, you'll be disappointed. Of course she can pick that stuff, but her direction on these two very nice albums is more in tune with her California raisin', with liberal touches of jazz, new acoustic, and world-music influences. These are good CDs to unwind with at the end of a working day.—N.V.R.

JIM ED BROWN & HELEN CORNELIUS
★★　Greatest Hits (RCA 55979-2) 1992
The title of this one should really be *Greatest Hit,* singular, since "I Don't Want to Have to Marry You" is the only song by Jim Ed and Helen that could accurately be described as either a hit, or, charitably, great. It's a pretty cool track, highly suggestive of Conway & Loretta (on a so-so recording day), but the others. . . .

Well, imagine Helen, multi-tracked to the point of sounding a lot more like Abba than Melba (Montgomery, that is: *the* female country duet partner), putting across the deathless Dean Dillon line: "At work they're thinking you're down with a bug/But all you've caught is a case of my love." And there's lots more true romance where that came from. Seven whole tracks here, in all. For fans only. —P.Ca.

MARTY BROWN
★★★★　High and Dry (MCA MCAD-10330) 1991
★★★★　Wild Kentucky Skies (MCA MCAD-10672) 1993
Many neotraditionalist country singers pay lip service to ol' Hank. Marty Brown, honky-tonking like a man possessed, sounds like it's Hank's own voice issuing from his lips. This is the guy, you may recall, who made his national debut in a

1991 Nashville segment on CBS-TV's "48 Hours"—a single-minded hayseed from Maceo, Kentucky, who slept on the streets of Music Row until someone finally listened. His career would be a freaky joke if his records weren't so good.

Produced by Richard Bennett and Tony Brown, the guys behind Steve Earle's and Marty Stuart's best work, Brown's albums take the basics of 1950s-style country music and prove that the lyrical themes (barrooms and broken hearts) and the basic sound (fiddle and steel) can be timeless, if handled right. Honestly, these songs never sound old; they just sound sincere. Though Marty loves to play Hank—the bouncy "Don't Worry Baby" from *High and Dry* brings "Hey Good Lookin'" right up to date— he's also capable of launching into the soaring Everly-esque harmony of "Every Now and Then." Both those songs appear on the solid debut. *Wild Kentucky Skies* may be even better. It's certainly more daring, attempting an honest-to-God chilling hillbilly death ballad ("She's Gone") and a lushly orchestrated ballad ("Wild Kentucky Skies") right alongside the homages to Hank and the Everlys that Brown keeps pulling off with unstudied ease. For added value, he even works against your expectations for the Nashville playbook. Just check out "Let's Begin Again," where Marty earnestly pleads, "Break his heart and let's begin again." When was the last time you heard a mean-spirited, selfish country love song on the radio?

Well, you may still have to wait. Gawky Marty can't match Hank's fabled sexual charisma, so he's got an uphill battle against neotraditionalist studs like Randy Travis, Alan Jackson, and Clint Black. In fact, given the exigencies of the marketplace, in years to come Marty will probably be known chiefly as a songwriter. But judged by these records alone, Marty's setting the pace for guys working within the sawdust hashmarks that Hank and Lefty drew.—P.K.

T. GRAHAM BROWN
★★½ **I Tell It Like It Used to Be** (Liberty C21K-46901) 1986
★★½ **Brilliant Conversationalist** (Liberty C21K-46773) 1987

★★½ **Come As You Were** (Capitol CDP 7 48621 2) 1988
★★½ **Bumper to Bumper** (Liberty C21S-91780) 1990
★★★ **Greatest Hits** (Liberty C21S-94166) 1990
★★½ **You Can't Take It with You** (Liberty C21S-93547) 1991
★★★ **The Best of T. Graham Brown** (Liberty C21Y-97520) 1992

T. Graham Brown is a flashy showman and an occasionally compelling vocalist whose serviceable but undistinguished Southern "beach music" (read: rhythm & blues) style has more good-timey grit and growl than it does soul. He's a countrified Joe Cocker who quite conceivably got in over his head when he rose past the level of bar bands.

On *I Tell It Like It Used to Be,* his debut album, Brown and producer Bud Logan struggled against uneven material and a haphazard sense of direction as they strove to package Brown for the country mainstream. Brown's subsequent albums were competent enough, but all seemed to run together and consistently missed finding a formula that might transform his over-stylized blue-eyed soul into anything that was more than vaguely compelling. Though Brown, thus far, has hardly had enough hits to fill a greatest hits compilation, that didn't stop Capitol (now Liberty) from releasing one.—B.A.

JANN BROWNE
★★★ **Tell Me Why** (Curb D2-77251) 1990
★★★★ **It Only Hurts When I Laugh** (Curb D2-77451) 1991

Try to imagine a singer with Emmylou Harris's delicate phrasing brimming with Webb Pierce's low-down, honky-tonk spunkiness, and you might approximate the allure of this underrated performer. *Tell Me Why* is the more hard-core country of these two efforts—"I Forgot More" features a duet with Wanda Jackson, and there's a strong bluegrass influence to be heard on "Lovebird." As a bid to expand her audience in 1991, however, *It Only Hurts* is even stronger, a collection that permits rock & roll backbeats to propel tunes like "Blue Heart in Memphis" and "I Don't Do Floors." *It Only Hurts* has already taken on the air of a neglected classic—mixing originals with shrewd covers ranging from Ray Price ("My Shoes Keep Walking Back to You") to John Hiatt ("Where Nobody Knows My Name"), there's not a weak song in the bunch, and they're sung with a tearful passion wiped dry by astringent wit.—K.T.

SONNY BURGESS

★★★★ We Wanna Boogie (Rounder CDSS 36) 1990
★★★ [with Dave Alvin] Tennessee Border (HighTone HCD 8038) 1992

On one level, Sonny Burgess sounds like the guy who gets drunk at a convention and barges up to sing with the band, but, for all the delicate shadings his voice lacks, it's a wonderful rock & roll instrument. Some of his Sun records were among the rawest on a label never noted for being slick, and the best of them are on We Wanna Boogie. Burgess has been dubbed a rockabilly, but, in truth, there's very little 'billy in his style. A roadhouse rock & roll album cut with Dave Alvin in 1992 showed that at age sixty Burgess still has the fire in his belly, but with a playing time of less than half-an-hour, it's hardly the bargain of the year.—C.E.

BILLY BURNETTE

★★ Coming Home (Capricorn 42007) 1993

Best-known as a rock & roll songwriter and a member of the last incarnation of Fleetwood Mac, Burnette used his 1993 debut as a vehicle to establish himself in the country market. Which is fair enough, considering that he's the son of rockabilly cat Dorsey Burnette. So it truly is a homecoming of sorts. Much of Coming Home stands as acceptable if not particularly challenging country-rock; its top tunes, like "Tangled Up in Texas," suggest that Burnette's visions may be more off-beat and interesting than the self-consciously straightforward ones that fill this disc.—J.G.

TRACY BYRD

★★★ Tracy Byrd (MCA MCAD-10649) 1993

Tracy Byrd has managed the nigh unthinkable in 1993: a neo-honky-tonk debut that still commands attention after all these years of unsortable big hats and boyish grins. A product of the Beaumont, Texas, club stages, Byrd's debt to George Strait is pronounced, but not oppressive. His "Back in the Swing of Things" has the right devil-may-care dance hall touch, while the lyrically understated "Why" returns dignity to a much-maligned (and nearly extinct) honky-tonk theme: got drunk and cheated. Byrd's cover of "Someone to Give My Love To," a former Top Five power ballad for Johnny Paycheck, is an inspired A&R choice. Byrd leans into the song as if he's been spinning the Paycheck 45 at home for years. Nothing is so rare among young country artists as plain sincerity.—D.C.

THE BYRDS

★★★½ Sweetheart of the Rodeo (Columbia CK09670) 1968

Sweetheart of the Rodeo was not the Byrds' first flight from folk-rock to country. Three years before, in 1965, they'd cut the Porter Wagoner hit, "Satisfied Mind." But it wasn't until Gram Parsons signed up and joined forces with fellow country fan Chris Hillman that the Byrds went Nudie, getting good and rhinestoned, and took off for Nashville to begin recording Sweetheart. The album is patchwork, some of it cut in Music City; the rest, and the mix, done in Hollywood. Legal hassles over Parsons's contract (he'd been signed to Lee Hazlewood's label) inspired Columbia to overdub Roger McGuinn on most of Parsons's lead vocals. The result: an erratic rodeo with some brilliant moments, in Parsons's evocative "Hickory Wind" and plaintive "You're Still on My Mind," Bob Dylan's "You Ain't Going Nowhere," and the Louvin Brothers' "The Christian Life," on which McGuinn straps on his best Southern accent. Overall, the Byrds, with considerable help from Nashville session players, are true to roots country, and the album stands as a landmark in the history of country-rock. But for the best version of Sweetheart, as well as the best overview of the band's entire career in rock & roll, invest in The Byrds, the four-CD set issued in 1990 by Columbia/Legacy, in which Parsons's vocals are restored, along with several out-takes.—B. F.-T.

THE CACTUS BROTHERS
★★★½ **The Cactus Brothers (Liberty 3217) 1993**

The Cactus Brothers willingly present a few prickly musical challenges. Can old-time string band music be electrified and psychedelicized? Can a bunch of ragged, long-haired stoners blend Scotch-Irish reels, sweet waltzes, bombastic country-rock, sentimental swing, and spaced out acoustic instrumentals that sound like Joe Venuti sitting in with the Grateful Dead?

For the most part, this motley crew pulls off its ambitiously eclectic musical juggling act, mostly because of its enthusiastic spirit and partly because of the sheer gall of it all. The Cacti originally began as a side project of Walk the West, a Nashville-based roots-rock band that released an under-appreciated album in 1986 on Capitol Records. Singer-guitarist Paul Kirby, guitarist-banjoist Will Golemon, bassist John Golemon, fiddler Tramp, and drummer David Kennedy began performing acoustic, unhinged hoedowns with dulcimer wizard David Schnaufer and dobro-pedal steel player Sam Poland. Eventually, the two bands melded, with the Cactus theme providing the guiding light.

The album celebrates the band's diversity. The cover of "Sixteen Tons" is swaggering and forcefully sinister, while "Devil Wind" opens with a guitar line that recalls the Doors' "Love Her Madly" before vamping into something hauntingly mystical. On the other side, there are dulcet waltzes ("Our Love," "Bubba, Bubba"), a traditional instrumental ("Fisher's Hornpipe"), and songs that blend the modern and traditional as seamlessly as Ricky Skaggs at his best ("Crazy Heart").—M.M.

TOY CALDWELL
★★½ **Toy Caldwell (Cabin Fever Music 9012) 1992**

On this solo album, the late singer-guitarist from the Marshall Tucker Band restages all the blues and country styles that made Southern rock groove and kick during in the Seventies. With his songs now mentioning Steven King novels and women who hide behind their answering machines, Caldwell tries to keep his beloved genre current. Unfortunately, the songwriting lacks the focused purpose of Caldwell's voice, an alternately easy going and brusque instrument that was clearly in no need of renewal on this, its last outing.—J.H.

GLEN CAMPBELL
★★★★★ **The Very Best of Glen Campbell (Capitol CDP 7 46483 2) 1987**

★★★ Greatest Country Hits (Curb/
Capitol Nashville D2-77362)
1990
★★★ Classic Collections (Capitol
Nashville CDP 7 94165 2) 1990
★★★ Walkin' in the Sun (Capitol
Nashville CDP 7 93884 2) 1990
★★★★ All-Time Favorites (Pair/CEMA
PCD-2-1089) 1992
★★★ Best of the Early Years (Curb/
CEMA D21K-77441) 1991
★★ Country Gold (Liberty C21Y-
94164) 1991
★★★ Still Within the Sound of My
Voice (MCA MCAD-42009) 1987
★★★ Light Years (MCA MCAD-42210)
1988
★★★ Letter to Home (Atlantic 82214-
2) 1991
★★ Old Home Town (Atlantic 82215-
2) 1991
★★★½ Merry Christmas (Liberty C21K-
96383) 1991
★★★ Somebody Like That (Liberty
DPRO 79354) 1993

Campbell has always worked that
perilous middle ground between country
and pop music—and with considerable
skill and effectiveness. From the early
Sixties through the mid-Seventies, he
appeared regularly on the pop charts—
although seldom quite as prominently as
he did on the country rankings, which he
continues to inhabit. A creamy smooth
balladeer and skilled guitarist, the
Arkansas native introduced mainstream
America to a variety of country music and
country music stars (including John
Hartford, Jerry Reed, and Carl Jackson)
in the late Sixties and early Seventies
through his popular CBS-TV show, "The
Glen Campbell Goodtime Hour." The
various greatest hits collections listed
here embrace not just the most popular
but also the artistically best of his work,
notably "Gentle on My Mind" (his
signature hit of 1967), "By the Time I
Get to Phoenix," "Galveston," "Wichita
Lineman," and "Rhinestone Cowboy."
Although the *All-Time Favorites* collection, with sixteen cuts, has one more song
than *The Very Best of Glen Campbell*, the
latter has fewer covers of other singers'
hits. Also worth a listen: the comfortably
traditional *Merry Christmas* and *Light
Years*, which is made up primarily of
Jimmy Webb compositions. —E.M.

STACY DEAN CAMPBELL
★★★ Lonesome Wins Again (Columbia CK
47872) 1992

Nashville's answer to ominous, doomy
rock & roll crooner Chris Isaak, Stacy
Dean Campbell is steeped in
neotraditionalism. Produced by Judds
helmsman Brent Maher, Campbell's
straightforward debut CD is modest and
spacious, rarely straying from comfortable
midtempo settings that showcase
Campbell's sweet, elegant vocals. When
he ups the tempo a bit, as on "Rosalee,"
Campbell is most convincing. But it'll
take more energetic songs and performances to make Campbell a convincing
comer.—J.G.

PAULETTE CARLSON
★★★ Love Goes On (Liberty C21S-97711)
1992

Carlson is an intriguing contradiction.
Perhaps the most ultrafeminine of
contemporary country singers, she has a
rose-petals-on-the-wind fragility in her
style. Yet her lyrics and overall musical
attitude have been consistently feisty and
assertive. As the fiery lead vocalist of
Highway 101 she had sass and country-
rock spunk.
   Her solo debut maintained her chin-
out, modern-woman image with such
tough-minded tunes as "I'll Start with
You," "Not with My Heart You Don't,"
and "The Chain Just Broke." But
something was missing. Producer Jimmy
Bowen smoothed out Carlson's rough
edges and took the bite out of her sound.
So instead of a tigress's snarl we got a
kitten's purr.—R.K.O.

MARY-CHAPIN CARPENTER
★★★ Hometown Girl (Columbia CK
40758) 1987
★★★★ State of the Heart (Columbia CK
44228) 1989
★★★★ Shooting Straight in the Dark
(Columbia CK 46077) 1990 ●
★★★★ Come On Come On (Columbia CK
48881) 1992 ▲

Country-folk songwriter and singer Mary-
Chapin Carpenter is four records into a
contradictory career. Skeptics note how
this one-time D.C. coffeehouse regular
clings progressively tighter to conventional Nashville methods and arrangements as each new record appears. But
those who listen to her that way miss

how her performances get stronger and wilder with each CD. Carpenter's debut record, her most overtly folk-oriented and singer-songwriterly, is a bit tentative, but every record since then has offered strong numbers that artfully mix Carpenter's folk instincts with country come-ons, forcefully moving forward. Especially worthwhile tracks include "Never Had It So Good" (from *State of the Heart*), *Shooting Straight in the Dark*'s "Middle Ground" and "You Win Again" (a tough original, owing nothing to the Hank Williams song), and "Passionate Kisses" (an ace, multilayered Lucinda Williams cover on *Come On Come On*). Her inevitable singles collection will be a knockout set. And on "I Feel Lucky," a sweet laugh from *Come On Come On*, she marries so many sundry influences— blues, Fats Domino style R&B, sassy country—that one comes away convinced that she's capable of resolving any contradiction.—J.G.

THE CARTER FAMILY
★★★★★ **Country Music Hall of Fame (MCA MCAD-10088) 1991**
★★★★ **Clinch Mountain Treasures (County CCS CD 112) 1991**
★★★ **Diamonds in the Rough (Copper Creek CD 107) 1989**

Their career began without fanfare, in 1927, when A. P. Carter drove all day over rough mountain roads to get to a field recording session the Victor Talking Machine Company had set up in Bristol, Tennessee. From those humble beginnings the original Carter Family went on to one of the most influential recording careers in country music history. From 1927 until their break-up in 1943, the Carters recorded their folk and folk-like songs for every major company, eventually amassing some 250 sides. A. P.'s ability to find and rewrite old songs, his wife Sara's high, forceful singing, and sister-in-law Maybelle Carter's guitar style made them the first really successful vocal group in county music—and also started a dynasty that still continues today in the persons of singers like June Carter Cash and Carlene Carter.

Few of the Carters' original Victor records (now controlled by RCA) are available on CD; a pair of gospel tunes show up on the anthology *Something Got a Hold of Me* (see Various Artists section).

More important is the group's entire first session for Ralph Peer, done in Bristol in 1927, which is available on the two-CD set *The Bristol Sessions* (also in Various Artists). Here, in their original versions, are "Bury Me under the Weeping Willow" and "The Storms Are on the Ocean," two songs that would become country standards. Here too is Sara Carter's incredible vocal tour de force "Single Girl, Married Girl," the piece that, in Sara's words, "tipped it off" and gave the trio their first immediate hit.

Their years with Decca, 1936-38, which many fans consider to have produced their most aesthetically satisfying records, are sampled in the *Country Music Hall of Fame* set. Here are originals of pieces that became bluegrass and country standards: "You Are My Flower," "Hello Stranger," "My Dixie Darling," and "Coal Miner's Blues." Richly detailed notes and a good discography complement the music in this CD. An odd but appealing collection is *Clinch Mountain Treasures*, which includes the entire final session the group did for the Okeh label in 1940. Here is the family near the end of their career, but in fine form and with a surprisingly modern sound. There are no seminal hits here, but you will find favorites like "Black Jack David," "Bear Creek Blues," and "Meeting in the Air." Notes by Bill Clifton, a close friend of A. P. Carter, add to the set.

About the only place to hear other early Carter classics, in the absence of any serious RCA Victor reissue, is *Diamonds in the Rough*. Taken from "border radio" transcriptions done in 1941, marred by inferior sound and shortened performances, the set is still the only place to hear the Carters do the songs that defined their music, such as "Little Moses," "Engine 143," and the album's title song.—C.K.W.

CARLENE CARTER
★★★★★ **I Fell in Love (Reprise 9 26139-2) 1990**
★★★★★ **Little Love Letters (Giant 9 24499-2) 1993**

After almost hitting it time after time— coming closest with *Musical Shapes* in 1980—Carlene just flat nailed it to the floor with *I Fell in Love*, fulfilling the promise of her bloodlines (she's Carl

Smith and June Carter's daughter) and, if anything, exceeding the expectations of fans and critics alike. She'd come back from some bad personal places to do this work (her first country effort after spending a decade in London), and that gave the album's quality extra value. *I Fell in Love* is a beautiful collection, as wisely reflective (the nostalgic "Me and the Wildwood Rose," the wondrous "Guardian Angel") as it's good-spirited and energized ("Come on Back," "Goodnight Dallas," the title track), and stylistically there's nothing quite like it. Working in L.A., Carlene and producer Howie Epstein (Tom Petty's bass player) built a wonderfully lush, moving, Carter-Family-meets-the-Bangles kind of sound. And the quality of her songwriting throughout is topnotch.

After *I Fell in Love,* there was a silence from Carlene which grew awkward, then ominous (was it going to be another decade?), but not to worry: just before this book went to press, *Little Love Letters* was released on the Giant label. The wait was worth it. Every bit as thoughtfully conceived and creatively produced as *I Fell in Love* (again in Hollywood with Howie Epstein), it's pure Carlene: such great good-humored bop ("Every Little Thing," "I Love You Cause I Want To"), such beautiful soul ("Unbreakable Heart," the lovely "World of Miracles"). Now all we need is a CD reissue of *Musical Shapes*. At the very least.—P.Ca.

LIONEL CARTWRIGHT

★★★ Lionel Cartwright (MCA MCAD-42276) 1989
★★ I Watched It on the Radio (MCA MCAD-42336) 1990
★★ Chasin' the Sun (MCA MCAD-10307) 1991

Cartwright arrived with the same young country class of '89 that produced Garth Brooks, Clint Black, Travis Tritt, and Alan Jackson. His early singles "Like Father Like Son" and "Give Me His Last Chance," both from the debut disc, got heavy rotation and gave every indication that Cartwright would accompany his classmates into the precious metal sales bracket. From the opening cut, *Lionel Cartwright* crackles with the fire of the singer's exuberant vocals—pitched halfway between

Appalachia and Santa Monica—and his multi-instrumental musicianship. The coproduction by Tony Brown and Telecaster-cowboy extraordinaire Steuart Smith couldn't be more sympathetic. If anything, the disc suffers from Smith's humility. A few more of his vigorous chops could have livened the intermittent dead spots where Cartwright's style drifts popward.

Strangely, Cartwright has yet to deliver on the promise of his debut—commercially or artistically. *I Watched It on the Radio* and *Chasin' the Sun* are not, on the surface, noticeably inferior to the first album. But there's an energy drain that may stem from Cartwright's faith in his pen. He writes most of his own material, and though he has a musician's ear for interesting changes, he's a distressingly uninspired lyricist. Many of his best melodies (*I Watched It on the Radio*'s "Playing It Safe," for instance) collapse under the weight of piled platitudes.—D.C.

JOHNNY CASH

★★★★★ Sun Years (Rhino R270950) 1990
★★★★★ The Fabulous Johnny Cash (CBS Special Products A-8122) 1959
★★★★ Ride This Train (Sony Special Products A-8255) 1960
★★★★ Greatest Hits, Vol. 1 (Columbia CK 9478) 1967 ▲³
★★★★★ Johnny Cash at Folsom Prison and San Quentin (Columbia CGK 33639) 1968 ▲² 1969 ▲²
★★★ Biggest Hits (Columbia CK 38317) 1987
★★★ Best of Johnny Cash (Curb D2-77494) 1991
★★★ Patriot (Columbia CK-45384) 1990
★★★★ Columbia Records 1958-1986 (Columbia CGK 40637) 1987
★★★★★ The Essential Johnny Cash (Columbia C3K 47991) 1992
★★★★ Johnny Cash Is Coming to Town (Mercury 832 031-2) 1987
★★★½ Classic Cash (Mercury 834526) 1988
★★★★ Mystery of Life (Mercury 848 051-2) 1991

Visitors from other planets might need to be told who Johnny Cash is and how he sounds, but you don't. Therefore let's get straight to consumer guidance. Cash's long, brilliant, erratic recording career has been picked apart, rearranged, and put back together—and abused, neglected, and abandoned—by all manner of packagers, reissuers, and re-recorders (including Cash himself), so wisdom dictates a cautious approach.

You can't go far wrong with Columbia's three-CD *The Essential Johnny Cash,* which does a more than respectable job of hitting the high points, from Cash's first single "Hey Porter," cut for Sun Records in March 1955, to his April 1983 recording of Bruce Springsteen's "Highway Patrolman" with "Ballad of a Teenage Queen," "I Walk the Line," "Ring of Fire," "Dirty Old Egg Suckin' Dog," "Jackson," "Folsom Prison Blues," "One Piece at a Time," "Sunday Morning Coming Down," and sixty-seven other inimitable artifacts in between. It's sort of staggering, really, when you get to the end, reflect on how many places Cash has been, and then realize that he isn't through traveling yet.

The Columbia set doesn't, of course, cover the whole trip, and neither do any of the other collections available. Rhino's eighteen-track *Sun Years* offers eight early cuts not included on the *Essential* package, though, and some of the lesser anthologies of his post-Sun work, particularly the twenty-track *Columbia Records 1958-1986,* offer a decent alternative for the more casual fan. Note, by the way, that *Classic Cash* is not an anthology, but (pretty good) 1988 recordings of all the old hard-core Cash tunes.

There are also three reissues of original albums: *The Fabulous Johnny Cash,* his first, great work for Columbia after leaving Sun in 1958; *Ride This Train,* the first of his thematic folk-myth collections; and *Johnny Cash at Folsom Prison and San Quentin,* which gives you both his wonderful 1968 prison concert and part of its somewhat less essential 1969 sequel. All three of these CDs are well worth having; the tragedy is that many more Columbia albums haven't been reissued as CDs, and they've been out of print on vinyl long enough to make them extremely hard to find in any condition. There are some true stars in this category, notably *Blood, Sweat, and Tears; Bitter Tears;* and *Ballads of the True West,* which continued the *Ride This*

Train approach to Americana (focusing on, respectively, the working man, the Indian, and the lore of the frontier); and, from his last years with Columbia, the magnificent *Rockabilly Blues,* wherein the Man in Black made a creative comeback of the first order, and *The Adventures of Johnny Cash,* which doesn't fall far short.

One rule of thumb about Cash is that more often than not, his sessions with producer Jack "Cowboy" Clement are more interesting than his other work. Clement was there at Sun in the beginning; he was behind *Rockabilly Blues* and *The Adventures of Johnny Cash;* and he's been on board for *Johnny Cash Is Coming to Town* and *Mystery of Life,* the two CDs available from Cash's post-Columbia career with Mercury. Nobody much noticed, but those last two albums were as honest, righteous, funky, funny, quirky, contrary, and just plain one-in-a-billion great as Cash himself. —P.Ca.

JOHNNY CASH, WAYLON JENNINGS, WILLIE NELSON, AND KRIS KRISTOFFERSON

★★★★ Highwayman (Columbia CK 40056) 1985 ●
★★★½ Highwayman 2 (Columbia CK 45240) 1990

Looked at one way, the subtitle of the first Highwayman album could have been *Old Outlaws Contemplating Extinction.* It's full of edgy farewells, swan songs, and laments for the passing of better, more adventurous days. But Cash's leadership ensured that it also featured plenty of moral depth and antiauthoritarian sentiment ("Deportee," "Welfare Line," "Committed to Parkview"—protest songs in the Reagan era!), so you could just as well call it *Still Stickin' It to 'Em after All These Years.* Either way, it's a coherent and heartfelt album, and quirky as all hell (and that's a compliment).

The sequel, released five years later, is less impressive. The song choices aren't as sharp, and the production is uneven at best, weird at worst; some of Willie's vocals, in particular, sound as if he phoned them in from Maui. But it definitely has its moments.—P.Ca.

ROSANNE CASH

★★½   **Right or Wrong (Columbia CK 36155) 1979**

★★★   **Seven Year Ache (Columbia CK 36965) 1981 ●**

★★½   **Somewhere in the Stars (Columbia CK 37570) 1982**

★★   **Rhythm & Romance (Columbia CK 39463) 1985**

★★★★   **King's Record Shop (Columbia CK 40777) 1987**

★★★½   **Hits 1979-1989 (Columbia CK 45054) 1989**

★★★   **Interiors (Columbia CK 46079) 1990**

★★★★   **The Wheel (Columbia ACC 52729) 1993**

From the start of her career, Rosanne Cash has projected such a strong personality that it's hard to separate her from her music. Like her father, Johnny Cash, she brings a streak of rugged individualism to everything she does; like her father, she has explored different styles that have taken her far outside country's boundaries. Her pro-woman stance has verged on feminism (a daring viewpoint amid country's conservatism), yet most of her records have been produced (and many of her songs written) by her former husband, Rodney Crowell. Repeated forays into pop and rock have shown her to be particularly anxious to break free from country's restraints. Ultimately, what sets her outside of country isn't production values but her punkish lack of reverence for tradition. Yet her country sides have been some of her most rewarding, while her stabs at pop and rock have proved inconsistent overall.

Cash's early albums suffer from an absence of cohesion. *Right or Wrong* moves from the warmed-over new wave of the title track to a couple of gorgeous country ballads, "Take Me, Take Me" and "This Has Happened Before." Then, like a kid who wants to see how much she can get away with, she tosses off the naked feminism of "Man Smart, Woman Smarter." On *Seven Year Ache,* it's the straight country material that is again most consistently rewarding, from Merle Haggard and Red Simpson's "You Don't Have Very Far to Go" to the sassy "My Baby Thinks He's a Train"; the cover of Tom Petty's "Home Town Blues" late in side two seems a bit precious.

Somewhere in the Stars is another uneven effort. The ersatz cocktail jazz of "I Wonder" arrives out of left field, but the coy naiveté in Cash's voice pulls it off. She's also irresistible amidst the plainspoken heartache of Tom T. Hall's "That's How I Got to Memphis." *Rhythm & Romance* flirts with disaster. The red spiked hair and pink lipstick on the cover display an ill-advised image makeover, and the synthed-out power pop of "Never Be You" and "I Don't Know Why You Don't Want Me" falls flat. To her credit, Cash is too intelligent to play the vampy siren, and acoustic moments like "Second to No One" point to future introspection.

On *King's Record Shop,* Cash finally melds her different sources. With its crisp slap of drums and ringing guitar, "Rosie Strike Back" stands as a fearless anthem for women who have been victims of abuse. Cash's cool, composed delivery on "The Way We Make a Broken Heart," John Hiatt's *abc*'s of cheating, is transcendent. *Hits 1979-1989* gives a faithful representation of her various moods and styles.

Interiors, produced by Cash, is an unapologetic diary of the breakup of her marriage to Crowell. With its numb, slow tempos and brooding arrangements, the album feels rather torpid and dense, long on catharsis but short on actual songs; it's as if Cash simply wrung out her emotions on the page and came up with words and melodies to suit them. From "On the Inside" to "Paralyzed," the album is intended as a portrait of collapse. Some critics called it Cash's watershed; newcomers to her music might find it rough going.

The Wheel is Cash's statement of renewal. The tempos have a buoyant optimism, and the production, by Cash with John Leventhal, offers a crisp pop-rock blend of electric and acoustic guitars, subtle percussion, and tasteful keyboards. Cash seems to have rejoined the land of the living: the romantic perspectives are less obsessively withdrawn, the language cleaner and more direct. In "Seventh Avenue" and "Sleeping in Paris," the singer finds strength in solitude; "The Truth about You" is a character sketch told with unflinching, Dylanish irony. —K.S.

JEFF CHANCE

★★ **Picture on the Wall (Mercury 846 615) 1991**

★★★ **Walk Softly on the Bridges (Mercury 314-512 274) 1992**

An entrant in the young-stud sweep-stakes, Jeff Chance has puppy dog eyes, a sad country croon, and oodles of sensitivity. *Picture on the Wall,* in fact, is too sensitive, overwrought with heartache after heartache: "Talkin' to Your Picture," "It Sure Is Cold in Here Tonight," "So Far Not So Good." After sitting through this litany of woe, you want to kick him just to see if he whimpers. *Walk Softly on the Bridges* has more oomph and point of view. Chance shows a knack with vocal phrasing in the title track, singing it loud and proud enough to reach across generations; the jouncy ditty "Alone in San Antone" is the album's goof song, allowing a now welcome Chance to lighten up.—K.S.

RAY CHARLES

★★★★★ **Modern Sounds in Country and Western Music (Rhino R2 70099) 1962, 1988 ●**

★★★★★ **Greatest Country and Western Hits (DCC Compact Classics. DZS040) 1988**

★★★½ **Friendship (Columbia CK 39415) 1984**

★★★★ **Seven Spanish Angels and Other Hits (Columbia CK 45062) 1989**

In one of the greater ironies of a career spanning five decades and embracing every genre of American pop song, Ray Charles, the High Priest of Rhythm & Blues, was nominated in 1983 for the Country Music Association's Horizon Award, the nook honoring promising newcomers. Charles was then making records aimed at the Nashville market and country radio, but he was, in his fifty-third year, no newcomer to country. He had redefined it in 1962 for a pop audience with a landmark ABC Para-mount label album, *Modern Sounds in Country and Western Music,* which stood tall on *Billboard*'s pop album charts for nearly two years and yielded such hits as "Born to Lose" and "I Can't Stop Loving You."

Modern Sounds wasn't a country album but rather a pop interpretation of country standards by a unique song stylist and arranger who knew that great songs transcend genres. Charles intuited the link between his gospel-drenched vocals and the emotional directness of such songs as Hank Williams's "You Win Again," plainly churchy in construction, but before Charles no one had explored vocal art rooted in the black church as a vehicle for country songs. Also, for Charles to lovingly embrace and at the same time reinvent this white Southern music at the height of the Civil Rights struggle was an act of subtle daring.

The arrangements for *Modern Sounds* are delightfully dated, relics of the time when LPs were an "adult" format (as opposed to the kid-friendly 45) and albums were auditory fireplaces, ambient make-out mood enhancers. Swirls of lush strings and ethereal choruses sweep through the ballads, while the kickier tunes have sassy brass which conjures images of a Cyd Charisse dance routine from a long ago "Ed Sullivan Show." But Charles's vocals are timeless, and the window dressing that frames them is of a piece with what producer Owen Bradley was doing with Patsy Cline during the same era: making adult-contemporary country records before there was a marketing niche for them.

Charles recorded two volumes of country's *Modern Sounds* and other albums featuring country standards between 1962-1965. DCC's twenty-song *Greatest Country & Western Hits* gives a full overview of these recordings, including such post-*Modern Sounds* classics as "Crying Time" and Ray's rubbery reading of Buck Owens's "Don't Let Her Know." The fifteen-song *Modern Sounds* on Rhino has six of the same songs that appear on DCC's set, though Rhino alone offers "Born to Lose." Either collection is a good buy with fine sound.

While exploring Charles's country recordings, his 1980s Columbia albums, especially *Wish You Were Here Tonight,* are worth a listen (check used LP bins) for a portrait of the Genius approaching country from an insider's vantage. *Friendship* was a welcome-to-Nashville collection of duets with ten Music City stars, among them George Jones ("We Didn't See a Thing"), Ricky Skaggs ("Friendship"), and the ubiquitous Willie Nelson ("Seven Spanish Angels"), who must hold the Nashville record for most duet cameos. *Seven Spanish Angels and Other Hits* is the best available collection of Charles's Columbia country recordings, though the absence of the drawling "3/4 Time" is a sin. He's such a consummate pro that there may be no such thing as a bad Ray Charles album, but 1986's *From the Pages of My Mind* (not yet on CD at press time) isn't an especially focused one, and one suspects that by then the eclectic Charles was chafing at the restraints of being marketed solely to country buyers. "Uh-Huh!" waited in the wings.—M.H.

MARK CHESNUTT

★★★★   **Too Cold at Home (MCA MCAD-10032) 1990 ●**
★★★★   **Longnecks and Short Stories (MCA MCAD-10530) 1992 ●**
★★★   **Almost Goodbye (MCA MCAD-10851) 1993**

Longnecks and Short Stories was about as close to perfect a country album as anything released during 1992. All artists say they're trying to create collections of ten potential hit singles. Mark Chesnutt actually did it. The ballads "I'll Think of Something" and "Old Country" resonate with hillbilly integrity. His reworking of Charlie Rich's "Who Will the Next Fool Be" shows him as a blues master. Chesnutt scampers and romps through "Old Flames Have New Names" and "Talking to Hank" (featuring Chesnutt's hero George Jones) like it's Saturday night in an East Texas roadhouse. And what can you say of the transcendently countrified "Bubba Shot the Jukebox"? If you have any feeling at all for country music, it will set you free.

Chesnutt became a gold record artist and a radio favorite on the strength of "Blame It on Texas," "Brother Jukebox," "Too Cold at Home" and the other tunes on his startlingly accomplished CD debut of 1990. By the way, it also included the first version of Garth Brooks's anthem "Friends in Low Places." Both albums showcase a pure-country voice that draws on the bent-note traditions of the past without being slavishly imitative of it. Chesnutt has a certain wiry, tense quality that vibrates through his music. It is a style that wears its blue collar with pride.

Almost Goodbye appeared as the third collection in mid-1993, with the exquisitely produced "It Sure Is Monday" as its introductory single. The tune was a textbook case of how you can update the elemental country sound without selling it out. Only Chesnutt, John Anderson, and a handful of others have this rare ability. And if everything else on *Almost Goodbye* didn't quite measure up to the fabulous "It Sure Is Monday," or to the two preceding albums, well, it was still better than most of the competition.

MCA Records is fond of billing this guy under a "Who's Gonna Fill Their Shoes?" banner to indicate that maybe, just maybe, Mark Chesnutt is the modern honky-tonk messiah, the one youngster who can step into the boots of George Jones, Merle Haggard, and Lefty Frizzell. For once, the hype might be justified. —R.K.O.

VIC CHESNUTT

★★★½   **Little (Texas Hotel 20) 1990**
★★★½   **West of Rome (Texas Hotel 21) 1992**

Vic Chesnutt, an Athens, Georgia-based singer-songwriter, is one of those iconoclastic artists who simply cannot be categorized: a little bit country, a little bit folk, and quite a bit off-kilter. One thing's for sure, though: Chesnutt writes intriguingly original lyrics, which are set to sad but catchy melodies and sung with a compelling twang. Both *Little* and *West of Rome* are sparse affairs, produced with a light hand by R.E.M. vocalist Michael Stipe. *Little*'s stark yet tuneful compositions about tangled up relationships ("Soft Picasso"), romantic dreams ("Isadora Duncan"), and childhood rebelliousness ("Speed Racer") are such powerful story songs that they don't need much more than simple acoustic guitar strumming for instrumentation. Chesnutt's second outing, *West of Rome*, is not quite as spare, with bass and drums throughout and moody sounds of cello, slide guitar, keyboards, and violin slipping in occasionally. As on the debut, the songs entice with their ethereal beauty, while intriguing with their colorfully painted lyrics. "Imports and altercations/My faculties on a shoe-string vacation/I settled down on a hurt as big as Robert Mitchum/And listen to Lucinda Williams," sings Chesnutt on "Lucinda Williams." You're not quite sure what the songwriter means—but there's no doubt about what the singer is feeling. —H.G.-W.

THE CHIEFTANS

★★★½ Another Country (RCA Victor
09026-60939-2) 1992

Recorded for the most part in Nashville,
Another Country shows how little
distance there really is between this
band's traditional Celtic airs and what we
call country. The music here doesn't
really sound like it came from Nashville
or Dublin, but instead some timeless
place unconcerned with fashion or trends,
where Don Williams is allowed to fret
lovingly over "I Can't Stop Loving You,"
where Ricky Skaggs gets to play Roy
Acuff on an Irish hoedown of "Wabash
Cannonball," where Chet Atkins manages
to sound simultaneously rootsy and jazzy
on "Tahitian Skies," and where Willie
Nelson once more brings everyone
together as only he can on "Goodnight
Irene." Another time, another country
indeed.—P.K.

THE CHUCK WAGON GANG

★★½ Greatest Hits, Vol. 1 (Arrival 753-2)
1991

★★½ Old Time Hymns, Vol. 2 (Arrival
3001-2) 1991

The Chuck Wagon Gang has endured in
one form or another since 1935 when
D. P. "Dad" Carter began singing with
his children, Anna, Rose, and Jim, on a
Lubbock, Texas, radio station. After 1936
their sound began reaching out to a much
larger American public through their
Columbia recordings and through their
daily broadcasts on WBAP in Fort Worth.
Despite frequent changes of personnel
after the mid-1950s, the Chuck Wagon
Gang sound and style never altered
substantially. After a brief experimentation with old-time country songs in 1936,
the Gang moved to the exclusive
performance of material drawn from the
gospel shape-note hymnbooks and from
the compositions of gospel songwriters
like Albert Brumley. Their performances
of songs like "I'll Fly Away" and "Jesus
Hold My Hand" ensured the endurance of
such numbers while also giving them
wide circulation among country audiences.

"I'll Fly Away" is included in *Greatest
Hits,* along with fifteen other songs that,
in one or two cases, may have been hits
for someone, though probably not for the
Chuck Wagon Gang. The Chucks did

perform "A Beautiful Life," "Echoes from
the Burning Bush," and "I'll Fly Away"
quite often, and their cumulative sales on
albums over the years may have been
quite substantial. For the most part,
though, the songs heard here come from
the familiar world of religious standards.
"Keep on the Sunny Side," the radio
theme of that other Carter Family, and
such venerable hymns as "Amazing
Grace," "Whispering Hope," and "When
the Roll Is Called Up Yonder" are
performed with songs of somewhat more
recent vintage such as "Tattlers' Wagon"
and "Looking for a City."

The other CD, *Old Time Hymns,* is
more honestly named. It includes no
songs that are particularly identified with
the Chuck Wagon Gang, nor any commercial hits, with the possible exception of
Red Foley's "Just a Closer Walk with
Thee." Instead, the collection includes
such classic religious pieces as "Softly
and Tenderly," "Keep on the Firing
Line," "Are You Washed in the Blood,"
and "I'll Live On." Although the
performances on these collections
preserve the familiar sound and style of
the Chuck Wagon Gang, only the most
confirmed fans or collectors will recognize the identities of the singers or the
dates of the recordings. No notes are
provided, but the music probably dates
from no earlier than the late 1960s. Fans
of the original Chuck Wagon Gang may
therefore be disappointed by what is
presented here. I'm sure that I hear the
golden alto of Anna Carter Davis on some
of the selections, but the other voices
remain unknown to me.—B.C.M.

GUY CLARK

★★★½ Old No. 1 (Sugar Hill SH-CD-1030)
1975

★★½ Texas Cookin' (Sugar Hill SH-CD-
1031) 1976

★★★½ Old Friends (Sugar Hill SH-CD-
1025) 1989

★★★★ Boats to Build (Asylum/American
Explorer 61442-2) 1992

A major influence among the Lyle Lovett
generation of Texas singer-songwriting
progressives, Clark has an uncommon gift
for the common touch, turning everyday
detail and conversational phrasing into
songs that sound like anyone could write
them, but no one else does. His best (and
particularly his later) recordings have the

acoustic ease of country blues or backporch picking sessions, with harmonies from long-time supporters such as Emmylou Harris and Rodney Crowell helping to take some of the rough edges off Clark's vocal delivery.

Highlighting 1975's *Old No. 1* debut for RCA (subsequently reissued by Sugar Hill) are "L.A. Freeway" and "Desperados Waiting for a Train," which had previously been popularized by Jerry Jeff Walker, along with "She Ain't Goin' Nowhere" and "Texas-1947," which continue to rank with Clark's songwriting best. As a singer, however, Clark didn't sound entirely comfortable with the recording process, a problem that would be even more pronounced amid the lesser material and more intrusive arrangements on the *Texas Cookin'* followup (also reissued by Sugar Hill).

After recording in the late Seventies and early Eighties for Warner Bros. (albums that are unavailable on CD and otherwise out-of-print), he found a sound that best matched his songs on the primarily acoustic *Old Friends* and *Boats to Build.* Where earlier albums served primarily as source material for other artists, it is hard to imagine anyone singing the title song of either of these albums, or the best of the rest contained herein, better than Clark. *Boats to Build* is Clark's most consistent effort to date as far as songwriting quality and vocal interpretation that does the material justice. —D.McL.

VASSAR CLEMENTS
★★★★　Hillbilly Jazz (Flying Fish FF-70101) 1974, 1986
★★★　Hillbilly Jazz Rides Again (Flying Fish FF-70385) 1986
★★★½　Grass Routes (Rounder CD 0287) 1991

Vassar Clements is well known as a bluegrass and progressive jazz fiddler and as one of Nashville's most requested session musicians. His *Hillbilly Jazz,* a 1974 collaboration with guitarist David Bromberg, has become a classic. Along with Vassar's performance on the Nitty Gritty Dirt Band's 1972 *Will The Circle Be Unbroken* album, *Hillbilly Jazz* helped introduce Clements to a wider musical audience. This CD reissue includes everything from the original double-LP release except "Cherokee," which was probably omitted due to space restrictions. *Hillbilly Jazz Rides Again,* recorded a decade later, is fine music but not as interesting as the first outing. *Grass Routes* returns to Clements's bluegrass roots and showcases his prowess as one of the best of bluegrass fiddlers.—C.H.S.

BILL CLIFTON
★★★★　The Early Years, 1957-58 (Rounder CD-1021) 1992

Clifton has been a goodwill ambassador for American old-time country and bluegrass music since his move to England in the 1960s. Before that he pioneered in other ways—as the sponsor of the first bluegrass festival in Luray, Virginia, in 1961; as the compiler of one of the best bluegrass songbooks; and as a champion of old-time music in his capacity as a director of the Newport Folk Festival. He also kept the flame of bluegrass burning during the ascendancy of rock & roll and country-pop in the late 1950s. His sound was always more mellow than that of other bluegrass musicians, but he competed favorably with them through his skillful selection of songs and employment of outstanding musicians.

Clifton is poorly represented on CD, but his Rounder collection, *The Early Years, 1957-58,* includes some of the best recordings from his Mercury period. Clifton's great knowledge of and respect for old-time country music is evident in his choice of such songs as "Girl I Left in Sunny Tennessee," "Dixie Darling," "Mary Dear," "Darling Corey," "Blue Ridge Mountain Blues," "Pal of Yesterday," and "Little White Washed Chimney." He was performing such material long before the urban folk revival discovered bluegrass music. Clifton's warm and sensitive singing is ably supported by a stellar group of musicians including his long-time banjo-playing sidekick, Johnny Clark, as well as Curley Lambert, Benny Martin, Tommy Jackson, George Shuffler, John Duffey, Mike Seeger, and Junior Huskey.—B.C.M.

PATSY CLINE
★★★★　Patsy Cline: Her First Recordings, Vols. 1-3 (Rhino R2 70048, R2 70049, R2 70050) 1989

★★½   **Great American Legends: Patsy Cline, Vols. 1-3 (LaserLight 15 407, 15 408, 15 409) 1991**

★★½   **The Legendary Patsy Cline (Pair PCD-2-1236) 1988**

★★   **More of the Legendary Patsy Cline (Pair PCD-2-1307) 1991**

★★★   **Today, Tomorrow, and Forever (MCA MCAD 1463) 1985**

★★★   **Stop, Look & Listen (MCA MCAD 1440) 1986**

★★★   **Country Spotlight (Dominion Entertainment 30112) 1991**

★★★   **Forever and Always (Epic EK 53018) 1992**

★★½   **The Legendary Patsy Cline (Special Music SCD-4927) 1988**

★★   **Let the Teardrops Fall (Special Music SCD 4959) 1991**

★★★   **Best of Patsy Cline (Curb D2-77518) 1991**

★★★   **Patsy Cline (MCA MCAD-25200) 1957, 1988**

★★★★   **Showcase with the Jordanaires (MCA MCAD-87) 1961, 1988**

★★★★   **Sentimentally Yours (MCA MCAD-90) 1962, 1988**

★★★½   **The Last Sessions (MCA MCAD-25199) 1988**

★★★★½   **The Patsy Cline Story (MCA MCAD-4038) 1963, 1988**

★★★½   **A Portrait of Patsy Cline (MCA MCAD-224) 1964, 1988**

★★★   **Here's Patsy Cline (MCA MCAD-738) 1965, 1988**

★★★★★   **12 Greatest Hits (MCA MCAD-12) 1967, 1988 ▲⁴**

★★½   **Songwriters' Tribute (MCA MCAD-25019) 1986**

★★★½   **Live at the Opry (MCA MCAD-42142) 1988**

★★★½   **Live, Vol. 2 (MCA MCAD-42284) 1989**

★★   **Sweet Dreams Original Motion Picture Soundtrack (MCA MCAD-6149 DIDX-424) 1985 ●**

★★★★★   **The Patsy Cline Collection (MCA MCAD4-10421) 1991 ●**

★   **Always (MCA MCAD-27069) 1988**

★★   **Patsy Cline & Jim Reeves: Remembering (MCA MCAD-1467) 1988**

★★   **Jim Reeves & Patsy Cline: Greatest Hits (RCA 5152-2-RRE) 1981**

It's hard not to hear a little bit of an angel in Patsy Cline's voice. From her early records in the mid-Fifties until her death in 1963, Cline sang with an exuberance and sophistication that set a new standard for generations to come. In the first half of her career, Cline was the archetypal country gal, dressed in fringed cowgirl outfits, exuding down-home spunk and sass, singing about honky-tonk merry-go-rounds and the rhythm in her soul as swinging fiddles and pedal steel played around her. Then, starting with her hit "I Fall to Pieces" in 1961, Cline matured into one of country's true stylists. Her voice blossomed to fill out ballads of slow heartbreak; her accompaniment became the lush orchestrations of producer Owen Bradley's Nashville Sound. Even her image changed, to a more refined look of furs and gowns. Like Frank Sinatra in pop, Cline reinvented her chosen form, giving it a new depth of artistry it didn't know it had. She didn't simply bring country uptown; she brought to it a piece of heaven.

The period preceding "I Fall to Pieces" was a developmental one for Cline. She recorded fifty-one sides for the 4 Star label, which then licensed the material to Decca; and although her work lacks the emotional impact she would later attain, she was never anything less than a very good country singer, able to belt for joy or sob a line of particular heartache. No matter what the lyric, Cline always sounded as though she loved to sing—one can feel her smiling as she revs into a crescendo. The early recordings have been endlessly packaged and repackaged for CD release by a variety of different labels. Rhino's three-CD set *Patsy Cline: Her First Recordings* is thorough and well annotated, collecting forty-one of the fifty-one original tracks and organizing them, roughly, by style. *Vol. 1: Walkin' Dreams* includes her first version of "Walkin' after Midnight," her only hit before 1961, and "Three Cigarettes in an Ashtray," which presages her later sensitivity with a ballad. *Vol. 2: Hungry for Love* contains some early and misdirected attempts at pop crossover, like "I Can See an Angel," on which the cluttered background vocals of the Anita Kerr singers prove just how subtle and delightful the Jordanaires can be. *Vol. 3: The Rockin' Side* shows Cline experimenting with more uptempo styles; "In Care of the Blues" is one step shy of rockabilly. For those interested in exploring Cline's early work, this set should do the trick.

The LaserLight three-CD series includes a few tracks left off the Rhino collection, but is less carefully packaged. Pair's *The Legendary Patsy Cline* and *More of the Legendary Patsy Cline* again draw from the original fifty-one tracks. *Legendary* contains twenty songs and more consistent material; *More's* eighteen tracks lead off with the underwhelming love song "Fingerprints." The four compilations *Today, Tomorrow and Forever, Stop, Look & Listen, Country Spotlight,* and *Forever and Always* are each solid, single-CD collections of Cline's early work. Special Music's *The Legendary Patsy Cline* is spotty; *Let the Teardrops Fall* is substandard. *Best of Patsy Cline* is downright misleading, filled as it is with singles which failed to chart in Cline's lifetime.

In late 1960, Cline's contract with 4 Star expired, and she signed directly with Decca. The change signaled a new freedom both for Cline and her producer, Owen Bradley. At the time, Nashville was looking for a way to re-establish itself after the rock & roll explosion, searching for a new direction that would keep the music vital. This was the era of the Nashville Sound, a hybrid that exchanged down-home fiddle and pedal steel touches for pop orchestrations. During her lifetime Cline suggested that she preferred the old-fashioned country fare to the hushed ballads for which she became famous. Yet her vocal quality on those later records is quite simply transcendent.

On "I Fall to Pieces," "Crazy," "Strange" and other Sixties hits, a fuller, richer tone can be heard in Cline's voice. Her phrasing, which in the past diligently abided by restrictions of rhythm and melody, now defines a song. Cline seems to be singing from the inside out: her voice could be raw and parched on an extended high note, broken in a lyric about betrayal, fragile and tentative as she begs for a love denied. She artfully handles the most advanced vocal tricks, but what shines through is as pure an emotional expression of the heart's pain as popular music has ever allowed.

Decca released only three albums by Cline before her death. The first, *Patsy Cline,* was simply a package put together in 1957 around the hit single "Walkin' after Midnight"; filler ranges from the forgettable ("Ain't No Wheels on This Ship") to the more pristine ("Then You'll Know"). By the time of her next LP, *Showcase with the Jordanaires,* in late 1961, she had accumulated much more substantial material. Opening with "I Fall to Pieces," the album proves Cline's new confidence and range. From the breathlessly soft pop of "The Wayward Wind" to the aching grandeur of "I Love You So Much It Hurts" and "Crazy," the singer transforms even the smallest turn of phrase into a statement of eloquence. Her next album, *Sentimentally Yours,* originally released in 1962, is even more concentrated. The potentially saccharine "You Belong to Me," a pop hit for Jo Stafford in 1952, becomes an understated promise of everlasting love; in "Strange," she effortlessly communicates a forced detachment.

Over four days in February of 1963, Cline recorded her last studio sessions. Ten of these twelve songs are collected in *The Last Sessions,* and they include material that begins to return to Cline's roots—"Blue Moon of Kentucky," "Bill Bailey Won't You Please Come Home"— although the arrangements remain softly refined. The pop standard "Always" practically feels like a farewell note.

After her death in a plane crash in March of 1963, Decca issued *The Patsy Cline Story,* a twenty-four-track compilation of her later work that drew on material from *Showcase* and *Sentimentally Yours* ("She's Got You," "Foolin' Round"), plus material that hadn't yet made it to LP: the boisterous "Tra Le La Le La Triangle" and the ballad "Leavin' on Your Mind," which was Cline's current single release at the time of the crash. *The Patsy Cline Story* remains a strong overview of her later career, mingling hits with less familiar tunes. Other collections released in the aftermath of the crash are *A Portrait of Patsy Cline,* which compiles material from 1962 and 1963; and *Here's Patsy Cline,* which dug up early material like "I've Loved and Lost Again" and "In Care of the Blues." Even the cover photo was a rehash—an out-take from the shoot for *Showcase.*

Standing as the only comprehensive overview of her career, the four-CD box set *The Patsy Cline Collection* is a rewarding and sensitively executed look at Cline's life and music. Starting with early radio transcriptions of "I'm Walking the Dog" and Kitty Wells's "It Wasn't God Who Made Honky Tonk Angels" (recorded in 1954, before Cline signed with 4 Star), the set contains the bulk of Cline's recorded material plus unreleased outtakes, radio appearances, and live performances. Because Cline's career was so brief, this box set has a completeness and manageability that most multi-CD collections lack. Unessential tracks are left off; breathtaking performances are placed in their chronological context. Even the graphic design is beautiful.

12 Greatest Hits, in turn, is a kind of mini-orgy of Cline's superlative moments: the later, 1961 version of "Walkin' after Midnight," "Sweet Dreams (Of You)," "Crazy," "So Wrong," "Why Can't He Be You." "Faded Love" is perhaps Cline's most emotional performance, full of anguish that could wrap around the listener's neck like a taut wire. *Songwriters' Tribute,* with material culled from 1961-63, is distinguished only by having liner notes from the writers of songs like "Crazy," "You're Stronger Than Me," and "Imagine That."

Live at the Opry and *Live, Vol. 2* are remarkable in that they contain songs that Cline was fond of but never recorded in the studio, as well as countrified versions of later material. *Opry* covers performances for the Grand Ole Opry from 1956 to 1962: pared-down readings of "She's Got You" and "I Fall to Pieces" that erupt with spontaneity, an unrecorded song "Loose Talk" that shows her at her spunkiest. *Live, Vol. 2* offers transcriptions of radio performances. Her version of Little Jimmy Dickens's "When Your House Is Not a Home" shows her innate ease with straight country; she even injects Connie Francis's "Stupid Cupid" with a dose of class.

The practice of posthumously overdubbing a singer's work is one that Nashville inexplicably condones; it has the effect of neutering the emotional intent of the performer and perversely bringing out a lifelessness in the original recordings. *Sweet Dreams,* the soundtrack to the Cline film biography starring Jessica Lange, adds unseemly trumpets, guitar, and backing singers to "Walkin' after Midnight" and "Foolin' Around," all under the watchful eye of original producer Owen Bradley! He also took part in the massacre that is *Always,* a thoughtless Eighties-style makeover of classics like "I Fall to Pieces" and "That's My Desire"; the jump-started "Faded Love" is particularly offensive. The two Jim Reeves-Patsy Cline collections, *Remembering* and *Greatest Hits,* each offer an overdubbed duet, again supervised by Bradley— "I Fall to Pieces" and "Have You Ever Been Lonely," respectively—plus solo hits by the two greatest exponents of the Nashville Sound (Reeves was killed in a plane crash in 1964). These albums have a freakish, Frankenstein feel, as though someone were trying to resurrect the peacefully sleeping dead.—K.S.

DAVID ALLAN COE

★★★★ **Greatest Hits (1974-78) (Columbia CK 35627) 1978 ▲**
★★½ **For the Record (The 1st Ten Years) (Columbia CGK 39585) 1984**
★★★½ **17 Greatest Hits (Columbia CBSCK-40185) 1985**
★★½ **Crazy Daddy (Columbia CK 45057) 1989**
★★★★ **Biggest Hits (Columbia/Legacy CK 38318) 1991**

David Allan Coe, an ex-con and biker turned country singer-songwriter, was one of the most outrageous, brazen, and talented figures to ride roughshod across country music's sleepy landscape in the mid- and late 1970s. A blatant self-promoter and name dropper (as in his quasi-hit, "Willie & Waylon & Me"), a gifted parodist (as in his hilarious hit version of Steve Goodman's "You Never Even Called Me by My Name"), this self-styled, self-proclaimed, and self-aggrandizing "Mysterious Rhinestone Cowboy" often rubbed Nashville's staid music establishment raw with his propensity for X-rated lyrics, musical references to drug use, and sarcastic digs at country's sacred cows. Yet Coe, for all his bluster, often backed up his bizarre larger-than-life musical image with some outrageously good music—particularly as heard on his first four Columbia LPs: *Once Upon a Rhyme, The Mysterious Rhinestone Cowboy, Longhaired Redneck,*

and *David Allan Coe Rides Again.*
Unfortunately, these obscure classics are
currently only available on CD as imports
from the Bear Family label in Germany.

Coe has never recaptured the ragged
intensity of his early Columbia recordings; as years went, he gradually lost the
fine balance between performance and
self-promotion that made his early
recordings so memorable. He has, from
time to time, continued to turn out
provocative music in the years since—
though little of it can be heard on *Crazy
Daddy,* one of the few more recent Coe
studio LPs available on CD. Here, Coe
has mellowed remarkably and certainly
sounds competent. But the delightful
poetics and bombast of his earliest and
best work is sadly missing.

CBS (now Sony), for whom Coe
recorded for more than a decade and a
half, has relentlessly shuffled, reshuffled,
and repackaged his catalogue with no
fewer than four single-CD hits packages,
despite the fact that only three of his
thirty-odd single releases ever even made
it into the country Top Ten.

Of these various compilations,
Columbia's *Greatest Hits* and *17 Greatest
Hits* offer the most bang for the buck and
the most solid samplings from Coe's early
vintage years. *Biggest Hits,* by contrast, is
a haphazard collection of material that is
really second- and third-rate Coe. *For The
Record: The First Ten Years* is two-thirds
classics and one-third dross, and contains
little not found on the two superior above-
mentioned *Greatest Hits* packages.—B.A.

MARK COLLIE
★★★★ **Hardin County Line (MCA MCAD
42333) 1990**
★★★ **Born and Raised in Black and
White (MCA MCAD-10321) 1991**
★★★★ **Mark Collie (MCA MCAD 10658)
1993**

Part of Mark Collie wants to be in *The
Girl Can't Help It* sandwiched between
Gene Vincent and Eddie Cochran. His
birthplace in Waynesboro, Tennessee,
halfway between Memphis and Nashville,
really defines his predicament. His first
album, *Hardin County Line,* was a serious
attempt to subvert the Nashville
mainstream with a jolt of rockabilly's
primal energy. It has half-a-dozen great
tunes graced by veteran rockabilly picker
James Burton. God crept into the credits

of the follow-up, *Born and Raised in
Black and White,* and much of the
dangerous edge was gone. Oddly, the
move toward center ground didn't pan out
commercially, and, realizing that the
third album was a do-or-die effort, Collie
pulled out all the stops. The visceral edge
is back with this self-titled disc, but
whether it has enough hooks for the
stern guardians of radio is as yet unclear.
The #5 hit "Even the Man in the Moon Is
Crying" was a good start, though.—C.E.

THE COLLINS KIDS
★★★★ **Introducing Larry and Lorrie . . .
the Collins Kids (Sony Music
Special Products A 38457) 1983**

What a talented pair of whippersnappers,
those Collins Kids! Lorrie, twelve, and
brother Larry, ten, debuted on the Grand
Ole Opry in 1954 and made quite an
impression: she a throaty belter and he a
precocious guitarslinger. Regulars on Tex
Ritter's "Town Hall Party" TV show, they
went on to record for Columbia Records
beginning in 1956, but their enthusiastic
rockabilly never made the charts. The
Oklahoma-born Kids have managed to
garner quite a cult following over the
years, however. Every song here is a
winner, from the Collinses' original
tunes—the rockin' "Hurricane," the
unforgettable "Whistle Bait," the sassy
"Hot Rod"—to charming covers of
"Walking the Floor over You" and
"Shortnin' Bread Rock." You can't go
wrong with the dozen songs included
(though you're left wanting more), and
the liner notes and photos bring back the
innocence of a musical era that's long
gone.—H.G.-W.

COMMANDER CODY & HIS
LOST PLANET AIRMEN
★★★½ **Lost in the Ozone (MCA MCAD-
31185) 1971**
★★★½ **Hot Licks, Cold Steel & Truckers
Favorites (MCA MCAD-31186)
1972**
★★★ **Country Casanova (MCA MCAD-
661) 1973**
★★★ **Live from Deep in the Heart of
Texas (MCA MCAD-659) 1974**
★★★½ **Too Much Fun (MCA MCAD-
10092) 1990**

Good timin' cosmic cowboys, Commander
Cody & His Lost Planet Airmen brought a
welcome dose of humor to the country-

rock genre in the late Sixties and early Seventies. The band's original tunes, along with its classic covers, cross the country boundaries, from western swing to Cajun to honky-tonk to rockabilly to boogie-woogie. Commander Cody's one and only Top Ten hit, "Hot Rod Lincoln," along with its infamous lament "(Down to) Seeds and Stems (Again)" are on 1971's *Lost in the Ozone* (the title track is the band's party-down theme song). Tongue-in-cheek trucker tunes make up the majority of the rambunctious second album, and Tex Williams's "Smoke! Smoke! Smoke! (That Cigarette)" is the high point of *Country Casanova*. Recorded at Austin's Armadillo World Headquarters in 1973, the live album shows the band at its rowdiest, and for the most part includes songs not found on the other LPs. *Too Much Fun* is a comprehensive sampling (fifteen tracks) of the first four albums, including all the aforementioned songs and chatty liner notes written by none other than Dr. Demento.—H.G.-W.

CONFEDERATE RAILROAD
★★★ **Confederate Railroad (Atlantic 82335-2) 1992 ●**

I've got to admit it: I had these guys pegged as just another bearded, sleeves-rolled-up, macho band out of Nashville. And after listening to their rowdy hit songs (with titles like "Time Off for Bad Behavior" and "Black Label, White Lies"), I realized that, yeah, that's what they are. But so what? I still keep popping this one into my CD player. The folks in (or behind) Confederate Railroad picked a great bunch of songs (mostly written by Nashville pros), put the guitars and the hooks way up front, and came out rockin'. Those big, burly guys on the back cover (there's a rebel flag on the front) may like their women "on the trashy side," but they've got big hearts under those leather vests. Sort of like a country version of Bachman-Turner Overdrive. Pretty dumb, but lots of fun.—P.Cr.

JOHN CONLEE
★★ **Rose Colored Glasses (MCA MCAD-31228) 1978**
★★ **Greatest Hits (MCA MCAD-31229) 1983**
★★ **Greatest Hits, Vol. 2 (MCA MCAD-31230) 1985**

★★ **Best of (Curb D21K-77437) 1991**
★★★ **20 Greatest Hits (MCA MCAD-5925) 1988**

When the clutter was kept to a minimum, this Kentucky-born ex-mortician and one-time Nashville DJ made some good records. Against the country-pop context of the late Seventies and early Eighties, the singer's high-in-the-throat vocal and blue-collar themes sounded traditional. "Rose Colored Glasses" had honky-tonk credibility; "Backside of Thirty" caught the confusion of dreams gone off the rail; and his recording of Harlan Howard's "Busted" offered boozy solace to those who found themselves in that predicament. Though not one of his biggest hits, "Nothing behind You, Nothing in Sight," a plaintive Harlan Howard-Ron Peterson tune, ranks as Conlee's best work.

The problem is, as his career moved into the Eighties, the production values of Conlee's records remained stuck in the Seventies, with strings, voices, even a harpsichord, thrown into the mix, while fiddles, steels, and Telecasters ushered in new traditionalists. More recent Conlee ballads such as "As Long as I'm Rockin' with You" or "In My Eyes," while agreeable enough melodically, drip with sap in their arrangements.

The twenty-hit collection on MCA gathers all the best early work, including "Nothing behind You," and chooses wisely such later, nostalgia-heavy hits as "Years after You" and "Old School." (All selections from *Greatest Hits*, save "Baby, You're Something," and from *Greatest Hits, Vol. 2*, save "Lifetime Guarantee, are included on *20 Greatest*.) The Curb *Best of* combines four late MCA hits ("Common Man" and "I'm Only in It for the Love" among them) with tracks Conlee cut for Opryland Music Group's now-defunct 16th Avenue Records. One of the Curb tracks, "Hit the Ground Running," became the basis of a popular ad campaign for Ford trucks, with Conlee's voice featured prominently.

In the age of video, short-and-wide Conlee lacks hunk credentials, but he continues to appear occasionally on the Grand Ole Opry, in support of farmers via Farm Aid, and in live concerts around the country.—J.O.

EARL THOMAS CONLEY

★★★½   Fire & Smoke (RCA 55981-2) 1981
★★★   The Best of Earl Thomas Conley (RCA 6700-2-R) 1988
★★★½   The Heart of It All (RCA 6824-R-2) 1988
★★★   Greatest Hits (RCA PCD1-7032) 1988
★★★   Greatest Hits, Vol. 2 (RCA 2043-2-R) 1990
★★★½   Yours Truly (RCA 3116-2-R) 1991

Despite his competent vocals and his clutch of #1 radio hits, Earl Thomas Conley is country music's invisible man. He's a strong, second-string singer whose straight-ahead country baritone often agreeably echoes that of George Jones. But he's been continually hampered by his lack of a discernible public image and perennially upstaged by more distinguished and charismatic contemporaries like John Anderson and his former labelmate, the late Keith Whitley.

Still, albums like *Yours Truly*—one of his best, most ambitious, and ironically his last for RCA—stand as a reminder that Conley, in his better moments, has turned out more than mere chart fodder. He's especially convincing with Jonesian songs of tortured love ("You Must Not Be Drinking Enough") and blue-collar blues ("Borrowed Money"). *Yours Truly* features a lovely duet with Keith Whitley on "Brotherly Love."

For those seeking the hits, there are three solid compilations of Conley's work available. *Greatest Hits, Vol. 1* and *Best of Earl Thomas Conley*, cover much of the same 1981-86 material and include such #1s as "Somewhere between Right and Wrong," "Holding Her and Loving You," and "Your Love's on the Line." *Greatest, Vol. 2* begins in 1986 and runs up through 1990, when Conley's hits began to tail off.—B.A.

COWBOY COPAS

★★   Tragic Tales of Love and Life (King KCD-714) 1960
★   Mister Country Music (Starday SCD-175) 1962
★   Opry Star Spotlight (Starday SCD-157) 1962

Lloyd "Cowboy" Copas was an Ohio-born singer and guitarist who performed on the Grand Ole Opry from 1944 until his death on March 5, 1963, in the same airplane crash that killed Hawkshaw Hawkins and Patsy Cline. Copas was best known for singing honky-tonk songs like "Filipino Baby" and "Tragic Romance," but fans also discovered that he was a top-notch flat-top guitarist when he recorded and made a hit of "Alabam" in 1960.

The available CDs will disappoint those who remember Cowboy Copas. Of the three songs mentioned above, only "Tragic Romance" is included. Where is "Tennessee Waltz"? "Kentucky Waltz"? "Signed, Sealed, and Delivered"? "From the Manger to the Cross"? *Tragic Tales of Love and Life,* a 1960 album gathering cuts from 1946 to 1955, will be most satisfying to old-time fans because it includes such venerable songs as "Those Gone and Left Me Blues" and Grandpa Jones's sentimental classic "Tragic Romance." "An Old Farm for Sale" has a nice nostalgic touch but is poorly recorded. The other songs are average at best, and "Hangman's Boogie," though a hit in 1949, is an embarrassment. *Opry Star Spotlight,* first released on LP in 1962, does include some of Copas's flat-top picking, but virtually all of the selections are covers of other people's songs, such as Ferlin Husky's "Wings of a Dove," Porter Wagoner's "A Satisfied Mind," and Carl Smith's "Loose Talk." *Mister Country Music,* also from 1962, offers "A Penny for Your Thoughts," which is both well written and well sung. Copas also does a good job on the "Alabam" sound-alike, "Sal," and on "How Do You Talk to a Baby" and "I Dreamed of a Hillbilly Heaven." His duet version of the 1890s parlor song, "There'll Come a Time Someday," though well performed, is marred by a radical alteration of the lyrics which completely changes the original meaning of the song. Both Copas and his fans deserve better treatment than they receive in these collections.—B.C.M.

CORBIN-HANNER

★★★   Black and White Photograph (Mercury 846 326-2) 1990
★★½   Just Another Hill (Mercury 314 512 288-2) 1992

On one of their album covers, Bob Corbin and Dave Hanner are pictured on a hill overlooking the skyline of Pittsburgh, their hometown. It's an appropriate image, for these two folk-rock veterans present tightly produced, slickly performed adult pop that balances images of urban, working-class life with struggles of the heart common to city and country dwelling baby boomers everywhere.

The duo, long a popular bar band in Pennsylvania, recorded a couple of independent albums in the early 1980s that led to a Nashville contract. Before Corbin-Hanner's country album debut, Alabama had a hit with Corbin's "Can't Keep a Good Man Down," which is a good representation of the duo's style: swaying, pop-inflected rhythms, sweet harmonies, hummable melodies, and a flair for light drama.

Black and White Photograph, their country debut, is the more consistent of the two albums. The two primarily write alone, each contributing five songs to the album. Corbin tends to pen gritty slices of urban Americana, while Hanner updates soft Sixties singalong pop, with his lyrics translating matters of the heart to fit aging couples.

Just Another Hill, the follow-up, also benefits from the same strengths: well-thought-out arrangements, nicely observant lyrics, and a winning vocal rapport elevate their work above the mundaneness of most harmony-driven pop-country. Interestingly, many of the best songs—"Any Road," "I Could Be the One," and the title tune—represent the duo's first recorded efforts at co-writing with each other. These two former high school pals prove the value of collaboration.—M.M.

LARRY CORDLE
★★★½ Larry Cordle, Glen Duncan, & Lonesome Standard Time (Sugar Hill SH-CD 3802) 1992

Larry Cordle ranks with the best of the new generation of bluegrass songwriters, and he has assembled a top-notch band that's precise yet energized. Fiddler Duncan earns his billing, while mandolinist Butch Baldassari provides some sharp accents, and bassist Wayne Southards and banjoist Mike Bub drive the rhythm with precise force. The only aspect that is average about the band's debut is Cordle's voice: he's an impassioned, earthy singer, but his range is as thin as a whisper.

Some of his material may sound familiar, since Cordle had a hand at writing several songs here that have been popularized by other artists. In addition to the Kathy Mattea hit that provides the band's name, there's "Highway 40 Blues" and "You Can't Take It with You When You Go," both done by Ricky Skaggs, "Lonesome Dove," which Trisha Yearwood recorded, and "Lower on the Hog," to which John Anderson gave his indelible stamp. Just as good, however, are such originals as "You Can't Do Wrong and Get By" and "The Fields of Home."—M.M.

ELVIS COSTELLO
★★ Almost Blue (Columbia CK 37652) 1981
★★★★★ King of America (Columbia CK 40173) 1986

Costello is one of the most intriguing songwriters and performers to emerge from the British punk eruption of the Seventies, and one of the most eclectic. The former Declan MacManus has thrived in many forms across his wide-ranging career, country music being one of his most interesting forays. *Almost Blue* was a half-hearted restatement of obvious country standards (among them songs originally associated with Hank Williams, Patsy Cline, George Jones, and Merle Haggard), with producer Billy Sherrill adding his usual shovelful of sweetening, an especially destructive move considering Costello's affinity for bare-bones production. Costello later reviled Sherrill, calling him "a complete and utter hack." But Costello still loved country, even if he hadn't yet figured out how to express his affection. *King of America* is far more successful, a sprawling blockbuster set on which he digs into America's root forms, New Orleans jazz, and traditional pop as well as rockabilly and hard country. Supported by the core of the other Elvis's TCB Band (guitarist James Burton, bassist Jerry Scheff, and drummer Ronnie Tutt), Costello emerged with the most straightforward and unpretentious music of his checkered career.—J.G.

COUNTRY GAZETTE
★★★ Hello Operator . . . This Is Country Gazette (Flying Fish FF-70112) 1991

★★★ **Keep on Pushing (Flying Fish FF-70561) 1991**

Back in 1971 when the Country Gazette spun off from the Flying Burrito Brothers, they were a high-energy fusion of Southwestern bluegrass picking and L.A. country-rock singing by Byron Berline, Alan Munde, Kenny Wertz, Roger Bush, and Herb Pedersen. If you see either of their first two long-out-of-print albums on United Artists, *A Traitor in Our Midst* (UAS-5596; disregard the obnoxious cover art) and *Don't Give Up Your Day Job* (UA-LA090-F-0598), grab them; you can hear the magic that made them big news in the bluegrass world in the early Seventies. After 1974 the band went through a number of changes and today is led by the only original member, banjoist Alan Munde.

Keep on Pushing features a recent version of the band; the title cut is a reprise of the hit track from their first United Artists album. Munde is a fine banjoist, one of the leaders in the post-Scruggs "melodic" style, and he contributes some neat picking to this album's mixed repertoire of newly composed and traditional numbers (Rounder CD 0311, *Festival Favorites Revisited,* is a good compilation of his instrumentals, originally released on the Ridge Runner label). Mandolinist Dawn Watson contributes some tasty picking along with her harmony vocals on this CD. *"Hello, Operator . . . This is Country Gazette"* is a retrospective collection taken from five albums made for Flying Fish between 1976 and 1987. There's some good music on it, but like many collections of this sort, it varies considerably in texture from cut to cut. I particularly enjoy the tunes from the earliest album like "Still Feeling Blue" and "Blue Light" because they have something of that distinctive multi-tracked vocal sound that producer Jim Dickson helped develop for them and for country-rock acts in the L.A. area. But for the bluegrass purists there are plenty of more mainstream numbers that help explain why this band has remained in demand over the years.—N.V.R.

THE COUNTRY GENTLEMEN

★★★★★ **Country Songs Old and New (Smithsonian/Folkways SF 40004) 1960**

★★★★ **Folksongs and Bluegrass (Smithsonian/Folkways SF 40022) 1961**

★★★★ **Bluegrass at Carnegie Hall (Hollywood HCD-112) 1962**

★★★ **Nashville Jail: Classic Country Gentlemen (Copper Creek CCCD 0111) 1990**

★★★★★ **The Award Winning Country Gentlemen (Rebel CD 1506) 1971**

★★★★ **Live in Japan (Rebel CD 1105) ca. 1972**

★★★½ **Featuring Ricky Skaggs on Fiddle (Vanguard VMD 73123) 1987**

★★★★★ **Calling My Children Home (Rebel CD 1574) 1977**

★★★½ **25 Years (Rebel CD 1102) 1986**

★★★ **Return Engagement (Rebel 1663) 1988**

★★★ **Duffey, Waller, Adcock & Gray: Classic Country Gents Reunion (Sugar Hill SH-CD-3772) 1989**

★★★★ **Let the Light Shine Down (Rebel CD 1675) 1991**

★★ **New Horizons (Rebel CD 1699) 1992**

In the Sixties, critics invented the term "progressive bluegrass" to describe the music of the Country Gentlemen, the band that established Washington, D. C.'s reputation as a bluegrass center. Formed in 1957 by guitarist-lead vocalist Charlie Waller and tenor singer-mandolinist John Duffey, the band has gone through many permutations. That a surprising number of its recordings have made it into the CD format is indicative of its popularity.

During the early Sixties, with banjoist Eddie Adcock and bassist Tom Gray, the incarnation of this group now known to their fans as the "Classic Country Gents" refined their sound. To a repertoire dominated by obscure folksongs and little-known early country music they applied techniques of bluegrass instrumentation, vocal style, and arrangement. Smithsonian/Folkways has reissued their first two albums, both of them a value with sixteen tracks and extensive notes. *Bluegrass at Carnegie Hall* is a reissue of a 1962 Starday album with the same band that preserves an inaccurate title: they did appear at Carnegie Hall (in a 1961 hootenanny) but these are studio recordings. The hokey liner notes of the original are gone (in fact there are none), but this is musically as strong as the Folkways albums. *Nashville Jail* was cut in 1964 as the band's second Mercury album but didn't see the light of day until 1990. They recut some of the material for other labels later. And their *Classic Country Gents Reunion* for Sugar Hill was voted "recorded event of the year" by the International Bluegrass Music Association in 1990. Except for the last-mentioned compilation, all of these are well-recorded in good old pure monaural.

At the end of the Sixties, Duffey and Adcock left the band (Gray departed earlier), and Waller rebuilt the band with another fine group of musicians—tenor singer Doyle Lawson on mandolin, Bill Emerson on banjo, and Bill Yates on bass. They won most of the bluegrass awards going in the early Seventies, redoing some of the earlier band's repertoire but adding some new numbers, like their recording of "Fox on the Run" that made the Manfred Mann song into a bluegrass war horse. Listening to all of these early recordings today makes clear that *The Award-Winning*—with "The Legend of the Rebel Soldier," Gordon Lightfoot's "Redwood Hill" and Bob Dylan's "Walking down the Line"—is the best of their albums. The CD reissue has as a bonus two strong cuts, from the original sessions, not included on the LP. The same version of the band does many of their most-requested numbers (including "Fox . . . " and the chilling ghost story of "Bringing Mary Home") on the *Live in Japan* (actually recorded in Japan: Waller told one interviewer "We are bluegrass in Japan," and he wasn't far from the mark). Selections from two later albums recorded for Vanguard while the young Ricky Skaggs was a band member have recently been issued as *Featuring Ricky Skaggs on Fiddle,* and include favorites like "The City of New Orleans," "Catfish John," and "House of the Rising Sun." In choosing just twelve cuts, Vanguard skimped on this one, leaving out some good material, particularly from the first album.

When bluegrass gospel albums began to catch on in the late Seventies, the Gentlemen were well served by Doyle Lawson's great talent in this field. The recently reissued *Calling My Children Home* from 1977 is a classic in that genre, with several fine a cappella quartets.

For a band with such a long period of creative recordings, retrospective anthologies make a lot of sense, and the two presently available are pretty good. The 1986 *25 Years,* with twenty-four selections—including quite a few of the "Classic" version of the band—is a pretty good buy, although the package has suffered in the transition from LP to CD in terms of information about the band and specific cuts. This is not a greatest hits compilation, though there are some nice lesser known performances on it. *Let the Light Shine Down* is a compendium of gospel cuts ranging from 1962 to 1976, mainly taken from now-unavailable albums.

Many of these albums get high ratings because this is a band fortunate to have had control over the production of almost all of their recordings. As recognized trailblazers in the field, they attracted good musicians and sought out distinctive material. If you like contemporary bluegrass and haven't checked out this band, by all means do so.—N.V.R.

BILLY "CRASH" CRADDOCK
★★ **Greatest Hits (Capitol CDP 7 91624 2) 1983**
★ **Back on Track (Atlantic 7 82013-2) 1989**

Craddock sang passable blue-eyed R&B in the Sixties, and a strange cajun/country/R&B hybrid in the early Seventies. The hybrid stuff wasn't as interesting as it sounds. By the late Seventies he'd gone pop, with an occasional lame rocker to remind you that his nickname is Crash. The Capitol disc is culled from the latter period. Devoid of real hits (only "If I Could Write a Song As Beautiful As You" cracked the Top Ten), it's probably best left to the fan club. *Back on Track* is a late comeback effort that no one involved seems to have taken too seriously.—D.C.

FLOYD CRAMER
★★★ **Best of Floyd Cramer (RCA Nashville 56322-2) 1964**
★★½ **Best of Floyd Cramer (RCA Pair PDC2-1210) N.D.**
★★ **Easy Listening Favorites (RCA Pair PDC2-1297) 1991**

★★ **Special Songs of Love (Step One Records SOR-0030) 1988**
★★ **Country Gold (Step One Records SOR-0031) 1988**
★★ **Just Me and My Piano (Step One Records SOR-0033) 1988**
★★ **Forever (Step One Records SOR-0042) 1989**
★★ **Originals (Step One Records SOR-0061) 1990**
★★ **Gospel Favorites (Step One Records SOR-0063) 1990**

Working alongside Chet Atkins during the Sixties, pianist Floyd Cramer was one of the cornerstones of the smooth, nonstick Nashville Sound. Cramer first stumbled upon his lazy, "slip-note" piano style on a demo of "Please Help Me, I'm Fallin'" that had been sent to Atkins by pianist-songwriter Don Robertson. After Cramer applied the style to that song and many other hit records, it became his trademark, and he used it on his own "Last Date," and on endless releases thereafter by everyone from Jim Reeves to Elvis Presley. Actually, Cramer had already met the King. Back in the late Fifties, after sharing a bill on the "Louisiana Hayride" with Elvis, the young pianist hit the road with his rockabilly band for a tour of the Southwest. Some of that influence rubbed off on Cramer's first single release, "Flip, Flop and Bop," with its silly rock & roll harpsichord. But since the bittersweet "Last Date" (and inferior follow-ups like "Your Last Goodbye" and "On the Rebound"), Cramer's music has devolved into an agonizingly mellow amalgam best described as country muzak. The majority of Cramer's records would sound more at home in an airport lounge than a honkytonk, and the pianist over the past several years has developed into a kind of country Lawrence Welk. Most of Cramer's records will appeal only to fans of the very bland. His RCA Nashville *Greatest Hits* collection is the best way to go and is actually a nice collection of Cramer at his best, before he became terminally relaxed.—P.Cr.

ROB CROSBY
★★★ **Solid Ground (Arista ARCD-8662) 1990**
★★★ **Another Time and Place (Arista 07822-18710-2) 1992**

The husky-voiced and folkish Crosby has yet to make an enduring mark on country music. But his intimate man-to-woman monologues and obvious sincerity seem well suited to the Nineties, particularly given the trailblazing Garth Brooks has done. Worth particular attention are "Love Will Bring Her Around" on the *Solid Ground* collection, and "Old News" and "When Hearts Agree" in *Another Time and Place.*—E.M.

J. D. CROWE
★★★★★ **J. D. Crowe & the New South (Rounder CD 0044) 1975**
★★★★ **Blackjack (Rebel REB-CD-1583) 1978**
★★★★½ **Model Church (Rebel REB-CD-1585) 1978**
★★★ **Straight Ahead (Rounder CD 0202) 1986**

At a time in life when many of his contemporaries were working at the local gas station or grocery store for pocket money, teenager J. D. Crowe was picking banjo for legendary bluegrass singer Jimmy Martin. Something of a legend himself for his solid, driving banjo and laconic personality, he put together his first band, the Kentucky Ramblers, in the late Sixties. Rebel has kept two of the Ramblers' Lemco albums from the Seventies in print. Both feature the lead singing of Doyle Lawson, and a smooth vocal trio with Lawson, Crowe, and mandolinist Larry Rice. *Blackjack*, the earlier of the two, mixes then-contemporary material, such as the Flying Burrito Brothers' "Sin City" and Tom Paxton's "Rambling Boy," with older bluegrass gems like Flatt & Scruggs's "I'll Stay Around." *Model Church* is often mentioned as a bellwether album that stimulated the growth of interest in gospel bluegrass albums by younger bands in the Seventies. With Doyle Lawson, a leader in that field today with his band Quicksilver, singing the title cut, this album still sounds good.

When Crowe changed the name of his band to the New South, he meant to indicate a move toward a more progressive sound. The album that survives from the first years of that move, *J. D. Crowe and the New South,* is one of the all-time bluegrass classics. It would be hard to find a better combination of musicians: Ricky Skaggs on fiddle and mandolin and tenor vocals, Jerry Douglas on dobro, and Tony Rice on lead vocals and guitar. And these guys, each a star in his own right today, were not just doing a studio gig; this was Crowe's road band. They all more than pull their weight: Rice's vocal stylings have never sounded better than on this album, in such contemporary singer-songwriter classics as Gordon Lightfoot's "Ten Degrees" and Ian Tyson's "Summer Wages," and Rice throws in hot lead acoustic guitar breaks every now and then, too. Skaggs, in addition to his tenor solos and mandolin, adds tastefully double-tracked fiddles and violas—part of what gives this album its warm sound, as does Jerry Douglas's steel on "You Are What I Am," the only non-acoustic aspect of this album. *Straight Ahead,* from 1986, is Crowe's latest release. It has more of a contemporary country sound, with drums and electric bass. Lead guitarist Tony King and drummer Randy Hayes contribute the vocal leads. As with all of Crowe's material, a strong vocal trio stands at the center. There's a nice version of Crosby, Stills & Nash's "Helplessly Hoping," a mix of newer country and older bluegrass tunes, and, as with most of his albums, several cuts that showcase Crowe's great banjo work.—N.V.R.

RODNEY CROWELL

★★★ **The Rodney Crowell Collection (Warner Bros. 25965) 1989**
★★½ **Street Language (Columbia CK 40116) 1986**
★★★★½ **Diamonds and Dirt (Columbia CK 44076) 1988 ●**
★★★★ **Keys to the Highway (Columbia CK 45242) 1989**
★★★½ **Life Is Messy (Columbia CK 47985) 1992**

A producer who helmed much of Rosanne Cash's best work, a songwriter who's been covered by everyone from the Oak Ridge Boys and Bob Seger to Jermaine Jackson and Foghat, a visionary bandleader (the remarkable groups he led around 1980, included three future producers—piano player Tony Brown, bassist Emory Gordy Jr., and guitarist Richard Bennett—as well as Albert Lee and Vince Gill on guitars), and one of Nashville's greatest live performers, Rodney Crowell has talents only hinted at in his albums. He's one of only a few

country artists—like Bob Wills, Buck Owens, Gram Parsons, and Emmylou Harris—who are important less for their singing than for their broad vision of country's history and future.

The Rodney Crowell Collection is a scattershot distillation of his first three albums, *Ain't Living Long Like This, But What Will the Neighbors Think,* and *Rodney Crowell.* The ragged spirit is a tonic from the discipline of current Nashville sessions, and several of the songs have become standards. But the new wave influences seem silly in retrospect—treading where an angel wouldn't dare, Crowell coproduced *But What Will the Neighbors Think* with Craig Leon, who'd handled the Ramones' debut four years earlier—and the compilation lacks the conceptual logic that distinguishes his best albums.

After five years away from recording, Crowell jumped to a new label and made *Street Language,* an ambitious, bombastic country-soul failure with more ace writing, including the storming celebration of female independence ("Let Freedom Ring") and the delicate admission of male insensitivity ("Past Like a Mask") that bookend the record. When former employee Tony Brown returned as a coproducer on *Diamonds & Dirt* and *Keys to the Highway,* Crowell wrote more bluntly about his stormy relationship with Rosanne Cash, whom he married in 1979, and his work peaked, both commercially and artistically. As a trilogy, his three most recent records offer a remarkable body of songs about the vicissitudes of marriage. *Diamonds & Dirt* begins by celebrating the sexy allure of instability and conflict, then returns Crowell to his Texas roots with Brown's handsome, lively honky-tonk production, which yielded five #1 singles. The pivotal song "After All This Time" acknowledges adversity but concludes with hopefulness.

The sentiment is reprised on *Keys to the Highway* in "The Faith Is Mine." But with the horny libertine joy of "We Gotta Go on Meeting Like This" ("Talk is cheap/Then again, so am I") and the grim humor of "If Looks Could Kill" ("There's a gun out in the hallway covered up in dust/That works well enough to turn a heartache into dust/Go on and let your lawyer make a deal"),

Crowell tilts the emotional balance towards resignation and solitude. On *Diamonds & Dirt,* he'd pledged, "I'll bring it home to you," but he fills *Keys to the Highway* with images of transit and escape, which peak on "Many a Long and Lonesome Highway," a meditation on family ties in which Crowell, like Frank Sinatra, stubbornly admits, "In the end, I'll do it my way."

Life Is Messy was released in the wake of Cash's celebrated *Interiors,* an unsparing account of the couple's conflicts. And while fans might have expected more confessionalism, the album has a meditative, almost cryptic focus. Disposing of steel guitars, Crowell uses a mix of Nashville and L.A. musicians to extend the previous album's folk-rock leanings. Despite several peppy uptempo tracks that celebrate new beginnings, the album turns on the disconnected imagery of "Alone But Not Alone," sung in the blue-hearted croon of Roy Orbison, and the wandering thoughts of the title song, which is summarized by the hysterical, endlessly suggestive couplet, "Life is messy/I feel like Elvis Presley." The record ends with "Maybe Next Time," a jarringly conclusive admission of romantic failure which seems to finalize the public discussion between Crowell and Cash, a dialogue which is unequaled in pop music for passion and honesty—R.T.

BILLY RAY CYRUS
★★ **Some Gave All (Mercury 314-510 635-2) 1992 ▲6**
★★★ **It Won't Be the Last (Mercury 314-514 758-2) 1993**

Poor Billy Ray Cyrus. He had the biggest selling album of 1992. He taught the world to dance again with his "Achy Breaky Heart." He stood up for his principles and recorded with his own band. He wrote six of his debut CD's songs himself. He had country-boy humility, aw-shucks politeness, and genuine decency. The fans loved him, but the Kentucky newcomer got absolutely no respect from the critics and precious little from his country-music peers.

OK: He's no Gary Morris as a singer. "Wher'm I Gonna Live?" was a chowderhead song, and maybe "These Boots Are Made for Walkin'" wasn't due for a revival just yet. His CD title tune, "Some Gave All," is rather bombastic and self-important, but you can't deny its sincerity. Other than that, what's the problem? "Never Thought I'd Fall in Love with You" rocks smartly. "She's Not Crying Anymore" and "Someday Somewhere Somehow" can stand shoulder to shoulder alongside any Music Row country ballad out there. And as for the much-maligned "Achy Breaky Heart," it is one of those feel-good songs that takes the music world by storm every now and then, the heir to a grand tradition that includes "Hound Dog," "Tutti Frutti," "Louie Louie," "Hanky Panky," "My Ding-a-Ling," "Kung Fu Fighting," "Le Freak," "Ring My Bell," "Wake Me Up Before You Go-Go," and "Walk Like an Egyptian." None of those were exactly epic poetry either. Fun doesn't have to make a statement.

And as if to prove that he was far more than a one-hit wonder, Cyrus came back strongly on his second CD, *It Won't Be the Last.* He roared its rockers with more confidence, and his producers gave the whole project enormous polish. "In the Heart of a Woman," "Talk Some," and "Right Face, Wrong Time" had some snarling guitar and rhythm work from Sly Dog, the Cyrus band, as well as some chesty, belting vocals from the star. Of the ballads, "When I'm Gone" was perhaps a rather too overt Elvis homage, but "Somebody New," "It Won't Be the Last," and "Words by Heart" picked up the pieces of his achy-breaky heart right where "She's Not Crying Anymore" had left them. The second collection's finest moment was unquestionably the "message" number "Dreamin' in Color, Livin' in Black and White," a song whose vividly painted lyrics were matched with a cool Euro-pop production and even some David Bowie-like phrasing from Cyrus.

On balance, these are more than respectable discs. I suspect that all the Billy bashing has more to do with the fact that his sexy wiggles and physical beauty make men uncomfortable than it does with the music itself. Lighten up, guys. —R.K.O.

D

LACY J. DALTON

★★★★ **Greatest Hits (Columbia CK 38883) 1983**

★★★ **Lacy J. (Capitol CDP 7-93912-2) 1990**

★★★ **Chains on the Wind (Liberty CDP-7-97931-2) 1992**

It is one of life's minor tragedies that Lacy J. Dalton (original name, Jill Byrem) has sung so eloquently yet had so little commercial or popular impact. Her wounded and smoky voice is a thing of wonder—an instrument that matches George Jones's clenched-teeth moaning for sheer drama. To her credit, she has seldom allowed her producers to saddle her with songs unworthy of her effort. Consequently, there is much to listen to, even in the relatively sparse collections so far available. To know the essential Lacy J. Dalton, attend to "Crazy Blue Eyes" and "Everybody Makes Mistakes" on *Greatest Hits* and the unrelievedly despairing title cut from *Chains on the Wind*. The former also contains the Music Row anthem, "16th Avenue," with which Dalton has become identified.—E.M.

DAVIS DANIEL

★½ **Fighting Fire with Fire (Mercury 848 291) 1991**

Davis Daniel has the uninspired vocal mannerisms of a third or fourth genera-

tion George Jones clone. That's not a moral offense in and of itself. Coughing up a weak, wimpy version of Elvis's gem "Love Me" is.—K.S.

CHARLIE DANIELS

★★★★ **Fire on the Mountain (Epic EK 34365) 1974 ●**

★★ **Saddle Tramp (Epic EK 34150) 1976 ●**

★★ **High Lonesome (Epic EK 34377) 1976**

★★ **Million Mile Reflections (Epic EK 35751) 1979 ▲²**

★★ **Full Moon (Epic EK 36571) 1980 ▲**

★★★ **A Decade of Hits (Epic EK 38795) 1983 ▲²**

★★ **Me and the Boys (Epic EK 39878) 1985**

★★ **Homesick Heroes (Epic EK 44324) 1988**

★★ **Simple Man (Epic EK 45316) 1989 ●**

★★ **Christmas Time Down South (Epic EK 46103) 1990**

★ **Renegade (Epic EK 46835) 1991**

★★★ **All-Time Greatest Hits (Epic EK 53743) 1993**

★ **America, I Believe in You (Liberty CDP0777-7-80477-2-8) 1993**

Charlie Daniels made his first impression as a session man (he played on

Dylan's *Nashville Skyline*); for the past two decades he has led an Allman Brothers-influenced band and come up with an occasional novelty hit, like 1973's "Uneasy Rider" and 1979's "The Devil Went Down to Georgia" (both are on *A Decade of Hits;* the latter is also on *Million Mile Reflections*). Daniels fancies himself a disciple of the Allmans and Lynyrd Skynyrd singer Ronnie Van Zant, but his extended jams are far more limited than those of Duane and Gregg, and he rarely rocks out with the abandon or concision of Van Zant's group (big exception: the Vietnam vet flashback "Still in Saigon," from the not-out-on-CD *Windows* but available on *All-Time Greatest Hits*). Daniels's albums are more adventurous than their recurrent jingoistic singles (titles like "What This World Needs Is a Few More Rednecks" and the unironic "Simple Man" tell half the story) as evidenced by his one genuinely solid Epic album, 1974's *Fire on the Mountain. Renegade* is docked an extra notch for its stultifying stumble through Derek & the Dominoes' "Layla" and its booklet's advertisement for a home video in which fans can see Daniels's "historic visit to Checkpoint Charlie and the Berlin Wall."—J.G.

GAIL DAVIES

★★★   **Pretty Words (MCA MCAD-42274) 1989**
★★★½ **The Best of Gail Davies (Liberty C21Y-94453) 1991**

An underrated Eighties singer-songwriter-producer whose firm assertiveness must have rubbed lots of male listeners and the Nashville good-ole-boy network the wrong way, Davies never had much commercial success and currently works primarily as a producer for other artists. But her rock-spiced country style in a series of Eighties albums remains notably distinctive and fresh; in compositions such as "Grandma's Song" and "Someone Is Looking for Someone Like You" (both on *The Best of),* there's a wealth of vivid narrative detail that never gets in the way of the shimmering melodies. Listening to her firm phrasing and carefully revealed emotions, you get the feeling that this is one country singer who's been as influenced by Joni Mitchell as by Wanda Jackson, and the result is an original,

brainy, feisty style. CD reissues of Davies Eighties Warner Bros. albums, especially 1984's *Where Is a Woman to Go,* would be well deserved.—K.T.

JIMMIE DAVIS

★★★★ **Country Music Hall of Fame (MCA MCAD-10087) 1991**

One of the more colorful figures in country history, Davis started his career with RCA in the late 1920s as an imitator of Jimmie Rodgers and a singer of off-color blues songs (some of which he recorded with black guitarists like Oscar Woods). After a flirtation with western-swing styled music, Davis moved into gospel music, and in the 1960s and 1970s became best known for mellow songs like "Supper Time." In between, he ran for and was elected Governor of Louisiana. At one point, he had dozens of LPs in the Decca catalogue, but the sole CD of his music is MCA's Hall of Fame set. Fortunately it is an excellent cross section of blues, western swing, gospel, and even a little honky-tonk. Here are the Davis classics, such as "You Are My Sunshine" and "Nobody's Darling But Mine" in their original readings, as well as efforts as diverse as "Supper Time" and "Mama's Getting Hot and Papa's Getting Cold." Great notes and complete recording data on the cuts.—C.W

LINDA DAVIS

★★ **In a Different Light (Liberty CDP-7-94829-2) 1991**
★★ **Linda Davis (Liberty CDP-7-97868-2) 1992**

As a country starlet under the aegis of omnipotent producer Jimmy Bowen, Linda Davis may have a bright future before her. Her past, though, at least as revealed on these two discs, cuts a little too close to the Bowen-produced Reba McEntire for comfort.—D.C.

MAC DAVIS

★★½ **Greatest Hits (Columbia CK 36317) 1979 ●**

You think country records that sound exactly like pop records are just a Nineties phenomenon? Here we have irrefutable proof that such is not the case. This collection of ol' Mac's early Seventies chartbusters—"Baby Don't Get Hooked on Me," "Stop and Smell the Roses," "I Believe in Music"—is oriented so clearly towards the Vegas/Hollywood end of the business that you wonder how the hell this guy ever got marketed the way he did. Oh, well. It's all here, complete with horns and gospel choruses and banks o' viols and the whole pumped-up shebang: the poor man's Elvis doing his thing.—P.Ca.

SKEETER DAVIS & NRBQ
★★★ **She Sings, They Play (Rounder CD 3092) 1986**

Skeeter Davis—born Mary Frances Penick—teamed with Betty Jack Davis as the Davis Sisters in the Fifties, blending Kentucky-bred, hillbilly voices in harmonies roughly the female equivalent of the Everly Brothers. The duo enjoyed a hit with "I Forgot More than You'll Ever Know" in 1953 before Betty Jack died in an auto accident.

Skeeter achieved pop and country solo success in 1963 with "The End of the World," the song she still sings often in her weekly appearances on the Grand Ole Opry. Unfortunately, none of her twenty-plus years with RCA are represented on domestic CD. We have others to thank for the opportunity to hear Davis on disc.

Terry Adams, keyboardist and songwriter for the eclectic rock group NRBQ, had treasured his Davis Sisters records for years when he and the band got a chance to hear Skeeter perform and meet her at a gig in New England. That encounter led eventually to this disc, cut in Rhode Island and released on Rounder in 1986. Combining tunes written by Davis ("Everybody Wants a Cowboy," "Everybody's Clown") and by members of the band with covers of "Someday My Prince Will Come," Hank Williams's "May You Never Be Alone," and the Carlisles' "Ain't Nice to Talk Like That," the record has plenty of humor—some of it ticklish and contagious ("Ain't Nice to Talk Like That"), some of it a little self-conscious (references to John "Travolty" and Donn Adams's "country trombone")—and a touch of country pathos. The real pleasure of the record, though, is the interplay of Davis's voice with NRBQ guitarist Al Anderson's savvy country guitar picking and with session man Buddy Emmons's moaning steel guitar. This works to best effect in the 4/4 version of "Someday My Prince Will Come." Emmons and Anderson each take tasty solos, and word is that Emmons went on to play twenty minutes of magnificent solos, which the band still has in the can.—J.O.

BILLY DEAN
★ **Young Man (Liberty 94302) 1990**
★★½ **Billy Dean (Liberty 96728) 1991 ●**
★★ **Fire in the Dark (Liberty 98947) 1992**

Like Garth Brooks, tall and long-haired Dean is a singer-songwriter out of the malls. But unlike Brooks, Dean has no winning eccentricities. His debut makes one silly point strongly: that his age qualifies him for a career in post-Garth country. But that's more of a marketing concern than a creative one. Remarkably, *Billy Dean* builds on his very inconsequential debut with confidence. A hit like "Billy the Kid" at least pushes the idea of Dean's youth toward everyday moral quandaries, and its rocklike momentum also leads the singer into his goofy appreciation of the mythic outlaw. *Fire in the Dark* longs to turn dramatic, offering atmospheric selections along the lines of a remake of Dave Mason's 1977 pop hit "We Just Disagree." Like so much of Dean's work, though, this cover is far too literal-minded and almost gleefully pedestrian. Mason's version completely disallowed the possibility that the fight was about the phone bill; Dean's encourages it.—J.H.

JIMMY DEAN
★★★ **American Originals (Columbia CK 45077) 1989**
★★ **Country Spotlight (Dominion 30042) 1991**

Whether selling country music or country sausage, Jimmy Dean seems to have a keen sense of popular taste. As a singer, he broke through in 1952 with "Bumming Around" on 4-Star Records, then reappeared on Columbia eight years later with the once-heard-never-forgotten story-song "Big Bad John." Later, he made a specialty of such recitations, most of them sugary enough to put a diabetic into a coma. His last Top Ten hit was in 1976 with "IOU," which still gets some airplay on Mother's Day. *American Originals* trawls through the Columbia years, while *Country Spotlight* comprises ten limp remakes that run the gamut from "Bumming Around" to "IOU."—C.E.

MARTIN DELRAY

★★½ Get Rhythm (Atlantic 82176-2)
1990
★★½ What Kind of Man (Atlantic 7
82439-2) 1992

Martin Delray is a hard-country singer whose heart is almost always in the right place. In the course of his first two albums, there are enough popped beer tops, neon-lit romances, and barroom5 dramas to make a veteran honky-tonker like Hank Thompson stand up and applaud. Unfortunately, Delray delivers these intriguing little slices of musical pathos with about as much verve as a swing-shift drinker with eight beers under his belt trying to mumble through the roar of a crowded barroom.

One of Delray's artistic—and commercial—high points thus far is the title tune to his first CD: a spirited duet with Johnny Cash on "Get Rhythm," the rockabilly chestnut which Cash himself wrote and popularized back in 1956. If nothing else, that cut proved Delray can get excited in the studio when the right fire is lit under him. Unfortunately too much of the rest of the time, Delray—even with the assistance of a veteran hard-country producer like Blake Mevis—is such a torpid vocalist that he may well be neo-honky-tonk's answer to Perry Como.—B.A.

IRIS DEMENT

★★★½ Infamous Angel (Warner Bros.
9 45238-2) 1992

This Arkansas-born singer-songwriter has a voice "like one you've heard before—but not really," writes John Prine in the insert booklet to DeMent's debut collection of nine self-penned songs and two gospel favorites. Hers is a voice that variously recalls Emmylou Harris and Nanci Griffith among her immediate foremothers, and, around the hard edges, Lucinda Williams or even Sara Carter (without the flint). More to the point, DeMent may be likened to a distaff Jimmie Dale Gilmore, a quavery nasal voice the vehicle for personal story songs from Small Town America that sound older than they (or the artist) really are. Like Gilmore, DeMent's performances are imbued with an appealing, slightly resigned beatific certainty. The bouquet of critical laurels heaped on her debut album is impressive and belies the fact

that DeMent's arrangements are too spare and her voice too quirky for the country mainstream. Only a few of her songs are apt to really wow the bluegrass crowd, while she seems too essentially country for the urban folksinger-songwriter audience. Despite which, DeMent is glorybound and hallelujahed—perhaps it's her Mona Lisa smile?—M.H.

JOHN DENVER

★★ I Want to Live (RCA 5192-2-R)
1971 ●
★★★½ Poems, Prayers and Promises
(RCA 5189-2-R) 1971 ●
★★ Rocky Mountain High (RCA 5190-
2-R) 1972 ●
★★½ Greatest Hits (RCA PCD1 0374)
1973 ▲⁷
★★★ Farewell Andromeda (RCA 5195-2-
R) 1973 ●
★★★ Back Home Again (RCA 5193-2-R)
1974 ●
★½ Some Days Are Diamonds (RCA
4055-2-R) 1981 ●
★★ Seasons of the Heart (RCA
PCD14319) 1982 ●
★★ Greatest Hits, Vol. 2 (RCA PCD1-
2195) 1983 ▲²
★★★ It's About Time (RCA PCD14740)
1983
★★ Greatest Hits Vol. 3 (RCA PCD1-
5313) 1984
★★ Dreamland Express (RCA PCD1-
5450) 1985
★★½ One World (RCA PCD1-5811)
1986
★ Take Me Home, Country Roads &
Other Hits (RCA 52160-2) 1990

Throughout his career, John Denver has vacillated between pop and country stylings—often within the same album—but otherwise his music has remained remarkably consistent. Cloying love songs dominate, along with nonthreatening overtures for environmental awareness and social harmony. He first struck gold with "Leaving on a Jet Plane," his winsome ballad that became a hit for Peter, Paul & Mary in the late Sixties; it has proved the template for what followed. Much of Denver's appeal stems from his ability to write "we are the world" sentiments with sing-along melodies that sound as if they were commissioned by the Campfire Girls.

Denver came to prominence as a recording artist in 1971 with *Poems,*

Prayers and Promises, a folk-styled period piece which includes the insufferably saccharine "Sunshine on My Shoulders" along with selections from the Beatles and James Taylor, and the antiwar poem, "The Box." The album also yielded his first big hit, "Take Me Home, Country Roads," a sort of anthem for the then-popular back-to-the-land movement.

Back Home Again was his break-through to a country music audience. Two songs from the album, the heavily orchestrated title track and the cartoonish "Thank God, I'm a Country Boy," hit #1 on the country chart. Then in 1975, the Country Music Association voted "Back Home Again" its Song of the Year and, amid a swirl of controversy, Denver was named Entertainer of the Year.

Despite the awards, Denver never equaled the success with his music that he achieved in 1975. He branched out into film and television and continued to release overproduced, forgettable albums that pressed his favorite themes of mellowed romance, country living, brotherhood, and environmentalism. Enticed by the golden goose of the Urban Cowboy fad, Denver laid an egg with *Some Days Are Diamonds,* a trifling hash of easy listening arrangements that includes Bobby Goldsboro's "The Cowboy and the Lady" and his own pastoral romance, "Country Love."

It's About Time is one of his most ambitious works, running the gamut from pop to rhythm & blues, to reggae and country. Prompted by the death of his father and the breakup of his marriage, it also boasts some of his most honest and compelling writing as he probes the mystery of death with the philosophical "On the Wings of a Dream," and candidly shares the aftershocks of love's decay in "Falling Out of Love." On *One World,* his most earnest recording, Denver makes an impassioned plea for an end to the arms race with "Let Us Begin (What Are We Making Weapons For?)," appeals for an end to suffering on "It's a Possibility," and eulogizes the crew of the Challenger on "Flying for Me."

His first collection of greatest hits, which has sold more than 7 million copies, was culled from his first six albums, before his cross-over into country music. *Take Me Home, Country Roads &*

Other Hits is a miserly thirty-minute disc of eight tracks from that same period.
—J.B.

THE DESERT ROSE BAND

★★★ **The Desert Rose Band (Curb D2-77570) 1987**
★★★½ **Running (Curb D2-77573) 1988**
★★ **Pages of Life (Curb D2-77567) 1990**
★★★★ **A Dozen Roses: Greatest Hits (Curb D2-77571) 1991**
★★ **True Love (Curb/CEMA D21K-77567) 1991**

The Desert Rose Band blew across country radio like a fresh wind from the California coast in 1987. Led by country-rock vet Chris Hillman, the DRB turned out a fine series of catchy singles about the trials and tribulations of love. Hillman handled most of the writing chores and supplied a manly lead vocal presence that had gone largely unnoticed in his previous bands, the Byrds and the Flying Burrito Brothers. What his writing lacked in lyrical originality on the early outings he more than made up for in melodic hooks. Surrounding himself with a band full of ace West Coast pickers like John Jorgenson, Herb Pedersen, and steel player Jay Dee Maness proved the smartest move of all.

With the band's debut album, all the elements of the DRB sound are in place—tart three-part harmonies, great gobs of twangy guitar riffs from Jorgenson, and infectious love songs from Hillman, such as "Love Reunited," "One Step Forward," and "He's Back and I'm Blue." A solid follow-up, *Running,* introduces smart covers of John Hiatt ("She Don't Love Nobody") and Buck Owens ("Hello Trouble") to the mix. The band's problems start here, though, with Hillman's stretch toward more topical writing on "For the Rich Man" and "Homeless." It's hard to fault the sentiment, but the execution is heavy-handed and pedantic. Unfortunately, Hillman's urge to lecture was a trend that would continue. Clearly with the next two studio albums, *Pages of Life* and *True Love,* the bloom was off this rose. Hillman had turned his back on silly love songs, Jay Dee Maness closed the book after *Pages of Life,* Jorgenson followed suit after *True Love,* and the band wilted. *A Dozen Roses* is the clear pick of the group's catalogue, filled as it is with all their meaningless, delightful Top Ten singles.—P.K.

DIAMOND RIO

★★★ **Diamond Rio (Arista ARCD-8673) 1991** ▲
★★★ **Close to the Edge (Arista 18656-2) 1992**

Is there such a thing as being too tight as a band? Diamond Rio has it all: A tenor lead singer with leap-from-the-speakers power, ensemble harmonies that are note perfect, sizzling instrumental ability, dazzling showmanship, and a sense of humor. And if all of that sometimes adds up to the squeaky-clean perfection of an Opryland theme park act, well, so be it.

Opryland is, in fact, where most of the six members honed their craft. But one listen to either of these albums is proof that Diamond Rio is way, way beyond the shallow, happy-face presentations generally offered in theme parks. For one thing, Jimmy Olander is one of the most refreshingly original lead guitarists in country music—his tricky twangs are the envy of the industry. For another, try singing high harmony above tenor Marty Roe as mandolinist Gene Johnson does—he makes the impossible sound effortless. Listen to the Grammy-nominated "Poultry Promenade" instrumental on the first CD, and you'll know you're in the presence of talent with a capital T.

Diamond Rio also has the remarkable ability to effectively mix bluegrass, honky-tonk, pop, and swing into the same stew. That's not an easy recipe to follow. Finally, start a new band and go looking for songs on Music Row to see if you can come up with anything anywhere nearly as terrific as "Norma Jean Riley," "Meet in the Middle" and "Nowhere Bound" (on the first CD), or "In a Week or Two," "Oh Me Oh My Sweet Baby" and "Calling All Hearts" (on the second). It ain't easy, folks. Being professional never is. —R.K.O.

HAZEL DICKENS

★★★★ **A Few Old Memories (Rounder CD-11529) 1988**

You will probably never hear Hazel Dickens on a Top Forty country radio station. Her hard, uncompromising vocal style and equally hard-hitting songs offer more realism than most program directors are willing to accept. She is definitely underrepresented on CDs, but the eighteen songs heard here provide a good sampling of her material. They come from five albums, three by Hazel alone, and two on which she appeared with other singers. Although she includes other people's songs, such as Harlan Howard's "Busted" and Billy Edd Wheeler's "Coal Tattoo," most of the songs describe Hazel's very personal views of working people's struggles, women's rights, and old-time ways. Worth special mention is the beautiful remembrance of her native state, "West Virginia, My Home."—B.C.M.

LITTLE JIMMY DICKENS

★★★½ **Take an Old Cold Tater & Wait (Richmond NCD-2131) 1988**

James Cecil Dickens came to the Grand Ole Opry in 1948 and has been a memorable mainstay there ever since. An effective ballad belter, Dickens's diminutive size and plucky personality inclined him toward novelty songs, and from 1949's "Take an Old Cold Tater (and Wait)" to 1965's "May the Bird of Paradise Fly Up Your Nose," several became hits for him on the Columbia label. This eight-song 1988 collection has Dickens reprising "Tater," "Bird," "Hillbilly Fever," "Out Behind the Barn," and other bucolic knee-slappers. An anonymous but effective group of Nashville Cats backs the man Hank Williams nicknamed Tater, who sounds much as he did when he and Hank barnstormed the hillbilly hustings. Those looking for Little Jimmy's spunky original Columbia recordings should seek out the Columbia Country Classics Series. *Vol. 2, Honky-Tonk Heroes,* has "Country Boy," "Take an Old Cold Tater (And Wait)," and "A-Sleepin' at the Foot of the Bed," while *Vol. 3, Americana,* offers "May the Bird of Paradise Fly Up Your Nose." Corny, yes, but not to be sneezed at. —M.H.

JOE DIFFIE

★★★ **A Thousand Winding Roads (Epic EK 46047) 1990**
★★★ **Regular Joe (Epic EK 47477) 1992**
★★ **Honky Tonk Attitude (Epic AEC 53002) 1993**

Ex-demo singer Joe Diffie commands a dizzying array of Jones and Haggard mannerisms—some that even George and Merle have forgotten. He either annoys you with their overuse, especially on *A Thousand Winding Roads,* or wins you with his joy in exercising them. Diffie's debut #1, "Home," for instance, is a triumph of vocal spirit over some wretchedly cloying Ma & Pa lyrics, whereas "New Way (To Light Up an Old Flame)" is the sort of cheap Jones pastiche better left to the guitar-and-casio set who entertain on Nashville's Lower Broadway. Smart enough to sense the need for his own identity, Diffie carves a more personal niche in the dramatic upper register on ballads like "If You Want Me To." At such moments he can almost sing circles around any hillbilly hunk in Nashville.

Regular Joe picks up where *A Thousand Winding Roads* leaves off. On "Startin' Over Blues," Diffie's self-proclaimed "overt reference to Jimmie Rodgers," he manages to lift from Rodgers, Hank, and Lefty, all in the same song. From there, he tones down the mimicry and sings it straight, as if he's learning to trust his voice on its own terms. The payoff is immense on "Ships That Don't Come In," a barstool moralizing tune written with uncommon philosophical restraint. If only Diffie didn't ruin the mood by rockin' out on the cheesy title cut. Why is it for all their talk about the Allman Brothers, young country so often sounds like they've absorbed more of Molly Hatchet?

Which brings us to *Honky Tonk Attitude,* on which the Kraft American rock & roll influence runs amok. "If I Had Any Pride Left at All" and a couple others are textbook soaring Diffie ballads. The rest is honky-tonk attitude badly in need of adjustment.—D.C.

THE DILLARDS

★★★★★ **There Is a Time (1963-70) (Vanguard VCD 131/132) 1991**
★★½ **Douglas Dillard: The Banjo Album (Sierra OXCD 6008) 1970**
★★★ **Homecoming & Family Reunion (Flying Fish CD 215) 1979**
★★★★ **Let It Fly (Vanguard VHD 79460) 1990**
★★★ **Rodney Dillard: Let the Rough Side Drag (Flying Fish FF 70537) 1991**

★★★ **Take Me Along for the Ride (Vanguard VCD 79464) 1992**

Douglas and Rodney Dillard, from down around Salem, Missouri, headed West with their picking buddies Dean Webb and Mitch Jayne in 1962 and hit the big time in Hollywood. As the mythical Darling Family, they appeared regularly on "The Andy Griffith Show," and as the Dillards, they recorded five albums for Elektra. The first two were in the progressive bluegrass mold, anchored by Rodney's guitar and lead vocals, Doug's powerful banjo work, Dean's mandolin, and Mitch's bass. The second LP, a live set, also featured Mitch's sophisticated down-home humor. A third album introduced the fiddle of Byron Berline to records. Then Doug left, and in the late Sixties the last two Elektra albums, including then-new bandmember Herb Pedersen's banjo and vocals (these days Herb is part of the Desert Rose Band), took the band in new directions with a sound that mixed folk, bluegrass, country, and rock in unique ways. *There Is a Time* anthologizes twenty-nine cuts from those five albums and gives today's listeners a chance to hear what made the Dillards an exciting band back in Sixties.

Doug's *Banjo Album,* a reissue of a rare album from 1970, includes an additional track with Byron Berline—not on the original—that is probably the strongest cut on it. Too bad it's the only in-print document of the band Doug formed with former Byrd Gene Clark after leaving the Dillards. I've always liked that band's The *Fantastic Expedition of Dillard & Clark,* the first of two A&M albums, a country-rock-bluegrass fusion quite different from the Dillards. Edsel, an English outfit, reissued a version with extra tracks from Dillard & Clark's second album a few years ago (ED 192), and copies of this LP might be lurking about still. Doug's more recent efforts on Flying Fish don't seem to have made it to CD. When the city of Salem celebrated Dillard Day in August 1979, Flying Fish recorded the event for *Homecoming and Family Reunion.* It's a fun event album, with several cuts each by the Dillard Family Band, including fiddling father Homer, re-creations of the original and late-Sixties Dillards, fellow Missourian and long-time friend John Hartford, and the contemporary version of the Dillards. That band, which carries on the group's late-Sixties sound (Vanguard is calling it "bluegrass sound gone electric," a contradiction in terms for bluegrass purists) with new material, can be heard on two recent Vanguard albums. Of those, *Let It Fly,* produced by Herb Pedersen, is the stronger. Rodney's 1991 solo effort, *Let The Rough Side Drag* is in much the same mold.—N.V.R.

DEAN DILLON

★★★½ **Out Of Your Ever Lovin' Mind (Atlantic 82183-2) 1991**
★★★ **Hot, Country, and Single (Atlantic 782438-2) 1993**

Dean Dillon has steadily contributed some of the best-written country songs to other stars for more than a decade: George Strait alone has recorded more than thirty of his tunes. Dillon apparently started saving a few of the best for himself. *Out of Your Ever Lovin' Mind* is a consistently winning, low-key gem. Dillon's voice, though narrow in range, works best on the excellent honky-tonk swing of "Holed Up in Some Honky Tonk" as well as on the jaunty title song and on "Her Thinkin' I'm Doing Her Wrong (Ain't Doin' Me Right)." But his lyrical talents also surface on the ballads "Holding My Own," which Strait later made into a title cut of an album, and on the smart social commentary of "Friday Night's Woman" and the crafty personal psychoanalysis of "The Umbrella Song."

His second Atlantic album, produced by Garth Fundis, revives "Holed Up in Some Honky Tonk" in an effort to get Dillon on the radio. For the most part, Fundis focuses Dillon on lighthearted swaying country with clever, concise wordplay, which comes off to good effect on "I Just Came Here" and "What'll I Do with It Now." The ballad "Old News" features Dillon at his melancholy best, while "Everybody Knows" proves that a good country lyricist still can explain better than any self-help book the psychosis of a hard drinking, lonely man. The only pitfall is "Hot, Country, & Single." Dillon might have thought it a good joke to write a song with a word twist on the one thing his career lacked— a hot country single—but the shallow sentiment of the tune is best left to less thoughtful artists.—M.M.

DIXIANA

★★★ **Dixiana (Epic EK 48620) 1992**

All the memorable parts of this vague, indecisive premiere come out of Cindy Murphy's mouth. The range and subtle intelligence of her interpretations highlight the album's three best songs. In "I Didn't Think You'd Care," she cites her lover's neglectfulness and placidly justifies her infidelity ("I know it isn't honest/But I believe it's fair"), reprising the defiant logic of country's first feminist song, Kitty Wells's "It Wasn't God Who Made Honky Tonk Angels." As she wonders whether romantic failure has left her with "A Heart That Can't Be Had," she builds pensively to the barely controlled, choked swells of the chorus, like an impassioned Crystal Gayle. And she unveils her sexuality to taunt a dismissive lover in the feisty "That's What I'm Working On Tonight." Unfortunately, producer Bob Montgomery believes that Murphy's modern sensibility merits an onslaught of synthesizers.—R.T.

DIXIE CHICKS

★★½ **Thank Heavens for Dale Evans (Dixie Chicks 000218) 1990**
★★★ **Little Ol' Cowgirl (Crystal Clear Sound CCR 9250) 1992**

Dressing in cowgirl garb and blending Western-themed songs with bluegrass instrumentation was the original schtick for this Dallas-based, all-woman group. Sisters Martie and Emily Erwin contribute solid, capable fiddle and banjo, respectively, while lead vocals on these discs are shared by bassist Laura Lynch and former member Robin Lynn Macy, who left the group in August 1992. Material on *Thank Heavens* ranges from Patsy Montana's cowgirl classic "I Want to Be a Cowboy's Sweetheart," to traditional fiddle tunes "Rider" and "Brilliancy," to Sam Cooke's "Bring It on Home to Me." Jon Ims, writer of Trisha Yearwood's hit, "She's in Love with the Boy," contributes "West Texas Wind."

Little Ol' Cowgirl is a more polished, diverse effort with the Western themes toned down a little. The title cut and "Two of a Kind" come from Ims again, while the bouncy "A Road Is Just a Road" is a find from Mary-Chapin Carpenter's first album. The band's rhythm & blues penchant is more pronounced, with another Cooke cover ("You Send Me"), Ray Charles's "Hallelujah, I Just Love Him So," and the Dixie Hummingbirds' "Standing by the Bedside." The Chicks also try Mick Hanly's "Past the Point of Rescue," recorded around the same time by Hal Ketchum. Of the original material, the jazzy pop of "Pink Toenails" is the standout.

Early in '93, the Chicks were sharing Nashville management with Riders in the Sky and entertaining major label overtures.—J.O.

MICHAEL DOUCET

★★½	Michael Doucet & Cajun Brew (Rounder CD 6017) 1987
★★★★★	Beau Solo (Arhoolie CD 32) 1989
★★★½	Le Hoogie Boogie (Rounder CD 8022) 1992

Michael Doucet has emerged as the premier exponent of Cajun fiddling, in the great tradition of his predecessors and mentors like Dewey Balfa, Dennis McGee, and Varise Connor. But he's much more than that. He sings, he writes, he picks guitar, he handles the accordion. A champion of traditional music and culture, Doucet has also been a progressive force in contemporary Cajun music, incorporating elements of other forms of contemporary music into his personal style. Doucet was a founding member of the first "cosmic Cajun" band to combine traditional Cajun music with Gulf Coast rock, Coteau, which was extremely popular and influential in the 1970s. Since then, he has been the leader of the very successful Cajun band Beausoliel. *Cajun Brew* is Doucet at his eclectic best with an ad hoc group of musician friends and heroes, doing almost tongue-in-cheek Cajunized versions of rock & roll chestnuts like "Wooly Bully" and "Louie, Louie." *Le Hoogie Boogie* is a really neat children's album that is by no means for children only. The extraordinary *Beau Solo* is a showcase for Doucet doing what he does best, offering a generous twenty-two cuts of exquisite Cajun music by today's finest Cajun fiddler. Just for fun he adds his own accordion to nine of the tracks, and throughout is accompanied only by his brother David on guitar and fiddle. The result is asolutely stunning.—C.H.S.

JERRY DOUGLAS

★★★★	Everything Is Gonna Work Out Fine (Rounder CD-11535) 1988
★★★½	Plant Early (MCA Master Series MCAD-6305) 1989
★★★★	Slide Rule (Sugar Hill SH-CD-3797) 1992

Ohio native Jerry Douglas emerged in the early Seventies as the bluegrass circuit's boy wonder of the dobro. His seemingly impossible facility on the instrument earned him the nickname "Flux," and would later make him one of Nashville's leading session players. Following the lead of mandolinist David Grisman, Douglas and his musical compadres began to incorporate jazz influences ranging from Joe Venuti to Django Reinhardt and pioneered newgrass music. Although that subgenre never quite jelled, Douglas made some really good records in the process. *Everything Is Gonna Work Out Fine,* a two-records-in-one Rounder rerelease finds him in the straight bluegrass mode (and few do it better) while his MCA Master Series release, *Plant Early,* features some of the better jazz-country fusion music on record. Douglas still finds time between production projects for artists like Maura O'Connell and Alison Krauss to make the occasional solo record, and his latest, *Slide Rule,* finds him returning somewhat to his bluegrass roots. The album's highlight is Douglas's slowed-down version of the Louvin Brothers' classic "I Don't Believe You've Met My Baby," featuring a gorgeous vocal by Krauss. —P.Cr.

HOLLY DUNN

★★	Holly Dunn (MTM D2-71052) 1986
★★★	Cornerstone (MTM CDP-71063) 1987
★★★½	Across the Rio Grande (MTM D2-71070) 1988
★★★	Heart Full of Love (Warner Bros. 9 26173-2) 1990
★★★	The Blue Rose of Texas (Warner Bros. 25939-2) 1989
★★★★	Milestones—Greatest Hits (Warner Bros. 9 26630-2) 1991
★★★	Getting it Dunn (Warner Bros. 9 26949-2) 1992

Let's face it: Somebody at MTM had their head up their butt when they recorded Holly Dunn's debut album back in 1986. Her voice is flavored with a natural Texas twang that was consistently downplayed in pop-ish arrangements. But there was one tune in the collection that let her be her country-folk self. It was "Daddy's Hands" and it launched her career. Doubtless realizing its error, the company rethought its approach and let her craft two minimasterpieces in succession. *Cornerstone* (1987) contained the keening heartache numbers "Strangers Again" and "Why Wyoming," while *Across the Rio Grande* (1988) included the soaring, sobbing "(It's Always Gonna Be) Someday," perhaps her finest songwriting and performing effort to date. This first era of her recording life was summed up on *Milestones—Greatest Hits,* one of the essential female-country collections of the 1990s.

Dunn's resilient soprano hurts in all the right places, and she is one of the finest female country songwriters on the scene. In recent years she has loosened up on stage and created a warmer public personality. Her best work may well lie ahead. She has issued a trio of CDs for Warner Bros. Records, of which 1989's *The Blue Rose of Texas* is the most satisfying. Not the least of its pleasures are background vocals by Dolly Parton and Joe Diffie.—R.K.O.

BOB DYLAN

⋀ ⋀ ★★★ **Blonde on Blonde (Columbia CGK 00841) 1966 ●**

★★★★ **John Wesley Harding (Columbia CGK 09604) 1968 ●**

★★★★ **Nashville Skyline (Columbia CK 09825) 1969 ▲**

Not country, you say? Think again. *Blonde on Blonde* is one of the greatest albums ever made in Nashville. Recorded at Columbia Recording Studios, right there on Music Row. Recorded with the strongest Nashville Cats going: Charlie McCoy, Wayne Moss, Kenny Buttrey, and Hargus "Pig" Robbins. The themes are spiritual, the approach is country metaphysical. The result is endearing and enduring. And greatly influential. Plus, this was when the Nashville Cats discovered that a song could stretch out past two and a half minutes (their minds were blown when Dylan launched into the eleven-minute-plus "Sad-Eyed Lady of the Lowlands" and then just kept going and going). As the first Sixties rocker who headed to Music City to rejuvenate

and expand his chops, Dylan's influence ran both ways: he was like a one-man underground railroad carrying passengers and baggage in both directions simultaneously.

By most accounts, Dylan had not thought before of recording in Nashville: producer Bob Johnston—who had finished Dylan's *Highway 61 Revisited* album when Dylan fell out with producer Tom Wilson—suggested Music City and its legendary session players when Dylan was casting about for inspiration. He found it in Nashville. The Nashville Cats were surprised when Dylan booked them and the session for a week rather than by the hour, which had been the traditional sort of assembly-line method. *Blonde on Blonde* took forty studio hours to complete: a long time by 1966 Nashville standards, but an incredibly short time by today's rock recording practices, when literally hundreds of hours produce much lesser works.

Dylan had a near-fatal motorcycle crash shortly after finishing *Blonde on Blonde* and after a long convalescence returned to Nashville a changed man. When he then went acoustic and cut two mellowed-out albums, country-rock was upon the land in earnest.

John Wesley Harding was recorded in three days in Nashville in late 1967, with Johnston producing and with only three other musicians: Charlie McCoy, Kenny Buttrey, and steel guitarist Pete Drake. The latter played on only two songs, so most of the album is Dylan on guitar, harmonica and piano, Buttrey on drums, and McCoy on bass. The result is a minimalist Dylan, attacking his new country-folk material with a gritty and simple musical approach. *John Wesley Harding* (Dylan has never discussed why he added the "g" to the last name of one of the Old West's most notorious outlaws) was recorded and mixed in six hours. If you listen, you can hear Hank Williams standing over Bob's shoulder in "I'll Be Your Baby Tonight."

Johnny Cash wrote the liner notes for *Nashville Skyline* and sang along on "Girl from the North Country," so that proved the country bloodlines were in place. It was finished in three days in Nashville in February of 1969, with Cash, Buttrey, McCoy, Drake, Charlie Daniels, Bob Wilson, and Norman Blake. *Skyline* is in fact a very *sweet* album: very romantic and introspective and very atypical of Dylan, without a single hard edge. The president of Columbia Records at the time, Clive Davis, reportedly fought Dylan every inch of the way on Dylan's decision to record and release a country album. Davis later did admit that he tried and failed to change the album's name—to delete the word *Nashville,* because Davis felt it was "too limiting." Fortunately, Dylan prevailed. His three Nashville albums stand up very well indeed against the test of time and represent much of the best of his work. But, all seriousness aside, country is as country does.—C.F.

E

THE EAGLES

★★★   **The Eagles (Asylum 5054) 1972** ●
★★★   **Desperado (Asylum 5068) 1973** ●
★★★★   **On the Border (Asylum 1004) 1974** ●
▲ ▲★☆   **One of These Nights (Asylum 1039) 1975** ●
★★ ☆ ▲   **Their Greatest Hits (Asylum 105) 1976** ▲[12]

In 1972, pop production in southern California had begun seriously taking on London, refining the revolutionary—yet often formally unsophisticated—sound of Sixties U. S. rock. Very significantly, *The Eagles* also appeared during this year. The record jumped on the proposition of country-rock (then a cool alternative choice in turn-of-the-decade Los Angeles) with an enormous arrogance that yielded an even greater stylistic acuity. On *The Eagles* and *Desperado,* a vague concept album that videos would have helped, the Eagles and English producer Glyn Johns coined a version of country-rock that would gain wide popularity and that, to this day, remains the envy of country musicians who crave country forms rendered with more of the attitude, energy, arrangement, and tonality of rock.

That tonality accounts for why the Eagles still sound rock, not country. In Nineties Nashville, some artists use the ideas in Eagles music: fiddles against speeded up blues rhythms, guitar lines that distort as they still basically behave, background vocals that rely more on personality than perfect pitch, cinematic song presentations. Yet country production rarely feels free to take in that relatively wild L.A. edge; only Dwight Yoakam and producer Pete Anderson, applying this studio sensibility to compositions much unlike Eagles music, really do it.

On the Border and *One of These Nights,* which replace Johns with producer-engineer Bill Szymczyk, become even more stylistically omnivorous and daring as the Eagles construct more coherent albums. Where early hits like "Take It Easy" and *Desperado*'s lovely title ballad are, at heart, refined renderings of organic melodic ideas, a song like the title tune from *One of These Nights* is as dependent on its bass lines as anything else.

Through *Greatest Hits,* the Eagles were drummer Don Henley, guitarist Glenn Frey, guitarist-mandolinist Bernie Leadon, and bassist Randy Meisner. As a widely influential songwriter whose work continues into the present, Henley is still stretching. Unfortunately, his superiority complex is as big as all outdoors, and in 1972-75 Eagles music it's around, even when the tunes sound as magnificent as, say, "You Never Cry Like a Lover" (from *On the Border*). Still, for country usages keyed into a compelling rock language, the Eagles' dramatic grasp remains peerless.—J.H.

STEVE EARLE
★★★★ Guitar Town (MCA MCAD-31305) 1986
★★★★ Exit 0 (MCA MCAD-5998) 1987
★★★★ Copperhead Road (Uni UNID-7) 1988
  ★★★ The Hard Way (MCA MCAD-6430) 1989
   ★★ Live: Shut Up and Die Like an Aviator (MCA MCAD-10315) 1991
  ★★★ The Essential Steve Earle (MCA MCAD-10749) 1993

Texan Steve Earle was perhaps the most interesting—and frustrating—talent to emerge from the Eighties neo-traditionalist pack. A songwriter with the ability to zero in consistently on telling, human details, Earle straddled two bases—hard country and hard rock & roll—but was so singular and fresh that he couldn't commit to just one, thus alienating narrow-casting radio formats. Earle's first two CDs (a 1986 LP of early, rushed neorockabilly tunes for CBS remains unreleased on disc) established him as a narrative master with the eye of Tom T. Hall and the anthemic power of Bruce Springsteen. *Guitar Town*'s "Someday" and "Fearless Heart" and *Exit O*'s "The Rain Came Down" and "I Ain't Never Satisfied" were prime work from an ambitious writer anxious to squeeze new ideas into familiar areas. From *Copperhead Road* on, Earle moved on to more straightforwardly rock & roll settings and except for that CD, his work also emerged a bit more simple, culminating with a throwaway live album built around a superfluous cover of the Rolling Stones' landmark country-rock tune "Dead Flowers." *Essential* is a border-line-acceptable single-disc compilation; the truly essential Steve Earle is found on his first three CDs.—J.G.

THE EDDIE ADCOCK BAND
★★★ Dixie Fried (CMH CD 6270) 1991

As a member of the Country Gentlemen, banjoist-mandolinist-guitarist Eddie Adcock helped make bluegrass a household word in the Sixties. His most recent outfit, in which he's joined by vocalist and rhythm guitarist Martha Hearon Adcock, upright bassist Missy Raines, and fiddler Glen Duncan, plays folky tunes a little closer to easy listening. But the Adcocks' lovely harmony singing and Eddie's masterful banjo picking keep the spirit of bluegrass alive on *Dixie Fried;* especially notable is the refreshing arrangement of the Allman Brothers' "Midnight Rider." Overall, the album is a pleasant, expertly performed collection of songs.—H.G.-W.

DON EDWARDS
★★★½ Songs of the Trail (Warner Western 9 26933-2) 1992

Don Edwards is a contemporary singing cowboy whose smooth vocal style is often compared to that of the late Marty Robbins. Accompanied by Nashville session musicians, Edwards performs fifteen songs ranging from traditional cowboy material like "Little Joe the Wrangler" to Marty Robbins's "The Master's Call" and recent compositions by Michael Martin Murphey, such as "An Old Cowboy's Dream." A polished and professional performer, Edwards has become a favorite on the growing cowboy and western music circuit.—C.H.S.

JONATHAN EDWARDS
★★★★ Jonathan Edwards (Atco 862-2) 1971
  ★★½ [& the Seldom Scene] Blue Ridge (Sugar Hill SH-CD-3747) 1984
   ★½ The Natural Thing (Curb/MCA MCAD-42256) 1989

Jonathan Edwards peaked early, but maybe not as early as you've been led to believe. In the fall of 1971, the then twenty-five-year-old singer-songwriter scored a #4 pop hit with a defiant, brilliantly propulsive single called "Sunshine." It turned out to be the only hit he ever had. It wasn't his only good record, though. The album it came from was every bit as charming and unpredictable as the single, achieving a confident balance between a natural, down-home feel and a good-natured folkie lyricism. Toe-tappers like "Athens County" and "Shanty," an FM radio favorite in its day ("We're gonna lay around the shanty, Mama, and put a good buzz on"), let the good times roll, while minor-key meditations like "Sometimes" and "The King" unfold nuances with repeated listenings. Throughout, Edwards's buoyant, boyish tenor carries the gorgeous melodies along with the refreshing purity of a swiftly flowing mountain steam.

Filled with youthful enthusiasm and enfused with confidence by "Sunshine"'s reception, Edwards threw caution to the wind and really got back to the country with the follow-up, *Honky-Tonk Stardust Cowboy,* in 1972. Or at least he got as close as a Virginia hippie living in Boston could. "Stop and Start It All Again," a pulsing celebration of life's renewing cycles, would have been a great follow-up to "Sunshine." Only problem is, Atlantic Records didn't release it as a single, then shrugged their shoulders when the album didn't sell. In short order, *Stardust Cowboy* was relegated to the cut-out bins and cult classic status, genus progressive country. It deserved better. Though its lyrics betray a bit more of the hippie's bucolic reveries than Edwards revealed on his debut, the appreciation of real country music is sincere and infectious. Needless to say, though, without a hit, it's unlikely to be released on CD anytime soon.

Afterwards Edwards put out a handful of desultory efforts for Atlantic and Warner Bros. with increasingly diminishing commercial prospects. In recent years, he has tried to approach country on its own terms with less than satisfying results. In 1984, he joined the bluegrass band the Seldom Scene for a gig at the Birchmere Club in Alexandria, Virginia. *Blue Ridge* is a mixed bag, sounding really more like a Seldom Scene album, filled as it is with bluegrass classics (Flatt & Scruggs's "Don't This Road Look Rough and Rocky," Ralph Stanley's "God Gave You to Me"). "Sunshine," gussied up in bluegrass trappings, is almost unrecognizable. In 1989, producer Wendy Waldman got Edwards to come to Nashville to do *The Natural Thing.* Of course, in Music City the natural thing is to cut songs assembled by Nashville's army of song carpenters. But part of the reason Edwards stood out on his first two albums was because of the cockeyed cleverness of his songwriting. Here, walled in by songs built to Nashville factory specifications and held back by his own voice (which has deepened at least a full octave and turned ordinary

with age), Edwards merely marks time.

Shortly after *The Natural Thing*'s release, Edwards was threatening to re-record the songs from *Honky-Tonk Stardust Cowboy* in hopes of giving them the hearing they deserve. Let's hope some generous exec at Atlantic beats him to the punch and reissues the original instead.—P.K.

DARRYL & DON ELLIS
★★½ **No Sir (Epic EK 48807) 1992**
Harmonizing brothers Darryl and Don Ellis could perhaps use a bit more of the Don and Phil Everly influence. Their debut album takes tentative steps towards rollicking tradition—"I Want to Be the First One" features background vocals by the famed Jordanaires—then heads right back into the middle of the road with soggy ballads like "No Sir." —K.S.

JOE ELY
  ★★★½ **Joe Ely (MCA MCAD-10219) 1977**
★★★★★ **Honky Tonk Masquerade (MCA MCAD-10220) 1978**
  ★★★½ **Down on the Drag (MCA MCAD-10221) 1979**
  ★★★½ **Live Shots (MCA MCAD-10816) 1980**
★★★★½ **Musta Notta Gotta Lotta (MCA MCAD-815) 1981**
  ★★★½ **Lord of the Highway (HighTone HCD-8008) 1987**
  ★★★★ **Dig All Night (HighTone HCD-8015) 1988**
  ★★★½ **Live at Liberty Lunch (MCA MCAD-10095) 1990**
  ★★★½ **Love and Danger (MCA MCAD-10584) 1992**

Forging a uniquely powerful synthesis that is steeped in the heart of Texas, Joe Ely makes music that is as difficult to resist as it is to categorize. His songwriting has earned comparison with that of Lubbock homeboy Buddy Holly, his onstage dynamism is a Lone Star match for Bruce Springsteen's, and his music has found common ground for western swing, roadhouse rock, Tex-Mex conjunto, and guitar-driven blues. Though Ely has never benefitted from popular exposure equal to the power of his music, he has proven a pivotal figure in the development of progressive country music (as an influence on artists such as Dwight

Yoakam and Steve Earle) and Texas music in general.

Ely bucked the Nashville studio system from the start, using his own band rather than session regulars on his self-titled debut and drawing material from Lubbock buddies Butch Hancock and Jimmie Dale Gilmore (who had previously recorded with Ely in a band called the Flatlanders). The next year's *Honky Tonk Masquerade* is a masterpiece of Texas music, one that shows how the state's divergent musical strains share common spirit. With the blazing interplay of guitarist Jesse Taylor, steel guitarist Lloyd Maines, and accordionist Ponty Bone, one never gets the sense of the band playing hybrid or hyphenated music. Instead, performances such as "Cornbread Moon" and "Boxcars" have the organic intensity of musicians who are rooted in country, raised on rock, and refuse to recognize any barriers between the two.

Down on the Drag found Ely and band recording in Seattle and moving even further from country convention. A subsequent tour of England, where punkish rockabilly was then the rage, found Ely embraced as an authentic spitfire and a hero to bands such as the Clash. The reception stoked the urgency of Ely's music, as 1981's *Musta Notta Gotta Lotta* put the pedal to the metal for his hardest rocking album to date, which further alienated country purists without attracting a sizable American rock following.

In its wake, the band broke up, leaving *Live Shots* from the British tour as a souvenir. Three years later, Ely emerged with a new band and a new direction on *Hi-Res,* now out of print, which reflected his infatuation with computer and synthesizer technology, and which alienated many of his fans even further.

Dropped by MCA, Ely formed a harder-rocking band that recorded a pair of albums for the independent HighTone label. *Lord of the Highway* introduces guitar firebrand David Grissom (who would later join John Mellencamp's band) and features the saxophone of Bobby Keys (a frequent Rolling Stones sideman). The subsequent *Dig All Night* finds the band even tighter (though without Keys) and the material from Ely

among the strongest and most direct of his career.

Ely was then re-signed by MCA, which issued *Live at Liberty Lunch* as a document of his barnstorming band through the late Eighties. With 1992's *Love and Danger,* Ely once again found his music in transition, moving away from the relentless rock of his hard touring days toward a more polished studio production. Whatever frustration Ely has felt in being ahead of his time or falling between the industry's categorical cracks, it has never affected the ebullience of his music.—D.McL.

BUDDY EMMONS
★★ **Steel Guitar (Flying Fish FF 70007) 1975**

For over thirty years as a road and session picker, Buddy Emmons has set standards for steel guitar in Nashville—which is saying everything. It's not just that he's consistently good; he's consistently inventive. His bluesy obbligato work on Ray Price's 1963 version of "Night Life" should be required listening for every pedal-pusher stepping off the Greyhound in Music City.

Unfortunately, Emmons is not inventive enough to overcome the inadequacies of steel guitar as a lead instrument. This 1975 release only illustrates how much better the steel functions as a mood-setter than as a pacesetter, standards such as "Steel Guitar Rag" notwithstanding. The compelling cuts here are not the hillbilly instrumentals, but the unusual takes on "Rose in Spanish Harlem" [sic] and Pachelbel's "Cannon In D Major" [sic], both of which are bolstered by the element of conceptual surprise.—D.C.

ALEJANDRO ESCOVEDO
★★★★ **Gravity (Watermelon CD 1007) 1992**

Melancholy and tragedy permeate the solo debut of cowpunk pioneer Alejandro Escovedo, who first merged indie-rock with country twang as a guitarist in Rank & File, before forming his own band True Believers. With the help of Austin-based country renegades, Escovedo has created a haunting, first-rate recording of rough-hewn country-meets-roots-rock. From the somberly beautiful "Paradise" with its eerie-sounding slide guitar to the bluesy

"Bury Me" to the piano-and-pedal-steel-driven ballad "Last to Know," each of the eleven tracks grabs hold and doesn't let go. Escovedo's husky voice has just the right amount of crackle to convey the deepest, darkest heartache—but steers clear of self-pity. "So pour me a drink from a broken bottle/And fill my glass with dirty water/What I've lost is gone/What I've gained has no name/And I'll take my leave once more," Escovedo sings in "Broken Bottle," artfully nudging honky-tonk into the twenty-first century.—H.G.-W.

THE EVERLY BROTHERS

★★★★ **The Everly Brothers (Rhino R2-70211) 1958, 1988**
★★★★★ **Songs Our Daddy Taught Us (Rhino R2-70212) 1959, 1988**
★★★★ **The Fabulous Style of the Everly Brothers (Rhino R2-70213) 1960, 1988**
★★★★★ **Cadence Classics (Rhino R2-5258) 1989**
▲▲▲ **All They Had To Do Was Dream (Rhino R2-70214) 1988**
★★★★★ **Golden Hits (Warner Bros. 1471-2) 1962**
★★ **The Very Best (Warner Bros. 1554-2) 1964 ●**
★★ **Highlights of the Reunion Concert (Mercury 824-479-2) 1985**

One of the half-a-dozen most successful rock & roll acts of the Fifties (the first, in fact, to be recorded and managed out of Nashville), the Everlys were essentially an old-time country brother duet in sharkskin suits. Gone, however, were the homilies to God, Mother, and Home; in their place were more pressing concerns: How can I meet her? Should we tell him? When will I be loved?

The classic Cadence recordings have been recycled in countless permutations, but the Rhino sets are the most reliable because of the superior audio. *The Everly Brothers* and *Fabulous Style* are essentially original Cadence albums from 1958 and 1960, highlighted by the two-minute, thirty-second confections that Felice and Boudleaux Bryant whipped up for them, like "Bye, Bye Love," "Wake Up, Little Susie," and "All I Have to Do Is Dream." *Cadence Classics* is a recap of everything in solid-gold rotation, whereas *All They Had to Do Was Dream* comprises rarities

and out-takes for the hard-core fan.

Songs Our Daddy Taught Us is something completely different. Their daddy, Ike, helped lay the foundation for the Merle Travis-Chet Atkins school of picking, and the album illuminates the Everlys' umbilical links to country music's past, drawing a straight line between them and the Blue Sky Boys in one charming old-time duet after another, making a case for them as consummate country performers. Its artistry is exquisite.

When the duo switched to Warner Bros. in 1960, they didn't miss a beat, and their big WB hits, like "Cathy's Clown," "Walk Right Back," and "Crying in the Rain," were at least as durable as the Cadences. All the stuff you know is on *Golden Hits,* whereas *Very Best* mixes in some remakes of the Cadence hits. The remakes, cut in 1964, used much the same session crew, so the sound is predictably close; only the indefinable edge that separates a hungry artist from a sated one was missing, along with the sparkle that comes from singing something for the first time as opposed to the thousandth.

The Beatles, whose harmonies were pure Everly Brothers, scuttled the duo with the result that many of their fine mid-to-late Sixties albums are neither available nor likely to be soon. In particular, *Roots,* another examination of their country heritage, deserves to be talked about in the same breath as Gram Parsons's *GP* or the Byrds' *Sweetheart of the Rodeo.* The brothers hung on until 1973, when they split. After re-forming ten years later, they recorded for Mercury in Nashville with middling success. The reunion concert is excerpted on *Highlights.* Maybe you had to be there.—C.E.

SKIP EWING

★★★½ **Coast of Colorado (MCA MCAD-42128) 1988**
★★★ **The Will to Love (MCA MCAD-42301) 1989**
★★★ **A Healin' Fire (MCA MCAD-42344) 1990**
★★★ **Greatest Hits (MCA MCAD-10356) 1991**
★★★ **Naturally (Liberty C215-96097) 1991**
★★★ **Homegrown Love (Liberty 80071) 1993**

Although still searching for his own niche as a vocalist and performer, Ewing is a songwriter whose observations are clearly steeped in wisdom—as evidenced by the developed narratives, near-photographic images, and digestible moralisms. His best efforts to date are "I Don't Have Far to Fall," "Autumn's Not That Cold," and "The Gospel According to Luke," all of which are models of observation and recounting—and all of which are on *Coast of Colorado.*—E.M.

EXILE

★★½   Exile (Epic EK 39154) 1983
★★   Hang on to Your Heart (Epic EK 40000) 1985
★★★   Exile—Greatest Hits (Epic EK 40401) 1986
★★   Still Standing (Arista ARCD-8624) 1990
★★   Keep It Country (Curb/CEMA D21Y-77295) 1990
★★   The Best of Exile (Curb/CEMA D21K-77296) 1990
★★½   The Complete Collection (Curb/CEMA D21S-77503) 1991
★★   Justice (Arista ARCD-8675) 1991

J.P. PENNINGTON
★★   Whatever It Takes (MCA MCAD-10213) 1991

LES TAYLOR
★★½   That Old Desire (Epic EK45329) 1990
★★   Blue Kentucky Wind (Epic EK 47096) 1991

This determinedly bland country-pop band once recorded a song called "Keep It in the Middle of the Road," which might as well have been its theme song. Exile's music has been so consistently competent, determinedly mainstream, and uniformly faceless that it's easy to imagine the group was dreamed up in some record company board room during a drowsy Monday morning meeting of under-adrenalized promo men. (Matters were not helped by the fact that their earliest LPs were produced by Buddy Killen, a brilliant music-publishing entrepreneur, but one of the least imaginative producers to ever blunder his way into a Nashville studio.) Actually, Exile began as a pop group from Kentucky; the disco dancin' "Kiss You All Over" was their one million seller. And when the well ran dry, they snuck under the fence to get at the green in the country field.

Like so many bands, Exile's earliest major-label country outings were its most promising. On the band's self-titled 1983 Epic debut, Exile proves it was often capable of infectious harmonies and melodically intriguing love ballads that ultimately earned them ten #1 hits during the 1980s—"Woke Up in Love," "I Don't Want to Be a Memory," "Give Me One More Chance," and "Crazy For Your Love"—quite a few of which are gathered on their 1986 Epic *Greatest Hits.*

Remarkably, Exile somehow managed to hold on in the charts, even after the departure of its most talented members, lead singers J.P. Pennington and Les Taylor. The group—sans Pennington and Taylor—found new lease, if not new life, on Arista, with background singer Sonny Lemaire stepping up to handle the lead vocals. Exile's two Arista albums—*Still Standing* and *Justice*—are pleasant enough, though ultimately forgettable.

All things considered, it's easy to understand why gifted singers like Pennington and Taylor would yearn to escape the confines of Exile's relentlessly anonymous style. So, finally free at last to seek and choose their own directions, what do these two come up with on their respective solo ventures? Answer: more relentlessly anonymous country pablum. There is very little on either Pennington's *Whatever It Takes* or Taylor's *That Old Desire* and *Blue Kentucky Wind* to either despise or to warm up to, though Taylor's *That Old Desire* displays moments when this soulful singer does manage to rise above the rote arrangements and ordinary material.—B.A.

CHARLIE FEATHERS

★★★★ **Uh Huh Honey (Norton CED 225)**
1992
★★★½ **Charlie Feathers (Elektra/**
Nonesuch/American/Explorer
Series 9 61147-2) 1991

Charlie Feathers hears an exotic, primal sound in his head. It comes partly from his own soul, partly from the cotton patch blues and high lonesome bluegrass music he heard growing up in Mississippi. He'll tell you that. He's more adamantly passionate and articulate about the origins of the Memphis sound than any of his rockabilly colleagues.

One need only listen to these recordings to understand what he means. Working as producer for the recalcitrant Feathers at Phillips Recording Service in Memphis, during the steamiest days of August 1990, rocker Ben Vaughan captured some of that heat on Feathers's self-titled major label debut, over thirty-five years after he made his first recordings for the Sun Records subsidiary, Flip. Vaughan wisely enlisted a corps of Sun veterans—guitarist Roland Janes, bass and steel guitarist Stan Kesler, and drummer J. M. Van Eaton—along with Feathers's son, guitarist Bubba Feathers, to provide authentic, spare instrumentation that pushes Feathers's expressive voice to the front.

Charlie Feathers finds the singer reworking country songs ("Fraulein," Hank Williams's "[I Don't Care] If Tomorrow Never Comes," George Jones's "Seasons of My Heart") or reaching back into his own Sun-era repertoire ("When You Come Around," "Defrost Your Heart"). Jack Guthrie's country-folk "Oklahoma Hills," becomes a jungle-rock rant. More often than not, Feathers is inventive, unpredictable, eccentric, and engaging. Indulging in hiccups, screams, phrases spoken instead of sung, abrupt changes in pitch from a falsetto to a growl, Feathers manages to tickle and tease something unexpected out of nearly everything he tackles.

The Norton reissue gathers various Feathers recordings from 1967 to 1979—everything from a TV show sound track to a single cut for a Los Angeles rockabilly independent to some releases from Feathers's own label to some late Sixties sides made for the purpose of reviving his dormant career. With twenty-eight tracks clocking in at over seventy minutes in length, the disc is a larger dose of Feathers-mania than most would care to swallow, but it provides a fascinating document of his stubborn allegiance to form in the face of changing musical fashion.

Not available currently on a domestic release are original versions of Feathers's classic early efforts for Flip, Sun, and King: "I've Been Deceived," "Peepin' Eyes," "Wedding Gown of White," "Tongue-Tied Jill," "Get with It," "Bottle to the Baby," and "One Hand Loose."

Sun Records founder Sam Phillips once told writer Colin Escott, "Had I stayed in country music alone and dedicated myself to it, then I had the nucleus of several fine artists who could have made it—in particular Ernie Chaffin and Charlie Feathers. I just love stylists. People you knew the minute you heard them on record."

Today, Feathers would be more at home in a David Lynch film sound track than on country radio. On the Norton reissue he sings, "I guess I'm crazy, but I'll never, never change." Let's hope he stands by that pledge.—J.O.

FREDDY FENDER
★★★★   **Freddy Fender Collection (Reprise 9 26638-2) 1991**
★★★   **Greatest Hits (Hollywood/IMG HCD-407)**

Often called the "Mexican Elvis," he was born Baldemar Huerta and later rechristened Freddy Fender (after the Fender guitar) the better to connect with his growing Anglo audience in Central and South Texas. Fender is best known for his lilting vibrato, his two million-sellers from 1975 ("Wasted Days and Wasted Nights" and "Before the Next Teardrop Falls"), and his membership in the Texas Tornadoes. He brings a true Chicano sensibility to the country ethos.—C.F.

FILÉ
★★★★   **Cajun Dance Band (Flying Fish CD418) 1987**
★★★   **2 Left Feet (Flying Fish CD 507) 1989**

Filé is one of several younger Cajun bands playing music firmly grounded in traditional French Cajun music while at the same time reaching out to incorporate elements of blues, rock, and country music. The members of Filé have added electric guitar, mandolin, and even an occasional saxophone to the more typical Cajun accordion, fiddle, acoustic guitar, drums, and electric bass to produce a progressive Cajun sound. Their repertoire ranges from bayou classics like "Pine Grove Blues" and "'Tit Gallop Pour

Mamou" to hard-driving renditions of rockers such as "Allons Rock and Roll" and "Sugar Bee." These guys play contemporary popular Cajun music at its best.—C.H.S.

CATHY FINK
★★★½   **Doggone My Time (Sugar Hill SH-CD-3783) 1982**
★★★★   **When the Rain Comes Down (Rounder CD 8013) 1988**
★★½   **Cathy Fink & Marcy Marxer (Sugar Hill SH-CD-3775) 1989**

Cathy Fink is a folk-based artist whose voice won't bowl you over, yet it's seldom not sincerely affecting, either. In its most fetching alto range (used winningly on the song, "When the Rain Comes Down," and on "I'm So Lonesome I Could Cry"), it's a mite reminiscent of Karen Carpenter without the darker earth tones. Fink is also an accomplished banjoist and guitarist, as well as a songwriter. Her 1982 debut, *Doggone My Time,* put all her talent to good use. Strong feminist feeling is drawn equally from Fink's "Coming Home," about a female Vietnam vet, and from the traditional "Cat's Got the Measles." If those performances frame Fink as a sister of the Seventies, there's a timeless luster to her moving interpretations of Stephen Foster's "My Old Kentucky Home" and Hank's "I'm So Lonesome I Could Cry" (turning the obvious on its head, Fink puts the guitar to Foster and the banjo to Hank).

For its range of material and because it splendidly showcases Fink's fine frailing, *Doggone* is a more satisfying collection than 1989's *Cathy Fink & Marcy Marxer,* an album shaped largely around the mandolin-guitar brother duo format much revived in recent years (see Tim and Mollie O'Brien). The vocal harmonies don't always sparkle with the high resolution that makes this sort of thing work best, and this followup just doesn't have the legs that made *Blue Rose* (Sugar Hill SH-3768), a Fink-Marxer collaboration with other sisters of the folk-grass sorority (Laurie Lewis, Sally Van Meter, and Molly Mason), such a strong pacer from the gate.

Fink's best album is basically for kids, but grownups can appreciate the variety, musicianship, and simple-but-heartfelt performances on 1988's *When the Rain Comes Down.* With a strong supporting cast of musicians, a children's chorus, and instruments ranging from mouthbow to steel drum to synthesizer, Fink performed a rollicking "Alphabet Boogie," a hip-hop tribute to "Cookies," some children's chestnuts ("Skip to My Lou"), and some country for kids of all ages (Roy 'n' Dale's "Happy Trails"). *When the Rain Comes Down* is just plain good music that kids especially will enjoy.—M.H.

THE FLATLANDERS
★★★½ **More a Legend Than a Band (Rounder CDSS-34) 1990**
Aptly titled, this album is the sole recording of a West Texas band featuring Jimmie Dale Gilmore, Butch Hancock, and Joe Ely, who disbanded shortly after this project was shelved in 1972. In light of Ely's subsequent emergence (though he played a supporting role to singer Gilmore and songwriter Hancock in the Flatlanders), the recordings were belatedly issued in England in 1980, though not in the United States until 1990.

With acoustic arrangements that emphasized spirit rather than slickness, the music initially sounded like a throwback to the era of Jimmie Rodgers, but ultimately anticipated the revitalizing country trends toward neotraditionalism and Western progressivism, Incorporating a streak of rustic mysticism and employing the musical saw as a featured instrument, the album presents the first recordings of Gilmore's "Dallas" and Hancock's "One Road More" among its highlights.—D.McL.

FLATT & SCRUGGS
★★★★★ **The Mercury Sessions, Vol. 1 (Rounder CDSS-18) 1988**
★★★★★ **The Mercury Sessions, Vol. 2 (Rounder CDSS-19) 1988**
★★★★ **The Complete Mercury Sessions (Mercury 512644-4) 1992**
★★ **20 Greatest Hits (Deluxe DCD-7787)**
★★★★ **Don't Get Above Your Raisin' (Rounder SSCD-08) 1992**
★★★★ **Golden Era (Rounder SSCD-05) 1992**
★★★★ **Blue Ridge Cabin Home (County CCS-CD-102) 1990**
★ **Golden Hits (Hollywood/IMG HCD-287) 1987**
★★★ **Columbia Historic Edition (CK-37469-E) 1982**
★★★★ **Foggy Mountain Banjo (Sony Music Special Products A-23392) 1961**
★★★ **Songs of the Famous Carter Family (Columbia CK-08464) 1961**
★★ **Live at Vanderbilt University (Sony Music Special Products A-8934) 1964**

After their departure from the fabled Bill Monroe band in 1948, singer-guitarist Lester Flatt and banjoist Earl Scruggs became the most highly visible and emulated bluegrass act in the nation. Until their split in 1969, Flatt & Scruggs and their band, the Foggy Mountain Boys, forged the sound that millions of listeners came to associate with bluegrass: the rolling three-finger banjo Scruggs played on "Foggy Mountain Breakdown"; the warm, lilting vocals of Flatt on "Why Did You Wander"; the surging gospel quartet sound of "Cabin on the Hill." After starting their careers on Appalachian radio stations, the band made it to the Grand Ole Opry in the mid-1950s, and soon had a following for their television and early morning radio shows. The use of their music as a theme for the hit film *Bonnie and Clyde,* as well as their involvement with the TV comedy "The Beverly Hillbillies," made them household names. They also fit nicely into the folk music revival of the late 1960s, recording both older traditional songs and newer pieces by the likes of Bob Dylan. For most of this time the band recorded for Columbia, producing more than thirty-five LPs and a host of singles, a dozen or so of which charted in the 1960s. Very little of this huge output is currently available on CD; the serious devotee should seek out the expensive imported sets of Germany's Bear Family (BCD 15472, containing the complete works from 1948 to 1959, and BCD 15539EI, with the recordings from 1959 to 1965).

The twenty-eight sides done for Mercury at the dawn of the Flatt & Scruggs career are rightfully considered the essential core of their music, and a large part of the core of classic bluegrass music. These 1948-50 masterpieces, recorded at various radio stations and makeshift studios around the South, include their first recordings of standards like "Foggy Mountain Breakdown," "My Cabin in Caroline," "We'll Meet Again Sweetheart," "Old Salty Dog Blues," and "Roll in My Sweet Baby's Arms." Over the years, these sides have been reissued in dozens of strange configurations, some with fake stereo added, few with decent notes. Finally, though, they have been issued in not one, but two, serious formats: Rounder's two volumes called *The Mercury Sessions, Vols. 1 and 2* and Mercury's own *The Complete Mercury Sessions*. Both have excellent notes, but the sound on the Rounder volumes is a bit better than that on Mercury's; either edition will serve as a juicy starting point for anyone wanting to explore the vast Foggy Mountain Boys repertoire.

The early Columbia years saw the band add to its raw talent and instrumental prowess a set of new songs and arrangements that became classics in their own right, still heard and played today. County's *Blue Ridge Cabin Home* includes some of the best of these 1951-54 efforts (including the title song), while Rounder's *Golden Era* offers more of the same—both with excellent notes. *Don't Get Above Your Raisin'* has the title song as well as the gospel "Get in Line, Brother," and 1952's "Why Did You Wander." Columbia's *Historic Edition* volume casts its net a bit more widely, including 1959's hit "Cabin on the Hill," as well as Scruggs's banjo workouts "Dear Old Dixie" and "Foggy Mountain Special." In 1961 the band released what would become its single most influential studio album, *Foggy Mountain Banjo*. Not a collection of earlier singles, the album was instead a showcase for the instrumental prowess of Scruggs, Flatt, fiddler Paul Warren, and dobroist Josh Graves. It included definitive versions of pieces like "Ground Speed," "Bugle Call Rag," and "Sally Ann." Widely applauded by folk and jazz enthusiasts (it actually got a five-star review in *Downbeat*), the album set the tone for much of the band's work in the 1960s. The CD reissue even captures the work of studio drummer Buddy Harman, whose presence was played down in the original LP for fear of offending bluegrass purists.

By the time the Foggy Mountain Boys did *Live at Vanderbilt University* in 1964, they were starting to lose some of their edge and were getting caught up in the folk music mania of the time. Just three years before, though, they proved they could still create classic music when they collaborated with Mother Maybelle Carter in *Songs of the Famous Carter Family*. Spotlighting Scruggs's unheralded guitar work, as well as Maybelle's guitar and autoharp, the session offered "You Are My Flower," "Keep on the Sunny Side," and "Foggy Mountain Top," among others. Josh Graves's dobro work, Curly Seckler's tenor, and Paul Warren's fiddle showed just how convincing the band could still be when they had good material.—C.K.W.

ROSIE FLORES
★★★½ **After the Farm (HighTone HCD8033) 1992**

After a now out-of-print album of progressive country for Reprise in 1987, Flores concentrates here on sturdy songcraft and emotional conviction regardless of musical category. Backed by the hard-twang of her roots-rocking Los Angeles band, she offers an emotional immediacy that is transparently sincere, with highlights ranging from the social conscience of "Price You Pay" to the lovelorn intimacy of "This Loneliness." Both the country traditionalism of "Dent in My Heart" (written with Jimmie Dale Gilmore) and the acoustic "West Texas Plains" confirm that, wherever she may live, the native Texan hasn't gone Hollywood.—D.McL.

FLYING BURRITO BROTHERS
★★★½ **Farther Along: The Best of (A&M 75021-5216-2) 1988**
★★½ **The Flying Burrito Bros. (Mobile Fidelity MFCD-10-00772) 1971**
★★ **Last of the Red Hot Burritos (A&M 75021-4343-2) 1972**

After spending five months countrifying the Byrds, Gram Parsons decided to form his own band—a country-gospel-rock band, as he envisioned it, that would turn mere songs into classics. The Flying Burrito Brothers, he said, would play "Cosmic American Music." Ragged as a live band, they pulled things together in the studio and, though falling short of creating standards, did come up with memorable originals like "Hot Burrito #1," "Hot Burrito #2," "Wheels," and "Sin City," which would later be covered by Elvis Costello, Emmylou Harris, and others. The Burritos also showed great taste in songs they chose to cover: "Dark End of the Street," "Do Right Woman," and, from Parsons's buddies, the Rolling Stones, "Wild Horses." The albums on which these songs appear are on CDs available only as Japanese and British imports, but they're all in *Farther Along,* a solid body of evidence that, although he never had a hit with what he called "Cosmic American Music," Parsons had the right ideas. After he left for a solo career, the Burritos carried on with guitarist Rick Roberts. The resulting *Flying Burrito Bros.* is solid country-rock, smoother and cleaner-cut than the Parsons edition. Maybe too much so. The thrill was gone. *Last of the Red Hot Burritos* is a live last gasp.—B.F.-T.

DAN FOGELBERG
★★½ **High Country Snows (Epic EK 39616) 1985**

Dan Fogelberg's records have often gently echoed the El Lay country-rock of his buddies the Eagles, although he tends to nurse a tremulous melancholy that is all his own. His roots have rarely shown on his other dozen or so albums, but on this effort Fogelberg pledges his love for traditional country, particularly bluegrass. Recorded in Nashville, this is a sincere effort from Fogelberg, issued the year that the *New York Times* said country was dead. So it's not trendy. But it is still, for better or worse, Fogelberg—replete with breathy, triple-tracked vocals that are more reminiscent of Queen's glam rock than classic King Records bluegrass. Happily, though, in contrast to his usual proclivity for playing everything but the drums, Fogelberg brings in top-notch country pickers, including Jerry Douglas, Doc Watson, and Herb Pedersen, who help keep the airy Fogelberg down to earth. Fogelberg also takes a couple of creditable stabs at Flatt & Scruggs's "Down the Road" and the Stanley Brothers' "Think of What You've Done," although a more representative cut is the gauzy pop hit "Go Down Easy," an apt description for this album. *High Country Snows* certainly won't win over bluegrass purists, but it's a pleasant entrée into the music for Fogelberg fans and lite-rock devotees.—P.K.

JOHN FOGERTY
★★★ **The Blue Ridge Rangers (Fantasy FCD-4502-2) 1973**
★★★ **John Fogerty (Asylum 5E-1046) 1975**
★★★½ **Centerfield (Warner Bros. 9 25203-2) 1985 ▲²**
★★★ **Eye of the Zombie (Warner Bros. 25449-2) 1987 ●**

After he broke up Creedence Clearwater Revival, Fogerty tested his independence with *The Blue Ridge Rangers,* a one-man-band project stuffed with loving treatments of a dozen country standards, such as Hank Williams's "Jambalaya" and Webb Pierce's "I Ain't Never." Fogerty's vocals are occasionally too agitated for the melodies they are fueling, but *The Blue Ridge Rangers* remains a pleasant, low-key extension of Fogerty's former band's country leanings. That charming if somewhat uneventful exercise out of the way, Fogerty released only one set, his eponymous 1975 collection that leaned toward Creedence-style rock & roll, before he disappeared for a decade. Fogerty returned with 1985's platinum *Centerfield,* a wily collection of rock & roll, country, and swamp-rock that brought him up-to-date in production methods if not in lyrical subjects. The following year's *Eye of the Zombie* rocked harder and was on the whole darker and more diffuse. Seven years later, a new CD is said to be imminent.—J.G.

RED FOLEY
★★★★ **Country Music Hall of Fame (MCA MCAD-10084) 1991**

Clyde Julian "Red" Foley may have been the most versatile singer in country music history. In a long career that included the "WLS Barn Dance," the "Renfro Valley Barn Dance" (which he co-founded), the Grand Ole Opry, and the "Ozark Jubilee," Foley demonstrated that he could do virtually everything demanded of a country entertainer. He was not noted for instrumental virtuosity, but he was a skillful comedian, master of ceremonies, straight man (for comics like Rod Brasfield and Minnie Pearl), and authoritative interpreter of any kind of song material that country audiences wanted to hear back in the Forties and Fifties. This compilation ably samples Foley's varied repertoire, which featured sentimental songs like "Old Shep," boogie tunes like "Tennessee Saturday Night" and "Chattanoogie Shoe Shine Boy," heart songs like "As Far As I'm Concerned," blues numbers like "Midnight" and "Deep Blues," hymns like "Just a Closer Walk" and "Peace in the Valley," and hit duets with Ernest Tubb and Kitty Wells. Even granting that Foley's smooth, Crosby-like style is now out of fashion, this once-popular performer is nevertheless seriously underrepresented on CD.—B.C.M.

TENNESSEE ERNIE FORD

★★★★ Sixteen Tons of Boogie (Rhino R2 70975) 1990
★★★★ Songs of the Civil War (Capitol C21Y-95705) 1991
  ★★   All-Time Greatest Hymns (Curb/ CEMA D21K-77326) 1990
  ★★   Country Gospel Classics, Vol. 1 (Liberty C21K-95849) 1991
 ★★★   Country Gospel Classics, Vol. 2 (Capitol Nashville C21K-95915) 1991
 ★★★   Favorite Hymns (Ranwood R-8229-CD) 1987
  ★★   The Heart of Christmas (Liberty C21K-96502) 1991
 ★★★   Red, White, and Blue (Liberty C21K-96677) 1991
★★★★ Collector's Series (Capitol C21Y-95291) 1991

For much of his long career, Tennessee Ernie Ford didn't sound much like a country singer. His strong, clear baritone was a popular alternative for those who couldn't stand the keening nasality of Hank Williams or the pedal-steel moans of George Jones. Though he was born and reared in the area around Bristol, Tennessee, the birthplace of old-time country music, Ford didn't make his mark in the music business until he settled on the West Coast after World War II and became a central figure in the burgeoning scene there. Braced by his successful network radio and television work ("Bless your little pea-pickin' hearts"), he had a huge number of hit singles and albums for Capitol during the 1950s and 1960s; his LP output alone totaled over eighty-five albums. He specialized in three types of song: the uptempo, finger-popping country boogie style of his #1 hit "Shotgun Boogie" (1950); the folk music style represented by his signature song, "Sixteen Tons"

(1955); and the hymns and gospel songs featured on his trend-setting album *Hymns* (1956). Fortunately, all three styles are well represented by the available CDs.

Two collections chronicle his early country boogie sound. Rhino's *Sixteen Tons of Boogie* focuses on uptempo tracks like "Blackberry Boogie" and "Kissin' Bug Boogie," and features stellar West Coast instrumentalists Merle Travis and Speedy West. The liner notes feature detailed comments by Ford himself about the songs. Overlapping the Rhino package, but casting a wider net for early Ford material, is Capitol's own *Collector's Series* anthology. Here, in addition to the boogies, are other early hits, including his haunting theme from *River of No Return*, duets with Kay Starr ("I'll Never Be Free"), folk songs ("The Ballad of Davy Crockett," "Sixteen Tons," "Nine Pound Hammer"), and gospel ("That's All," "His Hands").

In 1961, during the centennial of the Civil War, Ford and producer Lee Gillette released two excellent sets of vintage war songs from the conflict. Buoyed by spare arrangements from Jack Fascinato, Ford worked his way through beauties like "Lorena," "The Vacant Chair," and "Just Before the Battle, Mother." Originally issued as two LPs (one for the North, one for the South), all of these recordings have now been brought together in *Songs of the Civil War*—a splendid collection of songs that moved Ford to the front ranks of interpreters of old favorites. A related item is *Red, White, and Blue,* a set of patriotic songs done in Ford's powerful, straightforward manner.

Ford's 1956 *Hymns* album became one of the best-selling LPs in modern history, and set off a long string of gospel and sacred albums. Some of these early classic recordings are found in *All-Time Greatest Hymns,* but country fans may find them a bit stodgy and formal. Ford did several albums of gospel songs (including many sides with the Jordanaires), and some of these can be found in *Country Gospel Classics, Vol. 2.* Here are powerful folk hymns like "Wayfaring Pilgrim," gospel quartet favorites like "Precious Memories," and country favorites like "Peace in the Valley." The absolute absence of any liner notes makes it hard to tell just where these recordings came from, but in them Ford does a fine job of reminding us of why these songs became such staples in his repertoire.—C.K.W.

THE FORESTER SISTERS

★★ **You Again (Warner Bros. 9 25571-2) 1987**

★★ **A Christmas Card (Warner Bros. 2-25623) 1987**

★★★ **Sincerely (Warner Bros. 9 25746-2) 1988**

★★★½ **Greatest Hits (Warner Bros. 9 25897-2) 1989**

★★★½ **All I Need (Warner Bros. 25779-2) 1989**

★★ **Come Hold Me (Warner Bros. 9 26141-2) 1990**

★★½ **Talkin' 'Bout Men (Warner Bros. 9 26500-2) 1991**

★★½ **Got a Date (Warner Bros. 9 26821-2) 1992**

Signed in 1985 as Warner Bros.' answer to the Judds, the Foresters haven't even come close to the megaplatinum success that has made Wynonna and Naomi household names. Although pretty, none of them is the attention-grabbing equal of Mama Judd. More to the point, none of them can match the vocal firepower of Wynonna. Nevertheless, these four sisters from Lookout Mountain, Georgia—Kathy, Kim, June, and Christy—have proved durably entertaining on their own terms. Their church-trained, family-close harmonies remain an indelible vocal signature, regardless of who produces them. When applied to a strong song, those Forester harmonies can be as warm and comforting as a four-poster feather bed; given weak material, they can put you to sleep.

Generally, the Foresters have a good ear for songs, although they don't always play to their strengths: they cut a polite version of "These Lips Don't Know How to Say Goodbye" (*Sincerely*) two years before Doug Stone and a ponderous take (with the Bellamy Brothers!) on John Hiatt's "Drive South" (*Come Hold Me*) two years before Suzy Bogguss. The Foresters are at their best in quietly considered homilies about domestic life ("Letter Home"), sassy comments on the mating game ("Men"), or a smart revamp of an old classic (Brenda Lee's "Too Many Rivers"). Eldest sister Kathy generally dispenses the comforting down-home

wisdom on singles like "(That's What You Do) When You're in Love," while husky-voiced Kim tackles the uptempo, don't-tread-on-me cuts like "Leave It Alone"; June and Christy tend to get a track or two on each album.

Thanks largely to their distinctive harmonies, the Foresters' sound has remained remarkably consistent over the course of nine studio albums and one hits package. If you're a fan, you'll probably want all these albums. For those less committed, the *Greatest Hits* package is a solid (albeit brief) collection of ten hits, from their Top Ten debut with "(That's What You Do) When You're in Love" to their suitably lush remake of the McGuire Sisters' 1955 hit "Sincerely." (Their first two LPs from 1985 and 1986—*Forester Sisters* and *Perfume, Ribbons & Pearls*—are not available on CD, but pretty much all you'd want from them is collected on *Greatest Hits.*) Also worth singling out is the album that followed *Greatest Hits, All I Need.* Clearly a labor of love, this collection of gospel standards and contemporary Christian songs is tasteful and confident, but never prim.—P.K.

FOSTER & LLOYD

★★★★ **Foster & Lloyd (RCA 6372-2-R) 1987**

★★ **Faster and Llouder (RCA 9587-2-R) 1988**

★★ **Version of the Truth (RCA 2453-2-R) 1989**

★★★ **[Bill Lloyd] Feeling the Elephant (DB-97) 1987**

The 1987 debut CD by the duo of songwriters Radney Foster and Bill Lloyd was modest yet extremely promising, a sparkling mixture of midtempo rockabilly, Everly Brothers harmonies, Byrds-derived riffs, and straight-faced rock. The arrangements were lean, with nifty details sketched on many lyrics and riffs. It was as far as they got—both of their subsequent sets found them cooking up the occasional fiery track, although most of their numbers repeated the formula that they had perfected on their debut. It was especially distressing when their second CD, *Faster and Llouder,* was neither. Lloyd's solo set, recorded before the duo got started, for a label called Throbbing Lobster, has more to do with famous Memphis rock weirdo Alex

Chilton than anyone associated with country. The duo parted ways amicably in 1990.—J.G.

RADNEY FOSTER
★★ **Del Rio, TX, 1959 (Arista 18713) 1992**
Foster's solo debut offered a shuffle here ("Just Call Me Lonesome"), a rocker there ("Nobody Wins"), all pleasant enough but nothing that gained weight through repeated listenings. This disc suggests that Foster was the more conventionally minded member of Foster & Lloyd.—J.G.

GEORGE FOX
★★★ **With All My Might (Warner Bros. 9 26162) 1990**
★★ **Spice of Life (Warner Bros. 9 26566) 1991**
George Fox's debut *With All My Might* shows promise of a strong singer-songwriter in the John Prine mode. The sound is open-hearted acoustic rock tinged with folk and country. Fox's voice has a reassuring warmth, and his easy-handed observations on life and romance give a subtle grace to songs like "Bachelor Girl" and "Lonesome Avenue Goodbye (Goldmine)." *Spice of Life,* though, is more formulaic country fare, with Fox writing or co-writing only four of the ten tracks. It's hard to miss with a classic like Buck Owens's "There Goes My Love," but mild stompers like "Fell in Love and I Can't Get Out," while pleasant, lack personality.—K.S.

CLEVE FRANCIS
★★ **Tourist in Paradise (Capitol Nashville CDP 7 96498 2) 1991**
★★★ **Walkin' (Liberty C2-80033) 1993**

With Charley Pride exiled from the major labels in the early Nineties, Dr. Cleve Francis inherited the mantle as country music's most visible African American artist. His warm, enveloping tenor is most effective on the midtempo toe-tappers "Love Light" and "You Do My Heart Good." But most of the rest of his debut is curiously passionless, as though he was singing on automatic pilot. This is all the more disconcerting because the ballads "Those Were the Days, These Are the Nights" and "How Can I Hold You" suggest that there is much more heart in

this singing cardiologist than we're being allowed to hear.
Several critics pointed out that the overall song selection was weak. Cleve's 1993 *Walkin'* collection answered them. This time, the warmth and heart in his delivery were given freer rein, notably on the jaunty title tune, the uptempo "Run Like the Wind," and such big, robust ballads as "I Won't Let You Walk Away" and "Your Love Stays with Me." With progress like this, Cleve Francis remained in the running as one of country's most promising up and comers.—R.K.O.

JANIE FRICKE
★★★ **Greatest Hits (Columbia CK 38310) 1982**
★★★ **The Very Best of Janie Fricke (Columbia CK 40165) 1985**
★★★ **17 Greatest Hits (Columbia CK 40235) 1986**
★★★ **Saddle the Wind (Columbia CK 44143) 1988**
★★★ **Labor of Love (Columbia CK-45087) 1989**
Possessed of a fluid but undistinctive voice, this backup singer-turned-soloist scored several radio hits in that generally barren period of country music that stretched between the Urban Cowboy craze and the advent of the new traditionalists. And it was during this time that she twice earned the Country Music Association's Female Vocalist of the Year award (1982 and 1983), with such #1 hits as "Don't Worry 'Bout Me Baby," "It Ain't Easy Bein' Easy" and "He's a Heartache (Looking for a Place to Happen)." Being neither a songwriter nor a clearly defined persona, Fricke was inextricably tied to the level of the material she recorded. Her best and worst are evident, respectively, in "You Don't Know Love" and "Do Me with Love," both of which are available on *The Very Best* and *17 Greatest Hits* packages. Of her later albums, *Labor of Love* is among the best, containing as it does such memorable songs as Katy Moffatt and Tom Russell's "Walking on the Moon" and Steve Earle's "My Old Friend the Blues."—E.M.

LEFTY FRIZZELL
★★★★ **American Originals (Columbia CK-45067) 1990**
★★★★★ **The Best of Lefty Frizzell (Rhino R2 71005) 1991**

In the mid-Eighties, when country's new traditionalist movement pointed the music back to its staunchly hillbilly roots, Lefty Frizzell's name dominated discussion of what that tradition was all about. Young turks Randy Travis, George Strait, Dwight Yoakam, Keith Whitley, and John Anderson all acknowledged huge stylistic debts to Lefty. Merle Haggard had been singing his praises for years. Lefty's cascading vowels and throaty soul intimacy have informed so many young singers' styles it's tough to remember that hard country can mean anything else.

Yet far from being a cult hero, Frizzell was once the most explosively popular country singer in America. Between the fall of 1950 and Christmas of 1952, he scored five #1 hits and eight Top Tens. All thirteen songs, along with five later hits, are collected on the indispensable Rhino disc. They range from the racy "If You've Got the Money, I've Got the Time" to the celestially elegant "Forever (And Always)" to the novelty aplomb of "Saginaw, Michigan." The instrumentation is straight-up honky-tonk—fiddles, steel, and barrelhouse piano—all laid out behind Lefty's inimitable voice. He glides through each song with such apparent laid-back ease one can mistake his control for an artless native talent. Lefty won't raise your neck hairs with a Hank Williams howl; but on classics like "Always Late (With Your Kisses)" and "I Want to Be with You Always," he'll slide under your skin so quietly you won't even notice he's in there, till you find yourself returning to his music over and over again.

Lyrically, Lefty was a committed romantic with an occasional tendency to overstep the schmaltz line. He did love a good rounder's anthem, though; and he also had a mournful edge that showed up on early hits like "Don't Stay Away (Till Love Grows Cold)." That edge sharpened in self-directed ways as Lefty's personal life and career fell into disarray by the mid-Fifties. One can sense the oblique despair behind his eerie delivery of "The Long Black Veil," a seemingly impersonal story song that was his last hit of the 1950s. One can also hear his voice maturing, adding a profoundly weary resonance to his unique phrasing.

By limiting themselves to a greatest hits concept, the compilers of both these discs have barely tapped the final fifteen years of Lefty's life and career, during which he cut some outstanding music but less consistently, and with little chart success. The best window on that period (not counting Bear Family's sixteen-disc German import set) is on *American Originals*. Though it amounts to little more than an abridged, haphazardly sequenced version of *The Best of Lefty Frizzell*, the Columbia collection includes one 1960s obscurity not found on the Rhino disc. Called "A Little Unfair," it features Lefty in high-harmony tandem with his right-hand man, Abe Mulkey, their voices swirling around a bluesy arrangement in gloomy dismay at love's injustice.

There's so much more where "A Little Unfair" came from. Both of these discs are rim-to-rim some of the most important country music ever recorded. It's a tribute to Lefty that more would have definitely meant better.—D.C.

G

LARRY GATLIN & THE GATLIN BROTHERS

★★★½ **Greatest Hits (Columbia CK 36488) 1980** ●
 ★★★ **Greatest Hits Vol. II (Columbia CK 38923) 1983**
★★★★ **17 Greatest Hits (Columbia CK 40187) 1985**
 ★★★ **Biggest Hits (Columbia CK 44471) 1988**
★★★½ **Christmas with the Gatlins (Capitol Nashville CDP 7 94342 2) 1990**
 ★★★ **Greatest Hits Encore (Capitol Nashville CDP 7 95528 2) 1991**
 ★★★ **Adios (Liberty CDP 7 95759 2) 1992**

For pure vocal beauty and strength, few in country music come close to matching Larry Gatlin, especially when he blends his voice with those of his brothers Steve and Rudy. Gatlin has long been an inventive and occasionally brilliant songwriter as well, penning such cinematic masterpieces as "Broken Lady," "I Just Wish You Were Someone I Love" and "I've Done Enough Dyin' Today." To his own artistic detriment, Gatlin has also written and recorded a great deal of schlock, which he attempted to elevate to significance by surrounding it with gorgeous and intricate vocal harmonies. This ploy seemed to work well enough until the mid-Eighties, when country music turned toward the harder-edged new traditionalists. Still, Gatlin has left a legacy of dozens of songs that will survive the twists and trends. Fortunately, all his best work is now available on CD. The *17 Greatest Hits* package includes the lyrically exquisite "Broken Lady" and "I Just Wish You Were Someone I Love," plus the makeout masterpiece "What Are We Doin' Lonesome."—E.M.

CRYSTAL GAYLE

★★★½ **Classic Crystal (EMI Manhattan CDP 7 46549 2) 1979** ●
 ★★★ **Miss the Mississippi (Liberty C21K-95563) 1979** ●
 ★★★ **These Days (Liberty C21K-95565) 1980**
 ★★★ **Hollywood, Tennessee (Liberty C21K-95564) 1981**
★★★½ **Greatest Hits (Capitol Nashville CDP 7 95886 2) 1983**
 ★★★ **The Best of Crystal Gayle (Warner Bros. 25622-2) 1987**
 ★★★ **Nobody's Angel (Warner Bros. 25706-2) 1988**
 ★★★ **Ain't Gonna Worry (Liberty C21-94301) 1990**
 ★★★ **Three Good Reasons (Liberty C21-96507) 1992**

Gayle is basically a pop and jazz singer who flowered in the country format during one of its most artistically open periods. Her biggest country hits never really displayed her vocal range and stylistic influences. To witness these, one had to see her wide-reaching stage shows. More an interpreter than an originator, Gayle did her best work under the tutelage of producer Allen Reynolds, himself an emigré from pop music. Gayle's warm, liquid, precisely enunci-ated delivery and essentially country-free lyrics are showcased admirably on *Classic Crystal,* which contains such well-known songs as "Don't It Make My Brown Eyes Blue" and "Ready for the Times to Get Better," and *Greatest Hits,* which shows a little more of her range, via such cabaret proclamations as "Too Many Lovers" and "Livin' in These Troubled Times."—E.M.

CRYSTAL GAYLE & GARY MORRIS

★★ **What If We Fall in Love (Warner Bros. 25507-2) 1987**

This album is made up of adult love songs that emphasize Gayle and Morris's almost unearthly vocal harmonies. The arrangements and instrumentations are pure pop. None of these factors would of themselves imperil the album, but the lyrics are generally weak and undistin-guished.—E.M.

THE GEEZINSLAWS

★★★ **The Geezinslaws (Step One SOR-0052) 1989**

★★½ **World Tour (Step One SOR-0056) 1990**

★★ **Feelin' Good, Gittin' Up, Gittin' Down (Step One SOR-0074) 1992**

Semi-regulars on The Nashville Network's "Nashville Now" TV show, the Geezinslaws make laid-back, quasi-comedy records tailored for the boozy fog of barrooms. In the Geezinslaws' world, women are puzzling, fickle creatures. Men (read: the Geezinslaws) often are out of step with contemporary culture, fond of alcohol, and "old country songs," and victimized by women and by weirdos who don't share their worldview. Sam (Sammy Allred) and silent, straight man Son (Dewayne Smith) do have a pretty good eye for material, though, covering comic and slightly off-kilter songs by such talented writers as Robert Earl Keen Jr. ("Swervin' in My Lane,"

"Copenhagen"), John Prine ("Fryin' Pan [Never Leave My Wife at Home]"), Delbert McClinton ("Victim of Life's Circumstances"), John D. Loudermilk ("Life Can Have Meaning"), Paul Overstreet ("Lonely Heart"), and Shel Silverstein ("The Diet Song"). They also pound the funny bone with fractured, up-tempo versions of such ballad standards as "Night and Day," "Unchained Melody," "You Belong to Me," and "Somewhere over the Rainbow." *Feelin' Good, Gittin' Up, Gittin' Down* inter-sperses jokes, applause, and laughter between songs—the musical equivalent of prime-time TV's canned laughter. Audience prompting notwithstanding, the funny bits predictably lose their punch once they become familiar.

Chances are, this duo sounds funnier after a couple of beers, though some might argue that it takes as much as a six-pack to get the joke.—J.O.

BOBBIE GENTRY

★★★★½ **Greatest Hits (Curb 77387) 1990**

Only Nancy Sinatra ever managed Hollywood country as undeniable as this native of Greenwood, Mississippi, first heard from in 1967 when "Ode to Billie Joe" insinuated itself into the #1 position of the pop charts. Gentry's sound was scintillating: swamp rhythms and an occasional horn that, R&B-style, matched and extended the targeted sulk of her confident voice, all counterpointed by Jimmie Haskell orchestrations so tautly conversational that they sounded as down home as a washboard. But then songs like Gentry's come rarer still. In "Ode" she couches a smoldering tale of likely infanticide-suicide in mundane local details that build to evoke an everyday tragedy; the song unleashes a crack filmmaker's sense of visual editing and a novelist's command of time. The same is true of "Fancy," which is even better: the story of "poor white trash" striving from the point of view of a woman hardly sure that standard feminist indictments ought to apply to her particular strategies. Elsewhere on this well-coordinated compilation, Gentry does sexy stuff like "Slow Cookin'," which, like "Fancy," has influenced noncountry Southern songwriters like Cindy Wilson and Kate Pierson of the B-52s. Toward the end of

this disc's sequence (and not coinciden-
tally her career), Gentry sings folkie love
songs like "Let It Be Me" with Glen
Campbell. She always was a Hollywood
country singer.—J.H.

DON GIBSON

★★★★ All-Time Greatest Hits (RCA 2295-
2-R) 1990
★★★ Best of Don Gibson, Vol. 1 (Curb/
CEMA D21K-77440) 1991
★★★ 18 Greatest Hits (Curb/CEMA
D21S-77474) 1990

On December 3, 1957, when he took a
sparse back-up quartet into RCA's
Nashville studio, young singer-songwriter
Don Gibson made country music history
of sorts. Not only did two of the songs,
"Oh Lonesome Me" and "I Can't Stop
Loving You," become Top Ten hits and
country standards, but the production
style of the records was revolutionary.
Chet Atkins persuaded Gibson to record
without the obligatory fiddle or steel
guitar and to use a vocal quartet named
the Jordanaires. Though Gibson had
been recording for RCA, Mercury,
Columbia, and MGM since 1950, he never
really found his style until these 1957
sessions. These—and the sessions that
followed them for the next ten years—not
only made Gibson a major recording star,
but helped popularize the so-called
Nashville Sound: the spare, clean,
simple arrangements crafted by techni-
cians like Chet Atkins and Floyd Cramer.

Most of the great Gibson cuts from
this decade are on RCA's *All-Time
Greatest Hits,* a selection of twenty of the
best RCA sides that includes later
favorites like "Sea of Heartbreak," "Just
One Time," and "Lonesome Number
One." A good set of notes rounds out the
package. Unfortunately, very few of the
300-odd sides Gibson did for RCA before
1970 are in print, depriving listeners of a
chance to explore the legacy of one of the
modern era's seminal figures. During the
1970s Gibson continued to record, for the
Hickory label, and while many of his cuts
were remakes of earlier hits, he continued to create original songs like "Woman
Sensuous Woman." *18 Greatest Hits*
collects a number of the Hickory
remakes, as well as a few of the newer
pieces.—C.K.W.

GIBSON-MILLER BAND

★★★½ Where There's Smoke (Epic EK
52980) 1992

Here's Southern boogie distilled down to
its essence. It's a familiar formula, all
right, but what distinguishes these long-
haired good ol' boys from your Headhunters and Pirates is the crafty way they
have of reupholstering the most thread-
bare clichés in Southern rock and
country. Imagine the Trisha Yearwood hit
"She's in Love with the Boy" as rewritten
from rocker Ted Nugent's point of view,
and you've got the rip-roarin' "Your
Daddy Hates Me." Likewise, "High
Rollin'" could be the Juice Newton hit
"Queen of Hearts"—with its cylinders
rebored and a supercharger slapped on
top. (Unexpected bonus: its extended
card-playing metaphor for romance takes
the checkered flag, too.) "Texas Tattoo"?
That's ZZ Top's "Tush," with a sense of
humor. And as for "Where There's
Smoke" (punch line: "you'll find my old
flame") and "She's Gettin' a Rock" ("and
I'm gettin' stoned"), well, honky-tonk
phrases rarely come any more well turned
than those.

Of course, rebel rousers that they are,
these guys can't help but indulge in a few
of Southern boogie's more tiresome
routines: namely, the tribute to Hank and
Lefty ("Stone Cold Country") that owes
more to Charlie Daniels and the
obligatory ode to the unreconstructed
("Southern Man," not to be confused with
the Neil Young song). Still, give the GMB
credit for burying these two duds at the
very end of the disc.—P.K.

VINCE GILL

★★½ Way Back Home (RCA 5923-2-
RDJ) 1987
★★★ The Best of Vince Gill (RCA
9814-2-R) 1989 ●
★★★ I Never Knew Lonely (RCA
07863-61130-2) 1992
★★★★★ When I Call Your Name (MCA
MCAD-42321) 1989 ▲
★★ Christmas Favorites (MCA CD33-
3029) 1991
★★★★ Pocket Full of Gold (MCA MCAD-
10140) 1991 ▲
★★★★ I Still Believe in You (MCA
MCAD-10630) 1992 ▲

It was Vince Gill's irresistible, honey-
smooth voice that first got him on the
radio in 1980. "Let Me Love You Tonight"

was the song, back when he was lead singer for country-rockers Pure Prairie League. Considering the chart success of that song and the very untraditional bent of country radio at the time, it's not surprising that his first solo releases, also on RCA, leaned to the pop side. *Way Back Home* and *I Never Knew Lonely* are decent records, but they lack the fire of Gill's later Tony Brown-produced releases for MCA. Working with Brown and riding the burgeoning new traditionalist movement, Gill was able to focus more fully on his bluegrass roots and showcase his hot-shot guitar playing to arrive at a sound that was pleasing to traditionalists and radio programmers alike. *When I Call Your Name,* his first release for MCA, was the record that made him a country star and still stands as his most fully realized work. At its best, Gill's music deftly balances pop slickness with bluegrass chops he picked up as guitarist for Byron Berline, Rodney Crowell, and Emmylou Harris. Coming hot on the heels of his multi-platinum success with that record, much of *Pocket Full of Gold* sounds like a retread, although standout cuts like "Look at Us" and "Liza Jane" find Gill refining and perfecting his peerless pop-country blend. With 1992's *I Still Believe in You,* Gill returns fully to form and comes up with a batch of songs strong enough to rival those on *When I Call Your Name.*—P.Cr.

MICKEY GILLEY
★★★   **Greatest Hits, Vol. 1 (Playboy/CBS EK 34743) 1976**
★★★   **Biggest Hits (Epic EK-38320) 1982**
★★★½ **Ten Years of Hits (Epic-EGK 39867) 1984**

As a purveyor of conventional country sentiments, Mickey Gilley is even more effective than his mad-genius cousin, Jerry Lee Lewis. Although their vocal and piano-playing styles are similar, Gilley's voice has more of the tenderness and emotional nuance beloved by true country fans. It was Gilley's mixed fortune to become closely identified with the Urban Cowboy movement, which had its origins in the Pasadena, Texas, saloon named for him. While the identification gave Gilley a prominence he might never have otherwise received, it also sprayed him with the smell of trend. But Gilley was

turning out some memorable reworkings of country classics— "Room Full Of Roses," "Fraulein," "I Overlooked an Orchid," "City Lights"—well before the UC wave. Gilley's *Greatest Hits, Vol. 1* is the best collection of this early material, covering the 1974-75 period, but *Ten Years of Hits,* with its twenty cuts, is more fair and comprehensive, sampling his best work through 1982. The latter album contains the wonderfully raucous "Don't the Girls All Get Prettier at Closing Time" and a tastefully mournful reading of the Eddy Arnold classic "You Don't Know Me."—E.M.

THE GILLIS BROTHERS
★★★   **Down by the River (Hay Holler Harvest HHH-CD-301) 1992**
★★★   **Ice Cold Stone (Hay Holler Harvest HHH-CD-302) 1992**

The Gillis Brothers (& Their Hard-Driving Bluegrass Band) from Soperton, Georgia, turn back the clock with a highly spirited, hauntingly mournful style of bluegrass inspired by the pioneering bands of the late 1940s and early 1950s.

The influence of the Stanley Brothers on these young pickers is at once obvious in the quiveringly lonesome harmonies and soulful arrangements, and the preference for Stanley repertoire, which provides one half of the fourteen tracks on *Ice Cold Stone.* Five songs on *Down by the River* were written by Larry and John Gillis and add a personal dimension to the band's unfettered ancestor worship. However, the Gillis Brothers so closely approximate the Stanley Brothers' sound that even the originals seem derived from the Stanley's dusty catalog.

While neither album breaks new ground, together they offer a passionate and inspired tribute to a couple of bluegrass music's early architects, and they keep the fires burning decades after Ralph and Carter Stanley harmonized their last lonesome chorus together. —J.B.

JIMMIE DALE GILMORE
★★★½ **Fair & Square (HighTone HCD 8011) 1988**
★★★   **Jimmie Dale Gilmore (HighTone HCD 8018) 1989**
★★★★ **After Awhile (Elektra/Nonesuch/ American Explorer 9 61448-2) 1991**

A late bloomer, this West Texan first recorded in 1972 as a member of the Flatlanders (with boyhood buddies Joe Ely and Butch Hancock), but didn't release an album on his own until 1988. With a tremulous tenor that is the essence of high lonesome, he initially sounds like a throwback to the era of Jimmie Rodgers, but the streak of mysticism in his material helps make the music timeless. Ultimately, he's as much a maverick in his musical approach as he is a traditionalist.

Fair & Square features a strong sampling of progressive Texas songcraft— from Townes Van Zandt, Joe Ely, Butch Hancock, and David Halley in addition to Gilmore—though Ely's production occasionally overwhelms the reediness of Gilmore's vocals. Gilmore's self-titled followup is more conventionally country by the standards of Nashville (where it was recorded). Its material isn't as consistently inspired as on the debut, with Gilmore's "Dallas" and Hancock's "When the Nights Are Cold" highlighting the selections.

After Awhile finds Gilmore coming into his own, with the album focusing attention on the range and richness of his songwriting. The stripped-down production of Stephen Bruton complements the exquisite sense of longing in "Tonight I Think I'm Gonna Go Downtown" and "Treat Me Like a Saturday Night," and the sagebrush spirituality of "Go to Sleep Alone" and the title cut.—D.McL.

JOHNNY GIMBLE
★★★★ **The Texas Fiddle Connection (CMH CD-9027) 1989**
★★ **Texas Honky-Tonk Hits (CMH 2 CD-9038) 1987**

Johnny Gimble, who earned his wings with Bob Wills in the Texas Playboys, has established himself as the premier exponent of western swing fiddle. He began his early career playing with the Shelton Brothers, did a stint with Wills, and then moved on to Nashville to become a much sought-after session musician. He has been named the Country Music Association's "Instrumentalist of the Year" numerous times. Gimble has worked with many of country music's biggest stars, and his influence has been very important in the revival of interest in western swing. *The Texas Fiddle Collection* is a superb assortment of twenty-eight traditional and western-swing fiddle standards that reflect Gimble's wide ranging repertoire, performed in swing style with a band including the likes of fellow Playboy Eldon Shamblin and the legendary Cliff Bruner. *Texas Honky-Tonk Hits* assembles honky-tonk classics performed by members of CMH's stable of artists, including Merle Travis, Johnny Bond, and Mac Wiseman. Despite Gimble's able instrumental contributions, these recordings are weak compared to the originals.—C.H.S.

GOOD OL' PERSONS
★★★★ **Anywhere the Wind Blows (Kaleidoscope K-38) 1989**

A bluegrass band with a difference, the Good Ol' Persons, centered around lead singer and songwriter Kathy Kallick, played a big part in bringing women to center stage in bluegrass. Kallick can be heard in a recent reunion album with Persons co-founder Laurie Lewis; it's reviewed elsewhere under Lewis's name. Based in the San Francisco Bay area, the Good Ol' Persons incorporate elements of the locally popular new acoustic music along with swing, Latin rhythms, and old-time music in their sound. And somehow they get away with being a bluegrass band without having a full-time banjo player, although dobroist Sally Van Meter, widely acclaimed by bluegrass fans as one of the outstanding exponents of that instrument, adds banjo to one track on this CD. Another essential in bluegrass, a strong vocal trio (bluegrassers don't talk about "back-up vocalists"), they have in spades—either three female voices, as in the title cut, or in a mix of one male and two female vocals, like that on "Waking Up Alone." Two earlier Kaleidoscope albums are not available on CD, but their previous effort, *Part of a Story* (Kaleidoscope F-26 & C-26) is at least as good as this one, and worth looking for if you like their pleasing combination of subtlety and swing.
—N.V.R.

JOHN GORKA
★★★★ **I Know (Red House RHRCD-18) 1987**

★★★★ **Land of the Bottom Line (Windham Hill WD 1089) 1990**
★★★½ **Jack's Crows (High Street 10309) 1991**
★★★★ **Temporary Road (High Street 10315) 1992**

Though played on country radio and CMT, John Gorka is an unabashed folk singer with a keen understanding of the twists of life—those that gnarl as well as those that enlighten or confound. He's blessed with a mournful baritone that is masculine yet gentle and capable of wry whimsy. And his songs can be unassumingly charming, openly poignant, or bitingly pointed.

Raised in New Jersey, Gorka has resided in Bethlehem, Pennsylvania, since 1976. Part of what makes his songs so convincing is their strong sense of place: the gloomy, depressed setting of the industrial Northeast saturates his lyrics, and his songs make it easy to visualize the big-boned, emotional, close-knit clans that populate these areas. Despite the bleakness of his world, he manages to convey a sense of hope amid the decaying mills and cut-throat developers—or at least he digs up a laugh or two while watching neighborhoods disintegrate around him.

His debut album, *I Know,* is his least-known yet most passionately focused collection. Released in 1987, three years after he was named best new performer at the Kerrville Folk Festival, it's a stunning compilation that's rougher and bluesier than the albums that have followed. "Downtown Tonight" and "Blues Palace" represent Gorka at his grittiest, while "Winter Cows" and "B.B. King Was Wrong" prove that his contorted wit was in place from the start.

Two of the best songs from *I Know*—the brilliantly touching love songs "Love Is Our Cross to Bear" and "I Saw a Stranger with Your Hair"—are revived on *Land of the Bottom Line,* Gorka's first album for Windham Hill. Like its predecessor, it was produced by Bill Kollar, who highlights Gorka's percussive acoustic guitar style while giving the tunes a subtly dramatic sense of dynamics that suits the singer's voice and lyrics. *Land of the Bottom Line* is Gorka's darkest and angriest work, obviously inspired by the betrayal of a lover as well as his financial struggles and the theft of

his car. His talent shines in how directly and intimately he conveys his thoughts on the subjects, from the piercing bitterness of "Armed with a Broken Heart" to the sly truths of "Stranger in My Driver's Seat."

Jack's Crows finds Gorka in an experimental writing mood, and he occasionally abandons straightforward narratives for oblique poetics. It doesn't always work, and part of the blame may fall to producers Will Ackerman and Dawn Atkinson. The music is softer edged and the rhythms more diffuse, taking some of the force from Gorka's words. Nonetheless, "Houses in the Fields" and "Where the Bottles Break" represent Gorka at his best, spewing acidic protest songs about the changes he sees in the places he calls home. And "I'm from New Jersey" is a sardonic masterpiece that rates with Randy Newman's best.

On *Temporary Road,* Gorka not only regains his edge, he gives it a sharper, more menacing gleam. By now, he's writing more about movement and travel, and it appears his slowly evolving success has improved his outlook. He continues to offer caustic commentary about particular examples of greed and oppression, but he also presents a few songs that are upbeat, both in sound and meaning, as in the wondrous "Looking Forward to You" and "When She Kisses Me." Even the song about his second stolen car is light and humorous.—M.M.

VERN GOSDIN
★★★½ **The Best of Vern Gosdin (Warner Bros. 9 25775-2) 1988**
★★★★ **Rough around the Edges (RCA 58537-2) 1992**
★★★½ **It's Not Over (LaserLight 15 475) 1992**
★★★★★ **Chiseled in Stone (Columbia CK 40982) 1987 ●**
★★★★ **Alone (Columbia CK 45104) 1989**
★★★★½ **10 Years of Greatest Hits— Newly Recorded (Columbia CK 45409) 1990**
★★★★★ **Out of My Heart (Columbia CK 47051) 1991**
★★★ **Nickels and Dimes and Love (Columbia CK 52944) 1993**

It should stand as inspiration to late bloomers everywhere that Vern Gosdin was forty-two before he had a hit record. With roots in gospel, bluegrass, and the close harmony brother duet sound (he recorded with brother Rex in the 1960s), Gosdin brought a deeply felt authenticity to such bitterly understated ballads as 1983's "If You're Gonna Do Me Wrong (Do It Right)." Sharing a stylistic turf and temperament with George Jones, Gosdin's dramatic vocals earned him the nickname "The Voice," and a place of prominence among country's great prisoners of woe.

His 1976-1979 Elektra label hits (ten of 'em anyway) are showcased on *The Best of Vern Gosdin*. Producer Gary Sanford Paxton troweled on the strings, horns, and choruses thick 'n' heavy, and had the Voice singing an improbable array of covers: Donovan's "Catch the Wind," the Association's "Never My Love," even Big Joe Turner's "Shake, Rattle, and Roll." But damned if these don't often work, especially the unlikely R&B anthem! Gosdin always insisted on good harmony vocals on his records, and during his Elektra stint he often dueted with Janie Fricke or Emmylou Harris, who sounded especially Dolly-like on 1976's "Yesterday's Gone," Gosdin's first major hit. His Elektra recordings are dated by their Seventies glitz arrangements, but the Voice was essentially as it has been since.

Gosdin, who surely understands the virtue of patience, waited a few years more for the sort of material and production that framed the Voice to its best advantage. The early 1980s saw the resurrection of George Jones and the phenomenal success of "He Stopped Loving Her Today," Jones's Wagnerian weeper which proved classic country ballads were still viable in the days of mechanical bulls and *Urban Cowboy*. Gosdin may have lacked Jones's record for errant behavior, but he could give the Possum a run for the tragic money, and proceeded to do just that.

He began recording for A.M.I. in 1981, and his characteristic sound quickly came together. Songwriter Max D. Barnes, who has worked with Gosdin on many of his best songs, entered the picture, and the production (with a few exceptions) was pared back to contemporary honky-tonk dimensions. *Rough around the Edges* is an eight-song

collection of A.M.I. material with an emphasis on Jonesian ballads ("When Love Was All We Had to Share" finds Gosdin waxing nostalgic about candlelight and TV dinners). LaserLight's *It's Not Over* offers a dozen 1981-83 A.M.I. performances, including some suggesting the influence of Waylon Jennings ("Cowboys Are Common as Sin") and even Freddy Hart ("Your Bedroom Eyes"). Only three songs duplicate those on *Rough around the Edges,* and while *It's Not Over* is a fuller accounting of this stage of Gosdin's development, *Rough* is more consistent with the emerging balladeer with a knack for hard knocks.

From 1983 to 1986, Gosdin had a string of hits for the Compleat label, records which emphasized close harmony and heartache. (He also cut a fine gospel album during this period.) Gosdin's Compleat recordings are arguably his best work, but none of it is currently available on CD. After three years with Columbia, he recut seven of his Compleat hits (plus four other songs) on *10 Years of Hits—Newly Recorded.* "Today My World Slipped Away" (actually an A.M.I. hit in 1982) is one of the great *sturm und drang* divorce ballads, performed here with the sort of understated pathos Gosdin delivers better that anyone. "Was It Just the Wine" is another knockout performance that makes *10 Years* more than just a perfunctory career recap.

Gosdin's Columbia label debut album, *Chiseled in Stone,* opened with one of his most achingly authoritative ballads, "Do You Believe Me Now," and the laid back barroom vocal on "Set 'Em Up, Joe" is a thing of wonder. The title track, too, is a gem, and overall Gosdin hasn't made a more consistent album. *Alone,* released in 1989, offered ten songs imbued with the sting of Gosdin's recent divorce, and the chilling "I'm Only Going Crazy" ranks with the best of Gosdin's stunning ballad performances. Experience may be the best teacher but not necessarily the best songwriter: *Alone* is thematically strong but all the songs don't measure up to Gosdin's best work.

Out of My Heart (1991) returned to form with a classic tearjerker, "The Garden," and even a touching wedding song, "Once and for All," a surprising turn for this master of post-wedded woe. Fine songs and production buoyed the

Voice, who sang here like his career depended on it. He was, after all, swimming upstream against a flood of young Hats. Still afloat in 1993, Gosdin recorded *Nickels and Dimes and Love,* which found him wading safely close to shore in familiar shallows. While daring creative leaps are hardly expected of veteran country singers pushing sixty, each of *Nickels'* ten songs is numbingly derivative. Unless you're a completist, save your *Nickels* but ante up for *Chiseled in Stone* to hear how Gosdin carved his niche in the pantheon of great country ballad singers.—M.H.

THE GRATEFUL DEAD

★★★½   **Workingman's Dead (Warner Bros. 1869) 1970 ▲**
★★★★   **American Beauty (Warner Bros. 1893) 1970 ▲**

For all their jazz-rock pretensions and hippy-cult stature, the Grateful Dead actually hit their peak during a brief period in the early 1970s when they, like a lot of the California musical counterculture, concentrated on creating a distinctive brand of country-rock.

Workingman's Dead and its follow-up, *American Beauty,* feature the band at its most concise and tuneful. The fatalism that seeps through the group's songs over the decades has strong (albeit unintentional) ties to traditional country music, as does their bemusement with the odd and sometimes oppressive ways of the world. And singer-guitarist Jerry Garcia's limitations actually work to his advantage on these flower-child takes on country-folk. His coarse, wan vocals sound grittier and more animated, and his pseudo-jazz guitar playing works better within the tighter structures of these songs.

When all is said and done, nearly all of the memorable Dead tunes come from these two back-to-back albums. *Workingman's Dead,* the rougher and looser of the two, features "Uncle John's Band" and "Casey Jones," while *American Beauty,* which finds the band at its sweetest and most comprehensible, offers "Truckin'," "Friend of the Devil," "Sugar Magnolia" and "Ripple." The Dead never sounded more alive than when going back to the country. It's too bad they left so soon.—M.M.

GREAT PLAINS

★★★   **Great Plains (Columbia CK 48651) 1991**

Rising up like dust from the wheels of a pickup truck on a dirt road, Great Plains' gritty heartland sound borrows from the country, rock, and singer-songwriter tradition of folks like the Byrds, Green on Red, and Steve Earle. The songwriting isn't quite blue-ribbon level yet, but highpoints include an uplifting paean to the small farmer ("Iola"), a riveting outlaw tale ("Faster Gun"), and a sweeping, charming love song ("Oh Sweetness").—K.S.

LEE GREENWOOD

★★★   **Inside Out (MCA MCAD-31076) 1981 ●**
★★★   **Somebody's Gonna Love You (MCA MCAD-31026) 1983 ●**
★★   **You've Got a Good Love Comin' (MCA MCAD-31098) 1984 ●**
★★★   **Greatest Hits (MCA MCAD 5582) 1985 ▲**
★★★   **Christmas to Christmas (MCA MCAD-27135) 1985**
★★   **Streamline (MCA MCAD-5622) 1985**
★★   **Love Will Find Its Way to You (MCA MCAD-5770) 1986**
★★   **This Is My Country (MCA MCAD-42167) 1988**
★★   **Greatest Hits, Vol. 2 (MCA MCAD-42219) 1988**
★★   **If Only for One Night (MCA MCAD-42300) 1989**
★★   **Holdin' a Good Hand (Liberty C2-94153) 1990**
★★   **When You're in Love (Liberty C2-95527) 1991**
★   **American Patriot (Liberty CDP-7-98568-2) 1992**
★★   **Love's on the Way (Liberty C2-98834) 1992**

Lee Greenwood—he of the husky, Kenny Rogers-like voice—seems destined to be remembered principally for two songs: "It Turns Me Inside Out," the gut-wrenching Jan Crutchfield confessional that justifiably made him a star in 1981, and his own embarrassingly jingoistic composition, "God Bless the USA," which came three years later. Not content simply to write and perform the latter song, Greenwood used it to ingratiate himself as an unofficial minstrel for the Reagan and Bush administrations. Both the critics and the charts seem to agree that Greenwood's best work was in his early years of recording for MCA, essentially 1981-83, which is represented in the 1985 *Greatest Hits* package.—E.M.

RICKY LYNN GREGG

★ Ricky Lynn Gregg (Liberty CDP 0777-7-80135-2-5) 1993

Remember how a tearful Garth Brooks, receiving his first CMA Entertainer of the Year Award in 1991, dedicated it to his two heroes, George Jones and George Strait? Are you ready for the next wave— a guy who sounds like he's been studying George Jones and Billy Ray Cyrus? Enter Ricky Lynn Gregg, a long-haired, pumped-up Texan who briefly sang lead for third-rate rock band Head East. He's got a credible country voice and could probably handle "He Stopped Loving Her Today"—for a bar band in Dallas (which he also used to do). He's got a distinctive boom-crash sound, too, typified by the honky-tonk goose-step of "A Good Habit Is Hard to Break" and "Bring on the Neon," wherein sledgehammer drums and buzzsaw guitars march in martial lockstep while a fiddle hops around the mix like a yapping dog. The Ricky Lynn Gregg assault culminates in the pounding stomp of "If I Had a Cheatin' Heart," wherein the artist moans, "Oh, baby, you're makin' it hard"; this indiscreet admission is then hammered home by a stuttering guitar riff for the leering impaired. Music this pushy seems not so much artistically inspired as cynically calculated. Come back, Billy Ray, all is forgiven.—P.K.

CLINTON GREGORY

★★★ Music 'n Me (Step One SOR-0057) 1990
★★★ If It Weren't for Country Music (Step One SOR-0064) 1991
★★★ Freeborn Man (Step One SOR-0070) 1992

There is no justice. If there were, Clinton Gregory would be playing on a level field with Doug Stone, Mark Chesnutt, Randy Travis, and the rest of his country music peers. It is a hard, cold, cruel reality, however, that the others record for major international conglomerates while Clinton Gregory records for the tiny, Nashville-based Step One label. They have clout. He does not. It's that simple—and that unfair.

The boy has a yearning, straight-from-the-heart delivery that provides the plain satisfaction of well water in summertime. At his best, he brings Vern Gosdin to mind. And like Gosdin, Clinton Gregory is committed to country at its purest.

Who else would pay homage to Jimmie Davis's 1935 smash "Nobody's Darlin'" on his debut CD? Not to mention Mel Street's "Loving on Backstreets" and Merle Haggard's "I Can't Be Myself" alongside such superb hillbilly tunes as "Couldn't Love Have Picked a Better Place to Die," "She Put the Music in Me" and "Made for Loving You" (later a hit for Doug Stone).

The breakthrough single was "(If It Weren't for Country Music) I'd Go Crazy," the title track of Gregory's second CD. The collection's "Maybe I Should Have Been Listening" and "For Crying Out Loud" showed that he was growing as a stylist. "One Shot at a Time" was the most devastating alcohol indictment of 1991 and arguably one of the most devastating in country music history.

Freeborn Man, the third CD, was again produced by veteran studio master Ray Pennington, who has an uncanny ability to craft understated country perfection. Again, the song selection was flawless, from the country-rocking "Play Ruby Play" and "Look Who's Needing Who" to the aching, sobbing-in-the-dark ballads "Who Needs It" and "If a Broken Heart Could Kill."

If it's true that every puppy has his day, then one of them belongs to this gifted underdog.—R.K.O.

NANCI GRIFFITH

★★ There's a Light beyond These Woods (Philo CDPH-1097) 1982
★★½ Once in a Very Blue Moon (Philo CDPH-1096) 1984
★★½ Poet in My Window (Philo CDPH-1098) 1985
★★½ The Last of the True Believers (Philo CDPH-1109) 1986
★★★ Lone Star State of Mind (MCA MCAD-31300) 1987
★★★½ Little Love Affairs (MCA MCAD-42102) 1988
★★ One Fair Summer Evening (MCA MCAD-42255) 1988
★★ Storms (MCA MCAD-6319) 1989
★★½ Late Night Grande Hotel (MCA MCAD-10306) 1991

★★★★ **Other Voices, Other Rooms (Elektra 61464-4) 1993**
Griffith's little-girl soprano, earnest humorlessness, and fondness for winsome melodies regularly veers into annoying mannerism, especially on her earliest recordings. But this Texan gets more interesting—more tough-minded—as her career proceeds. Essentially a romantic folksinger with occasional outbreaks of country fever ("Lookin' for the Time" on *Last of the True Believers,* "Ford Econoline" on *Lone Star State of Mind,* the latter half of *Little Love Affairs),* Griffith is that rare musician whose literary influences—she's read deeply in writers ranging from Truman Capote to Larry McMurtry—actually enhance her music rather than just gussying it up. She's written songs that have become hits for more mainstream country artists—the bittersweet "Love at the Five and Dime" for Kathy Mattea, the yearning "Outbound Plane" for Suzy Bogguss—even as her own recordings seem to strike the Nashville establishment as uncommercially arty and precious. One big step in the direction of marketplace acceptance is *Other Voices, Other Rooms.* A series of rollicking, poignant folk-country collaborations with exemplars ranging from Emmylou Harris to Arlo Guthrie to Bob Dylan, it is some kind of breakthrough: Griffith's singing is looser and more passionate than it's ever been, and the variety of material—covers of her folk favorites, from Woody Guthrie's "Do Re Me" to Dylan's "Boots of Spanish Leather"—demonstrates her range in an unprecedented way—K.T.

WOODY GUTHRIE
★★★★ **Library of Congress Recordings, 3 Vols. (Rounder CD 1045, 1046, 1043; CD 1245) 1988**
★★★★★ **Dust Bowl Ballads (Rounder CD 1040) 1988**
★★★ **Columbia River Collection (Rounder CD 1036) 1987**
★★ **Golden Classics, Part 1, Worried Man Blues (Collectables COLCD-5098) N. D.**
★★★ **Golden Classics, Part 2, Immortal (Collectables COL CD-5098) N. D.**
★★★ **Greatest Songs of Woody Guthrie (Vanguard VCD-35/36) 1988**

★★★ **One of a Kind (Pair PCD2-1294) N. D.**
★★ **Worried Man Blues (Special Music Co. SCD 4824) N. D.**
★★★★ **Struggle (Smithsonian/Folkways SFCD-40025) 1990**
★★★ **Woody Guthrie Sings Folk Songs (Smithsonian/Folkways SFCD-40007) 1989**
★★★★ **[& Leadbelly] Original Vision (Smithsonian/Folkways SFCD-40001) 1989**
Though he is recognized as one of the country's great songwriters and as the dean of America's folksingers, Woody Guthrie's singing is for many country fans an acquired taste. He came from Oklahoma and was fascinated by the early recordings of the Carter Family; he also began his career as a radio entertainer in California. But as he traveled around the country during the Dust Bowl days of the Depression, he began to move away from traditional country fare to topical and protest songs of his own making—many of which he grafted to the melodies of older country songs. By the time he made it to New York in the late 1930s, he had acquired quite a following among folk music fans, and during the next decade he recorded prolifically, though seldom for major labels. As a result, the modern reissues of his work are a confusing jumble, with much overlapping among packages as well as multiple versions of seminal songs.

Two albums provide good starting points for someone wanting to explore the Guthrie legacy. One is *Dust Bowl Ballads,* the 1940 set done for RCA Victor, with classics like "Dust Bowl Refugee," "Talking Dust Bowl," "I Ain't Got No Home," "Do Re Me," and "So Long, It's Been Good to Know You." Framed by Guthrie's reedy voice, guitar, and harmonica playing, the songs make up the most impressive musical response to one of the most traumatic events in American history. Shortly before he entered the RCA Victor studios, Guthrie had traveled to Washington, D. C. to record for folklorist Alan Lomax and the Library of Congress. For several days he talked and sang into the microphone, discussing his own past, his travels, people he had known, and backgrounds of his songs; he also sang a wide variety of folksongs, as well as his own protest songs. The best of these are on *Library of Congress Recordings,* including several that would become Guthrie favorites: "Hard Times," "Pretty Boy Floyd," "Greenback Dollar," "Jolly Banker," and "Worried Man Blues." Many of the "Dust Bowl ballads" later done for RCA are also here.

About a year after the Dust Bowl album, Woody found himself in Portland, Oregon, commissioned to write songs for a film about the Columbia River and the Bonneville Power Administration. As always, he wrote more than he needed, but generated several favorites; these are found in *Columbia River Collection,* culled from a set of recently discovered acetates, and include "Roll on Columbia," "Ramblin' Blues," "Hard Travelin'," "Grand Coulee Dam," and "Pastures of Plenty." Later in the 1940s Woody began to record for Moe Asch's Folkways label, and with the Smithsonian Institution's recent acquisition of that label, three good digitally remastered sets of his material have emerged. *Folkways: The Original Vision* features well-known songs by Leadbelly and Woody, including Guthrie's "Philadelphia Lawyer," "This Land is Your Land," "Hobo's Lullaby," and "Vigilante Man"—all pieces that have been recorded dozens of times by later folk and country singers. *Woody Guthrie Sings Folk Songs* is just that—traditional songs, with a few Carter Family titles thrown in. Far more powerful is *Struggle,* a set of labor and protest songs that includes the favorite "A Dollar Down," as well as "The Dying Miner," "Ludlow Massacre," and "Union Burying Ground."—C.K.W.

H

MERLE HAGGARD

★★★★★ Capitol Collector's Series (Capitol CDP 7 93191 2) 1990
★★★★ Best of the Early Years (Curb D2-77438) 1991
★★★★ Best of the Best of Merle Haggard (Liberty C21Y-91254) 1072 ▲
★ Christmas Present (Curb D2-77352) 1973
★★★ Best of Country Blues (Curb D2-77368) 1990
★★★ 18 Rare Classics (Curb D2-77490) 1991
★★★ Country Boy (Pair PCD-2-1193) 1990
★★★★ More of the Best (Rhino R2 70917) 1990
★★★ Back to the Barrooms (MCA MCAD-31099) 1980
★★★ Back to the Barrooms/The Way I Am (MCA MCAD-5929) 1980
★★★ Rainbow Stew: Live at Anaheim Stadium (MCA MCAD-31101) 1981
★★★ Merle Haggard's Greatest Hits (MCA MCAD-5386) 1982
★★★★ His Greatest and His Best (MCA MCAD-5624) 1984
★★★ His Best (MCA MCAD-5573) 1985
★★★ Big City (Epic EK 37593) 1981 ●

★★½ [& Willie Nelson] Pancho & Lefty (Epic EK 37958) 1982 ▲
★★ Going Where The Lonely Go (Epic EK 38092) 1982
★★★ [& George Jones] A Taste of Yesterday's Wine (Epic EK 38203) 1982
★★ That's the Way Love Goes (Epic EK 38815) 1983
★★★ The Epic Collection (Recorded Live) (Epic EK 39159) 1983
★★ It's All in the Game (Epic EK 39364) 1984
★★★ His Epic Hits: The First 11 (Epic EK 39545) 1984 ●
★★ Chill Factor (Epic EK 40986) 1987
★★ 5:01 Blues (Epic EK 44283) 1989
★★★ Greatest Hits of the 80's (Epic EK 46925) 1990
★★★ Super Hits (Epic ET 53310) 1993
★★ Blue Jungle (Curb D2-77313) 1990

The most important thing to remember about Merle Haggard is not how much youthful time he spent behind bars, but how much time he spent escaping. He ran away from home as a childhood way of life and busted out of reform school seven times. When he graduated to San Quentin, he and a prison buddy planned a foolproof escape from those infamous confines. At 11:59, Haggard decided not to go. His friend got as far as San Jose, where he blew away a state trooper and was sent back to the gas chamber at San Quentin. Haggard fictionalized his friend's final walk into "Sing Me Back Home," a visceral honky-tonk prison dirge that will devastate you the second you hear it as more than clichéd jailhouse country.

At the peak of his powers, on Capitol in the late 1960s, Haggard and his band, the Strangers, could devastate—or elate—country fans almost at will. Better than any singer of his time, he has understood and tapped into one of the emotionally heroic battles of our culture: the working class's daily struggle with the temptation to run. The themes that established his country reputation—the honky-tonk destruction of "Swingin' Doors" and "The Bottle Let Me Down"; the convict's lament of "Sing Me Back Home" and "I'm a Lonesome Fugitive"; the hobo wanderlust of "I Take a Lot of Pride in What I Am"; the dust bowl shackles of "Hungry Eyes;" even the mean-spirited patriotism of "Fightin' Side of Me"—are all variations on the central theme of escape. Haggard's early work reached its thematic and musical apotheosis with "Workin' Man Blues." Direct, unsentimental, and driven by a Strangers rhythm guitar riff that has defied bar band exhaustion, "Workin' Man Blues" hits gut level with all the compact fury of "Jumping Jack Flash." Dogmatic Sixties rockers heard Hag as the voice of hard-hat reaction. More discerning ears heard a kindred spirit.

Of course, sorting out the music is a nightmare. Through the years, Capitol has revealed an outrageous disregard for the integrity of Haggard's catalogue—forever recombining his hit singles and deleting his back title albums. While there is talk of an eventual box set, the *Collector's Series* disc remains, for the time being, the essential Haggard compilation, thanks to his strength as a singles artist. The aforementioned songs are all included. *Collector's Series* offers the uninitiated a twenty-cut introduction to Haggard's fabled country soul voice and Bakersfield sound—an uncompromising honky-tonk style centered on the restrained, sputtering axe blows of lead guitarists Roy Nichols and James Burton.

Yet *Collector's Series* misses the point that Haggard, at his best, has had no peer as a country music album artist. He was the first—at times the only—mainstream country performer to exploit the LP as a medium for expanding the range of his work. Several of his Capitol albums cry out for reissue in their entirety. If nothing else, someone has got to take their eyes off *Billboard* long enough to resurrect Haggard's magnificent self-penned "Tulare Dust," a song that could have had Woody Guthrie bowing at Haggard's feet.

The Rhino, Pair, and Curb discs (other than *Blue Jungle*) add to the available Capitol material in slap-dash, overlapping combinations. Rhino provides "Mama Tried," with the immortal opening couplet: "The first thing I remember knowin'/Was a lonesome whistle blowin'." The other indispensable cut on *More of the Best* is "If We Make It through December," another brilliant Haggard original about blue-collar escape, and probably the most depressing Christmas song ever to hit the charts. (It's also the sole redeeming feature of Haggard's putrid *Christmas Present.*) The Rhino disc disappoints a completist, however, in that half the cuts come from Haggard's post-Capitol run on MCA—good stuff, but readily available elsewhere.

Haggard's switch to MCA breathed new life into what had started to sound like a very disinterested career. The core Strangers were still with him, though the addition of some ex-Bob Wills sidemen, a regular horn player, and an increasing reliance on electric piano changed the texture of many of his arrangements. A couple of Haggard's MCA albums were duds, but the label has done a fair job of keeping the best work in print. *Back to the Barrooms* finds Haggard in a defiantly honky-tonk mood at Urban Cowboy time. It spawned several hits, the most miraculous of which is "Leonard," a jaunty, acoustic country ballad about his songwriting mentor Tommy Collins. (You don't need *Back to the Barrooms* with *The Way I Am* attached, unless you're eager to hear Haggard's Ernest Tubb imitation.) The MCA hits collections tend to be redundant. For the economy-minded, buying The *Best of* and *Greatest Hits* separately gives you five more cuts than the single disc *His Greatest and His Best*. Either way, you don't want to miss "If We're Not Back in Love by Monday," a weekend pass to hopelessness.

Big City was Haggard's first and best Epic release. The title song is about— what else?—proletarian escapist fantasy. The fantasy turns to longing and private nostalgia with "My Favorite Memory," and to cranky moralistic nostalgia with "Are the Good Times Really Over (I Wish a Buck Was Still Silver)." The latter mood spoils too much of Haggard's late work. Ever since he joked his way to fame and riches with "Okie from Muskogee," Haggard's performances as peddler of homespun values have always come across a mite cynical.

After *Big City*, Haggard's musical high points started to turn epiphanic: the garrulous punch of his vocals as he enters for the final verse on "Pancho and Lefty," the disquieting self-referentialism of him singing wife Leona Williams's "You Take Me for Granted," the immediated devotion to Lefty Frizzell in his delivery of Frizzell's "That's the Way Love Goes," the poignancy added when he misses the high notes on the live "Sing a Sad Song." By the mid-Eighties, for the first time, the hits collections are the best way to buy his work. The other albums just aren't very interesting. The Strangers are often shunted aside in the studio, and Haggard sounds like he's finally running out of good songwriting ideas. After an unparalleled quarter-century run, that's to be expected. But Haggard hasn't been willing to let go a few writer's royalties for the sake of cutting strong records. One can't help fearing that if he doesn't adjust, the good times may really be over.—D.C.

TOM T. HALL
★★★★ Greatest Hits (Mercury 824 143-2) 1972

In spite of his gruff and monotonous vocals, Tom T. Hall has enriched country music immeasurably with his vision and his uncanny ability to turn that vision into words. Born and raised in eastern Kentucky, Hall early absorbed—and performed—the mournful bluegrass music so popular in that region. A stint abroad in the Army and a fascination

with American fiction helped him shed his provincialism and equipped him with the point of view and techniques to become a master storyteller in song. The elements that tend to set Hall's songs apart from those of other country songwriters are profuse and symbolic details, a strong conversational tone, and a near total absence of sentimentality. And even when his stories are longer than normal, they are still stripped of all verbal fat and filigree. His character sketches—"The Year Clayton Delaney Died," "Old Dogs and Children," "Ravishing Ruby," "Pamela Brown," "Turn It On, Turn It On, Turn It On"—are reminiscent of Sherwood Anderson's short stories, and his dramatic mono-logue, "Homecoming," is as fine an example of that difficult literary form as any of Robert Browning's best efforts. Hall is the most cerebral writer country music can boast. It is a pity that he is so poorly represented on CD, although his *Greatest Hits* package of eleven songs does contain some of his most memorable work. Other albums that should be re-released are his 1976 bluegrass album, *The Magnificent Music Machine*, and his 1982 album with Earl Scruggs, *Storyteller & the Banjo Man*.
—E.M.

BUTCH HANCOCK
★★★½ Own and Own (Sugar Hill SH-CD-1036) 1991

An uncompromising visionary even by the musical standards of his native Lubbock, Texas (home to Buddy Holly and Joe Ely), Hancock has been recording and distributing do-it-yourself albums since the late Seventies, with some of the best selections included within this seven-teen-cut compilation. Inspired by the populism of Woody Guthrie and the poetic ambitions of Bob Dylan, Hancock offers layers of linguistic revelation, combining down-to-earth whimsy with metaphysical flights, while paying scant attention to arrangements, production values, or vocal polish.

Among the highlights are Hancock standards such as "Fools Fall in Love," "If You Were a Bluebird," and "West Texas Waltz"—popularized by Joe Ely and Emmylou Harris—as well as four otherwise unavailable recordings with his Sunspots rock band, produced by Ely and

powered by former Ely guitarist Jesse
Taylor. —D.McL.

BUTCH HANCOCK AND JIMMIE DALE GILMORE

★★★½ Two Roads—Live in Australia
(Caroline Records CAROL-1726-2)
1992

Recorded on tour in 1990, this album
celebrates a West Texas musical kinship
dating back to the early Seventies, while
additionally paying homage to the very
beginnings of country music. Though the
styles of the two singer-songwriters
couldn't be more distinct—with
Hancock's Dylanesque rasp and lyricism
contrasting with Gilmore's aching vibrato
and open-hearted purity—they achieve an
almost brotherly blend. Original material
dominates the album, with Gilmore
proving to be one of Hancock's best
interpreters, while selections from the
songbooks of the Carter Family and
Jimmie Rodgers reflect the duo's
common roots. —D.McL.

EMMYLOU HARRIS

★★★★★ Pieces of the Sky (Reprise 2284-
2) 1975 ●
★★★★★ Elite Hotel (Reprise 2286-2)
1975 ●
★★★★★ Luxury Liner (Warner Bros.
3115-2) 1977 ●
★★★★ Quarter Moon in a Ten Cent
Town (Warner Bros. 3141-2)
1978 ●
★★★★★ Profile/Best of Emmylou Harris
(Warner Bros. 3258-2) 1978 ●
★★★★½ Blue Kentucky Girl (Warner Bros.
3318-2) 1979 ●
★★★★★ Roses in the Snow (Warner Bros.
3422-2) 1980 ●
★★★★★ The Christmas Album: Light of
the Stable (Warner Bros. 9
3484-2) 1980
★★★ White Shoes (Warner Bros. 9
23961-2) 1983
★★★★½ Profile II: The Best of Emmylou
Harris (Warner Bros. 9 25161-2)
1984
★★★½ The Ballad of Sally Rose (Warner
Bros. 25205-2) 1985
★★★★★ Angel Band (Warner Bros. 9
25585-2) 1987
★★★★½ Bluebird (Reprise 9 25776-2)
1988
★★★★ Duets (Reprise 9 25791-2) 1990

★★★★ Brand New Dance (Reprise 9
26309-2) 1990
★★★★★ At the Ryman (Reprise 9 26664-
2) 1992

Emmylou Harris's odyssey over the past
twenty-five years has taken her through
an array of roles, from coffee house
folksinger to sexy saint of hip country to,
a mite ironically, that of traditional
country matriarch (not in the same sense
as Kitty Wells, maybe, but an Honored
Elder nonetheless). Compared to many of
her sisters in country, her artistic vision
has been simultaneously wider in scope
and more conservative, in the sense that
her ear for what she believes to be classic
songs (and arrangements) is clearly
defined. Her early 1970s relationship
with Gram Parsons sensitized her to the
importance of luminous songs, and she
has always championed exceptional
songwriters. As a performer, "angelic" is
an adjective often tossed at her vulner-
able vibrato, and much of Harris's appeal
has unquestionably been derived from
her juxtaposition of qualities both sensual
and spiritual through her music and
personality.

All the elements that have characterized Harris as an artist were already in
sharp focus on her 1975 major label
debut, Pieces of the Sky. It opened with
the first of many Rodney Crowell songs
she would record, "Bluebird Wine," and
included a well-chosen handful of classic
country songs, among them a fine duet
with Herb Pedersen (late of the Desert
Rose Band) on the Louvin Brothers' "If I
Could Only Win Your Love," which
became Harris's first Top Ten country
chart record in the summer of 1975. It
also offered her own moving "Boulder to
Birmingham" and the first-class picking
of Hollywood's best Nashville Cats,
guitarist James Burton among them.

Hard on Pieces' heels came Elite
Hotel, with its Burrito Brothers covers
("Sin City" foremost), a performance of
the Crowell classic, "Till I Gain Control
Again," and the version of Buck Owen's
"Together Again" which became Harris's
first #1 hit in the spring of 1976. Luxury
Liner (1977) featured Harris's Hot Band
at full throttle (ace guitarist Albert Lee
had come aboard) and a brace of songs
from writers whose material you wouldn't
expect to work together: A. P. Carter,
Chuck Berry, Townes Van Zandt. But

work they did, and 1979's *Quarter Moon in a Ten Cent Town* harvested another crop of fine songs from the pens of Crowell ("I Ain't Living Long Like This"), Dolly Parton ("To Daddy"), and Delbert McClinton ("Two More Bottles of Wine") with the Hot Band again at no-holds-barred play.

Blue Kentucky Girl (1979) had a gently feminist slant with its trio of songs (all penned by men) about country women's experiences, including Crowell's "Even Cowgirls Get the Blues," on which Dolly Parton and Linda Ronstadt joined Harris. *Blue Kentucky*'s songs revolved in a somewhat narrower country orbit than some of Harris's prior albums (it earned a Grammy for Best LP by a Female Country Singer), and Hot Band fiddler Ricky Skaggs was at this point playing a prominent role as harmony vocalist. Skaggs's presence was stronger still on Harris's 1980 release, *Roses in the Snow,* which emphasized acoustic instrumentation and a bluegrass and old-time country repertoire. Harris's version of Jimmie Rodgers's "Miss the Mississippi and You" remains one of her loveliest performances, while her acoustic arrangement of Paul Simon's "The Boxer" shows her knack for taking an apparent wrong turn that works.

The *Roses in the Snow* session also yielded most of the tracks for Harris's gossamer snowflake of a Christmas album, *Light of the Stable.* (The title track, featuring ethereal harmony from Parton, Ronstadt, and Neil Young, actually dates from 1975.) The White sisters, Sharon and Cheryl, are among the harmonists who abet Harris in her pursuit of new ways into such standards as "The First Noel" (sung a cappella) and fresh takes on the Christmas repertoire via such unconventional songs as Rodney Crowell's "Angel Eyes (Angel Eyes)."

The next Harris album currently available on CD, 1983's *White Shoes,* offers an essentially new incarnation of the Hot Band and the first of several fine songs she would record written by future husband Paul Kennerley, "In My Dreams." The album overall has a more pop patina than her earlier work, and her voice sounds a bit frayed. It was Harris's final album with long-time producer (and husband) Brian Ahern. By 1985, her personal and professional relationship with Kennerley had yielded *The Ballad of Sally Rose,* a semi-autobiographical concept album widely interpreted as a fictionalization of Harris's relationship with Gram Parsons. Even if the concept was more inspired than its ultimate realization, it was good to see Harris stepping out of her role as interpreter and co-writing the album with Kennerley.

Following the stretch of *Sally Rose,* 1987's *Angel Band* was a warm retreat to familiar ground: old-time country and bluegrass gospel. Beautifully spare, *Angel Band* was Harris's most purely acoustic album to date and featured the dulcet tenor of Vince Gill in a strong supporting role. By contrast, *Bluebird* returned to a more aggressively commercial posture, à la *White Shoes,* but with greater vitality and purpose.

Harris then disbanded her Hot Band after nearly fifteen years and began the Nineties with the appropriately-titled *Brand New Dance.* Leave it to Harris to deliver a country album with both Uilleann (Irish) bagpipes and a Bruce Springsteen song, "Tougher Than the Rest." Then, in a typical move that suggests she now only does the hope-for-a-hit studio albums when prodded, Harris went to the Cathedral of Country to record 1992's relaxed retro concert album, *At the Ryman,* with a stellar group of acoustic pickers, the Nash Ramblers. Lovely stuff, and a Grammy winner besides.

Of the available hits packages, *Profile* draws from her Seventies albums while *Profile II* moves into the Eighties with such otherwise unavailable performances as Harris's kickin' live take on Hank Snow's "I'm Movin' On." The dozen *Duets* include such gems as "All Fall Down" with George Jones and the Everlys' "Love Hurts" with the man who first pushed Harris into country, Gram Parsons.—M.H.

EMMYLOU HARRIS, DOLLY PARTON, LINDA RONSTADT
★★★★★ **Trio (Warner Bros. 25491-2)**
1987 ▲

They'd been threatening to make this album for years, to the point where it was starting to sound like promises, promises—but then, by George they did it! Did they ever. *Trio* isn't just significant—for achieving the zenith of the new traditionalist movement, for setting a new standard in celebrity collaborations, for putting such wonderful singers together in the first place—it's also beautiful. The songs, by thoroughbreds like Jimmie Rodgers ("Hobo's Meditation"), Kate McGarrigle ("I've Had Enough"), Dolly herself ("Wildflowers" and "Pain of Loving You"), and even Phil Spector ("To Know Him Is to Love Him," the hit single), are enduringly great. The musicianship, arrangements, and production, overseen by George Massenburg, are purely exquisite, and the singing is simply lovely.

In one way, though, *Trio*'s release was a bittersweet delight. By demonstrating that Parton and Ronstadt could still outshine every other female on the planet when it came to pure country singing, it showed us exactly what their own relentlessly wrong-headed recording careers had been denying us for a decade or more (Emmylou, mostly singing backup to the divas on *Trio,* had nothing to prove in 1987 and doesn't now.) So don't hold your breath—the foolishness persists—but do pray for a sequel.—P.Ca.

JOHN HARTFORD
★★★★ **Mark Twang (Flying Fish FF 70020) 1976**
★★★★½ **Me Oh My, How the Time Does Fly: Flying Fish FF 70440) 1987**
★★½ **Down on the River (Flying Fish FF 70514) 1989**
★★★ **Hartford & Hartford (Flying Fish FF 70566) 1991**

"Gentle on My Mind" was the ubiquitous marriage of *Freewheelin'* era Dylan imagery with mainstream pop sensibilities that you could never escape in the late Sixties. Any self-respecting hack songwriter would've killed to have penned it, and would have continued to rewrite it *ad nauseum.* John Hartford, who wrote "Gentle on My Mind," chose not to milk the golden calf but instead sank his royalties into a riverboat and traversed the country as a back-to-the-earth hippie evangelist, singing the praises of the Mighty Mississippi along with weird and whimsical songs full of mouth noises and toe taps. It was an arch act, professional anti-showbiz, the hit songwriter playing at being the street-corner weirdo plunking for spare change, and Hartford was damn good at it. *Mark*

Twang was the culmination of his persona, a celebration of steamboats ("The Julia Belle Swain"), warped records ("Don't Leave Your Records in the Sun"), and even a stoned parody of the Lord's Prayer ("The Lowest Pair"). Hartford's flat molasses voice, banjo tuned low to give it a garbage-can resonance, and scraping fiddle were cut live (no overdubs), and while it's tempting to dismiss this warts-'n'-all album as an indulgence of its era, it's really a pretty convincing one.

By contrast, 1989's *Down on the River* smoothed down Hartford's quirks. The warts are airbrushed as he performs uncharacteristically straight songs, accompanied by four fiddles that tend to sound like a string section. The production leans towards a kind of schmaltzgrass complete with keening vocal choruses. *Hartford & Hartford* is a pleasant father-son outing, with son Jamie proving to be a fine mandolinist and an able singer-songwriter, albeit one targeting the Music City mainstream more than his dad ever did. Perhaps the best place to get a fix on Hartford's whimsical take on the River o' Life is *Me Oh My.* This eighteen-track overview draws from nine 1976-1987 Flying Fish albums and presents Hartford in a variety of settings, from the *Mark Twang* solo material to a stellar Nashville Cat recording of "Gentle on My Mind," the song that bought Hartford his riverboat fantasy.—M.H.

HAWKSHAW HAWKINS
★★★ **Hawkshaw Hawkins, Vol. 1 (King KCD-587) 1988**

Too often remembered as one of "the other two singers" who died in Patsy Cline's tragic 1963 plane crash, Harold F. "Hawkshaw" Hawkins was an important and influential singer of the 1940s and 1950s who has been all but forgotten by modern fans. A native of West Virginia, he held forth for years over radio station WWVA before moving on to Red Foley's "Jubilee U.S.A." and the Grand Ole Opry. Influenced by the style of Ernest Tubb, Hawkins helped forge the new style of love ballads and honky-tonk songs that defined postwar country music; he was one of a handful of stars who could merge the older Southeastern styles with the newer Southwestern styles of Tubb and company. His classic recordings for King from 1946 to 1953 are represented only by *Hawkshaw Hawkins, Vol. 1,* a set that contains hits like "Slow Poke" (1951), country standards like "Sunny Side of the Mountain" and "Rattlesnakin' Daddy," and a nice selection of heart songs like "I Am Slowly Dying of a Broken Heart" and "Picking Sweethearts." Though the complete absence of liner notes or recording information makes it difficult for a young fan to understand much about Hawkins, the music evokes a sense of style that will appeal to any age.—C.K.W.

RONNIE HAWKINS
★★★★ The Best of Ronnie Hawkins and the Hawks (Rhino R2 70966) 1990
An Arkansas native, Hawkins migrated to Canada in 1958 with the Hawks, a band of rockabilly razorbacks including Levon Helm. In his detailed liner notes, Colin Escott explains that Hawkins's decision to head north was based partly on word from fellow Arkansan Conway Twitty (known then as Harold Jenkins) that bar gigs were plentiful there, and partly on the results of a 1957 audition for Sun Records that left Hawkins with the impression that the waiting room for stardom in Memphis was too crowded.

A little tardy for the mid-Fifties rockabilly boom, Hawkins nevertheless landed a record deal with Morris Levy's Roulette label and scored a couple of modest hits—a reworking of Chuck Berry's "Thirty Days" (re-titled "Forty Days") and a cover of Young Jessie's rhythm & blues tune "Mary Lou"—in 1959. All but two of the eighteen selections on this album come from the Roulette years, 1959 to 1963, and all are rock & roll numbers. Hawkins cut an album of "folk" tunes—"John Henry," "I Gave My Love a Cherry," "A Wayfaring Stranger" among them—and he also recorded an album of Hank Williams tunes, but none of those tracks are included here.

Hawkins never found his way to the upper reaches of the charts, but he earned the lasting respect of rock & roll purists by making records that jumped with excitement and intensity, and by eventually assembling a band of capable Canadians—guitarist Jaime "Robbie" Robertson, bassist Rick Danko, pianist Richard Manuel, and organist Garth Hudson—to join Helm in backing him on the bandstand. That band—the Hawks from 1960 to 1963—accounts for the two most ferocious tracks on this album, covers of "Bo Diddley" and "Who Do You Love." That band also became The Band, later backing Bob Dylan before becoming established in their own right.

Hawkins continued to play Canadian clubs, and he mounted several more attempts at starting a recording career. Included here is "Down in the Alley" from a 1970 Muscle Shoals session, with Duane Allman playing slide guitar. Curiously, liner information puts the track length at 5:10, but actual length on the disc is 3:23, with a fade during an Allman solo.—J.O.

DON HENRY
★★★ Wild In the Backyard (Epic ECD 46034) 1991
Henry's commercial claim to fame is as the co-author of Kathy Mattea's big 1990 hit "Where've You Been," but his solo debut found him a delightful heir to eccentricity in the manner of Roger Miller and Ray Stevens. Singing intricately worded, oddly metered musical jokes ("Mr. God," "Into a Mall") in a charmingly scratchy voice, Henry is an offbeat upstart.—K.T.

HIGHWAY 101
★★★ Highway 101 (Warner Bros. 25608-2) 1987 ●
★★★ 101² (Warner Bros. 25742-2) 1988
★★★ Paint the Town (Warner Bros. 9 25992-2) 1989
★★★★ Greatest Hits (Warner Bros. 9 26253-2) 1990
★★ Bing Bang Boom (Warner Bros. 9 26588-2) 1991
Despite the best efforts of Linda Ronstadt, Emmylou Harris, and their peers, the California-bred fusion of country and rock never took hold on the country popularity charts of the 1970s. Instead, a whole line of second-generation country-rockers profited from the style a decade later in Music City. None were more stylish, more accomplished, or more successful than Highway 101.

The band was assembled by manager Chuck Morris to surround the sensuous, smoky vocals of Paulette Carlson. But when Highway 101 hit the stage or the recording studio the members sounded like they'd been together all their lives. The act was particularly associated with spunky, uptempo women's songs such as "The Bed You Made for Me," "Whiskey If You Were a Woman," "Just Say Yes," "Who's Lonely Now," "Setting Me Up," and "Honky Tonk Heart." The pattern was for Carlson and the rhythm section to set the tone on the verses with a full barrage of blazing guitars and robust male harmonies joining in on the choruses.

They were records with spit and polish that made you turn up the radio and sing along. They also defined their era, for Highway 101 came on the scene as country was turning left and embracing its new youth market in the late 1980s. The trend-setting look matched the sound, with the guys in earrings and nouveau-cowboy garb and Carlson in gaucho hats, flowing skirts, and a lion's mane of blonde hair.

The act simply doesn't make bad records. *Greatest Hits* is essential to any understanding of country's new youth appeal and stylishness in the late 1980s.

Carlson and her pals went their separate ways in 1990, and the boys recruited red-headed spitfire Nikki Nelson as their new front woman. The comeback CD was uneven, but Nelson matched her predecessor's vim on the "Bing Bang Boom" title tune as well as on "Wherever You Are," "Restless Kind" and especially "Baby I'm Missing You," all country-rock gems.—R.K.O.

CHRIS HILLMAN
★½ Morning Sky (Sugar Hill SH-CD-3729)
1982
★★ Desert Rose (Sugar Hill SH-CD-3743)
1984

Before he joined the Byrds as rock & roll bass player, Chris Hillman played bluegrass mandolin for such dimly remembered California outfits as the Scottsville Squirrel Barkers and the Golden State Boys, back in 1963-64. So the bluegrass feel of these efforts should not come as any great surprise to those who have been keeping up with Hillman all along. Those who are more familiar with his later work in the Desert Rose Band will be disappointed, though, at how puny and anemic Hillman's voice sounds on *Morning Sky*. The material

therein befits a former Byrd—country-rock songs (Danny O'Keefe's "Goodtime Charlie's Got the Blues," the Grateful Dead's "Ripple," Dan Fogelberg's "Morning Sky") done in an earnest, if unremarkable bluegrass style.

Desert Rose finds Hillman's voice bulked up considerably and supported by such capable old hands as Jay Dee Maness, Glen D. Hardin, and James Burton. The song selection hews more closely to classic country (Louvins, Wilburns, Johnnie & Jack covers) with good intentions and modest success. The sole embarrassment is Hillman's John Denver-like sacking of George Jones's golden "Treasure of Love." Two Hillman originals make their first appearance here, "Running the Roadblocks" and "Desert Rose." Taking a cue from these, he shrewdly capitalized on his pop-rock strengths in future work with the Desert Rose Band.—P.K.

BECKY HOBBS
★★★½ All Keyed Up (RCA 9770-4-R)
1988, 1989

Born in Bartlesville, Oklahoma, Beckaroo—as the name on her vanity license plate reads and as she calls herself in the title cut for this album—has made the rounds of record labels, recording for MCA and Tatoo in Los Angeles before shifting to Mercury and a country career in the late Seventies. Hobbs got off to a slow start in Nashville until she and Moe Bandy had a hit with "Let's Get over Them Together" in 1983.

The duet's success failed to boost Hobbs's career to the next level, however. Subsequent recordings for Liberty and EMI America stalled too, but her dynamic stage shows and her talent as a songwriter convinced MTM Records that Hobbs still had promise, and the fledgling label signed her to yet another deal in 1988.

Produced by Richard Bennett, *All Keyed Up* delivered on that promise. The ten originals by Hobbs sample a variety of styles including honky-tonk shuffles ("They Always Look Better When They're Leavin'" and "Jones on the Jukebox"), an Oklahoma swinger ("Are There Any More Like You [Where You Came From]"), a rockabilly number ("All Keyed Up"), a ballad ("She Broke Her Promise"), and a waltz ("Old Flame Burns Blue").

Around the time MTM went belly up, RCA bought Hobbs's contract and her album, resequenced it, dropped "It's Because of You," and added "Do you Feel the Same Way Too?" and "A Woman Needs," both written by Hobbs. But the makeover was of little avail, as country radio looked the other way. Meanwhile, the United States Information Agency has proved more daring than radio programmers: in recent years she has toured Africa as a cultural ambassador of the U. S.—J.O.

ROBIN HOLCOMB
★★★★ **Robin Holcomb (Elektra Musician 9 60983) 1990**
★★★★ **Rockabye (Elektra Musician 9 61289) 1992**

Pianist, singer, and songwriter Robin Holcomb has taken on the daunting task of merging an ancient rural tradition with a modern avant-garde sensibility. Her semitragic narratives and simple melodies have their roots in the ballads of the Civil War era, but her fractured perspectives and arrangements are progressive. Her concerns are deeply American: nature and the destruction of land, family, home, and loss. The production on her Elektra debut is spare, with few embellishments to her piano-vocal style, although "Troy" is a roots-rocker in the style of the Band; "The American Rhine," "So Straight and Slow," and "Deliver Me" are dark, distressed sketches of troubled landscapes. The bolder and more ambitious *Rockabye* includes the carnival atmospherics of "Dixie," and a beautiful rendition of Bruce "Utah" Phillips's "The Goodnight-Loving Trail."—K.S.

BUDDY HOLLY
★★★★ **The Chirping Crickets (MCA MCAD 31182) 1957, 1987**
★★★★ **Buddy Holly (MCA MCAD 25239) 1958, 1989**
★★★★★ **From the Original Master Tapes (MCA MCAD 5540) 1985**

The stat books tell us that Buddy Holly had three Top Ten hits and seven other chart entries while he was alive. It's hard to square that meager tally with the importance he has been accorded, an importance that revolves around the fact that he was a triple threat as one of rock & roll's first all-singing, all-picking,

songwriting stylists. He also extended hope to all geeky guys in glasses that they too could make it in the biz. Holly had sung hillbilly music on small stations in Texas and cut his first sessions in Nashville, but by the time he re-recorded "That'll Be the Day" in 1957, he had a new blend of everything he'd ever heard. Norman Petty's productions gave Holly another edge he never would have had in Nashville. The hits ("Maybe Baby," "Peggy Sue") occupy a cell or two in almost everyone's subconscious, but the depth of his catalogue repays investigation; unfortunately, warring widows (Buddy's and Norman Petty's) are likely to deny us that opportunity for a while. Two original albums, *The Chirping Crickets* and *Buddy Holly*, are skimpy but unreservedly recommended, as is a twenty-track compilation, *From the Original Master Tapes*, which includes one of the Nashville sides, "Rock Around with Ollie Vee."—C.E.

HOOSIER HOT SHOTS
★★★★★ **Rural Rhythm 1935-1942 (Columbia CK 52735) 1992**

One of the zaniest outfits ever committed to record, the Hoosier Hot Shots emerged from vaudeville to become a top novelty band of the Thirties and Forties. Although primarily a visual act whose eccentric instrumentation matched the whimsy of its songs, the band's Saturday night performances on Chicago's WLS "National Barn Dance" brought joy to Americans mired in the hardships of Depression and beginnings of world war.

Superior musicians who mastered an arsenal of homemade and specialty instruments including the slide whistle, washboard, clarinet, bells, fife, and horns, the Hot Shots recorded dozens of jukebox favorites between 1935 and 1942 for the American Record Corporation, Vocalion, and Okeh. This twenty-song collection includes some of their quirkiest and most popular numbers, including the nonsensical "I Like Bananas (Because They Have No Bones)," the alliterative "Connie's Got Connections in Connecticut," the blues standard "Taint Nobody's Business What I Do," and the slightly risqué "From the Indies to the Andes in His Undies," as well as the quasi-romantic pop ballads "Sweet Sue" and "What Is So Rare." Together, they provide for the modern listener a musical perspective on an earlier era. But most of all, they offer testimony to the resolve of the human spirit to laugh and smile its way beyond harsh realities.—J.B.

JOHNNY HORTON
★★★ Greatest Hits (Columbia CK-40665) 1961 ▲
★★★★ American Originals (Columbia CK 45071) 1989

Despite a few very good songs, like "I'm a Honky Tonk Man," "Honky Tonk Hardwood Floor," and "All For the Love of a Girl," Johnny Horton had only moderate success as a country singer until he recorded Jimmie Driftwood's "The Battle of New Orleans" in 1958. Thereafter, he became the premiere performer of saga songs, the pseudohistorical ballads that briefly dominated the country charts up into the early 1960s. Horton died at the apex of this fad, in an automobile accident near Milano, Texas, on November 5, 1960.

Originally released on LP just after Horton's death, *Greatest Hits* offers thirteen selections, eight of which, predictably, are saga songs, such as "Jim Bridger," "Comanche (The Brave Horse)," "Johnny Freedom," "Johnny Reb," as well as the better known "Battle of New Orleans," "Sink the Bismark," "North to Alaska," and "Springtime in Alaska." Fortunately, *Greatest Hits* also samples Horton's romantic side with "Whispering Pines" and the lovely "All for the Love of a Girl," while also including his classic "Honky Tonk Man" (which Dwight Yoakam later covered quite faithfully). Horton's rockabilly or country-boogie fans may still prefer the ten-cut *American Originals* which, along with his more commercial offerings, presents the singer at his high-energy best on numbers like "I'm a One Woman Man" and "Sleepy Eyed John."—B.C.M.

HOT RIZE
★★★ Hot Rize (Flying Fish FF 70206) 1979
★★★ Radio Boogie (Flying Fish FF 70231) 1981
★★★ Red Knuckles & the Trailblazers/Hot Rize (Flying Fish FF 70107) 1982/84

★★★★½ Traditional Ties (Sugar Hill SH-CD-3748) 1985
★★★½ Untold Stories (Sugar Hill SH-CD-3756) 1987
★★★½ Presents Red Knuckles & the Trailblazers: Shades of the Past (Sugar Hill SH-CD-3767) 1988
★★★★★ Take It Home (Sugar Hill SH-CD-3784) 1990

This Colorado-based bluegrass band released their first album, *Hot Rize,* in 1979, and their last, *Take It Home,* in 1990. During the twelve years they were together, they established a reputation as a dynamic stage band that captured the excitement of early bluegrass. Fiddler-mandolinist Tim O'Brien's strong lead singing (check out his fine performance of the Flatt & Scruggs standard "If I Should Wander Back Tonight" on *Traditional Ties)* and songwriting (try the title cut of *Untold Stories)* were at the center of a band that mixed their own compositions with bluegrass, folk, and country gems. Generally speaking, their albums got stronger as the band toured; their last, with the popular "Colleen Malone," rode the bluegrass charts for many months after their retirement.

The band took its name from an ingredient in Martha White Flour, long-time sponsors of Flatt & Scruggs. One of the most popular parts of their show was their comic alter-ego band, the retro-grade Fifties country band Red Knuckles & the Trailblazers (another inside joke: Trailblazer was Martha White's dogfood). With thirty tracks, *Red Knuckles & The Trailblazers/Hot Rize* gives a good idea of what the band sounded like in concert; it includes the complete contents of two albums: *Hot Rize Presents Red Knuckles and the Trailblazers* and *Hot Rize in Concert.* The Trailblazers can be heard on both; as on *Shades of the Past,* they offer not just comedy but also fine country singing by O'Brien on honky-tonk classics like "Always Late" and "The Window Up Above."—N.V.R.

DAVID HOUSTON
★★ American Originals (Columbia CK 45074) 1989

In the Sixties and Seventies, Columbia A&R man Billy Sherrill managed a stable of countrypolitan contenders that produced some real champions—Charlie Rich, Tanya Tucker, Tammy Wynette—

and more than a few also-rans. David Houston, a middlingly talented tenor, belonged in the latter category, and though we'll never know how he might have done without the worst of Sherrill's production excesses disfiguring his records, it's all too obvious what we've got here: semi-excruciating versions of "Almost Persuaded" and "My Elusive Dreams," plus eight much less memorable numbers from the bottomless pit where Sherrill kept his album filler. —P.Ca.

FERLIN HUSKY

★★½ **Capitol Collector's Series (Capitol C21Y-91629) 1989**
★★½ **Greatest Hits (Curb D2-77341) 1990**
★★ **With Feelin' (Pair PCD2-1301) 1992**
★ **Country Music Is Here to Stay (LaserLight 12 111) 1993**

Orthodox country history points to Jim Reeves and Patsy Cline as the two main superstars of the post-Elvis Nashville Sound. In fact, when the pop-oriented sound broke in 1957, neither Cline's "Walkin' after Midnight" nor Reeves's "Four Walls" hit the pop Top Ten. Ferlin Husky's "Gone," on the other hand, entered the pop charts a week after "Walkin' after Midnight" and rose to #4. At the time, Husky was a journeyman country singer with a comic alter ego (Simon Crum) and one monster hit to his credit—a hokey duet with Jean Shepard called "A Dear John Letter." The lushly arranged "Gone" catapulted Husky to the front ranks of hillbilly stardom, a position he solidified with the 1960 pop-gospel hit "Wings of a Dove."

"A Dear John Letter," "Gone," and "Wings of a Dove" belong on every compilation of classic country's greatest hits. The ten-cut Curb disc has all three. That may be all you need to know. Husky's vintage music has not worn well with age, and at times his sobbing vocals are overwrought to the point of high camp. Capitol's *Collector's Series* is top-heavy with overproduced singalong choruses, though it does include two of the three Husky smashes, and one out-of-nowhere dicey suicide number called "Draggin' the River." Beyond that, the Husky catalogue reduces to how much you can take of a grown man pretending to weep.—D.C.

ALAN JACKSON

★★★★   **Here in the Real World (Arista ARCD-8623) 1989** ▲

★★★   **Don't Rock the Juke Box (Arista ARCD-8681) 1991** ▲²

★★★   **A Lot About Livin' and a Little 'Bout Love (Arista 18711-2) 1992** ▲²

Jackson is both a skillful songwriter (of the old-fashioned hook-and-hum school) and an emotionally persuasive singer. These two strengths, showcased in a series of imaginative music videos, made him one of the best-selling and most-awarded members of the new traditionalist movement, along with his frequent co-writer, Randy Travis. Jackson is a throwback in both sound and theme to country's glory days of the early 1950s. His lyrics and values are framed in the innocent rural context that first gave country music its identity and name. Although he has mastered all their tricks, Jackson lacks the depth and urgency of such artistic mentors as Merle Haggard and George Jones. However, as a first taste for country music's newcomers, Jackson is an invaluable conduit to the works of the old masters. To date, his first album is his best, made so by such strong efforts as "Chasin' That Neon Rainbow," "I'd Love You All Over Again," "Wanted," and "Here in the Real World." That the follow-up, *Don't Rock the*

Jukebox, sold better is probably a testament to the popularity of the clever title track.—E.M.

STONEWALL JACKSON

★★★½   **The Dynamic Stonewall Jackson (Sony Music Spec. Prod. A-8186) 1959**

★★★½   **American Originals (Columbia CK 45070) 1989**

★   **Waterloo (LaserLight 12 113) 1993**

A terribly underrated honky-tonk stylist, Stonewall Jackson has never received proper respect—probably because in his prime he was a lunchpail singer who cut whatever tacky material Columbia handed him. One such song, included on both the Columbia and Sony discs, is "Waterloo," a 1959 crossover smash built around the chintzy percussive banjo that was all the rage in country production back then. (The LaserLight version is the usual dreary, budget-line remake.)

But when not saddled with trashy novelties and story songs, Jackson cut stout fiddle-and-steel weepers and sawdust chuggers. (The pace of his "Smoke along the Track" may surprise those only familiar with Dwight Yoakam's cover.) Jackson's voice has a Georgia red-clay presence that was perfectly suited to the Columbia echo chamber and equally suited to unpretentious ballads like

"Don't Be Angry" from *American Originals*. The Columbia and Sony discs overlap on four songs, and neither one is satisfying start to finish. (I don't know how the compilers of *American Originals* overlooked "I Washed My Hands in Muddy Water.") But individual cuts like "A Wound Time Can't Erase" are lunchpail country music at its best—three minutes of righteously undiluted heartache.—D.C.

WANDA JACKSON
★★★★ **Rockin' the Country (Rhino R2-70990) 1990**
★★★★ **Greatest Hits (Curb D2-77398) 1990**

Elvis and Wanda were sweethearts (albeit briefly), so she took his advice: ditched country music and cut rock & roll. "When I start eruptin', ain't nobody gonna make me stop," she proclaimed loudly and proudly on "Fujiyama Mama," but none of her releases clicked on the charts, so she went back to country. Then—out of the blue—one of her old album cuts, "Party," became a hit in 1960, so Wanda dusted off her rockin' shoes. Only then did she start scoring country hits like "Right or Wrong" and "In the Middle of a Heartache." Confused? Rhino's *Rockin' the Country* tries for an overview of her career, but it's flawed by omissions like her original versions of "Silver Threads and Golden Needles" and "Kickin' Our Hearts Around," a song she wrote for Buck Owens. Curb's *Greatest Hits* collates all eleven songs that Wanda placed in the pop and country Top Forty and rounds it out with a 1990 duet with Jann Browne on the old Davis Sisters' hit "I Forgot More Than You'll Ever Know." The early to mid-Sixties country sides are fine in their way, but give little sense of the incendiary quality she brought to her earlier work, a quality that changed the rules for women in country music. Miss Kitty Wells she wasn't.—C.E.

SONNY JAMES
★★★ **Capitol Collector's Series (Capitol C21Y-91630) 1990**
★★ **Young Love (Pair PCD-2-1310) 1991**
★★★ **Greatest Hits (Curb D2-77359) 1991**
★★ **American Originals (Columbia CK 45066) 1989**

Country chart tallies rate Sonny James one of the top twenty artists of all time. The sincere, pleading quality of his voice probably accounts in part for the strong showing there, but his habit of rehashing familiar songs certainly hasn't worn well. The mass audience first caught up with him in 1956 singing "Young Love," one of the first country songs to tap into the bubble gum market; thereafter, most of his success came from tepid revivals of other peoples' hits. James imparts a blank, rootless uniformity to songs as diverse as Roy Orbison's "Only the Lonely" and Jimmy Reed's "Bright Lights, Big City"—and that is perhaps his singular achievement. The hits collections have plenty to draw from, but, with the exception of the pimply innocence of "Young Love," little has endured. *Capitol Collector's Series* represents the best value, spanning the period from "Young Love" to 1972's "That's Why I Love You Like I Do." The Curb and Pair sets seem to have been compiled by sticking pins in chart books, and *American Originals* picks up where they leave off. By being so consistently mediocre, though, James can always be said to be at his best.—C.E.

JASON
★★★½ **One Foot in the Honky Tonk (Liberty 96797) 1991**

After punk-country rock band Jason & the Scorchers burned out, singer Jason Ringenberg decided to pursue his original dream of becoming a country singer and signed with Liberty Records. Though *One Foot in the Honky Tonk* turned down the gas on the rambunctious fire of the Scorchers' guitar attack, Jason's solo debut still carried more kick in its grooves than nearly anything else that surfaced in Nashville in the early Nineties. The songs focused attention on Jason's hard-country soul and his yearning vocal quality, with a couple of strong dashes of Buddy Holly-style rhythmic pop thrown in for balance. Outside of the rock press, where he received good reviews, Jason's solo shot still didn't earn him the notice he deserved, and Liberty dropped him without an opportunity for a second album.—M.M.

JASON & THE SCORCHERS

★★★★★ Essential Jason and the
Scorchers, Vol. 1 (EMI E21Y-
95321) 1992
★★★½ Thunder and Fire (A&M 5264)
1989

The Jason & the Scorchers story proves
once again the unpredictable greatness of
an unusual pairing—and the distressing
knack the music industry has for allowing
truly original, breathtaking music to slip
through the cracks.

Singer Jason Ringenberg, raised on an
Illinois pig farm, arrived in Nashville in
the early 1980s as a naive yet assured
vocalist who combined the sincere
fatalism of Hank Williams with the
spastic energy of rocker Iggy Pop. He met
up with a group of one-time punk rockers
who carried a flame for gutsy, no-holds-
barred honky-tonk. Together, they
created a dynamic force that combined
the visceral jolt of flat-out, high-energy
rock & roll with the mystical, knotty
truths of country music.

The group lasted through four albums
before imploding due to the wear-and-
tear of the road, the turbulence of the
rock & roll lifestyle, and the sheer
frustration that comes with a lack of
recognition. Their early albums on EMI—
Fervor, Lost and Found, and *Still
Standing*—are no longer available in their
original form. But *Essential Jason and the
Scorchers* contains the first two albums in
their entirety, as well as such previously
unreleased gems as a supercharged
version of Hank Williams's "Honky Tonk
Blues" and Neil Young's "Are You Ready
for the Country." *Thunder and Fire,* the
group's last album, lacks some of the raw
fire of the earlier work, but it shows that
the group was capable of smoothing its
edges while maintaining its provocative
center and dangerous swagger.—M.M.

WAYLON JENNINGS

★★★½ White Lightning (Laserlight 15
486) 1992
★★★★ The Early Years (RCA 9561-2-R)
1989
★★★★★ The Taker/Tulsa & Honky Tonk
Heroes (Mobile Fidelity MFCD-
10-007779) 1971/73
★★★ Are You Sure Hank Done It This
Way (RCA 07863-61156-2)
1992

★★★★ Greatest Hits (RCA 8506-2-RRE)
1979, 1986 ▲³
★★★★ Greatest Hits, Vol. 2 (RCA PCD1-
5325-RE) 1984
★★★★★ Collector's Series (RCA 07863-
58400-2) 1985
★★★★ Best of Waylon Jennings (RCA
6327-2-R) 1986
★★★★ Will the Wolf Survive (MCA
MCAD-31102) 1986
★★★ [& Willie Nelson] Take It to the
Limit (CBS CK 38562) 1987
★★★ A Man Called Hoss (MCA MCAD-
42038) 1987
★★★½ New Classic Waylon (MCA MCAD-
42287) 1989
★★★½ The Eagle (Epic EK 46105) 1990
★★★ [& Willie Nelson] Clean Shirt
(Epic EK 47462) 1991
★★★ Too Dumb for New York City, Too
Ugly for LA (Epic EK 48982)
1992

The man who boldly led what came to be
known as the Outlaw Movement in
modern country music got there via a
quiet and fairly circuitous route. Waylon
Jennings began his musical career as a
teen-aged protégé of Buddy Holly in the
West Texas of the late Fifties (Waylon, in
fact, gave up his seat on that ill-fated
small plane to J. P. "The Big Bopper"
Richardson the day the music died).
Holly produced Waylon's first record in
1959. The A-side of that single, "Jole
Blon," is now available on the *White
Lightning* CD. Waylon gives a spirited—if
often unintelligible—rendition of the
Cajun classic, accompanied by Holly as
well as by saxophone great King Curtis.
The rest of that CD contains other
fascinating early glimpses of Waylon,
including selections from his first album
Waylon Jennings at J. D.'s—J. D.'s being
a Phoenix club where he was the wildly
popular main draw for a year and a half
before moving to Nashville and signing
with RCA. His repertoire back then is
revealing of the course that lay ahead for
him: a Harlan Howard song, a Buck
Owens ditty, a rocker or two, a ballad, the
occasional quirky song. Nothing too
revolutionary, just a personal musical
vision. He was actually regarded as a
folk-country artist at first, recording Bob
Dylan songs and winning a Grammy for
"MacArthur Park" but it's worth noting
that the CD that represents that era (*The
Early Years*) includes songs by Waylon,

Chuck Berry, Harlan Howard, Mel Tillis, and Bobby Bare.

During the late Sixties and early Seventies, Jennings came up against the Nashville hierarchy, trying to make it in Nashville with his own peculiar brand of music but more importantly his own style of being a country star. The main struggle was over self-determination. He finally won production control from RCA in 1972—hardly a revolutionary topic now, but it was back then in Nashville. His record company did not fight him so much as it simply did not understand him. As an example, I cite a 1972 RCA promotional album called *Get into Waylon Jennings* (it would make an excellent CD) that contained sixteen songs, including Waylon's own versions of the Rolling Stones song "Honky Tonk Woman" and the Beatles' "Norwegian Wood." More attention went into that promo LP than to most of his commercial releases.

He discovered and championed the songs of Kris Kristofferson on *The Taker/ Tulsa* in 1971 and then devoted an album to the equally unconventional songs of then-unknown Texas writer Billy Joe Shaver with 1973's *Honky Tonk Heroes.* The two albums are now combined on a single brilliant, essential CD.

Waylon was in a hurry in those years. From the release of *The Taker/Tulsa* in February of 1971 until the progressive country movement reached its watershed with the first platinum-selling country album (*Wanted: the Outlaws,* a compilation which featured Waylon along with Willie Nelson, Jessi Colter, and Tompall Glaser) in January of 1976, Waylon put out fourteen albums, representing the core of his work.

The *Collector's Series* and *Greatest Hits* CDs cover much of this ground (although *Greatest Hits,* for no good reason, contains two fewer songs than did the original *Greatest Hits* record; "Ladies Love Outlaws" and "Only Daddy That'll Walk the Line" were dropped). They include such basic Waylon from that period as "Amanda," "Lonesome, On'ry and Mean," "Good Hearted Woman" (with Willie Nelson), "Bob Wills Is Still the King," "Luckenbach, Texas," "Are You Sure Hank Done it This Way," and "I've Always Been Crazy." I'd love to see a CD package of Waylon's true break-

through albums: 1974's *This Time* and *Dreaming My Dreams* the following year.

His personal vision of his sound began to emerge. It was defined by a highly individualistic lyric set against a heavy, drum-laden backbeat, accented by Jennings's West Texas-rockabilly guitar licks—sometimes likened to chicken scratching, because of their emphatic, forceful and seemingly random patterns. Above everything else rode his urgent vocals, a big, warm authoritative presence. When *Rolling Stone* magazine "discovered" Jennings for its audience, it referred to "the monster voice of Waylon Jennings"—his sound was that different from what the rock world expected of country singers.

The next few years saw Jennings hone his Outlaw persona until it almost took control of him and he finally made a conscious effort to pull back. He left RCA for MCA in 1986. *New Classic Waylon* is a sampling of his first four MCA albums. That work and his later Epic records and his duets with Willie and his *Highwayman* albums with Willie, Johnny Cash, and Kris Kristofferson represent the more introspective and mature Waylon Jennings. The younger, hell-bent-for-leather Jennings changed the face of country music.—C.F.

WAYLON JENNINGS, WILLIE NELSON, JESSI COLTER, AND TOMPALL GLASER

★★½ **Wanted! The Outlaws (RCA 5976-2-RRE) 1976, 1984 ▲²**

In its original LP incarnation, this sampler of tracks from four progressive country musicians earned country music's first platinum album certification. To fans and to the press, that sales milestone seemed to signal a breakthrough in Nashville. Finally, a new generation of country artists were getting their say! Nashville industry insiders knew better, of course. *Outlaws* wasn't a call to arms from Waylon, Willie, and company; it was a shrewd marketing ploy masterminded by RCA exec Jerry Bradley, who saw the new buzzword "outlaw" as an advertising slogan to sell more Waylon records. Bradley recycled five-year-old Waylon and Willie tracks, even combined the two in a fake live duet for "Good Hearted Woman," and licensed tracks from Capitol and MGM to get Waylon's wife

Jessi and his compadre Tompall on board.

Even if the packaging was disingenuous, the collection of tracks still proved a pretty good primer for newcomers. It had hits—two solid travelogues of the soul from Willie ("Yesterday's Wine," "Me and Paul"), Waylon & Willie's big number, Waylon & Jessi's "Suspicious Minds," and the two biggest hits Tompall ever had, his boogie rendition of the old Jimmie Rodgers favorite "T for Texas" and his smirking "Put Another Log on the Fire." Even the cuts that weren't hits, by Waylon and Jessi, worked in the mix.

Given the package's cut-and-paste origins, it seems ironically appropriate that the original LP has now been trimmed from eleven tracks to eight for CD and that the original track sequencing (pairing tracks by each artist and grouping the three duets) has been completely scrambled. Of course, it's also irritating as hell. The reason, according to a former RCA exec, is that RCA no longer has the rights to some of the licensed material. That explains why "Put Another Log on the Fire" is gone; it doesn't account for the absence of Waylon's "Honky Tonk Heroes" or "Suspicious Minds" or Chet Flippo's original liner notes. As it stands now on CD, consider *The Outlaws* tried and found wanting.—P.K.

JIM & JESSE

★★★★ The Jim & Jesse Story (CMH 2-CD-9022) 1990
★★★½ In the Tradition (Rounder CD 0234) 1987
★★★½ Music among Friends (Rounder CD 0279) 1991

Grand Ole Opry members since 1964, Jim and Jesse McReynolds carry on with flair in the venerable country music tradition of the brother duet. Contemporaries of the Louvin Brothers (their *Saluting the Louvin Brothers,* Epic BN26465, was issued in 1969), they added a bluegrass touch with lead singer Jesse's unique mandolin style, called "cross-picking," based on Earl Scruggs's banjo "roll" but using a flat-pick. Over the decades they've made many fine recordings. Their first ones, ten gospel songs for Cincinnati's Kentucky Records, have occasionally appeared on cheap

budget labels and contain perhaps Jesse's hottest mandolin picking, but probably won't appear on CD anytime soon. Their next twenty cuts, made for Capitol with a full bluegrass band, have recently been reissued on CD by the German Bear Family label (BCD-15635, *Jim & Jesse: 1952-1955)*. These introduced their band, the Virginia Boys. A late Fifties version of the Virginia Boys included hot fiddler Vassar Clements and ace banjoist Bobby Thompson; they made a few obscure records for Starday. Moving to Epic in 1960, Jim & Jesse had a string of hits on that label during the Sixties. Unfortunately none of these recordings are available on CD, but Rounder's *The Epic Bluegrass Hits* (SS 20), a recent LP reissue with some of their best music, is worth looking for.

Perhaps someone at Sony will see fit to dust off their 1965 bluegrass tribute to Chuck Berry, *Berry Pickin' in the Country* (Epic LN24144/BN26144)—along with Berry's liner notes. But meanwhile, of the available sets, *The Jim & Jesse Story* is the best buy, with twenty-four songs, including many of their best-known hits from "Are You Missing Me" to "Diesel on My Tail" and "Paradise." Produced by Bobby Thompson and featuring many of the most illustrious alumni of the Virginia Boys, it's a strong album. In fact some of these cuts sound more polished and assured than the originals. An added bonus with this set are the very detailed notes that, if you can hack the tiny print, offer the best single telling of the history of this long-lived outfit, now regarded as pioneers in the bluegrass field. Of their recent recordings for Rounder, *In the Tradition* from 1987 mixes new material with remakes of some older favorites, while *Music among Friends* from 1991 is a better than average collection of guest star performances, with some outstanding tracks like "The White Dove" with Ricky Skaggs, "Flower in the Desert" with Emmylou Harris, and "The Little White Church" with Mac Wiseman and Buck White.—N.V.R.

MICHAEL JOHNSON

★★★ That's That (RCA 6715-2-R) 1988
★★½ The Best of Michael Johnson (RCA 9958-2-R) 1990
★★½ Michael Johnson (Atlantic 82304-2) 1992

You may remember Michael Johnson as the voice behind "Bluer Than Blue," a late Seventies soft-rock staple. Since then, Johnson has turned his sleepy vocals and classical guitar in a country direction, scoring #1 hits with "Give Me Wings" (*Best of Michael Johnson*) and "The Moon Is Still over Her Shoulder" (*That's That*). Despite these successes, Johnson is less a country artist than a singer-songwriter in search of a format. Like a lot of latter-day James Taylors, Johnson has found a home in Nashville. *That's That* is the livelier of his two available studio CDs, ignited by a band that includes bassist Edgar Meyer and the flaming dobro of Jerry Douglas. His later eponymous release on the Atlantic label falls a little short, but strong songs like "Two Ships That Pass in the Moonlight" and "One Honest Tear" will please the faithful. Meanwhile, he remains on the commercial fringe in Nashville, an artist still searching for the material that could bring him some big hits.—P.Cr.

THE JOHNSON MOUNTAIN BOYS

★★★ **Favorites (Rounder CD-11509) 1987**
★★★★ **Let the Whole World Talk (Rounder CD-0025) 1987**
★★★ **Requests (Rounder CD-0246) 1988**
★★★★★ **At the Old Schoolhouse (Rounder 2-CD-0260/61) 1989**
★★★★ **Blue Diamond (Rounder CD-0293) 1993**

Throughout the 1980s, the Johnson Mountain Boys continued to win almost universal acclaim as the best traditional bluegrass band in the nation. Working out of the Washington, D. C., area, featuring the soulful singing of Dudley Connell, the mandolin picking of David McLaughlin, the fiddling of Eddie Stubbs, and the banjo work of Richard Underwood, and, later, Tom Adams, the Boys played with an emotional intensity and devotion to classic bluegrass style that won them countless awards and worldwide recognition. Throughout the 1980s, they did a series of LPs for Rounder that expanded the sometimes stale bluegrass repertoire (often by including older country honky-tonk songs); the best of these first four LPs is collected in

Favorites, the closest thing the band has to a greatest hits package. Probably their best studio album is *Let the Whole World Talk,* a landmark set done in 1987, which features a remarkable blend of modernism and traditionalism, especially in the way the band reinvents older songs with new arrangements. *Requests* (1988) was compiled by giving out request forms to fans at concerts, then winnowing suggestions down to a dozen sides. Though individual performances sparkle, the very method makes programming continuity odd. Far and away the best JMB album was the one intended to be their farewell concert when they had decided to break up in 1989: *At the Old Schoolhouse.* The drama of the moment, a sympathetic audience, and superb on-location recording all conspired to capture the band at its peak, and the farewell concert turned out to be a marathon set of eclectic performances. Here are bluegrass favorites like "John Henry" and "Daniel Prayed," old-time duets like "Sweetest Gift," string-band warhorses like "Going to Georgia." The set richly deserved its Grammy nomination and bluegrass association awards.

After a brief hiatus, the Johnson Mountain Boys began playing regularly again in 1990, and in 1993 produced *Blue Diamond,* in which they pushed the envelope of the bluegrass repertoire even further. Songs by Bob Dylan and Jean Ritchie jostled with songs by Carter Stanley; obscure pieces recorded by Little Jimmy Dickens and Buck Owens nested next to ancient murder ballads like "Christine LeRoy." Rested and as unpredictable as ever, the JMB here managed to challenge their own standards.—C.K.W.

DAVID LYNN JONES

★★★★ **Hard Times on Easy Street (Mercury 832 518-2) 1987**
★★★ **Wood, Wind, and Stone (Mercury 836 951-2) 1990**
★★★★ **Mixed Emotions (Liberty C21S-97251) 1992**

David Lynn Jones is one of modern country music's most gifted, visionary, and challenging songwriters. His lyrically provocative songs—which bear the influence of Dylan, Springsteen, and Kristofferson—seldom flinch from grappling with the sort of large-tapestry moral and religious dilemmas that mainstream Nashville songscribes routinely shy away from. Not surprisingly, Jones's uncompromising propensity for Dylanesque lyrics, rocked-up horn arrangements, and his tendency to wear his moralistic heart on his sleeve have pretty much kept him a stranger to the country record charts. *Hard Times on Easy Street,* Jones's first album, is his strongest and most conventional effort to date. It features—as do all three of his albums—all-original material, including his anthemic "Living in the Promiseland" (a hit for Willie Nelson), vivid character vignettes like "Billy Jean," and sweeping commentaries like the title tune, which is Jones's heartfelt ode to the American farmer. On the follow-up *Wood, Wind, and Stone,* Jones's lyric brilliance is in ample abundance, even if the material is, overall, more introspective, less focused, and often hampered by ponderous arrangements. (The album took many months to complete, was put on hold for a time, and suffered from misdirection and overproduction as Mercury briefly considered trying to break Jones as a pop artist.) With *Mixed Emotions,* Jones returned to his roots and reinfused his music with much of the fire of his debut album. Coproduced (with Richie Albright) in his own home studio in Bexar, Arkansas, *Mixed Emotions* is a riveting effort. Some of the tracks are infused with blistering rock & roll intensity and deal convincingly with such seemingly conflicting themes as romantic disillusionment and the absolving power of traditional values and relationships. Jones's seething moral indignation occasionally gives way to inveighing in apocalyptic anger (as in "Judgment Day" and "The Land of Ala"), giving the music on *Mixed Emotions* undeniable power. —B.A.

GEORGE JONES

★★★★★ Best of George Jones (Rhino R2 70531) 1991
★★★½ Best of George Jones: Vol. 1 (Mercury 848 978-2) 1991
★ Tender Years (LaserLight 15 488) 1992
★★★ 20 Greatest Hits (Deluxe DCD-7778) 1987
★ George Jones & Melba Montgomery (Hollywood HCD-111) 1987
★ 14 Greats (Hollywood HCD-389) 1988
★ Golden Hits (Hollywood HCD-103) 1989
★ Greatest Hits (Hollywood HCD-402) 1989
★ He Stopped Loving Her Today (Hollywood HCD-380) 1988
★ I'm a One Woman Man (Hollywood HCD-392) 1989
★ Sings the Great Songs of Leon Payne (Hollywood HCD-110) 1987
★★★ Best of George Jones (Epic EK 33352) 1975
★★ All Time Greatest Hits, Vol. 1 (Epic EK 34692) 1977
★★ My Very Special Guests (Columbia CK 35544) 1979
★★★ I Am What I Am (Epic EK 36586) 1980
★★★★★ Anniversary: Ten Years of Hits (Columbia EGK 38323) 1982
★★★ By Request (Epic EK 39899) 1984, 1987
★★★ First Time Live! (Epic EK 39899) 1985
★★★ Wine Colored Roses (Epic EK 40413) 1986
★★★ Super Hits (Epic CK 40776) 1987 ●
★★★ One Woman Man (Epic EK 44078) 1989
★★★ Greatest Country Hits (Curb D21K-77369) 1990
★★ Friends in High Places (Epic EK 45014) 1990
★★★ You Oughta Be Here with Me (Epic EK 46028) 1990
★★★ Hallelujah Weekend (Epic EK 46078) 1990
★★ And Along Came Jones (MCA MCAD-10398) 1991
★★★ Walls Can Fall (MCA MCAD-10652) 1992

George Jones may very well be the greatest country singer alive. Though the influence of others—the plaintive head-register phrasings of Roy Acuff, the raw straightforward lilt of Hank Williams—can be heard in his singing, Jones possesses a unique voice that stands alone in country music: a well of pure, natural power, capable of swooping from high tenor to deep baritone, of articulating emotion like no other, of weaving tapestries of hard-core honky-tonk, buoyant rockabilly, and back-country gospel.

But no one, great or otherwise, has ever recorded more junk, made more bad records than he. Since he first began recording, in 1954, the Jones corpus has grown to astounding size. Amid such a sea of recordings, packaged and repackaged again and again into a plethora of more than 270 albums, the devotee and casual listener alike will find the task of separating riches from dross to be truly herculean. It is a sad but simple fact that, for much of his estimable career, Jones was a complaisant victim of lackluster material and slipshod recording, circumstances that even his majestic voice could not overcome. However, when Jones is at his best, he is without peer; and there is enough available on CD to amply attest to that.

The Rhino anthology, *The Best of George Jones*, covers the years 1955-67 and includes some of Jones's earliest and finest work, the fierce, fresh energy and power of which even Starday's aboriginal recording technology could not obscure. Though not as intensive a sampling of his Starday (1954-57) and Mercury (1957-61) years as offered by the British CD *Don't Stop the Music* (Ace CDCH 912), the great early hits—"Why, Baby, Why" (1955), "White Lightning" (1959), "The Window Up Above" (1960), "She Thinks I Still Care" (1962), "The Race Is On" (1964), and the rest—are all here, making this Rhino set central to any overview of the Jones legacy. The album that belongs beside it is *Anniversary: Ten Years of Hits*, a grand, twenty-two-song retrospective of the years 1972-82, including such hits as "We Can Make It" (1972), "The Grand Tour" (1974), and "He Stopped Loving Her Today" (1980).

One should beware of the Hollywood and LaserLight albums. It is not so much the music itself that calls for warning. To be sure, the selections, drawn from United Artists (1961-64), Musicor (1965-71), and Epic (1971-90) recordings, are indeed uneven. But the real problem, beyond any issue of subjective taste, is that the CDs themselves are technically bad: egregious remasterings that sound far worse than the originals and are often downright unlistenable.

One Woman Man (1989) and *You Oughta Be Here with Me* (1990) are two of the best albums from Jones's final years with Epic. In perspective, like the *Anniversary* album, they also go far toward exonerating producer Billy Sherrill from once common charges of sweetening and diluting the essential Jones sound. While background voices and lush strings are often rendered ludicrous by Jones's own voice, his singing is undiminished by the questionable arrangements; and, all arguments of artistic merit aside, Sherrill kept Jones commercially alive at a time when country music was increasingly beset, and the old guard increasingly endangered, by the winds of a new era. As to Jones's recent work, there are moments in *Walls Can Fall*, his second MCA album (1992), that suggest there is a long and glorious coda to the Jones legacy yet to unfold. —N.T.

GRANDPA JONES
- ★★★ **16 Greatest Hits (Hollywood HCD-224) N.D.**
- ★★★★ **Hall of Fame Series (MCA MCAD-10549) 1992**
- ★★★½ **Grandpa Jones Live (Sony Music Special Products AK 52416)1992**

Best known for his boisterous banjo tunes and classic comedy, Louis M. "Grandpa" Jones is familiar to modern fans for his work on the Grand Ole Opry and "Hee Haw." Though he is a member of the Country Music Hall of Fame and has a recording career dating back to 1943, he is poorly represented on CD. The first stage of his recording career, when he helped King Records become one of the nation's leading independent labels, is reflected in *16 Greatest Hits*, which includes Grandpa's original versions of "Mountain Dew," "Old Rattler," and "Eight More Miles to Louisville." These 1940s sides are decently remastered, but the album's packaging lacks any liner notes at all, and the programming is so sloppy that the same recording of "Old Rattler" is included twice, once under the name "Here, Rattler, Here!"

In the mid-1950s, Grandpa did a brief stint with Decca, and his entire output there is found in *Hall of Fame Series*. These were not Grandpa's most dynamic records, not even his most representative, but the album features superb remastering and excellent, detailed liner notes. Jones himself has always thought that the Monument LPs he did for Fred Foster in the 1960s composed his best work, but only one of these is currently in print. This is *Grandpa Jones—Live,* a 1969 concert that features the singer's regular road band, as well as his talented wife, Ramona. It is the best single introduction to Grandpa's modern period and a good sample of his folk-based repertoire. —C.K.W.

WYNONNA JUDD

★★★½ Wynonna Judd (MCA MCAD-10529) 1992 ▲³
★★★★ Tell Me Why (MCA MCAD-10822) 1993 ▲

In the Judds, Wynonna's voluptuous voice always contrasted with the chaste instrumentation. But the first song on her solo debut, "What It Takes," a pointed lyric about restlessness and self-determination, contests her presence with steamy slide guitar and forces her most confident performance. With Judds' guitarist Don Potter playing and serving as associate producer to Tony Brown, there are clear links to Wynonna's past: the tender trembles of "My Strongest Weakness" (written by Naomi Judd and Mike Reid) and the inspirational homilies of "When I Reach the Place I'm Goin'" (with harmonies by Naomi Judd) could pass for Judds songs, and the leaving home images in "It's Never Easy to Say Goodbye" and "All of That Love from Here" are obvious and tiresome. But "No One Else on Earth" has the firm bump of Aretha Franklin's Muscle Shoals sessions, and that must be a deliberate Stax guitar lick in "A Little Bit of Love." Wynonna also begins to find more complex songs—"She Is His Only Need," a subtly disturbing story-song about a loner who falls in love and goes "over the line" to prove his devotion by buying gifts, features remarkable octave leaps that dramatize the theme of dependency.

Tell Me Why reveals a surer identity. Judd savors and stretches the wide melody of Karla Bonoff's title song and introduces a bittersweet tone to the despairing lyrics. With frequent contributions from a small choir, the album has a clear gospel influence, including the inspirational "Rock Bottom." Even her devotional themes have gained subtlety: the mystical imagery of the rousing "Father Sun" could have been written by

Prince, and though Jesse Winchester's "Let's Make a Baby King" calls for "a Lord to guide us," it also evokes Madonna's association of Christianity with sexual imagery. There are even two celebrations of rock & roll: "Just Like New," about Elvis's car fetish, and Mary-Chapin Carpenter's "Girls with Guitars," about the liberating power of an amplifier.—R.T.

THE JUDDS

★★★★ The Judds (RCA 8402) 1984 ●
★★★½ Why Not Me (RCA 5319) 1984 ▲²
★★★ Rockin' with the Rhythm (RCA 7042) 1985 ▲
★★½ Heart Land (RCA 5916) 1987 ▲
★★★ Christmas Time with the Judds (RCA 6422) 1987 ●
★★★★ Greatest Hits (RCA 8318) 1988 ▲²
★★★ River of Time (RCA 9595) 1989 ●
★★★ Love Can Build a Bridge (RCA 2070) 1990 ▲
★★★★ Greatest Hits Volume Two (RCA 61018) 1991 ●
★★★ The Judds Collection (RCA 66045) 1992

The Judds debuted early in 1984, midway through Ronald Reagan's reign, and became immediate stars. Although it would be foolish to discount the importance of their radically simple music, or Wynonna Judd's spectacular voice, it's also impossible to separate this mother-daughter duo's pious celebrations of fidelity ("Change of Heart," written by Naomi Judd), home ("Dream Chaser"), and the morality of rural life ("John Deere Tractor") from the decade of neoconservatism.

Janie Fricke and Barbara Mandrell were the dominant female singers in Nashville when the Judds patented a spare, warmly acoustic style that blended their roots in Kentucky and California, updating Appalachian harmony with Marin County folk-rock. Producer Brent Maher, who'd worked with Kenny Rogers, handled their entire career and built the songs around Don Potter's slippery acoustic guitar hooks. Consequently, the music gave the comforting illusion of being played on a front porch.

The Judds' first single was "Had a Dream (For the Heart)," an obscure Elvis Presley song, and that association helps describe the power and finesse of

Wynonna's voice. Her confident growls and melodic leaps in Harlan Howard's "Why Not Me" make the song as much a defining breakthrough as Patsy Cline's "Walkin' After Midnight." By *Rockin' with the Rhythm,* she'd become a great singer, handling the humorous honky-tonk yelps of "Have Mercy" as easily as the delicate entreaties of "If I Were You." Wynonna integrated blues (both Delta and lounge), jazz, and gospel influences, and even added layers of tension to the group's string of wounded and aggrieved lyrics; her bold delivery defies the description of a hometown girl "waiting patiently" in "Why Not Me," and on "Cry Myself to Sleep" she suggests a strength not contained in the defeated lyrics.

But mostly—when Wynonna stands against "these modern times" on Paul Kennerley's "One Man Woman," or announces that "women like men to make them feel alive" on "Maybe Your Baby's Got the Blues," or embraces fairy tales through the "handsome prince" of Don Potter's "Sleeping Heart"—the Judds promote traditional gender roles rejected by some of their female contemporaries. Never was this position clearer than in Jamie O'Hara's gorgeous but deceitful ballad, "Grandpa (Tell Me 'Bout the Good Old Days)." Like one of President Reagan's cozy, inaccurate anecdotes, the song offers a false equation: there was less divorce in the good old days because there was more faithfulness, honor, and, especially, prayer. More likely, rising divorce rates signify a greater number of women who refuse to suffer quietly, a fact the elder, divorced Judd should recognize.

The Judds' musical signature was so distinct and beautiful that they soon began to coast. The title hit from *Rockin' with the Rhythm* is cute alliteration passing for a song. By *Love Can Build a Bridge,* they were out of ideas: "This Country's Rockin'" recaps "Turn It Loose," while "Rompin' Stompin' Blues" just adds slide guitar to "Born to Be Blue," itself a reconstruction of Bruce Springsteen's "Pink Cadillac."

As a mother-daughter duo who could pass for sisters, the Judds were always ripe for gimmickry. The lyrical device of a young woman addressing her mom, for example, occurs three times on their introductory EP. Their catalogue was also muddied with shameless repetition: the EP was padded for CD release with two songs from *Rockin' with the Rhythm,* while *Why Not Me* was extended to ten songs by placing "Mama He's Crazy" on a second consecutive release, and *Love Can Build a Bridge* offers a second appearance of "John Deere Tractor." Both "Mama He's Crazy" and "Cry Myself to Sleep" appear on four different Judds albums. Furthermore, *Heart Land* inaugurated RCA's policy of nine-song albums, for which it's been docked a half-star. *The Judds Collection* is a three-CD package that expands the two definitive greatest hits volumes by adding a thirty-two-page booklet with photos and a cursory biography, plus a disc of "studio work tapes"—casual demos of the two singers accompanied by Don Potter's guitar. From the label that has repeatedly exhumed Elvis and Keith Whitley, that's actually quite discreet.—R.T.

K

ROBERT EARL KEEN JR.

★★½ **No Kinda Dancer (Philo CDPH-1108) 1986**

★★★ **The Live Album (Sugar Hill SH-CD-1024) 1989**

★★★½ **West Textures (Sugar Hill SH-CD-1028) 1989**

★★★ **A Bigger Piece of Sky (Sugar Hill SH-CD 1037) 1993**

The music of this Texas singer-songwriter offsets his boy-next-door folkishness with a bent toward danger, darkness, and occasional derangement. He first earned recognition through a collaboration with college buddy Lyle Lovett on "The Front Porch Song" (featured on each of Keen's first two albums and recorded by Lovett as well). Subsequently, he won a following of his own with the raucous humor of novelty numbers such as "Copenhagen," the antiromantic, snuff-dipping anthem from *The Live Album*.

Where *No Kinda Dancer* reflects the formative stage of a songwriter who is just beginning to find his voice, and *The Live Album* shows how engaging he can be in live performance, *West Textures* finds him truly coming into his own. While achieving a blend of the serious, the hilarious, and the bleak on the hard-boiled balladry of "The Road Goes on Forever" (later recorded by Joe Ely), thumbing his nose at Nashville in

"Leaving Tennessee," and offering a distinctive brand of bittersweet songcraft on "Mariano" and "Love's a Word I Never Throw Around," Keen confirms that he's a funny guy (in both senses of the term), but that humor's only half the story.

A Bigger Piece of Sky finds Keen dropping the "Jr." and shifting the balance even further toward the morbid and lethal (with humor that slashes the jugular), away from the lighter whimsy that marked his earlier fare. Though the album shows continued songwriting progression—particularly on the etiquette-by-gunfire balladry of "Whenever Kindness Fails" and the spooky, skeletal "Here in Arkansas"—some of the performances suffer from vocal flatness and the album's pacing fails to achieve the cohesiveness of *West Textures*.
—D.McL.

TOBY KEITH

★★ **Toby Keith (Mercury 314-514-421-2) 1993**

Hearing Toby Keith's debut single "Should've Been a Cowboy" on the radio, you might mistake it for the latest effort from the Bellamy Brothers or Brooks & Dunn. The song, written by Keith, craftily expresses every "Gunsmoke" fan's dream, and his strong, familiar voice sells it well. Unfortunately, though there's potential in Keith's songwriting, it's still undeveloped, and his first album peaks with that opening track. Still, with a little woodshedding—and if he doesn't try too hard to be the next David Bellamy or Ronnie Dunn—this young Oklahoman could be a winner.—P.K.

TOM KELL
★½ **One Sad Night (Warner Bros. 9 26508-2) 1991**
One Sad Night is one tedious, insignificant navel gaze. If Tom Kell's album seems like a lost work from the bottom drawer of 1970s Southern California folk pop, it could be because the whiny singer-songwriter receives lackadaisical support from such one-time Hollywood honchos as J. D. Souther, Timothy B. Schmidt, Bernie Leadon, and Dan Dugmore, as well as primary assistance from such close kin as the Dirt Band's Bob Carpenter and Jeff Hanna.

His debut manages only one moment of clear, compelling thought, and that's on the song Kenny Rogers later covered, "Walk Away," where Kell pleads with an emotionally abused female pal to ditch her cruel companion.

The rest of Kell's music is tender, sweet, and so irritatingly passionless that he seems to beg for a strong plate of red meat and a main course in assertiveness training. "Can't Tell You Why" offers a sample of the emotional complacency that sinks his solo debut: "You know how I get each time you lie/You treat me like a memory/Hung out to dry/So honey don't leave me/It's no surprise/Baby I still love you/Can't tell you why." Considering the sogginess of his sentiment, no wonder the woman finds the door so inviting.—M.M.

THE KENDALLS
★★★★ **20 Greatest Hits (Deluxe 7777) 1986**
★★ **Break the Routine (Step One 0023) 1987**
★★★ **Just Like Real People (Richmond 2263) 1988**
★★★ **Heaven's Just a Sin Away (Richmond 2294) 1988**
★★★ **It Don't Feel like Sinnin' (Richmond 2244) 1988**
The father-daughter duo of Royce and Jeannie Kendall seized the topic of adultery for everything it was worth with

"Heaven's Just a Sin Away," a 1977 country #1. Signed to the Chicago-based Ovation Records, the team continued to make spot-on singles about cheating. But because Jeannie executed her leads at such a high pitch of feverish dedication, the duo pushed songs like "It Don't Feel like Sinnin'" and "Sweet Desire" into pretty mind-boggling arenas of domestic sexual conflict. Without ever falling apart, Jeannie communicated moral panic.

20 Greatest Hits contains the two most intense selections from the Kendalls' uniformly intense Ovation recordings. In "Pittsburgh Stealers," Jeannie and Royce portray adulterous Northeastern factory workers for whom "it came too easy . . . to play the game." Equally forceful is "Just like Real People," a ballad, where Jeannie stops time begging a prospective husband to help her realize her dreams of romantic constancy, heartbreakingly careful to characterize herself as "no angel in white satin." It's one of country music's saddest tunes.

Moving to PolyGram and, briefly, Epic during the Eighties, the Kendalls' career gradually lost momentum. (Both PolyGram's *Thank God for the Radio . . . And All the Hits,* a 1985 LP which features a killer rendering of "The Dark Side of the Street," and Epic's *20 Favorites,* a 1989 mix of Ovation standards and good newer Buddy Killen-produced songs, are discontinued but recommended.) Still, as the Deluxe anthology and the Richmond repackages all demonstrate, the Kendalls consistently put their ace pop sense at the service of some unique honky-tonk. And never count a voice as resourceful as Jeannie Kendall's out.—J.H.

RAY KENNEDY
★★★ **What a Way to Go (Atlantic 82109-2) 1990**
★★½ **Guitar Man (Atlantic 82422) 1992**
In an age when even George Jones's voice is digitally recorded and edited, Ray Kennedy's do-it-yourself approach to music is refreshing. By working in his own home studio and playing any and every one of his zillion guitars (he credits 'em all in the liner notes), Kennedy arrives at a Merle Haggard-meets-Duane Eddy kind of country. It may take a few listens before the hooks start to sink in

on a song like "What a Way to Go" (his first Top Ten hit), but after they're absorbed, Kennedy's best songs wear very comfortably. On *Guitar Man,* his second effort, Kennedy carries the whole six-string schtick a little too far but still delivers a fairly solid bunch of songs, the hackneyed "No Way, Jose" notwithstanding.—P.Cr.

KENNEDY-ROSE
★★★½   **hai ku (IRS/Pangaea X21s-13011) 1990**

Mary Ann Kennedy and Pam Rose have written several top country hits for the likes of Alabama and Lee Greenwood, but their first effort as a duo is about as far from mainstream country music as two smart acoustic musicians can get. Like the style of Japanese poetry for which it's named, *hai ku* is simple, elegant, carefully structured, and ambitious in theme and essence.

Kennedy and Rose are former members of Calamity Jane, a band that deserved more than it received in its short life span. The same can be said for this project. The album was released in 1990 as one of the first offerings of a label partnership between British rocker Sting and I.R.S. Records. Sting personally pursued and promoted Kennedy-Rose's work, and it's easy to hear why: *hai ku* has much in common with the experimental nature and intellectual approach of the former chief of the Police.

On their lone release, Kennedy-Rose keep the music stripped down and percussive, setting an aggressively strummed acoustic guitar and mandolin against sensual, sturdy drum beats and atmospheric touches from electric guitars, synthesizers, simulated bagpipes, and an honest-to-God accordion.

At its best, as on "Love Like This," "Faithful," and "Who's Gonna Hold You," *hai ku* is passionate, bold, and honest. In some places, though, the album stretches the limits a bit too far, occasionally coming across too lyrically oblique and musically meandering.—M.M.

KENTUCKY COLONELS
★★★★★   **Appalachian Swing! (Rounder SS 31) 1964, 1993**
★★★½   **Long Journey Home (Vanguard VCD 77004) 1991**

This legendary bluegrass outfit was active in California during the late Fifties and early Sixties. At its center were the White brothers, Clarence and Roland. Mandolinist Roland went on to work with Bill Monroe, Lester Flatt, and the Country Gazette before settling in with the Nashville Bluegrass Band in the late Eighties. Younger brother Clarence went from bluegrass to the Byrds, where he translated his innovative lead acoustic guitar style to the electric. Occasionally the brothers reunited, and it was after one such gig in July 1973 that a drunken fan, driving through the parking lot outside a Southern California bar, plowed into both of them; Clarence died instantly.

Since then many bluegrass guitarists have worked at re-creating the magic of his style, and some, like Tony Rice and David Grier, have been acclaimed for the way in which they have built on it. But of course no one was quite like Clarence. His rhythm work—with runs in unexpected places behind the machine-gun precision of Billy Ray Latham's hard-edged banjo—cleverly subverted the bluegrass beat. Clarence's lead guitar on familiar old instrumentals—fiddle tunes like "Soldier's Joy" and gospel songs like "I Am a Pilgrim"—was subtle, original, and, when necessary, flashy. Although many albums of live appearances by the group were issued on LP, Vanguard's new compilation from the 1964 Newport Folk Festival is the only such set presently available. Not surprisingly virtually all of its contents are well-known old tunes, for the band recorded very little original material. Included are informal workshop performances, like Clarence and Roland demonstrating brother duets, and—perhaps the high spot—another with the two guitars of Doc Watson and Clarence. Clarence's magic is manifest in his lead work behind Doc's "Footprints in the Snow." Also present are four numbers featuring banjo whiz Bill Keith backed by the Colonels. *Caveat emptor:* these are all live performances, and some are pretty rough; also there is a fair amount of tape hiss on some cuts.

Rounder's CD reissue of the Colonels' 1964 classic LP, *Appalachian Swing,* is newly remixed from the original three-track recordings to highlight Clarence's guitar, which was already prominently

featured on much of the original release.
With its carefully crafted arrangements
and the polish of the studio it remains
the fullest document available of the
Kentucky Colonels and Clarence's
stunning guitar work. This all-instrumen-
tal album is unlike many bluegrass
instrumental collections in its
foregrounding of the guitar and mandolin
rather than the banjo and the fiddle—
although the latter are featured on some
cuts. The entire package is worth the cost
of hearing what Clarence does with Merle
Travis's "I Am a Pilgrim," but there are
plenty of other nice touches, like the
interplay between Roland's mandolin and
Clarence's guitar on "John Henry." With
familiar old-time material like "Listen to
the Mockingbird," "Faded Love," "Billy
in the Lowground" and others, this is an
album chockfull of tasty nuggets.—N.V.R.

KENTUCKY HEADHUNTERS
★★★★ Pickin' on Nashville (Mercury 838-
744) 1989 ▲
★★½ Electric Barnyard (Mercury 848-
054) 1991 ●
★★½ Rave On!! (Mercury 414-512 568-
2) 1993

Here's a cautionary tale about success.
The Kentucky Headhunters were a band
of woolly hillbillies united from two
different clans: guitarist Richard Young,
his brother Fred, a drummer, and their
cousin, guitarist Greg Martin, plus singer
Ricky Lee Phelps and his brother Doug, a
bassist. Proudly drawing on such oafish
Seventies influences as Black Oak
Arkansas and Cactus, they played
boisterous country-rock boogie typified by
"Walk Softly on This Heart of Mine," the
flagship single from *Pickin' On Nashville,*
and the wildest interpretation of a Bill
Monroe song since Elvis Presley liberated
"Blue Moon of Kentucky." It made the
band a sensation with Lynyrd Skynyrd
fans who loved Martin's slippery blues
solos, and with coastal tastemakers
delighted by the band's tacky buckskin
outfits. The group's originals were fine,
too: with its mysterious references to
slawburgers and marble-shooting,
"Dumas Walker" was one of the few
Southern-themed songs that sounded
like fun (even if the reference to a "six-
pack of Lite" didn't fit the group's image
or Richard Young's girth).

But you can only jump out of the closet
once. *Electric Barnyard* loses the giddy
spirit of the debut in blasts of feedback
guitar and turns the hillbilly theme to
shtick with a cover of "The Ballad of
Davy Crockett." The album fizzled and
the Phelps brothers left, replaced by
bassist Anthony Kenney and singer Mark
Orr. *Rave On!!* is more controlled and
coherent, but with Orr's rockabilly
howling replacing Ricky Phelps's jovial
finesse, it's difficult to recognize the
innocent and endearing band that made
Pickin' on Nashville.—R.T.

DOUG KERSHAW
★★★½ The Best of Doug Kershaw (Warner
Bros. 25964-2) 1989

Cajun wildman Doug Kershaw, along with
Jimmy C. Newman and Jo-El Sonnier, is
one of a handful of Cajun performers to
enjoy commercial success in mainstream
country music. Kershaw is known for his
frenetic stage demeanor, often going
through several fiddle bows in a single
performance as he sends horsehair flying
with the fierce attack on his instrument.
In childhood he began performing as an
accompanist for his mother, Mama Rita,
and then formed the Continental
Playboys with his brothers Rusty and Pee
Wee. Doug and Rusty then became a duo,
appeared for a while on the "Louisiana
Hayride," and briefly joined the Grand
Ole Opry. The material recorded as a
brother duet was generally better than
Doug's solo output, but *The Best of Doug
Kershaw* does a creditable job of
distilling his strongest cuts.—C.H.S.

SAMMY KERSHAW
★★★ Don't Go Near the Water (Mercury
314-510 161-2) 1991 ●
★★★ Haunted Heart (Mercury 314-514
332-2) 1993

Kershaw is upfront about his major
influence. He is unashamedly,
unapologetically, unmistakably George
Jones dipped in a light Cajun batter and
fried in corn oil. He makes the debt
explicit by reviving Jones's "What Am I
Worth" and moaning the ballads "Real
Old-Fashioned Broken Heart," "Yard
Sale," and "I Buy Her Roses" with
clenched-jaw, bent-note intensity. But on
his breakthrough hits "Don't Go Near
the Water," "Cadillac Style," and
"Anywhere But Here" he gave his

traditional leanings a country-rock kick in the pants. So he's a Possum with youth appeal.

Haunted Heart, the second CD, finds Kershaw stretching himself as a honky-tonk balladeer, notably on the exquisitely aching "Still Lovin' You" and in a remake of Jimmy C. Newman's classic "Cry Cry Darling." The radio-friendly uptempo tunes ("She Don't Know She's Beautiful") are present and accounted for. Taste takes a holiday on some downright cornpone numbers ("Queen of My Double-Wide Trailer," "Neon Leon"). But that's what we love about country music, isn't it?—R.K.O.

HAL KETCHUM
★★★ **Past the Point of Rescue (Curb D2-77450) 1991 ●**
★★★ **Sure Love (Curb D2-77581) 1992**

Ketchum is the cuddly bear of contemporary country, a singer-songwriter who wears his sensitivity on his sleeve, but whose best material taps into the resonant richness of everyday life. "Small Town Saturday Night" on 1991's *Past the Point of Rescue* provided his mainstream breakthrough with a song he didn't write (Pat Alger and Hank DeVito did), but bittersweet originals such as "Somebody's Love" and "I Miss My Mary" strike more deeply responsive chords.

On *Sure Love,* the production is slicker and the touchy-feely stereotypes even more pervasive, but the tunefulness of the title cut and the propulsive "Hearts Are Gonna Roll" find Ketchum extending the range of his music, while the tribute to the trucker's Annie ("Mama Knows the Highway") and a ballad of the unemployed ("Daddy's Oldsmobile") extend the range of his subject matter. Like former Doobie Brother Michael McDonald, Ketchum has a voice that's the aural equivalent of bedroom eyes, melting hearts like butter on the morning-after's toast.—D.McL.

KILLBILLY
★ **Stranger in This Place (Flying Fish FF70599) 1992**

In concert, the sight of a rough, irregular conglomeration of tattered punks and tattooed, long-haired biker types banging away at accelerated versions of bluegrass standards and original, acoustic mountain music has a certain engaging novelty effect. But, on their debut album, it becomes apparent that this Texas band relies on blustery energy and brash showmanship to camouflage its lack of any distinguishable musical talent.

Singer Alan Wooley struggles in vain to find a key, and the banjo and mandolin playing is barely serviceable. The original songs, especially those written by Wooley, are pale rewrites of sturdier classics. The lone cover is a herky-jerky, high-speed version of Chuck Berry's "Maybelline"; it is clumsily performed and apparently chosen because it seems unconventional rather than for any notion of creativity or inspiration. To make matters worse, Stephen Trued's banjo work would draw grimaces at any traditional music gathering.—M.M.

CLAUDE KING
★★★★ **American Originals (Columbia CK 45075) 1990**

Claude King was supposed to pick up where Johnny Horton left off. He was, like Horton, a "Louisiana Hayride" performer and was signed to Horton's label by Horton's manager right after Horton's death. He was no Johnny-come-lately, though; he'd been recording sporadically since 1947 in his virile, characterful voice. Once on Columbia, he was fed the songs that Horton might have done: movie title songs like "The Comancheros," ersatz folk like "Wolverton Mountain," and Horton's own "All for the Love of a Girl." *American Originals* is a hit-studded overview of King's peak years on Columbia; at best, he epitomized the undemanding, pop-flavored country music of the early Sixties.—C.E.

JEFF KNIGHT
★★½ **They've Been Talkin' About Me (Mercury 314 510 765-2) 1992**

On his debut, newcomer Jeff Knight employs his aw-shucks delivery to good advantage, turning in soulful readings of some decent (and some fairly weak) songs. If you can forget the tired Texas schtick of numbers like "Gettin' in to Goin' Out" and stick with the slow ones, his forte becomes clear. Knight knows how to lean back into a ballad, letting the spaces and phrasing say as much (or more) than the lyric.—P.Cr.

FRED KOLLER

★★★½ Songs from the Night Before
(Alcazar 107) 1989

★★½ Night of the Living Fred (Alcazar
108) 1989

★★★★ Where the Fast Lane Ends (Alcazar
112) 1990

Fred Koller is a former art student and rare-book seller who combines the bald, gruff ironies of Tom Waits and Randy Newman with the sentimental visions of Norman Rockwell and the coy wordplay of Cole Porter. After years of frustrating struggles, he suddenly emerged in the late 1980s as a song contributor to a wide range of artists (Jeff Healey, Kathy Mattea, Nanci Griffith, Dave Edmunds, Lowell Fulson, Lacy J. Dalton) and a favored collaborator of several highly respected writers (John Prine, John Hiatt, Pat Alger, John Gorka, Shel Silverstein, NRBQ's Al Anderson).

Beginning in 1989, Koller started issuing a series of hard-to-find but worth-seeking-out discs and tapes. Koller sings in a husky, guttural growl, sometimes assuming an animated style reminiscent of Louis Armstrong, at other times taking on a gentle, evocative whisper. When listening to him, amid all the unusual and brilliant images, it's hard to conceive that he's become a successful Music Row songwriter. The fact that he has speaks volumes about how country music (and Nashville) are much more adventurous than most people think.

Songs from the Night Before, his first solo effort, captures the eclectic nature of his work, combining the raw, hard-eyed insights of "Boom Town" and "This Guitar Is for Sale" with the sentimental melancholy of "Life as We Knew It" and "This Town" and the ribald, biting humor "The Hell We Created" and "Show Bizness." *Night of the Living Fred* emphasizes the broader, more absurd nature of his humor and experiments with an amazing array of musical styles. It has a more limited appeal than his other collections, but will be of interest to those who crave the intellectual side of Dr. Demento-style musical buffoonery. *Where the Fast Lane Ends* displays Koller's growth in stature. Everything from production values to musical guests to the details of his songcraft underscore the advancements that he has made in connections, eminence, style, and confidence. From the splendid insights he works into "Where the Fast Lane Ends" and "Goin' Gone" to the polished professionalism of "I Got Your Number" to the brilliantly idiosyncratic, disturbingly shrewd "Caught in the Spotlight" and "Patio Lights," it's obvious that Koller carries a peculiar genius that, with the right encouragement, can provide entertaining and troubling observations for years to come.—M.M.

ALISON KRAUSS

★★★★★ Too Late to Cry (Rounder CD-
0235) 1987

★★★★ Two Highways (Rounder CD-
0265) 1989

★★★★ I've Got That Old Feeling
(Rounder CD-0275) 1990

★★★★★ Every Time You Say Goodbye
(Rounder CD-0285) 1992

Bluegrass's newest superstar, Alison Krauss, is a powerful vocalist who's been compared to Emmylou Harris and Dolly Parton. She has that kind of high pure sound they do, though she cites as her model the less well-known Suzanne Cox of the Cox Family. In bluegrass, good singing isn't enough for stardom, and so it helps that she's also a first-rate soulful fiddler. She was a teenager when she made her first album, *Too Late to Cry.* A stunning debut, it stands up very well in comparison with her later efforts, in part because of the songs on it composed for her by John Pennell. She still features several, like "Foolish Heart," in her shows. Debuting her band Union Station on *Two Highways,* Krauss, then seventeen, showed there that she was not just a soloist but also a bandleader in the bluegrass tradition, doing some great vocal duets with guitarist Jeff White, a gospel number, and several instrumentals in addition to her solos. *I've Got That Old Feeling,* her second solo album, garnered her a Grammy. It's basically an acoustic album with lots of bluegrass feeling, but with piano on more tracks than banjo and even drums (heavens!) on several cuts, it caught the attention of mainstream country listeners. The title cut and "Steel Rails" will be familiar to those who follow country music videos.

While this album was selling like hotcakes, Krauss was touring with a new version of Union Station featuring three members of East Tennessee band Dusty

Miller—guitarist Tim Stafford, mandolin-ist Adam Steffey, and bassist Barry Bales—along with banjoist Ron Block. It's generally reckoned a hot band with vocal and instrumental talents that match and complement Alison's, and with them her latest album, another Grammy winner, *Every Time You Say Goodbye,* pulls together the best elements from earlier albums in a sound that reflects the confidence of a woman who, now in her early twenties, is a seasoned veteran. From the opening title cut, another John Pennell gem, to the closing number, a gospel number by Block, the band demonstrates the best in contemporary bluegrass. Nine of the fourteen cuts feature vocal trios, most of them showcasing Alison and Tim Stafford (Bales, Block, and Steffey all contribute third parts). The tunes range from hard-edged traditional bluegrass like the Stanley Brothers "Another Night" to soft-edged new material like Marshall Wilborn's "Heartstrings," a favorite of mine that's been getting a lot of airplay. The one instrumental is an intense version of the traditional fiddle tune (check out the half-measure in the second part) "Cluck Old Hen." Krauss has a bright future in country and bluegrass, and, for those who want to hear how good she really is, she has four strong albums from which to choose. —N.V.R.

KRIS KRISTOFFERSON

★★★★★	The Silver-Tongued Devil and I (Monument AK-44352) 1971 ●	
★★★★★	Me and Bobby McGee (Monument AK-44351) 1971 ●	
★★★	Jesus Was a Capricorn (Monument AK-47064) 1972 ●	
★★★	[with Rita Coolidge] Breakaway (Monument AK-47065) 1974	
★★	My Songs (Pair PCD2-1078) 1984	
★★★★	Songs of Kristofferson (Monument AK-44355) 1988 ●	
★★	Third World Warrior (Mercury 834 629-2) 1990	
★★★½	Singer/Songwriter (Sony Music Special Products A2K-48621) 1991	

A singer whose gruff, nonchalant singing style verges on tone-deaf and a songwriter of immense talent, Kris Kristofferson revolutionized country music of the 1970s

and briefly elevated the stature of the country singer-songwriter to that of king on Music Row. Kristofferson's evocative lyrics and too-true tales of hard times on 16th Avenue South ("Sunday Morning Coming Down," "The Pilgrim, Number 33," "Me and Bobby McGee") wedded the eloquent street poetry of Bob Dylan to mainstream country music in a way that's never been done before or since.

None of Kristofferson's original versions of the dozen or so classic songs he wrote and recorded on the Monument label in the late 1960s and early 1970s— "For the Good Times," "Help Me Make It through the Night," "Loving Her Was Easier (Than Anything I'll Ever Do Again)"—hit the charts, with the sole exception of "Why Me," a #1 in 1973. But these same songs were popularized by dozens of more vocally accessible artists, among them Johnny Cash, Jerry Lee Lewis, and Janis Joplin.

As Kristofferson's star began to rise as a performer and movie actor in the 1970s, and as he increasingly lost touch with the Nashville scene, his creative demiurge (which was best fueled, it seems, by the bleak poverty and recurring failure that this former Rhodes Scholar and Army captain faced as a minimum wage Music Row bartender and janitor) gradually shriveled. And as his original material grew less compelling and became increasingly leavened with his ultraliberal political sentiments (which went over with country audiences like a plutonium balloon), his ungainly voice became almost unlistenable.

Considering the unevenness of his recorded repertoire (which spans from 1968 to the early 1990s, and ranges from the magnificent to the barely palatable), Kristofferson is fairly well represented on CD. His two earliest, and by far best, albums on Monument—*Me and Bobby McGee* and *The Silver Tongued Devil and I*—are currently available on CD, as is *Jesus Was a Capricorn* and *Breakaway,* two of his later and somewhat more lackluster efforts for that label. *Third World Warrior,* one of a pair of earnest but plodding albums he more recently did for Mercury, is also available.

Kristofferson's music has also been gathered in a couple of interesting but flawed compilations. The more fascinat-ing of these is Kris *Kristofferson, Singer/*

Songwriter, a two-CD, thirty-six-song collection that's built on an intriguing marketing concept—that not enough listeners are willing to suffer two straight hours of Kristofferson's gravelly singing. Thus, this collection features Kristofferson's own renditions of seventeen of his classic (and some admittedly not so classic) compositions, along with somewhat more listenable covers of these same songs by everyone from Ray Price and Sammi Smith to Janis Joplin and Bob Dylan. *My Songs,* a sixteen-song, single-CD package, attempts to represent the full span of Kristofferson's career, but ends up leaving out some essential early tracks in favor of some second-rate later ones. —B.A.

L

SLEEPY LABEEF
★★★½ **Nothin' but the Truth (Rounder CD 3072) 1987**

Just before he launches into a roaring version of the Otis Blackwell-penned Jerry Lee Lewis hit "Let's Talk about Us," Sleepy LaBeef tells his raucous audience, "Here's one we're gonna do just 'cause I like this song here." In fact, every one of the selections on this live set, recorded in 1985 at Harper's Ferry in Allston, Massachusetts, sounds as though LaBeef chose it for that reason alone.

LaBeef has been called a human jukebox. He once told writer Peter Guralnick—who provides the liner notes for this disk and who has championed LaBeef's prowess as a live performer since first seeing him in 1977—that he estimates his repertoire at some six thousand songs. Sources for the performance captured on this disc include Hank Ballard, Junior Parker, Webb Pierce, Bo Diddley, Maybelle Carter, Jerry Lee Lewis, Hank Williams, and Johnny Cash, among others. The supporting band proves a capable bunch, though LaBeef, with his authoritative guitar playing and his commanding, basso profundo voice, takes them for a spirited, exhausting ride.

A native of Arkansas, LaBeef worked in Houston honky-tonks during the

Fifties, moved to Nashville in 1964, signed with Shelby Singleton's Nashville-based revival of Sun Records in 1968 and eventually found his way to New England, where he has entertained roadhouse audiences ever since. Those years of experience are reflected honestly on *Nothin' but the Truth.*—J.O.

k. d. lang
★★ **Angel with a Lariat (Sire 25441) 1987**
★★★½ **Shadowland (Sire 25724) 1988 ●**
★★★ **Absolute Torch and Twang (Sire 25877) 1989 ●**
★★★★ **Ingenue (Sire 26840) 1992 ▲**

Country music has made a lot of concessions to modern culture: drums onstage at the Opry, digital recording studios, songs in which women have careers and men do the dishes. But as k.d. lang learned, country music just isn't ready for a vegetarian lesbian from Canada who looks like the son Elvis Presley never had. There's little that's genuine about *Angel with a Lariat,* a camp collection of western-themed dance numbers played with the winking irony of performance art, both in the production by British guitarist Dave Edmunds and in lang's shrill, jumpy singing. A patent tribute to torch singing via Patsy Cline, *Shadowland* startles, and not only for Owen Bradley's exquisite production, best appreciated in a darkened room. Suddenly, lang learned to hold high notes and to build from her hearty alto to a clear, languid soprano. Bradley deploys several veterans of the sessions he produced for Cline, including his brother Harold, drummer Buddy Harman, and pianist Hargus "Pig" Robbins, and lang could have learned her newfound gracefulness merely by emulating the upward arc of Buddy Emmons's steel guitar on "Western Stars."

lang returned to her band, the Reclines, and coproduced *Absolute Torch and Twang* with Greg Penny and multi-instrumentalist Ben Mink. She tries to mingle a sincere devotion to classicism with a habitual overstatement that smacks of kitsch, an uncertain stance exacerbated by her band, which lacks the poise to play professional country music. After lang publicly opposed carnivorism, country radio stations formalized their opposition to her music with a boycott, and she abandoned the field. An enflamed version of Cole Porter's "So In Love" for the *Red Hot + Blue* AIDS benefit album led her to the lush, extravagantly swollen cabaret of *Ingenue*. As on *Shadowland,* she shows a brilliant grasp of concept and atmosphere, showering herself with clicking castanets, and broad, slow melodies. As merits a performer who doesn't distinguish between desire and obsession, lang's excesses won fanatical displays of adoration in concert. And she won a Grammy for "Constant Craving," a grand, swooning ballad about the loss of emotional balance and control, the unifying theme in lang's music.—R.T.

JIM LAUDERDALE

★★★★★ **Planet of Love (Reprise 9 26556-2) 1991**

Jim Lauderdale is a veteran of the same thriving Southern California country scene that made the world safe for Dwight Yoakam. Unlike Yoakam, however, Lauderdale draws from a wide range of pop and country traditions, good old-fashioned songcraft chief among them. Supported by the Dave Edmunds-meets-Owen Bradley coproduction of Rodney Crowell and John Leventhal, he managed to make one of the best records of 1991. Sadly, radio programmers (and hence record buyers) hardly noticed. That can probably be attributed to Lauderdale's eclectic vision of just what constitutes country music combined with a less-than-radio-friendly voice. What he lacks in vocal chops, however, he more than makes up for with the boyish charm and energy that lights up these tracks. "King of Broken Hearts," his loving tribute to George Jones, is simply one of the best damned country songs you're likely to hear, and George Strait's recent inclusion of that song and "Where the Sidewalk Ends," another Lauderdale original, on the million-selling sound track for the movie *Pure Country,* may open up a few more ears to this singer's far-reaching brand of country music. Let's hope Lauderdale can live up to the promise of this auspicious debut.—P.Cr.

TRACY LAWRENCE

★★★½ **Sticks and Stones (Atlantic 82326-2) 1991 ●**
★★★ **Alibis (Atlantic 7 82483-2) 1993 ▲**

This solid young neo-honky-tonker arrived on the scene with a pair of #1 ballads, "Sticks and Stones" and "Today's Lonely Fool," that lit up the country charts in 1991 and 1992. This was seemingly a most inauspicious time for a young (twenty-three when he first hit), unknown singer to be making a debut, since the charts were already glutted with better-than-average neo-honky-tonkers Mark Chesnutt, Alan Jackson, Sammy Kershaw, Doug Stone, and the like. Admittedly, Lawrence doesn't have the once-in-a-decade voice of a Randy Travis (though his baritone can scrape bottom rather nicely) or the dependable songwriting skills of an Alan Jackson (though he did co-write several choice cuts on *Alibis,* his second Arista album). Even if *Alibis* is a tad off the unusually high mark set by *Sticks and Stones* in terms of material and performances, this Arkansas-born singer still seems destined to enlarge upon the small but comfortable niche he's carved for himself with his winning, straight-ahead country baritone and his noteworthy debut.—B.A.

DOYLE LAWSON & QUICKSILVER

★★★★   The Gospel Collection, Vol. 1 (Sugar Hill SH-CD-9104) 1990
★★★★★   Rock My Soul (Sugar Hill SH-CD-3717) 1981
★★★½   I'll Wander Back Someday (Sugar Hill SH-CD-3769) 1988
★★★½   I Heard the Angels Singing (Sugar Hill SH-CD-3774) 1989
★★★   My Heart Is Yours (Sugar Hill SH-CD-3782) 1990
★★★½   Treasures Money Can't Buy (Brentwood CD-5303J) 1992
★★★   Pressing on Regardless (Brentwood CD-5304J) 1992

When Doyle Lawson formed Quicksilver in the late Seventies he'd paid his bluegrass dues, working in the bands of Jimmy Martin, J. D. Crowe, and the Country Gentlemen. His new band broke with tradition in progressive bluegrass by including an electric bass guitar instead of the acoustic string bass, a move that brought the censure of traditionalists but has been copied widely by a host of younger groups. Vocally, Quicksilver is distinguished by strong trios and quartets, the latter often featuring bass vocal leads. Lawson's albums for the Sugar Hill label alternated between all-gospel and secular (with a few gospel numbers on each of the latter), but it is with the religious music that he has built his reputation. His first gospel album, *Rock My Soul*, was a crossover hit in the Southern gospel field, something that almost never happens with bluegrass gospel. It set the standard for his gospel sound, with a cappella quartets like "Jesus Gave Me Water," borrowings from black gospel like the title cut, old bluegrass standards like the Stanley Brothers' "River of Death," and well-known gospel favorites like "Angel Band" and "A Beautiful Life." *I Heard the Angels Singing* is a later album in the same mold (it includes his version of Carl Jackson's popular "The Little Mountain Church House"), while *The Gospel Collection, Vol. 1* is a compilation of thirteen cuts from various earlier albums as well as two previously unissued numbers. It features some strong performances, like "A Lover of the Lord" and "Lay Your Burdens at His Feet," both by a version of Quicksilver including Terry Baucom, Jimmy Haley, and Randy

Graham, perhaps the most notable of the uniformly high quality Quicksilver aggregations. Of the two available non-gospel collections, *I'll Wander Back Some Day* seems the stronger, in part because of its distinctive material, much of which is drawn from older bluegrass bands like Bill Clifton, the Kentucky Travelers, the Kelley Brothers, Red Allen, and others.

Recently Lawson moved to Brentwood Music, an outfit known for its gospel products; it released two of his albums simultaneously. *Treasures Money Can't Buy* is an all-gospel effort with some interesting songs like "Buckle of the Bible Belt" and a version of "Just a Little Talk with Jesus" that has the feel of black gospel quartets. *Pressing on Regardless* is a secular package with some nice lead singing by John Bowman on songs like Mac Wiseman's "Let Me Borrow Your Heart." Quicksilver is a band that has had consistently high quality in its productions and has been much-praised, more for its sound than for specific songs or tunes. If you like good gospel quartet singing, give *Rock My Soul* half a chance and it'll convert you.
—N.V.R.

CHRIS LEDOUX

★★½   Songs of Rodeo and Country (Capitol CDP 7 97603 2) 1973, 1991
★★½   Rodeo Songs, Old and New (Capitol CDP 7 96594 2) 1973, 1991
★★★   Rodeo and Living Free (Capitol CDP 7 96595 2) 1974, 1991
★★   Life As a Rodeo Man (Capitol CDP 7 96872 2) 1975, 1991
★★½   Songbook of the American West (Capitol CDP 7 97602 2) 1975, 1991
★★½   Songs of Rodeo Life (Capitol CDP 7 96875 2) 1977, 1991
★★★½   Sing Me a Song Mr. Rodeo Man (Capitol CDP 7 97601 2) 1977, 1991
★★   Paint Me Back Home in Wyoming (Capitol CDP 7 97599 2) 1978, 1991
★★   Cowboys Ain't Easy to Love (Capitol CDP 7 97600 2) 1978, 1991
★★★½   Western Tunesmith (Capitol CDP 7 97597 2) 1980, 1991

★★★½ Old Cowboy Heroes (Capitol CDP 7 97595 2) 1981, 1991
★★½ He Rides the Wild Horses (Capitol CDP 7 97594 2) 1981, 1991
★★★½ Used to Want to Be a Cowboy (Capitol CDP 7 97593 2) 1982, 1991
★★★½ Old Cowboy Classics (Capitol CDP 7 96874 2) 1983, 1991
★★★ Thirty Dollar Cowboy (Capitol CDP 7 97596 2) 1983, 1991
★★ Melodies and Memories (Capitol CDP 7 96873 2) 1984, 1991
★★★ Wild and Wooly (Capitol CDP 7 97592 2) 1986, 1991
★★★ Gold Buckle (Capitol CDP 7 96869 2) 1987, 1991
★★½ Chris LeDoux and the Saddle Boogie Band (Liberty CDP 796870-2) 1988, 1991
★★★ Western Underground (Capitol CDP 96499 2) 1991
★★★ Watcha Gonna Do with a Cowboy (Liberty CDP 7 98818-2) 1992 ●

Chris LeDoux, "The Singing Bronc Rider," performs his own amalgam of cowboy country, rock, and western swing A genuine rodeo cowboy and former bareback bronc-riding champion, LeDoux spent almost twenty years recording and marketing his own records on an independent basis to a modest audience of admirers in the rodeo and cowboy subculture. He had released more than a score of these homemade albums between 1973 and 1991 when serendipity struck in the form of Garth Brooks. In "Much Too Young (To Feel This Damn Old)" from his 1989 debut album, Brooks made reference to "a worn out tape of Chris LeDoux"; it was only a matter of time before Garth's label boss, Jimmy Bowen, saw the light of the dollar sign and roped LeDoux for Capitol Records. Interestingly enough, Capitol chose to reissue almost the entire catalogue of LeDoux's independently released records on CD, as well as taking him into the studio for new recordings with Capitol's own producers. A prolific songwriter himself, LeDoux ranges from traditional cowboy songs to his own tales about rodeo life to contemporary cowboy songs by other writers. The early recordings have a nice homespun authenticity to them. Western Underground, the first recording he made for Capitol, has much more of a standard Nashville patina to it,

as his new producers try to make him sound and look like a more conventional country music hat act. Watcha Gonna Do with a Cowboy brings Brooks aboard for a duet on the hit title track. These new releases are still pretty good, but some of the innocent charm of LeDoux's earlier recordings is sacrificed.—C.H.S.

BRENDA LEE
★★★★ Brenda Lee Story (MCA MCAD-4012) 1973
★★★★★ Anthology, Vols. 1 & 2 (MCA MCAD2-10384) 1991
★★ Brenda Lee (Warner Bros. 9 26439-2) 1991
★★★ A Brenda Lee Christmas (Warner Bros. 26660-2) 1991

What Patsy Cline began, Brenda Lee took to its logical conclusion—moving the Nashville Sound of the Sixties into outright pop territory and taking it around the world. Brenda Mae Tarpley had begun her career in Georgia as a singing tot influenced equally by Hank Williams and Mahalia Jackson. By the time of her recording debut at age eleven in 1956, she'd fused the heart of Hank with the power of Mahalia to fashion an explosive vocal style. "Jambalaya," "Bigelow 6-200," "One Step at a Time," "Dynamite," "Let's Jump the Broomstick," and the unforgettable "Rockin' around the Christmas Tree," were cornerstone records of the female rockabilly style. Along with Wanda Jackson, Brenda Lee set the stage for distaff participation in the teen musical revolution of the day, matching the guys for musical aggression and sexuality. On her 1959 hit "Sweet Nothin's," for instance, the then-fourteen Lee shouts, pouts, and purrs over a steady beat in a way that can only be described as adult. She achieved similar effects on 1961's "Dum Dum" and 1960's "That's All You Gotta Do." Whether preteen or sweet sixteen, whenever Brenda Lee opened her mouth to sing, she was a woman.

If Lee's rockabilly work was exciting, her Nashville Sound performances were simply thrilling. The transition began with 1960's "I'm Sorry" and ran through a string of more than a dozen torrid torch tunes. Backed by Music Row's string section crescendos and subtle vocal backups, she gave throbbing passion to heart-stirring melodies and lyrics of exquisite melancholy. Even today, her pop performances sound so immediate, so smoldering with embers of emotion, so downright electrifying that it seems impossible that they came from a mere teenager. She could have been Edith Piaf emoting in a darkened Left Bank cafe on "All Alone Am I" (1962) or Frank Sinatra loitering in a smoky dancehall on "We Three" (1960). She was pleading, groveling, even desperate in "Break It to Me Gently" (1962). There was no more compelling Nashville Sound pop vocalist. Indeed, there were few singers in any era, in any field of music, who could grab you by your shirt collar and demand that you listen the way that Brenda Lee could. By the late Eighties she had sold more than 90 million records worldwide, more than any other woman singer in history.

Beginning with 1969's "Johnny One Time," she returned to her country roots, scoring major country hits in the Seventies with "Nobody Wins," "Rock on Baby," "Big Four Poster Bed," "Tell Me What It's Like," and "Broken Trust." She moved from her long time home at MCA to Warner Bros. Records in 1989, but neither of her first two projects for the new label fully captured her still potent vocal abilities.

Brenda Lee compilations are an essential part of any record collection. The *Story* set brushes over her rockabilly work lightly, goes deep into the Nashville Sound ballads, and ends its overview before Lee's country comeback. The two-volume *Anthology* is a must-have, for it contains the hottest rockabilly, has the best of the Nashville Sound performances, and brings Lee into the Eighties. These are performances to return to time and again. For when you close your eyes and imagine all the musicians gathered together playing live to create those extraordinary Nashville Sound classics, you can almost feel what a magical time in musical history that was.—R.K.O.

JOHNNY LEE
★★★   **Greatest Hits (Warner Bros. 23967-2) 1983**
★★   **New Directions (Curb CRBD-10617) 1989**

Lee's smooth, resonant, and reassuringly intimate vocals were a welcome relief amidst the dance hall clatter that marked the mercifully brief Urban Cowboy movement of the early Eighties. Like many other top singers of his era, Lee was not a strong songwriter and thus depended on others to provide him material. Consequently, some of his hits were substantial—notably "Lookin' for Love," "Cherokee Fiddle," and "Pickin' Up Strangers"—while others, such as "Be There for Me Baby" and "Hey, Bartender," were ephemeral, at best. All these songs are on Lee's *Greatest Hits* assemblage. His *New Directions* album fails to match even the modest level of his early Eighties work.—E.M.

ROBIN LEE
★   **Black Velvet (Atlantic 82085) 1990**
★★½   **Heart on a Chain (Atlantic 82259) 1991**

Named for her pallid version of the Alannah Myles pop smash, Lee's debut album can be fairly judged by the cover: inside are characterless productions of rock songs along the lines of Bonnie Raitt's "Love Letter." In fact, Lee only transcends pleasant vocals when she gets lightly under the skin of ballads like Rafe Van Hoy-Deborah Allen's "Something I Know I'm Gonna Love." *Heart on a Chain,* produced by a totally on-the-money James Stroud, regroups. It offers high-grade Nineties country tunes played with precision and nuance by a fine Nashville studio cast. Lee rises to the occasion, sounding much more alert and rocking than before.—J.H.

JERRY LEE LEWIS
★★★   **Jerry Lee Lewis (Rhino R2-70656) 1958, 1989**
★★★   **Jerry Lee's Greatest (Rhino R2-70657) 1961, 1989**
★★★★★   **Original Sun Greatest Hits (Rhino R2-70255) 1984**
★★★★   **Greatest Hits (Rhino RNCD 5255) 1989**
★★★★★   **Rare Tracks (Rhino R2-70899) 1989**
★★★   **Best of Jerry Lee Lewis (Curb D21K-77446) 1991**
★★★★   **Golden Rock Hits of Jerry Lee Lewis (Smash 826251) 1964, 1987**
★★   **Greatest Hits (Koch Present 399-538) 1991**
★★   **Heartbreak (Tomato R2-70656) 1992**

★★ **Rocket 88 (Tomato R2-70698) 1992**
★★ **Jerry Lee Lewis (Bella Musica BMCD-89916) 1990**
★★★★★ **Live at the Star-Club, Hamburg (Rhino R2-70268) 1992**
★★★ **Complete Palomino Club Recordings (Tomato 2696 742) 1991**
★★★★★ **Killer: The Mercury Years, Vol. I (Mercury 836935-2) 1989**
★★★★★ **Killer: The Mercury Years, Vol. II (Mercury 836938-2) 1989**
★★★★★ **Killer: The Mercury Years, Vol. III (Mercury 836941-2) 1989**
★★★★ **Rockin' My Life Away (Warner Bros. 26689-2) 1991**

Through a long and brilliant recording career, the legendary Jerry Lee Lewis has established himself as one of that rarest breed of American entertainers whose art transcends any and all categorical boundaries. As he himself will be the first to explain, with that characteristic megalomania rendered all the more disarming by its essential truth: "There's only been four of us. Al Jolson, Jimmie Rodgers, Hank Williams, and Jerry Lee Lewis." His music is a vortex of country, rock & roll, boogie-woogie, R&B, and Tin Pan Alley pop, transformed into a sound beyond their sum, a sound that is uniquely his.

It is a recording career than can be divided into two main periods: the Sun years (1956-63), during which he rose to rock & roll glory and fell into obscurity, and the Smash/Mercury years (1963-77), during which he rose anew, this time to the heights of country music, and faded yet again. Through fame and ignominy, fortune and ruin, Jerry Lee's music has remained remarkably consistent; and the same burning intensity that imbued his youthful Sun recordings still blazed true twenty years later in the darker and more mature Mercury recordings.

America has produced nothing in the way of Jerry Lee Lewis CD reissues to compare with the magnificent eight-CD set of Sun recordings, *Classic Jerry Lee Lewis,* issued in 1989 by Bear Family of Germany (BCD 15420). As for the Smash/Mercury years, nothing at all in the way of CDs can compare with Bear Family's 1986-87 three-volume, thirty-three-LP collection, *The Killer 1963-1977*

(BFX 15210, 15228, 15229). Though costly, these lavish sets constitute the only definitive Jerry Lee Lewis library.

That said, it should be noted that Jerry Lee Lewis is more than adequately represented by less extravagant CD reissues on his own side of the Atlantic. The Rhino albums are of exceptional quality: *Original Sun Greatest Hits* and *Rare Tracks* are fine collections that will go a long way toward satisfying the casual aficionado. The former contains the 1957-58 classics "Whole Lotta Shakin' Goin' On," "Great Balls of Fire," and "Breathless"; the latter, eighteen lesser known treasures. As for Rhino's reissues of Lewis's two original Sun albums, *Jerry Lee Lewis* and *Jerry Lee's Greatest,* the music is as startling a testimony today as it was thirty-odd years ago—to be sure, through digital remastering, it sounds better than ever—but there is a certain dissatisfaction in the very idea of mere LP-length CD reissues.

The three volumes of *Killer: The Mercury Years* present seventy-three of the best of Lewis's later recordings. Though these will likely be of more interest to the hard-line country enthusiast, they are no more country and no less rock & roll than the Sun recordings: Jerry Lee remains, always and ineffably, irrepressibly and maniacally, outrageously and sublimely, Jerry Lee. His wonderful 1968 comeback hit, "Another Place, Another Time," is only one of a slew of hits here; but this is a best of collection in the finest sense, and the uncharted beauties well outnumber the commercial landmarks.

Of special note is Rhino's *Live at the Star-Club, Hamburg,* which contains all but one of the tracks on Bear Family's CD of the same name. Recorded in the spring of 1964, it stands as perhaps the most wondrously berserk performance ever captured on tape. *Rockin' My Life Away,* from Warner Bros., brings together the best of Lewis's uneven but often surprisingly good 1979-82 Elektra recordings. —N.T.

LAURIE LEWIS
★★★ **Restless Rambling Heart (Flying Fish FF 70406) 1986**
★☆★½ **Love Chooses You (Flying Fish FF 70487) 1989**

★★★★ **Singing My Troubles Away (Flying Fish FF 70515) 1990**
★★★★ **[& Kathy Kallick] Together (Kaleidoscope K-44) 1991**

Winner of the International Bluegrass Music Association's 1992 award for female vocalist of the year, Lewis is a triple threat: fiddler, singer, and songwriter. She was cofounder, with Kathy Kallick, of the Good Ol' Persons, one of the first bluegrass bands to spotlight women. Her most recent effort as this review is written is *Together,* a reunion disc with Kallick that mixes older folk and country material like the Delmore Brothers' "Don't You See That Train" with powerful new songs, such as "That Dawn the Day You Left Me." Lewis is heard with her band Grant Street on *Singin' My Troubles Away,* with some really hard-hitting bluegrass in songs like "Raleigh and Spencer" and a softer country touch on "Miss the Mississippi and You" and others. Her own compositions are featured on *Love Chooses You,* a Nashville-recorded compilation that mixes mainstream county and bluegrass tracks with fine supporting work by such Nashville veterans as Jerry Douglas and Sam Bush. And *Restless Rambling Heart,* her first album, produced by Tim O'Brien, also features her compositions, as well as the first recording of O'Brien's "Hold to a Dream," later cut by the New Grass Revival and by O'Brien himself. Lewis is a talent to watch, a powerful vocalist who delivers movingly over a wide range of styles and feelings, and an excellent fiddler to boot. She recently signed with Rounder Records, and a new album, produced by Mike Marshall, is due out later in 1993. Look for it.—N.V.R.

LILLY BROTHERS
★★★★ **Early Recordings (Rebel CD 1688) 1971**

Everett and Bea Lilly, from Clear Creek, West Virginia, combined the close-harmony style of the brother duets with supercharged picking to create some of the most exciting tradition-based music ever heard in bluegrass. The Lillys contributed to the popularity of bluegrass music in the Northeast through their long tenure, along with banjo player Don Stover, at the Hillbilly Ranch in Boston from 1952 to 1970. The songs heard on this CD were recorded at the peak of

their performing years, in 1956 and 1957, for the Event label in Westbrook, Maine. "Tragic Romance" and "John Henry" serve as superb examples of their hard-driving bluegrass style, while Everett Lilly's solo performance of "Southern Skies" is a poignant fusion of nostalgia and unrequited love and a reminder that bluegrass music does not have to be performed at breakneck speed in order to be effective.—B.C.M.

LITTLE TEXAS
★★ **First Time for Everything (Warner Bros. 26820-2) 1992**
★★ **Big Time (Warner Bros. 45276-2) 1993**

It's one thing to find country artists who are partly influenced by James Taylor and Dan Fogelberg. But this breezy six-piece group, named during the post-Alabama craze for geographical monikers, sounds as though their idea of country begins and ends with Poco. For the full measure of the debt Nineties Nashville owes to mellow Seventies folk-pop, play Little Texas's pleasant hit "You and Forever and Me" (from *First Time*) next to England Dan & John Ford Coley's "I'd Really Love To See You Tonight."—R.T.

THE LOUVIN BROTHERS
★★★ **Songs That Tell a Story (Rounder CD 1030) 1992**
★★★ **Live at New River Ranch (Copper Creek CD) 1989**
★★★★ **Radio Favorites, 1951-1957 (CMF CD-009D) 1986**

CHARLIE LOUVIN
★★ **50 Years of Makin' Music (Playback PBCD-4505) 1990**
★★★ **And That's The Gospel (Playback PCD-4507) 1991**
★★ **[with Charles Whitstein] Hoping That You're Hoping (Copper Creek CC-0119) 1992**

Possibly the most influential harmony duet in country music history—they have affected everybody from Emmylou Harris to Vince Gill—Charles and Ira Louvin began their professional careers as gospel singers on radio stations in Memphis and Knoxville. Drawing on their rural Alabama background, they crafted a style of high, full-throat harmony that was more powerful and soulful that the softer sounds of their models, the Delmore

Brothers and the Blue Sky Boys. After signing with Capitol Records and joining the Grand Ole Opry in the mid-1950s, they began to do secular songs and soon had major hits with songs like "When I Stop Dreaming" and "You're Running Wild." In August 1963, the duo split up, each starting a career as a soloist; but in June 1965, Ira was killed in a car accident in Missouri. Charlie continued to record as a soloist for Capitol, actually racking up more hits by himself than he had had with Ira.

Tragically, not one of these solo efforts, nor any of the wonderful 200-plus Capitol duets, is currently available on domestic reissue. The true Louvin fan will have to seek out the imported German Bear Family boxed set *Close Harmony* (BCD 15561 HI), an eight-CD compilation containing the complete studio recordings of the Louvin Brothers. The more casual listener can sample the Louvin sound through a series of three albums of radio and live recordings. *Songs That Tell a Story* is very early Louvins—1952—and taken from an ill-fated radio show the boys began while working at Memphis. Gospel and old sentimental songs dominate here, along with a recitation or two. *Live at New River Ranch* offers an on-stage set from April 1056, with the brothers' regular back-up band of Paul Yandell and George McCormick performing hits like "When I Stop Dreaming" and "I Don't Believe You've Met My Baby." *Radio Favorites* is probably the best-rounded of the three sets, containing four cuts from 1951 and ten from Grand Ole Opry shows in the mid-1950s. Gospel favorites like "They've Got the Church Outnumbered" and "If We Forget God" are here, as well as secular hits like "Love Thy Neighbor," "You're Running Wild," and "Hoping That You're Hoping." Though none of the live cuts sound quite as sharp as the Capitol studio versions, the sound on all three CDs is surprisingly good.

The available Charlie Louvin solo albums all date from the early 1990s and all include various guest singers. The best is *And That's the Gospel,* which includes a powerful duet with Tammy Wynette on "If I Could Hear My Mother Pray Again." *50 Years of Makin' Music* pairs Charlie with his old duet partner Melba Montgomery, as well as George

Jones, Tanya Tucker, Willie Nelson, Waylon Jennings, and Charlie Daniels—generally doing newer songs instead of remakes of Louvin classics. *Hoping That You're Hoping* recaptures some of the old Louvin sound with fine tenor singer Charles Whitstein taking the place of Ira. Highlights include "Stormy Horizons," a "lost" Louvin song, and pieces like "Love and Wealth" and "Knoxville Girl."
—C.K.W.

PATTY LOVELESS

★★½ **Patty Loveless (MCA MCAD-5915) 1987**
★★★ **If My Heart Had Windows (MCA MCAD-42092) 1988**
★★★ **Honky Tonk Angel (MCA MCAD-42223) 1988 •**
★★½ **On Down the Line (MCA MCAD-6401) 1990**
★★★½ **Up Against My Heart (MCA MCAD-10336) 1991**
★★½ **Only What I Feel (Epic ET 53236) 1993**

Steeped in country tradition—as a Kentucky-born teen, she began her career singing behind country legends, the Wilburn Brothers—Loveless is also a student of Linda Ronstadt's throaty phrasing. All this can be heard on early efforts like *If My Heart Had Windows* (the title tune, a George Jones cover, became her first Top Ten hit) and *On Down the Line.* Thankfully, she doesn't share Ronstadt's self-pity; in her songs of tattered romance, Loveless opts for bitter defiance over meek rationalization, an attitude that has only strengthened the quality of her music as her career proceeds. Her first #1 hit was "Timber I'm Falling in Love" on 1988's *Honky Tonk Angel,* a silly title image redeemed by Loveless's firm conviction. Since then, she's turned out increasingly excellent collections—*Up Against My Heart* is particularly adroit. It includes "Jealous Bone," a thumping country-rocker that recycles the guitar hook from Creedence Clearwater Revival's "Green River," and features a corrosive version of Lyle Lovett's "God Will" that strips off all the ironic varnish that the author had applied in his own version. For all this, Loveless has remained a friendly if rather anonymous personality, with superstardom eluding her. In early 1993, she moved to Epic to release the glossy

Only What I Feel, her first collection after surgery on her vocal chords. Her voice sounded as strong and flexible as ever, but *Feel* belied its title—a self-conscious, timid album dominated by tritely upbeat tunes like the single "Blame It on Your Heart," it could have been entitled *Only What I Think Will Sell.*—K.T.

LYLE LOVETT
★★★★ Lyle Lovett (MCA MCAD-31307) 1986
★★★ Pontiac (MCA MCAD-42028) 1987
★★★½ Lyle Lovett and His Large Band (MCA MCAD-42263) 1989 ●
★★★★ Joshua Judges Ruth (MCA MCAD-10475) 1992 ●

Artists rarely arrive as fully formed as Lyle Lovett, a clever songwriter with a languid, knowing voice and a broad streak of eclecticism. From his startling first album, he began integrating the two poles of the Austin folk legacy—the sensuous delight of Guy Clark and the morbid stare of Townes Van Zant—with a big-band jazz and blues sensibility that recalls not only Bob Wills, but also that original rock & roll rascal, Louis Jordan. Lovett's debut was essentially a demo tape, recorded in Arizona with a Phoenix band he met while studying German in Luxembourg (eclectic, indeed). Guy Clark gave a copy of the tape to MCA executive and producer Tony Brown, who released it with just a few overdubs.

Adding remarkable twists to familiar images, the record established Lovett's central themes. The mythos of Texas cowboys provides a recurring contrast to musings on modern romance (each of the first two albums have three songs that mention cowboys). In "Farther Down the Line," a rodeo announcer's exhortations suddenly turn into a metaphor for love, while a similar trick transforms the card game in "If I Were the Man You Wanted" to a metaphor for infidelity. (Both songs were covered by Willie Nelson on his fine 1993 album *Across the Borderline.*) There are also three songs that mention food, another one of Lovett's great motifs. But the most memorable song is also the least flashy. Introduced by a deceptively classic steel guitar, "God Will," is a plainspoken declaration of judgmentalism, where Lovett reflects on forgiveness: "God does, but I don't/God will, but I

won't/And that's the difference between God and me."

"Farther Down the Line" also summarizes Lovett's view of female caprice: "One day she says she loves you/And the next she'll be tired of you." That view grew harsher on *Pontiac,* a bitter record, playful but still excessive, which peaks on the murderous "L.A. County." Comic relief comes only at the expense of women: the swinging "She's No Lady" ("she's my wife") rides a joke as old as vaudeville, "M-O-N-E-Y" warns against gold diggers, and "She's Hot to Go" unkindly salutes an easy lay who's "ugly from the front," and fit only for backdoor visits. Nearly lost in the midst is the title song, a taut, haunting character monologue Randy Newman would be proud to call his own.

Where *Lyle Lovett* opened with frisky western swing, *And His Large Band* begins with a strutting Clifford Brown instrumental, noting a gradual shift in the music's careful balance. The first half of the album is modern swing fired by a two-piece horn section and singer-shouter Francine Reed, while the second half downshifts into country. Lovett acknowledges his reputation for misogyny with a (fairly) straight-faced reading of "Stand by Your Man," Tammy Wynette's counter-liberation anthem. Cowboys reappear on "Which Way Does That Old Pony Run," a gorgeous ballad about female deceit, and yes, that's a PMS joke on "Good Intentions." Reviewing this album in the *Village Voice,* Robert Christgau wrote, "Concept: women, you can't live with 'em and you can't live without 'em—and it's their fault."

Lovett had been stonewalled at country radio and adopted by rock critics, so for *Joshua Judges Ruth,* he left MCA's Nashville division and recorded in L.A. for the first time. But while the album was viewed as a radical change because of the relocation, it was really another progression—Lovett even used many of the same musicians as before. More significantly, the record shows substantial emotional growth: the opening female joke—"Sherry she had big ones"—turns out to be an arch reference to children, there's an unprecedented tenderness to "Flyswatter/Ice Water Blues," and Emmylou Harris's vocal on "She's Leaving Me Because She Really Wants

To" makes Lovett the fool. The emotional generosity parallels the explicit gospel references, starting with "Church," a surreal yarn about a windy preacher who eats a dove, and extending to a death trilogy: "Since the Last Time" plays a funeral for laughs, "Baltimore" plays it for sorrow, and "Family Reserve" achieves both by fondly reciting the poetry of Southern names. The biggest small change may be in Lovett's voice—a cool modulation of blues phrasing that recalls Mose Allison—which begins to shed some of its detachment and shows a bit of passion.—R.T.

BOB LUMAN
★★★ **American Originals (Columbia CK 45078) 1989**
The late Bob Luman rocked hard as any 'billy out there in the Fifties and early Sixties. Though his career took a predictable countrypolitan turn when he later signed with Billy Sherrill's Epic empire, he had suffered the boogie disease for too long to make a complete transition à la Conway Twitty. On Epic hits like "Lonely Women (Make Good Lovers)," included on *American Originals,* Luman sounds like the missing link between Elvis and Ronnie McDowell. The best cut is "A Satisfied Mind," a stone country chestnut that Luman relivens as a harmonica-driven wail. The worst is "Let's Think about Livin'," a Nashville-slick rendition of what had once been Luman's signature rocker.—D.C.

LORETTA LYNN
★★★★½ **Loretta Lynn's Greatest Hits (MCA MCAD-31234) 1968**
★★★½ **Loretta Lynn's Greatest Hits, Vol. 2 (MCA MCAD-932) 1974 ●**
★★★★★ **The Very Best of Loretta and Conway (MCA MCAD-3126) 1979 ●**
★★★★½ **Coal Miner's Daughter (MCA MCAD-936) 1980 ●**
★★★★½ **Loretta Lynn's 20 Greatest Hits (MCA MCAD-5943) 1987**
★★★ **Who Was That Stranger (MCA MCAD-42174) 1988**
★★★★★ **Country Music Hall of Fame Series (MCA MCAD-10083) 1991**
For the better part of a decade, from 1966's "You Ain't Woman Enough" to 1975's "The Pill," Loretta Lynn ran roughshod over the crinoline-dressed and long-suffering image of country womanhood. City gals might then have ranted about a thing called Women's Lib, but theirs was a pale fury alongside that of a cracker wildcat who yowled, "I'm tearin' down your brooder house, 'cause now I've got *the pill!*" It's hard to imagine anyone *else* getting away with what Loretta wrought: frank songs about losin' it ("Wings upon Your Horns"), whompin' upside the empty, addled heads of no-'count husbands ("Your Squaw Is on the Warpath," "Don't Come Home A-Drinkin' with Lovin' on Your Mind"), and territorial catfights with rival women ("You Ain't Woman Enough," "Fist City"). Her spitfire spunk was leavened by a sparkly affability, which is why the country patriarchs just grinned sheepishly while Loretta became a singing Germaine Greer to the women of K-Mart America.

The four greatest hits collections currently in print cover songs from 1962's "Success" to 1981's "I Lie" with varied aplomb. The sixteen-song *Country Music Hall of Fame* set is the best starting place and the clearest overview of Lynn's career. All the pivotal songs that defined her persona (country gal with a heart of gold and a spine of steel) are here, plus duets with two of the important men in her career, Ernest Tubb ("Mr. and Mrs. Used to Be") and Conway Twitty ("After the Fire Is Gone"). The first MCA *Greatest Hits* collection has only eleven songs, but eight of them are 1962-66 gems (including the Viet Nam-era weeper, "Dear Uncle Sam") which aren't elsewhere in print. They reveal Loretta as a strong-voiced individualist from the get-go, though her debt to foremother Kitty Wells is more evident than it would later be. (Lynn, like Wells and Patsy Cline, worked with producer Owen Bradley at Decca). Also worth the ticket is the Sixties promo photo of Loretta resplendent in beehive 'do, gold lamé blouse, and million dollar 'howdy pardner' smile.

Greatest Hits, Vol. 2 collects eleven 1967-73 hits. Great songs, all right, but most of the winners here are available on more comprehensive sets except "What Sundown Does to You," a honky-tonk howler about a carousing hubby that wasn't really a hit but should've been. Given the brevity of *Greatest Hits* and *Greatest Hits, Vol. 2,* each about twenty-seven minutes long, you'd think MCA might simply combine them as a single twenty-two-song CD. Nope, but instead they offer *20 Greatest Hits,* which is more of the same and still somethin' else again. This is the only set to include Loretta's 1971 manifesto on behalf of divorcées, "Rated X," plus five 1976-1981 hits not on any other collection. Among them are the wonderfully woozy "Somebody Somewhere Don't Know What He's Missing Tonight" and Loretta's soulful "She's Got You," as good in its different way as Patsy Cline's original.

The early 1970s was the golden age of guy-gal country duos: George and Tammy, Porter and Dolly, and, at Decca, Conway and Loretta. Conway Twitty, master of the hard-country confessional, and tell-it-like-it-is Loretta were two of the most spectacular voices in that era of stellar country pipes. Between 1971 and 1981, Conway and Loretta scored a dozen Top Ten country hits, most of which can be heard on the fourteen-song *The Very Best of Loretta and Conway.* Their duets juxtaposed sexual tension ("Lead Me On") with country gospel structure, harmony, and sincerity. They echo the days when the notion of sin was a potent aphrodisiac. When those two flinty, intensely real voices commenced soaring entwined, it was a wonderment. Soulful country harmony doesn't come any finer than their "Feelins'."

"Coal Miner's Daughter" was the autobiographical song which inspired Lynn's book and the Sissy Spacek-starred bio-pic. The 1970 *Coal Miner's Daughter* album isn't a collection of similarly reflective "roots of my raisin'" songs but is a classic Loretta album of its era, what with the go-go country stomper (complete with fuzz and wah-wah guitars) "It'll Be

Open Season on You," where Loretta warns an encroaching female: "If you don't ease up on your matin' call, I'll nail your hide to the ol' barn wall." Eeee, doggies!

Last and frankly least, 1988's *Who Was That Stranger* is a Jimmy Bowen-produced album that frames Loretta in late-Eighties hard-country production values. Nothing wrong with that, though there's nothing classic here, either. "Survivor" is a spunky comeback anthem from a lady who still demanded attention and an admiring glance as one of Music City's sexiest grannies.—M.H.

SHELBY LYNNE

★★½ **Sunrise (Epic 44260) 1989**
★★½ **Tough All Over (Epic 46066) 1990**
★★½ **Soft Talk (Epic 47388) 1991**
★★½ **Temptation (Morgan Creek 2959-20018-2) 1993**

Lynne's work is for people sold on her big, athletic voice. She possesses a considerable vocal confidence, sort of like k.d. lang's although not that towering. Still, Lynne hasn't discovered a very meaningful approach for her chosen songs; whatever their subjects, they seem to be about her voice. *Tough All Over* tries to rough things up with soul and hints of down-home funk—in contrast with the more suburban Nashville plushness of her debut. On *Soft Talk,* Lynne goes simultaneously for a more acoustic country character and uptown torch. Her Morgan Creek debut, also formally accomplished, pursues period nightclub and pop-jazz flings, plus a few idiosyncratic tunes. But, as with all her records, a little less attention lavished on Lynne's vocal gymnastics might actually make her sound more essential.—J.H.

M

UNCLE DAVE MACON
★★★★ **Country Music Hall of Fame (MCA MCAD-10546) 1992**

If Jimmie Rodgers can lay claim to being the father of country music, then David Harrison "Uncle Dave" Macon can surely boast of being its grandfather. Born in 1870, coming from a background of folk music and nineteenth-century vaudeville, he described himself as a "banjoist and songster" and was country music's most important single link between its deep roots and modern mass media. By the late 1920s he was a recording star, a radio personality, and a vaudeville headliner. His strong, booming voice won him fans from Florida to California, and his banjo playing was a complex welter of finger picking and frailing styles.

Though he recorded almost 200 sides for virtually every major label, there is little of his prime work available on CD. The sole set, one produced by the staff of the Country Music Foundation for MCA, is drawn from late 1920s material done for the old Vocalion label. Though it contains few of Macon's most popular numbers, it does have some fine examples of his work with ace guitarist Sam McGee, as well as with his string band, the Fruit Jar Drinkers. Songs include "I'm the Child to Fight," "Kissing on the Sly," and "Late Last Night When Willie Came Home," as well as the rousing "Tennessee Jubilee." Though the sound of these 1920s recordings is not up to par with the CMF's usual work, the CD is a fitting tribute to the first real star of the Grand Ole Opry.—C.K.W.

ROSE MADDOX
★★★★★ **The Maddox Bros. & Rose, Vol. 1 (Arhoolie CD 391) 1993**
★★★★ **A Collection of Standard Sacred Songs (King KCD-669) 1960**
★★★★ **Rose of the West Coast Country (Arhoolie CD 314) 1990**

Rose Maddox was eleven when she began performing with her four brothers in 1937 and has been singing ever since. During their 1940s heyday, the Maddox Brothers & Rose were billed as "America's Most Colorful Hillbilly Band" and were noted for their flashy costumes and goofball antics onstage. Their 4 Star and Columbia recordings were rough-and-tumble affirmations of country spunk rife with cackles and yelps: the Maddoxes' reputation as the ancestors of cowpunk is well deserved, as Arhoolie's reissue of twenty-seven 1946-51 4 Star performances by the group illustrates. Their records were the aural equivalent of an Okie barroom brawl, spilling out with abandon in unhinged performances like their braying jackass version of "Honky Tonkin'."

Given their hellbent-for-hokum image, it's surprising to find the Maddoxes as performers of a generically-titled twelve-song *Collection of Standard Sacred Songs*. But that's truth in advertising, neighbors, what with "I'll Fly Away," "Farther Along," and "Tramp on the Street" here. Rose bellows robust as ever, though the brothers pull in their horns a mite and play close to the vest. Still, these performances (probably from the Fifties) are spirited and unpolished, and the overall effect is that of hearing a Sunday border radio broadcast from forty years ago. This isn't the Maddoxes in their demented glory, but it's untrimmed brush arbor country nonetheless.

Rose went solo in 1959, and made a host of great records for Capitol well into the mid-1960s. Many featured the wailing steel of Ralph Mooney and stand tall in the company of the classic Bakersfield Sound records of Buck Owens and Merle Haggard. For the best work of one of country's pioneer women to be unavailable on CD is akin to what Rose and Buck Owens, in a hit duet, called "Mental Cruelty."

The tireless Rose never quit performing, and *Rose of the West Coast Country* is a fine twenty-song collection of early 1980s performances by the unfaded Rose backed by bluegrass-oriented bands. It includes several of the songs most identified with her, including the Woody Guthrie song she's sung since she was eleven, "Philadelphia Lawyer."—M.H.

BARBARA MANDRELL

★★★½ **Best of Barbara Mandrell (MCA MCAD-31107) 1979** ●
 ★★★ **Christmas at Our House (MCA MCAD-5519) 1984**
★★★½ **Greatest Hits (MCA MCAD-5566) 1985**
  ★★ **I'll Be Your Jukebox Tonight (Capitol CDP 7 904162) 1988**
  ★★ **No Nonsense (Liberty C21S-94426) 1990**
  ★★ **Morning Sun (Capitol CDP7-91977-2) 1990**
  ★★ **Greatest Country Hits (Curb/CEMA D21K-77363) 1990**
  ★★ **Key's in the Mailbox (Liberty C21S-96794) 1991**
  ★★ **Best of Barbara Mandrell (Liberty C21Y-98491) 1992**

Always more of a live attraction and television entertainer than a recording great, Barbara Mandrell has nonetheless made some unforgettable discs. Her country-pop, show queen style fell precipitously out of favor when country went new-traditional in the late Eighties and early Nineties, leading many to dismiss her whole output. Yes, there were some frivolous records. But there were also some terrific moments when her blue-eyed soul style simply glowed in the studio.

Her early Columbia Records LPs are unavailable on CD, which is unfortunate. To hear "Burning the Midnight Oil," a breakthrough in frankness for female country singers in 1973, you'll have to go digging through Vol. 4 of the *Columbia Country Classics* anthology (see Various Artists). She echoed "Midnight Oil"'s power when she moved to the ABC/Dot/MCA fold in 1976 with the cheating two-stepper "Midnight Angel," and it's included on the *Best of* MCA set. That collection recaps her 1976-78 singles, ranging from the disposable ditty "Sleeping Single in a Double Bed" to the sublime love melody "Tonight."

The *Greatest Hits* MCA set picks up in 1979 and carries us to 1984. Again, there are clunkers like "Crackers" alongside excellent ballads such as "The Best of Strangers" and "There's No Love in Tennessee." Regrettably omitted are "Only a Lonely Heart Knows" and "Love Is Fair" in favor of her far less significant signature tunes "I Was Country When Country Wasn't Cool" and "(If Loving You Is Wrong) I Don't Want to Be Right." Her hoarse, soulful rasp was at its best on things like "In Times Like These" and "Wish You Were Here," both of which are present. For good or ill these Mandrell performances are among the records that defined an entire era of country music. They show Nashville musicians and songwriters in pursuit of metropolitan acceptance. They illustrate the sophisticated craftsmanship that took over the charts in the late Seventies and early Eighties. And despite critics' barbs, pop-country production king Tom Collins sometimes touched greatness, as with the whispered strings, sighing steel, and hushed harmonica in Mandrell's 1980 chart-topper "Years" (included on *Greatest Hits*).

Mandrell moved to Capitol/Liberty in 1987 and began sprinkling her albums and shows with country classics such as "The Key's in the Mailbox," "I Love You Because," and "I Wish That I Could Fall in Love Today," all of which are included on the Liberty *Best of* set. She'd always been a steel-guitar player, and this side of her began to show more. She also marketed a pair of nicely recorded gospel albums on TV. Curb Records' *Greatest Country Hits* is a ten-track summary of such otherwise available MCA and Liberty material as "I Was Country When Country Wasn't Cool" and "I Wish That I Could Fall in Love Today."

Country stars can be counted on for Christmas product, and Barbara Mandrell is no exception. Her *Christmas at Our House* collection from 1984 remains a CD favorite. Its standouts include a bluesy workout on "Santa, Bring My Baby Home" and an affectionate reading of "I'll Be Home for Christmas."—R.K.O.

THE MARCY BROTHERS
★ Missing You (Warner Brothers 9 26051-2) 1989
★★ Marcy Brothers (Atlantic 7 82213-2) 1991

This close harmony trio needs a hit to save them from Trivial Pursuit oblivion. *Missing You* was such an unabashed milquetoast failure—it'll renew your respect for the Gatlin Brothers—that they must have felt they needed to toughen things up for *Marcy Brothers*. Hence they brought in a song called "Don't Tell My Heart," which, under a different title, and in a different singer's version, but with near identical production, went on to become the country smash hit of the year in 1992. If you're stumped, here's a hint: "ass-wiggling." —D.C.

MARSHALL TUCKER BAND
★★½ A New Life (AJK Music A 636-2) 1974 ●
★★★½ Where We All Belong (AJK Music A 677-2) 1974 ●
★★★½ Searchin' For a Rainbow (AJK Music A 702-2) 1975 ●
★★½ Long Hard Ride (AJK Music A 727-2) 1976
★★★★ Greatest Hits (AJK Music A 799-2) 1978 ●

★★ Together Forever (AJK Music A 668-2) 1978 ●
★ Still Smokin' (Cabin Fever Music CFM-913-2) 1992

Combining country music with rock, blues, and jazz, the Marshall Tucker Band emerged from the smoky barrooms of Spartanburg, South Carolina, to reign as one of the leading Southern boogie bands of the Seventies. The band centered on the Caldwell brothers, bassist Tommy and lead guitarist and chief songwriter Toy, along with the whiskey-raw vocals of Doug Gray and the breathy reed work of Jerry Eubanks on flute and saxophone. Marshall Tucker built its reputation and its following with a grueling touring schedule, playing up to 300 shows in a single year. They carried their bar band persona into the studio, producing albums steeped in themes of rootlessness and persecution by women, and characterized by free-spirited jams anchored by Tommy Caldwell's peripatetic bass lines. The band reached a creative peak with *Where We All Belong*, a seventy-four-minute disc that includes the macho swagger of "This Ol' Cowboy," along with live cuts of "Take the Highway" and "Everyday (I Have the Blues)," a showcase for Toy Caldwell's lyrical guitar work. The momentum carried forward on *Searchin' For a Rainbow*, a groove-centered recording that features a live version of "Can't You See." But with *Long Hard Road* and *Together Forever*, the formulas had grown stale as the tough, exacting years in the bars had taken their toll. *Greatest Hits*, one of their best-selling albums, offers prime cuts from the early years without the rambling excesses that marred even their finest studio recordings.

Although Marshall Tucker continued to perform after Tommy Caldwell's death in 1980 from injuries he received in an auto accident, they never rekindled the spark that ignited their youthful flame. In the late 1980s, Gray and Eubanks attempted a comeback that spawned the regrettably derivative *Still Smokin'*.—J.B.

JIMMY MARTIN
★★★★ You Don't Know My Mind (Rounder CDSS-21) 1990
★★ 20 Greatest Hits (IMG Gusto DCD-7863)

★★ **Greatest Bluegrass (IMG Gusto HCD-213) 1978**

Bluegrass music never got any better than this. Martin, a product of Sneedville, Tennessee, began his professional career as guitarist and lead singer for Bill Monroe's Blue Grass Boys. With his high-pitched and hard-edged singing and dynamic guitar runs, Martin gave the Blue Grass Boys a new but equally compelling sound to replace the one earlier produced by Lester Flatt and Earl Scruggs. After Martin left Monroe he continued to make exciting music with his own band, the Sunny Mountain Boys. The Rounder CD is an anthology of Decca material recorded by Martin during his post-Monroe period, from 1956 to 1966, and every selection is a gem. Confirmed fans will be pleased to have in one collection such songs as the title cut, "Ocean of Diamonds," "Hit Parade of Love," "Sophronie," "Don't Give Your Heart to a Rambler," "Sunny Side of the Mountain," and "Prayer Bell of Heaven," while listeners who have never listened to bluegrass should marvel at the energy, intensity, musicianship, and high harmony heard on most of these cuts. With a superb supporting cast that included tenor singer Paul Williams on mandolin and J. D. Crowe on banjo (plus a variety of great fiddlers), Jimmy Martin set a standard with these recordings that fledgling bluegrass musicians long tried to reach.

After leaving Decca in 1974, Martin signed with Gusto Records in Nashville and re-recorded many of his earlier favorites. *20 Greatest Hits* and *Jimmy Martin Greatest Bluegrass Hits* date from this later period, and, though not on a par with his Decca material, do contain songs not heard on the Rounder anthology.—B.C.M. & C.K.W.

MATHEWS, WRIGHT & KING

★★½ **Power of Love (Columbia CK 48797) 1992**

When the hit group Shenandoah departed from Columbia Records a couple years ago, the label set about more or less manufacturing a replacement. Coproducers Steve Buckingham and Larry Strickland pooled the talents of singer Raymond Mathews, Nashville session singer Woody Wright, and Tony King, ex-lead singer for the premiere newgrass band J. D. Crowe & the New South and former harmony singer-acoustic guitarist in Vince Gill's band. On *Power of Love,* their debut, Mathews, Wright & King acquit themselves adequately, even though their music often has a derivative post-Eagles feel about it. Thus far they've yet to come up with the missing ingredient that would distinguish them from Restless Heart, Diamond Rio, and a half dozen other smooth-sounding latterday harmony ensembles that are competing for a berth in country's mainstream.—B.A.

KATHY MATTEA

★★ **Kathy Mattea (Mercury 818560) 1984**
★★★ **From My Heart (Mercury 824308) 1985**
★★★ **Walk the Way the Wind Blows (Mercury 830405-2) 1986**
★★½ **Untasted Honey (Mercury 832 793-2) 1987**
★★ **Willow in the Wind (Mercury 836 950-2) 1989 ●**
★★★½ **A Collection of Hits (Mercury 842330) 1990 ●**
★★ **Time Passes By (Mercury 846 975-2) 1991**
★★ **Lonesome Standard Time (Mercury 314-512 567-2) 1992**

Possessed of a warm, strong voice that landed her lots of back-up-vocal and demo work in Nashville before launching her own performing career, Mattea too often evinces the tidy unobtrusiveness of a back-up singer while doing lead-vocal work. This general lack of personality probably helps explain why her career got off to a slow start—the first two albums weren't significant successes, and singles like "You've Got a Soft Place to Fall" and "That's Easy For You to Say" are passive country tunes at their most generic. But she began scoring hits with *Walk the Way the Wind Blows,* and developed a bluegrass-shaded style that featured souped-up, catchy choruses ("Eighteen Wheels and a Dozen Roses," "Train of Memories") as an energy-boost to otherwise lackluster music. Fitting all-too-comfortably into both the folk and new traditionalist wings of country music, Mattea is a talented musician—twice named CMA Female Vocalist of the Year—who may be too mannerly for her music's own good.—K.T.

THE MAVERICKS
★★★½ From Hell to Paradise (MCA
MCAD-10544) 1992

This album debut represents a radical departure from conservative Nashville standards. The band hails from Miami (not known as a country hotbed), fills its songs with social issues and features the tremulous vocals of Raul Malo, whose quaver recalls the heightened drama in the Sixties rock of Del Shannon and Roy Orbison.

The album establishes its country credentials with tributes to Buck Owens ("Excuse Me [I Think I've Got a Heartache]") and Hank Williams ("Hey Good Lookin'"), while Malo's original material explores such uncharted country territory as the homeless, children of deprivation, and his family's flight from Cuba.
—D.McL.

MAC MCANALLY
★★ Simple Life (Warner Bros. 9 26136-2)
1990
★★ Live and Learn (MCA MCAD-10543)
1992

A music-biz pro, McAnally came to country from the pop world, where he scored a few innocuous, folksy hits, most notably "It's a Crazy World," a Top Forty single in 1977. Far too often, the voice and phrasing of singer-songwriter McAnally are dead ringers for those of a superior singer-songwriter, James Taylor—and Taylor isn't exactly a country-music touchstone. This may help explain why McAnally isn't a country star, and also why his meticulous craft as a composer has carried him through a series of beautifully wrought but emotionally inert albums.—K.T.

MARTINA MCBRIDE
★★★ The Time Has Come (RCA 66002)
1992

It's tempting to credit this crisp, handsome album to producers Paul Worley and Ed Seay, who handled Pam Tillis's similarly fine and enlightened debut a year earlier. But few new singers would have enough maturity to navigate the upper register yodeling of "True Blue Fool," keep up with Garth Brooks's harmonies on Emory Gordy Jr.'s "Cheap Whiskey," and accommodate John Hughey's downcast steel guitar in the vivid ballad "That's Me." McBride sings with a throttled tenderness, like her peers Tillis and Patty Loveless, and the addition of fiddle, mandolin, or steel guitar to each of these ten songs grants a rootsy authenticity to a singer who clearly grew up singing along to Linda Ronstadt's *Hasten Down the Wind.*—R.T.

MCBRIDE & THE RIDE
★★½ Burnin' Up the Road (MCA MCAD-
42343) 1990
★★★ Sacred Ground (MCA MCAD-
10540) 1992
★★★½ Hurry Sundown (MCA MCAD-
10787) 1993

Texas-born singer-songwriter Terry McBride, a former Delbert McClinton sideman, quickly proved that he was far more than a mere third of this mainstream country threesome, which has found chart success with middle-of-the-road ballads like "Can I Count on You," "Same Old Star," and "Sacred Ground." Guitarist Ray Herndon, a former Lyle Lovett band member, and drummer Billy Thomas (who previously worked the road with Emmylou Harris and Vince Gill) certainly make their contributions in the form of the Ride's formidable harmony sound. But it's really McBride's confident baritone and accessible original ballads that have thus far defined this trio's sound.

McBride is perhaps a trifle too much in abundance on *Burnin' Up the Road,* McBride & the Ride's tentative 1990 debut album on which he wrote or co-wrote nine of the ten unremarkable cuts and sang lead on all of them. *Sacred Ground* shows a maturation and new-found confidence in McBride's writing and singing. (This time he scaled back, including only six of his original songs, most of which were co-written with noted Nashville writers like Kostas, Gary Nichols, and Allen Shamblin.) Most important, *Sacred Ground* is also a significant step toward furnishing a bit more identity and edge to the engaging but faceless sound of the trio's first album. *Hurry Sundown* (1993), McBride & the Ride's most recent CD release, finds the band rounding out their sound with even more confidence and finesse, indicating that this may indeed be one of the few recent mainstream country ensembles that can go the distance.
—B.A.

THE MCCARTERS
★★★★★ The Gift (Warner Bros. 9 25737-
2) 1988
★★½ Better Be Home Soon (Warner
Bros. 9 25896-2) 1990

The McCarters, three young sisters from
Dolly Parton's Tennessee mountain
hometown, were a revelation when *The
Gift* introduced them in 1988. It was as if
Emmylou Harris's taste had been grafted
onto Linda Ronstadt's vocal chords, then
cloned into three and loosed upon the
marketplace to make it all really, really
country again. *The Gift,* in fact, sounds
like nothing less than the Parton-
Ronstadt-Harris *Trio* sequel that never
was. It's that good, or even better:
powerful songs, pristine production, and
blood-perfect harmonies. But there was a
tremor in the force, and by 1990, *Better
Be Home Soon* was offering more or less
conventional radio country with big sister
Jennifer up front and the twins almost
inaudible. Commercial success did not
ensue, and Warner Bros. dropped the act.
They're still working, though.—P.Ca.

CHARLY MCCLAIN
★★★ Biggest Hits (Epic EK 40186) 1985

McClain has never quite lived up to her
early expectations. In the late Seventies
and early Eighties, this Memphis vamp
was one of country music's bright spots.
She delivered her ballads and love songs
("That's What You Do to Me," "You're a
Part of Me," "Dancing Your Memory
Away") with a thin, crystalline, little-girl
voice that conveyed more youthful
distress than adult pain. She was one of
the relatively few women singers in
country at the time who enlivened her
stage shows with movement. Alas,
virtually all of her songs were of the sob-
and-toss variety—and her vocals were not
sufficiently compelling to overcome this
defect. *Biggest Hits* illustrates McClain at
her best and worst. There's surprisingly
little distance between the two.—E.M.

DELBERT MCCLINTON
★★★★ Live from Austin (Alligator ALCD-
4773) 1989
★★★ I'm with You (Curb D-277252)
1990
★★★★ Best of Delbert McClinton (Curb
D2-77415) 1991
★★★★ Never Been Rocked Enough (Curb
D2-77521) 1992

He invented a certain supercharged
roadhouse brand of Southern country
rhythm & blues, and he taught John
Lennon how to play harmonica when
Delbert was touring England with Bruce
Channel back before the Beatles had yet
to cross the ocean. He started out with a
hard apprenticeship as a teenager in Fort
Worth's legendary interracial blues joint
Jack's Place, where the equally mythic
Jimmy Reed and Buster Brown were his
mentors.

And Delbert McClinton is still rocking
as hard lo these three decades later. This
Lubbock, Texas-born journeyman country-
rocker, as vividly demonstrated on his
Best of, can blend his original songs with
material from Al Green or Otis Redding
and still produce a fresh sound. He's
earned his slot as a twenty-year overnight
sensation by writing such country
standards as "If You Really Want Me to,
I'll Go" and "Two More Bottles of Wine."
And he doesn't write all that much. His
"I Wanna Thank You Baby" from *Best of*
is vintage Delbert. That side of him, in a
refined bluesy vein, is preserved in *Never
Been Rocked Enough;* for highlights, try a
Bonnie Raitt duet on "Good Man, Good
Woman," a soulful interpretation of Bob
Marley's "Stir It Up," and some vintage
Delbert steam-heat songwriting with
"Cease and Desist."

And the Alligator album proves the
durability and intensity of one of the
better live performers going. Guaranteed
to liven up any party.—C.F.

DEL MCCOURY
★★½ I Wonder Where You Are Tonight
(Arhoolie CD-5006) 1967
★★½ Livin' on the Mountain (Rebel
REB-CD-1709) 1976
★★★½ Live in Japan (Copper Creek CC-
0118) 1979
★★★★★ Classic Bluegrass (Rebel CD-
1111) 1991
★★★★½ Don't Stop the Music (Rounder
CD-0245) 1990
★★★★½ Blue Side of Town (Rounder CD-
0292) 1992

In February 1963, Bill Monroe hired
North Carolina native Del McCoury as his
banjo picker. By the time Del got to
Nashville, Monroe had hired another
banjoist, so Del was invited to try out
instead as lead singer and rhythm
guitarist. That was the start of a career

that has led him to the top; in the three years that the International Bluegrass Music Association has been giving a male vocalist of the year award, McCoury has been the only winner. The archetypal bluegrass singer, Del cuts through the stratosphere with high lonesome notes in a style that builds on that of his mentor Monroe. And his much-praised rhythm guitar work, salted with modal runs, is the foundation of his band, the Dixie Pals.

Today McCoury's sound is centered around his sons, mandolinist Ron and banjoist Rob. Their two Rounder albums are strong statements of contemporary traditional bluegrass in songs like Steve Earle's "If You Need a Fool" on *Blue Side of Town* with its screaming twin fiddles and harmony choruses. On the same album, McCoury reprises the Ola Belle Reed song that's become his trademark piece, "High on a Mountain." Other treats on this album are a punchy version of "That's Alright Mama," the Big Boy Crudup blues that was one side of Elvis's first single, Ernest Tubb's "Try Me One More Time," and two soulful gospel quartets. The title cut of his previous Rounder album, *Don't Stop the Music,* is an old George Jones number, one of several Fifties and Sixties country numbers that McCoury has put his bluegrass touch to. Several duets with brother Jerry McCoury are an added bonus on this album, which, like the other Rounder CD, has a liberal dose of the blues, a genre Del likes.

Classic Bluegrass is an apt title for Rebel's McCoury anthology, based on albums made between 1974 and 1984. Its strength lies in the material—gems like the old ballad "Rain and Snow," Del's own "Don't Let My Love Get in the Way," and his version of the honky-tonk classic "Pick Me Up on Your Way Down."

With his recent popularity, several rather obscure McCoury albums have appeared in CD form. The best of these is the 1979 *Live in Japan* album, which includes good performances (including another "High on a Mountain") by a strong version of his band. Be warned that it is a live album; the balance is not always perfect. But on the other hand there's a sparkle to the performance, particularly in Del's singing and the late Sonny Miller's fiddling, not found in studio recordings. *Livin' on the Mountain,* a 1971 recording released on an obscure 1976 album, has good singing by McCoury, but the quality of the backup musicians is not up to the standards of his later albums. And *I Wonder Where You Are Tonight* is a reissue (with several previously unissued cuts from the original sessions) of his first album, from 1967. Some of my bluegrass friends think this showcases a certain purity in Del's vocal style. Maybe so, but he can sell a song a lot better today than he could then.
—N.V.R.

CHARLIE MCCOY

★★	**The Fastest Harp in the South (Monument AK-44354) 1973**
★★★	**Harpin' the Blues (Monument AK-47087) 1975**
★★	**The Real McCoy (Monument AK-47086) 1976**
★★½	**The Greatest Hits of Charlie McCoy (Monument AK-44353) 1978**
★★½	**Charlie McCoy's Thirteenth (Step One SOR-0038) 1988**
★★½	**Out on a Limb (Step One SOR-0067) 1992**

Charlie McCoy's name is familiar to any country music fan who takes the time to read liner notes. A multi-instrumentalist, it was McCoy's skillet-hot harmonica playing that, during the Sixties and Seventies, established him as one of Nashville's studio elite. McCoy was also that rare country musician that gained rock & roll credibility, playing on hits by everyone from Bob Dylan to Steve Miller. And he was cranking out his own records the whole time. If you're a harmonica lover, you'll find lots to like about McCoy's solo work. Otherwise these CDs won't convert you; they'll drive you nuts. He cites Little Walter as his biggest early influence, and on *Harpin' the Blues,* his best solo effort, McCoy pays tribute to the Chicago blues legend. Unfortunately, even for the harp lover, much of the music on McCoy's records is marred by a syrupy, Sixties-style production. A way-too-frequently recurring female chorus leaves a lot of these songs sounding more like a Bob Hope TV-special version of country music than the real thing. But when he avoids his schmaltzy side, McCoy's playing is exhilarating, and there are at least a few standout cuts ("Shenandoah" and "You Were Always on My Mind," on

Charlie McCoy's *Thirteenth,* for example) on each of these CDs.—P.Cr.

NEAL MCCOY

★ **At This Moment (Atlantic 82171) 1990**
★½ **When Forever Begins (Atlantic 82396) 1992**

Here's a revealing demonstration of Nashville's sense of roots during the Age of Garth: the title track to Neal McCoy's first album is a supper-club tear jerker written and recorded by Billy Vera and first popularized on an episode of the definitive Reagan-era sitcom, "Family Ties." Although McCoy is an able singer, with an affable, bluesy tone that hints at his Texas roots, these two albums are undisturbed by even one memorable song or compelling performance.—R.T.

MEL MCDANIEL

★½ **Greatest Hits (Capitol CDP 7 46867 2) 1987**

Outside of a little Oklahoma grit, McDaniel's voice has nothing distinctive about it. Most of the ten hits included here achieved success because of their radio-ready, hand-clapping, sing-along choruses. Cases in point: "Stand Up," "Let It Roll (Let It Rock)," "Baby's Got Her Blue Jeans On" (a #1 country single), and "Love Is Everywhere." McDaniel signed with the newly formed Branson Entertainment record label in 1993. —J.O.

RONNIE MCDOWELL

★★ **All Tied Up in Love (Curb/CEMA D21K-77517) 1986**
★★ **Older Women and Other Greatest Hits (Epic EK 40643) 1987**
★★ **I'm Still Missing You (Curb/CEMA D21Y-77279) 1988**
★★ **American Music (Curb/CEMA D21Y-77284) 1989**
★★ **The Best of Ronnie McDowell (Curb D2-77254) 1990**
★★★ **Your Precious Love (Curb D2-77507) 1991**
★★★ **Unchained Melody (Curb D2-77414) 1991**
★★ **When a Man Loves a Woman (Curb D2-77537) 1992**

More than fifteen years after McDowell made his recording debut with the Elvis Presley tribute, "The King Is Gone," the singer is still blighted by this identifica-

tion. He sounded uncannily like Presley then, and he still does—in spite of his best efforts at re-imaging himself. McDowell also suffers in critical esteem because of his tendency to record fluffy, feel-good pieces—such "Older Women," "Watchin' Girls Go By," and "She's a Little Past Forty"—that yield nothing substantial when stripped of their hooks and flourishes. Both *Your Precious Love* and *Unchained Melody* contain several listenable cover tunes, and the latter contains duets with Conway Twitty, Bobby Vinton, Jack Scott, and Jerry Lee Lewis. *American Music* and *I'm Still Missing* You number future Kentucky Headhunters Doug Phelps and Greg Martin, then members of McDowell's road band, among the backup musicians.—E.M.

REBA MCENTIRE

★★½ **You Lift Me Up to Heaven (PolyGram Special Products 846-496-2) 1980**
★★★★ **The Best of Reba McEntire (Mercury 824 342-2) 1985**
★★ **Reba Nell McEntire (Mercury 822455) 1986**
★★ **Behind the Scene (Mercury 812871-2) 1988**
★★ **Feel the Fire (Mercury 822887) 1990**
★★ **Unlimited (Mercury 822882) 1990**
★★½ **Forever in Your Eyes (PolyGram Special Products 836-692-2) 1992**
★★★ **My Kind of Country (MCA MCAD-31108) 1984 ●**
★★ **Just a Little Love (MCA MCAD-31081) 1985**
★★½ **Have I Got a Deal for You (MCA MCAD-31109) 1985**
★★★½ **Whoever's in New England (MCA MCAD-31304) 1986 ▲**
★★★ **What Am I Gonna Do about You (MCA MCAD-5807) 1986 ●**
★★½ **Last One to Know (MCA MCAD-42030) 1987 ●**
★★★★ **Greatest Hits (MCA MCAD 5979) 1987 ▲**
★★ **Merry Christmas to You (MCA MCAD-42031) 1987 ●**
★★★ **Reba (MCA MCAD-42134) 1988 ▲**
★★ **Live (MCA MCAD-8034) 1989 ●**
★★½ **Sweet Sixteen (MCA MCAD-8034) 1989 ●**

★★½ **Rumor Has It (MCA MCAD-10016) 1990** ▲²
★★★½ **For My Broken Heart (MCA MCAD-10400) 1991** ▲²
★★ **It's Your Call (MCA MCAD-10673) 1993** ▲²

Reba McEntire manages to combine spunkiness with maturity. A charming, energetic performer who cuts across all boundaries in country music, she has also served as an important transitional figure between the implied independence of a slightly earlier generation of female vocalists (Tammy Wynette, Loretta Lynn, Dolly Parton) and the forthright feminism of younger singers such as Kathy Mattea, Lorrie Morgan, and Wynonna Judd. Revisionist opinion holds that McEntire came into her own as an artist only when she was freed from the shackles of Mercury and producer Jerry Kennedy, and liberated into the benevolence of MCA and producer Jimmy Bowen; this is hogwash. As *The Best of Reba McEntire* proves, in her early-Eighties recordings she was already strong enough to defeat Kennedy's tendency to drown his artists in wet string sections, and commanding performances like "I Don't Think Love Ought to Be That Way," "I'm Not That Lonely Yet," and "Can't Even Get the Blues" reveal McEntire at her most beguiling.

With Bowen in the late Eighties as her coproducer, McEntire achieved a mass-appealing synthesis of country authenticity ("Have I Got a Deal for You") and pop prettiness ("Whoever's in New England") in her music, and she became a super-star: 1986 CMA Entertainer of the Year, roles in TV-movies (*The Gambler IV*) and films (*Tremors*). The thick Oklahoma twang that characterizes her earliest hits has been smoothed out on her later ones, but it's not a case of abandoning her roots. Instead, it's one measure of her ongoing development as a vocalist; her phrasing has become so flexible, so casually authoritative, that there's no sort of popular music McEntire cannot sing. The danger in this is that McEntire has been tempted to broaden her music into pop blandness, as the flaccid *It's Your Call* suggests. But most of the time, McEntire remains one of the most versatile, likable stylists in country.—K.T.

D. L. MENARD
★★★★ **No Matter Where You At, There You Are (Rounder CD 6021) 1988**
★★★★ **Cajun Saturday Night (Rounder CD 0198) 1989**

Nicknamed the "Cajun Hank Williams," D. L. Menard is one of the finest purveyors of Cajun music with a country edge. His uncanny vocal similarity to Hank's emphasizes the high lonesome twanginess inherent in the Acadian style. Sung entirely in Cajun-French, *No Matter Where You At* features a Mamou-style "Wildwood Flower," along with such rollicking numbers as "Lafayette Two Step." Menard and his percussive rhythm guitar are joined by fiddler Ken Smith and accordionists Eddie LeJeune and Blackie Forestier. *Cajun Saturday Night* takes Menard to Nashville, where he is backed up by country pros including Ricky Skaggs (fiddle), Buck White (piano), and original Drifting Cowboys Don Helms (steel) and Jerry Rivers (fiddle). With a full band, Menard pays tribute to the Hillbilly Shakespeare, recording six of Williams's songs in English, along with six of his own honky-tonk-style numbers. Whether you're a newcomer to Cajun or a die-hard two-stepper, you can't go wrong with either of Menard's Rounder recordings (each of which contain informative liner notes).
—H.G.-W.

TIM MENSY
★★ **Stone by Stone (Columbia CK 45088) 1990**
★★½ **This Ol' Heart (Giant 9 24463-2) 1992**

Mensy comes from a musical family. His mother was a regular on the "Old Dominion Barn Dance" out of Richmond, Virginia, and he played mandolin and sang with the family band throughout his youth. Moving to Nashville after high school, Mensy (known then as Tim Menzies) joined journeyman country group Bandana as a guitarist. In the early Eighties the band charted ten singles, mostly in the lower reaches of the charts.

Mensy's years of experience made him a savvy songwriter, able to turn a phrase or play on words with the best of them. Among the hits he's penned are Shenandoah's "Mama Knows," Doug Stone's "I Thought It Was You," Shelby

Lynne's "I Lie Myself to Sleep," and John Conlee's "Mama's Rockin' Chair."

His solo debut, produced by hard country specialist Bob Montgomery (Vern Gosdin) and featuring ten Mensy compositions, yielded three unsuccessful singles: the gently swinging "Hometown Advantage," "Stone by Stone," and "You Still Love Me in My Dreams." Mensy moved on to become one of the first country signings to Irving Azoff's Giant record label, and his prospects looked bright in 1992. Giant Nashville chief James Stroud produced *This Ol' Heart*. His successes with Clint Black, Tracy Lawrence, and John Anderson suggest Stroud knows what country radio will play. But Mensy's songs are a mixed bag. "She Dreams" works the disenchanted suburban housewife theme again; "Daddy's Shoes" and "The Grandpa That I Know" contemplate the shift of generations; "America for Sale" laments the liquidation of national treasures; "He'll Use His Wings" ponders death. "That's Good" is refreshingly different, with an easy swing feel coaxing the running dialogue between singer and chorus on what it takes to get straight A's in love. Mensy's Giant shot lasted only one album. In early 1993 he no longer had a record deal with the company, but his songwriting skills remained in demand. —J.O.

ROGER MILLER

★★★★ **The Best of Roger Miller, Vol. 1: Country Tunesmith (Mercury 848 977-2) 1991**
★★★★½ **The Best of Roger Miller, Vol. 2: King of the Road (Mercury 314 512 646-2) 1992**
★★★★★ **Golden Hits (Smash 826 261-2) 1965 ●**
★★★½ **Country Spotlight (Dominion 30062) 1991**
★★★½ **Best of Roger Miller: His Greatest Songs (Curb D2-77511) 1991**
★★★ **King of the Road (Epic EK 53017) 1992**
★★★½ **Dang Me! The Best of Roger Miller (LaserLight 15 479) 1992**

In 1965, Roger Miller was the King of the Road and the hottest thing going (excepting the Beatles) in pop music. Yes, in pop music, where he charted eleven songs, though he naturally did better still

in country. Miller (1936-1992) had an astonishing run between 1964 and '66, when nearly everything he wrote and recorded turned to gold and proved to the world that there *were* hip hillbillies. He scatted and spluttered and ran amok in a way that was irreverent but non-threatening and somehow at one with the zany zeitgeist of a time when Eng-a-land swung and the darker energies of the later 1960s had yet to manifest themselves. As lyrics were becoming more important, Miller tickled us with ones that were absurd yet rang askewly true. Was Bob Dylan's descent into the absurd at about the same time (compare "Subterranean Homesick Blues") a response to Roger Miller? Reckon not, though it's tempting to hear an affinity between Miller's stream-of-consciousness, especially in "My Uncle Used to Love Me But She Died," and Dylan's (legend has them both writing to the siren song of the methamphetamine muse). On another level, Miller's childlike fun with wordplay recalls another Okie singer-songwriter in his apolitical moments, Woody Guthrie. "Dang Me," after all, is basically a talking blues with a refrain.

Before stardom, Miller wrote some great honky-tonk songs for the likes of Ray Price and George Jones. Mercury's *Best of, Vol. 1* collects twenty-one 1957-70 performances by Miller of the hits he wrote for others ("Invitation to the Blues," "Half a Mind") as well as related songs in a more classic country vein than his mid-Sixties hits. Many are morose downers you wouldn't associate with ol' "Do-Wacka-Do" Roger, but all are informed by his crafty lyrical turns (as in "The Last Word in Lonesome Is Me"). Miller was a better hard country singer than you might imagine, and the three 1957 recordings, especially the tour de force vocal on "My Pillow," are a pleasant surprise.

Good as his hard country was, it was generic, while "King of the Road" was original, a collage of images from a drifter's world, neither pitying nor celebrating, set to fingerpops, bass, and acoustic guitar. Mercury's *Best of, Vol. 2* opens with a loopy 1957 novelty, "Poor Little John," and closes with a dismal bit of dreck from 1972, "Hoppy's Gone." Fifteen of its twenty tracks are prime

Miller time, but the remaining five could have been, too.

The old Smash *Golden Hits* package, the one you've seen crumpled in every used LP bin in the world, is briefer at eleven tracks but more on the money since everything's from Miller's 1964-66 heyday. It has two tracks, "In the Summertime (You Don't Want My Love)" and "Atta Boy Girl," that should have made Mercury's *Best of, Vol. 2,* though *Vol.2* offers the not-to-be-missed "My Uncle . . . ," Miller's unique take on folk-rock. Nowhere to be heard is his 1966 hit, "I've Been a Long Time Leavin' (But I'll Be a Long Time Gone)," and that's a shame.

Epic's ten-track *King of the Road* is Roger Sings Roger remakes of his Smash label hits. They're near Xerox-perfect, but you may as well have the originals. The ten-song *Country Spotlight* collection is more of the same, though it's less apparent from what source: "Chug-a-Lug" is surely the Smash hit recording, while the vocal on "My Uncle . . ." is notably rougher than on the '66 single, so go figure. LaserLight's *Dang Me!* is another Smash remake package (probably from the same source as *Country Spotlight*) with four ballads this time and minus "King of the Road." Curb's *Best of Roger Miller* has "King" and eleven more photocopies of his hits. (Given the slight variances in the time on these packages, Miller may well have revamped his catalogue more than once.) Anyway, Mercury's *Vol. 2* or Smash's *Golden Hits* offer more "Do-Wacka-Do" for your dough.—M.H.

RONNIE MILSAP

★★★	It Was Almost like a Song (RCA 5986-2-R) 1977	
★★★★★	Greatest Hits (RCA 8504-2-R) 1980 ▲²	
★★★	Keyed Up (RCA 5993-2-R) 1983	
★★★★	Greatest Hits, Vol. 2 (RCA PDC1-5425) 1985 ▲	
★★	Lost in the Fifties Tonight (RCA PCD1-7194) 1986 ●	
★★★½	Christmas with Ronnie Milsap (RCA 5624-2-R) 1986	
★★★½	Heart and Soul (RCA 7618-2-R) 1987	
★★	Stranger Things Have Happened (RCA 9588-2-R) 1989	

★★★★	Back to the Grindstone (RCA 2375-2-R) 1991	
★★★½	Greatest Hits, Vol. 3 (RCA 66048-2) 1992	

Like many contemporary country stars, Ronnie Milsap is well acquainted with the full spectrum of Southern music. Born in the North Carolina Appalachians, he has a natural feeling for gut-bucket country. But he came of age musically amid the gospel and soul sounds of the Sixties in Raleigh and Atlanta, then immersed himself in the rock & roll culture of Memphis. His long years as a piano lounge performer steeped him in pop-crooner standards. By the time he hit Nashville in the early 1970s, he had an act that wowed people by leap-frogging among all of these genres with ease.

But being a bundle of musical contrasts can have its disadvantages. Milsap's recorded work has been inconsistent and sometimes lacking in focus. He can be a soul shouter ("Let My Love Be Your Pillow"), a mainstream country balladeer ("A Legend in My Time") or a pop smoothie ("It Was Almost like a Song") with equal aplomb. He is capable of cheesy sing-alongs ("Back on My Mind") as well as devastating emotional essays ("Please Don't Tell Me How the Story Ends"). At his best he can be an inspiring hand-clapper who exhorts you to share his joy ("I'm a Stand by My Woman Man," "Pure Love," "Daydreams about Night Things") or ride the sonic highways ("Smoky Mountain Rain," "What a Difference You've Made in My Life"). The first volume of his *Greatest Hits* contained all of these tunes and effectively defined his range.

Or did it? By the time he'd assembled enough hits for *Vol. 2* in the series, he was reaching firmly into pop-rock territory with "Stranger in My House" and "(There's) No Gettin' over Me" as well as conjuring up the spirits of golden oldies in "Lost in the Fifties Tonight" and "Any Day Now." Alongside these were the gospel flavored toe-tapper "She Keeps the Home Fires Burning," a richly melodic ballad from composer Mike Reid titled "Inside," and a homage to Nashville Sound great Jim Reeves, "Am I Losing You."

Reid continued to supply deliciously evocative compositions in the Eighties, including "How Do I Turn You On,"

"Prisoner of the Highway," and "Where Do the Nights Go," all included on *Vol. 3* of the *Greatest Hits* series. By this time, Milsap was dabbling in electronic keyboard sounds, startling country listeners one minute with the modern pop romps "Button off My Shirt" and "L.A. to the Moon," then doing oldie about-faces such as "Snap Your Fingers" and "Happy, Happy Birthday Baby" the next.

Milsap apparently attempted to resolve the confusion with 1989's *Stranger Things Have Happened* CD by including the unmistakable country of "Houston Solution" and "Don't You Ever Get Tired of Hurting Me." But much on the set lacked conviction. The more eclectic *Heart and Soul* (1987) and *Keyed Up* (1983) collections were more honest presentations.

The blind dynamo has always been an enormously compelling live entertainer, capable of much more guts and fire than is evident on most of his recordings. Milsap finally allowed some passion into his sound on the excellent 1991 set *Back to the Grindstone.* With nary a concession to the prevailing neo-traditionalist country climate of the time, he tore into John Hiatt and Marshall Chapman's "Old Habits Are Hard to Break" with ferocity. He soared into the R&B stratosphere on a remake of the Skyliners "Since I Don't Have You," and barked an impassioned soul duet opposite Patti LaBelle on "Love Certified." He slipped into a sensuous rhythm groove in "Are You Lovin' Me Like I'm Lovin' You," rocked to "All Is Fair in Love and War," recaptured his country constituency with "Turn That Radio On," and addressed social issues in "Spare the Rod (Love the Child)." The album remains his most gripping to date.

Also recommended is Milsap's fine 1986 Christmas collection, wherein we find our hero fronting a full orchestra on standards and reprising Reid's moving brotherhood ode from the *Keyed Up* CD, "We're Here to Love."—R.K.O.

MOLLY & THE HAYMAKERS
★★½　Molly & the Haymakers (Reprise 26443) 1992

Led by Molly Scheer, who sings and plays fiddle and mandolin, this Wisconsin quartet plays ebullient, sometimes goofy country-rock with hard, booming drums.

The songs are unconventional, too—the narrator of Scheer's "Well Ran Dry" is a teenager who leaves the South with her family, after a drought that "raped our farm like a gang from the Upper West Side," then abandons her clan and returns to the Delta. Personal to Molly: there are no gangs on the Upper West Side.—R.T.

BILL MONROE
★★★★★　Mule Skinner Blues (RCA Victor 2494-2-R) 1991
★★★½　Columbia Historic Edition (Columbia CK 38904) 1984
★★★★　The Essential Bill Monroe and His Blue Grass Boys (Columbia C2K 52478) 1992
★★★　Bean Blossom (MCA MCAD-8002) 1973
★★★　Southern Flavor (MCA MCAD-42133) 1988
★★★　Live at the Opry: Celebrating Fifty Years (MCA MCAD-42286) 1989
★★　Cryin' Holy Unto the Lord (MCA MCAD-10017) 1991
★★★★　Country Music Hall of Fame (MCA MCAD-10082) 1991

Bill Monroe, the Father of Bluegrass music, is now in his eighties and still picking the fire out of his weathered Gibson mandolin and singing that high lonesome tenor so many have tried to emulate. He's been on the Grand Ole Opry since 1939, and his recording history stretches back to the mid-1930s when he and brother Charlie began together. Only a few of their classic duets are available on CD (see Various Artists, *Are You from Dixie* and *Something Got a Hold of Me)*, and for some reason, RCA seems to have let *Mule Skinner Blues*—a fine compilation of Monroe's first recordings with the Blue Grass Boys in 1940-41, before he'd added the five-string banjo to his sound—go out of print. This one is worth looking for, and someone at RCA ought to wake up and have it reprinted, for goodness sake!

The most influential Monroe recordings of all were made in the mid-Forties for Columbia. They feature the band that blew everyone away back then: guitarist-lead singer Lester Flatt, banjo ace Earl Scruggs, fiddler Chubby Wise, and bassist Cedric Rainwater. On first glance, *The Essential Bill Monroe* appears to deliver the goods, offering in a boxed set with a lavish booklet two CDs with every song and tune cut by Monroe and this band, as well as material from sessions before and after it. Unfortunately the poor condition of many of the original masters forced Columbia to use alternate takes—rejects, in other words—for nearly two-thirds of this material. If you are a long-time bluegrass collector and already own the three Harmony albums from the Sixties or the one Rounder and two County albums from the Seventies that reissued this stuff you can compare the cuts that actually established Monroe as the creator of this musical style with these rejects: some are just as strong as the originals. But if you're just getting started, the *Columbia Historic Edition,* with ten cuts, is the only alternative, and only half of those are not on *The Essential.*

Monroe moved to Decca (later MCA) in 1950 and still records for them. *The Country Music Hall of Fame* draws sixteen songs and tunes from his massive repertoire, a task of selection that surely was not easy. Included are some of his best numbers in their original versions, like "New Mule Skinner Blues," "Uncle Pen" (a tribute to his fiddling uncle), and "Scotland," in which his twin fiddlers pay homage to his Scottish heritage. Also included is Monroe's 1954 remake of his "Blue Moon of Kentucky," in response to the B side of Elvis's first record, and the original "Walk Softly on This Heart of Mine," later a hit for the Kentucky Headhunters. Any Monroe fan given the opportunity of choosing sixteen tunes from four decades of recording might disagree with other choices on the set, but luckily everything he recorded for this label between 1950 and 1969 has been issued on two four-CD sets, with complete documentation, by Bear Family (*Bill Monroe—Bluegrass 1950-58,* BCD-15423; *Bill Monroe—Bluegrass 1959-69,* BCD-15529); and a third set, for 1970-79, is in the works.

Other Monroe CDs are more recent: *Bean Blossom,* recorded in 1973 at the annual bluegrass festival at his country music park in Bean Blossom, Indiana, is a repackaging of a two-LP set that includes not only Monroe but also the bands of Jim & Jesse, James Monroe, Jimmy Martin, and Lester Flatt. As is

often the case with live productions, there are some problems; with this one it's some sloppy mixing. And the CD package omits descriptive material on the original album, including the fact that Monroe is only present on a fraction of the tracks. But *Bean Blossom* does capture the ambiance of the bluegrass festival movement at its height in the early 1970s, and at seventy-five minutes, it's a bargain. Another album, *Live at the Opry,* was recorded in 1989. It also includes one lively cut from a 1948 broadcast. All of the tunes are Monroe standards, and Monroe and the band are in pretty good form. *Southern Flavor,* a studio album from 1988, foregrounds instrumentals and gospel harmony numbers with lead singing by Blue Grass Boys guitarist Tom Ewing; Monroe chips in a rather thin solo on just one song. His most recent album is *Crying Holy unto the Lord,* an all-gospel collection that includes some high-profile guests: Ricky Skaggs, Ralph Stanley, the Osborne Brothers, Jim & Jesse, and Mac Wiseman. There are some good moments, like Ricky Skaggs's re-creation of Carter Stanley's part on "You're Drifting Away," but for this listener the mix is odd, often defeating the intention of blending in vocal quartets and trios.—N.V.R.

JOHN MICHAEL MONTGOMERY
★★ **Life's a Dance (Atlantic 82420) 1992** ▲

That's an obvious Hank Sr. tribute on the album-opening "Beer And Bones," followed by a Merle Haggard homage on "When Your Baby Ain't Around," a tip of the Stetson to George Strait on "I Love the Way You Love Me," and a George Jones imitation on "Taking off the Edge." Lots of people love those four singers, too. But they don't record an album to prove it. —R.T.

GEORGE MORGAN
★★★ **American Originals (Columbia CK 45076) 1990**

Father of Lorrie, George Morgan announced his arrival with "Candy Kisses" in 1949 and hung in there until his death in 1975 scoring ever-smaller hits. In fact, 1949 was Morgan's peak year—seven songs on the charts. His reading of "Candy Kisses" was very straight and smooth, modeled after Eddy Arnold, but he reversed the usual paradigm and became more country as he got older. *American Originals* collects a decade or so of Columbia hits, although they aren't (contrary to the album title) all originals: four of the ten recordings are actually 1959 remakes of 1949-52 originals. Regardless, Morgan had a fine tenor voice and an ear for a great song, although he hasn't weathered as well as some of the grittier hillbilly voices from the same era.—C.E.

LORRIE MORGAN

★★★★ Leave the Light On (RCA 9594) 1989 ●
★★ Something in Red (RCA 3021) 1991 ▲
★★½ Watch Me (BNA 66047) 1992 ●

Morgan's debut appeared a couple of years before the Nineties country explosion, anticipating the broadening of country's stylistic bases. An expert recording in every way, it lets Morgan's narrow yet expressive range put a glamorously twangy stamp on intimate Nashville balladry ("I'll Take the Memories"), attitude-rich uptempos ("Trainwreck of Emotion"), and seductive barroom confessions ("Out of Your Shoes"). The secret of the album, aside from Morgan's careful and elastic vocals, is producer Barry Beckett's sense of blues tonality and soul rhythms.

Something in Red presents an attractive rendering of George Jones's "A Picture of Me (Without You)." The album defines itself, however, with wild string arrangements that aren't well tailored to Morgan's particular vocal capabilities. This is true even if those orchestrations didn't stop the overly sentimental title song from becoming Morgan's career record. *Watch Me*—leaner, but still no *Leave the Light On*—is somewhat better, yet curiously flat all the same. Whether or not Morgan will again record in ways that suit her drive and demonstrated ability to communicate with her audience remains to be seen. Blessed with the pop instincts of her father, Grand Ole Opry veteran George Morgan, and the honky-tonk forthrightness of her late husband, Keith Whitley, Morgan certainly can do this if she wishes.—J.H.

GARY MORRIS

★★★½ Why Lady Why (Warner Bros. 23738-2) 1983 ●
★★★ Plain Brown Wrapper (Warner Bros. 25438-2) 1986
★★★ Hits (Warner Bros. 25581-2) 1987
★★★ Greatest Hits Vol. II (Warner Bros. 26305-2) 1990
★★★½ Every Christmas (Capitol Nashville CDP 7 90320-2) 1990
★★★ Full Moon, Empty Heart (Capitol Nashville CDP 7 96360-2) 1991

Morris's oak-shattering vocals were ideal for such oratorical set pieces as "The Love She Found in Me" and "Wind beneath My Wings." Even the light fare of "Baby Bye Bye" and "I'll Never Stop Loving You" had the sound of important proclamations. It was Morris's powerful and largely unaccented voice that earned him leading roles in the Broadway productions of *La Bohème* and *Les Misérables* during the mid-to-late Eighties; and it may well have been his excessively formal style, which sounded so stuffy alongside that of the hip new traditionalists, that accounted for his falling out of favor with the all-important radio programmers. Like many other thoroughly engaging live performers, Morris has never been able to translate his range, humor, and spontaneity onto records. But regardless of the trends he confronts, Morris is still golden for those who prefer the elevated to the casual. *Why Lady Why* contains Morris's artistically strongest hits. *Plain Brown Wrapper* illustrates that it takes more than traditional material to make a traditional artist.—E.M.

DUDE MOWREY

★★ Honky Tonk (Capitol CDP 7 95085 2) 1991
★★★ Dude Mowrey (Arista ACP-8678) 1993

With a name like Dude Mowrey and a title like *Honky Tonk,* this teen discovery's debut disc could have been a real straight-up country sleeper. It is, literally. Recorded when he was barely out of high school, *Honky Tonk* showcased Mowrey's classic Haggard-esque voice, but revealed none of Haggard's ability to deliver a line as though he lived it long before he sang it.

Two years later, Mowrey has lived a little and relaxed a little. He sounds less self-conscious, a feeling supported by the producers' generally deft honky-tonk touch. There's too much assembly-line action in the material, but the breezy, off-kilter "Dr. Wurlitzer" is one of the few listenable examples of what is fast becoming country's most dreaded subgenre: the ode to a hillbilly jukebox. Even more heartening is that Mowrey himself wrote the CD's most engaging tune, "View from the Bottom," a light-handed take on an otherwise equally dead thematic horse: a rummy geezer philosophizes.—D.C.

MOON MULLICAN
★★★ Sings His All-Time Greatest Hits (King KCD 555) 1958

Moon Mullican was something of an anomaly. A pianist, he started his career with western swing bands but ended up in Nashville in 1949 billing himself "King of the Hillbilly Piano Players" (in fact, just about the only hillbilly piano player then). He recorded some rollicking R&B-informed tunes like "Pipeliner's Blues" and "Cherokee Boogie," which were issued alongside sentimental parlor pieces like "The Leaves Mustn't Fall" and "Sweeter Than the Flowers." Mullican deserves a well-programmed anthology, but most of his well-known songs can be found in their original versions on *Sings His All-Time Greatest Hits*. It's lo-fi in places and ".Jole Blon" has been dreadfully overdubbed, but it's still a good primer. Mullican was quite unlike anyone else working in country music at that time, and he was one of the few artists cited as an influence by Jerry Lee Lewis. Consider that a recommendation, if you will.—C.E.

MICHAEL MARTIN MURPHEY
★½ Blue Sky Night Thunder (Epic EK 33290) 1975 ●
★ The Best of Michael Martin Murphey (EMI-USA CDP 7 92736 2) 1987
★½ The Best of Country (Curb/CEMA D21K-77336) 1990
★★ River of Time (Warner Bros. 9 25644-2) 1988
★★½ Land of Enchantment (Warner Bros. 9 25894-2) 1989
★★½ Cowboy Songs (Warner Bros. 9 26308-2) 1990
★★ Cowboy Christmas (Warner Bros. 9 26647-2) 1991

It's hard to remember that Michael Murphey (as he was then billed) was once one of the more promising singer-songwriters of the "cosmic cowboy" school—with his "Geronimo's Cadillac" among the more memorable anthems of the early Seventies—since his subsequent music has been sufficiently saccharine to make John Denver or Bobby Goldsboro wince. His output since the pop success of the insufferably mawkish "Wildfire" (featured on both *Blue Sky Night Thunder* and the EMI *Best of)* conjures a mild West of picture-perfect sunsets, impeccable grooming, and avid environmentalism. For a string of cowboy movies starring Alan Alda instead of John Wayne, Murphey would provide the perfect sound track.

Though *Best of* purports to offer the highlights of his Seventies and early Eighties output, the most familiar selections are re-recordings, and the reduction of the CD version to nine cuts (from twelve on the vinyl album) makes this an inexcusably cheesy compilation. The ten-cut *Best of Country* duplicates four songs from the earlier greatest hits package, while omitting the more crossover-oriented "Wildfire" and "Geronimo's Cadillac."

Land of Enchantment is the peppier of his more or less conventional country albums, while *Cowboy Songs* is a milestone of sorts, an album of traditional fare that attempts to put the "western" back into Country & Western. Though Murphey's renditions of "Tumbling Tumbleweeds," "The Yellow Rose of Texas," "The Streets of Laredo," and the like lack the grit to be definitive, at least the material doesn't cloy like so much of his own writing. The seasonal *Cowboy Christmas* follow-up suffers from a characteristic case of the cutes.—D.McL.

ANNE MURRAY
★★★★ Greatest Hits (Liberty C21Y-46058) 1980 ▲⁴
★★★½ Christmas Wishes (Liberty C21D-46319) 1981 ▲²
★★★ A Little Good News (Liberty C21K-46629) 1983 ●
★★★★ Anne Murray's Country Hits (Liberty C21D-46487) 1987
★★★ As I Am (Capitol CDP 7 48764 2) 1988

★★★½ **Christmas (Capitol CDP 7 90886 2) 1988**
★★★★ **Greatest Hits, Vol. 2 (Capitol CDP 7 92072) 1989**
★★★ **You Will (Liberty C21S-94102) 1990**
★★★ **Yes I Do (Liberty C21L-96310) 1991**
★★★★ **Fifteen of the Best (Liberty C21S-95954) 1992**

Anne Murray is a superb technician. Like her inspiration Patti Page, she is the mistress of flawless phrasing, exquisite musical taste, and precise execution. She simply does not make mistakes. On the surface that sounds like music without passion; yet somehow all of her attention to detail, the weight of her talent, the force of her delivery, and her undeniable vocal charisma add up to records that are quite moving, discs that stand the test of time to become classics, and performances that have served as the sound tracks for millions of lives and love affairs.

Let's face it: the lady has a lovely voice. This fresh-scrubbed Canadian beauty's resonant, stars-at-midnight alto has the ability to color and shade lyrics that few of her peers can match. Beneath the cool, still waters of her ballads are undertows of feeling and liquid depths of contemplation. You won't get lost in the throes of ecstasy listening, but you just might experience deep and abiding love.

Murray's *Greatest Hits* album has passed the four-million mark in world-wide sales, making it one of the most successful female albums in history. Why? It is the ultimate romance collection with "Could I Have This Dance," "You Needed Me," "A Love Song," "I Just Fall in Love Again," "Danny's Song," and "Shadows in the Moonlight" for starters. Not to mention the lilting "Snowbird" or the disconsolate "Broken Hearted Me." The *Vol. 2* hits collection shows that Murray lost none of her unerring artistic control. Its many pleasures include "Just Another Woman in Love" and "A Little Good News" as well as her synthesized, techno-pop experiments "Now and Forever" and "Time Don't Run Out on Me." Of the fifteen tracks compiled on the good-value *Country Hits* CD, only six are repeated from *Greatest Hits, Vol. 2*—"Blessed Are the Believers," "Nobody Loves Me Like You Do," "A Little Good News," "Time Don't Run Out on Me," "Just Another Woman in Love," and "Another Sleepless Night." The other nine are extremely well chosen, ranging from Murray's oldie remakes of "He Thinks I Still Care," "Walk Right Back," and "Hey Baby" to newer fare such as "Somebody's Always Saying Goodbye" and "Son of a Rotten Gambler."

By contrast, virtually all of *15 of the Best* songs are repeats from the earlier compilations. And of the nonrepeats only the stirring "Feed This Fire" of 1990 is really essential. Virtually anything this stylist has in print is worth listening to, for every Anne Murray collection is an exercise in class. But the Christmas albums are something special indeed. Both are huge sellers, for there's something in her shimmering style that fits the season. Murray's renditions of holiday standards are like candlelight reflections in the tree ornaments. And unlike so many who attempt these songs, she has the good sense to sing 'em straight, keep 'em simple, and let 'em breathe naturally. They'll have you sniffing for pine needles and eggnog in the middle of July.—R.K.O.

HEATHER MYLES
★★★½ **Just Like Old Times (HighTone HCD 8035) 1992**

Myles couldn't have picked a more apt title for her hard-country debut. With a voice that recalls Jean Shepard for its dusting of honest grit, Myles harks back effortlessly to the sounds of West Coast country, circa 1955. Though most of the songs are brand new, they fit snugly next to the faithful remake of Stonewall Jackson's 1960 classic "I'm Walkin'." Myles proves a capable songwriter, too, chipping in seven out of a dozen tracks. As titles like "Stay Out of My Arms" and "I Love You, Goodbye" suggest, her persona is that of a tough but tender-hearted single woman who's sadder but wiser, and just about ready to move on. Sparked here by members of Dwight Yoakam's band, Myles seems only a great song, and a major label, away from setting the woods on fire and heading for those big city lights.—P.K.

N

THE NASHVILLE BLUEGRASS BAND

★★★★   **The Nashville Bluegrass Band (Rounder CD-0232) 1987**

★★★★★   **To Be His Child (Rounder CD-0242) 1987**

★★★★½   **The Boys Are Back in Town (Sugar Hill SH-CD-3778) 1990**

★★★★½   **Home of the Blues (Sugar Hill SH-CD-3793) 1991**

★★★★★   **Waitin' for the Hard Time to Go (Sugar Hill SH-CD-3809) 1993**

If Alison Krauss is today's bluegrass superstar, the Nashville Bluegrass Band is the supergroup. Built around the vocal talents of guitarist Pat Enright and banjoist Alan O'Bryant, they're touted as the band that "put the blues back in bluegrass." With an earthy sound that recalls Bill Monroe's earliest years, they have built a new back-to-basics bluegrass sound. *The Nashville Bluegrass Band* combines tracks from their first two LPs on the Rounder label, a considerable number of which are older, often traditional, songs. But it also includes several newer pieces, including the haunting "The Train Carrying Jimmie Rodgers Home." O'Bryant has made Monroe's "Doghouse Blues," heard here, into a show stopper in their concerts. They have been leaders in the current trend of drawing upon the repertoires and styles of the great black gospel performers, and *To Be His Child* is a fine sampling of their work, with soulful a cappella quartets and an interesting selection of songs. This is one of the best three or four bluegrass gospel albums available.

In their current makeup, with award-winning fiddler Stuart Duncan, veteran mandolinist Roland White, and bassist Gene Libbea, they have three fine CDs on Sugar Hill. *Home of the Blues* is representative of what this band now offers. It includes "Blue Train," the 1992 bluegrass song of the year, and a live performance with the Fairfield Four, the pioneering black gospel quartet, of "Roll Jordan Roll." Strong new material like "Biggest Liars in Town" along with fresh versions of older material like the Bill Monroe tune "Old Daingerfield," make this a lively showcase for their rhythmic brand of bluegrass. Their previous album, *The Boys Are Back in Town,* is no dud either, with good gospel songs like "Get a Transfer" and "I'm Rollin' through This Unfriendly World," new story-songs like "Connie and Buster," and standards like Johnny Cash's "Big River." This is a band that just seems to get better; shortly before this book went to press I had a chance to hear their latest, *Waitin' for the Hard Times to Go*, a solid mix of great picking (like Texas fiddle favorite "Soppin' the Gravy"), moving black-style a cappella gospel singing, and eight old and new songs about love, work, and hard times (of which the title cut by Jim Ringer is my early favorite) that fulfills the promise of their earlier Sugar Hill albums.—N.V.R.

RICK NELSON
★★★   **All-Time Greatest Hits (Curb D2-77372) 1990**
★★★★   **Legendary Masters Series, Vol. 1 (EMI/Imperial CDP-7-92771-2) 1990**
★★★   **Legendary Masters Series, Vol. 2 (EMI E21Y-95219) 1991**
★★   **Rick Nelson Sings "For You" (MCA MCAD-31363) 1964, 1990**
★★★★   **The Best of Rick Nelson 1963-1975 (MCA MCAD-10098) 1990**
★★★   **Garden Party (MCA MCAD-31364) 1972, 1990**
★★★   **In Concert: The Troubadour, 1969 (MCA MCAD-25983) 1973, 1990**
★★★½   **Live, 1983-1985 (Rhino R2-71114) 1989**
★★½   **Best of Ricky Nelson (Curb D2-77484) 1991**

The first teen-idol created by a TV sitcom—"The Adventures of Ozzie and Harriet"—turned out to be a country fool who helped pave the way for country-rock in the late Sixties.

Nelson had a thin voice and a narrow range, and he worked in a diffident style—he had not one stage move—but he had a genuine love of roots music, a good ear, a talent for drawing top-rank session players around him, and a knack for writing simple, sincere songs himself ("Garden Party"). Most of his CDs are hits compilations, studio or live. For an overall survey of Nelson's career, the best of the best-ofs are EMI's two volumes, which miss his early Verve sides and his later Decca hits (including "Garden Party") but otherwise have everything and more, including false starts. *Volume 1* is the stronger, although EMI put Nelson's top two hits ("Travelin' Man" and "Poor Little Fool") on *Volume 2*, along with a radio spot and far too many flip sides and flops. The two Curb CDs are more concise, but beware: *Best of* consists of re-recordings made by a tired-sounding Nelson shortly before his death in 1985. *All-Time* has the Verve hits ("A

Teenager's Romance" and "I'm Walkin'") but is skimpy at ten songs (three of them duplicated on *Best of*). Rick's graceful journey into country-rock is best documented in MCA's *1963-75* set, featuring two versions of his Stone Canyon Band. A fine collection of Rick doing everything from rockabilly to country—and doing it with energy and affection—is *Live, 1983-1985.* Along with a generous helping of hits, he serves up "That's All Right" and "Honky Tonk Women." *Garden Party* displays a rockier Rick; the *Troubadour* concert showcases his tender ways with fine tunes by Bob Dylan and Eric Anderson. *For You*, a 1964 album, is for fanatics only.—B.F.-T.

WILLIE NELSON
★★★   **Best (EMI E21Y-48398) 1988**
★★★★★   **Nite Life: Greatest Hits and Rare Tracks, 1959-1971 (Rhino R270987) 1990**
★★★   **The Best of Willie Nelson (RCA 07863-56335-2) 1992**
★★★   **Willie (RCA 5988-2-R) 1986**
★★★   **All Time Greatest Hits, Vol.1 (RCA 8556-2-R) 1988**
★★★   **Willie Sings 28 Great Songs (Hollywood/IMG HCD-405) N.D.**
★★★   **Greatest Songs (Curb/CEMA D21K-77366) 1990**
★★★   **Super Hits (CSI Classics-40022) 1991**
★★★★★   **Shotgun Willie (Atlantic 7262-2) 1973**
★★★★★   **Phases and Stages (Atlantic 82192-2) 1974**
★★★★★   **Shotgun Willie/Phases and Stages (Mobile Fidelity UDCD581) 1974/75**
★★★★★   **Red Headed Stranger (Columbia CK 33482) 1975 ▲²**
★★★   **The Sound in Your Mind (Columbia CK-34092) 1976 ●**
★★★★   **To Lefty from Willie (Columbia CK-34695) 1977**
★★★★   **Stardust (Columbia CK-35305) 1978 ▲⁴**
★★★½   **Willie and Family Live (CBS G2K-35642) 1978 ▲²**
★★★   **[& Leon Russell] One for the Road (Columbia CGK-36064) 1979 ●**
★★★   **Willie Sings Kristofferson (Columbia CK-36188) 1979 ●**
★★★★   **[& Ray Price] San Antonio Rose (Columbia CK-36476) 1980 ●**

★★★   **Greatest Hits (& Some That Will Be) (Columbia CGK-37542) 1981 ▲³**

★★★   **Original Soundtrack: Honeysuckle Rose (Columbia CGK 36752) 1980 ▲²**

★★★   **Somewhere over the Rainbow (Columbia CK-36883) 1981 ▲**

★★★★   **Always on My Mind (CBS CK-37951) 1982 ▲³**

★★★   **Tougher Than Leather (Columbia CK-38248) 1983**

★★★   **Without a Song (Columbia CK-39110) 1983 ●**

★★★   **City of New Orleans (Columbia CK-39145) 1984 ●**

★★★   **Half Nelson (Columbia CK-39990) 1985 ●**

★★★   **Partners (Columbia CK-39894) 1986**

★★★   **The Promiseland (Columbia CK 40327) 1986**

★★★   **Island in the Sea (Columbia CK-40487) 1987**

★★★   **What a Wonderful World (Columbia CK 44331) 1988**

★★★   **Horse Called Music (Columbia CSK 45046) 1989**

★★★   **Born for Trouble (Columbia CK 45492) 1990**

★★★★★   **Who'll Buy My Memories (Sony A 22323) 1991**

★★★★   **Across the Borderline (Columbia CK 52752) 1993**

If there's a song—country or otherwise—that Willie Nelson hasn't at least attempted by now, I certainly haven't heard about it. And if there's a singer somewhere this side of heaven that Willie hasn't tried at least one duet with, then I don't want to know about it.

Willie Hugh Nelson from Abbott, Texas, has been everywhere, seen most of the rest of it, and done it all. And this holy man of the honky-tonks has left a lengthy trail of phonograph records to mark his progress. Many have made it to CD. You practically need a road map to tell them apart.

His early work, as with most inspired songwriters who also begin performing, still burns with an almost naive intensity. Few such writers also get the chance to perform their own work. Fortunately, while Willie was still an aspiring songwriter in Nashville, he made two albums for Liberty as well as several singles for that label and for RCA. Some

of those are preserved on the Rhino CD *Nite Life: Greatest Hits and Rare Tracks.* This is Willie the tortured artiste working at full bore; you can sense why traditional Nashville was almost afraid at the thought of this pale, pudgy, morose but intense little man trying to become a country star. This is the Willie Nelson who would twice revolutionize Nashville: first by his songs, later by his immense crossover appeal.

But this earlier Willie began by subverting songwriting, introducing a new humanistic literacy into a genre long dominated by formulaic songs. This is the Willie of "Half a Man," "Nite Life," "Hello, Walls," "Funny How Time Slips Away," "Touch Me," "Mr. Record Man," "One in a Row," and "Crazy." His first single, "Man with the Blues," from 1959 is here, on the Rhino disc.

In 1964, Nelson left Liberty for RCA, where Chet Atkins (as he did with Roy Orbison and Waylon Jennings) saw enormous potential but had difficulty in realizing it immediately. Several things happened in the early 1970s that radically changed Willie's life and career, as well as the face of country music. One: he left RCA for Atlantic, where he made two landmark conceptual country albums: *Shotgun Willie* and *Phases and Stages.* Two: he became depressed with life in Nashville, decided to move back to Texas, and settled in Austin in a little apartment near a fledgling hippie sound emporium called Armadillo World Headquarters. Three: he played there and discovered a crossover audience of what blossomed into armies of progressive country fans. Four: he decided to throw some little Fourth of July "picnics" as a sort of country Woodstock. Five: he went into a little studio near Dallas and put together a sparse and bleak album of love wronged and avenged.

That album, *Red Headed Stranger,* marked the debut date of modern country: 1975. He was soon at the White House and everywhere else, as country chic swept the country. It's impossible now to overstate the impact of *Stranger*—it legitimized country music and intellectualized it and immediately made it mainstream as no album had ever done. It is a brilliant saga-song Western epic album, a very minimalist work, but one which plucks every heartstring, wrings every emotion, subtly explores every aspect of the human condition. It was not for nothing that one review of *Stranger* was headlined "Matthew, Mark, Luke, and Willie."

All of that amounted to a musical revolution. He and his fellow radicals, Jennings and Kristofferson, have spent the ensuing years trying to keep up with the fallout from all that.

Never one to act with any predictability, Willie astounded everyone but himself in 1978 with his *Stardust* album, a collection of such Tin Pan Alley favorites as the title song, "Georgia on My Mind," "Moonlight in Vermont," and "Unchained Melody." Willie's warm, quavery voice wrapping itself around a standard like "Don't Get Around Much Anymore" endeared him to yet an even larger audience and pushed further the boundaries of country music.

He has continued to do so, nimbly leaping across almost every fixed category of music, like the leprechaun he has managed to become. Just when he seemed defeated by a back tax bill of many millions of dollars, he went back into the studio with just his voice and his guitar to re-record twenty-five of his best songs for a CD officially called *Who'll Buy My Memories?* but usually referred to as *The IRS Tapes.* The CD's purpose was to begin repaying Willie's massive tax debt. He produced it with Bob Johnston, who did Bob Dylan's three Nashville albums. Artistically, it is Nelson at his sparse and Biblical prophet-sounding best: the seductive voice of doom. (By 1993, his tax bill was reduced enough that the IRS finally settled with him).

On the eve of turning sixty in 1993, he sought to re-invent himself yet again and may well have done so with *Across the Borderline.* He combines some vintage Willie ("She's Not for You") with some current hip country songs by Lyle Lovett and reaches out to encompass the likes of a Mose Allison jazz hit of a Willie Dixon blues song, Paul Simon's "Graceland," new Bob Dylan works, and the title song by John Hiatt and Ry Cooder. Then he gets current hip producer Don Was to ramrod the project and herds in everybody from Dylan to Simon to Allison to play and sing on the thing. And it works.

The only thing that's really missing from Willie's body of CDs is some of his gospel recordings, and that problem could be speedily solved by reissuing the Columbia album *The Troublemaker.*—C.F.

MICHAEL NESMITH

★★★★ The Older Stuff: The Best of the Early Years (Rhino R2-70763) 1991
★★★ The Newer Stuff (Rhino R2-70168) 1989
★★★½ ". . .tropical campfires. . ." (Pacific Arts Audio PAAD-5000) 1992

One of the true pioneers of country-rock in the late Sixties was a Monkee. Michael Nesmith, a Texas native who'd been emceeing hoot nights at the L.A. folk club, the Troubadour, was picked to fill the John Lennon role—that is, to be the "smart" Monkee. Although the group's producers used session players behind them, Nesmith needed no help. He was an accomplished singer—the voice throaty, expressive and blues-based, echoing Stephen Stills—and writer, as evidenced by "Different Drum," which Linda Ronstadt took onto the charts.

After quitting the group, he formed the First National Band with several country players and scored a hit in 1970 with the ethereal "Joanne," a brilliant early moment in country-rock. He followed with "Silver Moon" on the album *Loose Salute,* wherein he included a lovely take on Patsy Cline's "I Fall to Pieces" and his Monkees-era "Listen to the Band." These, along with the classic "Tumbling Tumbleweeds" and Bob Wills's "Born to Love You," are highlights of *The Older Stuff,* covering a dozen post-Monkees years in which "the Nez" established himself as both a country boy faithful to his roots and as a musical visionary.

The *Newer Stuff* is essentially Nesmith of the Eighties, when he'd established his own record and video company. Suddenly, the songs are ultravisual; steel guitars give way to synthesizers, and Nesmith deserts the country for slick city dance floors, exotic islands, and fantasy trips to the moon. In the beautiful *"tropical campfires"* Nesmith again lets his roots show, bringing back the First National Band's steel player, Red Rhodes, to add country shadings to songs ranging from Brazilian to Cole Porter, along with a generous stack of new Nezmerizers.—B.F.-T.

NEW GRASS REVIVAL

★★★★ **Fly through the Country/When the Storm Is Over (Flying Fish CD-032) 1976/77**
★★★ **Barren County (Flying Fish FF-70083) 1979**
★★★ **Commonwealth (Flying Fish FF-70254) 1981**
★★★ **On the Boulevard (Sugar Hill SHCD-3745) 1985**
★★★ **Hold to a Dream (Capitol C2-46962) 1987**
★★½ **Friday Night in America (Capitol CDP 7 90739 2) 1989**
★★★½ **Live (Sugar Hill SHCD-3771) 1989**
★★★½ **Anthology (Capitol CDP 7 94624 2) 1990**

When they first appeared in the early Seventies, New Grass Revival was a real breath of fresh air. Here was bluegrass music being played by hip, young superpickers who grew up on rock & roll. Splitting vocal chores more or less evenly, the band— mandolinist Sam Bush, banjoist Courtney Johnson, guitarist Curtis Burch, and bassist John Cowan—specialized in bringing the joyous abandon and picking prowess of bluegrass to songs by young writers like John Hartford, Jackson Browne, and Bruce Cockburn. On *Fly through the Country/When the Storm Is Over,* a nice repackaging of two of their early releases, the formula works beautifully. The musicians keep one foot firmly in Bill Monroe territory, giving songs like "Good Woman's Love" and Rick Roberts's "Four Days of Rain" the understated efficiency they need to work. With the 1986 release of the now-out-of-print *New Grass Revival* album, the band made the leap—a big one for a bluegrass band these days—to a major label. Burch and Johnson were by this time replaced by guitarist Pat Flynn and banjo wizard Bela Fleck, with bassist Cowan taking over most of the lead vocals. Cowan's energy, an asset to the band's legendary live shows (check out their raucous *Live* set on the Sugar Hill label), tends to sink many of the band's in-studio rave-ups. On a song like the old Marvin Gaye hit "Ain't That Peculiar" (*Anthology),* Cowan's vocals sound not much like bluegrass and a whole lot like the guy from Styx. The band goes whole

hog on numbers like *Friday Night in America*'s title song, for example, and comes up sounding like they're trying way too hard. To be fair, you'll find great moments on every New Grass release—instrumentals like "Metric Lips" from *Anthology* and "County Clare" from *On the Boulevard,* and vocal workouts like "You Plant Your Fields" and "Hold to a Dream" (both available on *Anthology)*—but despite each member's undeniable virtuosity, or perhaps partially because of it, the band's Beatles-meet-Bill Monroe blend never got them the mass audience they'd hoped for. In 1989, after an incredible seventeen years together, New Grass Revival finally called it quits. —P.Cr.

NEW LOST CITY RAMBLERS

★★★★ **The Early Years, 1958-1962 (Smithsonian/Folkways SF CD 40036) 1991**

This disc pulls twenty-six tracks from a dozen albums released on Folkways between 1958 and 1962 by the most influential stringband of the urban folk music revival. Using many different acoustic instruments, the original New Lost City Ramblers—Mike Seeger, John Cohen, and Tom Paley—created authentic, skillfully played and sung renditions of tunes they found on older recordings and Library of Congress field tapes. *The Early Years* documents the Ramblers' exploration of a wide range of musical styles including old-time stringband music, early bluegrass, topical songs, ballads, dance tunes, children's songs, talking blues, and old-time ribaldry. The albums that yielded these selections provided a beginner's library for a second generation of musicians eager to learn to play in the same styles championed by the Ramblers. As the extensive liner notes for *The Early Years* point out, the Ramblers encountered a growing number of urban musicians playing in traditional styles as they traveled around the country during the years when these albums first appeared. In turn, the thousands of new converts created a market for album reissues of the original 78 rpm recordings that inspired the Ramblers.

Tagged "revivalists" by some scholars, the Ramblers nevertheless formed an important link between musical generations, and, more often than is acknowledged, they creatively expanded the music that inspired them. The trio's legacy endures. As the liner notes mention, the recordings on this album are now older than the 78 rpm discs were when the Ramblers learned their music from them.—J.O.

NEW RIDERS OF THE PURPLE SAGE

★★★ New Riders of the Purple Sage (Columbia CK 30888) 1971
★★ The Adventures of Panama Red (Columbia CK 32450) 1973
★★★ The Best of New Riders of the Purple Sage (Columbia CK 34367) 1976

A love child of the Grateful Dead's Jerry Garcia, New Riders of the Purple Sage were the ultimate hippie cowboys. Originally the band was a collaboration between Garcia, who wanted an outlet for his pedal steel playing, the Dead's bassist Phil Lesh and drummer Mickey Hart, and songwriter-guitarist John Dawson. The self-titled debut, written entirely by Dawson, was a Dead-ringer for that laid-back San Francisco sound. Garcia's steel guitar added just enough twang to make the album a bona fide country-rocker, and Dawson's cosmic cowpoke lyrics to such songs as "Portland Woman," "Henry," and "Last Lonely Eagle" guaranteed that New Riders material would appeal to Deadheads. Garcia and company left the band to its own devices after this initial outing, and Dawson and members David Nelson and Dave Torbert carried on with Buddy Cage and Spencer Dryden (ex-Jefferson Airplane). The only other original New Riders album available on CD is the gimmicky *Panama Red.* Though the title track is a clichéd but catchy outlaw anthem, the rest of the album consists of limpid rockers (both hard and soft). The anthology draws primarily from the first LP, along with a few later recordings, including "Panama Red," a live version of "Hello Mary Lou," and a soulless cover of Dylan's "You Angel You."—H.G.-W.

THE NEW TRADITION

★★½ Seed of Love (Brentwood CD-5231J) 1991
★★★½ Love Here Today (Brentwood CD-5285J) 1992
★★★★ Closer Than It's Ever Been (Brentwood CD-5286J) 1993

A Christian bluegrass quartet with roots in country, Southern gospel, and jazz, the New Tradition is one of the most promising progressive bluegrass bands to emerge in recent years. On the all-gospel *Seed of Love,* the band's signature traits of instrumental wizardry and sparkling vocals are in place, but they are diluted by a repertoire mired in tedious evangelical platitudes. The disappointing result is an unimaginative doctrinal tract of eight original songs mired in concerns about atonement, personal salvation, testimonies, and family values. The band fares better with *Love Here Today,* an animated and varied collection of secular songs featuring works from Bill Monroe ("Can't You Hear Me Calling"), the Beatles ("I Saw Her Standing There"), Merle Haggard ("Colorado"), Hazel Houser ("My Baby's Gone"), and others, along with three songs by band members Danny Roberts and Daryl Mosley.

The New Tradition returns to a gospel format with *Closer Than It's Ever Been,* a technically flawless album that glistens with maturity and confidence and exhibits dramatic advances in songwriting. While still focused on evangelical (and fundamentalist) issues, Mosley and Roberts's songs sound less like bluegrass versions of Gold City and the Kingsmen and more like the definitive, heartfelt gospel songs of Bill Monroe and Carl Story. With this fine album, the New Tradition has finally realized the potential that earned them the Best New Band award from the Society for the Preservation of Bluegrass Music in America in 1991.—J.B.

MICKEY NEWBURY

★★ Best of (Curb/CEMA D21K-77455) 1991

He's probably sick to death of hearing the words "cult hero," but after more than twenty years in the trenches that's what Mickey Newbury remains. Two generations of country fans have fallen for his smoky tenor, spare arrangements, and poignant songwriting. Each convert feels like this artist is a personal discovery, so Mickey has won his fans one by one.

Alas, none of his classic work for Mercury (late Sixties) or Elektra (early Seventies) is currently available. During a storm tossed odyssey through the music business, he has also recorded for MCA,

Airborne, and assorted other companies. Newbury sounds best when he's alone with a guitar, but most of his producers have yielded to the temptation to surround his immensely evocative voice with lush arrangements. This 1991 collection is no exception. What's worse, it's a best of that doesn't include his songwriter calling cards "Sweet Memories," "San Francisco Mabel Joy," "Just Dropped In (To See What Condition My Condition Was In)," "Love Look at Us Now," or "Why You Been Gone So Long." On the plus side, it does have "An American Trilogy" and "She Even Woke Me Up to Say Goodbye." And although it's gussied-up and schmaltzy, it is a Mickey Newbury album. So yet another wave of listeners will be captured. —R.K.O.

JUICE NEWTON

★★ [with Silver Spur] The Early Years (RCA 61142) 1992
★★½ Greatest Hits (Capitol C21Y-46489) 1987 ●
⅄ ⅄ ½ Can't Wait All Night (RCA PCD1-4995) 1984
★ Emotions (RCA 6371-2-R9) 1987
★★½ Ain't Gonna Cry (RCA 8376-2-R9) 1989
★★ Old Flame (RCA 6905-2-R9) 1989

After years of recording for two major labels, this Virginia-born pop-country belter hit in 1981 with a cover of Merrilee Rush's "Angel of the Morning." Like her slightly new wave-inflected pop rock hits that followed—Dave Edmunds's "Queen of Hearts" and the energetic "Love's Been a Little Bit Hard on Me," for example—Newton's most likable work draws on a real savvy. There's usually a cheese quotient, but she knows how to make a virtue of it, filling up spaces between hooks with a bold overstatement that still recognizes boundaries. For this Juice Newton, try *Greatest Hits* or *Can't Wait All Night,* a fairly tough pop-rock affair that's actually a little more sustained than the *Hits* collection.

After her brand of California country became unfashionable, Newton adjusted her music, with mixed results. *Emotions* is as generic as its title, but *Ain't Gonna Cry*—with touches like Cheryl Wheeler's excellent "I'm Only Walkin'" and good L.A.-in-Nashville session picking plus string arrangements by Jeremy Lub-

bock—is effective, mellow Newton. *Old Flame,* which features Newton's 1989 country hit of Timi Yuro's (and Elvis Presley's) "Hurt" falls between these two poles. *The Early Years* finds Newton sounding less focused, but what it really shows is how much she's progressed as a purveyor of vocal professionalism that can, sometimes, stick.—J.H.

OLIVIA NEWTON-JOHN

★★★ Come on Over (MCA MCAD-31092) 1976 ●
★★★ Making a Good Thing Better (MCA MCAD-1682) 1977
★★★ Warm and Tender (Geffen 24257) 1989
★★★½ Back to Basics: The Essential Collection 1971-1992 (Geffen 24470) 1992

Olivia Newton-John is a first-rate pop singer who has always been able to do articulate, often moving things with her voice, which triumphs on pitch, flow, and placement instead of heft or range. In the Seventies and early Eighties, she enjoyed pop-icon status, first as an English-style ingenue and later, after she donned leather in the film version of *Grease,* as a proto-Madonna stylist with hints of rock kink. It was in the mid-Seventies, though, that Newton-John's younger, more totally wholesome persona clicked on the country charts with tunes like "Have You Never Been Mellow" and "Please Mr. Please." She annoyed rockers and country traditionalists alike, but she claimed that she liked Kentucky whiskey.

As the two remaining in-print MCA albums demonstrate, Newton-John's country strengths lay not in her indifferent way with covers of, say, Dolly Parton's "Jolene," but in her own intimate balladry and dusky mid-tempo narratives. As perfectly produced by John Farrar as any pop singer in history has ever been rendered on tape, songs like "Don't Throw it All Away" (from *Come*) and the heartbreaking domestic blues of "Coolin' Down" (from *Making*) translated the Newton-John style into a language that the country audience immediately understood. She sang country, even if the accent was off.

No good compilation exists to argue this. *Warm and Tender,* which climaxes with an unimproveable version of

Bacharach-David's "Reach Out for Me," is a children's album of lullabies. *Back to Basics* contains minor pop-rock masterpieces like "Magic," the red-hot "A Little More Love," and "You're the One that I Want," the unhinged *Grease* rockabilly she cut with John Travolta. It ends with four country chart hits. *The Rumour* (1989), a deleted album produced by Davitt Sigerson, presents Newton-John once again as a country singer, with songs of mid-life reflection and a vocal approach that plays against her usual tonal flawlessness; it sold poorly but should be snapped up in bargain bins.

Newton-John was a pop icon during eras that, unlike the present, chose to belittle their pop icons. But it makes beautiful sense, in retrospect, that her worldview included some unforced country-pop. Newton-John's work on all fronts should continue to gain respect in the future.—J.H.

THE NITTY GRITTY DIRT BAND

★★★   Will the Circle Be Unbroken (EMI
         E22V-46589) 1972, 1986 ●
★★   The Best of the Nitty Gritty Dirt
         Band (EMI E21Y-46591) 1987
★★★   Twenty Years of Dirt: The Best of the
         Nitty Gritty Dirt Band (Warner Bros.
         9 25382-2) 1986
★★   Hold On (Warner Bros. 25573-2)
         1987
★★   Workin' Band (Warner Bros. 25722-
         2) 1988
★★   More Great Dirt: The Best of, Vol. 2
         (Warner Bros. 25830-2) 1989
★½   Will the Circle Be Unbroken, Vol. 2
         (Universal ULVD-12500) 1989
★½   The Rest of the Dream (MCA MCAD-
         6407) 1990
★★   Greatest Hits (Curb D21K-77357)
         1990
★★   Live Two Five Anniversary Package
         (Liberty C21Z-93128) 1991
★★   Not Fade Away (Liberty C21S-
         98564) 1992

Formed in the late Sixties, the Nitty Gritty Dirt Band is a country-rock outfit with strong ties to L.A.'s singer-songwriters of the Seventies (Jackson Browne was once a member; Linda Ronstadt has sung back-up vocals). The Dirt Band is best-known for two things: its lissome version of Jerry Jeff Walker's "Mr. Bojangles," which crossed over to

become a Top Ten pop hit in 1970, and *Will the Circle Be Unbroken,* the group's 1972 triple-record set (remember records?). *Will the Circle* was hailed at the time as a ground-breaking effort that bridged the country generation-gap, with the likes of Mother Maybelle Carter, Earl Scruggs, and Roy Acuff performing alongside these nonthreatening long-hairs; today, *Will the Circle* sounds merely quaint and well-intentioned. It wasn't until the mid-Eighties that the group shook its hippie-rockers-dabbling-in-country image sufficiently to become country-radio regulars with hit singles such as Rodney Crowell's "Long Hard Road (The Sharecropper's Dream)," "Modern Day Romance," and "Fishin' in the Dark." If *Will the Circle Be Unbroken, Vol. 2* shows how creatively bankrupt they can be—ripping off their own concept a decade later with lesser stars and lesser material, yet scoring a media coup nonetheless—*Twenty Years of Dirt* captures their skillful, utterly inconsequential music perfectly.—K.T.

NORMALTOWN FLYERS

★★   Normaltown Flyers (Mercury 848
         369-2) 1991
★★½   Country Boy's Dream (Mercury 314-
         512 247-2) 1992

Athens, Georgia, is better known as home to rock bands R.E.M. and the B-52s than as an incubator for country music bands. But this veteran college town trio has entertained the tweed-and-sandals crowd for more than a decade with home-grown compositions that tilt to the rock side of contemporary country.

While the group's first album suffers from tedious songwriting wrapped in arrangements that rock harder than they twang, *Country Boy's Dream* offers a more mature, acoustic production with fiddle, mandolin, and pedal steel at the fore. Unfortunately, the more compelling compositions are less than originally inspired. "This World Doesn't Turn for Me," a wizened if fatalistic take on life's burdens and woes, derives from early Springsteen, while the soft, mellow harmonies on "Anymore Than I Do" betray the band's roots in the Eagles and the Byrds.—J.B.

THE NOTTING HILLBILLIES
★★★ **Missing . . . Presumed Having a Good Time (Warner Bros. 26147-2) 1990**

Mark Knopfler, the creative leader behind Dire Straits, occasionally has shown a distant country influence in some of his songwriting, and his guitar work always has drawn upon the tasty, single-note stylings of Nashville studio pros, an inclination he later underscored in his duets with Chet Atkins.

With the Notting Hillbillies, Knopfler and a trio of like-minded British musicians—guitarist-vocalists Brendan Croker and Steve Phillips and keyboardist Guy Fletcher—fully indulge their love for old-time American roots music (with some help from Nashville-based pedal steel specialist Paul Franklin). The results are somewhat mixed. Though the musicianship is impeccable, the sessions are so low-key and relaxed that these Hillbillies sometimes seem on the verge of nodding off. Also, the band's reverence tends to drain the life from an extensive list of covers, turning vital songs by the Louvin Brothers ("Weapon of Prayer"), the Delmore Brothers ("Blues Stay Away from Me"), and Charlie Rich ("Feel Like Going Home") into listless history lessons. The original songs fare somewhat better.—M.M.

GARY P. NUNN
★★ **For Old Times Sake (A.O. AO-0001) 1989**

A honky-tonk favorite in his native Texas, Nunn is best known to the world at large for his Seventies stint in Jerry Jeff Walker's Lost Gonzo Band and for his writing of "London Homesick Blues" (the theme for the "Austin City Limits" PBS television series). This album mixes novelty numbers such as "Cut and Putt" (about Willie Nelson's recording studio/golf course combine), "Pickup Truck, Texas," and a reggae reworking of "London Homesick Blues" with warm-and-fuzzy reminiscences of favorite uncles and granddads playing dominos. Though the material might inspire a rousing sing along at some roadhouse's last call, its appeal on album wears as thin as Nunn's voice. —D. McL.

THE OAK RIDGE BOYS

★★★½ The Best of the Oak Ridge Boys (Columbia CK 35302) 1978

★★★½ Y'All Come Back Saloon (MCA MCAD-31084) 1977

★★★ Room Service (MCA MCAD-31113) 1978

★★★ The Oak Ridge Boys Have Arrived (MCA MCAD-31114) 1979

★★★ Together (MCA MCAD-31112) 1980

★★★ Greatest Hits, Vol. 1 (MCA MCAD-5150) 1980

★★½ Fancy Free (MCA MCAD-5209) 1981 ●

★★½ Bobbie Sue/Step On Out (MCA MCAD-5922) 1982 ●

★★ American Made (MCA MCAD-31126) 1983

★★½ Greatest Hits Vol. 2 (MCA MCAD-5496) 1984

★★½ Deliver (MCA MCAD-31125) 1985 ●

★★★ Oak Ridge Boys Christmas (MCA MCAD-5365) 1985 ●

★★½ Christmas Again (MCA MCAD-5799) 1986

★★½ Where the Fast Lane Ends (MCA MCAD-31301) 1987

★★★½ Monongahela (MCA MCAD-42205) 1988

★★ Greatest Hits, Vol. 3 (MCA MCAD-42294) 1989

★★★ American Dreams (MCA MCAD-42311) 1989

★★½ Unstoppable (RCA 3023-2-R) 1991

★★★½ The Long Haul (RCA 66004-2) 1992

Like the Statler Brothers before them, the Oak Ridge Boys successfully crossed over from gospel to mainstream country in the late 1970s. For the better part of a decade this quartet sustained immense popularity with its infectious, crowd-pleasing brand of country-pop which was fashioned from four-part gospel-style harmonies, retooled 1950s doo-wop, and a high-energy, entertainment-for-all-ages approach to record making. Frequently—with mixed success—the Oaks attempted to hitch a ride on the crossover wagon with good-timey remakes of Fifties hits like "So Fine," or clones of the same like "Bobbie Sue." Gradually, though, the Oaks' steadfast formula, which sounds so fresh and exhilarating on early albums like *Y'all Come Back Saloon* (1977), *Room Service* (1978), and *The Oak Ridge Boys Have Arrived* (1979), began to grow tired and hackneyed. By the time veteran member William Lee Golden officially departed the quartet in 1987, the group had sunk into a creative quagmire. Golden was replaced by Steve Sanders, a gifted singer who was promoted up to full-fledged membership in the quartet after playing rhythm guitar in their road band for several years. This led the group into a period of rejuvenation with inspired late efforts like *Heartbeat* (not on CD) and *Monongahela.* Ironically, *The Long Haul,* the Oaks' malappropriately titled swan song album for RCA, was a fine piece of work, even if it didn't capture country audiences.

The Oaks are extremely well represented on CD; nearly all of the dozen or so MCA albums (some of them memorable, some eminently forgettable) they recorded between between 1977 and 1990 are currently available, as are their two RCA discs. The many commercial high points of the Oaks' twelve-year tenure on MCA have been condensed into three meager compilations: *Greatest Hits, Vols.1-3.* Of these anthologies (none of which contains more than eleven cuts), *Vol. 1* best showcases the group at its creative prime. *Vol. 2* offers a worthwhile sampling of their fair-to-middlin' output in the early and mid-1980s, while *Vol. 3* is so patchy that it's padded out with a few nonhits, along with "Bobbie Sue," one of the group's monster hits, which, chronologically, really belongs on *Vol. 1* or *2. The Best of the Oak Ridge Boys* showcases the Oaks in an earlier, more steadfast gospel mode. These obscure cuts (recorded 1973-78) actually sparkle more than many of their later and far more commercially successful MCA recordings. What's sorely missing from the Oaks' extensive CD catalogue is one cohesive retrospective package that skims off the cream of their peak years with MCA.—B.A.

TIM O'BRIEN

★★★½	**Hard Year Blues (Flying Fish FF-70319) 1985**
★★★★★	**[& Mollie O'Brien] Take Me Back (Sugar Hill SHCD-3766) 1988**
★★★½	**Odd Man In (Sugar Hill SHCD 3790) 1991**
★★★½	**[& Mollie O'Brien] Remember Me (Sugar Hill SHCD-3804) 1992**
★★★★★	**[& the O'Boys] Oh Boy! O'Boy! (Sugar Hill SHCD-3808) 1993**

Tim O'Brien was a long-time member of the progressive bluegrass band Hot Rize before he left the group to attempt a solo career in country music. Thus far, his songs have found their way to country radio most frequently via Kathy Mattea,

who has had hits with "Walk the Way the Wind Blows" and "Untold Stories."

Eclectic is the word that best sums up *Hard Year Blues.* Supported by his buddies from Hot Rize, and by Buck White on piano and Jerry Douglas on lap steel, O'Brien tackles honky-tonk standards ("Good Deal Lucille," "Honky Tonk Hardwood Floor"), country gospel ("Cabin in Gloryland"), bluegrass ("Cora Is Gone"), and demonstrates his instrumental virtuosity throughout the album, most notably on his own tune, the Celtic-sounding "The High Road," where he is the whole show with mandolin, fiddle, and guitar.

Odd Man In marked O'Brien's debut as a solo entertainer independent of the Hot Rize band. It lacks the variety of *Hard Year Blues,* but its music is no less brilliantly performed. He sings two traditional songs, the confessional murder ballad "Flora, the Lily of the West," and a gently rocking version of "Handsome Molly," complete with electric guitar and a Cajun-sounding accordion. The real strength of the album, though, is the material written by O'Brien. He has demonstrated elsewhere that he can write commercial mainstream country songs, but with items like "One Way Street," "Circles around You," "Like I Used to Do," and "Lone Tree Standing," O'Brien projects a sensibility much like that of such folk-rock musicians as Gordon Lightfoot, James Taylor, and Jackson Browne. These songs evocatively conjure up vivid associations of intimacy, loss, longing, and self-absorbed restlessness.

Tastefully chosen songs and beautifully crafted harmonies characterize O'Brien's two collaborations with his sister. Mollie O'Brien has a remarkably supple voice and, like her brother, a sensitive feel for widely divergent genres of music. True to its title, *Take Me Back* harks back to the traditional and is totally acoustic. The material here ranges from black gospel to Tin Pan Alley to the songs of George Jones and Lefty Frizzell. Nevertheless, the O'Briens sound most inspired on the collection's newest song, John Prine's powerful and timely "Unwed Fathers."

On *Remember Me* the singing remains strong and versatile, but traditional songs are fewer, with the material more heavily weighted toward contemporary pop and rhythm & blues tunes like "That's the Way to Treat Your Woman." Consequently, some long-time followers may be a bit disappointed. I suspect, however, that most fans of Tim and Mollie O'Brien share their eclecticism and will respond positively to new masterpieces like "Floods of South Dakota" and the tender "Hush While the Little Ones Sleep."

O'Brien is at his eclectic and acoustic best in *Oh Boy! O'Boy!*, ranging freely and easily from traditional fiddle pieces and ballads to contemporary material written by himself and others. Old-time fans may prefer the traditional songs, "Run Mountain," "The Farmer's Cursed Wife," and "He Had a Long Chain On," which receive tasteful and compelling treatments. The best song on the collection, though, is the haunting and sensitively performed "Time to Learn," an O'Brien-Pat Alger original that confronts death and the need to accept that solemn and "strange finality."
—B.C.M.

MAURA O'CONNELL

★★★★ Helpless Heart (Warner Bros. 26016-2) 1989
★★★★ Just in Time (Philo PH-1124) 1988
★★★★ A Real Life Story (Warner Bros. 26342) 1990
★★★★★ Blue Is the Colour of Hope (Warner Bros. 45063) 1992

Maura O'Connell deserves to be recognized among the best vocalists and song interpreters working in the realm of popular music in the 1990s. A superbly honest and unaffected stylist, she chooses songs that seem genuinely to affect her emotionally, and she conveys the power she finds in the lyrics with brilliant, subtly dramatic artistry. That she isn't more widely known probably is a result of her independent vision. In an era of strict musical categorization, O'Connell is staunchly eclectic; her song selection and arrangements have nothing to do with what's trendy and everything to do with what works best for communicating the emotional center of a well-written lyric.

A native of Ireland, she first traveled to America as a singer with the Irish traditional group DeDanaan. She connected with a few outstanding Nashville-based acoustic musicians, including banjoist Bela Fleck and dobroist Jerry Douglas. Fleck produced her first solo album, *Western Highway,* for an Irish record label, Raglan, and it later became her 1989 Warner Bros. debut, *Helpless Heart.* The album set in motion O'Connell's itinerary. She brings together songs by writers of seemingly divergent styles and skillfully demonstrates how a good lyric is a good lyric, no matter where or when it was written or how it was originally performed. *Helpless Heart* features songs by Californian Karla Bonoff, Texan Nanci Griffith, Irish folk-rocker Paul Brady, British singer Linda Thompson, New Englander Cheryl Wheeler, and such little-known talents as Irishmen Charlie McGettigan and Henry Hipkins and Nashvillian Roger Brown.

Just in Time, also produced by Fleck, was actually O'Connell's American debut, coming out a year prior to her Warner Bros. reissue. It's the most wildly varied of her albums, blending everything from the Beatles ("I Will") to Edith Piaf ("If You Love Me") to traditional Irish ballads to an ancient Dixieland standard ("New Orleans"). The album features one of her crowning achievements, an unforgettable version of a Paul Brady song, "Crazy Dreams."

With *Real Life Story,* her first full-fledged studio production after signing with Warners, O'Connell makes a greater attempt at thematic consistency. Producer Greg Penny (k.d. lang, Rickie Lee Jones) nudges her on occasion into a more modern, synthesized, syncopated sound, but O'Connell's timeless qualities, her discerning taste, and her dead-center emotionalism remain intact, and the collection comes across as alternately grand and intimate. This time, there are works by John Hiatt, Shawn Colvin, Tom Waits, Janis Ian, Hugh Prestwood, newcomer Greg Trooper, and choice Lennon-McCartney.

With her fourth album, *Blue Is the Colour of Hope,* O'Connell weaves a flawless classic. Working with long-time collaborator Jerry Douglas as her producer, it's a thoroughly impassioned album that blends strength with pain, boldness with tenderness, and joy with loss. Unlike her previous albums, it never sounds like a throwback to another era, nor does it strain for a modern edge. It's relaxed, natural, and as powerful as it gets.—M.M.

MARK O'CONNOR

★★★½ Championship Years (Country Music Foundation CMF-015D) 1990
★★★ Retrospective (Rounder CD-11507) 1987
★★ Stone From Which the Arch Was Made (Warner Bros. 25539-2) 1987
★★½ Elysian Forest (Warner Bros. 25736-2) 1988
★★½ On the Mark (Warner Bros. 25970-2) 1989
★★★★ New Nashville Cats (Warner Bros. 9 26509-2) 1991

Mark O'Connor is one of those rare musicians who can play the living daylights out of just about any instrument he picks up. By the age of twelve, O'Connor was blowing veterans twice his age off stages at fiddle competitions across the country. Hand him a guitar, and he's a flatpicking wildman. Now in his thirties, the fiddle whiz made a living during the Eighties as a top-dog Nashville session player, before "retiring" from that lucrative trade in 1991 to make *New Nashville Cats,* a return to his roots and the best record of his career. The album's guest list includes virtually all of O'Connor's famous Music City pals. On his other Warner Bros. releases, he seems intent on shaking his just-a-hot-fiddler image. *Stone From Which the Arch Was Made* and *Elysian Forest* both find O'Connor and friends on somewhat shaky middle ground in a new age/jazz fusion (O'Connor also made a few records in the rock/jazz vein in the early Eighties, as a member of Steve Morse's Dixie Dregs). The one available Rounder release features O'Connor in his over-the-top bluegrass mode, while the CMF's *Championship Years* CD is an excellent overview of the prodigy busting loose in his adolescent, fiddle-contest prime. —P.Cr.

THE O'KANES

★★★ O'Kanes (Columbia CK 40459) 1986
★★★ Tired of the Runnin' (Columbia CK 44066) 1988
★★½ Imagine That (Columbia CK 45131) 1990

Songwriters Jamie O'Hara, from Ohio, and Kieran Kane, from New York, formed the O'Kanes in the late Eighties and scored a half-dozen Top Ten hit singles with their cross between the Monroe Brothers and the Everly Brothers: tight-harmonied, uncluttered new traditionalism with a rock sensibility ("Oh Darlin'," "Can't Stop My Heart from Loving You," "Blue Love"). Their beautiful-sounding fatalism had a tinge of "thirtysomething" self-pity; perhaps fed up by this quality in their music, they broke up in 1990.—K.T.

ROY ORBISON

★★★ The Sun Years (Rhino R2-70916) 1989
★★ Lonely and Blue (Monument A-21427) 1960
★★ Crying (Monument A-21428) 1962
★★ In Dreams (Monument A-21429) 1963
★★ Our Love Song (Monument AK-45113) 1989
★★★★ Legendary Roy Orbison, Vols. 1-4 (CBS Special Products A4K 46809) 1990
★★★★★ All Time Greatest Hits of Roy Orbison, Vols. 1-2 (CBS Special Products AGK 45116) 1989 ●
★★★★½ For the Lonely: A Roy Orbison Anthology (Rhino; R2-71493) 1988
★★★★ The Classic Roy Orbison (Rhino R2-70711) 1966, 1989
★★ Rare Orbison (Monument AK-45115) 1989
★★ Rare Orbison II (CBS Special Products AK-45404) 1990
★★★ Best of His Rare Classics (Curb/CEMA C21K-77481) 1991
★★ Best Loved Standards (CBS Special Products AK 45114) 1989
★★ Ride Away (Polygram Special Products 847-983-2) N. D.
★★★ The Singles Collection (Polydor 839234) 1989
★ Laminar Flow (Elektra 198-2) 1979
★★★★★ In Dreams (Virgin 90604-2) 1987 ●
★★★ Mystery Girl (Virgin 91058-2) 1989 ▲
★★★ Mystery Girl (Mobile Fidelity UDCD-01-00555) 1991
★★★ A Black and White Night (Virgin 91295-2) 1989

★★★ **King of Hearts (Virgin V2 86520) 1992**

For someone who lived and recorded in Nashville during most of his productive years, who made his records with the best Nashville Cats, who was a mainstay of the country music publishing giant Acuff-Rose, who lived next door to Johnny Cash and was close to most prominent country artists, and whose only Grammy during his life came for a country duet (with Emmylou Harris), Roy Orbison transcended categorization. He was, in the main, a brilliant ballad singer whose career was marked by a series of dramatic starts and stops, reflected in an uneven array of sometimes overlapping, sometimes repetitive, sometimes deficient CDs.

He was a reluctant rockabilly in his early days on Sun Records and was later furious when Sun's Sam Phillips released an album's worth of songs on him, some still unfinished. Those can be heard in Orbison's still-tentative vocal style on *The Sun Years*. Roy, then as always, thought of himself as a pop artist, for better or for worse.

That vision reached fruition quickly in his whirlwind years with Monument, when Orbison was one of the few American acts to successfully challenge the Beatles. His hits from that era, from "Only the Lonely" in 1960 to 1964's "Oh Pretty Woman," are gathered on CBS's two ten-cut discs *The All Time Greatest Hits* and Rhino's sixteen-cut *For the Lonely*. The scope of his work in those years is breathtaking. He defined and redefined the modern country-rock ballad and took the genre in directions no one expected. He thought it would never end.

Roy left Monument for MGM Records, for which he made some memorable as well as eminently forgettable recordings. Many of the good ones, alas, have never received their due. He was, it is easy to see with the benefit of hindsight, a singles artist who quickly became lost in the emerging album era. *The Classic Roy Orbison* includes such overlooked MGM cuts as "Ride Away," "Crawling Back," and "Breakin' Up Is Breakin' My Heart."

After leaving MGM, Orbison languished in a slough of ill-conceived singles and albums, best illustrated by the wretched *Laminar Flow*, a forced disco outing. Until his comeback on Virgin records in 1987, he was without a record label. His genius had always lain in the operatic two-and-a-half-minute song drama, and he made a superb re-recording of those hits with *In Dreams* for Virgin. His last works were for Virgin: *Mystery Girl*, while uneven, shows that his vocal talents remained undiminished and his writing skills were beginning to return in full force. *King of Hearts*, collected and released posthumously, lacks a sense of unity that Orbison would have undoubtedly sought to apply.

His two attempts at recording pure country albums are not available on CD, perhaps because the results are very mixed. *Roy Orbison Sings Don Gibson* (1967) mostly works well (two of the cuts are on the CD *Best Loved Standards*, and one is on *The Classic Roy Orbison* CD). But 1971's *Hank Williams: The Roy Orbison Way* is mainly a morbid curiosity. Orbison obviously felt some affinity with his friend and contemporary Gibson but clearly had none for the late Williams. Both albums were recorded at the insistence of Roy's manager Wesley Rose, and all the songs were Acuff-Rose copyrights. Even so, true Orbison fans would be fascinated by his approach to what he considered straight country.

The Orbison boxed CD set—*Legendary Roy Orbison*—is indeed big, but it may well be more than most Orbison fans need. A few obscure works go a very long way.—C.F.

ROBERT ELLIS ORRALL
★★★½ **Flying Colors (RCA 66090-2) 1993**
An erstwhile pop singer and veteran songwriter whose "Next to You, Next to Me" was a #1 single for Shenandoah, Orrall's country music debut pulses with buoyant enthusiasm and jubilant charm. His spirited vocal style, which straddles the fluid lyricism of Jonathan Edwards and the breathy soulfulness of former Exile member Les Taylor, is the perfect vehicle for his jaunty, optimistic songs of family and relationships, of loss and renewal.—J.B.

THE OSBORNE BROTHERS
★★★½ **From Rocky Top to Muddy Bottom (CMH CD-9008) 1977, 1991**
★★★½ **Bluegrass Collection (CMH CD-9011) 1978, 1989**

★★★½ **The Osborne Brothers and Mac Wiseman (CMH CD-9016) 1979, 1987**
★★★★ **Once More, Vols. 1 & 2 (Sugar Hill SH-CD-2203) 1991**
★★★ **Hillbilly Fever (CMH CD-6269) 1991**

The Osborne Brothers—Bobby and Sonny—have been working together since 1954 and on the Grand Ole Opry since 1965. During the Sixties they established their vocal trio, featuring Bobby's high tenor lead, as the best in bluegrass, and during the Seventies recognition of their vocal excellence spread through the world of country music, leading to an award as the CMA's Vocal Group of the Year for 1971. They always maintained a bluegrass oriented sound, anchored by Sonny's innovative banjo stylings and Bobby's underrated mandolin, but between 1965 and 1975 they worked at blending it with mainstream country. The result was a string of chart hits on Decca/MCA, the most memorable of which was "Rocky Top" in 1968. Incredibly, none of those Decca/MCA recordings are presently available, and only a few of their earlier (1956-62) MGM originals can be heard on a Mercury anthology reviewed elsewhere (see Various Artists, *Best of Bluegrass, Vol. 1*).

Once More, Vols. 1 & 2, combining two LPs made in the mid-Eighties, reprises some of their favorite numbers from the Decca years. The instrumental sound is more purely bluegrass than was heard on the original recordings, many of which included drums, electric bass, piano, steel guitar and, in some cases, Bobby and Sonny's electrified mandolin and banjo (heresy to bluegrass purists at the time). If the sound is somewhat different, the feeling is much the same, and strong trio harmonies remain at the heart of the music. You won't find their biggies like "Ruby" and "Rocky Top" on here, but quality of the material is uniformly high. With twenty-four tracks, this is a bargain, probably the best choice if you're going to have just one recording by this trend-setting group.

From Rocky Top to Muddy Bottom, the 1977 double album featuring twenty songs of Hall of Famers Boudleaux and Felice Bryant, does include "Rocky Top" and several of their other chart hits from the Seventies. And it is the only CD with

the award-winning Osborne Brothers bluegrass-country sound from that era now available, with fine support from Buddy Emmons on steel, "Pig" Robbins on piano, and Ray Edenton on guitar. With Dale Sledd, who was with them on most of their hit recordings, singing the third part, this set has some memorable performances like the Everly Brothers classic "All I Have to Do Is Dream" and Jimmy Dickens's "Country Boy."

Bluegrass Collection, recorded in 1978, is a heartfelt and respectful (but not copycat: listen to their special twist to "Rank Stranger," for example) tribute to the pioneers of bluegrass with the songs of Bill Monroe, Flatt & Scruggs, and the Stanley Brothers, as well as remakes of some of the Osbornes' early numbers. Produced by Sonny (who also contributes the great liner notes), its twenty-four numbers feature a traditional bluegrass sound with twin fiddles by Blaine Sprouse and Kenny Baker; Benny Birchfield, who helped Bobby and Sonny perfect their trio back in the early Sixties, is singing with them on this one. Recorded in 1979, *The Osborne Brothers and Mac Wiseman* is a collaboration with one of bluegrass music's pioneer figures. This CD set adds two songs that were not included in the original release, but does not include the detailed information that was included in that release about who is singing and playing on the various cuts. The repertoire is dominated by material Wiseman originally recorded for Dot in the Fifties like "Shackles and Chains" and "I Wonder How the Old Folks Are at Home," with a number of strong duets by Wiseman and Bobby Osborne. Instrumentally, it is closer to *Bluegrass Collection*, but unlike that album, includes drums. *Hillbilly Fever*, with its in-joke cover—a close copy of Flatt and Scruggs's first Mercury album cover—is the Osbornes' latest recording. It contains quite a few older numbers like "Out behind the Barn," and "The First Fall of Snow," and a good version of "Orange Blossom Special."—N.V.R.

K. T. OSLIN

★★★½ **80's Ladies (RCA 2193-2-R) 1987 ▲**
★★★ **This Woman (RCA 8369-2-R) 1988 ▲**

★★ **Love in a Small Town (RCA 2365-2-R) 1990 ●**

★★★½ **Greatest Hits: Songs from an Aging Sex Bomb (RCA 66138) 1993**

All over America, divorced or single fortysomething women were sitting around talking about their diet plans, their dating habits, and their trouble in finding a decent single man. K. T. Oslin spoke to these women as if through their own telephones. *80's Ladies* was one of the first true blossomings of the modern country era: against a mellow and sophisticated backdrop of synthesizers and adult-contemporary tempos, Oslin, in her husky, confident voice, dramatized the plight of the single professional woman. "80's Ladies" traces three friends from girlhood to women's lib to motherhood; "Younger Men" demands just that.

On her two subsequent albums, Oslin continued to mine the same themes. *This Woman* makes more demands for equal rights for older women: "Round the Clock Lovin'," "Hold Me." The production, again, emphasizes the urban pop gloss of keyboards over gentle acoustic guitar. By *Love in a Small Town,* Oslin is running out of ways to describe lonely weekends and caloric intakes, resorting to a smooth cover of Mickey and Sylvia's "Love Is Strange," as well as re-recording a selection from her first album, "Two Hearts." —K.S.

MARIE OSMOND

★★ **The Best of Marie Osmond (Curb D2-77263) 1990**

For most country fans, Marie Osmond is a guilty pleasure at best, and no wonder. Her producers invariably surround her with a consort of synthesizers and strings that leaves her stranded uptown in the middle of the road, while her girlish singing seems able only to express perkiness and glee, never anything darker or more complex. Yet there is still that guilty pleasure of hearing her on just the right song, preferably singing harmony. Emmylou Harris she's not, but "Meet Me in Montana," her 1985 duet with sensitive big-guy Dan Seals was a little pop-country gem that justly deserved its #1 status. Similarly, the gushy "There's No Stopping Your Heart" (another #1 for her in '85) won't appeal to country purists, but Marie's cascading double-tracked harmonies on the chorus are nevertheless a thing of beauty, vapid though the sentiment may be.

And that's about as good as Marie's been. Both of those cuts are on this ten-track CD in their original form, along with her two other #1s, "You're Still New to Me" and "Paper Roses." The latter is not the teen heartbreak MGM original from 1973 (Marie's million selling debut at age thirteen), but a fairly faithful 1990 remake. Four tracks, brand new in 1990, have yet to become hits. Don't hold your breath.—P.K.

PAUL OVERSTREET

★★★ **Sowin' Love (RCA 9717-2-R) 1989**
★★★ **Heroes (RCA 2459-2R) 1990**
★★★ **Love Is Strong (RCA 07863-66019-2) 1992**

Paul Overstreet is blessed with one of the great country voices, an instrument with a natural cry, a soft nasality, and an earthy twang that makes him an enormously effective communicator. As if that weren't enough, he stands as one of the premiere songwriters on the contemporary country scene. And to gild the lily, his albums are brilliantly produced tapestries of sound.

His Achilles heel is his tendency to be monochromatic in his song themes. Overstreet repeatedly drives home the same messages on his albums—happy family, clean living, domestic bliss, positive images, Christianity, monogamy. His music has a seamless tone that seldom admits life's doubts, fears, anger, misery, or pain.

But like Emily Dickinson, he manages to explore an entire universe within his homey perimeters. *Sowin' Love* (1989) defined the territory with the gentle tunes "Richest Man on Earth," "Seein' My Father in Me," "All the Fun," "Love Helps Those," and its title tune. The distinctive Overstreet touch came to maturity on *Heroes* (1990). Who among us country fans has not turned up the snappy backbeat of "Daddy's Come Around," swayed to the languid "If I Could Bottle This Up," and sung along to "Ball & Chain"? On the same album, Overstreet campaigned for literacy with "Billy Can't Read" and spoke up for the common man on "Heroes." With *Love Is Strong* (1992) the award-winning tunesmith took on styles from pop-rock ("Me and My Baby") to swing ("Still Out There Swinging") and country-rock ("Take Another Run"), and demonstrated that his basic messages could still be explored without being worn out ("There But for the Grace of God Go I"). Perhaps because of his zealous religious convictions, Overstreet is often overlooked or dismissed by music critics. But he is steadily building a body of work that places him in the front ranks of American singer-songwriters.—R.K.O.

BUCK OWENS

★★★★★ **The Buck Owens Collection (Rhino R2 71016) 1992**
★★½ **Live at Carnegie Hall (Country Music Foundation CMF-012-D) 1988**
★★★★ **All Time Greatest Hits (Curb/ Capitol D2-77342) 1990**
★★★ **Hot Dog! (Capitol CDP 7 91132 2) 1988**
★★★½ **Act Naturally (Capitol CDP 7 92893 2) 1989**

Some may think of him as that cornball on "Hee Haw," but musicians from George Harrison to Dwight Yoakam know differently: Alvis Edgar "Buck" Owens Jr., born on a farm outside Sherman, Texas, in 1929, is one of the major fountainheads of modern country music, right up there with Cash and Haggard. Beginning in the bars of Bakersfield, California, in the mid-Fifties, he and his buddy Don Rich developed a whole new thing, a kind of rockabillified honky-tonk or, as he himself put it, a "plain old drivin' country sound with a hell of a beat and a bunch of twangy guitars. It begins with a four-beat bass, a heavy shuffle with a heavy afterbeat—kinda reminds me of a runaway locomotive."

He first hit the charts in March 1959 and didn't look back for fifteen years; at his peak he had no fewer than fifteen *consecutive* #1 country hits. But the death of his right-hand man, guitarist-harmony singer Don Rich, in 1974, disheartened him immensely, and although he kept recording for a while, the fire had left him. The fans, over-Bucked anyway by his weekly "Hee Haw" appearances, passed, and by the end of the decade his recording career was trashed. He quit and went into business, building himself a very successful little empire in radio and publishing.

There's no question which package best tells the story of his years at the top: the Rhino box. With sixty-two tracks taken from the original masters and a wonderfully comprehensive booklet, it actually does the man justice. The whole of Buck's range is here, from the great and sublime ("Cryin' Time," "Together Again," "Love's Gonna Live Here," "Streets of Bakersfield") to the great and semi-ridiculous ("Act Naturally," "Made in Japan," "I Wouldn't Live in New York City If They Gave Me the Whole Dang Town"). The Curb/Capitol collection is also just fine if all you want is (some of) the big hits. The CMF album, on the other hand, is really for fans only. Carnegie Hall is no Bakersfield bloodbucket (ah, for a live album from those days), and Buck was heavy on the ham that night, light on the music.

And now for the happy ending. In 1988, Dwight Yoakam revived Buck's recording career—walked into his Bakersfield office and flattered him into it—and so we have *Hot Dog* and *Act Naturally* (and, floating around the discount bins somewhere, 1991's out-of-print *Kickin' In*). A blend of new material and judicious remakes of his classics (notably "Crying Time" with Emmylou Harris, "Act Naturally" with Ringo Starr, and "Streets of Bakersfield" and "Under Your Spell Again" with Yoakam), this new work is pretty damn lively. You could argue that it's as good as his Sixties stuff. It's certainly better than most other people's Nineties stuff.—P.Ca.

DAVID PARMLEY

★★★★ **I Know a Good Thing (Sugar Hill SH-CD-3777) 1989**

This scion of the justly celebrated Bluegrass Cardinals displays vocals that are reminiscent of—but more animated than—Paul Overstreet's. However, the elements that make this country-bluegrass album such a standout are its strong songs (including "Have You Come to Say Goodbye," "Someone Took My Place with You," "Sometimes Silence Says It All," "From Cotton to Satin") and the stellar lineup of musicians and harmony vocalists, among them the Osborne Brothers, Carl Jackson, Rhonda Vincent, Bela Fleck, Stuart Duncan, Jim Vest, Edgar Meyer, and Bobby Hicks. —E.M.

LEE ROY PARNELL

★★★★½ **Lee Roy Parnell (Arista ARCD-8625) 1990**
★★★★ **Love without Mercy (Arista ARCD-18684-2) 1992**

Lee Roy Parnell's debut album was one of the most confident and spirited admixtures of country, rhythm & blues, Texas soul, and rock & roll since the vintage *Victim of Life's Circumstances* days of Delbert McClinton. Parnell won deserved acclaim not only for his searing, soulful singing and whiplash slide guitar style, but also for his fine songwriting. (Even so, "There Oughta Be a Law," the most memorable cut from that album was provided by Gary Nicholson and soul vet Dan Penn.)

Love without Mercy, the follow-up, was a project born of artistic conviction, yet grounded in compromise, due to country radio's reluctance to air Parnell's first set of tracks. Thus, the punchy horn arrangements of the debut are replaced by a more predictable steel guitar as Parnell leans just a little more heavily on tried and true Nashville songwriters like Russell Smith, Mike Reid, and Bob DiPiero for his material.

Yet even though *Love without Mercy* lacks a little of the toughness and swagger that Parnell flashed in his debut, it's still fairly aggressive, gritty stuff. True, the second album is a little heavier on ballads, but, to his credit, Parnell also takes care to pay back some Texas roadhouse dues by bringing on mentor Delbert McClinton for a sizzling rock & blues duet on the autobiographical "Road Scholar."—B.A.

GRAM PARSONS

★★★½ **Gram Parsons' International Submarine Band: Safe at Home (Shiloh 4088) 1968**

★★★★ GP/Grievous Angel (Reprise 9
26108-2) 1973/74
★★★ Gram Parsons and the Fallen
Angels Live (Sierra OXCD 6003)
1992

Enormously influential in the history of
country-rock, Gram Parsons, a son of the
South (Waycross, Georgia, and Jackson-
ville, Florida), wasted his life away on
drink and drugs in 1973, on the eve of
turning twenty-seven. When he could
stand, though, he could write some
deeply affecting songs ("Hickory Wind,"
"In My Hour of Darkness") and sing
them—along with an encyclopedia of
country standards—in a spare, but
emotional tenor that broke the way his
heart often did. In 1966, he welded
country with rock instruments and
attitudes in the International Submarine
Band (the album, featuring several
Nashville cats, is hard to find but is a
gem). Parsons joined the Byrds and
pushed them into country, formed the
Flying Burrito Brothers, and brought
Emmylou Harris to the fore as his
partner in a series of stunning duets,
most of them captured on *GP/Grievous
Angel*, a set of his two solo albums.

To get the full range of Parsons's
work, we'd need a compilation including
out-takes of the Burritos doing pure
country and of the several duets with
Harris that were released, on vinyl, as
part of the Burritos' *Sleepless Nights* on
A&M; a couple of live tracks from the set
he and his touring band (including
Harris) did on Long Island's WLIR (the
entire broadcast is on the Sierra CD), a
few cuts from the Sub Band, and maybe a
track from his college-days folk group,
the Shilos. Actually, that CD exists. It's
called *Gram Parsons: Warm Evenings,
Pale Mornings, Bottled Blues,* on Raven
Records of Australia. This CD, along with
the Sub Band album and the WLIR live
album, is available in the U. S. through
Sierra Records, P.O. Box 5853, Pasadena,
CA 91117-0853, phone: 818-355-0181.
—B. F.-T.

DOLLY PARTON

★★★★ The World of Dolly Parton, Vol. 1
(Monument AK-44361) 1988
★★★★ The World of Dolly Parton, Vol. 2
(Monument AK-44362) 1988
★★★ Greatest Hits (RCA Victor
PCD14422) 1982 ▲

★★★ Great Pretender (RCA Victor PCD-
4940) 1984
★★★ [& Kenny Rogers] Once upon a
Christmas (RCA PCD1-5307-2)
1984
★★★ Collector's Series (RCA 6338-2-R)
1985
★★★ Best There Is (RCA Victor 6497-2)
1987
★★★ Best of, Vol. 3 (RCA 5706-2-R)
1987
★★★ Rainbow (Columbia CK-40968)
1987
★★★ White Limozeen (Columbia CK-
44384) 1989 ●
★★★ Home for Christmas (Columbia CK
46796) 1990
★★★ Eagle When She Flies (Columbia
CK-46882) 1991 ▲
★★★ Straight Talk (Holllywood
HR61303-2) 1992
★★★ Slow Dancing with the Moon
(Columbia CK 53199) 1993 ●

If there is a country artist more ill served
by her CD inventory than is Dolly Parton,
no name comes immediately to mind.
Granted, Dolly is not still churning out
such heartbreakingly beautiful and
haunting songs as "Coat of Many Colors,"
"Jolene," "Bargain Store" "Down from
Dover," "My Tennessee Mountain Home,"
and "Daddy Come and Get Me," but
that's still no reason to treat her backlog
of material as tainted goods.

If you judged Dolly Parton solely by
her CDs in print, you would conclude that
she is someone who once wrote a few
great songs—but so few that they overlap
on her many "greatest" and "best of"
CDs. And you would also conclude—
accurately, I'm afraid—that she no longer
makes great country albums. Furthermore, you would feel insulted to be
expected to buy CDs as short as some of
these "best ofs" are and as bare of
information and devoid of notes as these
are. Eight or nine songs and some nearly
blank paper do not a great CD make. She
is sadly overdue for a comprehensive box
set or compendium of her work. *The Best
There Is* CD is an adequate introduction
to some of her better work: it includes "9
to 5," "Here You Come Again," "Coat of
Many Colors," "I Will Always Love You,"
"But You Know I Love You," and
"Appalachian Memories" among others,
but it's still only a sketchy sampler. From
what's available, you might never know

that Parton is one of the most prolific and incisive country songwriters ever; or know that she was once one-half of the most intriguing duo in country music history; or learn that the other half of that duo was the redoubtable Porter Wagoner.

If you judged her only by what's available, you might conclude that her record company—and perhaps Dolly herself—was ashamed of her country past and now concentrated on a full-scale assault on the pop world. Her output since her conscious decision to cross over to pop music in the late Seventies has been erratic, with occasional glimpses of the old Dolly. *Eagle When She Flies* is good—but uneven—Dolly, as are *Rainbow* and *White Limozeen*. As with her latest, *Slow Dancing with the Moon,* there is a certain predictability to the formula: all-too-brief flashes of Dolly's writing, a self-consciously quasi-naughty song or two, a pop chestnut, a tearjerker or two, and a gospel closer. And, on the *Slow Dancing* CD, trendy dueting with Billy Ray Cyrus. Trendiness does not become her.

The two Monument *World of* CDs are faithful reissues of her earliest work, and, as such, are true time capsules. And, as for the *Trio* album with Linda Ronstadt and Emmylou Harris, (see entry at Harris) it would be hard to ruin that fine album. Which is more than can be said for the general treatment accorded Dolly's body of music.

P.S.: At presstime, RCA released a two-CD boxed set, called *The RCA Years, 1967-1986.* The announced song selections indicate that it will be a cursory Parton history, ranging from 1972's "The Letter" to the obligatory "Jolene" and to her duets with Kenny Rogers. All of the material has been previously released on other albums. It's a start, anyway.—C.F.

WAYLAND PATTON
★★ **Gulf Stream Dreamin' (Capitol Nashville CDP 7 93872 2) 1991**

Patton looks good on paper. He's a successful Nashville songwriter who's supplied peppy hits for Ricky Skaggs ("Something in My Heart") and Dwight Yoakam ("Turn It On, Turn It Up, Turn Me Loose"). He also used to be in Skaggs's band during that singer's mid-Eighties glory days. Too bad, then, that only the high-minded tone of Ricky's recent fare seems to have rubbed off on

Patton. Sounding like an exceedingly gentle disciple of James Taylor, Patton dispenses thinly veiled moral instruction disguised as contemporary country. The sermonettes run the gamut from Love Thy Neighbor ("Fellow Travelers"), to Prepare Ye the Way ("We Should Only Have Time for Love"), to Don't Get Above Your Raisin' ("One Horse Town"). Performances this slick and tidy make Paul Overstreet sound like a gritty realist.—P.K.

JOHNNY PAYCHECK
★★ **20 Greatest Hits (Deluxe DCD-7799) 1986**
★★★ **Biggest Hits (Epic EK 38322) 1987**
★ **Golden Hits (Hollywood HCD 106) 1987**
★★ **Take This Job and Shove It (Richmond NCD-2300) 1988**
★★ **Country Spotlight (Dominion 30052) 1991**

Johnny Paycheck suffers the misfortune of being most noted for his least typical work. His 1977 global smash "Take This Job and Shove It" secured his spot in the country outlaw pantheon, but offered no indication of the scope of his talent. He recorded his best music ten years earlier for Little Darlin' Records, a Nashville independent that thrived on the unfettered energy and studio iconoclasm that has driven all the best indie labels. Paycheck's Little Darlin' output includes some of the most riotous, downright twisted honky-tonk music you'll ever hear—if you can find it. *20 Greatest Hits* and *Take This Job and Shove It* both contain several tracks that sound like Little Darlin' overdubs. One track, "Don't Monkey With Another Monkey's Monkey," is the real McCoy—a 90 m.p.h. romp complete with screaming steel and ersatz primate laughter in the background. No one else has cut such wickedly funny stuff.

Buyer beware, though. The rest of the Deluxe and Richmond discs (and all of the Hollywood disc) offer nothing but atrocious low-budget remakes of Paycheck's hits. They sound like they were recorded in some Nashville warehouse with Paycheck getting paid in cigarettes. The Dominion disc takes the same tack, but having been recorded immediately after Paycheck's 1991 prison release, it finds the singer well involved in the project. It isn't bad, if you're a hardcore fan.

Biggest Hits covers Paycheck's eleven-year tenure on Epic, with an unfortunate emphasis on his outlaw posturing of the late Seventies. The real "Take This Job and Shove It" is included, of course, though for all its infamy it doesn't bear repeated listening. A duet with Merle Haggard on "I Can't Hold Myself in Line" has the proper beer-and-sawdust buddy appeal ("Tell 'em we're gone, Hag"), and Paycheck sings the lamenting "Yesterday's News Just Hit Home Today" with real conviction. But there's too much outlaw muscle-flexing collected at the expense of more durable, straight-ahead numbers left off. Only Paycheck's irrepressible humor saves the gruesome recitation "Colorado Cool-Aid," the moral of which is: Don't spit beer in a stranger's ear if you're ever out drinking in Texas.

A word to the wise—a 1991 Paycheck release called *The Last Outlaw* is available from Air Records, but not on disc. It's worth tracking down the cassette for his duet with George Jones on the title cut, and especially for "Big Bad Mama (On a Harley Hawg)." ("She can kick-start an Amtrak train.") I'm telling you, no one else would have sung it.—D.C.

CARL PERKINS
★★★★★   Original Sun Greatest Hits (Rhino R2-75890) 1986
★★★★   Honky Tonk Gal: Rare & Unissued Sun Masters (Rounder CDSS 27) 1060
★★★   Whole Lotta Shakin' (Sony Music Special Products A-1234) 1958
★★★★   Restless: The Columbia Years (Sony Legacy CK 48896) 1992
★★★   Jive after Five: The Best of Carl Perkins (Rhino R2-70958) 1990
★★★   [with NRBQ] Boppin' the Blues (Columbia CK 09981) 1969

There are those among Carl Perkins's fans who adamantly maintain that he could have been bigger than Elvis but for fortune. He not only started in the same place at the same time blending the same primordial musics, but he also wrote some anthemic songs and defined the vernacular of rockabilly guitar. The problem was that Perkins could never shake off the hillbilly edge—it informs all that's best in his music, hanging

especially heavy over his Sun recordings. *Original Sun Greatest Hits* is five-star, USDA Grade A Rockabilly; only the *s* on the end of *Hits* is a little misleading—Perkins only had one greatest hit, "Blue Suede Shoes" in 1956. *Rare & Unissued Sun Masters* is rawer and rougher, highlighted by a gloriously bibulous version of Louis Jordan's "Caldonia." In 1958 Perkins quit Sun for Columbia in Nashville, where the looseness and naturalness were replaced by self-conscious effort. The first album, *Whole Lotta Shakin'*, was a recap of other peoples' hits dashed off too quickly. The best tracks are on *Restless,* which culls through the early and late Columbia periods, reducing the hundred or so titles to a solid eighteen. In 1969 Columbia paired Perkins with NRBQ, two acts they didn't know what to do with, and the results are uneven. A sample solo instrumental from the NRBQ sessions appears on *Jive after Five,* compiled from his sojourns among various labels—Columbia, Decca, Mercury—between 1958 and 1978. Get in tune with the rough-cut brilliance of the Sun recordings first, though.—C.E.

WEBB PIERCE
★★   The One and Only (King KCD 648) 1988
★★★½   Sweet Memories/Sands of Gold (Mobile Fidelity MFCD 750) 1993

Judging by the record charts, Webb Pierce was arguably the most popular country singer of the 1950s: eleven #1 hits, thirty-three other chart entries. He later became a parody both of himself and of the hillbilly arriviste. Artifacts like his rhinestone-studded Pontiac and guitar-shaped pool survive in memory better than his music, possibly because many of his original Fifties recordings were only on long discontinued LPs. In general, his greatest hits LPs contained remakes, and there hasn't been a domestic hits CD because MCA's country reissues have been tied to the Hall of Fame, and—inexplicably—Pierce hasn't been elected. So, to obtain his classic early Fifties recordings, with their glorious, soaring off-key vocals, one needs to buy a four-CD Bear Family import boxed set (*The Wondering Boy,* Bear Family BCD 15522), which can't really be judged an entry level item but is an essential piece of Fifties country music history. Mobile Fidelity's *Sweet Memories/Sands of Gold* couples two complete albums from 1963 and 1965, a period when Pierce's career was beginning its downslide. Hits are here ("Don't Let Me Cross Over," "Wolverton Mountain," "Please Help Me I'm Falling"), but most of them aren't Pierce's. Still, this is the only domestically available CD of Pierce at—or near—his peak. Mobile Fidelity's CDs can't be had for budget prices, but the clear, warm transfers match the elegance of Owen Bradley's production. *The One and Only* consists of pre-Decca recordings for the 4-Star label, some of which were fine but only assume importance in light of his later work. —C.E.

PINKARD & BOWDEN
★★★ Live (Warner Bros. 9 266057-2) 1989
★★½ Cousins, Cattle, and Other Love Stories (Warner Bros. 26844-2) 1992

Continuing in the long tradition of hillbilly jokers, Pinkard & Bowden bring country comedy into the modern era with their redneck raunch. Their schtick is something like a cross between Homer & Jethro and George Carlin. They combine standup routines with parodies of well-known songs ("Libyan on a Jet Plane") and original compositions ("The Fifties Suck") with hysterical results. As they point out in "Censor Us," their songs often contain explicit language, and *Cousins, Cattle, and Other Love Stories* proudly sports a parental advisory sticker on the cover. If you are easily offended by barnyard humor, these guys will offend you. On the other hand, if you are like me, you will find them very funny. Their live recordings capture the essence of their comedy better than their studio recordings, because much of what they do involves interaction with an audience. You may not want to play these for Mom. —C.H.S.

PIRATES OF THE MISSISSIPPI
★★★½ Pirates of the Mississippi (Capitol 94389) 1990
★★½ Walk the Plank (Capitol Nashville 95798) 1991

★★ A Street Man Named Desire (Liberty 98781) 1992

It *could* be just a coincidence that Pirates of the Mississippi debuted shortly after the Kentucky Headhunters proved the commercial viability of a country-rock band with a Southern-identified name— or it could be crass commercial cynicism of the lowest order. Since the Pirates' debut opens with a crackling update of Hank Williams's "Honky Tonk Blues," just as the Headhunters' debut opened with a crackling update of Bill Monroe's "Walk Softly on This Heart of Mine," evidence favors the conspiracy theory.

Still, as long as they keep the wheels spinning fast, the Pirates' playful, contained boogie is sparked by Rich Alves's Duane Allman-inspired guitar leads and a spry rhythm section. Bill McCorvey's sly, sexy rasp is perfectly suited to the group's Delta-pride lyrics, as well as merry Guy Clark covers like "I Take My Comfort in You" and "Too Much." Although the Pirates distinctive character quickly dissipated under Jimmy Bowen's production, the debut gets an extra half-star for the progressive tolerance anthem "Feed Jake," one of the few country songs to mention homosexuality, and a reminder to Hank Jr. fans that redneck rock needn't be swinish. —R.T.

POCO
★½   Poco (Epic EK 26522) 1969
★   Deliverin' (Epic EK 30209) 1971
★★½ From the Inside (Epic EK 30753) 1971
★★   A Good Feelin' to Know (Epic EK 33537) 1972
★★½ The Forgotten Trail 1969-74 (Epic/Legacy EZK 46162) 1990
★★½ The Very Best of Poco (Epic EK 33537) 1975
★★★ Head Over Heels (MCA MCAD 31327) 1975
★★   Indian Summer (MCA MCAD 31353) 1977
★★½ Legend (MCA MCAD 31019) 1978 ●
★½   Under the Gun (MCA MCAD 31334) 1980
★★★ Crazy Loving: The Best of Poco 1975-1982 (MCA MCAD 42323) 1989
★½   Legacy (RCA 9694) 1989 ●

An early country-rock franchise, Poco's first records star ex-Buffalo Springfield players Jim Messina and Richie Furay, who left in 1971 and 1973, respectively. This music is less notable for its relaxed inclusion of country and bluegrass idioms than for its unfocused Sixties-rock splatter. Poco introduces the vocal-harmony expanses that this band (unlike Crosby, Stills & Nash or even the Bee Gees) never made distinct. Nevertheless, the debut retains a vague classic-rock significance; the live *Deliverin'* is far worse. *From the Inside,* Poco's first coherent album, is produced by Steve Cropper with a relatively heavy blues sense, which helps; *A Good Feelin' to Know* and most of the rest of the *Very Best* collection aren't as well done. Both, however, communicate the basis of the group's cult appeal: a smoky festival of ideas, quasi-passionate songwriting, a kind of light hippie-country buzz.

The rest of the records offer different degrees of decently crafted country-rock without any of the Eagles' sense of consequence or vocal aggression. At their best, Poco throws off laid-back sparks and nice glows. *Head Over Heels* is their definitive Seventies album; it's neither sidetracked by confusion or beguiled by post-Seventies changes in both rock and country that throw the band. *Legend*'s "Crazy Love" was a dusky hit, and that album's atypical "The Last Goodbye" (not on the *Crazy Loving* compilation) works up the melodic ingredient that Poco, for all its atmosphere, usually lacks: drama. Epic/Legacy's lavish *The Forgotten Trail* tries to make a case for rock connoisseurs, with an emphasis on acoustic authenticity. *Crazy Loving* better documents the band's affinities for ordinary country pleasure with a haze of rock credibility.—J.H.

PRAIRIE OYSTER
★★½ **Different Kind of Fire (RCA 2049-20R) 1990**
★★★ **Everybody Knows (RCA 07863-61013-2) 1991**

During the course of its brief, two-album stint for RCA in the early 1990s, this competent but unspectacular six-piece country band from Toronto demonstrated both genuine affection and smooth adeptness at reviving classic western swing and honky-tonk styles. *Different Kind of Fire,* the band's first U.S. offering, was an appealing work, even if it

lacked the pyrotechnics implied in the title. Stylistically, it showcased this youthful ensemble's infatuation with Fifties and Sixties country music, which is served up with a bit of Seventies country-rock attitude that always seems once removed from its original sources. *Everybody Knows,* the follow-up album, finds the band moving more into the realm of straight-ahead honky-tonk. But here, as on the first album, Prairie Oyster's obvious enthusiasm for their chosen genre is hampered by lead singer Russell deCarle's mannered vocals and the band's stiff and derivative instrumental licks. Despite their enthusiasm, these Oysters lack the grit necessary to produce a pearl.—B.A.

ELVIS PRESLEY—THE FIFTIES
★★★★★ **The Complete Fifties Masters (RCA 07863-66050) 1992**
★★★★ **The Complete Sun Sessions (RCA 6414-2-R) 1987**
★★★★ **Elvis Presley (RCA PCD1-1254) 1956**
★★★★ **Elvis (RCA PCD1-1382) 1956 ●**
★★★★ **The Million Dollar Quartet (RCA 2023-1-R) 1990**
★★★ **Loving You (RCA 1515) 1957 ●**
★★★★ **Golden Records, Vol. 1 (RCA PCD-1-5197) 1957 ▲[5]**
★★★ **Christmas Album (RCA PCD-1-5486) 1957, 1985 ▲[2]**
★★★ **Essential Elvis: The First Movies (RCA 6738) 1989**
★★★ **Stereo '57 (RCA 9589) 1988**
★★★ **King Creole (RCA 3733-2-R) 1958**
★★★ **Essential Elvis, Vol. 3: Hits Like Never Before (RCA 2229-2-R) 1990**
★★★★ **50,000,000 Elvis Fans Can't Be Wrong: Elvis' Gold Records, Vol. 2 (RCA PCD1-5197-RE) 1959 ▲[2]**
★★★ **For LP Fans Only (RCA 1990) 1959**
★★★★ **A Date with Elvis (RCA 2011-2-R) 1959**
★★★★ **The Rocker (RCA PCD-1-5182) 1984**
★★★★ **Reconsider Baby (RCA 5418) 1985**
★★★ **Return of the Rocker (RCA 5600) 1986**
★★★★ **The Number One Hits (RCA 6382) 1988**

★★★★ **The Top 10 Hits (RCA 6383) 1988 ●**
★★★★ **Sings Leiber and Stoller (RCA 3026) 1991**
★★ **Heartbreak Hotel, Hound Dog, and Other Top 10 Hits (RCA 2079) 1990 ●**
★★ **Remembering (Pair PDC2-1037) 1991**

Unless you've been mapping ice floes in Antartica for the last forty years, you know who Elvis Presley was, what he did, and maybe even how many Percodans he popped after supper. His posthumous role as a cultural icon may yet usurp his importance as the premier rock & roller, but so much of his music has sunk into our collective unconscious that almost everyone knows where they stand in relation to it. That makes it easier to recommend a boxed set as an entry level item. *The Complete Fifties Masters* confounds the premise that boxed sets contain an unacceptable ratio of dross to gold. Four of the five CDs contain every one of Elvis's studio masters from the Fifties, and there's nary a dud. The Sun sides on CD 1 re-emphasize that for the first two years of his career (1954-55) Elvis was a hillbilly circuit rider—but his was hillbilly music with an attitude. The key to understanding it is to appreciate that Elvis had perhaps the most catholic taste of anyone around. Yes, he loved country and blues, but he also loved the pop opera of Mario Lanza, the gospel harmonies of the Golden Gate Quartet— and more besides. All of the Sun masters are on *The Complete '50s Masters,* but for those who can't get enough of Elvis's rise at Sun, there is also *The Complete Sun Sessions.* Included with the masters are six more takes of "I'm Left You're Right She's Gone," several other alternate takes, and some false starts, all of them revealing and, in their way, essential. Sound quality on *Complete Sun Sessions* is a hit or miss affair, though.

Of course, *The Complete '50s Masters* goes beyond November 1955—when Elvis took his leave of Sun Records for the greener pastures of RCA—and, in cut after remarkable cut, he reminds us why he left everyone all shook up. Six months into his RCA contract, Elvis was the biggest act in the company's history, and the more mainstream side of his multiple personality began to assert itself. The

hillbilly diction was gone, but enough of the rough edges remained to ensure that virtually every one of his pre-Army recordings (up to 1958) is a gem. The other reason for purchasing the boxed set as an entry-level item is that the sound is the best yet on any Elvis compilation. The CD reissues of Elvis's original albums let you hear his music as it was originally programmed, but the sound quality of albums like *For LP Fans Only* or *Golden Records, Vol. 1* is often subpar.

Other permutations of Elvis's Fifties masters abound. For an overview, *The Top 10 Hits* runs from "Heartbreak Hotel" to "Burning Love"; *The Number One Hits* is the abridged version, and *Heartbreak Hotel* is a moronic compilation of eight Fifties hits with a late Sixties photo slapped on front. *Elvis's Christmas Album* is notable for the first punk Christmas song ("Santa Claus Is Back in Town") sitting cheek-by-jowl with the usual seasonal favorites. Two other items worth singling out from the cornucopia of Elvis issues are *Stereo '57* and *The Million Dollar Quartet.* By no means is *Stereo '57* for the novice; it contains multiple outtakes of various songs Elvis cut on the West Coast in January 1957, but we get a feel for him taking charge in the studio. *The Million Dollar Quartet* has much the same atmosphere, cut four weeks earlier at the Sun studio when Elvis returned to check on his ol' pals of yesterday. He found Carl Perkins in session and couldn't resist the temptation to join in. Elvis, Perkins, and Jerry Lee Lewis (Perkins's pianist that day) pluck songs from their subconscious, fool around with them, and briskly move on. It all amounts to a primer on the creation of rock & roll. The title is a bit of a misnomer, though; it's really a $750,000 Trio. Johnny Cash was there that afternoon, but not when the tapes were rolling.

Early Elvis—not everyone's idea of country music, but essential to understanding what happened to it after '56 and essential on its own terms, too.—C.E.

ELVIS PRESLEY—THE SIXTIES, SEVENTIES, AND BEYOND

★★★★★ **Elvis Is Back! (RCA 2231-2-R) 1960**
★★★ **G.I. Blues (RCA 3735-2-R) 1960 ▲**

★★★★★ His Hand in Mine (RCA 1319-2-R) 1960, 1988 ▲

★★★ Something for Everybody (RCA 2370-2-R) 1961

★★ Blue Hawaii (RCA 3683-2-R) 1961 ▲²

★★★ Pot Luck with Elvis (RCA 2523-2-R) 1962

★★★ Kid Galahad/Girls! Girls! Girls! (RCA 07863-66130-2) 1962/1962, 1993

★★★ It Happened at the World's Fair / Fun in Acapulco (RCA 07863-66131-2) 1963/1963, 1993

★★★★★ Elvis' Golden Records, Vol. 3 (RCA 2765-2-R) 1963 ●

★★★ Viva Las Vegas/Roustabout (RCA 07863-66129-2) 1964/1964, 1993

★★ Harum Scarum/Girl Happy (RCA 07863-66128-2) 1965/1965, 1993

★★★ Elvis for Everyone (RCA 3450-2-R) 1965

★★★★★ How Great Thou Art (RCA 3758-2-R) 1966, 1988 ▲²

★★★ Elvis' Gold Records, Vol. 4 (RCA 1297-2-R) 1968 ●

★★★★★ Elvis: NBC-TV Special (RCA 07863-61021-2) 1969, 1991 ●

★★★★★ From Elvis in Memphis (RCA 07863-51456-2) 1969 ●

★★★★ On Stage: February 1970 (RCA 07863-54362-2) 1970 ●

★★★★★ Elvis: 50 Worldwide Gold Hits, Vol.1 Part 1 & Part 2 (RCA 6401-2-R) 1970 ▲²

★★★★★ Back in Memphis (RCA 07863 61081-2) 1970

★★★ Elvis—That's the Way It Is (Mobile Fidelity UDCD-560) 1970, 1993

★★★★★ Elvis Country (RCA 6330-2-R) 1971 ●

★★★ Love Letters from Elvis (RCA 4530) 1971

★★★★ Elvis Sings the Wonderful World of Christmas (RCA 4579-2-R) 1971 ▲²

★★★ Elvis Now (RCA 4671-2-R) 1972

★★★★ He Touched Me (RCA 07863-51923-2) 1971 ●

★★★ Elvis As Recorded at Madison Square Garden (RCA 07863-54776-2) 1972 ▲²

★★★ Promised Land (RCA 0873-2-R) 1975

★★★ Elvis Today (RCA 07863-51039-2) 1975

★★★★ From Elvis Presley Boulevard, Memphis, Tennessee (RCA 1506-2-R) 1976 ●

★★★ Welcome to My World (RCA APL1-2274) 1977

★★★ Moody Blue (RCA 2428-2-R) 1977 ▲²

★★ Elvis in Concert (RCA 07863-52587-2) 1977

★★★★ Elvis Gold Records, Vol. 5 (RCA PCD1-4941)1984

★★★ Always on My Mind (RCA PCD1-5430) 1985

★★★★ A Valentine Gift for You (RCA PCD1-5353) 1985

★★★★★ The Memphis Record (RCA 6221-2-R) 1987

★★★★ The Great Performances (RCA 2227-2-R) 1990

★★★★ Collector's Gold (RCA 3114-2-R) 1991

★★★ The Lost Album (RCA 07863-61024-2) 1991

★★★ Great Performances (Pair CXD-3018) 1989

When Elvis Presley left the Army March 5, 1960, the pop music world had changed almost as dramatically as his first Army haircut changed Presley's appearance in 1958. The power and energy of blues-based rock & roll—Presley's initial calling card—had given way to the softer sound of pop crooners such as Frankie Avalon, Bobby Vee, Fabian, and Bobby Darin.

Elvis Is Back, recorded in Nashville within weeks of Presley's discharge, seemed to signal his refusal to slide into the compromising pop style of singers who tried to fill his civilian shoes. The album served every musical taste, from steamy blues to rock & roll, pop to a gospel-ly ballad, and showed that Presley could out-croon the crooners ("The Girl of My Best Friend," "I Will Be Home Again"). Presley would put things right again, his rock & roll fans must have felt.

G.I. Blues, however, suggested otherwise. Rather than blues and original rock & roll songs, the sound track featured lightweight pop tunes composed by the New York-based songwriting teams who would supply material for Presley's movies in the Sixties.

Presley's next release, *His Hand in Mine*, marked a foray into the Southern gospel field that provided much of his early musical inspiration. Firmly planted within his own culture, Presley relished the opportunity to sing with the Jordanaires, and the results were magnificent. The CD reissue of *His Hand in Mine* contains three extra cuts taken from sessions in 1957, 1967, and 1969. The additions go unexplained, since RCA has reissued this classic album without additional liner notes.

"Starting Today," featuring Floyd Cramer's slip-note piano, and "I'm Comin' Home," written by Charlie Rich, are highlights of *Something for Everybody*, a Nashville album that finds Presley more comfortable in the non-rock & roll mode, and showing himself in tune with the mellower sounds of the day.

With *Blue Hawaii,* Presley more or less vanishes into the soupy mist of the Sixties movie sound tracks, from which he would not re-emerge until his 1968 TV special. Presley's rock & roll fans must have shed tears to hear him interpreting such bizarre, celluloid dreck as "Ito Eats," "Slicin' Sand," and "Beach Boy Blues."

Pot Luck with Elvis could have been titled more aptly "Crap Shoot with the King," since it collects twelve very uneven tracks, most of the easy-listening variety, from the parlor pop of "I'm Yours" to the cha-cha "Fountain of Love." "Suspicion," which would be a hit for Presley soundalike Terry Stafford, appears here for the first time.

RCA reissued four double sets of movie sound tracks in 1993, perhaps reasoning that quantity would compensate for quality. Some of the sound track material has not been available before on an album, and there are decent songs scattered about: "King of the Whole Wide World" from *Kid Galahad;* "Where Do You Come From" and "Return to Sender" from *Girls! Girls! Girls!;* "One Broken Heart for Sale" from *It Happened at the World's Fair;* and "Viva Las Vegas" from the movie of that name.

Elvis Golden Records, Vol. 3 gathered hit singles from '60 to '62, including "Little Sister," "Good Luck Charm," and "Anything That's Part of You" (but not "Can't Help Falling in Love"). *Elvis for Everyone,* another grab bag, followed just under two years later, with tracks dating from 1957 to 1965, and including songs

from the movies *Wild in the Country, Follow That Dream,* and *Viva Las Vegas,* an overdubbed Sun-era track ("Tomorrow Night") and a Hank Williams cover, "Your Cheatin' Heart."

Presley's first album with producer Felton Jarvis was the gospel collection *How Great Thou Art,* another mix of upbeat traditional numbers and Southern gospel standards. The record won Presley his only Grammy. RCA's CD reissue adds an extra cut, "Peace in the Valley," from 1957.

Because his recent recording had been limited mostly to film music, *Elvis' Gold Records, Vol. 4* patched together seven B-sides and five A-sides from 1958 to 1966. It was a better album than the movie sound tracks, but in an era dominated by Bob Dylan, the Beatles, and the Rolling Stones, *Gold Records, Vol. 4* sounded almost irrelevant.

Then came the famous TV special, recorded in June 1968 for broadcast that December. Producer-director Steve Binder prevailed in his wish to have Presley make a statement about his music, rather than fall back on a formulaic Christmas script. Presley rediscovered himself, raw and vital, tapping into blues, gospel, and rock & roll for an infusion of new energy. Because the show is now available on home video, it might make more sense to recommend the entire package, visuals and all, but the sound track, *Elvis: NBC-TV Special,* offered proof that Presley still deserved respect as an entertainer. The CD includes eight bonus tracks not included in the original show.

If his TV show proved Presley still a consummate showman, his January and February 1969 Memphis sessions, the first in his home city since his days on Sun, showed Presley could recapture the magic as a recording artist. All the songs on *From Elvis in Memphis* also appear on *The Memphis Record,* a 1987 reissue with new liner notes from Presley biographer Peter Guralnick. *Back in Memphis,* originally released as the *From Vegas to Memphis* half of a Presley double album, contains more '69 Memphis recordings.

On Stage: February 1970, was Presley's only live album featuring all new—for him—songs. It nevertheless contained fare that was no doubt familiar to the Vegas audiences at the International Hotel in August 1969 and February 1970—"Yesterday" and "Proud Mary," for instance.

Filmmakers documented Presley's return to live performance in Vegas with *That's the Way It Is,* released in December 1970. The movie provides a fascinating glimpse of an anxious Presley, rehearsing for his show, then performing at the International Hilton. The sound track, *Elvis—That's the Way It Is,* loses some punch without the accompanying visuals. Only four songs actually were recorded before a live audience.

Recorded during a marathon sesion in June 1970, *Elvis Country* succeeds in every way, right down to the cover, a photo of Presley taken during his Tupelo childhood. As its name implies, *Elvis Country* acknowledged Presley's cultural grounding in hillbilly music in the same way his gospel albums paid homage to his gospel roots. Not all the songs come from the distant past. Anne Murray's "Snowbird" opens the album, then Presley goes on to tunes asssociated with Ernest Tubb, Eddy Arnold, Jerry Lee Lewis, Stonewall Jackson, and Bill Monroe, among others. Excerpts from "I Was Born About Ten Thousand Years Ago" join the songs together. That song appeared later in its unified form on *Elvis Now.*

Collected in a box with a booklet of pictures, *50 Worldwide Gold Hits* took stock of Presley's career up to 1970. Inserts for the CD reissue contain only song title, writer, and recording date information—no annotations.

Presley returned to familiar pastures with *Elvis Sings the Wonderful World of Christmas,* another strong collection of traditional and original seasonal material. Likewise, *He Touched Me* contains some of Presley's strongest gospel performances, including the title track, "I John" and "Lead Me, Guide Me." The gospel collection comes from Presley's last visit to a Nashville studio, in June 1971. On the front of the CD booklet, in white letters that did not grace the original LP, RCA notes: "original album art," an irritating practice that shows up on several other Presley reissues.

His first New York concerts, June 9-11, 1972, at Madison Square Garden, formed the basis of a marketing ploy in which RCA recorded, manufactured, and rush-released in just two weeks *Elvis As Recorded at Madison Square Garden,* the June 10 evening performance. Many of the tracks were already available on other live recordings.

Aloha from Hawaii Via Satellite, Elvis, Raised on Rock, Elvis: A Legendary Performer, Vol. 1, Good Times, Recorded Live on Stage in Memphis, and *Having Fun with Elvis on Stage* are not currently available on CD. *Aloha* should be, and *Elvis* contains the edited version of Bob Dylan's "Don't Think Twice, It's All Right."

Recorded at Stax Studios in Memphis, *Promised Land* aimed at the country market and yielded two Top Ten country hits, "Help Me" (written by Larry Gatlin) and "It's Midnight." *Elvis Today* marked Presley's last official studio dates, March 10-13, 1975, at RCA's Hollywood studio. He leaned toward country again, with standout cuts including Troy Seals's "Pieces of My Life" and Curly Putman's "Green Green Grass of Home."

From Elvis Presley Boulevard, Memphis, Tennessee and *Moody Blue* are primarily from the Graceland sessions of 1976 and 1977 and have been maligned as pitiful products of Presley's final retreat from creative courage. *Elvis Presley Boulevard,* however, with its nearly unrelenting focus on disillusion and heartache, is a fascinating document, achieving a more noticeable blues feel— in mood more than in music—than most blues albums. *Moody Blue* was the last album released during Presley's lifetime. Because of his reluctance to record, it contains tracks from both the 1976 and 1977 Graceland sessions supplemented with live tracks from concerts in Memphis and Saginaw, Michigan.

Presley's death on August 16, 1977, and the surrounding hoopla created a Presleyana growth industry. RCA fed the market with boxed sets, new collections of rarities and hits, overdubbed "updates" of older tracks, thematic song groupings, even deceptively repackaged albums.

Not all the reissues have come out on compact disc. Among those that have is *Elvis' Gold Records, Vol. 5,* ten hits stretching from the 1969 Memphis sessions up to the 1976 Graceland dates. *A Valentine Gift for You* collects romantic ballads. *The Great Performances* is the sound track for two home videos documenting Presley's performing career and notable for the inclusion of "My Happiness," the recording he made at Sun for his mother in 1953.

The Lost Album gathers fifteen recordings from a non-sound-track Nashville session in April 1963. The songs originally trickled out as singles, b-sides, and sound track album filler. The three-disc *Collectors Gold* contains alternate takes from the Sixties.

RCA has announced plans to release boxed sets for Presley's work in the Sixties and Seventies, a laudable but more challenging undertaking than the compilation of the Fifties masters.—J.O.

RAY PRICE

★★★   Greatest Hits (Columbia CK 8866) 1961

★★★   American Originals (Columbia CK 45068) 1989

★★★★★   The Essential Ray Price: 1951-1962 (Columbia/Legacy CK 48532) 1991

★★★★   Happens to Be the Best (Pair PCD2-1044) 1983

★★   Portrait of a Singer (Step One Records SOR-0009) 1985

★★½   Greatest Hits, Vols. 1-3 (Step One Records SOR-0012/13/14) 1986

★★   A Revival of Old Time Singing (Step One Records SOR-0016) 1986

★   Heart of Country Music (Step One Records SOR-0019) 1987

★   Just Enough Love (Step One Records SOR-0033) 1988

★★   Greatest Hits, Vol. 4 (Step One Records SOR-0050) 1989

★★   Hall of Fame Series (Step One Records SOR-0069) 1991

★★½   Sometimes a Rose (Columbia CK 48980) 1992

Ray Price is one of country music's great enigmas. How do you account for a honky-tonk hero whose music shows the influence of Hank Williams, Bob Wills, and Tony Bennett—not necessarily in that order? Never mind influences, though; the end result is some of the most energized, enduring hillbilly dance hall music ever waxed. Of all the stars who made their names in the honky-tonk 1950s, Price is the one whose work has aged the best. You could program his "Crazy Arms" or "Invitation to the Blues" onto today's playlists and blow the back windows out of every bass-boosted Chevy truck in sight.

The desert island disc is the *The Essential Ray Price*—twenty tracks that cover a wild eleven-year stretch during which Price sought, found, and cemented a hard-swinging country style that emptied the kegs in every honky-tonk he played. The early cuts trace Price's artistic development away from being a talented imitator of Hank Williams and toward roadhouse genius. Included are his original version of the now-standard "Release Me," and "Wasted Words," which is rumored to have the great Ira Louvin on high tenor harmony. Halfway through the disc, one arrives at the unforgettable "Crazy Arms," the country song of the year for 1956 and the place where (Price has acknowledged) he found his unique sound. Driven by a then-rare 4/4 bass line, and with a fiddle and steel guitar running roughshod over every preconception of clichéd country accompaniment, "Crazy Arms" delivers with expansive force all the more amazing given it came when country music was quailing before the gale-force rock & roll blowing out of Memphis.

Price spent the next six years fine-tuning his sound—adding a vibrant shuffle rhythm, in particular—and broadening the scope of his legendary tenor vocals. The last ten cuts on *The Essential Ray Price* (and most of Columbia's *Greatest Hits,* though at considerable loss in fidelity) cover the period when Price and his Cherokee Cowboys just about owned the two-steppin' barns and beer joints of America. Bob Wills may still be the king, but on cuts like "City Lights" and "Heart over Mind," you can hear what a worthy prince Ray Price has always been.

Now let's talk about Tony Bennett. Price's sound was slowing down and softening by the early 1960s. Though his old fans should have seen it coming, his string-sweetened 1967 version of "Danny Boy" was greeted with nothing less than hillbilly horror. Despite country radio silence, "Danny Boy" sold a lot of records—a lesson driven home for Price when his black-tie version of "For the Good Times" hit #11 on the pop charts in

1970. "For the Good Times" shows up on *American Originals* and *Happens to Be the Best,* both of which are recommended, with caution, to anyone looking to supplement *The Essential Ray Price.* The Pair disc is gangs of fun—sixteen tracks apparently selected and sequenced by an escapee from an "any monkey with a typewriter" experiment. The twenty-year leaps are jarring. But the disc is loaded with long-forgotten jewels like "Please Don't Leave Me." Incredibly, the original "Danny Boy" is nowhere in Price's CD catalogue. Paranoia strikes deep.

Price's Step One titles are of minimal interest except to those who enjoy him in a supper club setting. *Greatest Hits, Vols. 1-3,* a two-disc set, does offer surprisingly hopped-up remakes of his early hits, but *Heart of Country Music* and *Just Enough Love* are so narcoleptic they defy one's every impulse to give Price the benefit of the doubt. A better example of his latter-day work is *Sometimes a Rose.* The title cut integrates his many past styles in fine fashion, the rest of the disc segregates them back out.—D.C.

CHARLEY PRIDE

★★½ **The Best of Charley Pride (RCA 5968-2-RRE) 1969, 1985 ●**

★★ **Greatest Hits (RCA 6917-2-RRE) 1981, 1988**

★ **Best of Charley Pride (Curb/CEMA D21K-77471) 1991**

Granted, Charley Pride came along at just the right time in country music, but he didn't make it because of affirmative action. In fact, he slipped onto country radio without publicity in 1966, and by the time the home folks realized that that chicken-fried baritone was coming out of an African American (remember: no videos), it was too late: they loved him. As well they should have. In his early glory years, from 1966 to about 1974, Pride was the countriest of the country. Like Johnny Cash, his singing conveyed utter sincerity and hard working experience. He kept the faith with his hard-country fans by keeping his songs country well after Ray Price and others had pointed the way to crossover. During his twenty years on RCA, he issued more than forty LPs, and by 1975 his sales for that label were second only to Elvis Presley.

So how has RCA rewarded Pride and his fans? The two CDs that RCA has deigned to release in no way come close to doing justice to Charley Pride's recording career. Both are truncated, eight-cut versions of LP collections that originally consisted of eleven and twelve cuts. It's fair to say that what's missing from these twenty-minute CDs is better than what RCA has chosen to re-release. Among the definitive Charley Pride performances (and #1 hits) that you won't find on these CDs are the down-home musings of "Wonder Could I Live There Anymore," the country finger-popping of "Kiss an Angel Good Morning," and Pride's finest moment, "Is Anybody Goin' to San Antone," wherein a sadder but wiser Charley heads off down the highway to the rhythm of chicken-scratch fiddles.

Of the two RCA CDs at hand, you can listen to *Best of* for hard-country Pride (1966-69) on the brink of stardom. Though slathered with the sugary oohs and aahs of the Anita Kerr Singers, sides like "Just Between You and Me" and "The Day the World Stood Still" remain palatable thanks to Pride's consistently tart-as-lemon readings. But back then he had something to prove. In 1971, propelled by the undeniable power of "Is Anybody Goin' to San Antone" and "Wonder Could I Live There," Pride justly received the CMA's Entertainer of the Year award. Afterwards there were still occasional triumphs of taste—the almost autobiographical "Mississippi Cotton Pickin' Delta Town" (1974), an album of heartfelt Hank Williams covers (1980), and a towering performance on "Mountain of Love" (1981)—but through the Seventies you could hear Pride grudgingly making concessions to Nashville Sound formula. *Greatest Hits* offers a peek at a fat-and-sassy Charley succumbing to country-pop temptation (1976-81) and lazing on the hammocklike swing-and-sway of "You're My Jamaica" and "Burgers and Fries." Curb's *Best of* is a sneaky resurrection and repackaging of Pride's final LP for the now-defunct 16th Avenue Records, *Moody Woman,* from 1989. It should have been allowed to die quietly.—P.K.

JOHN PRINE

★★★★★ John Prine (Atlantic 19156-2) 1971

★★★★½ Diamonds in the Rough (Atlantic 7240-2) 1972

★★★ Sweet Revenge (Atlantic 81430-2) 1973

★★★ Common Sense (Atlantic 18127-2) 1976

★★★★½ Prime Prine (Atlantic 18202-2) 1976 ●

★★★★½ Bruised Orange (Oh Boy OBR-006CD) 1978

★★★ Pink Cadillac (Oh Boy OBR-007CD) 1979

★★★ Storm Windows (Oh Boy OBR-008CD) 1980

★★★ Aimless Love (Oh Boy OBR-002) 1984

★★½ German Afternoons (Oh Boy OBR-003) 1988

★★★★★ John Prine Live (Oh Boy OBR 005CD) 1988

★★★★½ Missing Years (Oh Boy OBR 009CD) 1991

This thoroughly unpretentious former Chicago mailman came out of nowhere in the early 1970s with a couple of LPs' worth of unforgettable country folk ballads so wryly humorous and chock-full of lucid social and emotional insight that they seemed the perfect marriage of country music and liberal commentary. Great Prine originals like "Sam Stone," "Illegal Smile," and "Your Flag Decal Won't Get You into Heaven Anymore" spoke with uncanny wit and perception to the preoccupations and alienation of the Seventies post-Vietnam era. The power of Prine's music quickly earned him a sizable live following, and his songs were eventually covered by dozens of other artists (Bonnie Raitt and Johnny Cash among them), even though he himself seldom made an impact in the country or pop charts, on account of his roughhewn voice and left-field style.

Prine has never quite matched the uniform lyric brilliance of his first two Atlantic LPs (*John Prine* and *Diamonds in the Rough*), and his material from that era is still the bedrock of his enduring appeal as a live performer. His later Atlantic albums—*Common Sense* and *Sweet Revenge*—were worthy enough efforts, but contained few songs of the caliber of the aforementioned gems. After a lengthy recording hiatus, Prine rebounded with *Bruised Orange* in 1978. With production assistance from his friend and fellow Chicago folkie, the late Steve Goodman, he began turning his prodigious power of metaphor and his unmatched flair for irony away from social commentary and more toward the affairs of the heart. *Pink Cadillac,* his 1979 foray into neo-rockabilly, is a fascinating experiment, but its manic instrumental settings too often drown his lazily drawling voice and obscure the laid-back charm of his original songs. After recording *Storm Windows* (1980), his noteworthy final Elektra LP, Prine released a pair of minimally produced yet eminently pleasant albums—*Aimless Love* and *German Afternoons*—on his own Oh Boy label. Unfortunately, they suffered in comparison to his brilliant early work on Atlantic.

Prine's muse rebounded dramatically on his Grammy-winning *Missing Years.* With its odes to ambivalent love ("Everybody Wants to Feel Like You") and its endearing wistfulness, *The Missing Years* is a work of heart, humor, and honesty that devastates listeners in all the right ways. *Prime Prine* is a dozen-cut, single-CD compilation of Prine's vintage early Atlantic material. But a better sampler is the nineteen-track *John Prine Live,* which contains fresher versions of many of the same Prime classics along with the bonus of Prine's irresistible offhand witticisms. —B.A.

PURE PRAIRIE LEAGUE

★★★½ Bustin' Out (RCA 4656-2) 1973 ●

★★½ Amie & Other Hits (RCA 52163-2) 1990

★★ Two Lane Highway (RCA 53669-2) 1975

★★ If the Shoe Fits (RCA 1247-2-R) 1976

★★½ Live! Takin' the Stage (RCA 2404) 1977

★★½ Firin' Up (Mercury 314 514 686-2) 1980

★★ Something in the Night (Mercury 314 514 684-2) 1981

Pure Prairie League, named after a ladies' temperance union in an Errol Flynn movie, started out as a determinedly quirky country-rock band. It ended up a brand name stamped with a Norman Rockwell cartoon cowboy.

In its earliest incarnation, Pure Prairie League took the then-fresh approach of infusing country picking with rock & roll dynamics to put across the tender-hearted, singer-songwriterly musings of singer-guitarists Craig Fuller and George Ed Powell. Fuller's is the limpid, gently countrified tenor you know from the band's one enduring hit, "Amie." He wrote and sang most of the band's material for the first two LPs, *Pure Prairie League* (now out of print) and *Bustin' Out.* The 1972 debut is well worth seeking out in used LP bins for the steel guitar pyrotechnics of John David Call and the band's second greatest song, the rousing kiss-off "You're between Me."

Bustin' Out lived up to its title both as a creative leap forward for the band and as a breakout onto the charts, though the latter didn't occur until two years after the album was released. Somehow, RCA noticed that *Bustin' Out*'s infectious celebration of romantic ambivalence, "Fallin' In and Out of Love"/ "Amie," had become a popular request on alternative FM stations across America. The label finally tried it as a single, and the band gained a Top Forty hit. By that time, though, Fuller had left, and the band was left in the ironic position of having a following and no leader. Consequently,

Two Lane Highway and *If the Shoe Fits* sound like an accomplished bar band sorely in need of some songs and a personality. *Live! Taking the Stage* mercifully shows more energy but the material is still thin, and the ragged renditions of Buddy Holly's "That'll Be the Day" and "Amie" fall far short of the originals.

Through the Seventies, the band drifted from gig to gig, lost and gained personnel, and, thanks to "Amie," kept recording. In 1980, a 23-year-old Vince Gill stepped up to microphone and into Fuller's shoes. "Let Me Love You Tonight," from *Firin' Up,* hit #10 on the pop charts, and the band had a new lease on life. But by the time of *Firin' Up* and *Something in the Night,* Pure Prairie League had drifted far, far away from the band's original sound and perilously towards twang-free pop. With guest artiste David Sanborn tootling away merrily on sax, the band was country only in Vince Gill's dreams.

Those hoping for a hits package to get the compact Pure Prairie League will only be disappointed; *Amie & Other Hits* is a bogus RCA scrambling of *Bustin' Out* minus that album's opening track, "Jazzman." The band is long gone, but the profits live on.—P.K.

R

EDDIE RABBITT

★★★½   **All Time Greatest Hits (Warner Brothers 26467-2) 1991**

★★★   **Greatest Country Hits (Curb/CEMA D21Y-77430) 1991**

★★★½   **Step by Step (Liberty C21K-90531) 1981 ●**

★★   **Radio Romance (Liberty C21K-94652) 1982**

★★   **Great Hits of Eddie Rabbitt (RCA 9756-2-R) 1989**

★★½   **The Best Year of My Life (Liberty C21K-94152) 1990**

★★   **Classics Collection (Liberty C21Y-95373) 1991**

★★   **Ten Years of Greatest Hits (Liberty C21S-94346) 1992**

Eddie Rabbitt, New Jersey's gift to modern country music, started out in the mid-1970s as a fairly conventional country crooner whose cheerfully infectious singing-songwriting style—as heard on early Rabbitt chart-toppers like "Two Dollars in the Jukebox," "Drinkin' My Baby off My Mind," and "Rocky Mountain Music"—imbued country music's stock jukebox clichés with a youthful edge and an ever-so-slightly urbane temperament.

By the early 1980s however, Rabbitt's music, under the direction of his long-time collaborators, producer David Malloy and co-writer Even Stevens, began to evolve into a rhythmically galvanizing and innovative neorockabilly sound that came to fruition on monster hits like "Drivin' My Life Away" and "I Love a Rainy Night." Unfortunately, the adventurous spirit of the Rabbitt/Malloy/Stevens team peaked rather quickly. By 1981's *Step by Step,* the fire was already beginning to burn down and the intriguing dance rhythms could no longer compensate for the trite moon-in-June lyrics. By 1982's *Radio Romance,* the spark of inspiration was gone. Rabbitt no longer seemed to be able to figure out if he wanted to be Neil Diamond with a heavy back-beat or Donny Osmond in tight pants. Since then, Rabbitt's music has more or less continued on a slow slide into the predictable and mundane—though occasionally the embers have flickered, as on his 1988 *I Wanna Dance* LP (RCA), which ironically is not on CD.

While most of Rabbitt's more recent and less interesting RCA and Liberty albums are readily available on CD, his all-time classic album, *Horizons* (1980) is nowhere to be found. However, fragments of them can be heard on *All Time Greatest Hits* (Warner Brothers) and *Greatest Country Hits* (Curb/CEMA), which are the strongest and most authentic of his various hits compilations. *Great Hits of Eddie Rabbitt* (RCA) and *Ten Years of Greatest Hits* (Liberty), on the other hand, are merely composed of tired, middle-aged, overly mannered remakes of some of Rabbitt's best musical moments from the 1970s and early 1980s.—B.A.

WILLIS ALAN RAMSEY
★★★★★ **Willis Alan Ramsey (Shelter/DCC Compact Discs SRZ-8008) 1972**
The J. D. Salinger of Austin's progressive country movement, Ramsey made just one dazzling album, when he was all of twenty-one years old. Then he disappeared like the rueful ramblers and rounders in his songs, as cleanly as if he'd hopped a freight.

Recorded in 1971 when the hubbub in Austin was at its height, this unheralded debut has withstood the indignities of time like little else from those Cosmic Cowboy days. In the bluesy color of his voice, singing with the conviction of a man twice his age, Ramsey recalls nothing so much as that archetypal country bluesman, Jimmie Rodgers. Like Rodgers, Ramsey goes for songs that have the conversational ease of classic blues. But Ramsey is no fussy revivalist, as his exhortation to "Praise the Lord and pass the mescaline" in "Satin Sheets" makes hilariously clear. Moreover, he goes Rodgers (and almost everybody else) one better by limning his lyrics with a novelist's eye for evocative, finely wrought detail, occasionally laced with a dash of whimsy for comic relief. In "Missoula" and "Ballad of Spider John," he spins spellbinding tales of love irretrievably lost because of the smallest misunderstandings. "Boy from Oklahoma" pays heartfelt tribute to Woody Guthrie, while the frisky "Painted Lady" turns the same trick for ladies of the evening. Not a one of the album's eleven tracks—all written by Ramsey—misses. And it wasn't long after the album was released that admiring artists like Jimmy Buffett ("Ballad of Spider John"), Waylon Jennings ("Satin Sheets"), and even America and the Captain & Tennille ("Muskrat Love") lined up to cover Ramsey's tunes.

Around 1989, Ramsey resurfaced after years of self-imposed exile in England. He's played a few songwriting festivals and sporadic gigs here and there, claiming that he is once again writing and looking forward to recording. We can only hope.—P.K.

EDDY RAVEN
★★½ **Best of Eddy Raven (RCA Victor 6815-2-R) 1988**
★★ **Temporary Sanity (Universal UVLD-76003) 1989**
★★ **Greatest Country Hits (Curb D2-77364) 1990**
★★ **Greatest Hits (Warner Bros. 26302-2) 1990**
★★ **Right for the Flight (Capitol Nashville CDP 7 94258 2) 1991**
A frustrating talent, this Eddy Raven. He's a terrific blue-eyed soul singer who understands that unteachable lesson about holding the emotion clenched in the back of his throat. Catch him with his guard down, on a spare ballad like *Temporary Sanity*'s "Island," and you know he could give your Steve Winwoods and Van Morrisons an understated run for their money.

Trouble is, Raven's productions and taste in material usually span either end of the car radio dial. His catalogue, from one label to the next, is littered with programmer-friendly dreck like the RCA collection's "Shine, Shine, Shine." The opening bars of this #1 hit (also included on the Curb disc) are bizarrely reminiscent of the Jackson Five's "I Want You Back." The Curb compilation features material leased from three different labels; it alone proves how consistently middle-of-the-road Raven's sound has remained through the years. Worse is the singer's tendency to trade on his Louisiana heritage with faux-Cajun arrangements on the uptempo numbers. There is no excuse for the shallow keyboard washes where an accordion belonged on *Temporary Sanity*'s "Bayou Boys."

But then, just as Raven's driven you into a self-righteous rage over his pop pandering, he hits you with the RCA disc's "Right Hand Man," a humble little beauty with tumbling metaphors on the right hand/left hand commitment theme. It's exquisite. Someone send this guy to Muscle Shoals with a five-piece pickup band.—D.C.

COLLIN RAYE
★★½ All I Can Be (Epic EK 47468) 1991 ●
★★ In This Life (Epic EK 48983) 1992

A singer with a pleasant, verging-on-bland high tenor, Raye is a likable lug whose debut yielded a mawkish #1 hit, "Love, Me" and a fabulous lesser success, the western swingin' "Every Second." Unfortunately, his follow-up album, *In This Life*, dominated by overripe ballads, suggested that mawkishness may be what Raye prefers.—K.T.

RED CLAY RAMBLERS
★★★★ Twisted Laurel/Merchant's Lunch (Flying Fish FF70055) 1976, 1977, 1991
★★★★ It Ain't Right (Flying Fish 70334) 1986, 1992
★★★ A Lie of the Mind (Rykodisc RCD 10034) 1986
★★ Far North, Original Soundtrack (Sugar Hill SH-CD-8502) 1989
★★★★ Rambler (Sugar Hill SH-CD-3798) 1992

An eclectic, original, and enduring string band, the Red Clay Ramblers draw their repertoire from an unusually wide variety of musical sources, including old-time fiddle tunes, early jazz and ragtime, Irish music, Tin Pan Alley pop, and their own, highly original, often humorous compositions.

Formed in 1972, the early Ramblers included Tommy Thompson of the Hollow Rock String Band, Bill Hicks of the Fuzzy Mountain String Band, Jim Watson, and Mike Craver. Skilled players and accomplished singers, the group grew popular in the Chapel Hill-Durham, North Carolina, area and did some recording before gaining wider exposure in an extended run of the hit Off Broadway play *Diamond Studs*.

By the time they cut *Twisted Laurel* and *Merchant's Lunch*, the Ramblers had added Jack Herrick, a versatile musician who greatly expanded the band's sound with his brass instruments, pennywhistle, and harmonica. Flying Fish has generously, if somewhat awkwardly, joined those two albums into one, but with no indication of where one record ends and the second begins and with liner notes that refer to photos not included in the CD packaging. At twenty-five cuts, the disc reflects the range of styles the Ramblers embraced by the mid-Seventies: a delicate reading of the Carter Family's "Will You Miss Me," jazzy humor in "The Ace," a breakneck fiddle tune in "Forked Deer," and spirited revivals of old songs by Uncle Dave Macon and Fats Waller.

The Ramblers' next two albums, the live *Chuckin' the Frizz* from 1979 and *Hard Times* from 1981 have not been reissued on CD and should be. The latter is the first with new fiddler Clay Buckner replacing Hicks. Both records include outstanding original songs.

It Ain't Right finds the quintet branching further. A new recording of the Thompson-Craver masterpiece, "Merchant's Lunch," is driven by a guest rhythm section of fretless bass and drums, and future member Chris Frank plays trombone with Jack Herrick in an expanded brass section on the title cut and on Rev. Robert Wilkins's "Jim Canaan's."

Around the time of *It Ain't Right*, playwright-actor Sam Shepard heard the Ramblers on radio while in Iowa to make the film *Country*. He enlisted the band to provide music for his New York play, *A Lie of the Mind*. The sound track features a combination of traditional tunes, original compositions by band members, and Lefty Frizzell's "I Love You a Thousand Ways." The group's association with Shepard led to work on the film sound track for *Far North*, written and directed by him. Though effective as a sound track, the largely instrumental work is more interesting as a document of the Ramblers' musical experimentation than as an engaging listening experience.

The Ramblers have continued to find their way into dramatic productions. Craver left the band to join a New York production of *Oil City Symphony*. Thompson has written and performed a one-man play, *The Last Song of John Proffitt*. The band took roles in another Shepard film, *Silent Tongue*, and in early 1993 they were appearing on Broadway in *Fool Moon*. Bland Simpson, co-author of *Diamond Studs*, joined the Ramblers in the late Eighties as pianist, vocalist, and songwriter. Frank signed on around the same time as a multi-instrumentalist capable of contributing a variety of sounds on brass and string instruments.

Rambler splits evenly between newly arranged traditional numbers, such as "Cotton-Eyed Joe" and "What Does the Deep Sea Say?" and band originals such as "Barbeque" and "Black Smoke Train." The record works on a larger scale by achieving an uncommonly successful synthesis of dramatic images, traditional melodies, and ambient moods ranging from romantic to raucous. —J.O.

JERRY REED

★★★★ The Best of Jerry Reed (RCA Nashville 07863-54109-2) 1972
★★ [& Chet Atkins] Sneakin' Around (Columbia CK 47873) 1992

When Chet Atkins gets all excited about a guitar player, people take notice. In the early Sixties that guitar player was Jerry Reed. The young gun became Atkins's protégé, his snapping Fender Telecaster throwing off some of the most fiery, inventive licks Nashville had heard in a while. He was the "Alabama Wildman" back then, and he busts with energy on self-penned classics like "Guitar Man," "Amos Moses," and "U. S. Male," all of which can be found on his *Best of*. His swampy picking and half-spoken vocals hold these rowdy songs together, and instrumentals like "The Claw" remind us that Reed was once the slinkiest guitar picker in Music City. But the real surprise is Reed's ballads. "A Thing Called Love" and "Today Is Mine" show an appealing (although apparently never fully developed) Jimmy Webb-ish side of his songwriting. After a career as a movie star, Reed's been laying low these past several years, and on *Sneakin' Around,* his laid-back comeback (with that most laid back of guitarists, Chet Atkins), it shows. The pair manage some effortlessly hot licks and catch fire briefly on a few tunes, but compared to Reed's (and Atkins's) earlier efforts, this is a pretty creaky affair.—P.Cr.

JIM REEVES

★★★ The Country Side (RCA Camden CAD-686) 1962
★★ Twelve Songs of Christmas (RCA 8326-2-R) 1963
★★ The Best of Jim Reeves (RCA Nashville 58451-2) 1964 ●
★★★★ Four Walls—The Legend Begins (RCA 2493-2-R) 1991
★★ I Guess I'm Crazy (RCA Camden CAD1-2652) N.D.
★★★ The Best of Jim Reeves, Vol. 3 (RCA-Camden CAD1-2702) 1969
★★★ Pure Gold, Vol. 1 (RCA Victor 3936-2-R) 1978
★★★★ Live at the Opry (Country Music Foundation CMF 008-D) 1986
★★★ He'll Have to Go & Other Favorites (RCA Nashville 52301-2) 1992
★★★★ Welcome to My World: The Essential Jim Reeves Collection (RCA 07863-66125-2) 1993

Though he was thoroughly capable of singing hard-driving honky-tonk songs and novelty pieces, as well as saga songs and crusty hymns, Jim Reeves is best remembered today for his mellow, velvet-voiced renditions of hits like "Four Walls" and "He'll Have to Go." Along with Eddy Arnold, he popularized the image of the country gentleman crooner—the sedate, tuxedoed singer, backed with soft vibes and piano, sometimes even strings, sounding more like Nat "King" Cole than Hank Williams. By the early 1960s, Reeves was appealing to a pop audience as much as a country one and was attracting a huge overseas audience in England and Africa. "I'm very grateful that you no longer have to be fish or fowl in this business," he told reporters who were always asking him about whether he thought of himself as country or pop.

A native of Panola County, Texas, Reeves gained his first fame over Shreveport's "Louisiana Hayride," and through a hit single he did for the independent Abbott label, "Mexican Joe." In May 1955, he switched to RCA Victor, and all his later records were done for them; these included over fifty hit singles between 1953 and 1971, the biggest coming in the early to mid-1960s. His tragic death in a plane crash in 1964 did little to diminish his popularity or slow his hit records. Indeed, he had half again as many Top Ten hits after his death as before, with some posthumous singles charting up through the 1980s. Throughout the decades since his death, RCA and Reeves's widow, Mary, have kept a fair sampling of his works in print.

One of the best of RCA's current crop of CD's is *Four Walls—The Legend Begins*. Beautifully packaged and annotated, this disc offers twenty prime cuts from the 1953-57 era, including "Mexican Joe" (in the original version, the masters of which had been bought by RCA), "Bimbo," "According to My Heart," and "Am I Losing You," some offered in alternate takes, or in stripped-down unoverdubbed takes. A more comprehensive and balanced set is the aptly named *Welcome to My World: The Essential Jim Reeves Collection*. Thirty cuts are spread over two CDs, and while there is some early overlap with the *Four Walls* CD, over half of *Essential* dates from the post-1957 era and includes many of the later favorites that modern Reeves fans associate with him, such as "I Missed Me" (1960), "I'm Gonna Change Everything" (1962), and "Is It Really Over" (1965). A lavishly illustrated and carefully annotated booklet complements the set.

Other early material is found on *The Country Side*, which features his bouncy "Yonder Comes a Sucker" from 1955, and "My Lips Are Sealed," from his second RCA session. Two RCA budget CDs, *The Best of Jim Reeves* and *He'll Have to Go and Other Favorites*, should receive some kind of award for the sloppiest reissues done in recent memory; in spite of their different covers and release numbers, they duplicate each other on five of the paltry eight selections. Though there are no notes or even recording dates, there are some excellent Reeves songs on both: "He'll Have to Go," "Four Walls," "Billy Bayou," and "Stand at Your Window." ("Danny Boy" and Harlan Howard's "The Blizzard" are found only in *The Best* set.)

A much better overview of Reeves's work, and one which has an excellent set of liner notes to introduce his music, is *Jim Reeves Live at the Opry*, a collection of on-the-air performances taken from Grand Ole Opry shows. Ranging from 1953 to 1960, they present Reeves in a more authentic country setting, backed up either by his touring band, the Blue Boys, or by an Opry pick-up band. Many of his big hits are repeated here (as well as some unusual gospel numbers), with adequate sound and occasional an-

nouncer introductions. An appealing oddity for unabashed fans is *Pure Gold,* which includes pop standards like "Mona Lisa" and "My Happiness."—C.K.W.

RONNA REEVES
★★ **Only the Heart (Mercury 848 260-2) 1991**
★★½ **The More I Learn (Mercury 314-510 847-2) 1992**

Texas-bred Reeves is a fine singer just one or two good songs shy of success. Selections on *Only the Heart* come from such hit factories as Bob McDill, Dickey Lee, and Wayland Holyfield, but the tunes aren't from their premium stock. The production, though adequate, never gets very interesting either. Reeves covers the Ernie Ashworth hit, "Talk Back Trembling Lips," and the album includes her version of Tony Arata's "Same Old Story," also done by Garth Brooks on his *No Fences* album.

Producer Harold Shedd (Alabama, K.T. Oslin) steps in for *The More I Learn,* and things improve some, but instrumental grandiosity and thunderous drum sounds nearly overwhelm Reeves's voice. That said, the chorus on McDill's "Honky Tonk Hearts" puts her in beautiful counterpoint to a steel guitar, and a duet with label mate Sammy Kershaw, "There's Love on the Line," finds its way to the soul of the song's emotions. As with her first outing, what keeps *The More I Learn* from distinguishing itself is the absence of an unforgettable song.
—J.O.

MIKE REID
★★ **Turning for Home (Columbia CK 46141) 1991**
★★ **Twilight Town (Columbia ACC 48967) 1992**

Reid is a former defensive tackle for the Cincinnati Bengals, and he sings in a tone as burly as his athletic frame. But he's a sensitive soul who's written pretty, treacly hits for Bonnie Raitt ("I Can't Make You Love Me") and Ronnie Milsap ("Inside"). On his own records, that husky voice too often seems wimpy—sensitive in an affected way, as are Reid's polite wordplay and melodies. *Turning for Home* yielded a #1 hit single, "Walk on Faith"; the wispy *Twilight*

Town faded from the charts quickly.—
K.T.

THE REMINGTONS
★★   **Blue Frontier (BNA 61045-2) 1992**
★★   **Aim for the Heart (BNA BADV66152-2) 1993**

For anyone who thinks too many current
country acts try to sound like the Eagles,
here's one that tries to sound like Poco.
Mighty audacious. Just to complicate
matters, one of the Remingtons used to
be a member of Bread. I suppose that
accounts for the cover of "Everything I
Own" on *Aim for the Heart*. New
traditionalism indeed.—D.C.

DON RENO & RED SMILEY
★★★★   **Good Old Country Ballads (King KCD-621) 1959**
★★★★   **A Variety of Country Songs (King KCD-646) 1959**

At the height of their popularity in the
late Fifties, Don Reno, Red Smiley, &
the Tennessee Cut-ups were generally
considered to be in the top four of
bluegrass, along with Bill Monroe, Flatt
& Scruggs, and the Stanley Brothers.
They recorded hundreds of songs for
King Records between 1952 and 1964,
and at one time most were available on
LP. The group disbanded in 1964 and
both men led their own groups separately for some years afterward. Smiley
died in 1972, Reno in 1984.

In the late Sixties, King became part
of the Starday Records empire and since
then Reno & Smiley's recordings have
moved from owner to owner as that
company has been sold and resold. The
new owners who created these CDs
don't seem to know much about the
material; each album is a straight
republication of an old King album from
the late Fifties, with no descriptive
notes, no composer credits. Although it's
good they are in print, it's a pity they
aren't in a package that does them
justice.

Both albums are collections of
material released on King singles in the
early Fifties and include some of the
strongest material recorded by this
band. Red Smiley plays rhythm guitar
and does most of the lead singing; Don
Reno plays banjo or lead acoustic guitar
and sings tenor most of the time. Reno
wrote many of the songs as well. If there

is any shortcoming with these sets, it is
the lack of instrumentals, for in his
heyday Reno was about the only banjoist
whose name was spoken seriously in the
same sentence with Earl Scruggs. If his
innovative picking is not spotlighted,
however, it can be heard to good effect
in solo breaks on many cuts. *Good Old
Country Ballads* includes Reno's much
copied composition "I Know You're
Married but I Love You Still" (Reno was
straightforward, even sentimental, about
sinful thoughts in his secular songs) and
his tour de force (lead vocal, lead guitar,
banjo) "Country Boy Rock 'n Roll." *A
Variety of Country Songs* has more
uptempo bluegrass-style numbers like
"Long Gone" as well as some good
gospel quartets, including "Since I've
Used My Bible for a Roadmap," a sequel
to their first very popular King single,
"I'm Using My Bible for a Roadmap." If
you're a serious collector of bluegrass
music, or just a fan of the good old
country music of the Fifties, you should
have at least one Reno & Smiley album
on the shelf, and either of these will do
just fine.—N.V.R.

RESTLESS HEART
★★★   **Restless Heart (RCA 5369) 1985**
★★★   **Wheels (RCA 5648) 1986 ●**
★★★   **Big Dreams in a Small Town (RCA 8317) 1998 ●**
★★★   **Fast Movin' Train (RCA 9961) 1990 ●**
★★★½ **The Best of Restless Heart (RCA 61041) 1991**
★★★   **Big Iron Horses (RCA 66049) 1992**

It's a rock critic fantasy that country
music ever seriously embraced the
notion of inspired amateurism. From the
Carter Family to Hank and Lefty, country
artists strove to have their recordings
sound as fully professional as possible.
So, in the Seventies and Eighties, with
the Eagles and, later, Toto setting
standards for technically pristine
playing, country musicians couldn't help
but be influenced.

Restless Heart certainly took a cue or
two from Toto. Technically able musicians, the original quintet—singer Larry
Stewart, bassist Paul Gregg, keyboardist
David Innis, guitarist Greg Jennings,
and drummer John Dittrich—won over
that segment of the country audience

impressed by chops. The band linked subtle, sometimes tricky rhythm and keyboard arrangements to romantic ballads and narratives. From the beginning, when they hit with a striking, syncopated tune called "(Back to the) Heartbreak Kid" that rode into the sunset (and towards the parking lot), they have melded crystalline harmonies, country comfort, and rock hooks. Critics have called their contemporary precision "cold." But that measurement doesn't account for Stewart's warm, soulful tenor, which always cuts intelligently against the so-called chill.

The band's albums, even when Stewart left for a solo career and Restless Heart regrouped with *Big Iron Horses* as a quartet, are assembly-line consistent. The drawback is that only their singles, well collected on *The Best of Restless Heart,* apply the band's strengths to songs that match the high level of production. The major exception is Restless Heart's record of Dave Loggins's song "Fast Movin' Train." One of the strongest Nashville hits of the Eighties, it's a highly detailed first-person account of falling in love that runs toward the obsessional and the hallucinogenic, and Stewart's vocal, time and again, is extraordinary. Still, it probably runs counter to Restless Heart's cool aesthetic to get that involved more than once over the course of a career.—J.H.

TONY RICE

★★★★ **Manzanita (Rounder CD-0092) 1979**
★★★ **Backwaters (Rounder CD-0167) 1982**
★★★★ **Church Street Blues (Sugar Hill SHCD-3732) 1983**
★★★½ **Cold on the Shoulder (Rounder CD-0183) 1984**
★★★½ **Me and My Guitar (Rounder CD-0201)1987**
★★★½ **Native American (Rounder CD-0248) 1988**
★★★ **Devlin (Rounder CD 11531) 1988**
★★★½ **California Autumn (Rebel CD-1549) 1990**
★★★½ **Guitar (Rebel REBCDJ-1582) 1991**

This superb musician's relative obscurity among the larger country music public is almost impossible to understand. His flat-picking guitar playing is dazzling,

his singing is soulful, and his choice of songs is sensitive and intelligent. After a lengthy apprenticeship in bluegrass music, the North Carolina-born and California-reared Rice moved on to master that amorphous and largely undefinable genre known as new acoustic music. Despite his eclectic experiments, Rice's singing and guitar work still strongly bear the imprint of his early bluegrass experience, and he freely admits the influence of such seminal country guitarists as Clarence White, Doc Watson, and Norman Blake.

The complete Tony Rice—judged by instrumental proficiency, singing, and choice of songs—is best displayed on the collections *Manzanita* and *Church Street Blues.* On the former, accompanied by a stellar cast of musicians including Ricky Skaggs, Sam Bush, and Jerry Douglas, Rice delves into an old-time acoustic feel. Most of the selections, whether instrumentals like "Blackberry Blossom" or "Stony Point," or a blues murder ballad like "Little Sadie," come from the realm of old-time music. "Midnight on the Stormy Deep" stands out; no brother duet ever gave a more powerful interpretation than the one heard here by Rice and Skaggs. *Church Street Blues,* in contrast, offers an almost exclusively solo performance. "The Gold Rush," "Church Street Blues," and "Cattle in the Cane" give Rice an opportunity to demonstrate his mastery of blues, hoedown, and Celtic styles of picking, while his vocal choices are equally eclectic, ranging from the traditional British ballad, "The House Carpenter," to the lovely contemporary piece about homelessness, "Streets of London."

Guitar concentrates primarily on instrumental treatments of songs like "Faded Love," featuring the fiddling of Bobby Slone, and "Lonesome Reuben," where Rice's virtuoso guitar playing competes with an equally breathtaking performance by J. D. Crowe on the five-string banjo.

Although *Cold on the Shoulder* has no instrumental selections at all, Rice and his accompanying musicians—which include the likes of Bela Fleck, Vassar Clements, Jerry Douglas, and Sam Bush—provide enough pyrotechnics on their respective instruments to please any fan of hot licks. Most of the material here comes from the pens of such contemporary writers as Gordon Lightfoot, Rodney Crowell, and Randy Newman, with Bob Dylan's "Fare Thee Well" standing out.

Me and My Guitar and *Native American* are Rice's most contemporary, introspective, and idiosyncratic albums. Between them, the two albums serve up seven Gordon Lightfoot compositions, including "Early Morning Rain" and "Fine as Fine Can Be" (both on *Me and My Guitar*). Rice's rather curious fascination with the Lincoln assassination reveals itself on the two CDs in the form of a ballad commissioned by Rice and written by Mary-Chapin Carpenter called "John Wilkes Booth" (on *Native American)* and an instrumental named "Port Tobacco" (on *Me and My Guitar)*. Both songs, though well performed, are forgettable, and theater historians will probably not agree with Tony that Booth was the "greatest actor of his day."

California Autumn offers a pleasing variety of tunes, both traditional and contemporary, but its main thrust is instrumental. Showing the influence of Doc Watson, Rice flat-picks three tunes borrowed from old-time fiddle music, "Billy in the Lowground," "Red Haired Boy," and "Beaumont Rag." This is one of the few Tony Rice collections that contains no Gordon Lightfoot song, but among five vocal performances, Tony gives excellent interpretations of "Good Woman's Love" and "You Don't Know My Mind."—B.C.M.

CHARLIE RICH

★★★★★ **The Complete Smash Sessions (Mercury 314-512643-2) 1992**
★★★ **Behind Closed Doors (Epic EK 32247) 1973 ▲**
★★★ **Greatest Hits (Epic EK 34240) 1976**
★★★ **American Originals (Columbia CK 45073) 1989**
★★★★★ **Pictures and Paintings (Sire 9 26730-2) 1992**

It's unfortunate that Charlie Rich is remembered chiefly for the crossover country hit "Behind Closed Doors," for this Memphis pianist and singer mastered a hybrid form of jazzy country soulful rockabilly gospel blues that will likely not pass this way again. He was too good to be restricted to any one musical genre and too private to be comfortable with stardom (and its attendant demand that he move toward the middle of the musical road) when it briefly beckoned.

This sometime farmer from Colt, Arkansas, was discovered in the late 1950s by Sun Records where he had a minor hit with his laconic country blues song "Lonely Weekends." From Sun, he moved on to RCA and to the modest success of "Big Boss Man," and then to Smash Records. He was most at home with the sort of quirky material best demonstrated on *The Complete Smash Sessions* CD: songs ranging from the novelty hit "Mohair Sam" to the quasi-folk-rock of "I Washed My Hands in Muddy Water" to Joe South's raucous "Let the Party Roll On" to the Dallas Frazier oddity "She's A Yum Yum." In these freewheeling 1965 and 1966 sessions, you can discern the seeds of what would become the later, "hip," countrypolitan Nashville records by Bob Dylan, Elvis, and all those that followed.

He went to Epic Records in 1968, and as both *Greatest Hits* and *Behind Closed Doors* attest, had his greatest commercial hits there once producer Billy Sherrill began working closely with him. Rich briefly became a country sensation, for "Behind Closed Doors," "The Most Beautiful Girl," "I Take It On Home," and the like. He looked superstardom in the eye—the private Convair plane, the "Silver Fox" public relations blitz, the Vegas bookings—and he walked away from it all.

Rich's is a marvelously private musical universe, and he emerged from his retirement in that distant Rich realm with 1992's *Pictures and Paintings*, at once a masterpiece of musical introspection and a looking glass into the many uncharted possibilities of country music. "Don't Put No Headstone on My Grave," "Feel Like Going Home," and the rest find this master of country blues back at the top of his form.

Much of his work is long since out-of-print on vinyl and also unavailable on CD. I would especially like to see resurrected his sole attempt to cut a pure country album. The 1967 *Charlie Rich Sings Country & Western* for Memphis's Hi Records sounds as if it were laid down in a single pass before a dusty two-track machine (with blowsy strings tacked on after), but it is one mind-blowing piece of country funk. Rich attacks and completely conquers eight Hank Williams songs and four other country standards. Eminently satisfying, it should be preserved on CD.—C.F.

ZACHARY RICHARD

★★★ Zack's Bon Ton (Rounder CD 6027) 1988
★★★½ Mardi Gras Mambo (Rounder CD 6037) 1989
★★★★ Women in the Room (A&M 75021 5302 2) 1990
★★ Snake Bite Love (A&M 75021 5387 2) 1992

The zydeco rocker has frequently been characterized as the "Cajun Mick Jagger," a tag that occasionally carries a touch of derision in his native Louisiana. Singing in French as well as English, mixing zydeco roots with rock dynamics, accordionist Richard has proven one of the region's most popular performers with audiences that care more about dance-floor propulsion than traditional purity.

Zack's Bon Ton attempts to capture the energy of one of Richard's roadhouse sets in the recording studio, mixing generic sounding originals with covers of familiar Louisiana fare such as "Jolie Blonde" and "The Battle of New Orleans." *Mardi Gras Mambo* boasts a bigger production and more of a New Orleans feel, with Richard putting his distinctive stylistic stamp on Mardi Gras staples such as "Iko Iko," "Big Chief," and the title cut.

As a major bid for mainstream attention beyond zydeco circles, *Women in the Room* is Richard's most artistically ambitious and convincingly soulful album, one where the richness of the material rewards more than dance-floor attention, while the fusion of styles makes a strong case for the contemporary vitality of zydeco. Its achievement makes the *Snake Bite Love* followup all the more disappointing—a slickly calculated crossover bid that waters down the zydeco influence for greater rock acceptance (which it failed to achieve).—D.McL.

RIDERS IN THE SKY

★★★★ Three on the Trail (Rounder CD-0102) 1980
★★½ Live (Rounder CD-0186) 1984
★★½ New Trails (Rounder CD-0220) 1986
★★★ Saddle Pals (Rounder CD-801) 1987
★★★★½ Best of the West (Rounder CD-11517) 1987
★★★★½ Best of the West Rides Again (Rounder CD-11524) 1987
★★★½ The Cowboy Way (MCA MCAD-31244) 1987
★★★ Riders Radio Theater (MCA MCAD-42180) 1988
★★ Riders Go Commercial (MCA MCAD-42305) 1989
★★★ Horse Opera (MCA MCAD-42338) 1990
★★★½ Prairie Serenade (Rounder CD-0170) 1991
★★★ Harmony Ranch (Columbia CK 48589) 1991
★★★½ Saturday Morning with Riders in the Sky (MCA MCAD-100495) 1992
★★★ Merry Christmas from Harmony Ranch (Columbia CK 52778) 1992

Riders in the Sky are the hottest act on today's burgeoning western music scene. In fact, they are largely responsible for the current revival of popular interest in western and cowboy music. They are direct heirs of the Sons of the Pioneers' legacy of close harmony trio singing and instrumental virtuosity. Many groups have emulated the Pioneers' style over the years, but no one has come as close to capturing the sound and feel of what has become a distinct genre of western music as have the Riders. Since they made their first recording, *Three on the Trail,* in 1980, they have had tremendous success, with their own show on National Public Radio, "Riders' Radio Theater," a CBS Saturday morning television show, and their status as members of the Grand Ole Opry. Sophisticated, hip comedy is as much a part of the Riders' persona as their superb musical abilities, and they are able to be funny in the western context without ever maliciously making fun of it. They convey a deep love and respect for their material that endears them to real working cowboys as well as to their more urban fans. The group has recorded prolifically, and there is some overlap in the material found on these discs. I personally recommend the two *Best of* compilations if you are just starting to buy their records. Their children's albums, like *Saddle Pals,* are great, and if you are a fan of their spoken humor, try *Riders Go Commercial* and *Riders Radio Theater.*—C.H.S.

BILLY LEE RILEY
★★★ **Blue Collar Blues (HighTone HCD 8040) 1992**
No one better captured rockabilly's pill-crazed bark than Billy Riley. He was present at its creation at Sun Records but quit in disgust more than once, never landing a better deal elsewhere. The Sun classics ("Flying Saucer Rock & Roll," "Red Hot") and more besides are on the import label Bear Family's *Classic Recordings 1956-1960* (BCD 15444), but the only domestically available CD is a recent outing on HighTone. The whiplash in Riley's voice has gone, but it has gained some appealing bluesy contours to compensate.—C.E.

TEX RITTER
★★★½ **Country Music Hall of Fame (MCA MCAD-10188) 1991**
★★ **Conversation with a Gun (Richmond NCD-2148) 1988**
★★ **Greatest Hits (Curb D2 77397) 1990**
★★★½ **Capitol Collector's Series (Capitol C21Y-95036) 1992**
Tex Ritter, along with Roy Rogers and Gene Autry, was one of the reigning triumvirate of musical cowboys of the movies. Ritter initially set out to study law at the University of Texas but was soon sidetracked into the entertainment business. After appearing in several Broadway plays, he began his recording career in 1932. Many of his earliest recordings were traditional cowboy folksongs, and they would always remain an important part of his repertoire. Later he increasingly leaned toward popular country songs or pieces written for his movies (he made seventy). Ritter's rich, rustic baritone voice made every song he sang unmistakably his and lent itself especially well to the sparsely accompanied cowboy songs of his early recordings. The *Country Music Hall of Fame*'s sixteen cuts give a good cross section of his Decca period between 1935 and 1939, and like all the CDs in this series, has an extensive booklet of notes. *Conversation with a Gun* includes only eight cuts, and songs like "Saginaw, Michigan" and "Conversation with a Gun" are not his best material. The *Greatest Hits* package from Curb contains twelve of his best known recordings, like "Rye Whiskey" and "Deck of Cards," but it overlaps a great deal with the much better *Capitol Collector's Series* disc. Ritter spent more than thirty years of his career recording for Capitol, and that is where most of his best-known work was done. This collection contains twenty-five well-chosen cuts from his Capitol period, including "You Two-Timed Me One Time Too Often," "High Noon," "I Dreamed of a Hillbilly Heaven," and "Blood on the Saddle," dating from the early 1940s to his last recording in 1973.—C.H.S.

DENNIS ROBBINS
★★★½ **Man with a Plan (Giant 9-24458) 1992**
Dennis Robbins keeps getting new opportunities as a recording artist because his talent is vital and obvious. Why his repeated recordings fail to break through to larger recognition can only be blamed on bad timing, poor marketing, or a simple lack of good luck.

Robbins, a North Carolina native, originally played lead guitar and sang with a gritty, underrated Detroit rock band, the Rockets. After moving to Nashville, he released a solid album under his own name on MCA that's no longer available. His stint as a member of Billy Hill also produced good music but fell short of its commercial potential.

Back to being a solo frontman, he comes up with yet another worthy, rockin' country effort, *Man with a Plan,* which features his slicing slide guitar work and animated vocals. Robbins falls into the John Anderson, Hank Williams Jr. school. He knows how to rock the joint, he has a sly sense of humor, and his drawling voice can bring a real, palpable emotion to a song.—M.M.

MARTY ROBBINS

★★★★   All Time Greatest Hits (Columbia CK 31361) 1972 ●
★★★   Biggest Hits (Columbia CK 38309) 1987
★★★   American Originals (Columbia CK 45069) 1989
★★★★★   The Essential Marty Robbins (Columbia/Legacy C2K 48537) 1991

Given a choice between country music or pop music, Marty Robbins would probably have opted for pop; instead, he had to choose between country music and a regular day job, so there was no contest. Still, Robbins's background in pop music seeped out—less so in the early days when he worked with a hillbilly string band, but increasingly so after 1955. He flirted briefly with rockabilly before he lucked out with "Singing the Blues." When it was covered for the pop market by Columbia label mate Guy Mitchell, Robbins threw a fit and was allowed to record in New York with pop arrangements ("A White Sport Coat"). Then, with faultless commercial instinct, he cut "El Paso" at the beginning of the vogue for folk and western songs. In the early Sixties he minted a string of country-pop hits which skipped with apparent effortlessness from style to style. By the time of his death in 1982, though, the hits were fewer, and he had more-or-less reverted to his first love, pop music.

Of Robbins, perhaps more than any other country artist, it can be said that there's something for everybody: sentimental hillbilly and folk songs, western ballads, rock & roll, pop, Hawaiian music, hymns, right wing polemics, and good journeyman country music. It's a tribute to his innate musicality that he puts his stamp on it all; they all sound like Marty Robbins records rather than Marty Robbins trying to sound like someone else. *The Essential Marty Robbins* is what it purports to be: an overview of his Columbia recordings (he was on the same label for almost his entire career), and it serves as an excellent starting place, tracing his career through its twists and turns and down occasional blind alleys. Unfortunately, at present it's almost a finishing place as well. *American Originals, All-Time Greatest Hits,* and *Biggest Hits* tread the same territory—the Sixties and Seventies hits in various reconfigurations, most on *The Essential*—some not. With twenty tracks, *All Time Greatest Hits* is the best value of the three. The overlooked Fifties recordings have been issued in their entirety on a Bear Family import boxed set (*Country 1951-1958,* BCD 15570) and a complementary single CD.—C.E.

JACK ROBERTSON

★   Honky Tonk Daze (Step One Records SOR-0071) 1992

More mannered, vocally, than Clint Black, but with the same Jones-'n'-Haggard honky-tonk point of reference, Robertson has had modest indie success, thanks mostly to his carefully groomed good looks as featured in videos. His voice won't win prizes for pitch perfection, but with a little soul or some good material Robertson might be worth some attention. Unfortunately, he's blessed with neither on these outings. Admitting that he's a "honky-tonkin', boogie foot stompin' jukebox jumpin' bootie bumpin' dancin' fool," or bemoaning the fact that the younger generation gets haircuts at the beauty salon on main street instead of from "The Old Country Barber" wins him no credibility. Robertson may be ready for the barroom but not the studio.—J.O.

JIMMIE RODGERS

★★★★★   First Sessions (Rounder CD-1056) 1990
★★★   Early Years, 1928-1929 (Rounder CD-1057) 1990
★★★   On the Way Up, 1929 (Rounder CD-1058) 1991
★★★   Riding High, 1929-1930 (Rounder CD-1059) 1991
★★★★   America's Blue Yodeler, 1930-1931 (Rounder CD-1060) 1991
★★★★   Down the Old Road, 1931-1932 (Rounder-1061) 1991
★★★★   No Hard Times, 1932 (Rounder CD-1062) 1991
★★★   Last Sessions (Rounder CD-1063) 1991
★★   Country Legacy (Pair PDC2-1248) 1989
★★   Jimmie Rodgers (RCA Camden CAD1-2717) N. D.
★★   Train Whistle Blues (ASV Living Era CDAJA-5042) 1992

During his short seven-year career (1927-1933), Jimmie Rodgers set the tone and direction for much of country music that followed. It is hard to imagine the music sounding as it does today had Rodgers not lived. Both singers and fans have instinctively recognized this for generations, and he has long been known as the Father of Country Music. A new listener coming to Rodgers's records today will be impressed with his pliant, expressive voice, his genuine fondness for the blues, his ability to yodel and break into spine-chilling falsetto runs, and his ability to make sentimental songs full of nineteenth-century diction sincere and appealing. While dozens of his hit songs have remained in the standard country repertoire, it was his singing style that fascinated so many of the music's best singers, from Lefty Frizzell to Merle Haggard to Hank Snow.

Rodgers's recorded legacy is surprisingly slender: 110 selections done for Victor between 1927 and 1933. The first sides reveal a nervous, thirty-year old singing Victorian-era parlor songs like "The Soldier's Sweetheart"; the last show us a consummate professional singing works given him by professional songwriters, though weakened by tuberculosis and within a bare thirty-six hours from death. In between are dozens of masterpieces, some sung only to the backing of Rodgers's guitar, others done to a bizarre variety of back-up bands that range from jazz combos to studio orchestras to Kentucky jug bands to a musical saw. Fortunately, all of these sides are currently in print, making the Rodgers legacy the best preserved of any prewar country performer.

Rodgers's complete works, including key alternate takes, are presented on a series of eight CDs issued by Rounder through a licensing arrangement with RCA Records. Mastered from the original metal parts, and containing detailed liner notes by Rodgers's biographer Nolan Porterfield, all eight albums are well worth having and, taken together, present a rich portrait of early country's rough and rowdy ways. *First Sessions, 1927-1928* contains the bulk of the familiar Rodgers classics on which he won his reputation: the original

"Blue Yodel" ("T for Texas, T for Tennessee") as well as "Away Out on the Mountain," his two biggest-selling discs; sentimental favorites like "Daddy and Home" and "Treasures Untold"; railroad songs like "Brakeman's Blues"; songs that were not such big hits in 1928 but became standards later, like "In the Jailhouse Now"; and the other two first blue yodels.

The Early Years, 1928-1929 contains the first efforts in which Rodgers is backed with an orchestra, such as "Desert Blues" ("Big Chief Buffalo Nickel"), "Waiting for a Train," and "My Carolina Sunshine Girl." *Ridin' High, 1929-1930,* as the title suggests, shows the singer at the peak of his powers, with a memorable session (which was recorded, for some reason, at the Atlanta Women's Club) in which he was backed only by his own guitar and that of Billy Burkes. Highlights include "Mississippi River Blues" and "Nobody Knows but Me." *America's Blue Yodeler, 1930-1931* contains his prophetic "T.B. Blues" as well as his famous side with jazz great Louis Armstrong, "Blue Yodel No. 9," while *Down the Old Road, 1931-1932* features a superb recording with the Louisville Jug Band—one of pop music's first integrated sessions—as well as "My Time Ain't Long" and "Roll Along Kentucky Moon."

No Hard Times, 1932 is easily the best of the later compilations; it contains a session in which the singer's producer, Ralph Peer, backed him with a small studio orchestra in an attempt to make him the music's first crossover star. The Depression defeated this plan, but the session yielded some of Rodgers's most evocative songs: "Miss the Mississippi and You," "In the Hills of Tennessee," and "Prairie Lullaby." Also here are most of the sides done with ace fiddler (and former Skillet Licker) Clayton McMichen and McMichen's innovative young guitarist Slim Bryant: "Peach Pickin' Time in Georgia," "Mother, the Queen of My Heart," and the spectacular "Whippin' that Old T. B.," which has what might be the finest blues fiddle solo on record.—C.K.W.

KENNY ROGERS
★★½ **The Gambler (EMI-Manhattan 48404) 1978 ▲**

★★½ Greatest Hits (EMI-America 46004)
1980 ▲
★ Christmas (EMI-America 46558)
1987 ▲
★★½ Twenty Greatest Hits (EMI 46106)
1987 ▲
★★½ 25 Greatest Hits (EMI-America
466731) 1987
★★½ Duets (EMI 46595) 1984
★★★ Eyes That See in the Dark (RCA
14697) 1983 ▲
★½ What About Me (RCA 5335) 1984 ▲
★★½ The Heart of the Matter (RCA7203)
1985 ●
★ They Don't Make Them Like They
Used To (RCA 5633) 1986
★★ I Prefer the Moonlight (RCA 6484)
1987
★★½ Greatest Hits (RCA 8371) 1988
★ Christmas in America (Reprise
25973) 1989 ●
★ Something Inside So Strong (Reprise
25792) 1989 ●
★ Love Is Strange (Reprise 26289)
1990
★ 20 Great Years (Reprise 26711)
1990
★ Back Home Again (Reprise 26740)
1991
★★ If Only My Heart Had a Voice (Giant
24490) 1993

Although he sang with the New Christy
Minstrels in the Sixties and later sexed
things up on "Something's Burning," his
1970 hit as Kenny Rogers & the First
Edition, this megasuccessful entertainer
remains best known as the most colossal
country crossover singer of the late
Seventies and early Eighties. Rogers
first won chart laurels with story songs
like "Lucille," "The Gambler," and
"Ruby Don't Take Your Love to Town"—
which are like Johnny Cash tunes with
all the narrative and none of the
consequence.

By 1980, Rogers had gone #1 with
"Lady," an elegant Lionel Richie tune
that showcases well Rogers's seemingly
nonexistent but actually very carefully
worked-out and deployed singing style.
It flows along, two-parts modesty to one-
part rough-hewn theatrical arc and vocal
pressure points. The ballads range from
"Lady," which as a declaration of
suburban love has aged well, to the
idiotic "You Decorated My Life." Rogers
would rework this middle-of-the-road
mode, with greater or lesser country

accents, on duets with female singers
like Kim Carnes, Sheena Easton, and
Dottie West. These records, similarly, go
from the commendably emotional "Don't
Fall in Love with a Dreamer," which
Rogers and Carnes and a highly-strung
orchestra push to a fairly scary MOR
edge, to a version of Bread's "Baby I'm a
Want You" that he and West just have no
business doing.

Moving from EMI to RCA after he
became the best-groomed pop star in the
U.S. of the early-Eighties, Rogers
adopted an ambitiousness befitting that
sort of giddy success. He made *Eyes
That See in the Dark* with the Bee Gees
team in Miami, and, later *The Heart of
the Matter* with Beatles producer George
Martin in London. The first yielded the
Rogers and Dolly Parton "Islands in the
Stream" smash, a pop-country hybrid
that merged Southern warmth with then
happening international dance beats.
The single worked, as did the Martin-
produced "Morning Desire," a handsome piece of scrupulously arranged and
recorded midtempo balladry. Elsewhere,
Rogers was more hit-and-miss. *What
About Me?,* an attempt at Quincy Jones-
style sound and drama, ended up all
foaminess and posturing. Neither
Christmas album persuasively adapts
Rogers's moody mellowness to the
holiday repertoire.

Rogers established himself as a
mass-market pop star before Michael
Jackson's *Thriller* forever changed the
playing field of American pop, and as
such, he is one of the last superstars to
make a commercial virtue of his
conventionality instead of his creative
idiosyncrasies. In the aftermath of his
glory days, when Randy Travis redi-
rected country careers towards rooted
virtuosity and Garth Brooks later
pursued his own path as boldly as
Madonna and Prince ever did theirs,
Rogers has recorded painstaking but
dull Nashville albums that give his
country suburbanite persona nothing to
play off of. The lowpoint is *20 Great
Years,* a collection of digital re-recordings of Rogers's big EMI records,
wherein every second is immaculate and
empty. Still, he continues to appear on
TV and was one of the industry powers
behind 1983's "We Are the World"
charity record and event. He's always

loved events, but lately he hasn't been able to link his career to one. In 1992, Rogers moved to Giant Records and released *If Only My Heart Had a Voice.* The album could have been named by his harshest critic, yet in fact it returned Rogers to some of his modest former strengths, arriving at a feel that was very familiar and a little new.—J.H.

ROY ROGERS

★★★½ **Country Music Hall of Fame (MCA MCAD-1005548) 1992**
★★ **Tribute (RCA 30224-2-R) 1991**

Roy Rogers, the "King of the Cowboys," probably more than any other pop-culture cowboy, has come to embody the white-hatted singing good-guy of the silver screen in the American collective psyche. Born Leonard Slye in Ohio in 1911, he later moved with his family to California where he became a founding member of the original Sons of the Pioneers. After performing with the group for several years, he moved into motion pictures in 1937 and eventually appeared in more than one hundred movies. Between 1951 and 1957 "The Roy Rogers Show" (co-starring wife Dale Evans) was the backbone of NBC's Saturday morning television schedule. Throughout his film and TV career, Rogers continued to be a major record-ing artist, first for Decca, and later for RCA, where he spent the bulk of his recording career. The MCA *Country Music Hall of Fame* disc spans his early recording career from his days with the Sons of the Pioneers to 1941. It includes some of his strongest material and is accompanied by an excellent booklet of notes by historian John Rumble. The 1991 *Tribute,* wherein Rogers performs with such current artists as Clint Black, the Oak Ridge Boys, and Lorrie Morgan, is great fun, and Rogers certainly deserves this kind of honor. However, the album suffers from the same problem that plagues most of these tributes: it is more a vehicle for promot-ing the careers of the participating contemporary artists than an attempt to make good music showcasing the honoree.—C.H.S.

LINDA RONSTADT

★★★★★ **Heart Like a Wheel (Capitol CDP 7 46073 2) 1974 ▲[2]**
★★★★ **Prisoner in Disguise (Elektra 1045-2) 1975 ▲**
★★★★ **Hasten Down the Wind (Asylum 1072-2) 1976 ▲**
★★★★ **Simple Dreams (Elektra 104-2) 1977 ▲[3]**
★★★★ **Greatest Hits (Asylum 106-2) 1978 ▲[4]**

Linda Ronstadt was a big-voiced pioneer of West Coast country-rock and folk music from the first, going back to her days with the Stone Poneys in Los Angeles in the early Sixties and her first hit, "Different Drum." After going solo—and hiring for her first backup group Glenn Frey and Don Henley, who would later form the Eagles—she began a steady climb to prominence. Her astute song selection began to pay off with the stellar *Heart Like a Wheel* album in 1974. She mixed songs by the likes of Hank Williams, Anna McGarrigle, James Taylor, Phil Everly, Paul Craft, and Lowell George to form a personal folk-country fusion with country-rock overtones. She became, in effect, an ambassador shuttling between and building alliances among different fields of music. Everly's "When Will I Be Loved" from that album became a #1 pop hit, as did the R&B remake "You're No Good." Her version of Hank Williams's "I Can't Help It (If I'm Still in Love with You)," also from *Heart Like a Wheel,* won for Ronstadt a 1975 Grammy Award for Best Female Country Vocal.

In addition to her savvy song selection, she relied on Peter Asher's (from the rock duo Peter & Gordon) production skills. Their next collabora-tion was 1975's *Prisoner in Disguise* album, which continued her pattern of picking songs from across the musical map. With that album, her big hit single was a remake of Motown's "Heat Wave," but she also sang a moving version of Dolly Parton's "I Will Always Love You," long before rock audiences knew about Dolly. Plus, her version of Neil Young's "Love is a Rose" actually made a splash on the country charts.

On 1976's *Hasten Down the Wind* album, she had pop and country hits with Willie Nelson's "Crazy" and Buddy Holly's "That'll Be the Day." The album also included "Lo Siento Mi Vida," one of her first self-penned songs and one that would start her to exploring her part-Mexican heritage.

The following year, her *Simple Dreams* album established a crossover pattern for her: a cover version of Roy Orbison's "Blue Bayou" that earned her a Grammy for best single, a country hit with "Poor Poor Pitiful Me," another country hit with a Dolly duet on "I Never Will Marry," and pop hits with the Rolling Stones' "Tumbling Dice" and Holly's "It's So Easy."

Ronstadt traveled easily from country to rock and back again, thanks to her sincere, guileless approach, warm vocals, and impeccable song picks. She managed to make it look much easier than it actually was—and, in the process, she paved the way for cross-overs by such sisters in song as Dolly Parton, Emmylou Harris, Tanya Tucker, and the legion of country artists who followed in their wakes. In her own quiet way, she transformed country music as much as anyone managed to in the past two decades.

Since then, she has turned out a series of consistently good records, increasingly drawing on her Latin roots for material and winning fistfuls of Grammys for best Latin and best Mexican-American songs and records. —C.F.

PETER ROWAN
  ★★ **Peter Rowan (Flying Fish FF-70071) 1979**
 ★★★½ **Walls of Time (Sugar Hill SH-CD-3722) 1982, 1991**
 ★★★★ **[& Nashville Bluegrass Band] New Moon Rising (Sugar Hill SH-CD-3762) 1988**
 ★★★½ **The First Whippoorwill (Sugar Hill SH-CD-3749) 1990**
  ★★★ **Dust Bowl Children (Sugar Hill SH-CD-3781) 1990**
 ★★★★ **All on a Rising Day (Sugar Hill SH-CD-3791) 1991**

Singer-songwriter Rowan, a Bostonian, began his musical odyssey as guitarist and lead singer with Bill Monroe's Blue Grass Boys—they co-wrote "Walls of Time"—in 1965. Then he spent a number of years in the rock band Seatrain, honing his skills as a songwriter. He returned to the bluegrass fold in the early Seventies in a couple of cooperative band projects on the West Coast—*Muleskinner,* with Clarence White (Kentucky Colonels, Byrds) and others; and *Old and in the Way,* with Jerry Garcia, David Grisman, and Vassar Clements. Both can be found on CD these days, the former on Sierra, the latter—which includes three of his best-known compositions, "Panama Red," "Midnight Moonlight," and "Land of the Navajo"—on Rykodisc. Versions of those three tunes are also on *Peter Rowan,* the 1979 album that consists mainly of live material along with three Tex-Mex cuts recorded in San Antonio with accordionist Flaco Jimenez and other local musicians. Overall, the quality of this recording is disappointingly uneven.

In the early Eighties, Rowan moved to Nashville to begin working as a songwriter and started recording for Sugar Hill. His first album was *Walls of Time;* the title cut reprised the song he and Monroe had authored, with Ricky Skaggs playing the part of Monroe. A new song from this album, "Thirsty in the Rain," has been covered by a number of bluegrass groups, and in general this is a strong album. Sugar Hill chose to add three tracks to the CD version taken from another album, recorded by Rowan in Japan with the Red Hot Pickers, a band assembled for that gig, and unfortunately these cuts don't match the others on the album in feeling or quality. *The First Whippoorwill* is a tribute to Bill Monroe with a band that includes Sam Bush, Alan O'Bryant, Bill Keith, and other highly regarded bluegrass pickers. The music is well sung and played with verve but seems just a bit too respectful to have the same impact as Monroe's original performances. With the exception of two Monroe songs, *New Moon Rising* consists entirely of Rowan's own compositions. A collaboration with the Nashville Bluegrass Band, it is an album of consistently high quality, his best to date, with strong songs like "One Way" and "That High Lonesome Sound" delivered powerfully. It was followed by *Dust Bowl Children,* a non-bluegrass solo effort showcasing his new songs with a Woody Guthrie-Southwestern theme and a roots feeling. *All on a Rising Day* again features Rowan's new compositions and includes a guest appearance by Alison Krauss for a fine duet on "Undying

Love." As a songwriter Rowan is a mystical romantic, and some of his best songs have been controversial because of this—some wonder, for example, if it is proper to speak in the voice of a Native American, as he does in "Trail of Tears" on *New Moon Rising.* Perhaps not, but here is a songwriter who deals in strong emotions and forbidden thoughts, delivering his own material in a style worth hearing. —N.V.R.

BILLY JOE ROYAL

★★ **Greatest Hits (Columbia CK 45063) 1989**

★★ **Greatest Hits (Special Music SCD-4815) 1989**

★★ **Greatest Hits (Hollywood HCD-418) N. D.**

★½ **Looking Ahead (Atlantic 90508-2) 1986**

★½ **The Royal Treatment (Atlantic 90658-2) 1987 ●**

★½ **Tell It Like It Is (Atlantic 91064-2) 1989**

★½ **Out of the Shadows (Atlantic 82104-2) 1990**

★★ **Greatest Hits (Atlantic 82199-2) 1991**

★½ **Billy Joe Royal (Atlantic 82327-2) 1992**

Royal sings professional pop-country, with only his first country chart hit, 1985's "Burned Like a Rocket" (on the Atlantic *Greatest Hits)* displaying much originality. Despite his attractively plaintive tenor croon, Royal remains most famous for his sole rock & roll hit, "Down in the Boondocks" in 1965, included on all the greatest-hits collections.—K.T.

RUN C&W

★★★ **Into the Twangy-First Century (MCA MCAD-10727) 1993**

With a band name and an album title like that, you'd expect these jokers to play their bluegrass versions of R&B classics strictly for laughs. Well, there are quite a few chuckles in store, especially on the "doing the dozens" version of "Sweet Soul Music," wherein the C&Ws manage to run down everyone in Nashville from Lee Greenwood to TNN's Ralph Emery ("Oh, Ralph has lost his memory!"). But these refugees from Music Row—Russell Smith, Bernie

Leadon, Jim Photoglo, and Vince Melamed—will also have you marveling at their juxtaposition of "Gentle on My Mind"-style banjo with the heart and soul of "Stop in the Name of Love" and grinning at the result. Do they like soul music? Yeah, yeah. Bluegrass too.—P.K.

LEON RUSSELL

★★★ **Hank Wilson's Back (Shelter/DCC Compact Classics SRZ-8009) 1973**

Although a contributor to such pop hits as Herb Alpert's "A Taste of Honey," Bob Lind's "Elusive Butterfly," Gary Lewis & the Playboys' "This Diamond Ring," and Harper's Bizarre's "Feelin' Groovy" when he made this record, Russell—real name Russell Bridges—was best known for his solo albums, for his work on Joe Cocker's "Mad Dogs and Englishmen" tour, and for his contribution to the Concert for Bangla Desh. Other rock musicians such as Bob Dylan, the Byrds, Linda Ronstadt, the Grateful Dead, and the Band already had dabbled in country and traditional music when Russell recorded this in February 1973 at Bradley's Barn outside Nashville. Working with established Nashville session players, and with long-time buddies guitarist J. J. Cale and bassist Carl Radle, from his native Oklahoma, Russell interpreted tunes associated with Hank Williams ("I'm So Lonesome I Could Cry," "Jambalaya," "Lost Highway"), Bill Monroe ("Uncle Pen"), George Jones ("The Window Up Above," "She Thinks I Still Care"), and Johnny Horton ("The Battle of New Orleans"), among others.

Russell's gritty drawl matched the material perfectly, even though, as he said later, his knowledge of country music was limited to the truck-stop tapes he picked up shortly before these sessions. Most successful are uptempo numbers such as "Truck Drivin' Man" and "A Six Pack to Go." The CD reissue includes two previously unreleased tracks: "Hey Good Lookin'" and "In the Jailhouse Now."

Russell's country connection became stronger some years later. He moved to Nashville (he still lives north of the city), recorded two albums with Willie Nelson, one with New Grass Revival, and a second volume of Hank Wilson country covers (released on an independent label and now out of print). During sessions for his 1992 rock release, *Anything Can Happen,* Russell cut a bluegrass version of Chuck Berry's "Too Much Monkey Business," which he made available to a Nashville radio station.—J.O.

TOM RUSSELL BAND

★★½   **Road to Bayamon (Philo 1116) 1987**
★★★½ **Hurricane Season (Philo 1141) 1991**
★★½   **Poor Man's Dream (Philo 1139) 1992**
★★   **Cowboy Real (Philo 1146) 1992**

Tom Russell is a cultural conservationist. His dedication to memorializing an endangered era yields lyrical references to bygone icons such as Betty Grable, Lightnin' Hopkins, Little Willie John, and Jack Johnson, plus a train song about "the last surviving hobo," and a deliberate anachronism like this couplet from *Road to Bayamon:* "I got George Jones on the record player/I got whiskey in a jar." An itinerant Texan who made a few albums not available on CD—even the liner notes to *Road to Bayamon* are unclear about the size of his catalogue— Russell records with a four-piece band that roams from Bakersfield twang to Mexican corridos. (He's best known in Nashville for co-writing "Outbound Plane" with Nanci Griffith, a big hit for Suzy Bogguss, which Russell first recorded on *Poor Man's Dream.)* With the drained sonority of Johnny Cash, Russell sings about the daily dramas of small towns, featuring barrels of booze and at least one waitress per album. His fascination with the male psyche peaks on *Hurricane Season,* a loose, engaged performance which combines the grim death of Bill Haley, a tabloid arsonist

with a broken heart, and the darkly funny title track, about a cute whirlwind devoted to gin-and-tonics. Russell then pursued authenticity on *Cowboy Real,* an acoustic tribute to cowboy ballads, complete with buckaroos, cockfighters, rustlers, whores, and—of course—a waitress.—R.T.

TIM RYAN

★★★ **Tim Ryan (Epic EK 45270) 1990**
★★★ **Seasons of the Heart (Epic EK 47822) 1991**
★★★ **Idle Hands (BNA 66122-2) 1993**

Now here's a cowboy you can take home to Mama. Montana-bred Tim Ryan has a wide-open-spaces innocence in his tenor, a gentle musical disposition, and a sweetness in his delivery that are quite appealing. You get the feeling that his parents raised him with plenty of love, milk and cookies at bedtime, church on Sunday morning, and respect for the land.

Neither of the Epic CDs became a hit. But both contain moments of magic. The enchanting whirligig "Dance in Circles" and the wounded whimper "Breakin' All the Way" were standouts on the first album. Ryan took on meatier productions with the oomph of "Seventh Direction" and "I Will Love You Anyhow" on his second effort, indicating perhaps that he was only beginning to grow as an act.

In 1993, Ryan moved to RCA's BNA Entertainment. Taking a cue from Vince Gill, his *Idle Hands* CD for the company showcased the bluegrassy shades in his tenor and his songwriting ability more than his earlier albums had. Now if only somebody would let him show off in the studio what a hotshot lead guitarist he is on stage.—R.K.O.

S

DOUG SAHM

★★★ **The Best of Doug Sahm & Friends: Atlantic Sessions (Rhino R2-71032) 1992**

This eclectic compilation of early Seventies recordings serves as a transition between Sahm's Sixties rock hits with the Sir Douglas Quintet and his country re-emergence in the Nineties with the Texas Tornados. From the sessions and out-takes of Sahm's two Atlantic albums (of the more than fifty he has recorded over the course of his career), it suffers from some material that isn't consistently as strong and from a spirit that isn't quite as loose as on his best work, while displaying the range of this renaissance man of Texas music.

Highlights in a country vein include his first recording of "(Is Anybody Going to) San Antone," featuring Flaco Jimenez on accordion and harmonies from Bob Dylan, and the previously unreleased "Box Car Hobo," dedicated to Jimmie Rodgers. For those interested in Sahm's work even further beyond country's borders, *The Best of Doug Sahm & The Sir Douglas Quintet, 1968-1975* (Mercury) is more inclusively representative.—D.McL.

SAWYER BROWN

★ **Sawyer Brown (Capitol 46660) 1985**
★ **Shakin' (Capitol 46468) 1985**
★ **Out Goin' Cattin' (Capitol 46328) 1986**
★ **Somewhere In the Night (Capitol 46328) 1987**
★½ **Wide Open (Capitol 90417) 1988**
★½ **The Boys Are Back (Capitol 90417) 1989**
★½ **Greatest Hits (Curb 77578) 1990**
★★ **Buick (Curb 77578) 1991**
★½ **The Dirt Road (Curb 77575) 1992 ●**
★½ **Cafe on the Corner (Curb 77574) 1992**

Here's an entrepreneurial turn that couldn't have been anticipated even by a cynic like George D. Hay, the Barnumesque founder of the Grand Ole Opry: Sawyer Brown gained their record contract thanks to Ed McMahon, who featured the quintet on "Star Search," his TV talent contest. This Hollywood connection would not be held against the group if it weren't also the most distinctive part of their career. Sawyer Brown's early records suffered from Randy Scruggs's plastic production and the band's annoying proclivity for the cutesy, as evidenced by a few titles from *Shakin'*: "When Your Heart Goes (Woo, Woo, Woo)," "That's a No No," and "Billy Does Your Bulldog Bite." Things improved some on *Somewhere in the Night,* as they moved to a more organic, almost dusty musical style that suits Mark Miller's prematurely creaky, constricted voice (for those who haven't heard Miller, imagine Gordon Lightfoot without a sense of modesty). Interesting only as a dimestore mirror of changing Nashville trends, they enjoyed substantial hits with the title tracks to *The Dirt Road* and *Cafe on the Corner,* each of which peddled the wholesome rural imagery then in fashion. Just in case anyone missed the point, Mark Miller even wears overalls on the cover of the former record.—R.T.

NORMAN LEE SCHAFFER
★ **Norman Lee Schaffer (Intersound CDI 9106) 1992**

The Lounge Lizard from Hell warbles through a lamentably ordinary repertoire of hurtin' and cheatin' songs that are long on formula and short on imagination. Quick, somebody! Grab that vibrato before he hurts himself.—J.B.

DAVID SCHNAUFER
★★★½ **Dulcimer Player Deluxe (S.F.L. 3) 1989**
★★★★ **Dulcimer Sessions (S.F.L. 5) 1992**

David Schnaufer turns a homely folk instrument into an eloquent, thoroughly beautiful voice. For some time now, the dulcimer has been an outdated instrument associated primarily with old-time music enthusiasts and dreamy folk singers. But Schnaufer has explored and expanded the instrument's range in much the same way Jerry Douglas has transformed the dobro or Bela Fleck and his peers have revolutionized the banjo. He's extended the dulcimer's melodic and harmonic capabilities far beyond its reputation as a limited, gently strummed instrument.

Dulcimer Player Deluxe combines Schnaufer's first two cassette releases on one CD. His song selection is similar to that of Chet Atkins (who makes a guest appearance) or most other instrumentalists drawn to lovely melodies rather than musical complexities. The twenty-six songs range from country tunes like "San Antonio Rose," "I'm So Lonesome I Could Cry," and "Wings of a Dove" to traditional standards like "Greensleeves," "Jesu Joy," and "Fisher's Hornpipe" to pop classics like "Somewhere over the Rainbow" and "Here Comes the Sun."

Dulcimer Sessions continues in the same vein, except the guest list celebrates Schnaufer's growing reputation among other artists. Among the eighteen musicians appearing alongside Schnaufer are Dire Straits leader Mark Knopfler, renowned guitarists Albert Lee and Sandy Bull, and Tex-Mex accordion master Flaco Jimenez. The songs range from a traditional fiddle tune, "Fisher's Hornpipe," to the country instrumental "Down Yonder" to such pop songs as "All I Have to Do Is Dream," "Lady Jane," and "Spanish Harlem," as well as several sparkling originals.—M.M.

JOHN SCHNEIDER
★★ **Too Good To Stop Now (MCA MCAD-31116) 1984**
★★½ **Memory Like You (MCA MCAD-31303) 1986**
★★★ **Greatest Hits (MCA MCAD-42033) 1987**

On the cover photo of his 1987 *Greatest Hits* release, a denim-clad, impishly grinning John Schneider is playing air guitar. Though I'm sure the symbolism is unintentional, the image nonetheless rings true. From the start, there seemed to be something slightly "pretend" about this lightweight TV star's short-lived incarnation as a country singer (who later decided he wanted to be a rock & roller instead). Surprisingly, as a brief listen to Schneider's slim catalogue attests, this former costar of the long-running TV comedy series "The Dukes of Hazzard" *could* sing a country song—sort of like Merle Haggard's wimpy, anemic baby cousin might. In fact, he scored four #1 hits in the mid-1980s, including such evanescent numbers as "I've Been Around Enough to Know," "Country Girls," and "What's a Memory Like You (Doing in a Love Like This")," all of which are featured on his MCA *Greatest Hits* CD. That compilation provides all but the most die-hard "Dukes" fans with a sufficient taste of Schneider's noncommittal but competent warbling. —B.A.

DAN SEALS
★★★ **Early Dan Seals (Liberty C21Y-95561) 1991**
★★★★ **The Best (Liberty C21Y-48308) 1987 ●**

★★★ **Rage On (Capitol CDP 7 46976-2) 1988**
★★★ **Love On Arrival (Liberty C21Y-91782) 1990**
★★★½ **Classics Collection, Vol. 1 (Liberty C21Y-95952) 1991**
★★★½ **Classics Collection, Vol. 2 (Liberty C21Y-96384) 1991**
★★★★ **Greatest Hits (Liberty C21S-95757) 1991**
★★★ **The Songwriter (Liberty C21Y-98481) 1992**
★★★ **Walking the Wire (Warner Bros. 9 26770-2) 1992**

Dan Seals has a voice that can reach down into your soul and massage away your spiritual pains. A big, strapping guy, he's got a tough but tender quality that accounts for at least part of his appeal. So "Everything That Glitters," "You Still Move Me," "One Friend," and the rest of his ballads have an extraordinary potency. But get this: he can rock like crazy, too. Is there anyone else in country music who can tear off his acoustic guitar, grab a saxophone, and honk rockers like "Bop," "Love on Arrival," and "Good Times"? And is there anyone else who has shown such consistently good taste in material? Seals writes a lot of what he sings ("The Wild Side of Me," "Three Time Loser," "God Must Be a Cowboy"), but he's not so ego involved that he can't hear someone else's heartbeat (Paul Davis's "Meet Me in Montana," Thom Schuyler's "My Old Yellow Car," Cheryl Wheeler's "Addicted").

Grab *The Best* or the *Greatest Hits* CD and you can't go wrong. The man just doesn't make bad records. Of the recent CDs, 1988's *Rage On* and 1992's *Walking the Wire* are particularly nourishing, the former for its open-road masterpiece "Big Wheels in the Moonlight" and the latter for its troubled-man saga "Maybe That's Why" and its ode to international brotherhood "We Are One."—R.K.O.

DAWN SEARS
★★★★ **What a Woman Wants to Hear (Warner Bros. 26442) 1991**
Sears's first and only album didn't make her a star, but it will leave its impression on any country fan who hears it. With an elastic voice that articulates blues authority whether she's singing a honky-tonk classic or an unusual "Ebb Tide"-like rendering of Mike Reid-Troy Seals's "Till You Come Back to Me," Sears never misses on this album, superbly produced by Barry Beckett. A contemporary country woman with an old-fashioned, frequently broken heart, Sears has a way with lines like "He's in Dallas/Without us." She is just as knowing when she rocks through a first-person tale about leaving the kitchen and hitting the road in an unapologetically thumping cover of Highway 101's "Good Goodbye."—J.H.

THE SELDOM SCENE
★★★ **Act 3 (Rebel REB CD-1528) 1973**
★★★½ **Old Train (Rebel CD-1536) 1974**
★★★★ **Recorded Live at the Cellar Door (Rebel CD-1103) 1975**
★★★½ **The New Seldom Scene Album (Rebel CD-1561) 1976**
★★★ **. . . At the Scene (Sugar Hill SH-CD-3730) 1983**
★★★½ **The Best of the Seldom Scene, Vol. 1 (Rebel CD-1101) 1986**
★★★½ **A Change of Scenery (Sugar Hill SH-CD-3763) 1988**
★★★ **Scenic Roots (Sugar Hill SH-CD-3785) 1990**
★★★★ **Scene 20: 20th Anniversary Concert (Sugar Hill SH-CD-2501/02) 1992**

Going strong for more than two decades, the Seldom Scene is made up of virtuoso musicians who've created their own style of bluegrass, playing not only traditional gospel and old-time Appalachian tunes, but also giving the newgrass treatment to contemporary country, folk, and even pop songs. Departing slightly from the usual bluegrass instrumentation, Seldom Scene has never used a fiddle, except when pal Ricky Skaggs sits in. The group was founded by mandolinist John Duffey, fresh from the Country Gentlemen, in 1971, with other like-minded musicians living in the Virginia outskirts of Washington, D. C. He was joined by guitarist-vocalist John Starling, dobroist-vocalist Mike Auldridge, banjoist-guitarist-vocalist Ben Eldridge, and upright bassist-vocalist Tom Gray. This lineup, which lasted until Starling's departure in 1977, can be found on *Act 3*, *Live at the Cellar Door*, *Old Train*, and *The New Seldom Scene Album*. *Act 3* consists primarily of traditional numbers and includes guest fiddler Ricky Skaggs; *The New Seldom Scene Album*, featuring

Linda Ronstadt on harmony vocals, finds the group performing a mix of standards and contemporary country, including two superb Rodney Crowell songs ("California Earthquake" and "Song for Life"). *Old Train,* with Skaggs and Ronstadt again taking guest turns, also combines traditionals with newer country material, such as "Through the Bottom of the Glass," written by guest guitarist Paul Craft. *The Best of the Seldom Scene* pulls selections from *Act 3, Old Train,* and other albums recorded by the original group. And the excellent twenty-one-track *At the Cellar Door* features some of the same songs and more, performed live in a Washington club by the gregarious combo. With Starling's departure came guitarist-songwriter Phil Rosenthal, whose smooth vocals took the lead on many of the group's harmonies. Rosenthal wrote several of the songs on *At the Scene,* some of which sound as if they could have been performed by the Louvin Brothers ("The Weary Pilgrim," for example). In 1986, Rosenthal and Tom Gray exited and were replaced by guitarist-vocalist Lou Reid and bassist-vocalist T. Michael Coleman, both of whom began to write compelling new songs for the band. *A Change of Scenery* shows the group at its most eclectic, performing compositions by rock guitarist Mark Knopfler, the Beatles, and contemporary country numbers. On *Scenic Roots,* the band returns to more traditional gospel and bluegrass material. *Scene 20* documents all three aggregations of the band, performing at the Birchmere in Arlington, Virginia, where the group has held a once-a-week residency for almost two decades. This lively two-night concert in 1991 demonstrates the Seldom Scene's virtuosity, personality, and eclecticism. Emmylou Harris makes a guest appearance, singing lead on "Satan's Jeweled Crown," and the band plays wonderfully. Consisting of twenty-eight tracks, the two-CD set is a marvelous representation of this extraordinarily talented outfit's musical legacy.—H.G.-W.

BILLY JOE SHAVER
★★★★★ **Tramp on Your Street (Zoo/ Praxis 72445-11063-2) 1993**

As a singer, Billy Joe Shaver ranks only a notch or two above Kris Kristofferson and Tom T. Hall, which is to say that it's a good bet he'll never be invited to sing the "Star Spangled Banner" anywhere. His homely Texas twang creaks and strains in ways only a mother could love. But like Kris and Tom T., Shaver has his own picturesque way with words. Although he's recorded half a dozen now out-of-print LPs for Monument, Capricorn, and Columbia, he's always had more success in passing along his off-beat loser's tales to guys like John Anderson and Waylon Jennings who have a lot more business stepping into a vocal booth.

That said, it's hard to imagine anyone delivering the songs on this remarkable album with anything approaching Shaver's conviction. Coming from that cracked and leathery tenor, *Tramp on Your Street* sounds like the life story of a rambler who's still struggling with the desire for sin and the need for salvation. Shepherded by producer R. S. Field (Sonny Landreth, John Mayall) and goaded by the sparks from son Eddy's guitar, old Shaver standbys like "Georgia on a Fast Train" and "Old Chunk of Coal" ring with new autobiographical resonance, while fresh efforts like "If I Give My Soul" and "Heart of Texas" give you something to think about even as they rip and snort. Masterful storyteller that he is, Shaver even provides comedic relief with the tongue-in-cheek, Dixieland tribute to the "Good Ol' USA." Abetting Shaver on two tracks each are outlaws old and new, in the person of Waylon and former Headhunters Doug and Ricky Lee Phelps. But this is clearly the old hombre's yarn to spin, as he searches restlessly for comfort in the strictures of religion ("If I Give My Soul") and the arms of faithless women ("The Hottest Thing in Town"). Ultimately, he comes closest to realizing redemption in the songs he sings. If you like to put some drive, and reflection, in your country, Shaver's fevered dreams of wrestling with angels will set you free.
—P.K.

RICKY VAN SHELTON
★★ **Wild-Eyed Dream (Columbia CK 40602) 1987 ▲**
★★½ **Loving Proof (Columbia CK 44221) 1988 ▲**
★★ **RVS III (Columbia CK 45250) 1990 ▲**

★★ Backroads (Columbia CK 46855) 1991 ▲
★ Don't Overlook Salvation (Columbia CK 46854) 1992
★★½ Greatest Hits Plus (Columbia CK 52753) 1992 ●

A sullen bruiser whose trademark is a big white cowboy hat offset by a teeny white t-shirt, Van Shelton has positioned himself as a country sex symbol while lacking a body of work to back up his pose. He's had hits with overwrought versions of Charlie Rich's "Life's Little Ups and Downs" and Jack Greene's "Statue of a Fool." Left to his own devices, he sings mostly countrypolitan-style schlock in a pop-operatic tenor, but hits his high-point with a fluke: an Elvis impersonation, crooning a solid "Wear My Ring" for a movie sound track (1992's *Honeymoon in Vegas*). His stab at gospel, *Don't Overlook Salvation*, is particularly egregious, imbuing humble gospel music such as "Family Bible" and "The Old Rugged Cross" with pompous solemnity.—K.T.

SHENANDOAH

★★★ The Road Not Taken (Columbia CK 44468) 1989 ●
★★★ Extra Mile (Columbia CK 45490) 1990
★★★½ Greatest Hits (Columbia CK 48885) 1992
★★★ Long Time Comin' (RCA 66001-2) 1992

Like the group Alabama, Shenandoah has carved out its own sizable niche on the country music charts by invoking a sentimental view of Southern rural life and relying on the appeal of a distinctive and charismatic lead vocalist. Marty Raybon, a former bluegrass singer, is the convincing narrator of such easy-going hits as "Mama Knows," "Church on the Cumberland Road," "Sunday in the South," "Next to You, Next to Me" and "Ghost in This House." Since the five members of Shenandoah write little of their own material, their albums tend to be a bit uneven, ranging from solid to frothy. *Greatest Hits* encapsulates not only the most popular but also the best songs the group has yet produced. —E.M.

T. G. SHEPPARD

★★ Biggest Hits (Columbia CK 44307) 1988

★★★ The Best of T. G. Sheppard (Curb D2-77545) 1992

Sheppard (original name William Browder) broke into country music in 1974 with the fairly hard-hitting "Devil in the Bottle." In the ensuing years, however, he and his producers usually opted for blander, feel-good lyrics. During the late Seventies and early Eighties, Sheppard turned out some of the most hummable songs available on country radio, few of which, alas, showed any staying power. His best efforts include the dreamy "Last Cheater's Waltz" and the doleful "Party Time." Sheppard also recorded duets of dubious value with Karen Brooks, Clint Eastwood, and Judy Collins. In spite of his considerable chart success, Sheppard has simply failed to attract the songwriters and producers who could take him to the level of artistic significance. The *Best of T. G. Sheppard* contains the original recordings of "Devil in the Bottle," "Last Cheater's Waltz" and "Party Time." *Biggest Hits* offers the chaff of his career.—E.M.

RICKY SKAGGS

★★★★★ [& Tony Rice] Skaggs & Rice (Sugar Hill CD-3711) 1980
★★★★ Sweet Temptation (Sugar Hill SHCD-3706) 1981
★★★★ Family and Friends (Rounder CD-0151) 1982
★★★★★ Waitin' for the Sun to Shine (Epic EK 37193) 1981 ●
★★★★★ Highways & Heartaches (Epic EK-3700C) 1002 ▲
★★★½ Don't Cheat in Our Hometown (Epic EK-38954) 1983 ●
★★★½ Country Boy (Epic EK-39410) 1984
★★★½ Favorite Country Songs (Epic EK-39409) 1985
★★★ Live in London (Epic EK 40103) 1985
★★★ Love's Gonna Get Ya! (Epic EK-40309) 1986
★★★½ Comin' Home to Stay (Epic EK 40623) 1988
★★ Kentucky Thunder (Epic ESK 1627) 1989
★★½ My Father's Son (Epic EK 47389) 1991

Neotraditionalism in country music began in earnest with Ricky Skaggs's recording of "Don't Get above Your Raisin'" in 1981. Before his ascent to superstardom in mainstream country music, however, Skaggs had served a long apprenticeship in bluegrass music, first as a teenage member of Ralph Stanley's Clinch Mountain Boys, and later with a number of other bands including his own group, Boone Creek. Although the CDs reviewed here concentrate on Skaggs's post-bluegrass career, they nevertheless demonstrate his debts to the bluegrass genre in his awesome instrumental virtuosity, his clear tenor vocal style, and in his selection of songs. They also reveal his dishearteningly steady movement away from these strengths towards a more generic, contemporary sound.

The absolute gem among these recordings is the simple collection of old-time duets performed with Tony Rice, *Skaggs and Rice.* Most of the songs, such as "Bury Me beneath the Willow," "Mansions for Me," and "Will the Roses Bloom Where She Lies Sleeping," feature only mandolin and guitar for backing, while "Talk about Suffering," which Skaggs includes in virtually all of his stage shows, is a lovely a cappella performance.

The immensely satisfying *Sweet Temptation* draws mostly from the venerable bluegrass and honky-tonk songbooks. The title cut comes from Merle Travis, "Little Cabin Home" from Bill Monroe, "Forgive Me" from Wiley Walker and Gene Sullivan, and "I'll Take the Blame" and "Could You Love Me One More Time" from the Stanley Brothers. In Skaggs's inspired interpretations, the songs emerge not as bluegrass nor as old-time country, but as modern country music with the old-time feeling.

With *Waitin' for the Sun to Shine,* Skaggs signed with Columbia Records and plunged confidently into mainstream country music. Except for "Waitin' for the Sun to Shine" and "You May See Me Walkin'," all of the songs are country music classics ("Don't Get Above Your Raisin'," "Crying My Heart Out over You,") or (in the case of the beautiful "Lost to a Stranger") seem like they ought to be.

Highways and Heartaches and *Don't Cheat in Our Hometown* proved to be Skaggs's last full-blown syntheses of traditional country music and modern sounds and sensibilities. Afterwards, the novelty of reviving old-time songs either

wore off, or Skaggs and his managers decided that he needed to project a more contemporary sound and image. *Highways* mixes old and new material smartly, with "Don't Let Your Sweet Love Die," "Can't You Hear Me Callin'," and "I Wouldn't Change You If I Could" reaching out to the tradition minded, whereas "Heartbroke," "Highway 40 Blues," and the very pretty "Nothing Can Hurt You" looked toward the charts. *Don't Cheat,* dedicated to the Stanley Brothers, focuses almost exclusively on bluegrass and honky-tonk country music for material. Despite the presence of such superior musicians as Albert Lee and Hank DeVito, the album serves as a showcase for Skaggs. He plays guitar, mandolin, and fiddle on "A Vision of Mother," and handles both vocal lead and harmony on "Keep a Memory" and "She's More to Be Pitied." It seemed, however, that as his confidence grew, he began to lose touch with his roots.

By the time of *Country Boy* and *Love's Gonna Get Ya!,* Skaggs had shifted the emphasis in his music rather clearly toward modernity. Though classics like "Window Up Above," "I'm Ready to Go," and "Wheel Hoss" make their appearance on the former album—as does the great fiddler, Bobby Hicks, who had endured in Skaggs's band as a link to the bluegrass tradition—most of the songs on these decidedly commercial efforts vacillated between rock and country.

With *Comin' Home to Stay* Skaggs made at least a partial return to traditional form. (The album includes an apologetic note to his fans saying, "Thanks for staying with me through some trial and error. I've come back home to stay.") Hard-country songs like "I'm Tired," "That's Why I'm Walkin'," and "Hold Whatcha Got" (complete with the hard-driving banjo of bluegrasser J. D. Crowe) provide the album's musical core, while treatises on traditional values like "If You Don't Believe the Bible" and "Old Kind of Love" furnish emotional underpinning.

Kentucky Thunder contains no surprises and little excitement. The music is competently performed, as one would expect, but there are no songs here that recapture the vitality and clear-toned beauty of his earlier recordings. "Hummingbird" sounds like a dozen other hard-driving train songs, while "Fields of Home" and "Kentucky Thunder" repeat the standard homilies about the old home place and the old home state.

Though he claimed he was coming home to stay, Skaggs once again courted a wider following with the eclectic and contemporary *My Father's Son*. Despite evocations of home, family, and old-fashioned morality ("Simple Life," "Father Knows Best," the title cut), the music here turned away from traditional country sounds. "Somebody's Prayin'," for example, is pure contemporary Christian pop in mood and style, while "From the Word Love" could make anyone's easy listening list.—B.C.M.

CARL SMITH
★★★ **The Best of (Curb D21K-77473) 1991**
★★★★½ **The Essential Carl Smith: 1950- 56 (Columbia/Legacy CK 47996) 1991**

A smoothie with deep emotions, Carl Smith is one of the finest Fifties honky-tonkers. Smith could take a piece of overwrought image making like Arthur Q. Smith's "I Overlooked an Orchid" and turn it into a small masterpiece of longing and regret. The Curb collection is impersonal, chart-driven, just-the-hits without a few of the nonhit songs that fill out the portrait Smith deserves as a master at crooning weepers without becoming a soggy singer; for this, you must get *The Essential Carl Smith*, carefully assembled by compilation producer Gregg Geller, with astute musical and biographical liner notes from Chet Flippo. On his best hits, Smith projected a sensitive masculinity that found its finest match in the songwriting of Boudleaux and Felice Bryant; "It's a Lovely, Lovely World," "Just Wait Till I Get You Alone," and especially "This Orchid Means Goodbye"—all included on *The Essential*—display Smith at his most charismatic. Smith stands at the center of modern country music: himself a protégé of both Hank Williams and Ernest Tubb, he was married briefly to June Carter, a union that produced singer Carlene Carter.—K.T.

CONNIE SMITH
★★★ **The Best of Connie Smith (Dominion 574-2) 1989**

Smith made her mark in the Sixties with throaty renditions of such Bill Anderson songs as "Once a Day" (her debut smash hit), "Then and Only Then," "Cincinnati, Ohio," and "Nobody But a Fool (Would Love You)." (Anderson discovered Smith at a talent contest and nurtured along her budding career.) By the mid-Seventies, in an attempt to cross the pop bridge with James Taylor ballads, she lost her knack for hitting the country charts. This compilation consists of re-recordings of the Anderson penned hits and such classics as "Ain't Had No Lovin'" and "Just One Time." Fairly faithful to the original versions, these remakes show that Smith can still sing her heart out. —H.G.-W.

DARDEN SMITH
★★½ **Native Soil (Watermelon CD 1009) 1992**
★★★ **Darden Smith (Epic EK 40938) 1988**
★★★½ **Trouble No More (Columbia CK 45289) 1990**
★★★½ **Little Victories (Columbia CK 45828) 1993**

Though the music of this Texas singer-songwriter was initially marketed as progressive country, his artistry equally incorporates pop tunefulness, folkish balladry, and rock dynamics, as it has progressed beyond conventional categories. On 1988's self-titled debut album, the production by Asleep at the Wheel's Ray Benson and the backing provided by members of his band nudged Smith's songcraft in a country direction, with harmony vocals from Nanci Griffith and Lyle Lovett helping align him with the music's emerging generation.

His musical development soon took him well beyond country's confines, however. A transitional effort paired him with Britain's Boo Hewerdine for a duo album titled *Evidence* (on Chrysalis), while the subsequent *Trouble No More* represents a fuller flowering of his popcraft. On songs such as "2000 Years," "Ashes to Ashes," and the title cut, the material explores a spirituality that reinforces the music's melodic grace. While not reissued nationally until 1992, *Native Soil* was actually Smith's independent Texas debut, incorporating some material that he would later record for Epic, though the skeletal arrangements are more like demo quality and much of the songwriting reflects more ambition than experience.

Little Victories is Smith's most thematically ambitious and stylistically consistent album to date, a song cycle of temptation, betrayal, and redemption. Recorded in New York with veteran pop producer Richard Gottehrer, it shows little trace of Smith's roots in country music.—D.McL.

RUSSELL SMITH
★★★★½ **This Little Town (Epic EK 40918) 1989**

Russell Smith, former lead singer of the Amazing Rhythm Aces, went solo in the early 1980s and made a handful of noteworthy but overlooked albums for various labels while gaining recognition as one of Nashville's leading songwriters. *This Little Town* is his most recent solo outing and the only one currently preserved on CD.

It's ironic that Smith was summarily given his walking papers by Epic when *This Little Town* failed to find a sufficient audience; the LP is an obscure masterpiece. Songs like the title track, "An American Tragedy," "Blue Collar Blues," "Writing on the Wall," and "When the Night Comes to Call" are replete with all the sly wit, wry social commentary, and rhythmic assurance ("rhythm and bluegrass . . . hillbilly harmony over a heavy backbeat," is how Smith himself has described it) that gave the Rhythm Aces' 1975 hit, "Third Rate Romance," such lasting power. If there's any prevailing sense of taste or aesthetic justice, more of Russell Smith's (and the Amazing Rhythm Aces'!) out-of-print back LP catalogue will eventually be reissued on CD.—B.A.

HANK SNOW
★★★★★ **I'm Movin' On and Other Great Country Hits (RCA 9968-2-R) 1990**
★★ **Collector's Series (RCA 07863-52279-2) 1992**

For more than thirty years there were five pillars of the Grand Ole Opry—Roy Acuff, Minnie Pearl, Bill Monroe, Ernest Tubb, and Hank Snow. Each represented a different country tradition. Acuff maintained the Appalachian mountain sound. Minnie was the essence of country comedy. Monroe was bluegrass. Tubb was honky-tonk.

And what of Hank Snow? Well, he was his own idiosyncratic self, one of the most individual stylists in the annals of country music. Part Jimmie Rodgers songster, part sentimental recitation specialist, part flat-top guitar wizard, part honky-tonker, and part bluesman, Snow has a vast repertoire that includes sea shanties, train songs, cowboy tunes, murder ballads, Victorian parlor melodies, and traditional folk songs. He is also the progenitor of that bizarre stylistic offshoot, the country rhumba. This Nova Scotian forged an arrestingly distinctive and unique performance style that made him the longest-tenured RCA Records act in history, the possessor of eighty-five chart hits between 1949 and 1980.

No matter what genre he's exploring at any given moment, he's got an addictive sound. Hank Snow records are marked by his trademark clipped diction and flat, back-of-the-palate vocal tone as well as by his jaunty, deft acoustic guitar picking. His Rainbow Ranch Boys band featured scampering steel work, good-time fiddle bowing, and a propulsive rhythm section. One of Snow's crowd-pleasing techniques was the rapid fire tongue twister, best exemplified by "Would You Mind" and his 1962 masterpiece "I've Been Everywhere." (The latter is criminally unavailable on a U.S. compact disc.) Similar in impact are his lickety-split uptempo romps such as "Music Makin' Mama from Memphis," "The Golden Rocket," "Unwanted Sign upon Your Heart," "The Gal Who Invented Kissin'," "The Gold Rush Is Over," and the career-making "I'm Movin' On." All are included on the *Great Country Hits* package. The set also reprises his sentimental "Marriage Vow" and "My Mother," includes the guitar instrumental showcase "Silver Bell," offers the truly delightful rhythm ditty "The Rhumba Boogie," and reminds us of Snow's origination of such standards as "I Don't Hurt Anymore" and "Let Me Go Lover." At twenty tracks, this set is also an outstanding value for the money.

The *Collector's Series* CD, by contrast,

offers a chintzy eight songs, fully half of which weren't even Hank Snow hits. The jacket bills 1953's "(Now and Then There's) A Fool Such as I" as being included, but all you get is an instrumental of the tune behind Snow's melodramatic reading of his biography. Similarly, the version of "I'm Movin' On" included is a schmaltzy Nashville Sound updating, not the 1950 original. "Sentimental Journey" is a decent guitar instrumental. But the only real highlight of the set is Snow's 1966 updating of the Buddy Knox teen classic "Hula Love."

So if that's a must to avoid, what are we left with? All too little. There is no domestic CD reissue of such masterpieces as "Bluebird Island," "The Next Voice You Hear," "Tangled Mind," "The Last Ride," "Miller's Cave," "Ninety Miles an Hour," "When Mexican Joe Met Jole Blon," "These Hands," "Honeymoon on a Rocket Ship," "Hello Love" or the aforementioned "I've Been Everywhere" or "A Fool Such as I." An artist of this stature deserves far better treatment.

For a properly respectful overview, the Snow devotee must turn to Europe, where record companies are not just respectful, but exhaustively worshipful. Germany's Bear Family label has packaged four boxed sets devoted to Snow's career. The first contains four CDs plus a booklet detailing everything he did between 1949 and 1953. The second is another four CDs spanning 1954-58. The third consists of twelve (!) CDs in a box containing all of Snow's music of the Sixties. There's also a five-CD Bear Family set that brings you 138 songs he recorded for radio shows in 1950-56. —R.K.O.

JO-EL SONNIER

★★★★ Cajun Life (Rounder CD 3049) 1980
★★★ Complete Mercury Sessions (Mercury 314-512645-2) 1992
★★★★ Come on Joe (RCA 6374-2-R) 1987
★★★½ Have a Little Faith (RCA 9718-2-R) 1989
★★ Tears of Joy (Liberty C21Y-95684) 1991
★★ Hello Happiness Again (Liberty CDP-7-98761-2) 1992

There are at least four Jo-El Sonniers on disc to date. He initially surfaced as a teenaged "Cajun Valentino" on tiny Louisiana labels in the Sixties. This roots musician, singing traditional bayou music in French, was recaptured on the 1980 Rounder album *Cajun Life,* which many still consider to be Jo-El's finest moment. But there is more to Sonnier than this. His influences range from rockabilly to Lefty Frizzell, from backwoods gospel to downtown R&B. He came to Music City to explore all of these.

Since few pure Cajun acts make the country charts, he initially hit Nashville as a mainstream honky-tonk stylist on Mercury Records. The label occasionally let him sing in French, as well. These generally well-produced sides of 1974-77 were rescued and reissued on the 1992 CD *The Complete Mercury Sessions.*

The musical chameleon achieved his greatest commercial success on RCA in the late 1980s. *Come On Joe* and *Have a Little Faith* blended his Cajun accordion playing, natural rhythmic sensibilities, top-notch country-rock songs, and eclectic musical heritage with a certain alternative music edge. They were zesty, totally original works that remain ear-opening exercises in musical fusion, as adventurous and ambitious as anything on the market then or now. The rollicking "Tear Stained Letter" and "The Scene of the Crime" were among the tunes that became audience favorites during this Sonnier incarnation.

Since then, Jo-El Sonnier has settled into a rootsy, R&B-tinged groove at Liberty, with little of his Cajun style in evidence. These are only moderate artistic successes.—R.K.O.

SONS OF THE PIONEERS

★★★★★ Country Music Hall of Fame (MCA MCAD-10090) 1991
★★★★ Columbia Historic Edition (Columbia CK-37439) 1982
★★★ Cool Water (RCA Nashville 07863-58406-2) 1960
★★★ Songs of the Trails (Pair PDC2-1217) 1990
★★★★ Sunset on the Range (Pair PDC2-1156) 1990
★★ Country & Western Memories (Pair PDC2-1298) 1991

Despite numerous personnel changes and a multitude of stylistic innovations in country music, the Sons of the Pioneers have not only remained intact since the group was first organized in 1934, they have also preserved a distinctive group-harmony sound that is remarkably similar to that first introduced by Bob Nolan, Tim Spencer, and Leonard Slye (Roy Rogers). The Sons have reached far and wide for songs, and have recorded pop, gospel, and country, but made-for-movies western material has always been central to their stage, radio, and recording repertoire. Both Spencer and Nolan were capable of writing superb songs, but with classic numbers like "Cool Water" and "Tumbling Tumbleweeds," Nolan bequeathed to us some of the finest material heard in any area of country music. The Sons of the Pioneers added still another appealing and commercial dimension to their style when the talented Texas brothers Hugh and Karl Farr joined the group with their fiddle and guitar and their taste for hot jazz music. This unlikely fusion of smooth, romantic vocalizing and swinging instrumental accompaniment helped to make the Sons of the Pioneers popular among a broad spectrum of listeners.

The Sons of the Pioneers are well represented on CDs, but one hears a good bit of duplication on songs, and most of the albums contain no liner notes. Consequently, the identities of the singers will not be clear except to the most ardent fans and collectors. MCA's *Country Music Hall of Fame* collection is the most satisfying in every respect. It covers their recording career from 1934 to 1954 and includes the original performances of such classic songs as "Way Out There," "Tumbling Tumbleweeds," "Cool Water," "Echoes from the Hills," and "One More Ride."

The *Columbia Historic Edition* is an excellent anthology of material recorded in 1937 for the American Record Corporation (the producer of such budget labels as Banner, Romeo, Oriole, and Perfect). These recordings came at a time when Tim Spencer was absent from the group, and when Lloyd Perryman had joined them. One finds here the usual Pioneer assortment of cowboy songs like "Hold That Critter Down," romantic love songs like "At the Rainbow's End," and prairie hymns like "The Touch of God's Hand." The high points of the album, however, are the swinging instrumental "Cajon Stomp," which showcases the

superb fiddling and single-string guitar picking of Hugh and Karl Farr, and the cowboy yodel songs "The Devil's Great Grandson" and "Cowboy Night Herd Song." When you hear the latter two songs, you'll know why many people think that Roy Rogers was country music's greatest yodeler.

The Pair CDs provide no notes on personnel, but they present the group doing a wide variety of songs that include their western classics, pop songs, and modern country and western numbers. *Sunset on the Range,* for example, has "Riders in the Sky," "High Noon," "Home on the Range," a bluegrassy version of "Jesse James," "Room Full of Roses," and "Kaw-Liga." *Songs of the Trail* offers similar diversity, ranging from songs like "South of the Border" and "Sierra Nevada" to "Columbus Stockade Blues," "That Lucky Old Sun," "San Antonio Rose," and Hank Williams's "I Can't Help It (If I'm Still in Love With You)."

Country and Western Memories—with only two cowboy songs, "Cattle Call Rondolet" and "Song of the Bandit"—instead concentrates on Fifties country and pop favorites like "Memories Are Made of This," "Mocking Bird Hill," "Four Walls," "Crazy Arms," and "Cold Cold Heart." The Pioneers' smooth adaptations are the ultimate in easy listening, and thus for fans only. *Cool Water* contains eight pleasant performances of standards like "Cool Water," "Tumbling Tumbleweeds, and "Riders in the Sky," plus such older cowboy songs as "Cowboy's Dream" and "Red River Valley." One song worth mentioning, because it seldom appears on Sons of the Pioneers's anthologies, is Vaughan Horton's "Teardrops in My Heart," a pretty love song that deserves revival. —B.C.M.

SONS OF THE SAN JOAQUIN
★★★ **A Cowboy Has to Sing (Warner Western 9 26935-2) 1992**

The Sons of the San Joaquin are a family singing group from California who specialize in re-creating the close-harmony style of the Sons of the Pioneers. Backed up by Nashville session musicians, they do an admirable job on ten classic Sons of the Pioneers songs, such as "Cool Water," "Timber Trail" and

"Way Out There." Maybe not the Sons of the Pioneers, but among the best you will hear today in that western harmony tradition.—C.H.S.

SOUTHERN PACIFIC

★★½ Zuma (Warner Bros. 25609-2) 1988
★★★ County Line (Warner Bros. 9 25895-2) 1990
★★½ Greatest Hits (Warner Bros. 9 26582-2) 1991

This Southern California-based country-rock band conjured up echoes of Poco, Buffalo Springfield, the Eagles, and other formative West Coast country-rock bands without ever achieving the same level of distinction or identity. Their taut instrumental sound, smooth harmonies, and generally unremarkable original songwriting resulted in a sound that was often a bit too streamlined and formulaic for its own good. County Line, Southern Pacific's fourth album and one of its strongest, saw the departure of guitarist and co-lead singer David Jenkins. This briefly inspired the remaining four members to reconfigure their sound in a slightly more adventurous way, with vocal assists from the likes of Carlene Carter and the Beach Boys. Southern Pacific's first two Warner Bros. albums, Southern Pacific and Killbilly Hill, on which they seemed freshest and most innovative, are not currently available on CD. However, a few cuts from these albums can be heard on the band's one and only Greatest Hits compilation. The fact that this hits package includes a couple of blatant rock remakes that weren't really hits for the band at all—Del Shannon's "I Go to Pieces" and Bruce Springsteen's "Pink Cadillac"—hints that Southern Pacific was already running out of steam long before the engine stopped.—B.A.

RED SOVINE

★★★ The Best of Red Sovine (Deluxe DCD-7828) 1986
★★½ Phantom 309 (Hollywood HCD-117) 1987
★★½ Teddy Bear (Hollywood HCD-118) 1987
★★★ The One and Only (Starday SCD-132) 1987
★★ Giddy-Up-Go (Hollywood HCD-116) 1987
★½ Cryin' in the Chapel (Hollywood HCD-413) 1989

★★ Famous Duets With Minnie Pearl, Johnny Bond, and Others! (Hollywood HCD-416) 1989
★★½ Golden Hits (Hollywood HCD-412) 1989

Best known for his tear-jerkin' trucker tales, Red Sovine started out at the "Louisiana Hayride" (on the heels of Hank Williams) and first topped the charts via a duet with Webb Pierce, "Why Baby Why." This and other early honky-tonk numbers can be found on the poorly recorded collection The One and Only. Too bad about the low-grade sound quality because the songs are classics. Famous Duets drags except for a couple of tracks with Jean Shepard. As for the rest of Sovine's catalogue, most are cheesy packages, each consisting of one Top Ten sixteen-wheeler recitation ("Giddy-Up-Go," "Phantom 309," or "Teddy Bear") surrounded by maudlin fodder. The Best of Red Sovine offers the meatiest selection, including all the hits and enough sentimental weepers to last a lifetime.—H.G.-W.

LARRY SPARKS

★★★★½ Classic Bluegrass (Rebel CD-1107) 1989
★★★★ Sings Hank Williams (Rebel CD-1694) 1977
★★★½ Silver Reflections (Rebel CD-1654 1991
★★★ Travelin' (Rebel CD 1700) 1992

Young Larry Sparks first came to the attention of the bluegrass world in 1967 when he took the place of Ralph Stanley's brother Carter as lead singer and rhythm guitarist in the Clinch Mountain Boys following Carter's death. What made this newcomer particularly noticeable was that he also took over the role of George Shuffler in re-creating the band's acoustic lead guitar sound. By 1970 when he went off on his own to start the Lonesome Ramblers, Sparks was considered one of the up-and-coming talents in the bluegrass movement, a soulful mountain-style singer with an intense guitar style.

Since then he's made many albums for a bewildering variety of companies and more than once has recorded the same song for different labels. Classic Bluegrass assembles material from earlier albums, most originally by Rebel but a few from masters purchased and reissued on Rebel. It's a good place to hear his powerful baritone vocals on solo masterpieces like "Smoky Mountain Memories" and "John Deere Tractor," bluegrass kickers like "Love of the Mountains" and "Girl at the Crossroads Bar," and his spare, bluesy, guitar picking on "Cannonball Blues." There's only one gospel number (the Keith Whitley-penned "Great High Mountain"), which is a shame, since Sparks cut some good gospel albums for Rebel but none are now in print. *Sings Hank Williams,* from 1977, is his oldest album now available on CD—it's a good one. Not only are the songs, which include well-known standards like "Mansion on the Hill" and "Singing Waterfall" as well as some slightly lesser-knowns, all Williams classics, but there's also a strong backup band that includes Ricky Skaggs on mandolin and Chubby Wise on fiddle.

Silver Reflections and *Travelin'* are his two most recent albums; they reflect his mixture of repertoire and instrumentation, and give a good picture of the Sparks sound today.—N.V.R.

THE STANLEY BROTHERS

★★★★   Vol. 3, No. 3 (Copper Creek CD5511) 1989
★★★★   Vol. 3, No. 4 (Copper Creek CD5512) 1992
★★★★   Hymns and Sacred Songs (King CD-645) 1959
★★★★   Long Journey Home (Rebel CD-1110) 1990

RALPH STANLEY

★★★★   Bound to Ride (Rebel REBCD-1114) 1991
★★★   Almost Home (Rebel CD-1707) 1992
★★½   Back to the Cross (Freeland FRC CD638) 1992
★★★★   Saturday Night and Sunday Morning (Freeland FRC CD-9001) 1993

Carter and Ralph Stanley were the most tradition-based of all bluegrass musicians. They often borrowed songs from such early hillbilly musicians as Grayson & Whitter, Mainer's Mountaineers, and the Monroe Brothers, and in fact often reached back earlier to perform songs heard only at home or in their mountain boyhood churches. Carter Stanley, however, was also an outstanding

songwriter who had the ability to fuse the pastoral images of country life with the themes of loneliness, loss, and separation. Ralph Stanley's high, lonesome tenor has made him a hero to both traditional bluegrass fans and such contemporary musicians as Emmylou Harris. After Carter's death on December 1, 1966, Ralph continued singing with a sound and repertoire that were even more traditional than before. He has been fortunate in attracting to his band such outstanding musicians as Keith Whitley, Ricky Skaggs, and Larry Sparks, as well as a long string of lead singers who sounded uncannily like his brother Carter.

Hymns and Sacred Songs, a CD reissue of a 1959 LP, is a wonderful collection of vintage bluegrass gospel music. It passes the test of all classic country music: it makes the hair stand up on your arms and it demands listening to again and again. Most of the performances (all recorded in a single February 1959 session) exhibit the powerful influence of Bill Monroe and particularly the vocal sound of Monroe's Blue Grass Quartet. One hears, for example, close four-part harmony, high tenor singing, and numerous breaks on the mandolin, an instrument which the Stanleys eventually discarded. The album includes rousing versions of the old shape-note standards "Daniel Prayed" and "He Said If I Be Lifted Up," a couple of Bill Monroe tunes ("The Wicked Path of Sin" and "I'll Meet You in Church Sunday Morning"), and the now-classic Carter Stanley original, "White Dove."

Long Journey Home collects sixteen songs recorded in the early 1960s for Ray Davis's Wango label and released under the name of John's Country Quartet. With material like "Pretty Polly," "East Virginia Blues," "Wild and Reckless Hobo," "Ramshackle Shack on the Hill," and "Will You Miss Me," the album is exclusively old-time in nature and features the singing of Carter, Ralph, and George Shuffler, a seminal bluegrass bass player and pioneer of guitar cross picking.

The Copper Creek recordings are wonderful assortments of live performances made by the Stanleys in 1958. *Vol. 3, No. 3* includes material recorded at Sunset Park in West Grove, Pennsylvania, on May 4, 1958, while *Vol. 3, No. 4* presents concerts given at New River Ranch in Rising Sun, Maryland, on September 7, 1958. The performances aren't flawless by any means. In some cases, the Stanleys tried out songs that they had only recently recorded, or, on a few occasions, did numbers that they only half-knew but which had been requested by the audience. Nevertheless, the forgotten lyrics, muffed vocals, less-than-crisp instrumental breaks, and false starts only add to the charm of these vintage concerts. Ably supported by a talented cast of musicians, the Stanleys present a vibrant collage of vocal and instrumental music, powerfully combining the feeling and soul of traditional balladry with the dynamic musicianship of modern acoustic bluegrass. It is no wonder that Alan Lomax was thinking of the Stanleys when he called bluegrass "folk music in overdrive."

With *Bound to Ride,* a rich bonanza of twenty songs, Ralph Stanley demonstrates the strong pull of tradition that shaped his music after the death of his brother. The collection features the lead singing of Roy Lee Centers, who was probably the best of the Carter Stanley replacements, but one also hears Ricky Skaggs and Keith Whitley and a guest appearance by Country Gentleman John Duffey who takes the high baritone on "Lonesome River." Ralph plays two clawhammer banjo tunes learned from his mother, "Shout Little Lulie" and "Little Birdie," and he and the Clinch Mountain Boys reach back to do exciting versions of old country songs such as "Maple on the Hill," "I'll Remember You Love," and "Gold Watch and Chain," plus some Stanley Brothers favorites.

Back to the Cross, a collection of original gospel material rumored to have been cut in a single day, sounds rushed and a little weary. Thankfully, the two-disc set *Saturday Night and Sunday Morning* proves a refreshing return to form. Joined by an all-star cast that includes George Jones, Bill Monroe, Tom T. Hall, Emmylou Harris, Ricky Skaggs, Vince Gill, Dwight Yoakam, Patty Loveless, Alison Krauss, and Larry Sparks, Stanley and company breathe new life into old Stanley Brothers warhorses as well as other favorites from the secular (*Saturday Night)* and sacred (*Sunday Morning)* realms of bluegrass.

Among the many highlights in these thirty-one tracks are Dwight Yoakam's passionate rendition of "Down Where the River Bends" and Emmylou Harris's sensitive reading of Keith Whitley's gospel song "Great High Mountain."

Almost Home may very well be the most traditional-sounding collection of music now available on commercial recordings. Ralph Stanley and his Clinch Mountain Boys sing twelve religious songs, both gospel hymns and the much older "white spirituals," in an austere, a cappella style that is most commonly identified with Stanley's home region of southwestern Virginia and neighboring East Tennessee. Employing stylistic devices that are even older than Appalachia, Stanley lines out the verses on some songs and the Clinch Mountain Boys sing responsively in a slow, long-metered style that would have been familiar to hymnist Isaac Watts in the early eighteenth century. This style of music may not be everyone's cup of tea, but when Stanley performs such haunting songs as "Village Churchyard," "The Day Is Past and Gone," and "God Put a Rainbow in the Clouds," he does more than simply return to the culture of his youth. He takes all of us back to one of the great sources of country music.—B.C.M.

THE STATLER BROTHERS

★★	**World of the Statler Brothers (Columbia CGK-31557) 1972**	
★★★★★	**Best of, Vol. 1 (Mercury 822524-2) 1975 ▲²**	
★	**Holy Bible: Old Testament (Mercury 826267-2) 1975**	
★★	**Holy Bible: New Testament (Mercury 826268-2) 1975 ●**	
★★	**Christmas Card (Mercury 822743-2) 1978 ▲**	
★★★★	**Best of, Vol. 2 (Mercury 822525-2) 1979 ●**	
★★★	**Today (Mercury 812184-2) 1983 ●**	
★★★★	**Atlanta Blue (Mercury 818652-2) 1984**	
★★★	**Christmas Present (Mercury 824785-2) 1985**	
★★★	**Partners in Rhyme (Mercury 824420) 1985**	
★★	**Four for the Show (Mercury 826782-2) 1986**	
★★★	**Maple Street Memories (Mercury 832-404-2) 1987**	

★★★ Greatest Hits (Mercury 834626-2) 1988
★★★★ Live and Sold Out (Mercury 838231-2) 1989
★★★★ Radio Gospel Favorites (Mercury 826710-2) 1990
★★ Music, Memories, and You (Mercury 842518-2) 1990
★★★ All American Country (Mercury 848 370-2) 1991
★★★★ Gospel Favorites (Heartland HC 2012) 1992

"America's poets" novelist Kurt Vonnegut called them, in deference to their evocative songs about baby boomer nostalgia like "Class of '57." But the Statler Brothers are also arguably the most distinctive vocal group in modern country music. Their personnel has been remarkably stable, with only one major change since their professional start back in 1963, and their soft, close-harmony gospel quartet style has remained amazingly consistent through four decades of country trends. Even their back-up arrangements, produced mainly by Jerry Kennedy, have a character of their own: single-string guitar solos set off by a light dusting of violins and a pumping piano.

The Statlers (named jokingly for the now-defunct Statler Tissue company) began their career as an opening act for Johnny Cash, and throughout the 1960s recorded for Cash's label, Columbia. The act first consisted of only two brothers—Harold and Don Reid—along with Lew DeWitt and Phil Balsley, and specialized in punning songs like "Flowers on the Wall" and "You Can't Have Your Kate and Edith Too." The best of these efforts are found in 1972's *The World of the Statler Brothers*. After they signed with Mercury in 1970, they really hit their stride with a series of nostalgia-oriented songs like "Class of '57," "What Ever Happened to Randolph Scott," and "Pictures." These and others from this era are in *The Best of the Statler Brothers*. Efforts from the later 1970s, like "The Official Historian of Shirley Jean Berrell" and "How to be a Country Star," are in an equally satisfying package, *The Best of the Statler Brothers Rides Again, Vol. 2*. About as good as a retrospective is *Statler Brothers Live and Sold Out*, a 1989 concert recorded in Wheeling, West Virginia.

In 1982 Lew DeWitt left the group for health reasons and was replaced with Jimmy Fortune, whose soaring tenor was soon heard on later albums like *Atlanta Blue* (1984) and *Pardners in Rhyme* (1985). Throughout their career, the Statlers have kept in touch with their gospel music roots (they started as a gospel quartet called the Kingsmen), and this has lead to odd experiments, like two concept albums built around the Scriptures—*The Holy Bible: Old Testament* and *The Holy Bible: New Testament* (1975). Far more successful are two anthologies of gospel pieces from various albums, *Radio Gospel Favorites* and the mail-order set *Gospel Favorites*. There's a good deal of overlap between the two, but both have the stunning "There is Power in the Blood" and "When the Roll is Called Up Yonder."—C.K.W.

RAY STEVENS
★★★½ Greatest Hits (RCA 5153-2-R) 1983
★★ Everything is Beautiful & Other Hits (RCA 52161-2) 1992
★★★ Greatest Hits (MCA MCAD-5918) 1987 ●
★★½ Crackin' Up! (MCA MCAD-42020) 1987
★★ Greatest Hits, Vol. 2 (MCA MCAD-42062) 1987
★★★½ His All-Time Greatest Comic Hits (Curb D2-77312) 1990
★★½ Lend Me Your Ears (Curb/Capitol CDP 7 94374 2) 1990
★★ Greatest Hits (Curb D2-77464) 1991
★★ #1 With a Bullet (Curb/Capitol CDP 7 95914 2) 1991

Stevens began his career as a novelty singer whose early hit, "Ahab the Arab," coincided with the popularity of 1962's Oscar-winning film, *Lawrence of Arabia*. Later in his career, he turned to contemporary social issues, sometimes with the plodding earnestness of "Everything Is Beautiful," but more often with good-natured satire or cynical wit. Stevens is at his best when exposing whimsical contradictions or destructive hypocrisies that lie beneath society's glossy veneer. "Shriner's Convention," his brilliant satire on the fez-topped secret society, and "The Mississippi Squirrel Revival," his hilarious send-up of evangelical sanctimony, cut right to the soul of

American character. At his worst, Stevens's recordings are loud and boorish, with all the subtlety of a Saturday night TV sitcom sound track.

All of these greatest hits packages include some of Stevens's classics along with works of lesser merit. Except for the Erroll Garner jazz standard, "Misty," Stevens wrote all the songs on the RCA *Greatest Hits* set, which features several of his most enduring early recordings, including "Ahab," "The Streak," "Guitarzan," "Shriner's Convention," and "Everything Is Beautiful." *His All-Time Greatest Comic Hits* includes the novelty songs named above, plus "Mississippi Squirrel Revival" and "Would Jesus Wear a Rolex," a reflection on the excesses of televangelism. Stevens's recent studio recordings contain a rare knee-slapper, such as "Sittin' Up with the Dead" (*Lend Me Your Ears*), "I'm My Own Grandpa" (*Crackin' Up*), and "The Pirate Song (I Want to Sing and Dance)" (*#1 With a Bullet*), but little else to compare with the cracked genius of his earlier creations.—J.B.

GARY STEWART
★★★★★ **Out of Hand (HighTone HCD 8026) 1975**
★★★★ **Brand New (HighTone HCD 8014) 1988**
★★★ **Battleground (HighTone HCD 8023) 1990**
★★★★★ **Gary's Greatest (HighTone HCD 8030) 1991**

Gary Stewart assured his place in country music history with his first album, *Out of Hand.* Justifiably, critics regard the record, produced by Roy Dea, as a honky-tonk classic, a hard stare into the darkness of adultery, jealousy, alcoholism, and crime. Stewart's trembling voice conveys tortured guilt, disillusion, and dissolution. *Out of Hand* is remarkable too, for being packed with quality songs at a time when country albums more commonly contained three hits and cover songs for filler. Though it clocks in at less than thirty minutes, the disc delivers more passion than most longer collections. Not currently available is Stewart's 1977 album, *Your Place or Mine,* also produced by Dea. On it, Stewart tackles quality songs by Rodney Crowell and Guy Clark, among others, and Emmylou

Harris, Nicolette Larson, and Crowell supply backing vocals on some tracks.

Stewart ended a recording hiatus of several years with *Brand New,* another Dea production. Though his voice has a little less power, Stewart still sings with the growling, trembling passion of his earlier work. That country radio—suddenly turned puritanical—would not play "An Empty Glass" is a crime. With eight strong songs written by Stewart and wife Mary Lou, *Brand New* deserved a better reception than it got. On *Battleground* Stewart attacks on another front, deploying the Southern rock side of his arsenal on some cuts. "Bedroom Battleground," "Nothing Cheap about a Cheap Affair," "Woman in Demand," and "Seeing's Believing" retain the classic country feel, but "Let's Go Jukin' " and "Nothin' but a Woman" lean more toward rock. A cover of Bobby Darin's "You're the Reason I'm Living" misfires badly.

Gary's Greatest contains selections from 1973 (his recording of "Ramblin' Man," which should have been left off this set) to 1990 ("Let's Go Jukin'"). Stewart maintains consistently high standards, and his vocal work seldom wavers. Particularly welcome in this package are the bluesy "Little Junior," the slide-guitar graced "Flat Natural Born Good-Timin' Man," "She's Got a Drinking Problem," and "Single Again." To hear this collection is to be amazed that country radio won't play Stewart's songs. Get *Gary's Greatest* and weep. —J.O.

LARRY STEWART
★★½ **Down the Road (RCA 07863 66210-2) 1993**

The cover photo of *Down the Road* shows Larry Stewart sitting in a beat-up lounge chair on the side of the road, with an electric guitar in his lap. It's a fitting image for this former lead singer for country smoothies Restless Heart, who drove right down the middle of the road for most of the late Eighties. On this first solo outing, the agreeably rough-voiced singer edges toward danceable country-rock at times while offering enough familiar sounding romantic ballads ("When I Close My Eyes," "Brittany") for old fans to fall back on. Stewart sounds freshest and most inspired, though, when he swings into modern dancehall numbers like "Alright Already" and "I'll Cry Tomorrow." Musically, *Down the Road* proves to be a two-step in the right direction. Now, if he could just find some really distinctive material. . . . —P.K.

LISA STEWART
★★ **Lisa Stewart (BNA 66040-2) 1993**
This Mississippi-born brunette has a nice ache around the edges of her dusky alto, which comes off particularly well in her sensitive remake of Jeannie Seely's classic ballad "Don't Touch Me." But the production and song choice here try to be all things to all listeners—obligatory fiddle and steel on a heartbreak song here; a backdrop of strings, chorus oo-ahs, and cocktail piano on a Patsy pastiche there—with the result that Stewart emerges with no distinct vocal identity. Unfortunately, all you'll remember about this album is that there was a good voice lurking in there somewhere.—P.K.

DOUG STONE
★★ **Doug Stone (Epic 45303) 1990 ▲**
★★ **I Thought It Was You (Epic 47357) 1991 ●**
★★★ **From the Heart (Epic 52436) 1992**
★★ **The First Christmas (Epic 52844) 1992**

Singers who don't write their own material rarely develop a persona as quickly and clearly as Doug Stone. Starting with the Spectoresque grandeur of "I'd Be Better Off (In a Pine Box)," from his first album, Stone's tender entreaties delivered the words of lovestruck losers in a style so soft and trembly he made Garth Brooks sound like Waylon Jennings. As befits a singles artist, Stone expanded his signature with a few honky-tonk novelties: "A Jukebox with a Country Song" peddles the same reactionary blue-collar jingoism that marked Randy Travis's "A Better Class of Losers," while "Warning Labels" cautions about the depressive effect of a barroom hit parade with an unexpected wit, and typifies the spare production that fired *From the Heart.*—R.T.

GEORGE STRAIT
★★★ **Strait Country (MCA MCAD-31087) 1981 ●**
★★★ **Strait from the Heart (MCA MCAD-31117) 1982 ●**
★★★½ **Right or Wrong (MCA MCAD-5450) 1983 ●**
★★★★ **Does Fort Worth Ever Cross Your Mind (MCA MCAD-31032) 1984 ▲**
★★★★★ **Greatest Hits (MCA MCAD-5567) 1985 ▲²**
★★★★ **Something Special (MCA MCAD-5605) 1985 ●**
★★★ **#7 (MCA MCAD-5750) 1986 ●**
★★★½ **Merry Christmas Strait to You (MCA MCAD-5800) 1986 ●**
★★½ **Ocean Front Property (MCA MCAD-5913) 1987 ▲**
★★★★½ **Greatest Hits, Vol. 2 (MCA MCAD-42305)**
★★ **If You Ain't Lovin' You Ain't Livin' (MCA MCAD-42114) 1988 ▲**
★★★★½ **Beyond the Blue Neon (MCA MCAD-42266) 1989 ▲**
★★½ **Livin' It Up (MCA MCAD-6415) 1990 ▲**
★★★½ **Ten Strait Hits (MCA MCAD-10450) 1991 ●**
★★★ **Chill of an Early Fall (MCA MCAD-10204) 1991 ▲**
★★★ **Holding My Own (MCA MCAD-10532) 1992 ●**
★★★½ **Pure Country (MCA MCAD-10651) 1992 ▲²**

During the Eighties, Randy Travis and Dwight Yoakam coaxed the notion of being a traditional country singer into the realm of the cool. But George Strait, whose career had about a half-decade headstart on them both, outfitted the occupation with a sleek new modernity, showing the way. Without the immediacy of Travis's head-turning vocal presence, and with a sweeping disregard for Yoakam's rock touches, Strait steered his own streamlined course. He became one of country's largest stars, a laid-back yet staunch believer in minimalism who nevertheless didn't limit his music.

Strait's first albums, produced by Blake Mevis, introduced the sort of tune—subtle, often wry-minded, immi-nently hummable—on which he would long rely: "If You're Thinking You Want a Stranger (There's One Coming Home)," "A Fire I Can't Put Out." There are, of course, outstanding stylistic exceptions to this Strait rule, as the rockabilly-ready "Unwound" and the luxurious ballad "Marina Del Ray" suggest in their ways. But *Strait Country* and *Strait from the*

Heart bank on a concise yet very lush instrumental style from which Strait decidedly backed off. That kind of sound seemed inconsistent with his ultimate goal of stripping away anything that could be construed as extraneous to the *songs.* Even *Right or Wrong,* which brings on his rhythmically expansive, soon-to-be-trademark western swing rhythms, pares back. That Ray Baker-produced album, a hair away from being Strait's finest, invites a listener to appreciate how less instrumental clutter brings out more in Strait's singing. Note how comfortably Strait can stretch out on, say, "A Little Heaven's Rubbing Off on Me."

This success pointed the way for the future. With the title track of *Does Fort Worth Ever Cross Your Mind,* Strait, who had put out crackerjack records before, released a masterpiece working for the first time with producer Jimmy Bowen. Every element of the track—the Texas rhythm section, the major impact of the ever-shifting points of emphasis of Strait's carefully nuanced vocal of subtle pain and sarcasm, the steel-and-fiddle crosstalk—advances the lyric. Continuing in a seven-year association with Bowen, this approach would yield albums that blended modern roots-country with classic pre-rock American pop. Here was a Lefty Frizzell fan who listened to, and learned from, Frank Sinatra and Perry Como. (That background makes Strait's Christmas collection, for example, into a fine negotiation between urban and rural Americana.)

Other times, when Strait's material wasn't quite as transcendent as, say, *Fort Worth's* "You're Dancin' This Dance All Wrong," *Something Special's* "The Chair" and "Lefty's Gone," or "Overnight Success," from 1989's magnificent *Beyond the Blue Neon,* the Strait line came out just too dry. That's because Strait, the most sophisticated traditional country singer of his generation, is lousy at persona; if, when he's done with it, the song doesn't seem like something special, he has little flash, attitude, or emotive power to salvage anything. His seeming faith in pure musicianship is the only true sense in which Strait is a throwback.

Since the late-Eighties, Strait has enjoyed a full-fledged platinum-plus career, with #1 singles, well-attended live performances, CMA Entertainer of the Year awards, and all the usual perquisites. In 1992, after three albums that had their moments but coasted on past accomplishments, Strait teamed up with producer Tony Brown for *Pure Country.* Although it's a big departure in style that makes little stylistic sense for Strait apart from the film for which it served as the sound track, the album still sold very well indeed. More importantly, it led Strait back toward a fuller, more commercially competitive sound. This approach, with better material, is doubtless where he'll be aiming in future.—J.H.

STRENGTH IN NUMBERS
★★★★ Telluride Sessions (MCA MCAD-6293) 1989

Sam Bush, Jerry Douglas, Edgar Meyer, Bela Fleck, and Mark O'Connor—the members of this occasional aggregation of session pickers—first got together at the Telluride Bluegrass Festival. Each is an acoustic virtuoso known in his own right for pushing the envelope of his individual instrument. So it's no surprise that they venture out into the newgrass stratosphere on this, their only recorded effort. What is surprising is just how listenable these off-the-wall musical excursions can be.—P.Cr.

MARTY STUART
★★★ Busy Bee Cafe (Sugar Hill SH 3726) 1982
★★★ Marty Stuart (Columbia CK 52960) 1986
★★½ Let There Be Country (Columbia CK 40829) 1992
★★★ Hillbilly Rock (MCA MCAD-42312) 1989
★★★★ Tempted (MCA MCAD-10106) 1991
★★★★½ This One's Gonna Hurt You (MCA MCAD-10596) 1992 ●

For Marty Stuart, country is the gospel, and he's spent most of his career trying to spread the word. He drives Ernest Tubb's tour bus, owns one of Hank Williams's guitars, and wears rhinestoned Nudie suits. A member of Lester Flatt's band when he was only thirteen years old and a sometime guitarist for Johnny Cash, among others, Stuart is "country to the bone," as he says on one album, although his habit of injecting his songs with a rock & roll attitude has caught some flak around Nashville. Yet his solo work is steeped in tradition: he always includes a few vintage numbers on his albums, and studio guests have included his mentor Cash, Duane Eddy, and members of the Sun Records stable. Many of Stuart's peers hark back to the singer-songwriters of the Seventies, but Stuart clearly has his feet planted in the classic country of the Forties and Fifties.

Less than a solo debut, *Busy Bee Cafe* is more a side project that showcases Stuart's bluegrass roots. The informal jam session setting finds Stuart trading off vocals with Cash and others, while renowned pickers like Earl Scruggs and Doc Watson jump in and out of old-timey tunes like Bill Monroe's "Watson's Blues," Flatt & Scruggs's "Down the Road," and the traditional "Soldiers Joy."

Marty Stuart, his major-label debut, is a bit scattered, with the melancholy pluck of Stuart's mandolin at war with an occasional overload of synthesizers. The album dashes from rockabilly ("Arlene") to bar-band boogie ("Do You Really Want My Lovin'") to Springsteenish rockers ("Hometown Heroes"). Yet Stuart seems at home in almost any style. *Let There Be Country* was recorded as a follow-up but never released until 1992, when Stuart was seeing greater chart success with MCA. In the title track he attempts to articulate his philosophy but comes off sounding arrogant; nevertheless the album has some great moments, like the bluegrass instrumental "Old Hat" and a wacked-out, mega-spiritualized version of Bill Monroe's "Get Down on Your Knees and Pray."

Before switching to MCA, Stuart dropped out and honed his image, and *Hillbilly Rock* kicks his attitude into action. From the revved-up twang of the title track to the rumbling guitar on Cash's "Cry, Cry, Cry" (yet another love letter to his hero), Stuart proves himself a true revivalist, dedicated to the preservation of country's rebel heart. Not a track on his next album, *Tempted,* misses. It's classic country in a contemporary setting: "Paint the Town Tonight" and "Burn Me Down" could set the honky-tonk afire, while "Till I Found You" is a soft whisper in the ear. Stuart

even dares to end the album with "Get Back to the Country," an anthem by that ornery California rocker Neil Young.

This One's Gonna Hurt You is nothing less than a concept album about the meaning of country music. Rife with allusions to Hank and Elvis, rusted trucks and old front porches, the album presents a seamless narrative about the music, the lifestyle, and the characters that people its history. The opening track, "Me & Hank & Jumpin' Jack Flash," is a surreal spoken piece that sets the stage; "High on a Mountain Top" is a supercharged bluegrass tune. In "Honky Tonk Crowd," the singer dumps his girlfriend because "she didn't like hillbilly music/And that was more than I could take." Stuart understands the heart of country music—its glitz and its grime, its roots, and its living traditions— and he conveys its truths masterfully. —K.S.

JERRY AND TAMMY SULLIVAN
★★★★ **A Joyful Noise (Country Music Foundation CMF-016D) 1991**
The Sullivans are a father-daughter evangelical duo who deliver polished but spirited Pentecostal gospel bluegrass. Their friendship with Marty Stuart led to this 1991 album, which features eight songs written (or rewritten) by the senior Sullivan and Stuart, who lends a hand as singer and mandolinist-guitarist. But the lion's share of vocal leads are ably handled by Tammy Sullivan, who has an emotionally expressive voice many a mainstream country chanteuse might envy. A host of talented Nashville Cats play on this largely acoustic-supported songfest of ten toetappers designed to send the most unrepentant sinner to the prayer bench.—M.H.

DOUG SUPERNAW
★ **Red and Rio Grande (BNA 07863 66133-2) 1993**
According to publicity from his record company, this rugged-sounding young Texan got his record contract because he and his band, Texas Steel, played to packed dancehalls back in Tyler, Texas. So what does the record company do? They take away his band, surround him with the usual gang of overworked studio pros, and leave him in the hands of BNA

staff producer Richard Landis, whose previous credits include Juice Newton and Ronnie Milsap. Is it any wonder, then, that Supernaw sinks like a stone under formulaic country-pop arrangements and tedious material? Musts to avoid include the slobbering "I Would Have Loved You All Night Long" and the ridiculous "Honky Tonkin' Fool," wherein a barfly gets his dying wish: a jukebox for a tombstone.—P.K.

SWEETHEARTS OF THE RODEO

★★★ **Sweethearts of the Rodeo (Columbia CK 40406) 1986**
★★★½ **One Time, One Night (Columbia CK 40614) 1988**
★★★ **Buffalo Zone (Columbia CK 45373) 1990**
★★★★ **Sisters (Columbia CK 47358) 1992**

With their winning two-part harmonies, rollicking upbeat tunes, and songs about the moments of freedom that occur in the blush of love, Sweethearts of the Rodeo present a version of the country life that's hard to resist. Naming themselves after the famous 1968 Byrds album, sisters Kristine Arnold and Janis Gill (who is married to singer-guitarist Vince Gill) never get too heavy: "We stop off at the ice cream stand/One shake, two straws, holding hands," they rhapsodize in "Chosen Few," from their debut album. But when the time comes, Sweethearts are more than able to show some backbone. They don't get weepy; they get tough.

The debut album is short—eight songs that clock in under twenty-five minutes— but easily sets the Sweethearts' pace. "Hey Doll Baby" and "Since I Found You" are pure confection, updates of the Everly Brothers' crisp, friendly country-pop blend. *One Time, One Night* fleshes out the sound with guests like Augie Myers on accordion and Mark O'Connor on fiddle; background singers add more depth to the sisters' harmonies. Their version of the Everlys' "So Sad (To Watch Good Love Go Bad)" boasts pretty piano and pedal steel, while a cover of the Beatles' "I Feel Fine" betrays the girls as sweet hearts indeed.

As if the good times were running out, *Buffalo Zone* feels a bit more somber. Kristine Arnold's dark vocal blues take the lead on several tracks, and the tunes have less of a carefree bounce. From the stoic struggle of "Uphill All the Way" to the breakup tears of "Hard Road to Go," Sweethearts examine the shadowy side of romance. "He Doesn't Tell Me Anything" poignantly captures the helplessness one feels when love grows silent and cold.

On *Sisters,* Arnold and Gill return with some hard-earned maturity. The pace remains a bit deliberate, but the lyrics are a testament to a woman's particular breed of strength. Sweethearts' habit of eschewing self-pity is one of their most admirable traits. "Why Should I Stay Blue" and "I Don't Stay Down for Long" are plainspoken statements of resilience. As Arnold sings in the latter, "Had a real good cry after you had left/ Went out the next mornin', bought a brand new dress."—K.S.

SYLVIA

★★ **Greatest Hits (RCA 5618-2-R) 1987**

Sylvia Allen, the discovery and former secretary of producer Tom Collins, was a lovely poster girl for country music in the early Eighties with her cherry-lipped pout and long, long auburn tresses. Alas, her album covers, shot by the likes of glamor photographers Francesco Scavullo and Mario Casili, have worn better than her brief string of hits. That's probably because Sylvia's pop-country style is hopelessly unfashionable now, bringing to mind a less accomplished, less emotionally committed version of Crystal Gayle. Sylvia's breathy vocals do have the charming habit, though, of occasionally wobbling on the edge of true pitch, which keeps her from sounding overly polished even when the arrangements have the high gloss of a Madison Avenue office tower. *Greatest* collects most of Sylvia's Top Ten hits—the cotton candy of "Tumbleweed" (1980), the squeaky clean double entendres of "Nobody" (1982), the Gayle-force of "Cry Just a Little Bit" (1985). At just under thirty minutes, this CD version of a 1987 LP is about all you'd ever want from Sylvia.—P.K.

T★U★V

TEXANA DAMES

★★★ **Texana Dames (Amazing AMCD-1018) 1990**

With their breezy swing and buoyant harmonies, this Austin, Texas, trio sounds like the Andrews Sisters singing Bob Wills. The good time eclecticism of this album debut encompasses everything from jazzy saxophone to Tex-Mex accordion, and the songs of Conni Hancock offer pointed humor in their social observations. —D.McL.

TEXAS TORNADOS

★★★★ **Texas Tornados (Reprise 9 26251-2) 1990**

★★★★ **Los Texas Tornados (Reprise 9 26472-2) 1990**

★★★½ **Zone of Our Own (Reprise 9 26683-2) 1991**

★★★½ **Hangin' On by a Thread (Reprise 9 45058-2) 1992**

A triumph of diverse styles, the Texas Tornados capture the beauty as well as the grit of the multicultural mix that is Tex-Mex music. Doug Sahm and Augie Meyers are the Anglos, coming out of the Sixties' Sir Douglas Quintet. Freddy Fender and Flaco Jiminez are Chicano legends: Jiminez as reigning king of the conjunto accordion and Fender as balladeer numero uno.

As a quartet, the mix is irresistible: good-time rhythm & blues and waltz and corrida and two-step blend with polka and Gulf Coast Sound triplets and shuffles to capture most of Texas's musical styles over the past few decades. Dominated by Meyers's reedy Vox organ and Jiminez's majestic accordion runs, this is guaranteed good party music. The *Los Texas Tornados* CD is the unit's debut CD recorded in Spanish. Their latest, *Hangin' on by a Thread,* continues their exploration of the Tex-Mex themes of food, as in "Guacamole," and drink, as with "Ando Muy Borracho," and frolic, as exemplified by the raucous "A Mover El Bote." The latter is loosley translated as "Shake Yer Booty." But the CD also includes a version of Dylan's "To Ramona" that is transformed by the Tex-Mex sensibility to a melody as delicate as lace, as intricate as filigree. —C.F.

B.J. THOMAS

★★ **The Best of B.J. Thomas (Dominion CD 6713) 1987**

★★★ **16 Greatest Hits (Deluxe DCD 7902) 1987**

★★ **The Best of B.J. Thomas (Hollywood HCD-134) 1987**

★ **At His Best (Richmond NCD-2302) 1988**

★★★½ **Greatest Hits (Rhino R2 70752) 1990**

Born in Oklahoma and raised near Houston, Billy Joe Thomas was weaned on a diet of early rock & roll and classic country music, but made his first mark on the pop charts. Ironically, his Top Ten debut, in 1966, came with a cover of Hank Williams's immortal song-poem "I'm So Lonesome I Could Cry."

Gifted with rugged good looks and a soulfully romantic tenor, Thomas continued to enjoy modest success with ballads like the treacly sentimental "Mama," the rhapsodical "Eyes of a New York Woman," and the playfully innocent "Hooked on a Feeling." Then, in 1970 he topped the chart with his career-making single, "Raindrops Keep Falling on My Head," the Oscar-winning theme song from the film *Butch Cassidy and the Sundance Kid.*

Minor hits followed, including "Mighty Clouds of Joy" and "Rock and Roll Lullaby," but five years elapsed before receiving his next breakthrough. In 1975, "(Hey Won't You Play) Another Somebody Done Somebody Wrong Song" hit #1 on the country chart, establishing Thomas as a country music star for the years surrounding Nashville's Urban Cowboy era.

These greatest hits packages cover recordings from Thomas's pop years. Each includes "I'm So Lonesome I Could Cry," but only the Rhino disc extends to "(Hey Won't You Play)." Missing are the songs from Thomas's gospel period (for which he earned five Grammys) and his country hits from the Eighties.

The Rhino collection is the best of the best. Its eighteen songs are chronologically sequenced from earliest to most recent, and its liner notes provide a brief but serviceable summary of Thomas's early recording history. The Deluxe disc offers sixteen songs, all but two of which are provided by Rhino. Sequencing is random with respect to recording dates, and notes are not included. All eleven tracks on the Hollywood disc appear on Rhino, and all but "I Can't Help It (If I'm Still in Love with You)" appear also on Deluxe. The ten songs on Dominion clock in at thirty-one minutes and offer nothing of value that's not available on the more complete anthologies. At the opposite pole from Rhino is the Richmond disc, a shameful twenty-two-minute, eight-song teaser that culls deservedly obscure

recordings from Thomas's catalogue, including such toss-offs as "Love Is a Hurting Thing," "Plain Jane," and a laughingly tepid cover of the Doors' "Light My Fire."—J.B.

HANK THOMPSON

★★★★   **Capitol Collector's Series (Capitol C21Y-92124) 1989**
★★★   **20 Greatest Hits (Deluxe DCD-7807) 1987**
★★★½   **Country Music Hall of Fame (MCA MCAD-10545) 1992**
★★   **Here's to Country Music (Step One SOR-0027) 1987**

Henry "Hank" Thompson from Waco, Texas, sang honky-tonk songs with a western swing band to create a commercial sound all his own. While his Brazos Valley Boys set down an infectious, danceable beat, Thompson sang in a clear, crisply articulated style that few country singers could match. And when he was at his best, Thompson wrote some of country music's most imaginative lyrics, marked by the use of internal rhymes and clever word play.

The twenty-track *Capitol Collector's Series* is by far the strongest assortment of Thompson material now available on CD. The anthology includes a good sampling of Thompson's stylistic strengths over the period ranging from 1947, beginning with his first Capitol release, "Humpty Dumpty Heart," to 1960, when he recorded "Oklahoma Hills" and "Hangover Tavern." His "The Wild Side of Life," presented here with some of the studio patter that preceded its recording, inspired Kitty Wells's famous answer song, "It Wasn't God Who Made Honky Tonk Angels." Despite such crucial contributions to the honky-tonk genre, Thompson was a multi-faceted entertainer equally at ease with novelty songs ("Wake Up, Irene," "Squaws Along the Yukon") and romantic pieces ("Don't Take It Out on Me," "Breakin' the Rules"). These are original recordings that every real fan of country music will want to possess.

Like the *Capitol Collector's Series,* Deluxe's *20 Greatest Hits* includes Thompson's most popular songs, such as "Wild Side of Life," "Humpty Dumpty Heart," "A Six Pack to Go," "Blackboard of My Heart," "Oklahoma Hills," and "Yesterday's Girl." Unlike the Capitol anthology, though, in most cases these are not the original recordings.

MCA's *Country Music Hall of Fame* samples the varied song styles that Hank continued to pursue through the Sixties and Seventies for the Dot and ABC labels. "On Tap, in the Can" and "Smoky the Bar" bring his honky-tonk style up to date, while "Most of All," "Tomorrow Night," and "Swing Wide Your Gate of Love" are lovely songs about the heartbreak of romance. Although these recordings have not had the lasting impact of his earlier work for Capitol, fans will want to have them, for Thompson remains in fine voice here.

The Step One CD, *Here's to Country Music,* has a few good moments, but most of the songs are largely forgettable. Age and the many years on the road seem to be taking their toll on Hank, and he frankly sounds a bit tired on several of the cuts. His singing doesn't have quite the sharp-edged vigor for which he is famous, and a few of the songs, like "Cowgirl Cutie," are just downright silly.—B.C.M.

MARSHA THORNTON
★½   **Marsha Thornton (MCA MCAD-42319) 1990**
★★★★   **Maybe the Moon Will Shine (MCA MCAD-10142) 1991**

What a difference a producer can make! Thornton's debut, produced by grizzled veteran Owen Bradley, is a soggy attempt to replicate the smooth country flavor of vintage Patsy Cline. (It's even got a song called "A Bottle of Wine and Patsy Cline," in case you weren't hip to the musical allusions.) The picking here sounds as tired as a lounge act at last call, leaving even a talented singer like Thornton little to play against. Those who can't believe Owen Bradley's responsible in the least should give a listen to "Don't Tell Me What to Do," a song that producers Paul Worley and Ed Seay made into a declaration of independence and a well-deserved #1 hit for Pam Tillis. On Thornton's version you'll recognize the lyrics and the tune, and marvel at what's still missing.

In contrast, *Maybe the Moon Will Shine* is a revelation. Led by the inspired nouveau honky-tonk vision of steel player-producer Steve Fishell (the man behind Jann Browne), ace pickers Albert Lee,

Ray Flacke, and Jerry Douglas deal out some delightfully kickin' licks, and, spurred by them, Thornton cuts loose like the honky-tonk thoroughbred she is. Her voice echoes Patsy Cline's sensitivity ("Always Believin'") and Reba McEntire's sassiness ("Why Cry") in the best ways without ever sounding imitative. Though the material is standard Nashville issue, the performances manage to wring some sweat and tears out of them. None of these cuts were hits, though, and Thornton has since been dropped by MCA. It's a pity that Thornton didn't get out of the gate with her sophomore effort; this is really a wonderful album that got away.—P.K.

MEL TILLIS
★★★   **American Originals (Columbia (CK 45079) 1990**
★★★★   **Greatest Hits (Curb D2-77482) 1991**

A clever songwriter and competent singer, Tillis hit his peak commercially in 1976 when he was named the Country Music Association's Entertainer of the Year. By that time, he had already logged eighteen years of chart activity. Although he had a few Top Ten hits along the way, Tillis did not really make waves as a recording artist until the early Seventies, when he turned out such classics as "Sawmill," "Midnight, Me and the Blues," and "Best Way I Know How." Tillis began appearing on various syndicated and network television shows in the late Sixties. He was a regular on "The Glen Campbell Goodtime Hour" and did much to develop and spread his comic stuttering persona on that show. Beginning in the mid-Seventies, with *W. W. & the Dixie Dance Kings,* Tillis also embarked on a movie career, appearing in a number of B-grade films. While singing and acting were important elements in Tillis's broad range of talents, his place in country music has been unquestionably secured by the enduring songs he has written or co-written. His "Detroit City," a career-making hit for Bobby Bare in 1963, remains the definitive lament of the displaced Southern laborer, as well as an insight into a larger cultural upheaval. "Ruby, Don't Take Your Love to Town" not only established Kenny Rogers as a country singer in 1969, it also gave voice to American frustration with "that old crazy Asian war" in Vietnam, and, in so doing, became a Top Ten pop hit. Other of his standards include "I Ain't Never," "Lonely Street," "Heart over Mind," "No Love Have I," and "Tupelo County Jail." The albums listed above barely touch the breadth and richness of Tillis's contributions to country music. Nonetheless, they are a good start. The *American Originals* tribute to Tillis showcases him singing ten of his own compositions. The *Greatest Hits* package is, except for two selections, made up of the singer's interpretations of other people's songs, including "Coca Cola Cowboy," "I Believe in You," "Lying Time Again," and "New Patches," all from his fruitful late Seventies-early Eighties period.—E.M.

PAM TILLIS

★★★½ **Put Yourself in My Place (Arista ARCD 8642) 1991 ●**
★★★★ **Homeward Looking Angel (Arista 18649-2 07822) 1992 ●**

For most of the Eighties, Nashville music bizzers pegged Pam Tillis as the Gal Most Likely to Succeed. She could write, having provided songs for Conway Twitty, Highway 101, and Chaka Khan. When other songwriters needed a soulful voice to help sell their songs on demo tapes, Pam and her soaring, scorching soprano often got the call. ("There was a time," she has said, "when I prided myself on being a mockingbird.") And, as the daughter of countrypolitan star Mel Tillis, she had great bloodlines. But as the decade closed, a hit recording career still hadn't materialized for Pam Tillis, despite a five-year stint with Warner Bros. And Dad's career overshadowed Pam's so completely that talk-show hosts on more than one occasion got ahead of themselves and introduced her as Mel Tillis.

Finally, after nearly a decade of trying, she's fulfilling her great potential. One of only two women signed to Arista's Nashville division when it opened in 1989, Tillis connected with her first single, the defiant, supercharged honky-tonk number "Don't Tell Me What to Do." It went straight to #1. Of the disc's three subsequent Top Ten singles, two are topnotch examples of hard-country craftsmanship co-written by Tillis ("Put Yourself in My Place" and "One of Those

Things"), while the other, the incandescent country-rocker "Maybe It Was Memphis," though written by Michael Anderson, has become a signature song for Tillis. All of those hits can be found on *Put Yourself in My Place,* the album where Pam finally decides that her place is in country.

As good as that album was, though, it was only a warm-up for *Homeward Looking Angel.* Where the debut sounded like a collection of smart singles—some hard country, some country-rock—*Angel* is a more focused, consolidated effort that allows her to assert her tough but tender personality. On track after track, Tillis (who co-wrote five cuts) achieves an effortless synthesis of country and rock elements that many newer country acts—heck, rock acts—would kill for. "Shake the Sugar Tree," a lover's plea for attention, starts off like a bluegrass ballad with mandolin and fiddle and then spills out into an irresistible undertow of pop rhythm. "Fine, Fine, Very Fine Love" is a great soul workout that somehow smoothly incorporates pedal steel and Hammond organ licks. "Cleopatra, Queen of Denial" is a modern woman's joke that really rocks. It's a tribute to Tillis's considerable abilities as a singer (as well as to producers Paul Worley and Ed Seay) that the entire album sounds stone country, even though it's got more hooks than a tackle box. The album's only misstep is a crass cross-promotional duet between Tillis and singer Marty Roe of Diamond Rio, another big act from Arista. (What, Alan Jackson said no?) It's a bland, generic misfit in the midst of an otherwise stellar effort from one of new country's most distinctive voices. Luckily CDs can be programmed.—P.K.

FLOYD TILLMAN

★★★ **The Country Music Hall of Fame (MCA MCAD-10189) 1991**

As a songwriter, few outdistanced Floyd Tillman in the late Forties and early Fifties. He wrote "Slippin' Around," "It Makes No Difference Now," "I Love You So Much It Hurts," and "This Cold War with You," but, beginning with his original version of "Slippin' Around" in 1949, Tillman found a maverick half-spoken vocal style in which the world seemed to be viewed through the bottom of a shot glass. It was too weird for radio that year—and every year since. Many of his nonhit records, like "Small Little Town" and "Blood on the Moon," were splendidly eccentric, but the only person he seems to have influenced was Willie Nelson. Unfortunately, Tillman's solitary CD, *The Country Music Hall of Fame,* catches him on Decca before his prime on Columbia in the late Forties and early Fifties, but it still contains a few nuggets like "Each Night at Nine." His old Columbia and Harmony LPs should be bought on sight.—C.E.

AARON TIPPIN
★★★ You've Got to Stand for Something (RCA 2374-2-R) 1991
★★ Read Between the Lines (RCA 61129-2) 1992 ▲

Tippin gets the most out of a baleful howl of a voice—if you can imagine a coyote with a profound respect for Hank and Lefty, you're close to Tippin's trademark sound. His debut is, as its title suggests, a sterling statement of honky-tonk principles, as can also be heard on such *Stand for Something* songs as "She Made a Memory Out of Me," "Ain't That a Hell of a Note" and "Many, Many, Many Beers Ago." The follow-up features vocals just as strong, but the songs, most of them by the singer, are weaker, displaying a fondness for meaningless novelty ("There Ain't Nothin' Wrong with the Radio"—er, right, Aaron) over deeper emotions.—K.T.

KAREN TOBIN
★★★½ Carolina Smokey Moon (Atlantic 7 82323-2) 1991

Following in the footsteps of Emmylou Harris, Karen Tobin is one of the new breed of female country singers. Her lilting soprano does justice to a selection of well-chosen, well-played old-timey-style country songs. Hints of bluegrass sneak into the lovely "Carolina Country Moon," and the ballad "Pictures of Your Daddy" pulls on the heartstrings without being sappy. Healthy doses of fiddle, mandolin, and dobro give a down-home feel to the album, and Tobin's emotive vocals never give way to cliché. Every song rings true, making the album a very impressive debut.—H.G.-W.

WAYNE TOUPS
★★★ Zydecajun (Mercury 846 584-2) 1986
★★½ Johnny Can't Dance (Mercury 846 585-2) 1988
★★★ Blast from the Bayou (Mercury 83366518-2) 1989
★★★ Fish Out of Water (Mercury 848 289-2) 1991

Wayne Toups and his band Zydecajun perform high-energy, tradition-based Cajun music, incorporating much of the feel of zydeco, as well as other contemporary musical forms. Driving the band with his athletic accordion playing and singing the lead vocals, Toups can range from rock to bluesy zydeco to what I can only describe as Cajun soul. Wayne's live performances regularly send his audiences into dancing frenzies, and if you are looking for progressive Cajun boogie, these discs will no doubt do the same for you.—C.H.S.

THE TRADITIONAL GRASS
★★★★ Howdy Neighbor Howdy (Rebel REB CD-1698) 1992

As its name suggests, this Ohio-based quintet finds its inspiration in the old-time, bluesy roots of Bill Monroe, Flatt & Scruggs, Reno & Smiley, and other patriarchs from bluegrass music's formative years. The band receives discerning leadership from Paul Mullins, a journeyman fiddler who served with the Stanley Brothers and the Boys from Indiana, and emotionally potent singing from guitarist Mark Rader, a rangy tenor who wields Appalachian urgency with studied control.

For this album, Traditional Grass looks to old standards ("Lover's Quarrel," "Katy Kline") and the bluegrass canon ("Six White Horses," "The Shuffle of My Feet") for part of its repertoire, and contributes three original songs ("My Memories Aren't Precious Anymore," "The Blues Are Still the Blues," and "Lord, Lead Me On Home") that add depth, personality, and timelessness to a masterful set of uncommonly good bluegrass.—J.B.

MERLE TRAVIS
★★★ The Best of Merle Travis (Rhino R2 70993) 1990
★★★★ The Merle Travis Story—24 Greatest Hits (CMH CD-9018) 1989

Merle Travis (1917-83) was a gifted song craftsman with a sure wit and a poetic streak that ran deepest when recalling his Kentucky coal-country youth in such songs as "Dark as a Dungeon" and "Sixteen Tons." More influentially, Travis was the fountainhead (not the creator, but the primary disseminator) of a blues-and-jazz-tinged country guitar fingerstyle dubbed "Travis picking." Without Merle, there would have been no Chet, and without those two, it's hard to imagine Scotty Moore or Carl Perkins or at least two subsequent generations of country and rockabilly guitarists. Given Travis's reputation as a seminal guitarist foremost and a singer-songwriter secondarily, Rhino's eighteen-track *Best of Merle Travis* is revisionist history. Its emphasis is squarely on Travis's late 1940s Capitol hits, songs in which lyrical cuteness ("I Like My Chicken Fryin' Size") winks and elbows insistently while the chunk-twang of Travis's guitar is discreet or nonexistent. "Best of" and "Biggest Hits" aren't always synonymous. Travis's twenty-three-year stint with Capitol yielded many fine instrumental recordings, only one of which ("Cannon Ball Rag") appears on the Rhino set. To its credit, Rhino includes three performances ("Sixteen Tons" among them) from Travis's legendary 1947 *Folk Songs of the Hills* album, none of which charted, along with "Re-enlistment Blues," the song Travis wrote for the 1953 film *From Here to Eternity.* But the lion's share of the performances are the novelties which were Travis specialties in the late Forties ("Divorce Me C.O.D."), fun in small doses but marred by asthmatic trumpet, grin-'n'-bear-it accordion, and other Forties Hollywood dudebilly dressings that grate when clumped more than two at a time. Rhino's collection offers Travis's chart hits to the detriment of his artistic reputation. Capitol has plenty of guitaristic gems in its vaults and would do well to compile a more balanced overview of the hit singer-songwriter and the guitarist.

It's heresy to recommend late re-recordings over originals, but in the case of the two currently available Travis collections, the twenty-four 1979 recordings on CMH's *The Merle Travis Story* have an edge: Travis's guitar. By the time CMH re-recorded most of the songs on the Rhino set (plus a few more and four instrumentals), Travis picking

had become a buzzword among country and folk guitarists, and Travis a revered rediscovered elder statesman, so the maestro's guitar, incidental to many of the early Capitol performances, was wisely given prominent play. His voice was frayed by then, but Travis was always more storyteller than singer anyhow, and there's a warm warts-and-all informality to this reprise session of a remarkable career, even if the players at times re-create too faithfully the corncrib chintz of the early Capitol sides. It's clearly the artist, not the sometimes cloying wink and nudge songs, who's center stage here, and for that the CMH set is a better introduction to the Travis legacy.—M.H.

RANDY TRAVIS

★★★★★	**Storms of Life (Warner Bros. 9 25435-2) 1986** ▲[3]
★★★½	**Always & Forever (Warner Bros. 9 25568-2) 1987** ▲[5]
★★★★	**Old 8x10 (Warner Bros. 9 25738-2) 1988** ▲
★★★★	**No Holdin' Back (Warner Bros. 9 25988-2) 1989** ▲
★★★	**An Old Time Christmas (Warner Bros. 9 25972-2) 1989** ●
★★½	**Duets—Heroes & Friends (Warner Bros. 9 26310-2) 1990** ▲
★★	**High Lonesome (Warner Bros. 9 26661-2) 1991** ●
★★★★	**Greatest Hits, Vol. 1 (Warner Bros. 9 45044-2) 1992** ●
★★★½	**Greatest Hits, Vol. 2 (Warner Bros. 9 45045-2) 1992** ●

His fervent defenders will tell you he was the Lone Ranger who singlehandedly saved country music from its postcrossover/pre-Hat Act doldrums. Like the Masked Man of yore, Travis proved reliable if a mite bland over the long haul and was soon replaced by flashier heroes. (So much for the lifelong loyalty of the country fan.) But there was something refreshingly right and real about Travis's Leftyish hook as "Opera-tor, please connect me . . . with 1982" oozed from radios early in 1986. Of all the so-called new traditionalists of the 1980s, none emerged with such a stunning debut album as *Storms of Life,* a work Travis has yet to surpass. Along with "1982," it had "On the Other Hand," a Paul Overstreet-Don Schlitz song that was a new "Almost Persuaded" in theme crafted to sound like a classic George Jones performance of an earlier era (Jones himself copied it in 1987 with "The Right Left Hand"). All *Storms'* songs and performances reached for this timeless quality, new country that tasted vintage, and most all of it worked. A young guy with an old soul (it showed through the songs he wrote, like the weary "Reasons I Cheat," as well as in his vocals), Travis's debut redefined the expectations of the new country singer.

The followup, *Always & Forever,* became Travis's best-selling album (over five million copies), though it failed to deliver the goods as stunningly as *Storms.* As its title implied, *Always* was essentially for the ladies, Travis's most supportive fans. The songs were largely earnest pleas of fidelity pledged "Forever and Ever, Amen," the title of one of the album's hits. The formula worked commercial wonders, but only "I Won't Need You Anymore" rang with the classic resonance that washed through *Storms.*

Old 8x10 was half as successful but artistically stronger than *Always.* The production was more low-key, and Travis asserted himself as co-writer of the understated stunner, "Promises," performed with just voice and acoustic guitar. *No Holdin' Back* was likewise a solid collection with a couple of pleasant surprises, such as a nice "Singing the Blues" and a laconically soulful performance of Brook Benton's "It's Just a Matter of Time." Travis closed out the Eighties with *An Old Time Christmas,* a pleasant stocking stuffer which included a fine loser's ballad, "White Christmas Makes Me Blue," and an unexpectedly moving "God Rest Ye Merry Gentlemen."

Travis ushered in the Nineties with a collection of duets, *Heroes & Friends,* which probably worked better as a concept than it does as an album. The notion of having the new country classic croon with such veterans as Merle Haggard, Dolly Parton, and Loretta Lynn (a dozen duets in all), seems like a natural, but the difficulty of finding precisely the right material and developing any artistic rapport on short notice renders this a patchwork that is only intermittently woven tight. The hit duet with George Jones, "A Few Old Country Boys," probably works best, along with

Tammy Wynette's gorgeous harmony to "We're Strangers Again."

High Lonesome is an exceptionally unexceptional album. Travis co-wrote five of its ten songs, and while "Better Class of Losers" (co-written with Alan Jackson) is an assertive kick from the often diffident Travis, "I'd Surrender All" (also co-penned with Jackson) makes you wish singin' stars had editors when Travis mopes aloud, "I never thought I'd miss the early morning smell of hairspray in the air." Open a window! And for the Smart Bomb set, here's the Bush league anthem, "Point of Light."

Travis's two *Hits* packages bait his loyal fans (the ones with every album) with two songs not on any previous collection on each. The newcomer who might assume his best songs are on *Vol. 1* is likewise foiled, as the packages aren't chronological and a couple of songs from *Storms* are on *Vol. 2. Vol. 1* has a slight edge, offering the early career makers, "1982" and "On the Other Hand," and the best new performance, a kicker called "If I Didn't Have You."
—M.H.

TRAVIS TRITT

★★★½ **Country Club (Warner Bros. 9 26094-2) 1990 ▲**

★★★★ **It's All About to Change (Warner Bros. 9 26589-2) 1991 ▲²**

★★★½ **A Travis Tritt Christmas: Loving Time of the Year (Warner Bros. 9 45029-2) 1992**

★★★ **T-R-O-U-B-L-E (Warner Bros. 9 45048-2) 1992 ▲**

1989 was the year most of the young men who came to be called the Hat Acts were unveiled like a fleet of new cars. But the most impressive newcomer that year didn't wear a hat, and there was no cowboy fringe to his more hardcore honky-tonk. Travis Tritt's debut single, "Country Club," was a wry anthem of Southern blue-collar solidarity delivered with the sort of grits-'n'-gravel voice Kenny Rogers might have had if he lived in a trailer park and pumped gas for a living. Tritt either wrote or co-wrote five of the *Country Club* album's ten songs, including the right-to-rock manifesto, "Put Some Drive in Your Country," and the Hank Jr.-style "Son of the New South." Tritt's writing wasn't as focused as it would later become, and the album's best song, "If I Were a Drinker," came from other pens (it remains his single best ballad performance).

It's All About to Change was Tritt's career-maker, an album that delivered four #1 hits, including the barroom buddies duet with Marty Stuart, "The Whiskey Ain't Workin'," and the emphatic kiss-off, "Here's a Quarter (Call Someone Who Cares)." Tritt penned all but three of the album's songs, including the classic-sounding title track, and his writing had become more confident than on *Country Club*. He sharpened his new-kicker-with-an-edge image and proved that he had the pipes to do pretty much whatever he wanted, from the pseudo-Garth ballad, "Nothing Short of Dying," to the pseudo-metal cruncher, "Homesick."

Come time for album number three, *T-R-O-U-B-L-E*, and it was pretty plain to Tritt what worked: soulful ballads for the ladies ("Can I Trust You with My Heart"), Monday night football keg party boogie for the dudes ("Blue Collar Man"), and an occasional old-style country kicker, especially good if it carries a toast-the-drones class solidarity message ("Lord Have Mercy on the Working Man").

Tritt's Christmas album, *Loving Time of the Year,* genially offered something for everyone, from a cocktail lounge doo-wop version of "Have Yourself a Merry Little Christmas" to a Dixie boogie "Winter Wonderland," which conjures images of the Kentucky Headhunters staggering through snowdrifts. Despite the big truck overkill of some tracks, Tritt underotated others and was even brave enough to present a couple of dry (sans reverb) vocals, a rarity that works wonders on "O Little Town of Bethlehem."

Tritt had stretched from his first to his second album, and there found his formula. *T-R-O-U-B-L-E* includes a photo of Tritt striking a muscle pose in a buckskin jacket in front of a huge American flag, and he looks for the world to have become the new Hank Jr. minus Bocephus's one admirable trait, his unpredictability.—M.H.

ERNEST TUBB

★★★★½ **Country Music Hall of Fame (MCA MCAD-10086) 1991**

★★★★ **Ernest Tubb Live 1965 (Rhino R2 70902) 1989**

★★ **The Ernest Tubb Collection with Guests, Parts I and II (Step One Records SOR 0049) 1989**

★★½ **Ernest Tubb and Friends, Vols. 1-5 (LaserLight 12 115) 1992**

E. T., the founding spirit of honky-tonk music—predating and inspiring every white man's blues singer from Hank Williams to George Jones to Dwight Yoakam—was shamefully underrepresented on vinyl for the last quarter century of his career (he died in 1984), and his American CD catalogue is even skimpier. On the other hand, we do have two high-quality takes on this almost mythic figure, and by fortunate happenstance they complement each other rather nicely.

First, though, the less compelling items: *Ernest Tubb and Friends* and *The Ernest Tubb Collection with Guests* are basically the same material—E. T. towards the end of his career doing overdubbed duets with everyone from Willie Nelson and Merle Haggard to Razzy Bailey and Boxcar Willie—except that the five-disc LaserLight package has twenty more of 'em. Is that a blessing or a curse?

The MCA *Hall of Fame* compilation, on the other hand, is unequivocally worthy: sixteen studio tracks recorded between April 1941 (his first hit, "Walking the Floor over You") and April 1965 ("Waltz across Texas"). The good news is that unlike most of the Tubb collections you'll find at the flea market, all the tracks here are taken from the original masters, not successive generations of remakes and remixes. The bad news, of course, is that there are only sixteen tracks, and some of the very best stuff (the original cuts of "Driving Nails in My Coffin" and "Blue Eyed Elaine," for instance) is missing. So if you want the whole picture of the man at his peak, you need an import: the massive five-CD box *Let's Say Goodbye Like We Said Hello* (Bear Family BCD 15498), which offers all but five of the studio tracks cut between 1947 and 1953—114 sides of unadulterated E. T., including the wilder and woolier moments of which he was clearly capable (Ol' Ernest was as legendary a good-timer as he was a gentleman).

He was also a great road warrior, crisscrossing the country with the many incarnations of his Texas Troubadours until as late as 1982, and Rhino's *Ernest Tubb Live 1965* captures one of those thousands of nights. It wasn't a wild one, and Ernest was already a little past his prime (though such judgments approach meaninglessness when you're talking about a man who never had more than two tempos and a voice like a bucket of sand inside a Caterpillar transmission), but he did more than adequate versions of some of the great songs missing from the MCA collection.

More importantly, though, *you are there* where he was, band chat and crowd noise and everything, and y'know, every self-respecting country fan should be able to spend an evening in a place like that. After all, the kindest spirits of the music are still there for us at the feet of Ernest Tubb.—P.Ca.

TANYA TUCKER

★★★★½ Greatest Hits (Columbia CK 33355) 1975 ●
  ★½ TNT (MCA MCAD-31152) 1978 ●
  ★★★ Greatest Hits (MCA MCAD-31153) 1978
  ★★ The Best of Tanya Tucker (MCA MCAD-31166) 1982
  ★★½ Love Me Like You Used To (Liberty C21Y-46870) 1987
  ★★ Strong Enough to Bend (Capitol CDP 7 48865 2) 1988
  ★★★ Greatest Hits (Liberty C21S-91814) 1989
  ★★½ Tennessee Woman (Liberty C21S-91821) 1990
  ★★ Greatest Hits Encore (Liberty C21 Y-94254) 1990
  ★★★½ Greatest Country Hits (Curb D21Y-77429) 1991
  ★★★ What Do I Do with Me (Liberty C21S-95562) 1991 ▲
  ★★★ Can't Run from Yourself (Liberty CDP-7-98987-2) 1992 ●

Tucker is Thelma without Louise: tough, worldly wise, secure in the knowledge that you can surrender to romance and heartbreak without being a victim or a sucker. A star since the age of thirteen, when the hit singles "Delta Dawn" and "Will You Lay with Me (In a Field of Stone)" made her a country Lolita to producer Billy Sherrill's cornpone Humbert Humbert (ponder them and

much more on the Columbia *Greatest Hits*), Tucker has spent her career overcoming—with remarkable grace, skill, humor, and resilience—potentially poor image make-overs and spotty material. Tucker has had her share of turkeys, most notably 1978's *TNT*, a silly excursion into rock & roll that found her turning Elvis-impersonator on "Heartbreak Hotel" and applying a superfluously white, female spin to Chuck Berry's "Brown-Eyed Handsome Man." But since signing with Capitol/Liberty in 1986, Tucker has staked out her turf as a mature singer whose implied feminism gives backbone to even her most sentimental songs, and her best latterday hits, such as "Down to My Last Teardrop" and "What Do I Do with Me"— what she has called "women's songs"— radiate an easy assurance and power that few country stars achieve. Of her more recent releases, *Tennessee Woman* and *Love Me Like You Used To* showcase Tucker at her most eager and eclectic, casting about for a grown-up-woman's fresh career style; *What Do I Do with Me* and *Can't Run from Myself* at her most serious and confident. With these last two, it appears she's found the music she wants to make.—K.T.

SHANIA TWAIN

  ★★ Shania Twain (Mercury 314-514 422-2) 1993

Forgettable soap opera fluff from this one-time Canadian resort singer who counts among her inspirations Gladys Knight and Karen Carpenter. A bold and gritty stylist who can belt out a bopper and ache on a weeper, Twain has potential that smothers beneath the detritus of ordinary, inconsequential songs. If there's gold in her future, it will come only after digging for better material and refining her artistic focus.— J.B.

CONWAY TWITTY

  ★★ It's Only Make Believe (PolyGram Special Products 837-668-2) 1992
★★★★★ Best of Conway Twitty, Vol. 1 (Mercury 849 574-2) 1991
★★★★★ Greatest Hits, Vol. 1 (MCA MCAD-31239) 1972 ●
  ★★★★ Greatest Hits, Vol. 2 (MCA MCAD-31240) 1976 ●

★★★★ Very Best of (MCA MCAD-31238) 1978 ▲
★★★★ Number Ones (MCA MCAD-1488) 1982 ●
★★★★★ 20 Greatest Hits (MCA MCAD-5976) 1987
★★★★ No. 1's: The Warner Bros. Years (Warner Bros. 2577-2) 1988
★★★ Borderline (MCA MCAD-5969) 1987
★★★ Still in Your Dreams (MCA MCAD-42115) 1988
★★★ House on Old Lonesome Road (MCA MCAD-42297) 1989
★★★★★ Silver Anniversary Collection (MCA MCAD-8035) 1990
★★★ Crazy In Love (MCA MCAD-10027) 1990
★★★★★ Greatest Hits, Vol. 3 (MCA MCAD-6391) 1990
★★★ Even Now (MCA MCAD-10335) 1991
★★★ Final Touches (MCA MCAD-10882) 1993

Here he is folks, the Big Kahuna, the High Priest of Country Music, the man with more #1 hits than anyone in history. Conway Twitty didn't play politics in Music City, so you rarely saw him on the big awards shows. He wasn't a publicity whore, so you didn't find him on the cover of *People* or hawking his wares on "Entertainment Tonight." Although he was one of the greatest songwriters in country music history, he was incredibly low-key about it. He could out-sing most of the competition, but never hogged the limelight. No flash. No fuss. Twitty was a man who knew his job and how to do it. His job was to please the lady fans, and he made no apologies for aiming straight at their hearts, for saying the things they wish their boyfriends and husbands would say, for giving them three-minute fantasies of unbridled passion.

His vocals throb with desire as he rumbles from his growled bass range on up to his tenor shouts of florid ecstasy. The band pounds soul rhythms, moans in honky-tonk misery, or sizzles in country-rock grooves. Whatever the musical context, Twitty is the evangelist of blue-collar desire and the testifying apostle of working-class temptation.

Our saga begins in the 1950s when Twitty was one of the rockabilly heroes. "Shake It Up," "Danny Boy," "I Need Your Lovin'," "I Vibrate," and "Got My

Mojo Workin'" found him mining teen tunes in the shadow of Elvis. His urgent-voiced ballads "It's Only Make Believe" and "Lonely Blue Boy" were among Nashville's finest contributions to the pop radio airwaves back then. These are compiled along with gems like "Mona Lisa," "Platinum High School," "Long Black Train," "Is a Bluebird Blue," and "What a Dream" on the Mercury Records *Best of* set, subtitled *The Rockin' Years*.

By the mid 1960s, Twitty's rock & roll dream was over. He begged producer Owen Bradley to take him on as a country singer at Decca/MCA. Beginning in 1966 the former rockabilly idol was releasing singles that were state-of-the-art honky-tonk masterpieces, many of them self-composed. "The Image of Me," "Next in Line," "To See My Angel Cry," and his other 1968-69 efforts were songs of the heartbroken loser. Then in 1970 he growled "Hello Darlin'" and set female hearts fluttering. "You've Never Been This Far Before" (1974), "I See the Want-To in Your Eyes" (1974), "Linda on My Mind" (1975), "Touch the Hand" (1975), "I Can't Believe She Gives It All to Me" (1976), and "I've Already Loved You in My Mind" (1977) trembled with lust as the star became ever more daring. But Twitty was never one dimensional, and he always had the wisdom to shift stylistically to hold listeners' interest.

"Play Guitar Play," for instance, was a prison song that became a major hit for him in 1977. "The Grandest Lady of Them All" (1978) was a salute to the Grand Ole Opry. "Boogie Grass Band" (1978) was a smokin', Allman Brothers-style, Southern-rock rave up. "Don't Take It Away" (1979) was an apocalyptic shout of hoarse, fevered urgency. He returned to sexy lyrics in the stripped down sounds of "I'd Love to Lay You Down" and "Tight Fittin' Jeans" in the early Eighties. But during the same period he looked to sources as diverse as Bette Midler ("The Rose"), the Bee Gees ("Rest Your Love on Me"), Lionel Richie ("Three Times a Lady"), and the Pointer Sisters ("Slow Hand") for inspiration. Twitty adopted a mature, worldly wise tone for 1984's "I Don't Know a Thing About Love," 1985's "Don't Call Him a Cowboy," and 1987's "That's My Job." The story-song "Saturday Night Special" and the wistful "I Wish I Was Still in Your Dreams" took him to the end of the decade. He quit smoking and discovered a hair-raising tenor range for the electrifying "She's Got a Single Thing in Mind," the hit that carried him into the 1990s.

Alone among his 1950s contemporaries, Twitty was still cutting Top Ten hits in 1990-91 ("Crazy in Love," "I Couldn't See You Leavin'"). The most enduring star of his generation noted the profusion of newcomers on the charts and opted to sit out 1992 while planning the CD that would make him their competitor. That collection, *Final Touches,* became his swan song when he died suddenly of an abdominal aneurism at the age of fifty-nine. He'd enlisted the aid of hot producer Don Cook (Brook & Dunn, Mark Collie) and gathered a strong set of tunes ("I Hurt for You," "An Old Memory Like Me," "Two Timin' Two Stepper"). He was at the peak of his vocal powers.

His career had well over one hundred hits, and with any body of work that large there are bound to be omissions in the reissues. On the plus side, there are so many major hits that virtually every compilation is studded with historic performances. Because of his stylistic shifts, Conway Twitty isn't the kind of artist that will bore you through numerous *Best of* sets. The three volumes of the *Greatest Hits* on MCA, plus the Mercury and Warner Bros. packages give you the full overview. If you don't want to invest that kind of time and money, the twenty-five-song *Silver Anniversary* or *20 Greatest Hits* collections on MCA are both superb encapsulations of his remarkable work.—R.K.O.

IAN TYSON
★★★★ **Cowboyography (Sugar Hill SHCD 1021) 1986**
Western music seemed rooted in a mythic past until the late Eighties when several people tried to drag it kicking and screaming into the modern age. One such was Ian Tyson. Once half of the Canadian folk duo Ian & Sylvia, he fulfilled the promise he made in his hit "Four Strong Winds" and moved out to Alberta to become a rancher. When he began playing again, he celebrated his new lifestyle in a series of albums for the Canadian Stony Plain label. The best of those, *Cowboyography,* is available here, and it's a mosaic of contemporary western

life, as if North America divided vertically rather than horizontally. Immemorial themes (horses, cattle, the big sky, isolation) are filtered through a modern sensibility.—C.E.

DONNA ULISSE
★★ **Trouble at the Door (Atlantic 82282) 1991**
As a kind of backlash against all those feisty independent gals—the Wynonnas and Mary-Chapins and Trishas—comes Donna Ulisse, a weeper from the old, old, old school. Ulisse has a sweet molasses voice, an adequate way with a dance-floor ballad, and a sensibility that could set country women back twenty years. On *Trouble at the Door,* she finds a hundred ways to say her heart's broken, and then she finds one more: "My Broken Heart's Breaking All Over Again." She's also happy to play the victim, as in "You Always Take Her Memory Out on Me." —K.S.

UNCLE WALT'S BAND
★★★ **Girl on the Sunny Shore (Sugar Hill SH-CD-1032/33) 1991**
★★★ **An American in Texas Revisited (Sugar Hill SH-CD-1034/35) 1991**
Formed in the early Seventies, this progressive acoustic trio of Walter Hyatt, David Ball, and Champ Hood combines harmonies reminiscent of Crosby, Stills & Nash with the pop melodicism of a Paul McCartney and the virtuosity of string-band swing. While the results aren't exactly country, the musical blend is too eclectic for classification as anything else. Before disbanding in the early Eighties, the trio found a kindred spirit in Lyle Lovett, who produced a solo album by Hyatt and wrote liner notes for these 1991 reissues.—D.McL.

TOWNES VAN ZANDT
★★★★ **At My Window (Sugar Hill SH-CD-1020) 1987**
★★★½ **Live and Obscure (Sugar Hill SH-CD-1026) 1989**
A laconic singer and a lyricist of bitter-sweet subtlety, Van Zandt has long been revered by many of his songwriting peers (particularly in his native Texas), while remaining an acquired taste with the public at large. His range extends from rambling songs to talking blues to love songs that are caught between spiritual

yearnings and the despair of almost metaphysical loneliness, occasionally laced with deadpan humor.

At My Window features a re-recording of "For the Sake of the Song," long one of his signature tunes, along with more recent material in a folkish, bluesy vein. *Live and Obscure* offers a representative club set, highlighted by "Pancho and Lefty" (a duo hit for Willie Nelson and Merle Haggard). From the late Sixties through the Seventies, he released more than a half-dozen earlier albums on the financially beleaguered Tomato label (subsequently issued on CD), which are harder to find but worth the effort, particularly the cult classics *Our Mother the Mountain* and *The Late Great Townes Van Zandt.*—D.McL.

GENE VINCENT
★★★ **Capitol Collector's Series (Capitol C21Y-94074) 1990**

Known almost exclusively for his 1956 smash "Be-Bop-a-Lula," Vincent was one of the few to ride in on Elvis's ducktails who occasionally went the King one better; along with ace guitarist Cliff Gallup, the now breathy, now hiccupping Vincent was responsible for some of rockabilly's most lascivious recordings. Early on, Vincent and His Blue Caps often aped the Sun sound of Elvis, Scotty, and Bill; in the Sixties he expanded, often with strange, persuasive results. The single-disc Capitol set collects Vincent's handful of hits along with lesser-known gems, like the salacious "Woman Love." Fans should search out the British import boxed set from EMI (EMI CDS 7 94593 2), which offers six CDs stuffed with Vincent's complete 1956-1964 recordings for Capitol and Columbia. —J.G.

RHONDA VINCENT
★★★½ **A Dream Come True (Rebel REB CD 1682) 1990**
★★★ **New Dreams and Sunshine (Rebel REB CD 1665) 1991**
★★★½ **Timeless and True Love (Rebel REB CD 1697) 1991**

For decades, bluegrass was such an exclusively male lodge that the appearance of anomalies like Rose Maddox's mid-1960s *Sings Bluegrass* album was greeted as a wonder of the talking dog variety. Nowadays, most of the bluegrass performers who gain a glance beyond that insular world's purview are women, and Rhonda Vincent, a fine mandolinist and fiddler, is arguably the best singer of the lot. Her prodigious pipes actually present a problem: bluegrass is her home base, but she delivers knockout renditions of country ballads in the grand rafter-rattling manner of Connie Smith. *A Dream Come True* (1990) is purely contemporary bluegrass in instrumentation, but Vincent's two 1991 albums are a mixture of grass-based pickin' and singin' with production and material more in the Nashville mainstream, albeit with a traditionalist bent (if you didn't know better, you might think you *were* hearing a Connie Smith record of twenty-five years ago). Vincent may be the first artist to record with piano, steel guitar, and drums for the bluegrass purist Rebel label. Hearing her genre jump on *New Dreams* and *Timeless* isn't at all jarring, but she has a ways to go in establishing a clear artistic identity. The fact that some of the songs she does best are identified with chart-topping artists ("Timeless and True Love" was a hit for the McCarters and "I'm Not That Lonely Yet" for Reba McEntire) suggests a need to seek fresh material that highlights Vincent's grass-country hybrid in a way that uniquely defines her considerable talents.—M.H.

RICK VINCENT
★★★★ **A Wanted Man (Curb D277586) 1993**

No hat trick here, just stone-solid country music, West Coast style. While a Bakersfield influence is discernible in the occasional turn of a Haggard phrase or in a dreamy lick of the pedal steel, Vincent gleams as a singer with an intuitive hold on honky-tonk principles and country soul. Equally impressive as a songwriter, Vincent wrote or co-wrote all ten tracks. Recalling the craftsmanship and Old West motifs of Guy Clark, he writes compellingly about outlaws and trains, valleys and streams as metaphors for relationships, desire, and change in this inviting debut by a hugely talented artist.—J.B.

W ★ Y

PORTER WAGONER

★★ Heartwarming Songs (Hollywood HCD-419)
★★★ Pure Gold (PW-1991-CD) 1991
★★★ [with Dolly Parton] Sweet Harmony (Pair PCD2-1013) 1992

So far, Wagoner has been ill-served on compact disc. For a time, the twenty-five-minute throwaway *Heartwarming Songs* was the only domestic CD available from this popular Grand Ole Opry star. (Germany's Bear Family has released *A Satisfied Mind,* BCD 15499-DI, a four-CD set of his earlier recordings.) RCA, Wagoner's label from 1952 to 1980, should release a comprehensive set that includes his trio harmony beginnings, his sweet-and-sexy hits with Dolly Parton (and, before her, Norma Jean), and especially his frank sermonizing, as found in "Skid Row Joe," "The Cold Hard Facts of Life," "The Second Mrs. Jones," and "Rubber Room," some of the most startling popular music of the Sixties, country or otherwise. For now, the short-but-better-chosen *Pure Gold* offers ten of Wagoner's liveliest performances, and *Sweet Harmony* is an adequate showcase of his duets with protégé Parton. But we ought to have much more.—J.G.

JERRY JEFF WALKER

★★★ Driftin' Way of Life (Vanguard VMD-73124) 1969
★★★ Viva Terlingua! (MCA MCAD-919) 1973 •
★★★ Ridin' High (MCA MCAD-920) 1975
★★★★ Great Gonzos (MCA MCAD-10381) 1991
★★★ Gypsy Songman (Rykodisc RCD 20071) 1988
★★★★ Live at Gruene Hall (Rykodisc RCD 10123)1989
★★★ Navajo Rug (Rykodisc RCD 10175) 1991
★★★ Hill Country Rain (Rykodisc RCD 10241) 1992

Texas songman Jerry Jeff Walker (born Ronald Clyde Crosby in New York) enjoys a cult following not unlike those of Townes Van Zandt and Guy Clark. Walker, who wrote the story-song standard "Mr. Bojangles," recorded by everyone from the Nitty Gritty Dirt Band to Sammy Davis Jr., travels the same road of "progressive" writing and close-to-the-ground singing and playing: his Seventies accompanists, the Lost Gonzo Band, were as tight and rollicking a country live unit as any that decade, save Merle Haggard's Strangers. Only eight of Walker's twenty-three LPs have made it to CD, although what is available gives a good sense of his strengths and limitations. The Vanguard set from 1969 includes some fine playing from Nashville stalwarts Charlie McCoy (harmonica) and Hargus "Pig" Robbins (piano), and it coasts pleasantly if not too strenuously between introspective country and folk tunes. *Viva Terlingua!* and *Ridin' High,* both from the mid-Seventies, are a tad more spirited, witty, and diverse, though the writing is sometimes a bit too precious for the arrangements; together they contribute eight of the fourteen tracks to the representative retrospective *Great Gonzos.* The more recent collections for Rykodisc are characteristically low-key, modest, and chummy. *Gypsy Songman* mixes old and new compositions; *Gruene Hall* is a smooth live album with a live band nearly the supportive equals of the Lost Gonzos and a brief vocal assist from Willie Nelson; *Navajo Rug* and *Hill Country Rain* each offer up a handful of pointed, world-weary tunes that will bulk up his next *Best of.*—J.G.

CHRIS WALL

★★★ **Honky Tonk Heart (Rykodisc RCD 10179) 1990**
★★★ **No Sweat (Rykodisc RCD 10219) 1991**

Listening to this shot-and-a-beer songwriter (a discovery and protégé of Jerry Jeff Walker) is like having a barstool conversation with a particularly witty good old boy, one who's convinced that the redemptive power of whiskey can counter even the most painful broken heart. "Trashy Women" from his album debut represents Wall's best bid for a honky-tonk classic, while the *No Sweat* followup finds him more assured in the studio as a vocalist, producer, and bandleader, with something of a theme song offered on the closing "I'm Not Drinking Any More" ("and I'm not drinking any less").—D.McL.

STEVE WARINER

★★ **Greatest Hits (RCA 5326-2R) 1985**
★★ **The Best of Steve Wariner (RCA Nashville 07863-52321-2) 1990**
★★½ **One Good Night Deserves Another (MCA MCAD-31137) 1985**
★★½ **Life's Highway (MCA MCAD-31002) 1986**
★★½ **It's a Crazy World (MCA MCAD-31299) 1987**

★★★ **Greatest Hits (MCA MCAD-42032) 1987**
★★½ **I Should Be with You (MCA MCAD-42130) 1988**
★★½ **I Got Dreams (MCA MCAD-42272) 1989**
★★★ **Laredo (MCA MCAD-42335) 1990**
★★★½ **Christmas Memories (MCA MCAD-10067) 1990**
★★★½ **Greatest Hits, Vol. 2 (MCA MCAD-10357) 1991**
★★★ **I Am Ready (Arista 07822-18691-2) 1991**

It's got to be frustrating being Steve Wariner. A hot guitarist and proficient singer and writer of clever, slick-sounding, but ultimately faceless country music, Wariner's been crankin' 'em out for fifteen years now, scoring the occasional Top Ten record, but never really breaking out of the pop-country pack. Listen to his numerous releases, and you'll hear an occasional gem like "Lynda" (*It's a Crazy World*) or "The Tips of My Fingers" (*I Am Ready*) sandwiched between songs that range from merely pleasant to fairly mediocre. Working with top producers like Tony Brown and Jimmy Bowen, Wariner's music has moved from the pop side to the more traditional side as the times dictate, but his career, like most of his records, has never really caught fire. Maybe because Christmas is his birthday (yes, his middle name is Noel) Wariner's holiday CD is something special, and one of his best records, period. Working with Maura O'Connell, Nanci Griffith, Chet Atkins, and the Chieftans, Wariner really poured it on and made a really good Christmas album, of all things. In the final analysis, the *Greatest Hits* collections from MCA contain his best stuff. While his career (and the quality of his music) has been on a slow-but-steady climb, Wariner gives the overall impression of being a genuinely talented guy who works awfully hard, only to come up sounding like the poor man's Vince Gill.—P.Cr.

B. B. WATSON

★½ **Light at the End of the Tunnel (BNA 61020-2) 1991**

A howling exercise in barroom and blue collar clichés. Like most of these tracks, the shuffle beat of the title tune and lilting swing of "Honkytonk the Town

Tonight" are standard hardwood fare, while the boozy ballads "Hank Drank" and "Bottle of Whiskey" add nothing to the canon of country music drinking songs. And Watson's blatant impersonations (of Merle Haggard on Hag's own "Good Intentions," and of Hank Sr. on "Hank Drank") are, ironically, more appealing than the clatter of his own loud and plodding style.—J.B.

DOC WATSON

★★★★   The Doc Watson Family (Smithsonian/Folkways CDSF-40012) 1990

★★   Jean Ritchie and Doc Watson at Folk City (Smithsonian/Folkways CDSF-40005) 1990

★★★★   The Essential Doc Watson (Vanguard Twofer VCD 45/46) 1986

★★★   Treasures Untold (Vanguard VCD-77001) 1991

★★★   Doc Watson (Vanguard VMD-79152) 1964

★★★★★   Southbound (Vanguard VMD-79213) 1966

★★★   Doc Watson on Stage (Vanguard Twofer VCD 9/10) 1988

★★★   [with Merle Watson] Red Rocking Chair (Flying Fish FF-70252) 1981

★★★★   [with Merle Watson] Pickin' the Blues (Flying Fish FF-70352) 1983

★★★★   [with Merle Watson] Guitar Album (Flying Fish FF-70301) 1983

★★★   [with Merle Watson] Down South (Sugar Hill SHCD-3742) 1984

★★★   Riding the Midnight Train (Sugar Hill SHCD-3752) 1985

★★★   Portrait (Sugar Hill SHCD-3759) 1987

★★★   [with Merle Watson] Ballads from Deep Gap (Vanguard VMD-6576) 1989

★★   On Praying Ground (Sugar Hill SHCD-3779) 1990

★★★   Doc Watson Sings Songs for Little Pickers (Sugar Hill SH 3786) 1990

★★★   [with Merle Watson] Remembering Merle (Sugar Hill SHCD-3800) 1992

★★★★★   My Dear Old Southern Home (Sugar Hill SHCD-3795) 1992

Doc Watson hasn't really ever made a bad album. His acoustic guitar work—probably the most distinctive and recognizable in American music today—and his warm, lazy voice are heard to best advantage in small, informal groups, with minimal studio arranging. Whether fans think of him as a folk musician, a bluegrasser, an old-time picker, or simply an acoustic guitarist, Doc has managed for three decades to enchant audiences with his flat-top picking. Although he has often been associated with traditional or old-time country music, his guitar style is in many ways quite unique and innovative: he uses picking techniques borrowed from mandolin playing and likes to adapt guitar tunes from unlikely sources, such as fiddle breakdowns.

Doc's first recordings were done for folksong collectors during the folk revival movement of the early 1960s and emphasize the mountain ballads and traditional tunes he grew up on. *The Doc Watson Family,* the album that introduced Doc to the musical world, features him in various combinations with his large family, many of whom are impressive musicians in their own rights. *The Essential Doc Watson* and *Treasures Untold* are drawn from stage performances at the Newport Folk Festival in 1963-64, and are filled with songs drawn from the 1920s country music era and from acts like Jimmie Rodgers, Grayson & Whitter, and the Carter Family. *Southbound,* released in 1966, is a landmark album on several counts: it contained new, original tunes, some fascinating adaptations of modern country songs, and some of the first cuts to feature Doc's son Merle. In his self-penned liner notes, Doc felt the need to apologize to his folk music fans, but he needn't have: *Southbound* showed the world that Doc was far more than a folk revivalist.

After a decade of not entirely satisfying experiments with commercial labels like Poppy and United Artists (some of which surrounded Doc's music with Nashville sidemen and even string arrangements), Doc signed with the folk label Flying Fish and from 1981 to 1983 recorded several albums for the Chicago-based label. In these, Merle really came into his own as a blues guitarist, and Doc began working with a small combo that occasionally included drums. *Guitar Album* (1983) and *Pickin' the Blues* (1983) are the best of these, and they offer some of Watson's grittiest picking. By 1984 Doc had found a home at the Sugar Hill label of North Carolina and began with them a series of albums in which he took more direct control, with production chores being handled by Merle or long-time Watson sideman T. Michael Coleman. *Down South,* the first Sugar Hill release, was devoted to traditional old-time country music, with mellow songs like "Bright Sunny South," "Fifteen Cents," and "Hello Stranger"; the sparse back-up and superb sound make it possibly Doc and Merle's best studio album. It was followed by a bluegrass album, *Riding the Midnight Train,* in which Doc was backed by a stellar set of young bluegrass stars like Bela Fleck, Sam Bush, and Mark O'Connor. Unfortunately, this was the last studio album on which Merle appeared; he died in a farming accident in October 1985.

After a brief recording hiatus, Doc began returning to the studios in 1990, doing an all-gospel album, *On Praying Ground,* and a children's set, *Songs for Little Pickers,* with Jack Lawrence playing second guitar. Far more successful, though, was 1992's *My Dear Old Southern Home,* another tour of Doc's own roots, dedicated to Merle. Backed by another all-star cast that features the Nashville Bluegrass Band's Alan O'Bryant, ace session men Sam Bush and Jerry Douglas, and fiddler Stuart Duncan, Doc infuses wonderful new life into chestnuts like "Silver-Haired Daddy of Mine," "No Telephone in Heaven," and "Dream of the Miner's Child"—as well as his original "Life Is Like a River." There are no flashy instrumentals here, but fine singing and tasteful back-up work. *Remembering Merle* is an anthology compiled from various live and informal recordings that feature Merle's immense talent, both on banjo, guitar, and slide guitar.—C.K.W.

GENE WATSON
★★★★ **Greatest Hits (MCA MCAD-31128) 1985**
★★★★ **Greatest Hits (Curb/CEMA D21K-77393) 1990**

★★★★ **Back in the Fire (Warner Bros. 25832-2) 1989**
★★★ **At Last (Warner Bros. 9 26329-2) 1991**

Gene Watson, born in Palestine, Texas, but identified usually with Houston, has kept the Texas style of honky-tonk music alive through successive fads and fashions in country music. A traditionalist before Ricky Skaggs and George Strait made such a posture fashionable, Watson has stepped often to the edge of stardom, but has never quite crossed the threshold. This is a pity, because he is one of country music's finest singers, with a clear and soulful tenor voice that retains just enough hard edge to keep it from being saccharine.

Watson's best CD, the Curb *Greatest Hits* package, is accurately named. Included are Watson's first hit, the sultry "Love in the Hot Afternoon," Johnny Russell's cleverly written "Got No Reason Now for Goin' Home," as well as other strong cuts like "Nothing Sure Looked Good on You," and "Paper Rosie." "Farewell Party" is in a class by itself. In one of the great vocal performances in modern country music, Watson demonstrates how a marvelous singer can turn a mediocre, bathetic song into a transcendent experience.

Supplementing the Curb CD, MCA's *Greatest Hits* contains such gems as "14 Carat Mind," "Speak Softly," and "What She Don't Know Won't Hurt Her." *Back in the Fire* is also a very strong collection, and several cuts—such as the title song, "She Found the Key," "The Great Divide," and "Dreams of a Dreamer"— would all be hits if Watson had not been buried in the avalanche of neo-traditionalists.

At Last has a few nice moments, but on the whole, the collection sounds like someone was trying to blunt Watson's hard edge and present him to a middle-of-the-road audience. The effort doesn't work, and Watson is left in a kind of stylistic no-man's land that should not be altogether satisfying to any group of listeners.—B.C.M.

KEVIN WELCH
★★★★ **Kevin Welch (Reprise 9 26171-2) 1990**
★★★★★ **Western Beat (Reprise 9 26823-2) 1992**

To think of him as Carlene Carter's male equivalent would be sexist, of course, but the prolifically singing-songwriting Welch *does* have Carlene's advanced urbane-country kind of consciousness, inventiveness, and class, plus some virtues all his own—significantly, a poet's eye for an image and a mystic's touch with meaning. There are in fact those who finger him as the pick of the Nineties alternative-country litter, and they might be right. Both his albums are packed with smart songs superbly performed—ranging from infectiously rhythmic movers like "Happy Ever After (One Day at a Time)" and "The Mother Road," his instant classic hymn to Route 66, to songs as quietly intense as you could wish for, like "A Letter to Dustin." And he seems to be getting better as he goes.

A native Oklahoman, Welch comes by his "Western Beat" tag honestly (explaining, by the way, that "beat" carries Kerouackian connotations as well as its obvious meaning, and also denying authorship of the handle; he heard it, he says, from an observer at the Montreux Jazz Festival—which should tell you something all by itself). His band, the Overtones, plays on the albums and is almost as good as he is.—P.Ca.

KITTY WELLS

★★★   **The Country Music Hall of Fame Series (MCAD-10081) 1991**
★★★★   **Greatest Hits, Vol. 1 (Step One SOR-0046) 1989**
★★½   **Greatest Hits, Vol. 2 (Step One SOR-0047) 1989**
★★½   **Country Spotlight (Dominion 30262) 1991**

In our enlightened age of nasty rap and Madonna, it seems beyond our ken that there once was a time, not quite prehistoric (1952, to be precise), when Kitty Wells's "It Wasn't God Who Made Honky Tonk Angels" was briefly banned by CBS radio as, well, more than the public ought to hear. So vast is the chasm between our time and the early 1950s—when a humble housewifely singer born Muriel Deason became a sensation on the strength of an answer song to Hank Thompson's "The Wild Side of Life"— that Kitty Wells, whose name was borrowed from an old folk song, takes some explaining. What made her popular and, in the Greater Scheme of Things,

important? She was the first female country singer to meet her male counterparts on adult terms. Wells was a severely limited vocalist, but an emotionally sincere one, who struck a nerve with country audiences in the 1950s, when she was dubbed Queen of Country Music. She was an important early role model for Patsy Cline and Loretta Lynn, both indisputably better singers than Wells, but it was Kitty who opened the door for women onto the thematic turf of post-World War II country, proving that both sexes could sing frankly of heartache and honky-tonk hardwood floors.

The Country Music Hall of Fame set reissues sixteen of Wells's 1952-65 Decca recordings. To the artist's detriment, the compilation exaggerates Wells's reputation for whipped keening, weepy lyrics, and lachrymose monotony. It includes "Icicles Hanging from Your Heart," frosty treacle that Decca and MCA Records refrigerated unissued for decades, and "My Cold, Cold Heart Is Melted Now," a sorry juxtaposition of Hank Williams's "Cold, Cold Heart" and "Your Cheatin' Heart." Granted, *Hall of Fame* does collect the original "Honky Tonk Angels" and nine other Top Ten hits ("Making Believe" is and ever will be one of the great country songs, and Wells's definitive recording is here), but nowhere to be heard is anything remotely upbeat, such as Wells's 1953 hit, "Hey Joe." Likewise absent are any of her fine duets with Red Foley, Roy Acuff, and Webb Pierce. What should be a definitive collection paints this artist in drab hues and argues against taking her seriously, but there was really more to Wells than the weary, woeful stereotype reinforced here.

Wells was better served by Rounder's 1982 *The Golden Years* (Rounder SS-13), containing a dozen 1950s Decca recordings; it's still available on cassette or LP. It presented her as a more varied and vital artist by including some of her duets and balancing ballads with uptempo songs. *The Golden Years* is arguably all the Kitty Wells anyone needs, though the truly devout can still find the German Bear Family label's six-LP box, *The Golden Years, 1949-57* (Bear Family LP 15239). It includes all ninety-five of Wells's Decca recordings from her reign as unchallenged Queen of Country, a completist's delight.

Like many veteran country performers, Wells has re-recorded her hits in recent years. If the notes to *Country Spotlight* are accurate, this ten-song set (eight re-create Decca hits on the *Hall of Fame* collection) is as recent as 1991. If so, she was in good voice for a woman of seventy-two, though that's the sole exceptional thing here. The playing and production are workmanlike but uninspired. Far more enjoyable are the 1989 performances for Ray Pennington's SOR label, *Greatest Hits, Vol. 1*. Pennington went to the trouble to do something other than the obvious with Wells. Only three of the twelve songs duplicate selections from *Hall of Fame*, and the playing is top drawer, with plenty of crying steel guitar throughout. Pennington recast "Honky Tonk Angels" as a slow Ray Price shuffle, a nice variance from the original. "I Don't Claim to Be an Angel" actually kicks, and this is the most fun you'll hear Kitty having on the available CDs. Alas, SOR's *Vol. 2* falters from the gate. This ten-song set duplicates none of the *Hall of Fame* Deccas, but there's little to crow about unless your idea of heaven is hearing Kitty Wells cover Olivia Newton-John ("If You Love Me Let Me Know"). SOR would've done better to raid Kitty's Decca catalogue once again.—M.H.

CHERYL WHEELER

★★½   Cheryl Wheeler (North Star W0001) 1986
★★★★   Circles & Arrows (Capitol 92063) 1990
★★★★   Half a Book (North Star WS0005) 1991

Cheryl Wheeler is an intelligent singer-songwriter based in southern New England who writes sensitive, direct, sometimes humorous songs about the capricious conflicts of love and other absurd, undeniably important whims of life. A former member of Jonathan Edwards's backup band, Wheeler began performing in folk clubs in the mid-1970s and has built a strong following along the Eastern Seaboard.

With the 1986 release of her first full-length album, Wheeler's reputation as a sharp songwriter and engaging performer started to spread. Several country artists picked up on her songs: Dan Seals, for example, had a hit with "Addicted," one of the best songs from her first album.

Wheeler's debut revealed her talent; unfortunately, Jonathan Edwards's synthesized adult-pop production and the intricate arrangements sap passion and intimacy from her songs. In addition, tunes like the corny "Lethal Detective" and the predictable environmental diatribe, "Paradise in Troubled Waters," don't measure up to her later work.

With *Circles and Arrows,* her lone major label effort so far, Wheeler continued to hone her talents. Produced to intimate perfection by Kyle Lehning, it includes the darkly humorous "Estate Sale" as well as the superb "Aces" (later a hit for Suzy Bogguss) and the piercing insights of "Arrow," a song that originally appeared on her debut and which benefits from a splendidly lyrical fiddle solo by Mark O'Connor.

Wheeler returned to the North Star label for her third album, *Half a Book,* and the warmer, more acoustic arrangements cash in all of her strengths, and her songs have grown into well-crafted gems. By now, Wheeler's warm, compelling voice has grown more mature and supple, and her subtly theatrical touches present the perfect instrument for her sensitive lyrical portrayals, including the fine "Tell Him Goodbye" and "Summerfly," which Maura O'Connell later recorded.—M.M.

JOY WHITE

★★★½   Between Midnight & Hindsight (Columbia CK 48806) 1992

There's nothing timid about Joy White. She has a hair-raising vibrato that can be tough or tender and a fearlessness in the way she stomps a roadhouse beat. Her debut album features a few standout tracks—"Little Tears," "True Confessions"—that could easily hold their own against hillbilly boys like Dwight Yoakam or Marty Stuart, with whom she shares an unmistakable reverence for the honky-tonk tradition.—K.S.

LARI WHITE

★★★½   Lead Me Not (RCA 07863-66117-2) 1993

This talented newcomer's debut album is a richly textured pastiche of musical styles reflecting both the extent of her musical interests and the range of her abilities. Eight of ten songs were written or co-written by White, who also coproduced with Rodney Crowell and Steuart Smith. Together, they provide a showcase for White's mastery over an impressive array of musical styles, including steamy torch songs, gospel, pop ballads, heart-broke honky-tonk, and contemporary country. Both her gospel styled "Lead Me Not" and "What a Woman Wants," her spunky manifesto for gender equity, will likely become signature songs for what promises to be a long and prosperous career.—J.B.

MICHAEL WHITE
★★½ **Familiar Ground (Reprise 9 26816-2) 1992**

"I wanted it to sound a little bit different than anyone else," said Michael White of his debut album. He achieved that effect: his deft, minor league middle-brow country pop sounds a little bit different from Garth Brooks, a little bit different from Clint Black, a little bit different from . . . well, whomever. Which isn't surprising, given White's past as a cover-band rocker and Nashville demo singer, but it isn't very interesting, either. There's potential—an unusual curve or two, an elegant idea (the title track, the clever "Professional Fool") but mostly this is all-too-familiar ground.—P.Ca.

THE WHITES
★★★ **Greatest Hits (MCA MCAD-31227) 1986**

Buck White and his daughters, Cheryl and Sharon, created a sound that combined the swing music of their native Texas with smooth vocal harmonies borrowed from pop, gospel, and bluegrass music. With Buck alternating between piano and mandolin, and Jerry Douglas adding his innovative dobro styles to their early performances, the Whites built a large following in both bluegrass and mainstream country music.

Like too many of the CDs that have become available in country music, though, the Whites' MCA collection is grossly mistitled. The songs are pleasant and competently performed, but few of them were genuine hits. The Whites exhibit their versatility on the western-swing style "Hangin' Around," the bluegrassy "If It Ain't Love," and the pop-contemporary "Give Me Back That Old Familiar Feeling." The real source of the Whites' popularity, however, was the

rich mellow sound of their trio singing, and it is heard to best advantage in romantic songs like "Hometown Gossip," "Forever You," and "You Put the Blue in Me."—B.C.M.

KEITH WHITLEY
★★ **Second Generation Bluegrass (Rebel 1504) 1971, 1990**
★★ **L.A. to Miami (RCA 5870) 1985**
★★★ **Don't Close Your Eyes (RCA 6494) 1988 ●**
★★★★½ **I Wonder Do You Think of Me (RCA 9809) 1989 ●**
★★★★ **Greatest Hits (RCA 2277) 1990 ▲**
★★★ **Kentucky Bluebird (RCA 3156) 1991**

In retrospect, it's possible to spot some of Keith Whitley's genius in his first two RCA albums. His version of "On the Other Hand" bears little similarity to the song that was subsequently a hit for Randy Travis; Travis glides along this tale of temptation resisted as though he's recounting it safely after the event, while Whitley's muted, halting reading seems to come during the troubled moment of decision. He established his themes early, too, from the lovelorn resignation of "I Get the Picture" ("Last night when I met you at your lawyer's house/I wondered 'bout the guy who dropped you off") to the unrepentant fatalism of "I'm No Stranger to the Rain" and David Halley's "Hard Livin'."

Everything improved when Garth Fundis took over production from Blake Mevis and fashioned a music with the same relaxed intensity as Whitley's voice. As a measure of ambition, they cut Lefty Frizzell's "I Never Go around Mirrors," and it's a revealing performance. Whitley illustrates the sense of lost time by dragging out syllables ("where heart-aches hay-ay-ang around") in a tart Kentucky twang. While country was moving towards pop-influenced, middle-American tenors, Whitley, like John Anderson but few others, held on to his deeply Southern accent.

Whitley's singing grew even more generous and expansive on *I Wonder Do You Think of Me.* The songs constitute a classic honky-tonk identity, especially the despondent solitude of "Between an Old Memory and Me," the macho self-deceit of "I'm Over You," and the barroom self-knowledge of "Tennessee Courage." There are a lot of bars and a few juke-boxes in the lyrics, but ultimately all of the songs are about love, which is occasionally seen as salvation, but more often depicted as a cursedly eternal bond that yields only undying regret. Helped by Paul Franklin, whose nuanced steel guitar bolsters the melodies, Whitley made one of the best country albums of the Eighties. Just before completing his breakthrough, he died of alcohol poisoning.

And so, this dead country superstar became the Jimi Hendrix of Nashville, his catalogue repackaged and his unreleased sessions revamped. *Greatest Hits* doesn't disguise its bathos, concluding with "'Til a Tear Becomes a Rose," an old-timey duet between Whitley and wife Lorrie Morgan, and "Tell Lorrie I Love Her," a scratchy home demo of an unreleased song filled with portents of death. *Second Generation Bluegrass*, a two-day session with Ricky Skaggs and Ralph Stanley, among others, was recorded in 1971, when Whitley was fifteen. And *Kentucky Bluebird* opens with an even younger Whitley singing Hank Williams on a local radio show, then mixes good album tracks like "I Never Go around Mirrors" with TV and radio interviews, plus unreleased songs and publishing demos given additional production by Garth Fundis (including "Brotherly Love," a duet with Earl Thomas Conley). Inevitably, perhaps, RCA scheduled a late 1993 release for the 1984 EP *Hard Act to Follow*, Whitley's label debut.—R.T.

THE WILBURN BROTHERS

★★ Wonderful Wilburn Brothers (King KCD-748) 1988
★★★ Retrospective (MCA MCAD-25990) 1990

Doyle and Teddy Wilburn are best known for bringing the brother duet style into the modern Nashville era. During the 1960s and 1970s, they released more than twenty-five LPs for Decca and had over a dozen Top Twenty singles, including "Which One Is to Blame" (1959) and "Trouble's Back in Town" (1962). Though the Wilburns lacked the soulful edge of the Louvin Brothers or the vitality of Johnnie & Jack, they gained great popularity through their syndicated

television series and Grand Ole Opry appearances. Both Wilburns became active in publishing and promotion as well. Sadly, very little of their huge catalogue of recordings is currently available. *Retrospective* collects a good sampling of the chart hits, while *The Wonderful Wilburn Brothers* spotlights a number of earlier, more traditional efforts, such as "Bugle Call from Heaven" and "Are You Lonely Too."—C.K.W.

WILD JIMBOS

★★ Wild Jimbos (MCA MCAD-10279) 1991

This slight but intermittently endearing trio is a side project of Nitty Gritty Dirt Band singer and guitarist Jimmy Ibbotson. Their sole CD offers some low-key guilty pleasures, such as Fred Koller and John Prine's "Let's Talk Dirty in Hawaiian." But nobody on this disc is counting on this unit for his livelihood. —J.G.

DON WILLIAMS

★★★★ Greatest Hits, Vol. 1 (MCA MCAD-31249) 1975
★★★ The Best of Don Williams, Vol. 2 (MCA MCAD-31172) 1979 ●
★★★½ I Believe in You (MCA MCAD-31122) 1980 ▲
★★★½ Especially for You (MCA MCAD-31123) 1981
★★★½ The Best of Don Williams, Vol. 3 (MCA MCAD-31247) 1984 ●
★★½ Greatest Hits, Vol. 4 (MCA MCAD-31248) 1985
★★★★ 20 Greatest Hits (MCA MCAD-5944) 1987
★★ Prime Cuts (Capitol CDP7914442) 1989
★★★ Greatest Country Hits (Curb/CEMA D21K-77361) 1990
★★★½ One Good Well (RCA 9656-2-R) 1989
★★★ True Love (RCA 2407-2-R) 1990
★★★½ Currents (RCA 07863-61128-2) 1992

As a vocalist, Texas-born Don Williams (a founding member of the Sixties folk group the Pozo Seco Singers) has always been a one-trick pony. But, ah, what a wonderful trick it has often been. His warm, laconic baritone, backed by tastefully minimal productions—as heard on memorable hit recordings like "Amanda," "'Til the Rivers All Run Dry,"

"Tulsa Time," "Rake and Ramblin' Man," and "I'm Just a Country Boy"—suggest all the positive power of enduring love, faith, and inner direction. Williams's music has often been a font of calm and gentleness amidst the splashiness of the country mainstream and represents some of the best music made in Nashville during the 1970s. And although Williams's output from the 1970s remains his best, he's never really put out a bad album. In more recent years, Williams has, on his somewhat more commercially obscure RCA releases, strayed little from his instantly recognizable stick-to-the-basics approach, even when the hits have been harder to come by.

Currently there are no fewer than seven different Williams hits collections available on CD; sadly, early classic Williams albums, like *You're My Best Friend, Harmony, Visions,* and *Country Boy,* haven't yet made the transfer. *Prime Cuts,* a half-baked anthology of his few years with Capitol is mostly quasi-hits and uninspired out-takes. Thus, for the time being, the various collections (the strongest of which are MCA's *Greatest Hits, Vols. 1-4* and *20 Greatest Hits)* and Williams's three very worthwhile recent RCA albums—*True Love, One Good Well,* and *Currents*—will have to suffice.—B.A.

HANK WILLIAMS
★★★★★ **40 Greatest Hits (Polydor 821 233-2) 1978**
★★★★★ **I Ain't Got Nothin' But Time— December 1946-April 1947, Vol. 1 (Polydor 825 548-2) 1985**
★★★★★ **Lovesick Blues—August 1947- December 1948, Vol. 2 (Polydor 825 551-2) 1985**
★★★★★ **Lost Highway—December 1948- March 1949, Vol. 3 (Polydor 825 554-2) 1986**
★★★★★ **I'm So Lonesome I Could Cry— March 1949-August 1949, Vol. 4 (Polydor 825 557-2) 1986**
★★★★★ **Long Gone Lonesome Blues— August 1949-December 1950, Vol. 5 (Polydor 831 633-2) 1987**
★★★★★ **Hey, Good Lookin'—December 1950-July 1951, Vol. 6 (Polydor 831 634-2) 1987**
★★★★★ **Let's Turn Back the Years—July 1951-June 1952, Vol. 7 (Polydor 833 749-2) 1987**
★★★★★ **I Won't Be Home No More—June 1952-September 1952, Vol. 8 (Polydor 833 752-2) 1987**
★★★★★ **The Original Singles Collection... Plus (Polydor 847 194-2) 1990**
★★★★★ **Rare Demos: First to Last (Country Music Foundation CMF-067-D) 1990**
★★★★★ **Health & Happiness Shows (PolyGram 314 517 862-2) 1993**

Hank Williams (1923-1953) was either the Hillbilly Shakespeare or a crude, semi-literate plagiarist, depending on which biographer you believe. Since he shuffled off this mortal coil in the back seat of a Cadillac bound for a New Year's Eve comeback gig (no other American death-cult hero exited with such piquant poetic flair), Williams has been the subject of countless legends and counterlegends. Some yarns are attached to specific songs and the turmoil that inspired them; like any good Romantic poet, Williams was an artist whose life and work were closely interwoven. But even if you hadn't heard the juicy tales of drink and drugs and a Lost Highway littered with ex-wives and squabbling heirs of varying legitimacy, all of it is somehow implied when you hear him sing. Measured by the Richter scale of either his mentor, Roy Acuff, or his artistic heir, George Jones, Williams's voice was no great shakes, yet it rang with an emotional conviction and resonance somehow in this world but not of this world. Like a meager handful of recorded artists, Williams managed both to epitomize the genre in which he worked and to transcend it in a manner that makes his best work timeless and universal. Alongside such an accomplishment, the issue of whether he swiped a few songs seems irrelevant.

Williams's recorded legacy has endured clumsy posthumous meddling: band tracks were added to home demos when MGM rifled its vaults for fresh Hank product in the 1950s. In the countrypolitan Sixties, stereophonic strings added an urbane touch of class to ol' Hank. By the early 1980s, some ninety LPs had been culled from not quite that many commercial recordings and a dizzying jumble of demos. Hank had been variously marketed as Folk Singer, Gospel Singer, and the Original Outlaw. Given that background, it's a wonder he isn't now packaged as the First Hat Act, the Ur-Garth.

In 1978, PolyGram's *40 Greatest Hits* was a milestone double LP, for it restored the central performances of Williams's career to monophonic purity, free of overdubs. It confirmed that these recordings were more than mere product and deserved to be heard in the form in which the artist left them during his lifetime. This two-CD set is still the best place to begin a Williams collection—everything essential, familiar, and much covered is here, though the sound isn't as crisp as it might be.

Guided by Colin Escott and Hank Davis, PolyGram then launched the most ambitious Hank reissue program to date in 1985 with the first of eight double LPs, which boldly displayed a "statement of purpose" on the back cover of each: "This series is intended to present all of Hank Williams' studio recordings: in chronological order; in original undubbed mono; remastered for the clearest possible sound."

The series achieved its goals, eventually issuing 168 performances, including a handful of previously unreleased demos. The double LPs are now single CDs of twenty-one to twenty-two tracks and present a deservedly detailed portrait of Williams's artistic evolution on record. If you want to sample the series, start with *Vol. 1* (it includes "Honky Tonkin'" and the haunting "Alone and Forsaken") and see if you want more. The eight-CD series is comprehensive though not exhaustive: radio performances, live recordings, and still-unissued demos exist that aren't on CD. And while the chronology of the demos is less certain than that of the session recordings, there are moments of sloppiness: if Hank wrote "Weary Blues from Waitin'" for Ray Price in 1952, as Escott tells us in the notes for *Lovesick Blues,* why is Hank's demo of it on that collection of material from 1947-48?

As an attractive compromise between *40 Greatest Hits* and the eight-CD motherlode, PolyGram issued *The Original Singles Collection . . . Plus,* a three-CD, eighty-four-song boxed set, in 1990. But it doesn't really offer all Hank's singles. Only two of the pseudonymous "Luke the Drifter" performances are here, and his duets with first wife Audrey are omitted because, compiler Escott tells us, she couldn't sing! Not many would argue with that, but Audrey and Hank's "Lost on the River" duet is a masterpiece anyway and, as a comprehensive singles collection, this box is sixteen tracks shy of a load. Caveats aside, the audio restoration is superb. The superior presence and clarity make *The Original Singles Collection* by far the best-sounding set of Hank's commercial recordings.

Rare Demos: First to Last is the Country Music Foundation's CD issue of two remarkable LPs, *Just Me and My Guitar* and *The First Recordings.* The twenty-four Williams demos include such standards as "Jambalaya" and "Honky Tonk Blues," and sound far clearer on CD than on the 1985-86 vinyl releases. The intense performance of "Your Cheatin' Heart," muffled on vinyl, is much brighter here. The moving "House of Gold" has so much presence it's downright spooky. More that mere sketches, Hank's demos bear stark witness to the emotional power of the country genre's most compelling genius.

Along with his studio recordings and demos, Hank's radio performances present yet another dimension of his legend, and the eight 1949 *"Health & Happiness Shows"* are wonderful snapshots from a long-gone era, one where radio ruled and could make a regional star of an affable hayseed like Hank. Aside from the music, much of what's appealing here is Hank's relaxed between-song patter and assured sense of his role as bandleader. The fabled Hank-Audrey relationship is captured in some good-natured verbal sparring, and Audrey's vocal solos live up to her legend as a hillbilly Yoko Ono. Long-time collectors of Hank bootlegs and imports may quibble with the "Complete and Undubbed for the First Time" claim on the shrinkwrap of this two-CD box, but it's great anyway to have this Truman-era time capsule of the Hillbilly Shakespeare's eight *"Health & Happiness Shows"* together in a handsome little box.—M.H.

HANK WILLIAMS JR.

★★★   Hank Williams Jr.'s Greatest Hits (Polydor 811903-2) 1987
★★★   The Best of Hank Williams Jr., Vol. 1 (Mercury 849575-2) 1992
★★★½ Living Proof The MGM Recordings, 1963-1975 (Mercury 314-517 320-4) 1992
★★★★ Family Tradition (Warner Bros. 194-2) 1979
★★★★ Habits Old and New (Warner Bros. 278-2) 1980
★★★½ Whiskey Bent and Hellbound (Elektra 237-2) 1981 ●
★★★★ Rowdy (Warner Bros. 330-2) 1981 ●
★★★½ The Pressure Is On (Warner Bros. 535-2) 1981 ▲
★★★★ Hank Williams Jr.'s Greatest Hits (Warner Bros. 9 60193-2) 1982 ▲²
★★★★ High Notes (Warner Bros. 60100-2) 1982 ●
★★★   Man of Steel (Warner Bros. 23924-2) 1983 ●
★★½   Strong Stuff (Warner/Curb 9 60223-2) 1983 ●
★★★   Major Moves (Curb/Warner Bros. 25088-2) 1984 ●
★★★   Five-O (Warner Bros. 25267-4) 1985 ●
★★★   Hank Williams Jr.'s Greatest Hits, Vol. 2 (Curb/Warner Bros. 25328-2) 1985 ▲
★★   Montana Cafe (Warner Bros. 925412-2) 1986 ●
★★½   Hank "Live" (Warner Bros. 25538-2) 1987 ●
★★   Born to Boogie (Warner Bros. 25593-4) 1987 ▲
★★½   Wild Streak (Warner Bros. 9 25725-2) 1988 ●
★★½   Hank Williams Jr.'s Greatest Hits, Vol. 3 (Warner Bros. 25834-2) 1989 ▲
★½   America (The Way I See It) (Warner Bros. 9 26453-2) 1990
★★★   Lone Wolf (Warner Bros. 9 26090-2) 1990 ●
★★★   Pure Hank (Warner Bros. 9 26536-2) 1991
★★★   The Bocephus Box: The Hank Williams Jr. Collection, 1979-1992 (Curb/Capricorn 9 45104-2) 1992
★★½   Maverick (Capricorn 9 26806-2) 1992
★★★   Hank Williams/Hank Williams Jr. (K-Tel 3049-2) 1992
★★★   The Best of Hank and Hank (Curb/CEMA D21K-77552) 1992
★★★½ Out of Left Field (Capricorn 4-45225) 1993

Since he turned his back on being a talented but feckless imitator of his illustrious father, Hank Jr. has embarked upon one of the most amazing cases of musical self-invention that country music has ever seen. In the process, he's established a formidable rock & roll-oriented audience quite apart from the older devotees who bought his earliest records in slavish devotion to his father's memory. He's proven to be an even more versatile singer than his father, and he's composed some of the most compellingly topical country songs ("A Country Boy Can Survive," "I Got Rights," "The Coalition to End Coalitions") this side of Merle Haggard. Hank Jr. has also recorded some of the finest country-blues, Dixieland, and Southern boogie heard in the last twenty years.

On the flip side, Williams—whose musical vocabulary is extensive, but whose lexicon doesn't seem to include the notion of subtlety—has exploited his father's legend incessantly in his music, all the way from his 1966 confessional, "Standin' in the Shadows," to 1989's "There's a Tear in My Beer," an electronically simulated hit duet with his father, dead some forty years. And, in more recent years, Hank Jr.'s music has suffered heavily from its preponderance of thematically redundant redneck anthems. Recently, the righteous anger that first fueled his best topical songs has slowly given way to dull cynicism—as best typified in *America (The Way I See It)*, a compendium of his musical opinions which are, too often, heavy on attitude but light on perception. All this said, Williams nonetheless surprised everyone with his 1993 release *Out of Left Field*. It is the first Hank Jr. album in recent memory that didn't include at least one gratuitous reference to his father or some sort of self-serving self-reference to "Ol' Bocephus." Instead, it's a mellow, soulful R&B-influenced collection of songs in which Hank Jr. cools his rowdy musical persona and segues into middle age much more smoothly than anyone might have imagined.

None of Williams's numerous early MGM albums (1963-75) have yet resurfaced intact on CD. Most sorely missing are early MGM and Warners gems like *Hank Williams Jr. & Friends* (1975)—a brilliant exercise in country-rock fusion—*Living Proof* (1974), *The New South* (1977), and *Bocephus* (1975). However, most of his dozen and a half or so more recent albums on Elektra, Warners, Warner-Curb, and Capricorn, are available.

Predictably, the bins are flooded with single-CD Hank Jr. best of collections—nearly a dozen at last count. There are also two boxed collections: *The Bocephus Box: The Hank Williams Jr. Collection, 1979-1992,* and *Living Proof—The MGM Recordings (1963-1975).* These two packages demonstrate the liabilities of having two record companies trying simultaneously to box the same artist. Neither set is definitive, although *Living Proof,* drawn from Williams's earlier and more obscure MGM recordings, is the more interesting and the one that showcases the many sides of early Hank Jr. (Hank Sr. clone, young rock & roller, aspiring pop crossover artist, etc.) *The Bocephus Box,* on the other hand, offers an adequate survey of Hank Jr.'s prolific post-MGM output. But with its numerous out-takes, live cuts, and second-rate previously unreleased tracks, it strives for eclecticism at the expense of comprehensiveness. In this case, the boxes aren't even necessarily the best buy. *The Best of Hank Williams Jr., Vol. 1* is a credible single CD anthology of his MGM years. And *Greatest Hits,Vols. 1-3,* compile the Elektra/Warner Brothers years adequately enough for all but the most die-hard fans.

For novice country fans, there are a couple of interesting single-CD collections—*Back to Back* and *The Best of Hank and Hank*—which showcase the younger Williams right alongside the paterfamilial shadow he's never quite escaped.—B.A.

JASON D. WILLIAMS
★ **Tore Up (RCA 9782-2-R) 1989**
★½ **Wild (Sun SCD 1037) 1993**
What does it say about an artist when he has built an entire career out of impersonating Jerry Lee Lewis? A popular nightclub performer in Little Rock and Memphis, Williams has yet to make any impression on the wider public, which is probably just as well. Oh, he's got the act down pat, all right. He duplicates every nuance of Jerry Lee Lewis's classic idiosyncrasies—he even looks a little like a youthful Lewis—and reduces them to meaningless mannerisms. Fittingly, he provided the flying fingers in close-ups for the fictionalized Jerry Lee movie bio *Great Balls of Fire.* And that's about as close to mass appeal as he'll get if he continues to serve up warmed-over covers of classic R&B and rockabilly numbers ("Slow Down," "Caldonia," "Red Hot") performed flatly in the style of you-know-who. *Tore Up* is a much sleepier affair than its title suggests. *Wild* rates a little higher for occasionally rocking.

To be fair, Jason D. does add one noticeable twist to the classic Jerry Lee sound. He tosses in an occasional bit of movie theme music—"Dueling Banjos" as "Dueling Pianos," the undead "Theme from the Exorcist"—and then plays it strictly for laughs. Somewhere in the shadows, the Killer is gnashing his teeth and howling at the moon.—P.K.

LUCINDA WILLIAMS
★★ **Ramblin' (Smithsonian/Folkways SF 40042) 1979, 1991**
★★★ **Happy Woman Blues (Smithsonian/ Folkways SF 40003) 1980, 1990**
★★★★ **Lucinda Williams (Chameleon 61387-2) 1988, 1992**
★★★½ **Sweet Old World (Chameleon 61351-2) 1992**
Williams works well outside the country mainstream. *Ramblin'* is primarily a collection of blues standards, *Happy Woman Blues* is—contrary to its title— her most folk-rocky effort, and many of her songs show a strong rock and Cajun influence. But Williams nonetheless has a country sensibility, writing tales of heartache and cheating, singing them in a flat twang whose emotional shading and suppleness is a constant nice surprise. She's written at least two great songs— the urgent "I Just Wanted to See You So Bad" and the overpowering "Passionate Kisses," both on *Lucinda Williams*—and for the sustained quality and sensuousness of her tight wordplay and crisp melodies, she's as strong a singer-songwriter as the late Eighties produced, with a Nineties career of enormous

promise, judging from the continued potency of her songwriting on the long-delayed *Sweet Old World.*—K.T.

KELLY WILLIS

★★★ **Well Traveled Love (MCA MCAD-6390) 1990**

★★★½ **Bang Bang (MCA MCAD-10141) 1991**

★★★★ **Kelly Willis (MCA MCAD-10789) 1993**

The cover art for *Well Travelled Love* shows a torn ticket from a concert by Janis Martin, the teen-aged rockabilly firecracker of the late Fifties. And at a time when most girl singers sang demurely, with a thin, pretty tone, Willis's throaty, boiling passion recalled Martin, Wanda Jackson, and the Patsy Cline of "Turn the Cards Slowly." Thus, her career turned into an ironic dilemma: how to promote a singer whose notion of traditionalism has been eradicated from Nashville's vocabulary. An Austinite by way of Annandale, Virginia, Willis was twenty-one when her debut album came out. "You can test the water, now it ain't no sin/Sometimes it's better just to dive right in," she sings boldly in "River of Love," racing alongside Richard Bennett's tumbling guitar solo. More than anything, her sense of dynamics seems to come from Texas blues guitarists, especially the sustained redlining of Stevie Ray Vaughan. The album mixes rockabilly, Tex-Mex, and honky-tonk with a few emphatic ballads, none of which cracked country radio. Interestingly, it also includes John Hiatt's "Drive South," subsequently a big hit for Suzy Bogguss, one of those girl singers who sings thin and pretty.

While Willis's four-piece band, Radio Ranch, played on her debut along with studio aces, the group is nearly gone from *Bang Bang,* represented only by a few contributions from drummer Mas Palermo and bassist Brad Fordham. Despite her rockabilly devotions, the uptempo jumpers—Joe Ely's "Settle for Love" and the title track—are overshadowed by slower numbers like Jim Lauderdale's majestic "Not Afraid of the Dark" and Kostas-Mas Palermo's "The Heart That Love Forgot," which presents Willis as a female Roy Orbison. Struggling to find a place for her at country radio, producer Tony Brown discharged

Radio Ranch for the third album and sought assistance from Don Was, who produces Bonnie Raitt (not to mention Iggy Pop). The excesses of the first two albums have been trimmed: there are no stomping tempos, and Willis minimizes the sobbing notes and athletic vibrato she'd used to signify intensity. Her increased subtlety is satisfying, as are the beefy power-twang runs of Billy Bremner, the British guitarist for Rockpile and the Pretenders. By its smart mixture of musicians and songs, *Kelly Willis* gracefully integrates West Coast influences into a Nashville structure. And it's hard to imagine another singer who'd cover the Kendalls' hard-country "Heaven's Just a Sin Away" on the same album as Detroit popster Marshall Crenshaw's "Whatever Way the Winds Blows."—R.T.

BOB WILLS

★★★★★ **Anthology: 1935-73 (Rhino R2 70744) 1991**

★★★★ **Columbia Historic Edition (Columbia CK-37468E) 1982**

★★★ **The Essential Bob Wills (Columbia CK 48958) 1992**

★★★★ **Tiffany Transcriptions, Best of the Tiffanys, Vol. 2 (Kaleidoscope K-19) 1984**

★★★★ **Tiffany Transcriptions: In the Mood, Vol. 9 (Kaleidoscope K-36) 1991**

★ **[& the McKinney Sisters] Tiffany Transcriptions (Kaleidoscope K-6002) 1991**

★★★ **21 Golden Hits (Hollywood/IMG HCD-411) N. D.**

★★★ **Country Music Hall of Fame (MCA MCAD-10547) 1992**

★★★ **Best of Bob Wills (MCA MCAD-5917) 1973**

It is good to report that the music of Bob Wills is well represented on CDs. This legendary Texas fiddler, singer, and bandleader, along with his fabulous band, the Texas Playboys, helped to forge a jazz-blues-country amalgam now known as western swing. Like some of his jazz-minded fans, Wills may have been uncomfortable with being labeled country, but his music touched and shaped the styles of many of the most important country musicians of the past fifty years.

The best available collection of Wills's material is the two-volume Rhino *Anthology, 1935-73*. Selections include the songs most associated with Wills, such as "Steel Guitar Rag," "New San Antonio Rose," "Take Me Back to Tulsa," "Faded Love," and "Maiden's Prayer" (performed without a vocal), as well as a sampling of tunes, like "Jo-Bob Rag," "Heart to Heart Talk," and "Blue Bonnet Lane," that only collectors will recognize. The material is heavily skewed toward the Playboys' jazzy and swing material; consequently, few "heart songs" such as "I Wonder if You Feel the Way I Do" will be heard here. Since this collection spans the entire recording career of Wills and the Texas Playboys, some listeners may be disappointed that more of the band's vocalists are not represented. Everyone should be pleased that the great Tommy Duncan dominates most of the vocal tracks and that Bob Wills can be heard on such cuts as "Corinne, Corinna," and "My Confession." But the collection would have been more representative, to cite one example, if the outstanding voice of Leon Rausch had been featured.

The *Columbia Historic Edition* is an outstanding short anthology sampling Wills's tenure with the Columbia label from 1935 to 1947, with eight of the ten cuts coming from the period before 1941. Tommy Duncan is the featured singer on several selections and is nothing short of sensational on "I Ain't Got Nobody" and "Right or Wrong." Although the Playboys shine on every selection, "Cowboy Stomp" is the only pure instrumental on the album.

Likewise, Columbia's *Essential Bob Wills* also covers the period from 1935 to 1947 but with a much heavier concentration of instrumental material. Classic Wills tunes, such as "Steel Guitar Rag," "New San Antonio Rose," "Time Changes Everything," and "Take Me Back to Tulsa," are here along with a few lesser known performances like "Sugar Moon," "Fat Boy Rag," and "Bob Wills Boogie." Swing fans will particularly like "Bob Wills Special," which features the twin guitars of Eldon Shamblin and Leon McAuliffe, and "Maiden's Prayer," which adds two clarinets, two saxophones, and two trumpets to the usual complement of Playboy instruments. The only peculiar feature of this album is the problem of

incomplete and occasionally misleading notes. A good bit of studio laughter and conversation precedes at least four of the songs, and one of the tunes ("New Spanish Two Step") begins with a false start. Tommy Duncan is also listed as vocalist on two songs which have no vocals at all. The album's annotator, Rich Kienzle, provides no explanation.

The *Tiffany Transcriptions* were recorded in Oakland, California, during the period from mid-1945 to 1947 and then sold to radio stations around the nation. The Playboys' personnel had changed substantially since the band's glory days at Tulsa from 1934 to 1942, but it was still a great band which could play everything from hoedowns to pop standards and jazz classics. There are no surprises on the transcriptions, for they convey the same spirit and the same varied repertoire of songs that were heard on their recordings and radio broadcasts and at their dances.

The McKinney Sisters collection, however, presents a sound sure to be unfamiliar to most Bob Wills fans. Duet singers Dean and Evelyn McKinney sounded a good bit like the Girls of the Golden West and could be passably good yodelers, but they were essentially pop singers. At least one of their songs, "Betcha My Heart," won some popularity with the larger country music public, but with the exceptions of a few songs like "Jealous Hearted Me" (a bluesy version of the old Carter Family song), "I Dreamed of an Old Love Affair," and "Echoes from the Hills," most of their song selections came from the realm of pop music.

Although grossly misnamed, *21 Golden Hits* nevertheless is a collection that all Bob Wills fans should own. Except for Tommy Duncan's vocal on "San Antonio Rose," all of the music comes from recordings made on Dewey Groom's Longhorn label in Dallas in 1964 and 1965. Frankly, the tracks recorded by the full Playboy band are undistinguished, but twelve of the recordings feature Bob Wills in a loving return to his roots. Chatting informally with a small group of friends, he sings his favorite gospel song, "There's No Disappointment in Heaven," and, backed only by guitar, tenor banjo, and upright bass, he fiddles eleven hoedowns, including the first tune he ever learned. It is a charming set of recordings and a refreshing reminder that jazz was not the only defining component of his music.

The Country Music Hall of Fame CD is a rather uneven collection of thirteen songs recorded for Decca, from 1955 to 1957, and three songs for its Kapp subsidiary, from 1965 to 1967. As Bob Pinson's excellent short history and liner notes indicate, the Texas Playboys were greatly reduced in size by the mid-1950s, with usually no more than eight members, and Wills had been unable to find a new vocalist to equal the departed Tommy Duncan. The band, though, could still swing as on "Cornball Rag" and "Texas Two Step," and Jack Loyd and Lee Ross did some nice singing, respectively, on "Don't Keep It a Secret" and "My Shoes Keep Walking Back to You." Wills's effort to stay current with Cindy Walker's "So Let's Rock," however, is misguided. The high point among the three Kapp recordings is Leon Rausch's singing of "A Big Ball in Cowtown."

The Best of Bob Wills presents twelve songs recorded in Nashville for the Kapp label from 1966 to 1969. They are, in fact, the last recordings he ever made. The Texas Playboys had been disbanded by 1965, and, except for Tag Lambert who traveled with him and acted as his chief vocalist, Wills now performed only with local or studio musicians. Consequently, virtually all of the musicians heard on the Kapp recordings were Nashville sessions musicians, including the superb fiddlers Buddy Spicher, Tommy Jackson, and Shorty Lavender. Along with Wills, and visiting Texas musician Gene Gassaway, the fiddlers do an excellent job of re-creating the Texas Playboys' style, even though their music on some sessions submerged under the sound of as many as nineteen musicians. Except for the popular old-time fiddle tune "Silver Bells," and "Milk Cow Blues," which features the scat singing of fiddler Johnny Gimble, all of the songs heard on this CD have a Southwestern theme or flavor. The best vocal moments on these selections comes in the singing of the visiting ex-Playboy Leon Rausch, on such western standards as "Deep in the Heart of Texas," "My Adobe Hacienda," and "A Big Ball in Cowtown."—B.C.M.

MAC WISEMAN

★★★★ **Early Dot Recordings, Vol. 3 (MCA-County CCS CD 113; MSD-35153) 1992**
★★★ **Classic Bluegrass (Rebel CD-1106) 1989**
★★ **24 Greatest Hits (Highland Music DCD-7790) 1987**
★★★ **Grassroots to Bluegrass (CMH CD-9041) 1990**

Mac Wiseman has recorded successfully in bluegrass, country, and even rockabilly, but is best known for the way his pure mountain tenor graces old favorites like "Jimmy Brown the Newsboy" and "Don't Let Your Sweet Love Die." Though he worked in his early years with country and bluegrass stars like Molly O'Day and Bill Monroe, he also brought to the music a voice that had had formal training, and a penchant for delving into older pop material for his repertoire. The solo records that won him his initial fame—and the ones many fans still consider his best—were done in a makeshift studio in Gallatin, Tennessee, for Randy Woods's Dot Label in 1952-55. These include songs like "I'll Still Write Your Name in the Sand," "The Waltz You Saved for Me," "Reveille in Heaven," and "Don't Let Your Sweet Love Die," all of which are available on *Early Dot Recordings, Vol. 3.* (*Volumes 1* and *2* came out on LP only.)

Few of the later major label sides Wiseman did for RCA, MGM, King, and Capitol are still in print, but two albums done for the independent label Vetco in the mid-1970s are combined on *Classic Bluegrass.* Backed by a good bluegrass band that includes Tater Tate on fiddle and Billy Edwards on banjo, Mac works his way through twenty-two old favorites like "Letter Edged in Black" and "Footprints in the Snow." *24 Greatest Hits,* bereft of any sort of annotation or explanation, appears to be compiled of late 1970s Gusto material which features remakes of many early songs and backing by the Shenandoah Cut-Ups. *Grassroots to Bluegrass,* a 1990 effort, finds the singer still in fine voice and able to reenergize old chestnuts like "Little Rosewood Casket" and "I'm Just Here to Get My Baby Out of Jail." An added bonus is a set of superb notes by Wiseman and scholar Paul Wells, in which the singer comments at length on his repertoire and early influences. (See also Osborne Brothers for the *Osborne Brothers and Mac Wiseman* CD.)—C.K.W.

THE WOOD BROTHERS
★★★ **The Wood Brothers (K-Tel 1042-2) 1992**
Generic boot-scootin' shufflers and hug me, I'm hurtin' ballads of the lounge variety, but done with a flair and a sense of timing that suggest that these guys have twirled around a hardwood floor a time or two. Ably assisted by producer-fiddler Glen Duncan (and with an ear for a good song, such as Merle Haggard's "Shelly's Winter Love" and Fleetwood Mac's "Say You Love Me") the Wood Brothers have put together a disarmingly pleasant album. Now, if only chances had been taken. . . . —J.B.

TOM WOPAT
★★ **Learning to Love (Epic EK 47874) 1992**
Like his co-star John Schneider, Wopat turned from TV's "Dukes of Hazzard" toward a country singing career in the early 1980s. He enjoyed a Top Twenty single in 1987 with "The Rock and Roll of Love," before dropping off the charts and out of sight. Although he is a credible vocalist with middle-of-the-road appeal, this album flounders in the fluff of bubble-gum ballads ("Learning to Love," "How the Other Half Lives") that ooze the cloying sentimentality of a Harlequin romance, while his genuflections toward the working class ("Too Many Honky Tonks [On My Way Home]," "Red Hot Love [In a Blue Collar Town]") are brazen attempts to create image where none exists.—J.B.

CURTIS WRIGHT
★★★ **Curtis Wright (Liberty CDP-7-97825-2) 1992**
Curtis Wright sings beautifully, like a slightly huskier version of Ricky Skaggs, and his sincere back-country tenor brings lovely conviction to sad songs like "I Don't Know How Love Starts" ("but I sure know how it ends") and scoots easily into the classic shuffle style of "I Can't Stand to Watch My Old Flame Burn." Melody, in fact, seems to be his strong point. The nine tracks he had a hand in writing here show that he's got a firm

grasp on Nashville lyrical conventions without being able to come up with a single memorable twist. When he's got a great tune, though, as on the minor-key beauty "If I Could Stop Lovin' You," you can almost forgive him for wasting your time.—P.K.

MICHELLE WRIGHT
★★★½ **Michelle Wright (Arista 8627) 1990**
★★★ **Now and Then (Arista 8685) 1992**
Although she's from Canada, Michelle Wright's voice is closer to the traditions of Memphis than to those of Nashville. Using a raspy melisma and singing behind the beat, she swells up from her husky bottom to create passionate peaks. At times, the showy leaps and dramatic growls overwhelm the songs. But wisely, Wright deploys lively, soulful productions and chooses lyrics that express a strength and emotional hunger suited to that huge, questing voice. Her best songs are usually written by men, which may say something about the prominence of gender roles in Nashville songwriting. "Show me where it says a woman's got to be/The one who waits home so patiently," she demands on "New Kind of Love," written by coproducers Rick Giles and Steve Bogard. The sentiment is reprised on the second album in her signature hit, "Take It Like a Man," which mourns the state of modern manhood. "One wants a maid, one needs his mother/They either want space, or they want to smother me," typifies country music's ability to summarize in one couplet what psychiatrists express in three hundred pages.—R.T.

WYLIE
★★½ **Wylie and the Wild West Show (Cross Three Records CTR 9210-2) 1992**
There's nothing remotely commercial about this eccentric West Coast creation which has more in common with self-produced recordings from the Fifties than a contemporary studio job. But what it lacks in polish it more than makes up for with the idiosyncratic charm of Wylie Gustafson, "The Yodeling Fool," and cattle lowing in the studio. And what perverse joy there is in hearing a lyric proclaim, in rhyme, "She came from Alabama in her funky Tony Lamas." You

don't (and probably shouldn't) hear *that* on the radio every day.—J.B.

TAMMY WYNETTE

- ★★★★ **Greatest Hits, Vol. 1 (Epic EK 26486) 1969** ▲
- ★★★★ **[& George Jones] Greatest Hits (Epic EK 34716) 1977**
- ★★★½ **[& George Jones] Greatest Hits, Vol. 2 (Epic EK 48839) 1992**
- ★★★ **Biggest Hits (Epic EK 38312) 1982**
- ★★★★★ **Anniversary: 20 Years of Hits (Epic EGK 40625) 1987**
- ★★★ **Higher Ground (Epic EK 40832) 1987**
- ★★ **Next to You (Epic EK 44498) 1989**
- ★★½ **Heart Over Mind (Epic EK 46238) 1990**
- ★★ **Best Loved Hits (Epic EK 48588) 1991**
- ★★★★ **Tears of Fire: The 25th Anniversary Collection (Epic E3K 52741) 1992**

Tammy Wynette believes in happy endings. Happily for us, though, she seldom celebrates them, preferring instead to sing about the heartache and tears that often stand between a dreamer and her dreams. The tension between Wynette's fondest wishes and her bitterest disappointments is what drives all her best material. In the grand tradition of Hank Williams and Patsy Cline, Tammy Wynette can hurt you bad in a real good way.

When her first record, "Apartment #9," hit the charts in 1966, she was just twenty-four years old. Already, she had endured a lifetime of adversity—losing her father when she was less than a year old, picking cotton on a hardscrabble farm, fleeing into a deadend marriage at seventeen, raising three daughters by herself on a beautician's salary. Every little hurt that she'd been holding inside seemed to pour out with exquisite sadness when she harmonized with herself on that first brilliantly gloomy record. She did it so well, in fact, that producer Billy Sherrill made sure that almost everything she did afterwards expressed some kind of longing. After a Loretta Lynn-like fling with the feisty "Your Good Girl's Gonna Go Bad," Tammy concentrated that throbbing voice, brimming with tears and womanly ache, on songs more fitting to her special abilities.

Greatest Hits, in addition to collecting those first two hits, shows Wynette and Sherrill skillfully working out the ground rules for roles she would re-create again and again: the mother whose broken marriage into sharp focus ("I Don't Want to Play House," "D-I-V-O-R-C-E"); the lover intoxicated on her worshipful obsessiveness ("Too Far Gone," "Take Me to Your World"); and the patient, devoted wife. Duetting with David Houston on the trail-of-tears vignette "My Elusive Dreams" proved a good dress rehearsal for this last role, which Wynette soon perfected on the incomparable 1968 hit "Stand By Your Man," co-written with Sherrill. Even those who can't abide the song's sexual politics must admit that it's a transcendent performance, with Tammy's soaring high notes challenging the steel for supremacy on the choruses. That record brought down the house—5 million people bought the single—but it also typecast Wynette so thoroughly as the male chauvinist's doormat that, twenty-three years later, Hillary Clinton felt justified in knocking Wynette to make a point.

Anniversary, a solid twenty-cut collection, and, to a lesser extent, the ten-cut *Biggest Hits* find Wynette willingly embracing the role at first; she follows "Stand By Your Man" with such minor variations on the theme as "Singing My Song" (1969), "We Sure Can Love Each Other" (1971), and "Good Lovin' (Makes It Right)" (1971), where she lovingly explains the do's and don'ts for keeping a man satisfied. Likewise, "Bedtime Story" (1972) and "Kids Say the Darndest Things" (1973) bring those familiar lumps to Mommy's throat again. Wynette begins to stretch a little, though, with "Run, Woman, Run" (1970) and "Woman to Woman" (1974), in which she plays the part of the older, more wiser sister counseling the younger, more impetuous woman to "go back to him and try to fix things up the very best you can."

True, these records were the very essence of formula, and, no, they don't exactly celebrate women's rights. But they do point to women's strengths (regardless of how they choose to use them) and, in every case, these records work because Wynette, a strong woman herself and a consummate actress, imbues them with the breath of real life. *Greatest Hits* was the first album by a woman in country to be certified platinum, a testament to her popularity with country record buyers, most of whom (subsequent market research has confirmed) were women.

During her six-year marriage to George Jones, Wynette closed the distance between records and real life until you could hardly tell the singer from the song on confessional masterpieces like "'Til I Get It Right" (1972) and "'Til I Can Make It on My Own" (1976). Meanwhile, in their duets, she and Jones kept fans informed as to the progress of their rocky marriage—from its first romantic stirrings ("Take Me," 1971) to a hokey re-enactment of their wedding vows ("The Ceremony," 1972) to a grim pledge of loyalty ("We're Gonna Hold On," 1973) to a sorry tale of love come full circle ("Golden Ring," 1975); these triumphs of co-dependency all are collected on their *Greatest Hits,* an album just as enjoyable for its music as it is for autobiography. *Vol. 2,* though it offers only two hits, "A Pair of Old Sneakers" and Tammy's own "Two Story House," is almost as strong.

Wynette reached her confessional peak with "Til I Can Make It on My Own," recorded a year after Jones walked out on her. Thereafter, her soap opera life began to look more like the fairy tales she'd always sung so longingly about, and her recordings—which had been gradually trading in steel guitars for string sections ever since "'Til I Get It Right"—finally succumbed to glamorous complacency. Since her 1978 marriage to songwriter-producer George Richey, she has written little and left a steadily diminishing impact on the charts. It seems that Billy Sherrill, who stopped producing her in 1980, had the right idea all along: she was meant to sing sad songs. For this reason and because her voice has lost some power in its upper register, her three recent albums and the late Eighties collection *Best Loved Hits,* though offering thoroughly polished performances, are best left to confirmed fans. Of the bunch, *Higher Ground* has the added enticement of hearing Tammy get back to a rootsier sound with help from Vern Gosdin, Vince Gill, and Ricky Skaggs.

Through its first two discs, the three-disc *Tears of Fire* boxed set does a marvelous job of recapping Wynette's triumphs (nearly every hit cited so far can be found herein). It also goes a little way towards making the case for Wynette as a self-determined artist and not the pawn of mix master Sherrill (who is reported to have said that if he asked Wynette to record "Three Blind Mice" for her next single, she'd reply with only three words: What key, Billy?). As the previously unreleased 1966 track "She Didn't Color Daddy" suggests, this single mother had been ready to sing those tear-jerking children songs from the beginning. Similarly, the opening 1964 demo track "You Can Steal Me" reveals Wynette's vocal style as fully developed and ready for the charts. Unfortunately, the superficial, fawning booklet of notes to the boxed set won't tell you that Wynette herself brought "She Didn't Color Daddy" to Sherrill to record for her first session (he liked the song enough to cut it, but released the superior "Apartment #9" instead). You'll have to read her 1979 autobiography for that fact. In addition, Wynette's book makes clear (though the boxed set doesn't) that she must have recorded the "You Can Steal Me" in Birmingham as a songwriter's demo for her DJ friend Fred Lehner before she ever visited Nashville.

Except for "Two Story House," the main reason to own the third CD of this set is to hear Wynette's improbable, and delightful, comeback singing "all bound for Mu-Mu Land" on the KLF's campy Euro-dance hit "Justified and Ancient." Without doubt, she's always been a trouper. Now that she's found her happy ending, it's just too bad for us.—P.K.

TRISHA YEARWOOD
★★★★ **Trisha Yearwood (MCA 10297) 1991** ▲
★★★★★ **Hearts in Armor (MCA 10641) 1992** ▲

No one in the Nineties—not Garth Brooks, not Wynonna Judd, not the far more critically correct Rosanne Cash—brought pop style into country with a more easy command than Trisha Yearwood, a former demo singer from Monticello, Georgia. "She's in Love with the Boy," her giant #1 country single debut from *Trisha Yearwood,* set the stage, then *Hearts in Armor* became the most critically lauded Nashville album since Randy Travis's *Storms of Life.*

In retrospect, Travis is the best comparison for Yearwood, an enormously gifted country singer whose work happened entirely within the Nashville system. The difference was that Yearwood had internalized more noncountry styles—Linda Ronstadt and the Eagles as well as Johnny Cash and Emmylou Harris and Yearwood's own Georgia girl's reading of Elvis Presley—than Travis did. Granted, producer Garth Fundis revealed inspired notions of how much rock aggression country could take and still remain a music that kicked and hit like honky-tonk. Yet the main reason Yearwood's synthesis of Ronstadt-like surges and intimate Rosanne Cash-style line readings could triumph on initial singles as different as the sorrowful "The Woman Before Me" and the spunky "That's What I Like about You" was Yearwood's confidence that the mainstream country format could accommodate all her creative wishes. And, as *Hearts in Armor* proves, she had great ones. From cinematic turns like "Walkaway Joe" to hard-country testaments like "Woman Walk the Line," the album is a tour de force of text and music. Fans also shouldn't miss Yearwood's knowing way with Presley's "You're the Devil in Disguise," from 1992's *Honeymoon in Vegas* sound track. As with Travis, two classic albums into his great Nashville career, it's not too much to say of Yearwood's work so far that it will last. —J.H.

DWIGHT YOAKAM

★★★★   **Guitars, Cadillacs Etc. Etc. (Reprise 9 25749-2) 1986** ▲

★★★★   **Hillbilly Deluxe (Reprise 9 25567-2) 1987** ●

★★★★   **Buenos Noches from a Lonely Room (Reprise 9 25749-2) 1988** ●

★★★★★   **Just Lookin' for a Hit (Reprise 25989-2) 1989** ●

★★★★★   **If There Was a Way (Reprise 9 26344-2) 1990** ▲

★★★★★   **This Time (Reprise 9 45241-2) 1993** ●

If you like modern country because it doesn't have pedal steel guitars and guys who sing through their noses about hard luck and trouble, stop right here. That's what Dwight Yoakam does.

He does it brilliantly and honestly too. Although in many ways he's the least likely inheritor of the honky-tonk mantle—he's a highly educated, health-food-eating teetotaller who lives in the Hollywood hills and hangs out with alternative movie stars—in many ways he fits the bill just perfectly. He's a misfit, he's a rebel, he's lonesome, he's got blood in his veins that's 100 percent Kentucky hillbilly, and, most of all, he's a man totally smitten by the righteousness and beauty of Hank, Lefty, Johnny, Buck, and Merle. And of course he's also a leading retro-Western fashion hunk, and he's been a powerful kid magnet for good ol' country music for a lot longer than most young Hats. When the EP that became *Guitars Cadillacs Etc Etc.* first aired on L.A. radio, bracketed by rock music from Dead Kennedys and the Butthole Surfers, it was way back in the giddy, far-off days of mid-Eighties California cowpunk.

All Dwight's work—done completely outside the Nashville system—makes it on every level. It's a body of work at once supremely adventurous and utterly classic. Only Emmylou Harris can match him as an innovator-preserver of the country form; only Rosanne Cash's auteur odyssey has progressed with such undistracted momentum. At his best, he's approaching Hank Williams as a writer and George Jones as a singer.

Basically, his catalogue breaks down into one completed trilogy (*Guitars, Cadillacs Etc Etc, Hillbilly Deluxe,* and *Buenos Noches from a Lonely Room*); one greatest-hits-with-extras package (*Just Lookin' for a Hit*); and two installments of a second trilogy-in-progress (*If There Was a Way* and *This Time*). The first trilogy offers a dazzlingly developing artist on a cultural-emotional journey from Ohio in the Fifties (as recounted in "Guitars, Cadillacs" and "Readin', Rightin', Rt. 23," covers of Johnny Horton's "Honky Tonk Man," and Elvis's "Little Sister") to a lonely room in Hollywood anytime ("I Sang Dixie," "Streets of Bakersfield" dueted with Buck Owens, Johnny Cash's "Home of

the Blues"). The next trilogy is an ever
deepening, ever more stylish exploration
of anguish, alienation, despair, and self-
destructiveness—all the Hankly verities,
in other words, done to a T. Numbers like
"The Heart That You Own" and "Home
for Sale" (from the last two albums,
respectively) are as gorgeously painful as
any Hank or Lefty sang. Meanwhile,
country-rock piledrivers like "Takes a Lot
to Rock You" and "Fast As You" come on
strong without ever betraying this guy's
deep hard-country roots. Dwight started
out a diamond in the rough. Now he's just
a gem.—P.Ca.

FARON YOUNG

★★★½ All-Time Greatest Hits (Curb D2-
    77334) 1990
★★ 20 Best Hits (Deluxe DCD-7879)
    1987
★★ Here's to You (Step One SOR-
    0040) 1988
★★½ Greatest Hits, Vols. 1-3 (Step One
    SOR-0043/44/45) 1989
★★½ [& Ray Price] Memories That Last
    (Step One SOR-0068) 1991
★ Country Spotlight (Dominion
    30272) 1991
★★ Live in Branson, MO, USA
    (LaserLight 12 137) 1993

Signed to Capitol Records in 1951, Faron
Young hit the honky-tonk hardwood floor
sporting a randy grin and a Shreveport
twang that broke like a major league
slider—nasty! Hear it once, you can't
wait for it to happen again. Young Faron
wore his Hank Williams influence on one
sleeve and his utter disdain for Hankish
morbidity on the other as he built his
career on hillbilly ribaldry like "Live
Fast, Love Hard, Die Young" and "Alone
with You" (which clocks in at a rollicking,
guitar-happy 1:56). The latter fabulous
cuts appear on the Curb disc, along with
other vintage Capitol gems such as
"Sweet Dreams" (very pre-Patsy Cline)
and "Hello Walls," the royalties from
which saw struggling songwriter Willie
Nelson through hard times. At ten quick
tracks, including a couple of overproduced clinkers, *All-Time Greatest Hits*
is more of a budget-line teaser than a
definitive collection. But short of shelling
out a hundred-plus dollars for Bear
Family's import box set (and I wouldn't
discourage a serious fan from doing so),
the Curb disc is the best available

introduction to Faron's fast-livin', hard-
lovin' early years.

Young switched to Mercury during the
Kennedy administration and greeted
Camelot with a broader tone and
Nashville Sound. Though he never
roamed as far uptown as his buddy Ray
Price, the years rounded the edge off his
killer twang, and his most memorable hit
from midcareer was a colossal 1971
ballad called "It's Four in the Morning."
It's all moot, however, as nothing from
Young's fifteen-year Mercury association
has surfaced on disc. Instead, you have
your pick of re-recorded versions of "It's
Four in the Morning" on either
Dominion's *Country Spotlight* or Step
One's *Greatest Hits, Vols. 1-3* (a two-disc
set). Both titles, as well as the Deluxe
collection, feature rehashed hits that get
less interesting with each new version.
The SOR set has the virtue of sound
Music Row production, whereas the
Dominion disc tries hardest to duplicate
the original takes—with predictably flat
results. The duets with Ray Price have
their charm, as does Young's between-
song banter on the Branson set. But on
the whole, the latter day material is a sop
to Young's long-time fans. New ones
aren't likely to wriggle and blush when
middle-aged Faron sings "Goin'
Steady."—D.C.

NEIL YOUNG

★★★★ After the Gold Rush (Reprise
    2283-2) 1970 ▲²
★★★ Harvest (Reprise 2277-2) 1972 ▲⁷
★★★ Comes a Time (Reprise 2266-2)
    1978 ●
★★★ Lucky Thirteen (Geffen GEFD
    24452) 1993
★★★ Harvest Moon (Reprise 45057-2)
    1992 ▲

Although Neil Young is most persuasive
as a ferocious hard rocker with his
sometime band Crazy Horse, the
incessant quick-change artist has also
spent much time in the orbit of country
music, with mixed results. Young's
alternately precise and formless version
of country, anxious to take in elements of
sundry other forms, dovetails with the
Southern California variety of country-
rock (as on the big hit from *Harvest*
"Heart of Gold"), though he usually
approaches the fusion with ideas much
more barbed than his laid-back contem-

poraries. But if country is just another one of Young's masks, it's one behind which he is often comfortable being himself. And the list of country artists who have covered his songs—Waylon Jennings, Emmylou Harris, and Marty Stuart, to name a few—continues to grow. Note: Young's most conventional yet intruguing country LP, *Old Ways,* remains available on CD only in Japan, though some of its songs appear on *Lucky Thirteen* (which is devoted mostly to noncountry excursions) and Willie Nelson's *Half Nelson.*—J.G.

STEVE YOUNG
★★★½ **Solo/Live (Watermelon CD 1004) 1991**
Somewhere along the way, this talented singer-songwriter's work has fallen through the cracks. *Solo/Live,* recorded acoustically at a Houston restaurant, collects the best of Steve Young's compositions, along with some of his favorite covers ("Tobacco Road," "Don't Miss Your Water"). Young's spirited, stripped down performances of such school-of-hard-knocks classics as "All Her Lovers Want to Be the Hero," "Montgomery in the Rain," and "Seven Bridges Road" showcase his rootsy folk-country-blues style. Though audiocassettes of *Seven Bridges Road* and *Honky Tonk Man* are available on Rounder, Young's other recordings from the Seventies (like the excellent *Renegade Picker)* are out of print. It's a shame, too, because *Solo/Live* makes you want to go back and hear these compelling songs in their original context.—H.G.-W.

Various Artists

General Interest

★★★★★ **Columbia Country Classics, Vol. 1: The Golden Age (CK 46029) 1990**

★★★★★ **Columbia Country Classics, Vol. 2: Honky Tonk Heroes (CK 46030) 1990**

★★★★ **Columbia Country Classics, Vol. 3: Americana (CK 46031) 1990**

★★★★ **Columbia Country Classics, Vol 4: The Nashville Sound (CK 46032) 1990**

★★★ **Columbia Country Classics, Vol. 5: A New Tradition (CK 46033) 1990**

When the CD was introduced as a sound carrier, the prospect of ever hearing something like Wiley & Gene's 1941 original of "When My Blue Moon Turns to Gold Again" on CD seemed impossibly remote, but it's here along with 127 other titles that pretty much run the gamut of recorded country music. Drawn from the venerable Columbia catalogue, these five volumes (sold separately) bear the eccentric imprint of the compiler, Gregg Geller, who brought thematic organization to the series rather than a chronological array of hits.

The first volume, *The Golden Age,* starts at a logical entry point, the Carter Family, then recaps the other styles that fit under the broad rubric of "country and western." Hillbilly tradition is represented by the likes of Roy Acuff and Molly O'Day, western swing by Bob Wills and Spade Cooley, cowboy music by Gene Autry and Patsy Montana, and bluegrass by Bill Monroe, Flatt & Scruggs, and the Stanley Brothers. All of the artists are at the top of their game, and the selections include either the original or best-known versions of songs like "Great Speckled Bird," "Pistol Packin' Mama," "Back in the Saddle Again," "Born to Lose," "Blue Eyes Crying in the Rain," and "Blue Moon of Kentucky." It all amounts to a compelling primer on the roots of country music, essential for anyone with even fleeting curiosity about where it all came from.

The second volume, *Honky Tonk Heroes,* centers on the Columbia roster built up by A&R man Don Law in the late Forties and Fifties: Lefty Frizzell, Carl Smith, Jimmy Dickens, Marty Robbins, Johnny Horton, Ray Price, Charlie Walker, and Carl Butler. The honky-tonk classics here include "If You've Got the Money I've Got the Time," "Honky Tonk Man," "Crazy Arms," "Pick Me Up on Your Way Down," "Heartaches by the Number," and "Don't Let Me Cross Over." Unequivocally recommended as a twenty-two chapter course on how to make a country record.

The third volume, *Americana,* is meant to be America celebrating itself—its history, traditions, and mythology, but with "The Ballad of Davy Crockett" as the kick-off, it's clear that genuine folklore is taking a back-seat to commercial exigencies. Johnny Cash, Marty Robbins, Lefty Frizzell, and Johnny Horton are here with some of their folksier outings. This is the first volume of this series to touch more-or-less current times: Charlie Daniels, Merle Haggard with Willie Nelson, and the Highwaymen round out the set. A few titles, like the Statler Brothers' "Flowers on the Wall" and Cash's "Boy Named Sue," strain the concept, ranking as Americana only by virtue of being American.

The Nashville Sound, is another loose garment that covers a multiplicity of styles. Chiefly, it's Columbia's Nashville A&R men (primarily Don Law and Billy Sherrill) in search of a good commercial groove—and finding it. Stylistically, it runs the gamut from the minimalism of Johnny Cash's "I Still Miss Someone" to the bloated excess of Ray Price's "For the Good Times." Along the way, there's Tammy Wynette's "Stand by Your Man," and George Jones's "The Grand Tour" for good measure. The problem is that someone who likes Cash's "I Still Miss Someone" probably won't like "For the Good Times" (and vice versa). More than anything, the set emphasizes that "The Nashville Sound" is a nebulous term.

A New Tradition covers too many bases. Consider this: Johnny Cash, Bob Dylan, the Byrds, Ricky Skaggs, Asleep at the Wheel, Crystal Gayle, Ricky Van Shelton . . . and others. Dylan and the Byrds helped make country music hep, but it's uncomfortably far from them to Crystal Gayle and late period George Jones. Still, there are some hot tunes here: Ray Price redeeming himself on "Faded Love" with Willie Nelson, Moe Bandy's "Hank Williams You Wrote My Life," and Marty Robbins's cowboy parable "El Paso City." Inevitably, the set also includes Willie Nelson's "Blue Eyes Crying in the Rain," the keynote address for Hillbilly Nouveau.

Taken as a whole, these five CDs are what history should be all about—opinionated, eccentric, and well signposted. Any fool can look at a chart book and compile a CD; this is a stab at something different.—C.E.

★★★★½ **Hillbilly Holiday (Rhino R2 70195) 1988**

This collection of Christmas songs is so delightful that you'll want to listen to it all year round. The folks at Rhino dug up some real gems, most of which haven't been played a million times on the radio every December. Selections cross all styles of traditional country music. Standouts include Bill Monroe's bluegrassy "Christmas Time's A-Comin'," the cowboy-inspired "Christmas Carols by the Old Corral" by Tex Ritter, Brenda Lee's "I'm Gonna Lasso Santa Claus," and George Jones's twistin' "My Mom and Santa Claus." Holiday versions of hits are lots of fun, too: Ernest Tubb's "I'll Be Walkin' the Floor This Christmas" and Bill Anderson's "'Po' Folks Christmas." If there's a message here, though, it's that the yuletide season is no guarantee of domestic bliss, e.g. Faron Young's "I'm Gonna Tell Santa on You," Loretta Lynn's "To Heck with Ole Santa Claus," and Commander Cody's "Daddy's Drinking Up Our Christmas." And there's plenty more: Every song on this eighteen-tune compilation, accompanied by an amusing, informative booklet of illustrated liner notes, is a joy.—H.G.-W.

★★★★ **Classic Country Music (Smithsonian RD 042) 1991**

The original LP/cassette version of this set, released in 1981, still stands as the definitive introduction to the form, an ideal companion to compiler Bill C. Malone's ground-breaking history of the genre, *Country Music U.S.A.* But this four-CD set falls short of the original—151 cuts down to 100. It's not just smaller, though; it's less comprehensive (no Merle Haggard, thanks to legal hassles; much less bluegrass); and what it does include is occasionally suspect, like Dolly Parton's "9 to 5," a pop tune that has little to do with classic country music. Significant flaws notwithstanding, most of what's here skims off the best of the last six decades of country, going all the way back to the music's commercial beginnings and marking the major signposts. As always, Malone's extensive historical notes are top-notch. This is an acceptable primer, though not the ultimate one it should have been.—J.G.

★★★★ **Hillbilly Music, Thank God!**
(Capitol C22Z-91346) 1989

The country grooves cut for Capitol were some of the best and deepest drawn during a significant thirty-year span (1942 to roughly 1972). The Louvin Brothers, Hank Thompson, Buck Owens, Wanda Jackson, and Merle Haggard all did their best work for Capitol, as did plenty of others. It's a crying shame, then, that there are—to this reviewer's knowledge anyway—no comprehensive overviews of the country side of a label which, for the influence and enduring impact of its artists, easily beggars comparison to the blues roster at Chess. Is a *Capitol Country* boxed set too much to ask?

Instead we have this quirky 1988 set, compiled by rocker Marshall Crenshaw and leaning hard on 1940s-50s novelties and a cartoonish Nudie-suited nasality. There's no denying the fun of this set, and it's probably crabby to criticize *Hillbilly Music* for gleaning vintage country kitsch from the Capitol vaults. Jaws still drop at the gimmicky guitar-and-steel pyrotechnics of Jimmy Bryant and Speedy West, and eyes surely roll at the high octane hokum of Ernie Ford and Ella Mae Morse singing "Hog-Tied over You." The Farmer Boys, Gene O'Quin, and Skeets McDonald are wonderful goofs, and Jean Shepard's "Two Whoops and a Holler" is a spunky feminist rant which predates Loretta Lynn's similarly spirited manifestos by at least a decade. Faron Young, Hank Thompson, Merle Travis, Rose Maddox, and Buck Owens all make memorable cameos, though the three classic Louvin brothers performances ("You're Learning," "Great Atomic Power," and "I Wish It Had Been a Dream") stick out in this company like Rembrandts in a gallery of Looney Tune cels. *Hillbilly Music* is scarcely representative of the best Capitol country, but it is a lot of fun.—M.H.

★★★★★ **Country U.S.A., 23 Vols., 1950-**
72 (Time-Life CTD 01-23) 1988-
91

For those who long for the days when jukeboxes played one solid country hit after another, this series from Time-Life is a godsend. Here's the hook: twenty-four of the top country hits from a given year, in their original versions, all together on one disc, and lovingly remastered so that the tracks sound better than you remembered. Looking for the Fifties hits of Eddy Arnold, back when Little Roy Wiggins was playing steel? Time-Life has got sixteen of them here, from the 1950's "Take Me in Your Arms and Hold Me" to 1959's "Tennessee Stud." And they've included his Sixties pop crossovers—"Make the World Go Away" and "What's He Doing in My World"—for good measure. Looking for Hank Snow's classics? They're here too, from 1951's "I'm Movin' On" through 1963's "Ninety Miles an Hour (Down a Dead End Street)." In fact, you can just about go down the list of every big star from the Fifties and Sixties—Hank Williams, Lefty Frizzell, Kitty Wells, Webb Pierce, Ray Price, Patsy Cline, Buck Owens, Merle Haggard, Johnny Cash, Loretta Lynn, Conway Twitty, Charley Pride—and what's here amounts to a greatest hits collection for each. (Plus the folks at Time-Life have gone the extra mile and salted discs here and there with the odd rarities that lend just a little more flavor: Leon Payne's "I Love You Because," Ramblin' Jimmy Dolan's "Hot Rod Race," Slim Whitman's "Indian Love Call," Jimmy Skinner's "I Found My Girl in the U.S.A."—and my favorite, Loretta Lynn's original recording of "Honky Tonk Girl" from Zero Records.) If you own one of those CD changers that can handle five or more CDs and shuffle tracks, you've got your own instant classic country jukebox.

The catch? You have to buy the whole series, and at $19 and change for each CD in the twenty-three disc set, that'll set you back nearly $500. The good news is that you don't have to cough up that wad of cash all at once; Time-Life sends you the CDs about every other month. So you can budget for it. You can't pick and choose with this series, however. They'll send you the disc for 1961 first, then 1957, then 1962, hopscotching through the years to keep you hooked. You can listen to these on a trial basis, but once you say no to one, say goodbye to the rest of the series. So if you've been moaning the blues about how bad you miss those classic country hits from the Fifties and Sixties, here's your chance to put up or shut up. Time-Life's toll-free number is 1-800-621-7026.—P.K.

★★★½ **Contemporary Country, 15 Vols., Early '70s-Late '80s (Time-Life CCD 01-15) 1991-93**
Time-Life picks up where it left off with its last series (see previous entry) and takes you to the present. Instead of chronicling individual years, though, this series groups hits under the broader headings *Early Seventies, Mid Seventies, Early Eighties, Mid Eighties,* and *Late Eighties.* Also, where the last series went twenty-four cuts deep on each CD, these just go to twenty-two. Again, these CDs will cost you around $20 each. At press time, the *Contemporary Country* series was already fifteen CDs along (and projected to go to a total of twenty), so you can see right there it's gonna cost you. All the Time-Life caveats mentioned in regard to the *Country U.S.A.* set apply here. For my money, this series—though nicely programmed within its chart-hit limitations—is not the goldmine that the previous one is, since most of these hits are still fairly easy to find on CD, not to mention still being played on the radio. Besides, for every sharp cut by Waylon or Willie or Dwight or Randy, you get dull efforts from the likes of Dave & Sugar, Anne Murray, and Kenny Rogers. Which, I guess, makes it a pretty faithful representation of country radio over the past twenty years, though not necessarily everybody's idea of essential country listening.—P.K.

  ★★★ **Billboard Top Country Hits, 1959 (Rhino R2 70680) 1990**
  ★★½ **Billboard Top Country Hits, 1960 (Rhino R2 70681) 1990**
  ★★★½ **Billboard Top Country Hits, 1961 (Rhino R2 70682) 1990**
  ★★★ **Billboard Top Country Hits, 1962 (Rhino R2 70683) 1990**
  ★★★½ **Billboard Top Country Hits, 1963 (Rhino R2 70684) 1990**
  ★★★½ **Billboard Top Country Hits, 1964 (Rhino R2 70685) 1990**
  ★★★ **Billboard Top Country Hits, 1965 (Rhino R2 70686) 1990**
  ★★★½ **Billboard Top Country Hits, 1966 (Rhino R2 70687) 1990**
  ★★★½ **Billboard Top Country Hits, 1967 (Rhino R2 70688) 1990**
  ★★★½ **Billboard Top Country Hits, 1968 (Rhino R2 70689) 1990**
This is a more modest version of the Time-Life hit series reviewed earlier in this section. Like the Time-Life set, each CD features original hit recordings. Unlike the Time-Life, there are only ten cuts per CD, which works out to less than thirty minutes a disc—not a great value. Still, if the whopping subscription cost of the Time-Life series poses a threat to your marriage, the price may be right. Besides, the Rhino compilations are readily available in stores, and the audio fidelity is top-notch.

Mostly the tracks on the Rhino sets are among the biggest hits of their representative years. Occasionally, though, a decidedly odd selection crops up. The 1960 disc offers both Jeanne Black's answer song "He'll Have to Stay" *and* Skeeter Davis's answer song "(I Can't Help You) I'm Falling Too" in addition to the original hits by Jim Reeves and Hank Locklin, which is two versions of those tunes too many. The 1962 disc gives us Walter Brennan's maudlin recitation "Old Rivers." Such questionable selections can quickly diminish the value of these brief compendiums—unless you're a collector of Brennan-alia or answer songs. Also, across the series the programming leans distressingly toward the mellow side of country, with Sonny James and Eddy Arnold getting more than their fair share of slots. On the other hand, it's worth noting that these discs are also convenient places to sample some gleaming hard-country nuggets from the likes of George Jones, Buck Owens, and Merle Haggard. Just pay close attention to the track listings before you buy.—P.K.

Old-Time

★★★★★ **Are You from Dixie? Great Country Brother Teams of the 1930s (RCA Heritage Series 8417-2-R) 1988**
As radio became the dominant medium for country music in the 1930s, close-harmony brother duet teams proliferated and dominated the radio airwaves. Using a simple acoustic back-up (usually two

guitars, or guitar and mandolin), these acts featured two youthful voices of similar pitch and timbre, a repertoire of sentimental songs and gospel songs, and an earnestness that belied their years and the various snake-oil tonics they often sold on the air.

Though RCA Victor didn't record every major duet act (they missed the Callahan Brothers, Karl & Harty, and Wiley & Gene), they managed to get most of the best on their venerable Bluebird label. *Are You from Dixie* collects eighteen cuts from six different groups (three cuts each), dating from 1930 to 1939. Four of the groups are superb. The Shelton Brothers, who later worked extensively for Decca, appear here as the Lone Star Cowboys, doing their signature songs "Just Because" and "Deep Elm Blues." The Delmore Brothers, plying their intricate blues-flavored original songs, do "Blow Yo' Whistle, Freight Train" and "The Nashville Blues." The Monroe Brothers, Bill on mandolin and Charlie on guitar, race through "Roll in My Sweet Baby's Arms," later to become a bluegrass standard, while the Blue Sky Boys offer the title song and their version of the Karl & Harty hit, "I'm Here to Get My Baby Out of Jail." Lesser groups like the Allen Brothers and the Dixon Brothers round out the set, and compiler Billy Altman's generous booklet of notes provides a fine introduction to the brother duet style.—C.K.W.

★★★ **Ragged but Right: Great Country String Bands of the 1930s (RCA Victor 8416-2R) 1988**

The problem with this anthology is that Victor never had on their roster many of the truly great, wild, influential bands like Charlie Poole's group or the McMichen-Stokes Skillet Lickers or the Earl Johnson-John Carson groups. This set, beautifully remastered from metal parts and well annotated, sports decent samplings from four string bands: Gid Tanner's Skillet Lickers, the Prairie Ramblers, J. E. Mainer, and his brother Wade Mainer. Only the Prairie Ramblers really strike fire here. Though they later became a smooth, slick pussy-cat band who backed Gene Autry, on these 1933 sides they were lean and hungry, and

their six sides, driven by Tex Atchison's fiddle, go like an Arkansas dog race. —C.K.W.

★★★ **Songs of the Civil War (Columbia CK 48607) 1991**

An offshoot of the Ken Burns PBS series about the Civil War, *Songs of the Civil War* is a newly recorded set of songs and tunes from the era, generated by a follow-up PBS program of the same name. The twenty-five selections actually make better listening than the original series sound track and range from quicksteps by the United States Military Academy Band to the haunting theme from the series, "Ashokan Farewell," played by folk fiddler Jay Ungar. Country artists who participated in the project include Waylon Jennings, Kathy Mattea, Hoyt Axton, and John Hartford, but only the latter two really get into the spirit of things. Hartford's "Aura Lee" and "Lorena" are moving, and Axton's "Oh I'm a Good Old Rebel" is sung with rare conviction. —C.K.W.

★★★★★ **Altamont: Black Stringband Music from the Library of Congress (Rounder CD 0238) 1989**

This recording presents two exemplary old-time black stringbands that were active in south-central Tennessee in the early decades of this century. Nathan Frazier and Frank Patterson, a banjo-fiddle duet, played in an ornamented style influenced, perhaps, by Frazier's years as a street musician in Nashville where he entertained passersby with banjo tricks like those of Uncle Dave Macon. The fiddle-banjo-guitar trio of John Lusk, Murph Gribble, and Albert York, played more straightforward square dance music rooted in the fiddling of Lusk's grandfather, a slave who had been sent to New Orleans in the 1840s to learn to play for white folks' dances, and in Gribble's three-finger banjo picking, a precursor to the bluegrass style of Earl Scruggs.

Frazier and Patterson were recorded on a glass disc-cutting machine in 1942, and the Lusk band was captured in 1946 and 1949 on a disc cutter and a wire recording machine. Hisses and pops and other surface noises interfere at times but otherwise lend an antique authenticity to the lively, archaic strains of these rural African-American string bands. —J.B.

★★★★★ **The Bristol Sessions (Country Music Foundation CMF-011-D) 1987**

It is impossible to overestimate the musical and historical importance of these thirty-five cuts, recorded by Victor talent scout Ralph Peer in Bristol, Tennessee, in July and August 1927. These sessions yielded the first recordings by Jimmie Rodgers and the Carter Family, as well as cuts from twenty-one other performers, such as Blind Alfred Reed, B.F. Shelton, and the venerable Stoneman Family. Throughout these two CDs, folk culture warily ambles up to the microphone and bravely enters mass culture. This set doesn't chronicle the birth of country music—that event escaped recording—but this is as close as we'll ever get. On the cover of this disc, Johnny Cash is quoted as calling these recordings "the most important event in the history of country music." Are you going to argue with the Man in Black? —J.G.

Gospel

★★ **Jubilation!, Vol. 3, Country Gospel (Rhino R270290) 1992**

The idea behind this collection is a great one. Religion has been one of the strongest underpinnings of country music, and the country singer who has not recorded gospel songs is rare indeed. Some of the essential recordings are here—Hank Williams's "I Saw the Light," the Louvin Brothers' "The Family Who Prays," Roy Acuff's "The Great Speckled Bird," and Martha Carson's "Satisfied." But a religious collection is seriously flawed conceptually if its liner notes assert that "white country gospel came out of Appalachian folk music," and if it does not include the Chuck Wagon Gang, Red Foley, Tennessee Ernie, Stuart Hamblen, Jimmie Davis, the Bailes Brothers, the Blue Sky Boys, the Brown's Ferry Four, Molly O'Day, Wilma Lee Cooper, or Ralph Stanley.—B.C.M.

★★★★★ **Something Got a Hold of Me: A Treasury of Sacred Music (RCA Victor 2100-2R) 1990**

In spite of the *Reader's Digest* type of title, this is in reality an appealing collection of prewar country gospel recordings, programmed and annotated by Billy Altman as part of RCA's excellent Heritage Series. The Carter Family, the Monroe Brothers, the Blue Sky Boys, Wade Mainer, and Blind Alfred Reed all get two cuts each, and Uncle Dave Macon, Bill Monroe, and Bill Carlisle have single entries. While there is little continuity in programming, highlights include some of the seminal songs of country gospel: the Monroes' "What Would You Give in Exchange for Your Soul," Grady Cole's "The Tramp on the Street," the Dixon Brothers' "I Didn't Hear Nobody Pray" (the original version of Roy Acuff's "The Wreck on the Highway"), Wade Mainer's "Further Along," and the Blue Sky Boys' "Only One Step More." The sound, taken from these original metal masters, is as good as 1930s vintage recording gets. —C.K.W.

★★★ **Favorite Sacred Songs (King KCD-556) 1958**

One measure of the importance of sacred music in white Southern culture is the variety of musical styles in which worshippers have rendered their songs of praise. While this brief twelve-song reissue does not exhaust the stylistic range of church music, and the sound quality extends from good to poor, it does offer a tantalizing sample of old-time country gospel singing at its inspirational best.

Highlights include Cowboy Copas's "From the Manger to the Cross," which transposes honky-tonk music from the bar to the altar; Grandpa Jones's old-time salvation tract "144 Thousand Were There"; the Delmore Brothers' close-harmony duet "The Wrath of God"; "Gloryland Boogie" by the Swanee River Boys, whose pumping bass vocal technique and jazz inclinations were inspired by the Golden Gate Quartet and other African-American gospel groups of the Thirties and Forties; and the fervor of Brother Claude Ely's testimony, "There Ain't No Grave Gonna Hold My Body Down," as uplifting and spirit-filled as any gospel song ever recorded.—J.B.

Cajun

★★★★ Cajun: Vol. 1, Abbeville Breakdown 1929-1939 (Columbia CK 46220) 1990

This album is part of Columbia's excellent "Roots 'n' Blues" series. It includes twenty-two cuts of vintage Cajun recordings by two seminal aggregations of Cajun musicians. The first of these is the Breaux family, brothers Amedee, Ophy, and Clifford, their sister Cleoma, and her husband Joe Falcon. In various combinations these musicians made some landmark early recordings of traditional Cajun music featuring fiddle, accordion, and guitar. Cleoma and Joe Falcon are responsible for the first commercially released recording of Cajun music in 1928. The other group featured on this disc is the Alley Boys of Abbeville, a somewhat lesser known band whose music was more progressive than the Breaux's, reflecting jazz, blues, and western swing influences. For recordings from this period, the sound quality is excellent. Aficionados of Cajun music will find this disc a must-have, while less devoted listeners may find these highly authentic performances a little too rustic and difficult to listen to.—C.H.S.

★★★★ Louisiana Cajun from the Southwest Prairies, Vol. 1 (Rounder CD 6001) 1989
★★★★ Louisiana Cajun from the Southwest Prairies, Vol. 2 (Rounder CD 6002) 1989

Both volumes of this series from Rounder are excellent samplers of the impassioned, rhythmic music created by Louisiana's Acadian-French community. Recorded in the field by the great musicologist Alan Lomax during the years 1964 to 1967, these discs feature the music at its most raw—and heartfelt. Each CD is accompanied by thorough liner notes that give biographical information about the artists, most of whom are quite obscure. *Vol. 1* opens with the best-known progenitors of traditional Cajun, the Balfa Freres, led by fiddler Dewey Balfa, who passed away in 1992. The brothers' seven tracks include the strangely mournful classic "Danse de Mardi Gras" as well as a selection of waltzes and uptempo tunes. Filling out this volume are Austin Pitre & the Evangeline Playboys, whose instrumentation includes electric guitar and drums (unusual among traditional Cajun groups), and the then-72-year-old fiddler-singer Edius Nacquin. *Vol. 2* begins with the bluesy music of "Bois Sec" Ardoin (accordion) and Canray Fontenot (vocals-fiddle). This black duo leans a little more toward zydeco than their white counterparts on the disc. Cousins Adam (vocals-fiddle) and Cyprien (vocals-accordion) Landreneau describe the stories told in their traditional songs in the liner notes. And the threesome of Isom Fontenont, Aubrey DeVille, and Preston Manuel offer up two compelling tracks, including the harmonica-driven "La Bataille dans le Petit Arbre." Both discs are highly recommended to anyone interested in Cajun sounds.—H.G.-W.

★★★★ Cajun Spice: Dance Music from South Louisiana (Rounder CD 11550) 1989

A compilation of the past fifteen years' worth of Cajun music, this CD will keep your toes tappin'. It ranges from traditional artists like the Balfa Brothers to honky-tonkin' D. L. Menard to contemporary performers Beausoleil and Bruce Daigrepont—nine different artists all together. If this flavor of music from the land of Tabasco is new to you, *Cajun Spice* offers a well-rounded sampling of the Acadian genre's divergent styles. Instrumentation varies from the Balfas' stripped-down, classic fiddle and acoustic guitar, to Jo-El Sonnier's spritely accordion, to saxophone and electric mandolin and guitar on Beausoleil fiddler Michael Doucet's solo offerings. Especially rockin' is Doucet's "Bayou Pon Pon," where he is joined by British guitar wiz Richard Thompson. All twenty-one tracks on *Cajun Spice* are culled from the artists' Rounder solo LPs, so if your appetite is whetted and you want to gorge yourself, you're in luck. —H.G.-W.

★★★★½ Le Gran Mamou, Vol. 1 (Country Music Foundation CMF-013) 1990
★★★★½ Raise Your Window, Vol. 2 (Country Music Foundation CMF-017) 1993
★★★★½ Gran Prairie, Vol. 3 (Country Music Foundation CMF-018) 1993

The three volumes of this superb series collect the earliest Cajun music recorded for the Victor/Bluebird labels. With excellent sound quality (digital remixes of archival recordings), the lengthy discs—more than twenty tracks each—feature an array of Cajun musicians performing in southwest Louisiana between 1928 and 1941. Informative liner notes explain the origins of the music, the stylistic changes within the genre, and what little biographical details exist about the artists. Especially helpful are the printed song lyrics, in French with English translations. It is the music, though, that makes all three volumes of the anthology indispensible. From the mournful ballads of Leo Soileau and Mayuse Lafleur (among the first Cajun artists to be recorded) to the good-timey country string-band feel of the Hackberry Ramblers, the series demonstrates the music's richness and diversity. Elements of western swing, blues, Jimmie Rodgers-style yodeling, and early country music pepper the collections' musical gumbo, serving as a reminder of the genre's rightful place in country music history. These discs showcase an astonishing range of instrumentation: the streamlined combo of Creole accordion pioneer Amedee Ardoin and seminal fiddler Dennis McGee (*Vol. 1,* an overview of the music); the solo harmonica player and vocalist Arteleus Mistric's (*Vol. 2,* focusing on the earliest recordings); the steel guitar, dual fiddles and guitars, washboard, and harmonica of the boisterous Rayne-Bo Ramblers (*Vol. 3,* which concentrates on various string bands). The waltzes, two steps, and mournful ballads, though more than half a century old, effectively transport the listener to a hot and smoky dancehall where the floorboards rhythmically creak and the swamps outside are filled with crawfish.—H.G.-W.

Cowboy

★★★★★ **Back in the Saddle Again (New World NW314/315-2) 1983**
This is a marvelous collection, skillfully conceived and planned, with full and perceptive notes by Charlie Seemann. It encompasses the entire range (no pun intended) of cowboy singing in this century: the early commercial performances of such sometime cowboys as Haywire Mac, Carl Sprague, and Jules Verne Allen; movie cowboys like Gene Autry, Tex Ritter, and Rex Allen; radio acts like Tex Owens and the Girls of the Golden West; rodeo cowboys like Chris LeDoux and Glenn Ohrlin; and modern revivalists like Riders in the Sky. Their songs illustrate both the hard, and often grim, reality of cowboy life as well as the romance that most of us prefer.—B.C.M.

★★★★ **Cowboy Songs on Folkways (Smithsonian/Folkways CD SF 40043) 1991**
This CD is a compilation of cowboy songs recorded over the years for the Folkways label. It includes a generous twenty-six cuts, with a few by authentic cowboy singers like Harry Jackson and Ray Reed, but focuses more on stalwarts of the folk revival such as Pete Seeger, Woody Guthrie, Cisco Houston, and even folk-bluesman Leadbelly. This is a solid collection of interesting performances with an excellent booklet of notes by compiler Guy Logsdon.—C.H.S.

Bluegrass

★★½ **20 Bluegrass Originals: Hymns (Deluxe DCD-7911) 1987**
Twelve different artists are represented on this uneven collection of bluegrass gospel songs, most of which seem to have been recorded originally during the 1950s and 1960s. The Stanley Brothers, Reno & Smiley, and the Lewis Family are given three songs each, while Carl Story and Moore & Napier each have two songs. The remaining artists—Reno & Harrell, Wade Mainer, the Acorn Sisters, Jimmy Martin, the Bailes Brothers, Jim & Jesse, and Wilma Lee & Stoney Cooper—have single entries.

There is no information given on recording dates, or on how and why these particular songs and artists were chosen for this compilation. While the Stanley Brothers' "Rank Stranger" and Reno & Smiley's "I'm Using My Bible for a Roadmap" are among the finest examples of bluegrass gospel ever written or recorded, other selections are less compelling. And, contrary to what the album title suggests, not all songs are originals: "I'll Fly Away" (Reno & Harrell), "Amazing Grace" (Reno & Smiley), "Unclouded Day" (Lewis Family), and "Precious Memories" (Carl Story) have been gospel standards for far longer than bluegrass has been sung. —J.B.

★★★ **Fifty Years of Bluegrass Hits (CMH CD-9033-9036) 1992**
Despite the panoramic premise of the title, the songs on this four-CD, 100-track boxed set were culled from albums recorded on the CMH label in the Seventies and Eighties. Many of the selections consist of up-dated versions of earlier recordings by the featured artists, and of songs popularized by other bluegrass musicians.

In general, the sound quality is better than on the earlier recordings. But the gains in fidelity are countered by the loss of passion heard in the originals recorded when bluegrass was new and its artists were young and on fire. For example, Reno & Harrell's tranquil rendering of "I'm Using My Bible for a Roadmap" lacks the urgency of Reno & Smiley's recording of the same song in 1952. Similarly, the Osborne Brothers' insouciant take on the Stanley Brothers' "Rank Stranger" pales next to the Stanley's own longingly lonesome version. And how could Rose Lee Maphis (or anyone, for that matter) improve on "Uncle Pen," Bill Monroe's loving tribute to his own uncle, Pendleton Vandiver?

Regardless of these shortcomings, the collection does offer a wide-ranging sample of some absorbing performances by many of the music's legends. Contributors include Merle Travis ("Dark as a Dungeon"), Jim & Jesse McReynolds ("Johnny B. Goode"), Mac Wiseman ("Jimmy Brown the Newsboy"), Donna Stoneman ("Life's Railway to Heaven"), Grandpa Jones ("She Was Always Chewing Gum"), Carl Story ("Somebody Touched Me"), Lester Flatt ("Father's Table Grace"), and others.—J.B.

★★★★★ **Best of Bluegrass, Vol. 1: Standards (Mercury 848 979-2) 1991**
Over the years Mercury did indeed record some of the best bluegrass, and now that MGM is part of the same PolyGram stable, they have a lot of good material to draw on. This album includes, for example, five of the best early Flatt & Scruggs numbers from 1949-50, including "Foggy Mountain Breakdown," "Old Salty Dog Blues," and "Roll in My Sweet Baby's Arms." Here too is the original "Feudin' Banjos," the 1955 Don Reno-Arthur Smith duet that was the model for "Dueling Banjos," the hit theme from the 1972 movie *Deliverance*. Perhaps the rarest cuts are five from the Stanley Brothers' mid-Fifties Mercury sessions, some of the best bluegrass ever recorded, including the classic "Angel Band." Also represented are the ground-breaking early MGM recordings by the Osborne Brothers and Red Allen, including "Once More," the song that launched the Osbornes' vocal trademark, the high lead trio, and their first hit, the driving "Ruby, Are You Mad." Other well-known groups represented here are the Country Gentlemen and the Lonesome Pine Fiddlers. If you don't own any bluegrass, this collection, with its informative notes, is a good place to start, particularly if you want to hear the classics. —N.V.R.

Western Swing

★★★★★ **Okeh Western Swing (CBS Special Products A 37324) 1982**
This is a great cowboy jazz collection, concentrating on relative unknowns who recorded for the trailblazing Okeh label from 1927 to 1950, although Bob Wills & His Texas Playboys contribute seven typically wild tracks. Wills towers over the competition like Bill Monroe over his bluegrass progeny; nonetheless, all the other performers make indisputable cases, among them Emmett Miller, a tremendous influence on Merle Haggard's periodic western swing excursions, and Spade Cooley, who played a similar role, albeit much lesser known, for Jerry Lee Lewis. More than any other multiple-performers set, *Okeh Western Swing* traces the form's varying styles and ties them together. Consumer alert: although this CD preserves John Morthland's ace notes from the original double LP, nowhere in the booklet or the disc are the performers listed.—J.G.

Honky-Tonk

★★★★ **Memphis Ramble (Rhino R2-70963) 1990**

This is a distillation of Bear Family's epic eleven-LP import set *Sun Records: The Country Years.* There's a token track apiece from Johnny Cash and Jerry Lee Lewis, but—in the main—it's given over to artists who were barely household names in their own households, such as Howard Seratt, Harmonica Frank, Doug Poindexter, and Mississippi Slim. More than anything, it shows how Sun owner Sam Phillips was drawn to individualists. This is music sharply at odds with the Nashville mainstream; still, it's raw and engaging stuff, and the real surprise is that Cash and Lewis don't overshadow their forgotten labelmates.—C.E.

★★★★★ **Hank Williams Songbook: 20 Songs by 11 Artists (Columbia/ Legacy CK 47995) 1991**

The best corrective to the ongoing debate over Hank's skill as songwriter (one biography depicts him as a near-illiterate rube who bought, stole, or was helped with his best songs) is the simple fact that he came to Nashville largely on the strength of his writing. Between the legend of Hank as Hillbilly Shakespeare and the revisionist view of a drunken plagiarist is a more pragmatic picture of a song craftsman working in a burgeoning Southern Tin Pan Alley. That's the Hank revealed by this collection of Williams's songs sung by his peers and written, in many cases, with other artists in mind.

The first is Molly O'Day's intense 1946 performance of "When God Comes and Gathers His Jewels," and the last from Hank's lifetime is Jimmy Dickens's "I Wish You Didn't Love Me So Much," the sort of fractured romance novelty that is inevitably interpreted as an account of the Hank and Audrey saga. In between are such gems as Ray Price's "Weary Blues from Waiting" and such trifles as Curley Williams's "Honey Do You Love Me, Huh?" The diversity of sacred songs, uptempo novelties, and balladic weepers is bound by the unity of Hank's unmistakable signature, an unabashed sincerity and straightforwardness.

Six of the songs are covers waxed after Hank's death, and they neatly encapsule the range of approaches his songs have invited over the past forty years. Anita Carter's "There'll Be No Teardrops Tonight" is artfully pretty, with strings and precise phrasing, while Marty Robbins's "Long Gone Lonesome Blues" is raucous, raw, and rockin'. As a bonus, Colin Escott's notes neatly frame this balanced portrait of one of American popular music's greatest songwriters. —M.H.

Rockabilly

★★★★ **Get Hot or Go Home (Country Music Foundation CMF-014-D) 1989**

Why would a label that had Elvis Presley want any other rockabillies? That's a question that the RCA sales and promo people answered by neglecting every one of the tracks on this set. Of the seventeen acts represented here, Pee Wee King, Homer & Jethro, and Roy Orbison were just flirting and soon reverted to what they did best. Anonymity beckoned the rest shortly after RCA did. Joe Clay gets the lion's share of tracks with nine; his "Did You Mean Jelly Bean (What You Said Cabbage Head)" defines the delightful folly that was rockabilly. Whammy bars are thrashed, larynxes seared, but for two-and-a-half glorious minutes these guys were standing where Elvis stood. Unlike many European rockabilly anthologies, this is wall-to-wall good stuff.—C.E.

★★★ **Honeymoon in Vegas (Epic Soundtrax EK52845) 1992 ●**

Elvis Presley's music, as performed by country, rock, and pop stars, provides the musical backdrop for this 1992 film comedy. Performances range from faithful reproductions of the originals (Ricky Van Shelton's "Wear My Ring around Your Neck," which he told interviewers he hadn't heard before recording it here; Billy Joel's "All Shook Up" and "Heartbreak Hotel") to liberally creative interpretations (Bryan Ferry's Euro-dance recasting of "Are You Lonesome Tonight," Jeff Beck's trash-guitar instrumental take on "Hound Dog," U2 lead singer Bono's ghostly "I Can't Help Falling in Love," the only track not in the movie).

Other performances by country artists include Travis Tritt's incendiary "Burning Love," Dwight Yoakam's driving update of "Suspicious Minds" (a hit for him between albums, thanks to a sexy video featuring the lanky one), Trisha Yearwood's growly "(You're the) Devil in Disguise," Vince Gill's "That's All Right" (in which Gill takes Scotty Moore's trademark guitar licks a step or two further), and Willie Nelson's nasally, luscious "Blue Hawaii." Nashville-based pop singer Amy Grant adds a breathy "Love Me Tender." Missing on this disc is Bruce Springsteen's animated version of "Viva Las Vegas," used to introduce the first scenes of Vegas in the movie. Springsteen recorded the song for *The Last Temptation of Elvis,* a two-disc set of Presley movie tunes released in 1990 in England by *New Musical Express* magazine to benefit the Nordoff-Robbins Music Therapy Centre in London.—J.O.

★★★ **Get with the Beat: The Mar-Vel Masters (Rykodisc RCD 20126) 1989**

Throughout the Fifties, Harry Glenn's Mar-Vel label supplied some of the wildest and most unbuttoned rockabilly records this side of Sun, with just enough side trips to western swing, novelty, and straight country to clue in listeners that these crazy folk had more in common with the Nashville zeitgeist than the Memphis competition. (This was indicated mostly through Mar-Vel's guitar styles, built around earlier achievements by Chet Atkins and Les Paul, rather than those of Scotty Moore and Carl Perkins.) Only specialists are familiar with names like Shorty Ashford, Lorenzo Smith, and Mel Kimbrough, but every forceful-yet-unassuming number on this set (twenty-seven in all) moves forward with enough energy to suggest that these unknowns deserved better.—J.G.

★★★½ **Legends (Garland/DCC Compact Classics GRZ015) 1986**
★★★★★ **The Sun Story (Rhino RNCD 75884) 1987**
★★★★ **Sun's Greatest Hits (RCA 66059-2) 1992**

As recently as fifteen years ago, it was still necessary for music critics to undertake an explanation what Memphis's Sun Records did. That's because a lot of that label's earthshaking singles got lost in the Sixties and Seventies as LPs became the popular music format. Now, thanks to fanatical European labels and (more recently) the boom in CD reissues, a lot of this stuff is readily available, and Sun's legacy is well known. But if you haven't heard the news, there's good rockin' here, for Sun Records is the Big Bang of rock & roll. True, that country-R&B amalgam wasn't actually created at Sun during the Fifties, but everything important flowed from it. The roll call of names that Sun owner/producer Sam Phillips recorded there ought to be enough to clue you in: Elvis Presley, Carl Perkins, Jerry Lee Lewis, Johnny Cash, Roy Orbison, Charlie Rich, to name only the most prominent. Though an undercapitalized independent label, Sun was much more than the minor leagues for these guys. It represented a fighting chance for them to be heard with music that was too edgy to fit comfortably in Nashville, or anywhere else. And for many of them—Perkins, Lewis, arguably Presley—Sun Records represents their artistic peak.

But the Sun rockabillies were still country. When Elvis first got airplay, it was largely on country shows. When he first toured, it was in country package shows. When he began charting, it was country. The same for Perkins, Lewis, and most of the rest. Only when they became so big—so popular—that they couldn't be contained by country, did they make it to the wider pop world and get stamped as rock & roll. You won't hear fiddle and steel on these records, but you will hear voices that are nothing but country.

Each of the three readily available domestic discs is a good vantage point for learning what all the commotion was about. Rhino's *Sun Story,* although an abridged version (Sam Phillips recorded blues and straight country too), provides a virtual primer on the Sun rockabilly sound in twenty tracks, ranging from the primal thrills of Elvis's "Good Rockin' Tonight" and Jerry Lee's "Whole Lotta Shakin'" to the inspired lunacy of Billy Riley's "Flyin' Saucer Rock 'n' Roll" and Warren Smith's "Ubangi Stomp." Presley, Lewis, Perkins, Cash, Orbison, and Rich weigh in with two classic tracks apiece here, while lesser lights like Carl

Mann and Bill Justis supply the enjoyable oddment.

Although not as ambitious in terms of breadth, RCA's seventeen-cut *Sun's Greatest Hits* does a good job of concentrating on the label's stars—Presley, Perkins, Cash, and Lewis, each of whom rates at least three classic tracks. Bill Justis ("Raunchy"), Carl Mann ("Mona Lisa"), and Charlie Rich ("Lonely Weekends") round out the set.

Legends might look like product of a fly-by-night label, but actually it comes from the dependable folks at DCC Compact Classics. Elvis, the Sun King, doesn't show up here, but Cash, Rich, Orbison, Perkins, and Lewis all do, filling out twenty tracks. Since Cash's boom-chicka-boom sound scored the most hits while on the label, it makes a certain amount of sense that he gets the lion's share of the cuts (six), among them the immortal "I Walk the Line" and "Folsom Prison Blues." Orbison and Rich merit only two apiece, but that's to be expected, since they did their best work elsewhere, at Monument and Smash, respectively. Among the surprising rarities also offered here are Carl Perkins's very faithful cover of "Roll Over, Beethoven," Jerry Lee's pointlessly tame reworking of "Good Rockin' Tonight," and the *piece de resistance,* mild-mannered Orbison's delightful freakout on "Mean Little Woman."

All of these sets come with informative historical sleevenotes. For any rock fan looking to get back to the country, these seminal Fifties recordings provide the aural equivalent of a thrilling ride down a country road with the top down. Get back and get with it.—P.K.

★★★★ **Rock This Town: Rockabilly Hits, Vol. 1 (Rhino R2 70741) 1991**
★★★½ **Rock This Town: Rockabilly Hits, Vol. 2 (Rhino R2 70742) 1991**
These two discs, sold separately, make the case for rockabilly being more than a blip in the time line in Memphis between 1954 and 1959. Rockabilly, they argue, is a state of mind. *Vol. 1* makes the more conservative, satisfying argument, confining the reach of its eighteen tracks strictly to the Fifties. Along with the expected, seminal records (Carl Perkins's "Blue Suede Shoes," Billy Riley's "Red Hot," the Rock & Roll Trio's "Train Kept

A-Rollin'"), you get such exhilirating rarities as Jimmy Edwards's "Love Bug Crawl" and Jimmy Lloyd's "Rocket in My Pocket" as well as Bill Haley's trailblazing "Rock the Joint," released two years before Elvis got started at Sun.

Vol. 2 goes the riskier route, splitting its offerings between Fifties rockabilly and later revivals by the likes of Robert Gordon, Tex Rubinowitz, and the Stray Cats. Though not as consistent as the first volume, it's got the almost irresistible allure of three country acts getting down: Wanda Jackson delivers the scorching invitation "Let's Have a Party," Johnny Horton rocks on his "Honky Tonk Hardwood Floor," and Conway Twitty swings wildly through a crazy version of "Danny Boy."—P.K.

Instrumental

★★ **The World's Greatest Country Fiddlers (C.M.H. CD-5904) 1989**
This compilation of thirty-six performances ranges from bluegrass to western swing to old-time, and it includes country fiddle tunes by artists like Johnny Gimble, Buddy Spicher, Ramona Jones, Paul Warren, Kenny Baker, Vassar Clements, and Chubby Wise. It's an interesting collection, but the performance quality is uneven. Although there are some excellent cuts, such as Tater Tate's "Fiddlin' Cricket" and Kenny Baker's "Dusty Miller," too many come up lame or just outright bizarre.—C.H.S.

★★★★★ *Guitar Player* **Presents Legends of Country Guitar Vols. 1 & 2 (Rhino RS 70718 and RS 70723) 1990, 1991**
Guitar Player magazine's "Legends" series is an excellent multi-CD overview of all kinds of guitar music, and the two CDs that constitute the country segment of this collection are among the best of the bunch. While two CDs are obviously not enough to do full justice to the many guitar styles that are the instrumental heart of country music, it's a rare compilation that succeeds on most every level the way this one does. Individual cuts like the Carter Family's "Wildwood Flower" and Hank Garland's "Sugarfoot Rag" just burst with the excitement of discovery. And while all these tracks,

from Arthur Smith's "Guitar Boogie" to Chet Atkins's "Chinatown My Chinatown" to Albert Lee's "Country Boy," serve as useful stylistic signposts, either one of these CDs played all the way through makes for a hell of a good listen. These are a must.—P.Cr.

Contemporary

★★★★ **The Best of Mountain Stage, Vol. 1 Live (Blue Plate Music BPM-001CD) 1991**

★★★★ **The Best of Mountain Stage, Vol. 2 Live (Blue Plate Music BPM-002CD)1991**

★★★½ **The Best of Mountain Stage, Vol. 3 Live (Blue Plate Music BPM-003CD)1992**

★★★★ **The Best of Mountain Stage, Vol. 4 Live (Blue Plate Music BPM-004CD) 1992**

★★★★ **The Best of Mountain Stage, Vol. 5 Live (Blue Plate Music BPM-005CD) 1993**

Let's say you've got a CD-changing player that can access several different discs; let's say your player has a random-play button; and let's say you own all five of these discs. Load 'em up all at once, hit the shuffle button, and—presto—you have the equivalent of a radio station better than just about any you'll hear in America. Culled from broadcasts of West Virginia Public Radio's excellent weekly music show "Mountain Stage," the live performances on these discs cover a blessedly wide range of styles including country, blues, Tex-Mex, rock, alternative, traditional gospel, rhythm & blues, songwriter/folk, and zydeco. The first three volumes tend to feature alternative and singer-songwriter heroes. *Vol. 4* moves into blues, rhythm & blues, and gospel. All are intelligently assembled groupings. Some performers choose to "unplug" (e.g., Mary-Chapin Carpenter, R.E.M.). Others keep a full band but with the looser feel of a live set (Marshall Crenshaw, Delbert McClinton).

Only a small percentage of the selections come from artists working primarily in country music. *Vol. 2* includes Kathy Mattea doing her Grammy-winning "Where've You Been," and Jimmie Dale Gilmore wailing "These Blues." *Vol. 3* has Carpenter doing

"Never Had It So Good," the Texas Tornados' "Soy de San Louis," and Jo-El Sonnier's recording of Richard Thompson's "Tear Stained Letter." *Vol. 5* includes Kevin Welch's "Early Summer Rain." A number of other Nashville-based artists who work outside or on the edges of country music also appear including Joey Spampinato and Al Anderson, with their band NRBQ, John Prine (whose management company and record label are responsible for issuing these discs), Maura O'Connell (with accompaniment from Nashvillians Jerry Douglas and Russ Barenberg), Delbert McClinton, Steve Forbert, the Fairfield Four, and Tracy Nelson.—J.O.

★★★ **Rig Rock Jukebox (Diesel Only/First Warning 72705-72510-2) 1992**
Diesel Only Records is a feisty Brooklyn label that does more to keep the honky-tonk aesthetic alive than most of the Nashville-based majors. Specializing in 45-rpm singles for the jukebox market (this is the label's only CD release), Diesel Only has cornered the market on ersatz Hanks and Leftys whose love for the harder side of Fifties country is complemented by a familiarity with rock & roll. But few of the ten groups on this sixteen-tune set let the rock & roll side of the equation hold sway, even on tracks like the Blue Chieftains' "Punk Rockin' Honky Tonk Girl" that verge on camp: Hank gets mentioned in two song titles and his influence shows up in a half-dozen more. It's unlikely that many of these spirited acts will last for a second edition of this volume, though many of them—particularly Courtney Lee Adams's group Courtney and Western—deserve a wider hearing.—J.G.

★★★½ **Points West: New Horizons in Country Music (HighTone XCD 8021) N. D.**
There's diesel fuel, hot whiskey, and hell fire running through the blood of the artists on this CD, a kind of introductory guide to alternative country. From Texas troubadours Joe Ely and Jimmie Dale Gilmore to plaintive songster Heather Myles to bar band stompers the Lonesome Strangers, *Points West* showcases fringe folks whose voices don't quite fit on country radio and whose styles owe as much to the roots tradition as the country

method. Highlights include Gilmore's "Red Chevrolet," a carefree look at a romantic joyride; Myles's "Rum and Rodeo," a sourmash tale of fun gone awry; and Gary Stewart's honky-tonkin' "Rainin', Rainin', Rainin'." —K.S.

★★ **White Mansions (A&M 75021-6004-2) 1978**

Cor, blimey. Talk about bizarre. Here we have one of the very strangest concept albums ever: the story of the Southland's struggle through the Civil War as imagined by an Englishman in the Seventies. Not just any old Englishman, mind you, but Paul Kennerley, who later moved to Nashville, became a pretty decent songwriter, and married Emmylou Harris. Back then, though, his writing was somewhere between immature and just plain dreadful ("When the only guts and brains you've got/Are the ones that are stuck to your boot . . ." sings poor Steve Cash of the Ozark Mountain Daredevils, sounding relieved to encounter lines with at least a singable syllable count and no mention of the Southern, Yankee-threatened "lifestyle" poor Waylon has to keep gritting his teeth around). The whole project, complete with star rockers (Eric Clapton on guitar, Glyn Johns producing) and pseudo-antique photos lovingly posed in famous Civil War locations like Chipping Sodbury, Berkshire, has the surreal obsessiveness of a *major* shootout at the hash factory (talk about a period piece). Which leaves you to wonder: How did this happen? Did he get a grant? When is Harlan Howard going to retaliate with a rock opera about the Blitz?—P.Ca.

★★★★½ **A Town South of Bakersfield, Vols. 1 & 2 (Restless 72575-2) 1988**
★★★½ **A Town South of Bakersfield, Vol. 3 (Restless 72592-2) 1992**

To call Los Angeles "a town south of Bakersfield" is a cheeky tribute to the prevailing myth of Bakersfield as a kickin' California alternative to the more tightly buckled Bible Belt country dominated by "the Athens of the South," as Nashville was once known. An alternative-country scene flourished in L.A. in the Eighties (it flickers dimly in the Nineties), here documented by *Town South of Bakersfield* anthologies, which offer wildly disparate versions of alternative country as played in Valley and Hollywood bars in the late Eighties (the performances span the years 1985 through 1991).

Pete Anderson's presence as producer and guitarslinger hangs heavily over *Bakersfield 1 & 2* (now available on a single twenty-cut CD), and they are more cohesive for it, though cohesion is scarce in this company. *Bakersfield 1* is noted for having unleashed Dwight Yoakam on the world, heard yodeling his one-night stand stomp, "I'll Be Gone." But it's more striking, in retrospect, for such should-have-beens as the Lonesome Strangers, whose "Lonesome Pine" crackles with a skewed humor that characterized the best element of L.A.'s short-lived hip hillbilly scene. Little of that survived the scrambles for major label deals, though likable Jim Lauderdale, whose Buckish drawl tore open *Vol. 2* with "What Am I Waiting For," is the rule-proving exception.

Arguably L.A.'s hip country scene peaked in 1988, and the performances waxed that year for *Vol. 2* witness artistic growth both in producer Anderson and in the artists he recorded. Along with Lauderdale, Lucinda Williams was on track, her "Dark Side of Life" sounding like a female Luke the Drifter homily. The quirky humor shines again through the song and performances of the Crazy Hearts and Re Winkler, true talents who sank with few traces. Conversely, Jeffrey Steele's overblown country-rock ("Driftin' Man") is a blueprint for his subsequent success with Boy Howdy. Country marketing moguls evidently feel more secure peddling the rank rather than the wry.

Yoakam's success fueled much of the action chronicled by these anthologies, but by the end of the Eighties it was apparent that his Nudie coattails were incredibly short. Nashville viewed what was happening in L.A. as an anomaly it wasn't sure it could sell to the Corn Belt and needn't try, what with polite young men like Randy Travis arriving from small Southern towns daily. Come the Nineties, many of the best of L.A.'s alternative country performers had called it quits, and the sixteen acts on *Bakersfield 3* have a shaggy diffuseness that suggests a scene on the wane. That's not to say the energy has abated. An admirable crash-and-burn abandon roils through much of this stuff, even as the Hollywood cartoon cowboy imagery wears a mite thin. Many of these acts don't take country too seriously (not a bad thing necessarily), even as their pseudo-drawls and Western suits surely brand them *country*. There's little danger of the Neon Angels' cowthrash ever being unleashed on country radio, though its rock credibility is hampered by the Twang Factor. Struggling for a toehold in a marketing niche that just doesn't exist, L.A.'s remaining country upstarts have a quixotic pluck going for them, even as their other talents (as these tracks attest) vary widely. Wish them luck (they'll need it), and check these out if you're at all curious about the health of L.A.'s country-rock underground twenty-plus years after the Flying Burrito Brothers.—M.H.

FOUR-STAR CDs

Roy Acuff The Essential Roy Acuff (Columbia/Legacy)

John Anderson Greatest Hits (Warner Bros.)

John Anderson Seminole Wind (BNA)

Chet Atkins Pickin' On Country (RCA Pair)

Mike Auldridge Treasures Untold (Sugar Hill)

Gene Autry The Essential Gene Autry: 1933-1946 (Columbia/Legacy)

Dewey Balfa Dewey Balfa, Marc Savoy And D.L. Menard: Under A Green Oak Tree (Arhoolie)

Moe Bandy Greatest Hits (Columbia)

Beausoleil Hot Chili Mama (Arhoolie)

Beausoleil Allons à Lafayette (Arhoolie)

Beausoleil Bayou Deluxe: The Best Of Michael Doucet & Beausoleil (Rhino)

Matraca Berg Lying To The Moon (RCA)

Clint Black The Hard Way (RCA)

Norman Blake [with Nancy Blake] Natasha's Waltz (Rounder)

Norman Blake [with Nancy Blake] Blind Dog (Rounder)

Norman Blake Fields of November/Old & New (Flying Fish)

Blue Sky Boys In Concert (Rounder)

Blue Sky Boys Radio Shows, Vol. 1 (Copper Creek)

Blue Sky Boys Radio Shows, Vol. 2 (Copper Creek)

James Blundell Hand It Down (Capitol)

Simon Bonney Forever (Mute/Elektra)

Boone Creek One Way Track (Sugar Hill)

Garth Brooks Garth Brooks (Capitol)

Garth Brooks Ropin' The Wind (Capitol Nashville)

Garth Brooks The Chase (Liberty)

Alison Brown Simple Pleasures (Vanguard)

Alison Brown Twilight Motel (Vanguard)

Marty Brown High And Dry (MCA)

Marty Brown Wild Kentucky Skies (MCA)

Jann Browne It Only Hurts When I Laugh (Curb)

Sonny Burgess We Wanna Boogie (Rounder)

Glen Campbell All-Time Favorites (Pair/CEMA)

Mary-Chapin Carpenter State of the Heart (Columbia)

Mary-Chapin Carpenter Shooting Straight In The Dark (Columbia)

Mary-Chapin Carpenter Come On Come On (Columbia)

Carter Family Clinch Mountain Treasures (County)

Johnny Cash Ride This Train (Sony Special Products)

Johnny Cash Greatest Hits, Vol. 1 (Columbia)

Johnny Cash Columbia Records 1958-1986 (Columbia)

Johnny Cash Johnny Cash Is Coming To Town (Mercury)

Johnny Cash Mystery Of Life (Mercury)

Johnny Cash, Waylon Jennings, Willie Nelson, and Kris Kristofferson Highwayman (Columbia)

Rosanne Cash King's Record Shop (Columbia)

Rosanne Cash The Wheel (Columbia)

Ray Charles Seven Spanish Angels And Other Hits (Columbia)

Mark Chesnutt Too Cold At Home (MCA)

Mark Chesnutt Longnecks And Short Stories (MCA)

Guy Clark Boats To Build (Asylum/American Explorer)

Vassar Clements Hillbilly Jazz (Flying Fish)

Bill Clifton The Early Years, 1957-58 (Rounder)

Patsy Cline Showcase With the Jordanaires (MCA)

Patsy Cline Sentimentally Yours (MCA)

Patsy Cline Patsy Cline: Her First Recordings, Vols 1-3 (Rhino)

David Allan Coe Greatest Hits (1974-78) (Columbia)

Mark Collie Hardin County Line (MCA)

Mark Collie Mark Collie (MCA)

The Collins Kids Introducing Larry And Lorrie . . . the Collins Kids (Sony Music Special Products)

The Country Gentlemen Bluegrass At Carnegie Hall (Hollywood)

The Country Gentlemen Live In Japan (Rebel)

The Country Gentlemen Let The Light Shine Down (Rebel)

The Country Gentlemen Folksongs And Bluegrass (Smithsonian/Folkways)

J.D. Crowe Blackjack (Rebel)

Rodney Crowell Keys To The Highway (Columbia)

Charlie Daniels Fire On The Mountain (Epic)

Lacy J. Dalton Greatest Hits (Columbia)

Jimmie Davis Country Music Hall Of Fame (MCA)

Desert Rose Band A Dozen Roses: Greatest Hits (Curb)

Hazel Dickens A Few Old Memories (Rounder)

The Dillards Let It Fly (Vanguard)

Jerry Douglas Everything Is Gonna Work Out Fine (Rounder)

Jerry Douglas Slide Rule (Sugar Hill)

Holly Dunn Milestones—Greatest Hits (Warner Brothers)

Bob Dylan John Wesley Harding (Columbia)

Bob Dylan Nashville Skyline (Columbia)

Eagles On The Border (Asylum)

Eagles One Of These Nights (Asylum)

Eagles Their Greatest Hits (Asylum)
Steve Earle Guitar Town (MCA)
Steve Earle Exit 0 (MCA)
Steve Earle Copperhead Road (Uni)
Jonathan Edwards Jonathan Edwards (Atco)
Joe Ely Dig All Night (HighTone)
Alejandro Escovedo Gravity (Watermelon)
The Everly Brothers The Everly Brothers (Rhino)
The Everly Brothers The Fabulous Style Of The Everly Brothers (Rhino)
Charlie Feathers Uh Huh Honey (Norton)
Freddy Fender Freddy Fender Collection (Reprise)
File' Cajun Dance Band (Flying Fish)
Cathy Fink When The Rain Comes Down (Rounder)
Flatt & Scruggs Foggy Mountain Banjo (Sony Music Special Products)
Flatt & Scruggs The Complete Mercury Sessions (Mercury)
Flatt & Scruggs Don't Get Above Your Raisin' (Rounder)
Flatt & Scruggs Golden Era (Rounder)
Red Foley Country Music Hall of Fame (MCA)
Tennessee Ernie Ford Sixteen Tons Of Boogie (Rhino)
Tennessee Ernie Ford Songs Of the Civil War (Capitol)
Tennessee Ernie Ford Collector's Series (Capitol)
Foster & Lloyd Foster & Lloyd (RCA)
Lefty Frizzell American Originals (Columbia)
Larry Gatlin & the Gatlin Brothers 17 Greatest Hits (Columbia)
Don Gibson All-Time Greatest Hits (RCA)
Vince Gill Pocket Full Of Gold (MCA)
Vince Gill I Still Believe In You (MCA)
Jimmie Dale Gilmore After Awhile (Elektra/Nonesuch/American Explorer)
Johnny Gimble The Texas Fiddle Connection (CMH)
Good Ol' Persons Anywhere The Wind Blows (Kaleidoscope)
John Gorka I Know (Red House)
John Gorka Land Of The Bottom Line (Windham Hill)
John Gorka Temporary Road (High Street)
Vern Gosdin Alone (Columbia)
Vern Gosdin Rough Around The Edges (RCA)
Grateful Dead American Beauty (Warner Bros.)
Nanci Griffith Other Voices, Other Rooms (Elektra)
Woody Guthrie Library Of Congress Recording. 3 vols. (Rounder)
Woody Guthrie [& Leadbelly] Original Vision (Smithsonian/ Folkways)
Woody Guthrie Struggle (Smithsonian/Folkways)
Merle Haggard Best Of The Best Of Merle Haggard (Liberty)
Merle Haggard His Greatest And His Best (MCA)
Merle Haggard More Of the Best (Rhino)
Merle Haggard Best Of The Early Years (Curb)
Tom T. Hall Greatest Hits (Mercury)
Emmylou Harris Quarter Moon In A Ten Cent Town (Warner Bros.)

Emmylou Harris Duets (Reprise)
Emmylou Harris Brand New Dance (Reprise)
John Hartford Mark Twang (Flying Fish)
Ronnie Hawkins The Best of Ronnie Hawkins and the Hawks (Rhino)
Highway 101 Greatest Hits (Warner Brothers)
Robin Holcomb Robin Holcomb (Elektra Musician)
Robin Holcomb Rockabye (Elektra Musician)
Buddy Holly The Chirping Crickets (MCA)
Buddy Holly Buddy Holly (MCA)
Johnny Horton American Originals (Columbia)
Alan Jackson Here In The Real World (Arista)
Wanda Jackson Rockin' The Country (Rhino)
Wanda Jackson Greatest Hits (Curb)
Waylon Jennings Greatest Hits (RCA)
Waylon Jennings Greatest Hits, Vol. 2 (RCA)
Waylon Jennings Will The Wolf Survive (MCA)
Waylon Jennings Best Of Waylon Jennings (RCA)
Waylon Jennings The Early Years (RCA)
Jim & Jesse The Jim & Jesse Story (CMH)
The Johnson Mountain Boys Let The Whole World Talk (Rounder)
The Johnson Mountain Boys Blue Diamond (Rounder)
David Lynn Jones Hard Times On Easy Street (Mercury)
David Lynn Jones Mixed Emotions (Liberty)
Grandpa Jones Hall Of Fame Series (MCA)
Wynonna Judd Tell Me Why (MCA)
The Judds The Judds (RCA)
The Judds Greatest Hits (RCA)
The Judds Greatest Hits Volume Two (RCA)
The Kendalls 20 Greatest Hits (Deluxe)
Kentucky Headhunters Pickin' On Nashville (Mercury)
Claude King American Originals (Columbia)
Fred Koller Where The Fast Lane Ends (Alcazar)
Alison Krauss Two Highways (Rounder)
Alison Krauss I've Got That Old Feeling (Rounder)
Kris Kristofferson Songs Of Kristofferson (Monument)
k. d. lang Ingenue (Sire)
Doyle Lawson & Quicksilver The Gospel Collection, Vol. 1 (Sugar Hill)
Brenda Lee Brenda Lee Story (MCA)
Jerry Lee Lewis Golden Rock Hits Of Jerry Lee Lewis (Smash)
Jerry Lee Lewis Greatest Hits (Rhino)
Jerry Lee Lewis Rockin' My Life Away (Warner Bros.)
Laurie Lewis Singing My Troubles Away (Flying Fish)
Laurie Lewis & Kathy Kallick Together (Kaleidoscope)
Lilly Brothers Early Recordings (Rebel)
The Louvin Brothers Radio Favorites, 1951-1957 (CMF)
Lyle Lovett Lyle Lovett (MCA)
Lyle Lovett Joshua Judges Ruth (MCA)
Uncle Dave Macon Country Music Hall Of Fame (MCA)
Rose Maddox A Collection Of Standard Sacred Songs (King)

Rose Maddox Rose Of The West Coast Country (Arhoolie)

Marshall Tucker Band Greatest Hits (AJK Music)

Jimmy Martin You Don't Know My Mind (Rounder)

Delbert McClinton Live From Austin (Alligator)

Delbert McClinton Best Of Delbert McClinton (Curb)

Delbert McClinton Never Been Rocked Enough (Curb)

Reba McEntire The Best Of Reba McEntire (Mercury)

Reba McEntire Greatest Hits (MCA)

D. L. Menard No Matter Where You At, There You Are (Rounder)

D. L. Menard Cajun Saturday Night (Rounder)

Roger Miller The Best Of Roger Miller, Vol. 1: Country Tunesmith (Mercury)

Ronnie Milsap Greatest Hits, Vol. 2 (RCA)

Ronnie Milsap Back To The Grindstone (RCA)

Bill Monroe Country Music Hall Of Fame (MCA)

Bill Monroe The Essential Bill Monroe And His Blue Grass Boys (Columbia)

Lorrie Morgan Leave The Light On (RCA)

Anne Murray Greatest Hits (Liberty)

Anne Murray Fifteen Of The Best (Liberty)

Anne Murray Anne Murray's Country Hits (Liberty)

Anne Murray Greatest Hits, Vol. 2 (Capitol)

Nashville Bluegrass Band The Nashville Bluegrass Band (Rounder)

Rick Nelson Legendary Masters Series, Vol. 1 (EMI/Imperial)

Rick Nelson The Best of Rick Nelson 1963-1975 (MCA)

Willie Nelson To Lefty From Willie (Columbia)

Willie Nelson Stardust (Columbia)

Willie Nelson [& Ray Price] San Antonio Rose (Columbia)

Willie Nelson Always On My Mind (CBS)

Willie Nelson Across The Borderline (Columbia)

Michael Nesmith The Older Stuff: The Best Of the Early Years (Rhino)

New Grass Revival Fly Through The Country/ When the Storm Is Over (Flying Fish)

New Lost City Ramblers The Early Years, 1958-1962 (Smithsonian/ Folkways)

The New Tradition Closer Than It's Ever Been (Brentwood)

Maura O'Connell Just In Time (Philo)

Maura O'Connell Helpless Heart (Warner Bros.)

Maura O'Connell A Real Life Story (Warner Bros.)

Mark O'Connor New Nashville Cats (Warner Bros.)

Roy Orbison The Classic Roy Orbison (Rhino)

Roy Orbison Legendary Roy Orbison; Vols. 1-4 (CBS Special Products)

The Osborne Brothers Once More, Vols. 1 & 2 (Sugar Hill)

Buck Owens All Time Greatest Hits (Curb/ Capitol)

David Parmley I Know A Good Thing (Sugar Hill)

Lee Roy Parnell Love Without Mercy (Arista)

Gram Parsons GP/Grievous Angel (Reprise)

Dolly Parton The World Of Dolly Parton, Vol. 1 (Monument)

Dolly Parton The World Of Dolly Parton, Vol. 2 (Monument)

Carl Perkins Honky Tonk Gal: Rare & Unissued Sun Masters (Rounder)

Carl Perkins Restless: The Columbia Years (Sony Legacy)

Elvis Presley Elvis Presley (RCA)

Elvis Presley Elvis (RCA)

Elvis Presley 50,000,000 Elvis Fans Can't Be Wrong: Elvis' Gold Records, Vol. 2 (RCA)

Elvis Presley A Date With Elvis (RCA)

Elvis Presley Golden Records, Vol. 1 (RCA)

Elvis Presley The Complete Sun Sessions (RCA)

Elvis Presley The Million Dollar Quartet (RCA)

Elvis Presley The Rocker (RCA)

Elvis Presley Reconsider Baby (RCA)

Elvis Presley The Number One Hits (RCA)

Elvis Presley The Top 10 Hits (RCA)

Elvis Presley Sings Leiber And Stoller (RCA)

Elvis Presley On Stage: February 1970 (RCA)

Elvis Presley Elvis Sings The Wonderful World Of Christmas (RCA)

Elvis Presley He Touched Me (RCA)

Elvis Presley From Elvis Presley Boulevard, Memphis, Tennessee (RCA)

Elvis Presley Elvis Gold Records, Vol. 5 (RCA)

Elvis Presley A Valentine Gift For You (RCA)

Elvis Presley The Great Performances (RCA)

Elvis Presley Collector's Gold (RCA)

Ray Price Happens To Be The Best (Pair)

Red Clay Ramblers Twisted Laurel/Merchants Lunch (Flying Fish)

Red Clay Ramblers It Ain't Right (Flying Fish)

Red Clay Ramblers Rambler (Sugar Hill)

Jerry Reed The Best of Jerry Reed (RCA Nashville)

Jim Reeves Live at the Opry (CMF)

Jim Reeves Four Walls (RCA)

Jim Reeves Welcome to My World: The Essential Jim Reeves Collection (RCA)

Don Reno & Red Smiley Good Old Country Ballads (King)

Don Reno & Red Smiley A Variety Of Country Songs (King)

Tony Rice Manzanita (Rounder)

Tony Rice Church Street Blues (Sugar Hill)

Zachary Richard Women In The Room (A&M)

Riders in the Sky Three On The Trail (Rounder)

Marty Robbins All Time Greatest Hits (Columbia)

Jimmie Rodgers America's Blue Yodeler, 1930-31 (Rounder)

Jimmie Rodgers Down The Old Road, 1931-1932 (Rounder)

Jimmie Rodgers No Hard Times, 1932 (Rounder)

Linda Ronstadt Prisoner In Disguise (Elektra)

Linda Ronstadt Hasten Down The Wind (Asylum)

Linda Ronstadt Simple Dreams (Elektra)

Linda Ronstadt Greatest Hits (Asylum)

Peter Rowan [& Nashville Bluegrass Band] New Moon Rising (Sugar Hill)

Peter Rowan All On A Rising Day (Sugar Hill)

David Schnaufer Dulcimer Sessions (S.F.L.)
Dan Seals The Best (Liberty)
Dan Seals Greatest Hits (Liberty)
Dawn Sears What A Woman Wants To Hear (Warner Bros.)
The Seldom Scene Recorded Live At The Cellar Door (Rebel)
The Seldom Scene Scene 20: 20th Anniversary Concert (Sugar Hill)
Ricky Skaggs Sweet Temptation (Sugar Hill)
Ricky Skaggs Family And Friends (Rounder)
Jo-El Sonnier Come On Joe (RCA)
Jo-El Sonnier Cajun Life (Rounder)
Sons of the Pioneers Columbia Historic Edition (Columbia)
Sons of the Pioneers Sunset On The Range (Pair)
Larry Sparks Sings Hank Williams (Rebel)
Stanley Brothers Long Journey Home (Rebel)
Stanley Brothers Hymns And Sacred Songs (King)
Stanley Brothers Vol. 3, No. 3 (Copper Creek)
Stanley Brothers Vol. 3, No. 4 (Copper Creek)
Ralph Stanley Bound To Ride (Rebel)
Ralph Stanley Saturday Night & Sunday Morning (Freeland)
The Statler Brothers Best Of, Vol. 2 (Mercury)
The Statler Brothers Atlanta Blue (Mercury)
The Statler Brothers Live And Sold Out (Mercury)
The Statler Brothers Radio Gospel Favorites (Mercury)
The Statler Brothers Gospel Favorites (Heartland)
Gary Stewart Brand New (HighTone)
George Strait Does Fort Worth Ever Cross Your Mind (MCA)
George Strait Something Special (MCA)
Strength in Numbers Telluride Sessions (MCA)
Marty Stuart Tempted (MCA)
Jerry and Tammy Sullivan A Joyful Noise (CMF)
Sweethearts of the Rodeo Sisters (Columbia)
Texas Tornados Texas Tornados (Reprise)
Texas Tornados Los Texas Tornados (Reprise)
Hank Thompson Capitol Collector's Series (Capitol)
Marsha Thornton Maybe The Moon Will Shine (MCA)
Mel Tillis Greatest Hits (Curb)
Pam Tillis Homeward Looking Angel (Arista)
The Traditional Grass Howdy Neighbor Howdy (Rebel)
Merle Travis The Merle Travis Story—24 Greatest Hits (CMH)
Randy Travis Old 8x10 (Warner Bros.)
Randy Travis No Holdin' Back (Warner Bros.)
Randy Travis Greatest Hits, Vol. 1 (Warner Bros.)
Travis Tritt It's All About To Change (Warner Bros.)
Ernest Tubb Ernest Tubb Live 1965 (Rhino)
Conway Twitty Greatest Hits, Vol. 2 (MCA)
Conway Twitty Very Best Of (MCA)
Conway Twitty Number Ones (MCA)
Conway Twitty No. 1's; The Warner Bros. Years (Warner Bros.)

Ian Tyson Cowboyography (Sugar Hill)
Townes Van Zandt At My Window (Sugar Hill)
Rick Vincent A Wanted Man (Curb)
Jerry Jeff Walker Live At Gruene Hall (Rykodisc)
Jerry Jeff Walker Great Gonzos (MCA)
Doc Watson [with Merle Watson] Pickin' the Blues (Flying Fish)
Doc Watson [with Merle Watson] Guitar Album (Flying Fish)
Doc Watson The Essential Doc Watson (Vanguard)
Doc Watson The Doc Watson Family (Smithsonian/Folkways)
Gene Watson Greatest Hits (MCA)
Gene Watson Greatest Hits (Curb/CEMA)
Gene Watson Back In The Fire (Warner Bros.)
Kevin Welch Kevin Welch (Reprise)
Kitty Wells Greatest Hits, Vol. 1 (SOR)
Cheryl Wheeler Circles & Arrows (Capitol)
Cheryl Wheeler Half A Book (North Star)
Keith Whitley Greatest Hits (RCA)
Don Williams Greatest Hits, Vol. 1 (MCA)
Don Williams 20 Greatest Hits (MCA)
Hank Williams Jr. Family Tradition (Warner Bros.)
Hank Williams Jr. Habits Old And New (Warner Bros.)
Hank Williams Jr. Rowdy (Warner Bros.)
Hank Williams Jr. Hank Williams Jr.'s Greatest Hits (Warner Bros.)
Hank Williams Jr. High Notes (Warner Bros.)
Lucinda Williams Lucinda Williams (Chameleon)
Kelly Willis Kelly Willis (MCA)
Bob Wills Columbia Historic Edition (Columbia)
Bob Wills Tiffany Transcriptions, Best Of The Tiffanys, Vol. 2 (Kaleidoscope)
Bob Wills Tiffany Transcriptions: In The Mood, Vol. 9 (Kaleidoscope)
Mac Wiseman Early Dot Recordings, Vol. 3 (MCA-County)
Tammy Wynette Greatest Hits, Vol. 1 (Epic)
Tammy Wynette Tears Of Fire: The 25th Anniversary Collection (Epic)
Tammy Wynette & George Jones Greatest Hits (Epic)
Trisha Yearwood Trisha Yearwood (MCA)
Dwight Yoakam Guitars Cadillacs Etc. Etc. (Reprise)
Dwight Yoakam Hillbilly Deluxe (Reprise)
Dwight Yoakam Buenos Noches From A Lonely Room (Reprise)
Neil Young After The Gold Rush (Reprise)

Various Artists— General Interest

Classic Country Music (Smithsonian)
Columbia Country Classics, Vol. 3: Americana (Columbia)
Columbia Country Classics, Vol. 4: The Nashville Sound (Columbia)
Hillbilly Music, Thank God! (Capitol)

Various Artists—Contemporary

The Best Of Mountain Stage, Vol. 1 Live (Blue Plate Music)

The Best Of Mountain Stage, Vol. 2 Live (Blue Plate Music)

The Best Of Mountain Stage, Vol. 4 Live (Blue Plate Music)

The Best Of Mountain Stage, Vol. 5 Live (Blue Plate Music)

Various Artists—Cajun

Cajun: Volume 1, Abbeville Breakdown 1929-1939 (Columbia)

Louisiana Cajun From The Southwest Prairies, Vol. 1 (Rounder)

Louisiana Cajun From The Southwest Prairies, Vol. 2 (Rounder)

Cajun Spice: Dance Music From South Louisiana (Rounder)

Various Artists—Honky-Tonk

Memphis Ramble (Rhino)

Various Artists—Rockabilly

Get Hot Or Go Home (CMF)

Sun's Greatest Hits (RCA)

Rock This Town: Rockabilly Hits, Vol. 1 (Rhino)

Various Artists—Cowboy

Cowboy Songs On Folkways (Smithsonian/Folkways)

FOUR-AND-ONE-HALF-STAR CDs

Dewey Balfa The Balfa Brothers: J'ai Vu Le Loup, Le Renard, et La Belette (Rounder)
Norman Blake Blake And Rice (Rounder)
Norman Blake Norman Blake And Tony Rice Two (Rounder)
Norman Blake Slow Train Through Georgia (Rounder)
Patsy Cline The Patsy Cline Story (MCA)
Garth Brooks In Pieces (Liberty)
J.D. Crowe Model Church (Rebel)
Rodney Crowell Diamonds And Dirt (Columbia)
Joe Ely Musta Notta Gotta Lotta (MCA)
Bobbie Gentry Greatest Hits (Curb)
Vern Gosdin 10 Years Of Greatest Hits—Newly Recorded (Columbia)
Emmylou Harris Blue Kentucky Girl (Warner Bros.)
Emmylou Harris Profile II: The Best Of Emmylou Harris (Warner Bros.)
Emmylou Harris Bluebird (Reprise)
John Hartford Me Oh My, How The Time Does Fly: A John Hartford Anthology (Flying Fish)
Hot Rize Traditional Ties (Sugar Hill)
Loretta Lynn Loretta Lynn's Greatest Hits (MCA)
Loretta Lynn Coal Miner's Daughter (MCA)
Loretta Lynn Loretta Lynn's 20 Greatest Hits (MCA)
Del McCoury Don't Stop The Music (Rounder)
Del McCoury Blue Side Of Town (Rounder)
Roger Miller The Best Of Roger Miller, Vol. 2: King Of The Road (Mercury)
Nashville Bluegrass Band The Boys Are Back In Town (Sugar Hill)
Nashville Bluegrass Band Home Of The Blues (Sugar Hill)

Roy Orbison For The Lonely: A Roy Orbison Anthology (Rhino)
Lee Roy Parnell Lee Roy Parnell (Arista)
John Prine Diamonds In The Rough (Atlantic)
John Prine Prime Prine (Atlantic)
John Prine Bruised Orange (Oh Boy)
John Prine Missing Years (Oh Boy)
Riders in the Sky Best Of The West (Rounder)
Riders in the Sky Best Of The West Rides Again (Rounder)
Carl Smith The Essential Carl Smith: 1950-56 (Columbia/Legacy)
Russell Smith This Little Town (Epic)
Larry Sparks Classic Bluegrass (Rebel)
George Strait Greatest Hits Vol. Two (MCA)
George Strait Beyond The Blue Neon (MCA)
Marty Stuart This One's Gonna Hurt You (MCA)
Ernest Tubb Country Music Hall Of Fame (MCA)
Tanya Tucker Greatest Hits (Columbia)
Keith Whitley I Wonder Do You Think Of Me (RCA)
Don Williams Greatest Hits, Vol. 1 (MCA)

Various Artists—General Interest

Hillbilly Holiday (Rhino)

Various Artists—Contemporary

A Town South Of Bakersfield, Vols. 1 & 2 (Restless)

Various Artists—Cajun

Le Gran Mamou, Vol. 1 (CMF)
Raise Your Window, Vol. 2 (CMF)
Gran Prairie, Vol. 3 (CMF)

FIVE-STAR CDs

Kenny Baker Master Fiddler (County)

Dewey Balfa The Balfa Brothers Play Traditional Cajun Music, Vols. 1 & 2 (Swallow)

Clint Black Killin' Time (RCA)

Norman Blake The Norman And Nancy Blake Compact Disc (Rounder)

Suzy Bogguss Somewhere Between (Liberty)

Garth Brooks No Fences (Capitol)

Glen Campbell The Very Best Of Glen Campbell (Capitol)

Carlene Carter I Fell In Love (Reprise)

Carlene Carter Little Love Letters (Giant)

Carter Family Country Music Hall of Fame (MCA)

Johnny Cash The Fabulous Johnny Cash (CBS Special Products)

Johnny Cash Johnny Cash At Folsom Prison And San Quentin (Columbia)

Johnny Cash Sun Years (Rhino)

Johnny Cash The Essential Johnny Cash (Columbia)

Ray Charles Modern Sounds In Country And Western Music (Rhino)

Ray Charles Greatest Country And Western Hits (DCC Compact Classics)

Patsy Cline 12 Greatest Hits (MCA)

Patsy Cline The Patsy Cline Collection (MCA)

Elvis Costello King Of America (Columbia)

The Country Gentlemen Country Songs Old And New (Smithsonian/Folkways)

The Country Gentlemen The Award Winning Country Gentlemen (Rebel)

The Country Gentlemen Calling My Children Home (Rebel)

J. D. Crowe J. D. Crowe & The New South (Rounder)

The Dillards There Is A Time (1963-70) (Vanguard)

Michael Doucet Beau Solo (Arhoolie)

Bob Dylan Blonde On Blonde (Columbia)

Joe Ely Honky Tonk Masquerade (MCA)

The Everly Brothers Golden Hits (Warner Bros.)

The Everly Brothers Songs Our Daddy Taught Us (Rhino)

The Everly Brothers Cadence Classics (Rhino)

Flatt & Scruggs The Mercury Sessions, Vol. 1 (Rounder)

Flatt & Scruggs The Mercury Sessions, Vol. 2 (Rounder)

Lefty Frizzell The Best Of Lefty Frizzell (Rhino)

Vince Gill When I Call Your Name (MCA)

Vern Gosdin Chiseled In Stone (Columbia)

Vern Gosdin Out Of My Heart (Columbia)

Woody Guthrie Dust Bowl Ballads (Rounder)

Merle Haggard Capitol Collector's Series (Capitol)

Emmylou Harris Pieces Of The Sky (Reprise)

Emmylou Harris Elite Hotel (Reprise)

Emmylou Harris Luxury Liner (Warner Bros.)

Emmylou Harris Profile/Best Of Emmylou Harris (Warner Bros.)

Emmylou Harris Roses In The Snow (Warner Bros.)

Emmylou Harris The Christmas Album: Light Of The Stable (Warner Bros.)

Emmylou Harris Angel Band (Warner Bros.)

Emmylou Harris At The Ryman (Reprise)

Emmylou Harris, Dolly Parton, Linda Ronstadt Trio (Warner Bros.)

Buddy Holly From The Original Master Tapes (MCA)

Hoosier Hot Shots Rural Rhythm 1935-1942 (Columbia)

Hot Rize Take It Home (Sugar Hill)

Jason & the Scorchers Essential Jason And the Scorchers, Vol. 1: Are You Ready For The Country (EMI)

Waylon Jennings The Taker/Tulsa & Honky Tonk Heroes (Mobile Fidelity)

Waylon Jennings Collector's Series (RCA)

The Johnson Mountain Boys At The Old Schoolhouse (Rounder)

George Jones Anniversary: Ten Years Of Hits (Columbia)

George Jones Best Of George Jones (Rhino)

Kentucky Colonels Appalachian Swing! (Rounder)

Alison Krauss Too Late To Cry (Rounder)

Alison Krauss Every Time You Say Goodbye (Rounder)

Kris Kristofferson The Silver-Tongued Devil And I (Monument)

Kris Kristofferson Me And Bobby McGee (Monument)

Jim Lauderdale Planet Of Love (Reprise)

Doyle Lawson & Quicksilver Rock My Soul (Sugar Hill)

Brenda Lee Anthology Vols. 1 & 2 (MCA)

Jerry Lee Lewis Original Sun Greatest Hits (Rhino)

Jerry Lee Lewis Rare Tracks (Rhino)

Jerry Lee Lewis Killer: The Mercury Years, Vol. I (Mercury)

Jerry Lee Lewis Killer: The Mercury Years, Vol. II (Mercury)

Jerry Lee Lewis Killer: The Mercury Years, Vol. III (Mercury)

Jerry Lee Lewis Live At The Star-Club, Hamburg (Rhino)

Loretta Lynn The Very Best Of Loretta And

Conway (MCA)

Loretta Lynn Country Music Hall Of Fame Series (MCA)

The Maddox Bros. & Rose Vol. 1 (Arhoolie)

The McCarters The Gift (Warner Bros.)

Del McCoury Classic Bluegrass (Rebel)

Roger Miller Golden Hits (Smash)

Ronnie Milsap Greatest Hits (RCA)

Bill Monroe Mule Skinner Blues (RCA)

Nashville Bluegrass Band To Be His Child (Rounder)

Nashville Bluegrass Band Waiting For The Hard Times To Go (Sugar Hill)

Willie Nelson Shotgun Willie (Atlantic)

Willie Nelson Phases And Stages (Atlantic)

Willie Nelson Shotgun Willie/Phases and Stages (Mobile Fidelity)

Willie Nelson Red Headed Stranger (Columbia)

Willie Nelson Nite Life: Greatest Hits And Rare Tracks, 1959-1971 (Rhino)

Willie Nelson Who'll Buy My Memories (Sony)

Tim & Mollie O'Brien Take Me Back (Sugar Hill)

Maura O'Connell Blue Is The Colour Of Hope (Warner Bros.)

Roy Orbison In Dreams (Virgin)

Roy Orbison All Time Greatest Hits Of Roy Orbison, Vols. 1-2 (CBS Special Products)

Buck Owens The Buck Owens Collection (Rhino)

Carl Perkins Original Sun Greatest Hits (Rhino)

Elvis Presley The Complete Fifties Masters (RCA)

Elvis Presley Elvis Is Back! (RCA)

Elvis Presley His Hand In Mine (RCA)

Elvis Presley Elvis' Golden Records, Vol. 3 (RCA)

Elvis Presley How Great Thou Art (RCA)

Elvis Presley Elvis: NBC-TV Special (RCA)

Elvis Presley From Elvis In Memphis (RCA)

Elvis Presley Back In Memphis (RCA)

Elvis Presley Elvis: 50 Worldwide Gold Hits, Vol.1 Part 1 & Part 2 (RCA)

Elvis Presley Elvis Country (RCA)

Elvis Presley The Memphis Record (RCA)

Ray Price The Essential Ray Price: 1951-1962 (Columbia/Legacy)

John Prine John Prine (Atlantic)

John Prine John Prine Live (Oh Boy)

Willis Alan Ramsey Willis Alan Ramsey (Shelter/DCC Compact Discs)

Charlie Rich The Complete Smash Sessions (Mercury)

Charlie Rich Pictures And Paintings (Sire)

Marty Robbins The Essential Marty Robbins (Columbia/Legacy)

Jimmie Rodgers First Sessions (Rounder)

Linda Ronstadt Heart Like A Wheel (Capitol)

Billy Joe Shaver Tramp On Your Street (Zoo/Praxis)

Ricky Skaggs [with Tony Rice] Skaggs & Rice (Sugar Hill)

Ricky Skaggs Waitin' For The Sun To Shine (Epic)

Ricky Skaggs Highways & Heartaches (Epic)

Hank Snow I'm Movin' On And Other Great Country Hits (RCA)

Sons of the Pioneers Country Music Hall Of

Fame (MCA)

The Statler Brothers Best Of, Vol. 1 (Mercury)

Gary Stewart Out Of Hand (HighTone)

Gary Stewart Gary's Greatest (HighTone)

George Strait Greatest Hits (MCA)

Randy Travis Storms Of Life (Warner Bros.)

Conway Twitty Greatest Hits, Vol. 1 (MCA)

Conway Twitty 20 Greatest Hits (MCA)

Conway Twitty Silver Anniversary Collection (MCA)

Conway Twitty Greatest Hits, Vol. 3 (MCA)

Conway Twitty Best Of Conway Twitty, Vol. 1 (Mercury)

Doc Watson Southbound (Vanguard)

Doc Watson My Dear Old Southern Home (Sugar Hill)

Kevin Welch Western Beat (Reprise)

Hank Williams 40 Greatest Hits (Polydor)

Hank Williams I Ain't Got Nothin' But Time—December 1946-April 1947, Vol. 1 (Polydor)

Hank Williams Lovesick Blues—August 1947-December 1948, Vol. 2 (Polydor)

Hank Williams Lost Highway—December 1948-March 1949, Vol. 3 (Polydor)

Hank Williams I'm So Lonesome I Could Cry—March 1949-August 1949, Vol. 4 (Polydor)

Hank Williams Long Gone Lonesome Blues—August 1949-December 1950, Vol. 5 (Polydor)

Hank Williams Hey, Good Lookin'—December 1950-July 1951, Vol. 6 (Polydor)

Hank Williams Let's Turn Back The Years—July 1951-June 1952, Vol. 7 (Polydor)

Hank Williams I Won't Be Home No More—June 1952-September 1952, Vol. 8 (Polydor)

Hank Williams The Original Singles Collection... Plus (Polydor)

Hank Williams Rare Demos: First To Last (CMF)

Hank Williams Health & Happiness Shows (PolyGram)

Bob Wills Anthology: 1935-73 (Rhino)

Tammy Wynette Anniversary: 20 Years Of Hits (Epic)

Trisha Yearwood Hearts In Armor (MCA)

Dwight Yoakam Just Lookin' For A Hit (Reprise)

Dwight Yoakam If There Was A Way (Reprise)

Dwight Yoakam This Time (Reprise)

Various Artists— General Interest

Columbia Country Classics, Vol. 1: The Golden Age (Columbia)

Columbia Country Classics, Vol. 2: Honky-Tonk Heroes (Columbia)

Country U.S.A., 23 vols., 1950-72 (Time Life)

Various Artists—Honky-Tonk

Hank Williams Songbook: 20 Songs By 11 Artists (Columbia/Legacy)

Various Artists—Western Swing

Okeh Western Swing (CBS Special Products)

Various Artists—Bluegrass

Best Of Bluegrass, Vol. 1: Standards (Mercury)

Various Artists—Rockabilly

The Sun Story (Rhino)

Various Artists—Instrumental

Guitar Player Presents Legends Of Country Guitar
Vols. 1 & 2 (Rhino)

Various Artists—Cowboy

Back In The Saddle Again (New World)

Various Artists—Gospel

Something Got A Hold Of Me: A Treasury Of Sacred
Music (RCA)

Various Artists—Old-Time

Are You From Dixie? Great Country Brother Teams
Of The 1930s (RCA)
Altamont: Black Stringband Music From The
Library Of Congress (Rounder)
The Bristol Sessions (CMF)

#1 HITS

This index to *Billboard's* #1 country hits (1944-92) shows where those songs can be found on CD. Each entry begins with the #1 song, followed (in order) by the year it topped the chart, the artist who made the #1 recording, the CDs that offer recordings of this song by this artist (various artist packages are indicated by "VA"), and the record labels that issue these discs.

The index is confined strictly to #1 *recordings*. Thus, for example, Buck Owens's original 1960 version of "Above and Beyond," which predates Rodney Crowell's #1 hit but got no higher than #3 on the chart, is not listed. Also note that in some cases the CDs listed may not contain the original hit version but a later re-recording by the same artist. Finally, even where there is no current CD version of the #1 hit, we have still listed the #1 song for the sake of completeness. Consult the individual reviews for more detailed information. Happy hunting.

Abilene (1963) George Hamilton IV: VA—*Country USA 1963* (Time Life); VA—*Billboard Top Country Hits—1963* (Rhino)

Above and Beyond (1989) Rodney Crowell. *Diamonds & Dirt* (Columbia)

Ace In The Hole (1989) George Strait: *Ten Strait Hits* (MCA); *Beyond The Blue Neon* (MCA)

Achy Breaky Heart (1992) Billy Ray Cyrus: *Some Gave All* (Mercury)

Act Naturally (1963) Buck Owens: *Live At Carnegie Hall* (CMF); VA—*Billboard Top Country Hits—1963* (Rhino); *All-Time Greatest, Vol. 1* (Capitol-Curb); *The Buck Owens Collection, 1959-1990* (Rhino); VA—*Country USA 1963* (Time Life)

Addicted (1988) Dan Seals: *Greatest Hits* (Liberty); *Rage On* (Liberty)

After All The Good Is Gone (1976) Conway Twitty: *Greatest Hits, Vol. 2* (MCA)

After All This Time (1989) Rodney Crowell: *Diamonds & Dirt* (Columbia)

After The Fire Is Gone (1971) Conway Twitty & Loretta Lynn: *Loretta Lynn Country Music Hall Of Fame* (MCA); *The Very Best Of Loretta Lynn & Conway Twitty* (MCA); VA—*Country USA 1971* (Time Life); VA—*Contemporary Country: The Early '70s—Pure Gold* (Time Life); VA—*Classic Country Music* (Smithsonian)

Ain't Misbehavin' (1986) Hank Williams Jr.:

Greatest Hits III (Warner-Curb); *Five-O* (Warner-Curb); *The Bocephus Box* (Curb/Capricorn)

Ain't She Somethin' Else (1985) Conway Twitty

Alabam (1960) Cowboy Copas: VA—*Country USA 1960* (Time Life)

All For The Love Of Sunshine (1970) Hank Williams Jr.: *Living Proof: The MGM Recordings 1963-1975* (Mercury)

All I Ever Need Is You (1979) Kenny Rogers & Dottie West: *Classics* (EMI)

All I Have To Do Is Dream (1958) The Everly Brothers: *The Reunion Concert* (Mercury); *The Very Best Of The Everly Brothers* (Warner Bros.); *All They Had To Do Was Dream* (Rhino); VA—*Country USA 1958* (Time Life); *Fabulous Style Of The Everly Brothers* (Rhino); *Cadence Classics—Their 20 Greatest Hits* (Rhino); *All-Time Greatest Hits* (Capitol-Curb)

All I Have To Offer You Is Me (1969) Charley Pride: *The Best Of Charley Pride* (RCA); VA—*Country USA 1969* (Time Life)

All My Ex's Live In Texas (1987) George Strait: *George Strait Greatest Hits, Vol. II* (MCA); *Ocean Front Property* (MCA)

All My Rowdy Friends (Have Settled Down) (1981) Hank Williams Jr.: *Hank 'Live'* (Warner-Curb); VA—*Contemporary Country: The Early '80s—Pure Gold* (Time Life); *Hank Williams, Jr.'s*

Greatest Hits (Warner Bros.); *The Pressure Is On* (Warner-Curb)

All Roads Lead To You (1981) Steve Wariner: *Greatest Hits* (RCA)

All Shook Up (1957) Elvis Presley: *Elvis—In Person* (RCA); *Top Ten Hits* (RCA); *Elvis' Golden Records, Vol. 1* (RCA); *The King Of Rock & Roll: The Complete 50s Masters* (RCA); *Elvis—NBC-TV Special* (RCA); *Elvis Presley As Recorded Live At Madison Square Garden* (RCA); *Number One Hits* (RCA)

All The Gold In California (1979) Larry Gatlin & The Gatlin Brothers: *Greatest Hits Encore* (Capitol); *Live At 8:00* (Capitol); *17 Greatest Hits* (Columbia); *Greatest Hits, Vol. II* (Columbia)

All The Time (1967) Jack Greene: VA—*Billboard Top Country Hits—1967* (Rhino)

All These Things (1976) Joe Stampley: VA—*Contemporary Country: The Mid-'70s—Pure Gold* (Time Life)

Almost Persuaded (1966) David Houston: VA—*Columbia Country Classics, Vol. 4: The Nashville Sound* (Columbia); VA—*Country USA 1966* (Time Life); VA—*Billboard Top Country Hits—1966* (Rhino); *American Originals* (Columbia)

Alone With You (1958) Faron Young: VA—*Country USA 1958* (Time Life); *All-Time Greatest Hits* (Curb); *Greatest Hits, Vol. 1-3* (Step One)

Already It's Heaven (1968) David Houston: *American Originals* (Columbia)

Always Have Always Will (1986) Janie Frickie

Always Late (With Your Kisses) (1951) Lefty Frizzell: *The Best Of Lefty Frizzell* (Rhino); *American Originals* (Columbia); VA—*Country USA 1951* (Time Life)

Always On My Mind (1982) Willie Nelson: *Greatest Hits and Some That Will Be* (Columbia); *Always on My Mind* (Columbia); VA—*Contemporary Country: The Early '80s—Hot Hits* (Time Life)

Always Wanting You (1975) Merle Haggard: *Capitol Collector's Series* (Capitol); *Very Best Of Merle Haggard* (Capitol)

Am I Blue (1987) George Strait: *Ocean Front Property* (MCA); *Greatest Hits, Vol. II* (MCA)

Am I Losing You (1981) Ronnie Milsap: *Greatest Hits, Vol. 2* (RCA)

Amanda (1979) Waylon Jennings: *Greatest Hits* (RCA); VA—*Contemporary Country: The Late '70s—Pure Gold* (Time Life)

Amazing Love (1973) Charley Pride

American Made (1983) The Oak Ridge Boys: VA—*Contemporary Country: The Early '80s* (Time Life); *American Made/Deliver* (MCA); *Greatest Hits, Vol. 2* (MCA); *The Oak Ridge Boys Collection* (MCA)

Among My Souvenirs (1976) Marty Robbins: *Essential Marty Robbins, 1951-1982* (Columbia)

Angel Flying Too Close To The Ground (1981) Willie Nelson: *Greatest Hits & Some That Will Be* (Columbia); *Honeysuckle Rose* (Columbia)

Angel In Disguise (1984) Earl Thomas Conley: *Greatest Hits* (RCA)

Another Lonely Song (1974) Tammy Wynette: *Anniversary: 20 Years Of Hits* (Epic); *Tears Of Fire—The 25th Anniversary Collection* (Epic)

Any Day Now (1982) Ronnie Milsap: *Greatest Hits, Vol. 2* (RCA); *Inside Ronnie Milsap* (RCA); VA—*Contemporary Country: The Early '80s—Hot Hits* (Time Life)

Anymore (1991) Travis Tritt: *It's All About To Change* (Warner Bros.)

Anytime (1948) Eddy Arnold: *The Best of Eddy Arnold* (RCA)

Are You Ever Gonna Love Me (1989) Holly Dunn: *Blue Rose Of Texas* (Warner Bros.)

Are You Happy Baby (1981) Dottie West

Are You On The Road To Lovin' Me Again (1980) Debby Boone

Are You Sure Hank Done It This Way (1975) Waylon Jennings: VA—*Contemporary Country: The Mid-'70s* (Time Life); *Greatest Hits* (RCA)

Are You Teasing Me (1952) Carl Smith: VA—*Country USA 1952* (Time Life); *Essential Carl Smith, 1950-1956* (Columbia)

As Long As I'm Rockin' With You (1984) John Conlee: *John Conlee's Greatest Hits, Vol. 2* (MCA); *Best Of John Conlee* (Capitol/Curb)

As Soon As I Hang Up The Phone (1974) Conway Twitty & Loretta Lynn: *The Very Best Of Loretta Lynn & Conway Twitty* (MCA)

At Mail Call Today (1945) Gene Autry

B.J. The D.J. (1964) Stonewall Jackson

Baby, Baby (I Know You're A Lady) (1970) David Houston: *American Originals* (Columbia)

Baby Blue (1988) George Strait: *If You Ain't Lovin' (You Ain't Livin')* (MCA); *Ten Strait Hits* (MCA)

Baby Bye Bye (1985) Gary Morris: *Hits* (Warner Bros.)

Baby, What About You (1983) Crystal Gayle: *The Best Of Crystal Gayle* (Warner Bros.)

Baby's Got A New Baby (1987) Schuyler-Knobloch-Overstreet

Baby's Got Her Blue Jeans On (1985) Mel McDaniel: *Greatest Hits* (Capitol); VA—*Contemporary Country: The Mid-'80s* (Time Life)

Baby's Gotten Good At Goodbye (1989) George Strait: *Ten Strait Hits* (MCA); *Beyond The Blue Neon* (MCA)

Back Home Again (1974) John Denver: *Back Home Again* (RCA); *John Denver's Greatest Hits, Vol. 2* (RCA)

Back Street Affair (1952) Webb Pierce: VA—*Country USA 1952* (Time Life)

Backside Of Thirty (1979) John Conlee: VA—*Contemporary Country: The Late '70s—Pure Gold* (Time Life)

Ballad Of A Teenage Queen (1958) Johnny Cash: *The Essential Johnny Cash* (Columbia); *The Best Of Johnny Cash* (Capitol/Curb); VA—*Sun's Greatest Hits* (RCA); VA—*Country USA 1958* (Time Life); VA—*Legends* (Dunhill); *Sun Years* (Rhino)

The Ballad Of Jed Clampett (1963) Lester Flatt & Earl Scruggs: VA—*Columbia Country Classics, Vol. 3: Americana* (Columbia); VA—*Country USA 1962* (Time Life)

Bar Room Buddies (1980) Merle Haggard & Clint Eastwood

The Bargain Store (1975) Dolly Parton: *The Best Of Dolly Parton* (RCA); *Collector's Series* (RCA)

The Battle Of New Orleans (1959) Johnny Horton: VA—*Billboard Top Country Hits—1959* (Rhino); *Greatest Hits* (Columbia); VA—*Columbia Country Classics, Vol. 3: Americana* (Columbia); VA—*Country USA 1959* (Time Life); VA—*Classic Country Music* (Smithsonian); *American Originals* (Columbia)

Bayou Boys (1989) Eddy Raven: *The Best Of Eddy Raven* (Liberty); *Temporary Sanity* (Liberty)

Bedtime Story (1972) Tammy Wynette: *Tears Of Fire—The 25th Anniversary Collection* (Epic); *Anniversary: 20 Years Of Hits* (Epic); *Biggest Hits* (Epic)

Before The Next Teardrop Falls (1975) Freddy Fender: VA—*Contemporary Country: The Mid-'70s* (Time Life); *Freddy Fender Collection* (Reprise)

Before You Go (1965) Buck Owens: VA—*Country USA 1965* (Time Life); VA—*Billboard Top Country Hits—1965* (Rhino); *The Buck Owens Collection, 1959-1990* (Rhino); *All-Time Greatest, Vol. 1* (Capitol/Curb)

Begging To You (1964) Marty Robbins: VA—*Billboard Top Country Hits—1964* (Rhino); *Essential Marty Robbins, 1951-1982* (Columbia); VA—*Country USA 1963* (Time Life)

Behind Closed Doors (1973) Charlie Rich: *American Originals* (Columbia); VA—*Contemporary Country: The Early '70s* (Time Life); *Greatest Hits* (Epic); *Behind Closed Doors* (Epic)

Behind the Tear (1965) Sonny James: VA—*Billboard Top Country Hits—1965* (Rhino); VA—*Country USA 1965* (Time Life)

Beneath Still Waters (1980) Emmylou Harris: VA—*Classic Country Music* (Smithsonian); *Profile 2: The Best Of Emmylou Harris* (Warner Bros.); *Blue Kentucky Girl* (Warner Bros.)

The Best Year Of My Life (1985) Eddie Rabbitt: *The Best Year Of My Life* (Liberty)

Bet Your Heart On Me (1981) Johnny Lee

Better Man (1989) Clint Black: *Killin' Time* (RCA); VA—*Contemporary Country: The Late '80s* (Time Life)

Big Bad John (1961) Jimmy Dean: VA—*Columbia Country Classics, Vol. 3: Americana* (Columbia); VA—*Billboard Top Country Hits—1961* (Rhino); VA—*Country USA 1961* (Time Life); VA—*Classic Country Music* (Smithsonian); *American Originals* (Columbia)

Big City (1982) Merle Haggard: *His Epic Hits—First Eleven* (Epic); VA—*Columbia Country Classics, Vol. 5: A New Tradition* (Columbia); VA—*Contemporary Country: The Early '80s* (Time Life); *Big City* (Epic)

Big Wheels in The Moonlight (1989) Dan Seals: *Rage On* (Liberty); *Greatest Hits* (Liberty)

Billy Bayou (1959) Jim Reeves: *He'll Have To Go & Other Favorites* (RCA); *The Best Of Jim Reeves* (RCA); *Welcome To My World: The Essential Jim Reeves* (RCA); VA—*Billboard Top Country Hits 1959* (Rhino); *Live At The Opry* (CMF)

Bimbo (1954) Jim Reeves: *Four Walls (The Legend Begins)* (RCA); VA—*Country USA 1953* (Time Life); *Live At The Opry* (CMF)

Bird Dog (1958) The Everly Brothers: *Fabulous Style Of The Everly Brothers* (Warner Bros.); *The Very Best of The Everly Brothers* (Warner Bros.); *Cadence Classics—Their 20 Greatest Hits* (Rhino); *All-Time Greatest Hits* (Capitol/Curb); VA—*Country USA 1958* (Time Life)

Birmingham Bounce (1950) Red Foley: VA—*Country USA 1950* (Time Life)

Black Sheep (1983) John Anderson: *Greatest Hits* (Warner Bros.)

Blanket on The Ground (1975) Billie Jo Spears

Bless Your Heart (1972) Freddie Hart

Blessed Are The Believers (1981) Anne Murray: *Anne Murray's Country Hits* (Liberty); *15 Of The Best* (Liberty); *Greatest Hits, Vol. II* (Liberty)

Blood Red and Goin' Down (1973) Tanya Tucker: *Tanya Tucker's Greatest Hits* (Columbia); *Greatest Hits Encore* (Liberty)

Blue Blue Day (1958) Don Gibson: *18 Greatest Hits* (Capitol/Curb); VA—*Country USA 1958* (Time Life); *All-Time Greatest Hits* (RCA)

Blue Christmas (1950) Ernest Tubb: VA—*Billboard Greatest Country Christmas Hits* (Rhino)

Blue Eyes Crying In The Rain (1975) Willie Nelson: *Red Headed Stranger* (Columbia); *Greatest Hits & Some That Will Be* (Columbia); *Honeysuckle Rose* (Columbia); VA—*Contemporary Country: The Mid-'70s* (Time Life)

Blue Moon With Heartache (1982) Rosanne Cash: *Seven Year Ache* (Columbia); VA—*Contemporary Country: The Early '80s—Pure Gold* (Time Life); *Hits 1979-1989* (Columbia)

Blue Side of Lonesome (1966) Jim Reeves: VA—*Country USA 1966* (Time Life)

Blue Skies (1978) Willie Nelson: VA—*Contemporary Country: The Late '70s* (Time Life); *Stardust* (Columbia)

Blue Suede Shoes (1956) Carl Perkins: VA—*Sun Story* (Rhino); VA—*Sun's Greatest Hits* (RCA); VA—*Country USA 1956* (Time Life); VA—*Rock This Town: Rockabilly Hits, Vol. 1* (Rhino); VA—*Legends* (Dunhill); *Original Sun Greatest Hits* (Rhino)

Blues Stay Away From Me (1950) Delmore Bros.

Bluest Eyes In Texas (1988) Restless Heart: *Big Dreams In A Small Town* (RCA); *The Best Of Restless Heart* (RCA); VA—*Contemporary Country: The Late '80s* (Time Life)

Bobbie Sue (1982) The Oak Ridge Boys: VA—*Contemporary Country: The Early '80s—Hot Hits* (Time Life); *Greatest Hits 3* (MCA); *Greatest Hits, Vol. 2* (MCA); *Bobbie Sue* (MCA)

Boot Scootin' Boogie (1992) Brooks & Dunn: *Brand New Man* (Arista)

Bop (1986) Dan Seals: *The Best Of Dan Seals* (Liberty); *Greatest Hits* (Liberty); *I Won't Be Blue Anymore* (EMI); VA—*Contemporary Country: The Mid-'80s* (Time Life)

Born To Be With You (1968) Sonny James

Born To Boogie (1987) Hank Williams Jr.: *The Bocephus Box* (Curb/Capricorn); VA—*Contemporary Country: The Late '80s—Pure Gold* (Time Life); *Greatest Hits III* (Warner/Curb); *Born To Boogie* (Warner/Curb)

Both To Each Other (Friends & Lovers) (1986) Eddie Rabbitt & Juice Newton: *Juice Newton Old Flame* (RCA)

Bouquet Of Roses (1948) Eddy Arnold: *The Best Of Eddy Arnold* (RCA)

A Boy Named Sue (1969) Johnny Cash: VA—*Country USA 1969* (Time Life); *The Best Of Johnny Cash* (Capitol/Curb); *The Essential Johnny Cash* (Columbia); VA—*Columbia Country Classics, Vol.3: Americana* (Columbia); *Johnny Cash At Folsom Prison & San Quentin* (Columbia); *Columbia Records 1958-1986* (Columbia); *Biggest Hits* (Columbia)

Brand New Man (1991) Brooks & Dunn: *Brand New Man* (Arista)

Branded Man (1967) Merle Haggard: *More Of The Best* (Rhino); VA—*Country USA 1967* (Time Life)

The Bridge Washed Out (1965) Warner Mack

Bright Lights, Big City (1971) Sonny James: *Greatest Hits* (Capitol/Curb); VA—*Country USA 1971* (Time Life)

Bring It On Home To Me (1976) Mickey Gilley: *Ten Years Of Hits* (Epic)

Broken Down In Tiny Pieces (1977) Billy "Crash" Craddock

Broken Hearted Me (1979) Anne Murray: *15 Of The Best* (Liberty); *Songs Of The Heart* (Capitol);

Greatest Hits (Liberty)

Brother Jukebox (1991) Mark Chesnutt: *Too Cold At Home* (MCA)

Buckaroo (1965) Buck Owens & The Buckaroos: *Live At Carnegie Hall* (CMF); VA—*Billboard Top Country Hits—1965* (Rhino); *The Buck Owens Collection, 1959-1990* (Rhino)

Burnin' Old Memories (1989) Kathy Mattea:*Willow In The Wind* (Mercury)

But You Know I Love You (1981) Dolly Parton: *The Best There Is* (RCA); *Greatest Hits* (RCA)

Bye Bye Love (1957) The Everly Brothers: *Everly Brothers* (Rhino); VA—*Classic Country Music* (Smithsonian); VA—*Country USA 1957* (Time Life); *All-Time Greatest Hits* (Capitol/Curb); *Cadence Classics—Their 20 Greatest Hits* (Rhino); *The Very Best Of The Everly Brothers* (Warner Bros.); *The Reunion Concert* (Mercury)

Cajun Moon (1986) Ricky Skaggs: *Live In London* (Epic)

Candy Kisses (1949) George Morgan: *American Originals* (Columbia)

Can't Even Get The Blues (1983) Reba McEntire: *The Best Of Reba McEntire* (Mercury); VA—*Contemporary Country: The Early '80s—Pure Gold* (Time Life); *Unlimited* (Mercury)

Can't Keep A Good Man Down (1985) Alabama: *Forty Hour Week* (RCA); *Alabama 'Live'* (RCA)

Can't Stop My Heart From Loving You (1987) The O'Kanes: *The O'Kanes* (Columbia)

Caribbean (1953) Mitchell Torok

Carolyn (1972) Merle Haggard: *Very Best Of Merle Haggard* (Capitol); VA—*Country USA 1971* (Time Life)

Cathy's Clown (1989) Reba McEntire: *Sweet Sixteen* (MCA)

Cattle Call (1955) Eddy Arnold: *The Best Of Eddy Arnold* (RCA); *Last Of The Love Song Singers: Then & Now* (RCA); VA—*Classic Country Music* (Smithsonian); VA—*Country USA 1955* (Time Life)

Chains (1990) Patty Loveless: *Honky Tonk Angel* (MCA)

The Chair (1985) George Strait: VA—*Contemporary Country: The Mid-'80s—Hot Hits* (Time Life); *Something Special* (MCA); *Greatest Hits, Vol. II* (MCA)

Chance Of Lovin' You (1984) Earl Thomas Conley: *Treadin' Water* (RCA); *Greatest Hits, Vol. II* (RCA)

Change Of Heart (1989) The Judds: *The Judds Greatest Hits* (RCA); VA—*Contemporary Country: The Late '80s—Pure Gold* (Time Life); *The Judds Collection 1983-1990* (RCA); *The Judds (Wynonna & Naomi)* (RCA)

Chantilly Lace (1972) Jerry Lee Lewis: *Rocket 88* (Tomato)

Charlie's Shoes (1962) Billy Walker: VA—*Columbia Country Classics, Vol. 4: The Nashville Sound* (Columbia); VA—*Country USA 1962* (Time Life)

Chattanoogie Shoe Shine Boy (1950) Red Foley: VA—*Country USA 1950* (Time Life); *Country Music Hall Of Fame* (MCA)

Cherokee Maiden (1976) Merle Haggard: *Capitol Collectors Series* (Capitol)

The Church On The Cumberland Road (1989) Shenandoah: *Greatest Hits* (Columbia); VA—*Contemporary Country: The Late '80s—Pure Gold* (Time Life); *The Road Not Taken* (Columbia)

City Lights (1958) Ray Price: *Ray Price's Greatest Hits* (Columbia); *Greatest Hits, Vols. 1-3* (Step

One); *Essential Ray Price, 1957-1962* (Columbia); VA—*Country USA 1958* (Time Life)

City Lights (1975) Mickey Gilley: *Ten Years Of Hits* (Epic); *Gilley's Greatest Hits, Vol. 1* (Epic)

City Of New Orleans (1984) Willie Nelson: *City Of New Orleans* (Columbia)

Close Enough To Perfect (1982) Alabama: *Mountain Music* (RCA)

Closer You Get (1983) Alabama: VA—*Contemporary Country: The Early '80s—Pure Gold* (Time Life); *The Closer You Get* (RCA); *Greatest Hits, Vol. II* (RCA)

The Clown (1982) Conway Twitty: *No. 1's: The Warner Bros. Years* (Warner Bros.)

Coal Miner's Daughter (1970) Loretta Lynn: VA—*Contemporary Country: The Early '70s* (Time Life); VA—*Country USA 1970* (Time Life); *Coal Miner's Daughter* (MCA); *Loretta Lynn's Greatest Hits, Vol. 2* (MCA); VA—*Classic Country Music* (Smithsonian); *Country Music Hall Of Fame* (MCA)

Coca Cola Cowboy (1979) Mel Tillis: *Greatest Hits* (Curb)

Cold, Cold Heart (1951) Hank Williams: *40 Greatest Hits* (Polydor); *The Original Singles Collection...Plus* (PolyGram); VA—*Country USA 1951* (Time Life); *Long Gone Lonesome Blues (Aug. 1949-Dec. 1950)* (Polydor)

Come From The Heart (1989) Kathy Mattea: *Willow In The Wind* (Mercury)

Come Live With Me (1973) Roy Clark

Come Next Monday (1990) K. T. Oslin: *Love In A Small Town* (RCA)

Come With Me (1979) Waylon Jennings: *Waylon's Greatest Hits, Vol. 2* (RCA)

Common Man (1983) John Conlee: VA—*Contemporary Country: The Early '80s—Hot Hits* (Time Life); *Best Of John Conlee* (Capitol/Curb); *John Conlee's Greatest Hits* (MCA)

Convoy (1975) C. W. McCall: VA—*Contemporary Country: The Mid-'70s—Pure Gold* (Time Life)

Could I Have This Dance (1980) Anne Murray: *Contemporary Country: The Early '80s* (Time Life); *15 Of The Best* (Liberty); *Greatest Hits* (Liberty)

Country Boy (1985) Ricky Skaggs: *Country Boy* (Epic); *Live In London* (Epic); VA—*Contemporary Country: The Mid-'80s* (Time Life)

Country Bumpkin (1974) Cal Smith: VA—*Contemporary Country: The Mid-'70s—Pure Gold* (Time Life)

Country Girl (1959) Faron Young: *Greatest Hits, Vols. 1-3* (Step One); VA—*Billboard Top Country Hits—1959* (Rhino); *All-Time Greatest Hits* (Capitol/Curb); VA—*Country USA 1959* (Time Life)

Country Girls (1985) John Schneider: *Greatest Hits* (MCA); *Too Good To Stop Now* (MCA)

Country Is (1974) Tom T. Hall

Coward Of The County (1980) Kenny Rogers: *Kenny Rogers' Greatest Hits* (EMI); *Twenty Greatest Hits* (EMI); *20 Great Years* (Reprise); *Greatest Country Hits* (Capitol/Curb)

Cowboys And Clowns (1980) Ronnie Milsap

Crazy (1985) Kenny Rogers: *What About Me* (RCA); *Greatest Hits* (RCA)

Crazy Arms (1956) Ray Price: *Ray Price's Greatest Hits* (Columbia); VA—*Columbia Country Classics, Vol. 2: Honky Tonk Heroes* (Columbia); *Greatest Hits, Vols. 1-3* (Step One); *The Essential Ray Price, 1951-1962* (Columbia); VA—*Country USA 1956* (Time Life)

Crazy For Your Love (1985) Exile: *Greatest Hits* (Epic)

Cry (1986) Crystal Gayle: *The Best Of Crystal Gayle* (Warner Bros.); VA—*Contemporary Country: The Mid-'80s—Pure Gold* (Time Life)

Cry, Cry, Cry (1988) Highway 101: *Greatest Hits* (Warner Bros.); *Contemporary Country: The Late '80s* (Time Life); *Highway 101* (Warner Bros.)

Cry Myself To Sleep (1987) The Judds: *The Judds Greatest Hits* (RCA); VA—*Contemporary Country: The Late '80s* (Time Life); *The Judds Collection 1983-1990* (RCA); *Rockin' With The Rhythm* (RCA)

Crying My Heart Out Over You (1982) Ricky Skaggs: *Waitin' For The Sun To Shine* (Epic); VA—*Contemporary Country: The Early '80s* (Time Life)

Daddy Frank (The Guitar Man) (1971) Merle Haggard: *Capitol Collector's Series* (Capitol); VA—*Country USA 1971* (Time Life); *Best Of The Best Of Merle Haggard* (Capitol)

Daddy Sang Bass (1969) Johnny Cash: VA—*Columbia Country Classics, Vol. 5: A New Tradition* (Columbia); VA—*Country USA 1969* (Time Life); *The Essential Johnny Cash* (Columbia)

Daddy's Come Around (1991) Paul Overstreet: *Heroes* (RCA)

Dallas (1992) Alan Jackson: *Don't Rock The Jukebox* (Arista)

The Dance (1990) Garth Brooks: *Garth Brooks* (Capitol)

Dancin' Cowboys (1980) The Bellamy Brothers: VA—*Contemporary Country: The Early '80s—Hot Hits* (Time Life); *Greatest Hits* (MCA)

Dang Me (1964) Roger Miller: VA—*Country USA 1964* (Time Life); *Golden Hits* (Smash); *The Best Of Roger Miller, Vol. 2—King Of The Road* (Mercury); VA—*Billboard Top Country Hits—1964* (Rhino)

Darlene (1988) T. Graham Brown: VA—*Contemporary Country: The Late '80s—Pure Gold* (Time Life); *Come As You Were* (Capitol); *Greatest Hits* (Capitol)

Daydreams About Night Things (1975) Ronnie Milsap: *Collector's Series* (RCA), *Greatest Hits* (RCA)

Daytime Friends (1977) Kenny Rogers: *Twenty Greatest Hits* (EMI); *Ten Years Of Gold* (EMI)

A Dear John Letter (1953) Jean Shepard & Ferlin Husky: *Ferlin Husky Greatest Hits* (Curb); VA—*Country USA 1953* (Time Life)

Deeper Than The Holler (1989) Randy Travis: *Old 8x10* (Warner Bros.); *Greatest Hits, Vol. 1* (Warner Bros.); VA—*Contemporary Country: The Late '80s—Pure Gold* (Time Life)

Desperado Love (1986) Conway Twitty: VA—*Contemporary Country: The Mid-'80s—Pure Gold* (Time Life); *No. 1's: The Warner Bros. Years* (Warner Bros.)

Devil In The Bottle (1975) T. G. Sheppard

The Devil Went Down To Georgia (1979) The Charlie Daniels Band: *Million Mile Reflections* (Epic); *Decade Of Hits* (Epic); VA—*Columbia Country Classics, Vol. 3: Americana* (Columbia); VA—*Contemporary Country: The Late '70s* (Time Life); VA—*Classic Country Music* (Smithsonian)

Devil Woman (1962) Marty Robbins: *Lifetime Of Song (1951-1982)* (Columbia); VA—*Country USA 1962* (Time Life); *Essential Marty Robbins, 1951-1982* (Columbia); VA—*Billboard Top Country Hits—1962* (Rhino); VA—*Columbia Country Classics, Vol. 4: The Nashville Sound* (Columbia);

Marty Robbins' All-Time Greatest Hits (Columbia)

Diggin' Up Bones (1986) Randy Travis: VA—*Contemporary Country: The Mid-'80s—Pure Gold* (Time Life); *Greatest Hits, Vol. 2* (Warner Bros.); *Storms Of Life* (Warner Bros.)

Distant Drums (1966) Jim Reeves: VA—*Billboard Top Country Hits—1966* (Rhino); VA—*Country USA 1966* (Time Life)

D-I-V-O-R-C-E (1968) Tammy Wynette: VA—*Country USA 1968* (Time Life); *Tears Of Fire—The 25th Anniversary Collection* (Epic); *Biggest Hits* (Epic); *Tammy's Greatest Hits, Vol. 1* (Epic); *Anniversary: 20 Years Of Hits* (Epic)

Divorce Me C.O.D. (1946) Merle Travis: *The Best of Merle Travis* (Rhino)

Dixie On My Mind (1981) Hank Williams, Jr.: *Hank Williams, Jr.'s Greatest Hits* (Warner Bros.); *Rowdy* (Warner/Curb); *The Bocephus Box* (Curb/Capricorn)

Dixie Road (1985) Lee Greenwood: *Greatest Hits* (MCA); VA—*Contemporary Country: The Mid-'80s* (Time Life)

Dixieland Delight (1983) Alabama: *Greatest Hits, Vol. II* (RCA); *The Closer You Get* (RCA)

Do Ya' (1987) K. T. Oslin: *80's Ladies* (RCA); *Contemporary Country: The Late '80s—Pure Gold* (Time Life)

Do You Know You Are My Sunshine (1978) The Statler Brothers: *The Best Of The Statler Brothers Rides Again, Vol. 2* (Mercury); VA—*Contemporary Country: The Late '70s—Pure Gold* (Time Life)

Do You Love As Good As You Look (1981) The Bellamy Brothers: *Greatest Hits* (MCA)

(Do You Love Me) Just Say Yes (1988) Highway 101: *Greatest Hits* (Warner Bros.); *Highway 101²* (Warner Bros.)

Do You Wanna Go To Heaven (1980) T. G. Sheppard: *All-Time Greatest Hits* (Warner Bros.)

Does Fort Worth Ever Cross Your Mind (1985) George Strait: *Does Fort Worth Ever Cross Your Mind* (MCA); *George Strait Greatest Hits, Vol. II* (MCA); VA—*Contemporary Country: The Mid '80s* (Time Life)

Don't Be Cruel (1956) Elvis Presley: *'Heartbreak Hotel,' 'Hound Dog' & Other Top Ten Hits* (RCA); *Great Performances* (RCA) *Collector's Gold* (RCA); *The King Of Rock & Roll: The Complete 50s Masters* (RCA); *Million Dollar Quartet* (RCA); *Elvis—In Concert* (RCA); *Worldwide 50 Gold Award Hits, Vols. 1 & 2* (RCA); *Number One Hits* (RCA); *Elvis Presley As Recorded Live At Madison Square Garden* (RCA); *Top Ten Hits* (RCA); *Elvis' Golden Records, Vol. 1* (RCA); *Elvis—NBC-TV Special* (RCA)

Don't Break The Heart That Loves You (1978) Margo Smith

Don't Call Him A Cowboy (1985) Conway Twitty: *No. 1's: The Warner Bros. Years* (Warner Bros.); *Greatest Hits* (Capitol/Curb); *Silver Anniversary Collection* (MCA)

Don't Cheat In Our Hometown (1984) Ricky Skaggs: *Don't Cheat In Our Hometown* (Epic)

Don't Close Your Eyes (1988) Keith Whitley: *Don't Close Your Eyes* (RCA); *Greatest Hits* (RCA); VA—*Contemporary Country: The Late '80s—Pure Gold* (Time Life)

Don't Come Home A' Drinkin' (With Lovin' On Your Mind) (1967) Loretta Lynn: *Greatest Hits* (MCA); VA—*Country USA 1966* (Time Life); *Country Music Hall Of Fame* (MCA); *Loretta Lynn's Greatest Hits* (MCA)

Don't Fight The Feelings Of Love (1973)
Charley Pride
Don't Go To Strangers (1987) T. Graham Brown:
Greatest Hits (Capitol); *I Tell It Like It Used To Be*
(Capitol)
Don't It Make My Brown Eyes Blue (1977)
Crystal Gayle: VA—*Contemporary Country: The
Late '70s* (Time Life); *All-Time Greatest Hits*
(Capitol/Curb); *Classic Crystal* (EMI)
Don't Just Stand There (1952) Carl Smith:
Essential Carl Smith, 1950-1956 (Columbia); VA—
Country USA 1952 (Time Life)
Don't Keep Me Hangin' On (1970) Sonny James:
The Best Of Sonny James (Capitol/Curb)
Don't Let Me Cross Over (1962) Carl & Pearl
Butler: VA—*Columbia Country Classics, Vol. 2:
Honky Tonk Heroes* (Columbia); VA—*Billboard Top
Country Hits—1963* (Rhino); VA—*Country USA
1962* (Time Life)
Don't Let Our Love Start Slippin' Away
(1992) Vince Gill: *I Still Believe In You* (MCA)
Don't Let The Stars Get In Your Eyes (1952)
Slim Willet
Don't Let The Stars Get In Your Eyes (1952)
Skeets McDonald: VA—*Country USA 1952* (Time
Life)
Don't Make It Easy For Me (1984) Earl Thomas
Conley: *Greatest Hits* (RCA)
Don't Rob Another Man's Castle (1949) Eddy
Arnold
Don't Rock The Jukebox (1991) Alan Jackson:
Don't Rock The Jukebox (Arista)
Don't Take It Away (1979) Conway Twitty: VA—
Contemporary Country: The Late '70s—Pure Gold
(Time Life); *Number Ones* (MCA)
Don't Take Your Guns To Town (1959) Johnny
Cash: *Johnny Cash's Greatest Hits* (Columbia);
The Fabulous Johnny Cash (Sony); *The Essential
Johnny Cash* (Columbia); VA—*Country USA 1959*
(Time Life); VA—*Columbia Country Classics, Vol.
3: Americana* (Columbia)
**Don't The Girls All Get Prettier At Closing
Time** (1976) Mickey Gilley: *Ten Years Of Hits*
(Epic); VA—*Contemporary Country: The Mid-'70s*
(Time Life)
Don't Underestimate My Love For You (1986)
Lee Greenwood: *Streamline* (MCA); *Greatest Hits,
Vol. 2* (MCA)
Don't We All Have The Right (1988) Ricky Van
Shelton: *Greatest Hits Plus* (Columbia); *Wild-Eyed
Dream* (Columbia)
Don't Worry (1961) Marty Robbins: *Marty
Robbins' All-Time Greatest Hits* (Columbia); VA—
Country USA 1961 (Time Life); *Essential Marty
Robbins, 1951-1982* (Columbia); *More Greatest
Hits* (Columbia); VA—*Billboard Top Counrty Hits—
1961* (Rhino)
Don't Worry 'Bout Me Baby (1982) Jane
Frickie: *17 Greatest Hits* (Columbia); *Greatest Hits*
(Columbia)
Don't You Ever Get Tired (Of Hurting Me)
(1989) Ronnie Milsap: *Stranger Things Have
Happened* (RCA)
Don't You Know How Much I Love You (1983)
Ronnie Milsap: *Greatest Hits, Vol. 2* (RCA); *Keyed
Up* (RCA)
The Door (1975) George Jones: VA—*Contemporary
Country: The Mid-'70s—Pure Gold* (Time Life);
Anniversary (Ten Years Of Hits) (Epic)
The Door Is Always Open (1976) Dave & Sugar
Down Home (1991) Alabama: *Pass It

On Down* (RCA)
Drifter (1981) Sylvia: *Greatest Hits (RCA)*
Drinkin' My Baby (Off My Mind) (1976) Eddie
Rabbitt: *Greatest Country Hits* (Curb/CEMA)
Drivin' My Life Away (1980) Eddie Rabbitt: *Ten
Years Of Greatest Hits* (Liberty); *All-Time Greatest
Hits* (Warner Bros.)
Easy Loving (1971) Freddie Hart: VA—
Contemporary Country: The Early '70s (Time Life);
VA—*Country USA 1971* (Time Life)
Easy On The Eyes (1952) Eddy Arnold: VA—
Country USA 1952 (Time Life)
Eddy's Song (1953) Eddy Arnold: VA—*Country
USA 1953* (Time Life)
Eighteen Wheels And A Dozen Roses (1988)
Kathy Mattea: *Untasted Honey* (Mercury); VA—
Contemporary Country: The Late '80s (Time Life);
A Collection Of Hits (Mercury)
El Paso (1959) Marty Robbins: *Marty Robbins' All-
Time Greatest Hits* (Columbia); VA—*Billboard Top
Country Hits—1960* (Rhino); *Gunfighter Ballads &
Trail Songs* (Columbia); VA—*Columbia Country
Classics, Vol. 3: Americana* (Columbia); *More
Greatest Hits* (Columbia); VA—*Classic Country
Music* (Smithsonian); *Biggest Hits* (Columbia);
VA—*Country USA 1959* (Time Life); *Essential
Marty Robbins, 1951-1982* (Columbia); VA—
Legends Of Country Guitar, Vol. 1 (Rhino)
El Paso City (1976) Marty Robbins: VA—*Columbia
Country Classics, Vol. 5: A New Tradition*
(Columbia); VA—*Contemporary Country: The Mid-
'70s* (Time Life); *Essential Marty Robbins, 1951-
1982* (Columbia)
Eleven Roses (1972) Hank Williams Jr.: VA—
Country USA 1972 (Time Life); *Living Proof: The
MGM Recordings 1963-1975* (Mercury); *The Best
Of Hank Williams, Jr., Vol. 1—Roots & Branches*
(Mercury)
Elizabeth (1984) The Statler Brothers: VA—
Contemporary Country: The Mid-'80s—Pure Gold
(Time Life); *The Statlers Greatest Hits* (Mercury);
Today (Mercury)
Elvira (1981) The Oak Ridge Boys: *Fancy Free*
(MCA); VA—*Contemporary Country: The Early
'80s—Pure Gold* (Time Life); *Greatest Hits, Vol. 2*
(MCA); *The Oak Ridge Boys Collection* (MCA)
Empty Arms (1971) Sonny James: VA—
Contemporary Country: The Early '70s (Time Life);
The Best Of Sonny James (Capitol/Curb); VA—
Country USA 1971 (Time Life)
Endlessly (1970) Sonny James: VA—*Country USA
1970* (Time Life); *The Best Of Sonny James*
(Capitol/Curb)
Even Tho' (1954) Webb Pierce: VA—*Country USA
1954* (Time Life)
Every Time Two Fools Collide (1978) Kenny
Rogers & Dottie West
Every Which Way But Loose (1979) Eddie
Rabbitt
Everybody's Had The Blues (1973) Merle
Haggard: *More Of The Best* (Rhino); *Very Best Of
Merle Haggard* (Capitol)
Everyday (1984) The Oak Ridge Boys: *Greatest
Hits, Vol. 2* (MCA)
Everything That Glitters (Is Not Gold) (1986)
Dan Seals: *The Best Of Dan Seals* (Liberty);
Greatest Hits (Liberty)
Face To Face (1988) Alabama: *Just Us* (RCA)
Faking Love (1983) T. G. Sheppard & Karen
Brooks: *T. G. Sheppard All-Time Greatest Hits*
(Warner Bros.)

Fallin' Again (1988) Alabama: *Just Us* (RCA); *Greatest Hits, Vol. 2* (RCA)

Famous Last Words Of A Fool (1988) George Strait: *If You Ain't Lovin' (You Ain't Livin')* (MCA); *Ten Strait Hits* (MCA)

Fancy Free (1981) The Oak Ridge Boys: *Fancy Free* (MCA); *Greatest Hits, Vol. 2* (MCA); *The Oak Ridge Boys Collection* (MCA)

Faster Horses (The Cowboy And The Poet) (1976) Tom T. Hall: VA—*Contemporary Country: The Mid-'70s—Pure Gold* (Time Life)

Feelin's (1975) Conway Twitty & Loretta Lynn: *The Very Best Of Loretta Lynn & Conway Twitty* (MCA)

Feels So Right (1981) Alabama: *Feels So Right* (RCA); *Greatest Hits* (RCA)

Fifteen Years Ago (1970) Conway Twitty: *Greatest Hits, Vol. 1* (MCA); VA—*Country USA 1970* (Time Life)

The Fightin' Side Of Me (1970) Merle Haggard: *Best Of The Best Of Merle Haggard* (Capitol); VA—*Contemporary Country: The Early '70s* (Time Life); *Very Best Of Merle Haggard* (Capitol); VA—*Country USA 1970* (Time Life); *All American* (Liberty); *Capitol Collector's Series* (Capitol)

Finally (1982) T. G. Sheppard: *All-Time Greatest Hits* (Warner Bros.)

Fire & Smoke (1981) Earl Thomas Conley: VA—*Contemporary Country: The Early '80s—Hot Hits* (Time Life); *Greatest Hits* (RCA); *Fire & Smoke* (RCA)

Fire I Can't Put Out (1983) George Strait: *Greatest Hits* (MCA); *Strait From The Heart* (MCA)

The First Thing Ev'ry Morning (And The Last Thing Ev'ry Night) (1965) Jimmy Dean: *American Originals* (Columbia); *Country Spotlight—Best Of Jimmy Dean* (Dominion)

Fishin' In The Dark (1987) Nitty Gritty Dirt Band: *Hold On* (Warner Bros.); VA—*Contemporary Country: The Late '80s* (Time Life); *More Great Dirt (Best Of The Nitty Gritty Dirt Band, Vol. II)* (Warner Bros.)

Fist City (1968) Loretta Lynn: *Loretta Lynn's Greatest Hits, Vol. 2* (MCA); *Country Music Hall Of Fame* (MCA); VA—*Country USA 1968* (Time Life)

Five Minutes (1990) Lorrie Morgan: *Leave The Light On* (BNA)

Flesh And Blood (1971) Johnny Cash: *Biggest Hits* (Columbia); *The Essential Johnny Cash* (Columbia); VA—*Contemporary Country: The Early '70s—Pure Gold* (Time Life)

Folsom Prison Blues (1968) Johnny Cash: VA—*Sun Story* (Rhino); *Sun Years* (Rhino); *Johnny Cash At Folsom Prison & San Quentin* (Columbia); *The Essential Johnny Cash* (Columbia); *The Best Of Johnny Cash* (Capitol/Curb); VA—*Sun's Greatest Hits* (RCA); VA—*Country USA 1968* (Time Life); *Columbia Records 1958-1986* (Columbia) VA—*Classic Country Music* (Smithsonian); VA—*Legends* (Dunhill)

Fool For Your Love (1983) Mickey Gilley

Fool Hearted Memory (1982) George Strait: *Strait From The Heart* (MCA); *Greatest Hits* (MCA)

For All The Wrong Reasons (1982) The Bellamy Brothers: *Greatest Hits* (MCA)

For Loving You (1967) Bill Anderson & Jan Howard: VA—*Billboard Top Country Hits—1967* (Rhino)

For My Broken Heart (1991) Reba McEntire: *For My Broken Heart* (MCA)

For The Good Times (1970) Ray Price: VA—*Contemporary Country: The Early '70s* (Time Life);

VA—*Classic Country Music* (Smithsonian); VA—*Country USA 1970* (Time Life); VA—*Columbia Country Classics, Vol. 4: The Nashville Sound* (Columbia); *Greatest Hits, Vols. 1-3* (Step One)

Forever And Ever, Amen (1987) Randy Travis: *Greatest Hits, Vol. 2* (Warner Bros.); *Always & Forever* (Warner Bros.)

Forever Together (1991) Randy Travis: *High Lonesome* (Warner Bros.)

Forever's As Far As I'll Go (1991) Alabama: *Pass It On Down* (RCA)

Forgiving You Was Easy (1985) Willie Nelson: VA—*Contemporary Country: The Mid-'80s—Hot Hits* (Time Life)

Forty Hour Week (For A Livin') (1985) Alabama: *Forty Hour Week* (RCA); *Greatest Hits* (RCA); VA—*Classic Country Music* (Smithsonian)

Four Walls (1957) Jim Reeves: *Welcome To My World: The Essential Jim Reeves* (RCA); *Four Walls (The Legend Begins)* (RCA); *Pure Gold* (RCA); *The Best Of Jim Reeves* (RCA); VA—*Country USA 1957* (Time Life); *Greatest Hits* (RCA); *He'll Have To Go & Other Favorites* (RCA); *Live At The Opry* (CMF)

Fourteen Karat Mind (1982) Gene Watson: VA—*Contemporary Country: The Early '80s—Pure Gold* (Time Life); *Greatest Hits* (MCA)

Fraulein (1957) Bobby Helms: VA—*Country USA 1957* (Time Life)

Friends (1981) Razzy Bailey

Friends In Low Places (1990) Garth Brooks: *No Fences* (Liberty)

From A Jack To A King (1989) Ricky Van Shelton: *Greatest Hits Plus* (Columbia); *Loving Proof* (Columbia)

The Fugitive (1967) Merle Haggard: *Capitol Collectors Series* (Capitol); *Rainbow Stew* (MCA); VA—*Billboard Top Country Hits—1967* (Rhino); VA—*Country USA 1967* (Time Life)

A Full Time Job (1952) Eddy Arnold: VA—*Country USA 1952* (Time Life)

Funny Face (1972) Donna Fargo

Galveston (1969) Glen Campbell: *The Best Of The Early Years* (Capitol/Curb); VA—*Country USA 1969* (Time Life); *Classics Collection* (Liberty); *The Best Of Glen Campbell* (Liberty)

The Gambler (1978) Kenny Rogers: *The Gambler* (EMI); *Kenny Rogers' Greatest Hits* (EMI); *Greatest Country Hits* (Capitol/Curb); *20 Great Years* (Reprise); *Twenty Greatest Hits* (EMI)

The Games That Daddies Play (1976) Conway Twitty: *Greatest Hits, Vol. 2* (MCA)

Georgia On My Mind (1978) Willie Nelson: VA—*Contemporary Country: The Late '70s—Pure Gold* (Time Life); *Stardust* (Columbia); *Greatest Hits & Some That Will Be* (Columbia); *Willie & Family Live* (Columbia)

Giddyup Go (1966) Red Sovine: *Giddy-Up-Go* (Hollywood)

Girl On The Billboard (1965) Del Reeves: VA—*Country USA 1965* (Time Life); VA—*Billboard Top Country Hits—1965* (Rhino)

Girls Night Out (1985) The Judds: *The Judds Greatest Hits* (RCA); *Why Not Me* (RCA); *Rockin' Country Hits* (RCA); *The Judds Collection 1983-1990* (RCA)

Give Me More, More, More (Of Your Kisses) (1952) Lefty Frizzell: VA—*Country USA 1952* (Time Life); *The Best Of Lefty Frizzell* (Rhino)

Give Me One More Chance (1984) Exile: *Greatest Hits* (Epic)

Give Me Wings (1987) Michael Johnson: *The Best Of Michael Johnson* (RCA)

Goin' Gone (1988) Kathy Mattea: *Untasted Honey* (Mercury); *A Collection Of Hits* (Mercury)

Going, Going, Gone (1984) Lee Greenwood: *Greatest Hits* (MCA); *Somebody's Gonna Love You* (MCA)

Going Where The Lonely Go (1983) Merle Haggard: *Going Where The Lonely Go* (Epic); *His Epic Hits—First Eleven* (Epic)

Golden Ring (1976) George Jones & Tammy Wynette: *Greatest Hits* (Epic); *Tammy Wynette Tears Of Fire—The 25th Anniversary Collection* (Epic); *Tammy Wynette Anniversary: 20 Years Of Hits* (Epic)

The Golden Rocket (1951) Hank Snow: VA—*Country USA 1951* (Time Life); *I'm Movin' On & Other Great Country Hits* (RCA)

Golden Tears (1979) Dave & Sugar: VA—*Contemporary Country: The Late '70s—Hot Hits* (Time Life)

Gone (1957) Ferlin Husky: *Greatest Hits* (Capitol/Curb); VA—*Country USA 1957* (Time Life); *Capitol Collector's Series* (Capitol)

Gone Too Far (1980) Eddie Rabbitt: *Ten Years Of Greatest Hits* (Liberty); *All-Time Greatest Hits* (Warner Bros.)

Gonna Take A Lot Of River (1988) The Oak Ridge Boys: *Greatest Hits 3* (MCA); *Monongahela* (MCA)

Good Hearted Woman (1976) Waylon Jennings & Willie Nelson: *The Outlaws* (RCA); *Willie Nelson Greatest Hits & Some That Will Be* (Columbia); *Waylon Jennings Greatest Hits* (RCA)

Good Lovin' (Makes It Right) (1971) Tammy Wynette: VA—*Country USA 1971* (Time Life); *Anniversary: Twenty-Five Years of Hits* (Epic); *Tears of Fire—The 25th Anniversary Collection* (Epic)

Good Times (1990) Dan Seals: *On Arrival* (Liberty); *Greatest Hits* (Liberty)

Good Woman Blues (1976) Mel Tillis: *Greatest Hits* (Capitol/Curb)

Goodnight, Irene (1950) Ernest Tubb & Red Foley: VA—*Country USA 1950* (Time Life)

Got My Heart Set On You (1986) John Conlee

Got The All Overs For You (All Over Me) (1972) Freddie Hart

The Grand Tour (1974) George Jones: VA—*Columbia Country Classics, Vol. 4: The Nashville Sound* (Columbia); VA—*Contemporary Country: The Mid-'70s* (Time Life); *Classic Country Music* (Smithsonian); *First Time Live* (Epic); *Super Hits* (Epic); *Anniversary (Ten Years Of Hits)* (Epic)

Grandma Harp (1972) Merle Haggard: *18 Rare Classics* (Capitol/Curb)

Grandpa (Tell Me 'Bout The Good Old Days) (1986) The Judds: *The Judds Collection 1983-1990* (RCA); *The Judds Greatest Hits* (RCA); *Rockin' With The Rhythm* (RCA); VA—*Classic Country Music* (Smithsonian)

Great Balls Of Fire (1958) Jerry Lee Lewis: *Rocket 88* (Tomato); VA—*Sun's Greatest Hits* (RCA); *Original Sun Greatest Hits* (Rhino); VA—*Sun Story* (Rhino); VA—*Legends* (Dunhill); *Jerry Lee Lewis: Live At The Star Club—Hamburg, 1964* (Rhino); *Jerry Lee's Greatest* (Rhino)

Guess Things Happen That Way (1958) Johnny Cash: *The Best Of Johnny Cash* (Capitol/Curb); *The Essential Johnny Cash* (Columbia); *Sun Years* (Rhino); VA—*Legends* (Dunhill); VA—*Country USA 1958* (Time Life)

Guitar Man (1981) Elvis Presley: VA—*Contemporary Country: The Early '80s—Hot Hits* (Time Life); *Elvis In Nashville* (RCA); *Elvis—NBC-TV Special* (RCA)

Guitar Polka (1946) Al Dexter

Hang On To Your Heart (1985) Exile: *Hang On To Your Heart* (Epic); *Greatest Hits* (Epic)

The Happiest Girl In The Whole U.S.A. (1972) Donna Fargo: VA—*Contemporary Country: The Early '70s* (Time Life); VA—*Country USA 1972* (Time Life)

Happy Birthday Darlin' (1979) Conway Twitty: *Number Ones* (MCA); VA—*Contemporary Country: The Late '70s* (Time Life)

Happy, Happy Birthday Baby (1986) Ronnie Milsap: *Lost In The Fifties Tonight* (RCA); *Greatest Hits, Vol. 3* (RCA)

Hard Rock Bottom Of Your Heart (1990) Randy Travis: *Greatest Hits, Vol. 1* (Warner Bros.); *No Holdin' Back* (Warner Bros.)

Harper Valley P.T.A. (1968) Jeannie C. Riley: VA—*Country USA 1968* (Time Life)

Have A Little Faith (1968) David Houston: *American Originals* (Columbia)

Have Mercy (1985) The Judds: *The Judds Collection 1983-1990* (RCA); VA—*Contemporary Country: The Mid-'80s—Pure Gold* (Time Life); *Rockin' With The Rhythm* (RCA); *The Judds Greatest Hits* (RCA)

He Got You (1982) Ronnie Milsap: *Inside Ronnie Milsap* (RCA)

He Loves Me All The Way (1970) Tammy Wynette: VA—*Country USA 1970* (Time Life); VA—*Contemporary Country: The Early '70s* (Time Life); *Tears Of Fire—The 25th Anniversary Collection* (Epic)

He Stopped Loving Her Today (1980) George Jones: VA—*Classic Country Music* (Smithsonian); VA—*Contemporary Country: The Early '80s* (Time Life); *Anniversary (Ten Years Of Hits)* (Epic); *First Time Live* (Epic); *I Am What I Am* (Epic); VA—*Columbia Country Classics, Vol. 5: A New Tradition* (Columbia); *Super Hits* (Epic)

He Thinks I Still Care (1974) Anne Murray: *Anne Murray's Country Hits* (Liberty)

A Headache Tomorrow (Or A Heartache Tonight) (1981) Mickey Gilley: *Biggest Hits* (Epic); *Ten Years Of Hits* (Epic)

Heart Healer (1977) Mel Tillis

Heartbeat In The Darkness (1986) Don Williams: *Greatest Country Hits* (Capitol/Curb); *Prime Cuts* (Capitol)

Heartbreak Hotel (1956) Elvis Presley: *Great Performances* (RCA); *'Heartbreak Hotel', 'Hound Dog,' & Other Top Ten Hits* (RCA); *Top Ten Hits* (RCA); *Number One Hits* (RCA); *Collector's Gold* (RCA); *The King Of Rock & Roll: The Complete 50s Masters* (RCA); *Elvis Presley As Recorded Live At Madison Square Garden* (RCA); *Country USA 1956* (Time Life); *Elvis' Golden Records, Vol. 2* (RCA); *Elvis—NBC-TV Special* (RCA); *Elvis' Golden Records, Vol. 1* (RCA)

Heartbreak Hotel (1979) Willie Nelson & Leon Russell: *One For The Road* (Columbia)

Heartbreak U.S.A. (1961) Kitty Wells: *Country Music Hall Of Fame* (MCA); VA—*Country USA 1961* (Time Life)

Heartbreaker (1978) Dolly Parton: VA—*Contemporary Country: The Late '70s—Hot Hits* (Time Life)

Heartbroke (1982) Ricky Skaggs: *Live In London* (Epic); *Highways & Heartaches* (Epic); VA— *Contemporary Country: The Early '80s—Pure Gold* (Time Life)

Hearts Aren't Made To Break (They're Made To Love) (1986) Lee Greenwood: *Greatest Hits, Vol. 2* (MCA); *Streamline* (MCA)

Heaven Says Hello (1968) Sonny James

Heaven's Just A Sin Away (1977) The Kendalls: VA—*Contemporary Country: The Late '70s* (Time Life); *20 Favorites* (Epic)

Hell And High Water (1986) T. Graham Brown: *I Tell It Like It Used To Be* (Capitol); *The Best Of T. Graham Brown* (Liberty); *Greatest Hits* (Capitol)

He'll Have To Go (1960) Jim Reeves: *The Best Of Jim Reeves* (RCA); *Greatest Hits* (RCA); VA— *Billboard Top Country Hits—1960* (Rhino); VA— *Country USA 1959* (Time Life); *He'll Have To Go & Other Favorites* (RCA); VA—*Classic Country Music* (Smithsonian); *Welcome To My World: The Essential Jim Reeves* (RCA); *Live At The Opry* (CMF)

Hello Darlin' (1970) Conway Twitty: *Greatest Hits, Vol. 1* (MCA); VA—*Country USA 1970* (Time Life); VA—*Contemporary Country: The Early '70s* (Time Life); *Greatest Hits* (Capitol/Curb); *Silver Anniversary Collection* (MCA); *The Very Best Of Conway Twitty* (MCA)

Hello Love (1974) Hank Snow

Hello Vietnam (1965) Johnny Wright

Hello Walls (1961) Faron Young: VA—*Classic Country Music* (Smithsonian); VA—*Country USA 1961* (Time Life); *Greatest Hits, Vols. 1-3* (Step One); VA—*Billboard Top Country Hits—1961* (Rhino); *All-Time Greatest Hits* (Capitol/Curb)

Help Me Hold On (1990) Travis Tritt: *Country Club* (Warner Bros.)

Help Me Make It Through The Night (1971) Sammi Smith: VA—*Contemporary Country: The Early '70s* (Time Life); VA—*Country USA 1971* (Time Life); *Kris Kristofferson Singer/Songwriter* (Columbia)

Here Comes Honey Again (1971) Sonny James: *The Best Of Sonny James* (Capitol/Curb)

Here You Come Again (1977) Dolly Parton: *The Best There Is* (RCA); VA—*Contemporary Country: The Late '70s* (Time Life); *Greatest Hits* (RCA)

Here's Some Love (1976) Tanya Tucker: *Tanya Tucker's Greatest Hits* (MCA); *Greatest Hits Encore* (Liberty); *Tanya Tucker Collection* (MCA)

He's A Heartache (Looking For A Place To Happen) (1983) Janie Frickie: *17 Greatest Hits* (Columbia)

He's Back And I'm Blue (1988) The Desert Rose Band: *The Desert Rose Band* (Curb); *A Dozen Roses: Greatest Hits* (MCA/Curb)

Hey Good Lookin' (1951) Hank Williams: *40 Greatest Hits* (Polydor); *The Original Singles Collection...Plus* (PolyGram); VA—*Country USA 1951* (Time Life); *Hey Good Lookin' (Dec. 1950-July 1951)* (Polydor)

Hey, Joe (1953) Carl Smith: VA—*Country USA 1953* (Time Life); VA—*Columbia Country Classics, Vol. 2: Honky Tonk Heroes* (Columbia); *Essential Carl Smith, 1950-1956* (Columbia)

(Hey Won't You Play) Another Somebody Done Somebody Wrong Song (1975) B. J. Thomas: *Greatest Hits* (Rhino); VA—*Contemporary Country: The Mid-'70s* (Time Life)

High Cotton (1989) Alabama: VA—*Contemporary Country: The Late '80s* (Time Life); *Greatest Hits, Vol. 2* (RCA); *Southern Star* (RCA)

Highway 40 Blues (1983) Ricky Skaggs: *Highways & Heartaches* (Epic)

Highwayman (1985) Jennings, Nelson, Cash, Kristofferson: VA—*Contemporary Country: The Mid-'80s* (Time Life); VA—*Columbia Country Classics, Vol. 3: Americana* (Columbia); *The Highwayman* (Columbia)

Hold Me (1989) K. T. Oslin: *This Woman* (RCA)

Holding Her And Loving You (1983) Earl Thomas Conley: *Greatest Hits* (RCA)

Home (1990) Joe Diffie: *A Thousand Winding Roads* (Epic)

Honey (1968) Bobby Goldsboro: *All-Time Greatest Hits* (Capitol/Curb); *Great Records Of The Decade—60's Hits—Country* (Capitol/Curb); *EMI Legends Of Rock 'N' Roll Collection—24 Greatest Hits Of All Time* (EMI); *Honey, The Best Of Bobby Goldsboro* (EMI); *Bobby Goldsboro's Greatest Hits* (EMI)

Honey (Open That Door) (1984) Ricky Skaggs: *Live In London* (Epic); *Don't Cheat In Our Hometown* (Epic)

Honky Tonk Blues (1980) Charley Pride: *Greatest Hits* (RCA)

Honky Tonk Moon (1988) Randy Travis: *Greatest Hits, Vol. 1* (Warner Bros.); *Old 8x10* (Warner Bros.)

Honky Tonk Song (1957) Webb Pierce: VA— *Country USA 1957* (Time Life)

Honky Tonkin' (1982) Hank Williams Jr.: *Greatest Hits, Vol. 2* (Warner/Curb); *High Notes* (Warner/Curb); *Living Proof: The MGM Recordings 1963-1975* (Mercury)

Honor Bound (1985) Earl Thomas Conley: *Treadin' Water* (RCA)

Hope You're Feelin' Me (Like I'm Feelin' You) (1975) Charley Pride

Hound Dog (1956) Elvis Presley: *Elvis—NBC-TV Special* (RCA); *Elvis—In Person* (RCA); *Aloha From Hawaii (Via Satellite)* (RCA); *The King Of Rock & Roll,' The Complete 50s Masters* (RCA); *Heartbreak Hotel,' 'Hound Dog' & Other Top Ten Hits* (RCA); *Top Ten Hits* (RCA); *Elvis—In Concert* (RCA); *Rocker* (RCA); *Elvis Sings Leiber & Stoller* (RCA); *Elvis' Golden Records, Vol. 1* (RCA); *Alternate Aloha* (RCA); *Number One Hits* (RCA); *Elvis Presley As Recorded Live At Madison Square Garden* (RCA)

Houston (Means I'm One Day Closer To You) (1983) Larry Gatlin & The Gatlin Brothers: VA— *Contemporary Country: The Early '80s* (Time Life); *17 Greatest Hits* (Columbia); *Greatest Hits, Vol. II* (Columbia); *Greatest Hits Encore* (Capitol); *Live At 8:00* (Columbia); VA—*Columbia Country Classics, Vol. 5: A New Tradition* (Columbia)

How Blue (1985) Reba McEntire: *Greatest Hits* (MCA); *My Kind Of Country* (MCA)

How Can I Unlove You (1971) Lynn Anderson

How Do I Turn You On (1987) Ronnie Milsap: *Greatest Hits, Vol. 3* (RCA); *Lost In The Fifties Tonight* (RCA)

How Long Will My Baby Be Gone (1968) Buck Owens: *The Buck Owens Collection, 1959-1990* (Rhino); VA—*Country USA 1968* (Time Life)

How Much More Can She Stand (1971) Conway Twitty: VA—*Contemporary Country: The Early '70s—Pure Gold* (Time Life); VA—*Country USA 1971* (Time Life); *Greatest Hits, Vol. 1* (MCA)

100% Chance Of Rain (1986) Gary Morris: *Hits* (Warner Bros.)

Hungry Eyes (1969) Merle Haggard: VA—*Country*

USA 1969 (Time Life); *Best Of The Best Of Merle Haggard* (Capitol); *Capitol Collectors Series* (Capitol)

Hurt (1986) Juice Newton: *Old Flame* (RCA)

I Ain't Living Long Like This (1980) Waylon Jennings: *Waylon's Greatest Hits, Vol. 2* (RCA); VA—*Contemporary Country: The Early '80s—Pure Gold* (Time Life)

I Ain't Never (1972) Mel Tillis: *American Originals* (Columbia); VA—*Contemporary Country: The Early '70s—Pure Gold* (Time Life)

I Always Get Lucky With You (1983) George Jones: *By Request* (Epic); VA—*Contemporary Country: The Early '80s—Pure Gold* (Time Life)

I Am A Simple Man (1991) Ricky Van Shelton: *Greatest Hits Plus* (Columbia); *Backroads* (Columbia)

I Believe In You (1978) Mel Tillis: *Greatest Hits* (Capitol/Curb)

I Believe In You (1980) Don Williams: VA—*Contemporary Country: The Early '80s* (Time Life); *Best Of Don Williams, Vol. 3* (MCA); *Greatest Country Hits* (Capitol/Curb)

I Can Help (1974) Billy Swan: VA—*Rock This Town: Rockabilly Hits, Vol. 2* (Rhino); VA—*Contemporary Country: The Mid-'70s—Pure Gold* (Time Life)

I Can Tell By The Way You Dance (You're Gonna Love Me Tonight) (1984) Vern Gosdin: *10 Years Of Greatest Hits Newly Recorded* (Columbia); VA—*Contemporary Country: The Mid-'80s* (Time Life)

(I Can't Believe) She Gives It All To Me (1977) Conway Twitty: *The Very Best Of Conway Twitty* (MCA)

I Can't Believe That You've Stopped Loving Me (1970) Charley Pride

I Can't Get Close Enough (1988) Exile

I Can't Stop Loving You (1972) Conway Twitty: VA—*Country USA 1972* (Time Life); *The Very Best Of Conway Twitty* (MCA)

I Can't Win For Losin' You (1987) Earl Thomas Conley: *Greatest Hits, Vol. II* (RCA)

I Care (1975) Tom T. Hall

I Cheated Me Right Out Of You (1979) Moe Bandy: *Greatest Hits* (Columbia); VA—*Contemporary Country: The Late '70s—Hot Hits* (Time Life)

I Could Get Used To You (1986) Exile: *Greatest Hits* (Epic); *Hang On To Your Heart* (Epic)

I Couldn't Leave You If I Tried (1988) Rodney Crowell: *Diamonds & Dirt* (Columbia); VA—*Columbia Country Classics, Vol. 5: A New Tradition* (Columbia); VA—*Contemporary Country: The Late '80s—Pure Gold* (Time Life)

I Cross My Heart (1992) George Strait: *Pure Country* (MCA)

I Don't Believe You've Met My Baby (1956) The Louvin Brothers: *Radio Favorites '51-'57* (CMF); VA—*Country USA 1956* (Time Life)

I Don't Care (1955) Webb Pierce: VA—*Country USA 1955* (Time Life)

I Don't Care (1982) Ricky Skaggs: *Waitin' For The Sun To Shine* (Epic)

I Don't Care (Just As Long As You Love Me) (1964) Buck Owens: *The Buck Owens Collection, 1959-1990* (Rhino); *Live At Carnegie Hall* (CMF); VA—*Country USA 1964* (Time Life)

I Don't Hurt Anymore (1954) Hank Snow: VA—*Country USA 1954* (Time Life)

I Don't Know A Thing About Love (The Moon Song) (1984) Conway Twitty: *No. 1's: The Warner Bros. Years* (Warner Bros.)

I Don't Know Why You Don't Want Me (1985) Rosanne Cash: *Rhythm & Romance* (Columbia); VA—*Contemporary Country: The Mid-'80s—Hot Hits* (Time Life); *Hits 1979-1989* (Columbia)

I Don't Mind The Thorns (If You're The Rose) (1985) Lee Greenwood: *Greatest Hits, Vol. 2* (MCA); *Streamline* (MCA)

I Don't Need You (1981) Kenny Rogers: *Greatest Country Hits* (Capitol/Curb); *Twenty Greatest Hits* (EMI)

I Don't See Me In Your Eyes Anymore (1974) Charlie Rich

I Don't Wanna Play House (1967) Tammy Wynette: VA—*Country USA 1967* (Time Life); *Anniversary: 20 Years Of Hits* (Epic); VA—*Billboard Top Country Hits—1967* (Rhino); *Tammy's Greatest Hits, Vol. 1* (Epic); *Tears Of Fire—The 25th Anniversary Collection* (Epic)

I Don't Want To Be A Memory (1984) Exile: *Exile* (Epic); *Greatest Hits* (Epic)

I Don't Want To Have To Marry You (1976) Jim Ed Brown & Helen Cornelius: *Greatest Hits* (RCA)

I Don't Want To Spoil The Party (1989) Rosanne Cash: *Hits 1979-1989* (Columbia)

I Fall To Pieces (1961) Patsy Cline: VA—*Billboard Top Country Hits—1961* (Rhino); VA—*Country USA 1961* (Time Life); *Always* (MCA); *Greatest Hits* (MCA); *Sweet Dreams* (MCA); *Showcase (With The Jordanaires)* (MCA); *Remembering* (MCA); *Live At The Opry* (MCA); *The Patsy Cline Story* (MCA); *The Patsy Cline Collection* (MCA)

I Feel Like Loving You Again (1981) T. G. Sheppard

I Fell In Love Again Last Night (1985) The Forester Sisters: VA—*Contemporary Country: The Mid-'80s—Pure Gold* (Time Life); *Greatest Hits* (Warner Bros.)

I Forgot More Than You'll Ever Know (1953) The Davis Sisters: VA—*Country USA 1953* (Time Life)

I Forgot To Remember To Forget (1955) Elvis Presley: VA—*Country USA 1955* (Time Life); *The King Of Rock & Roll: The Complete 50s Masters* (RCA); *Complete Sun Sessions* (RCA)

I Get The Fever (1966) Bill Anderson: *The Best Of Bill Anderson* (Curb); VA—*Billboard Top Country Hits—1966* (Rhino); VA—*Country USA 1966* (Time Life)

I Got Dreams (1989) Steve Wariner: *I Got Dreams* (MCA); VA—*Contemporary Country: The Late '80s—Pure Gold* (Time Life); *Greatest Hits, Vol. 2* (MCA)

I Got Mexico (1984) Eddy Raven: *The Best Of Eddy Raven* (RCA); VA—*Contemporary Country: The Mid-'80s—Pure Gold* (Time Life); *Greatest Country Hits* (Capitol/Curb)

I Guess I'm Crazy (1964) Jim Reeves: *Welcome To My World: The Essential Jim Reeves Collection* (RCA); VA—*Country USA 1964* (Time Life); VA—*Billboard Top Country Hits—1964* (Rhino)

I Guess It Never Hurts To Hurt Sometimes (1984) The Oak Ridge Boys: *Deliver* (MCA); *Greatest Hits, Vol. 2* (MCA); *Ozark Mountain Jubilee* (MCA); *The Oak Ridge Boys Collection* (MCA)

I Just Can't Get Her Out Of My Mind (1975) Johnny Rodriguez

I Just Fall In Love Again (1979) Anne Murray:
15 Of The Best (Liberty); *Greatest Hits* (Liberty)

I Just Want To Love You (1978) Eddie Rabbitt:
Greatest Country Hits (Capitol/Curb)

I Just Wish You Were Someone I Love (1978)
Larry Gatlin & The Gatlin Brothers: *17 Greatest
Hits* (Columbia); *Greatest Hits* (Columbia);
Greatest Hits Encore (Capitol)

I Keep Coming Back (1981) Razzy Bailey

I Know How He Feels (1988) Reba McEntire:
Reba (MCA)

I Know Where I'm Going (1987) The Judds:
Heartland (RCA); *Greatest Hits, Vol. II* (RCA)

I Let The Stars Get In My Eyes (1953) Goldie
Hill: VA—*Country USA 1953* (Time Life)

I Love (1974) Tom T. Hall: VA—*Contemporary
Country: The Mid-'70s* (Time Life)

I Love A Rainy Night (1981) Eddie Rabbitt: VA—
Contemporary Country: The Early '80s (Time Life);
All-Time Greatest Hits (Warner Bros.); *Ten Years
Of Greatest Hits* (Liberty)

I Love My Friend (1974) Charlie Rich: *Greatest
Hits* (Epic)

I Love You A Thousand Ways (1951) Lefty
Frizzell: VA—*Classic Country Music* (Smithsonian);
The Best Of Lefty Frizzell (Rhino); VA—*Country
USA 1950* (Time Life); VA—*Columbia Country
Classics, Vol. 2: Honky Tonk Heroes* (Columbia)

I Love You Because (1950) Leon Payne: VA—
Country USA 1950 (Time Life)

I Love You More Today (1969) Conway Twitty:
Greatest Hits, Vol. 1 (MCA)

I Love You So Much It Hurts (1949) Jimmy
Wakely

I Loved 'Em Every One (1981) T. G. Sheppard:
All-Time Greatest Hits (Warner Bros.)

I May Never Get To Heaven (1979) Conway
Twitty: *Number Ones* (MCA)

I Need More Of You (1985) The Bellamy
Brothers: *Restless* (MCA); *Greatest Hits, Vol. 2*
(MCA)

I Overlooked An Orchid (1974) Mickey Gilley:
Gilley's Greatest Hits, Vol. 1 (Epic), *Ten Years Of
Hits* (Epic)

I Really Don't Want To Know (1954) Eddy
Arnold: VA—*Country USA 1954* (Time Life); *Last
Of The Love Song Singers: Then & Now* (RCA); VA—
Classic Country Music (Smithsonian); *The Best Of
Eddy Arnold* (RCA)

I Really Got The Feeling (1979) Dolly Parton

I Sang Dixie (1989) Dwight Yoakam: *Just Lookin'
For A Hit* (Reprise); *Buenas Noches From A Lonely
Room* (Reprise)

I Saw The Light (1992) Wynonna: *Wynonna*
(MCA/Curb)

I See The Want To In Your Eyes (1974) Conway
Twitty: VA—*Contemporary Country: The Mid-'70s—
Pure Gold* (Time Life); *Number Ones* (MCA)

I Still Believe In You (1989) The Desert Rose
Band: *Running* (Curb); *A Dozen Roses: Greatest
Hits* (MCA/Curb)

I Still Believe In You (1992) Vince Gill: *I Still
Believe In You* (MCA)

I Think I'll Just Stay Here And Drink (1981)
Merle Haggard: *Back To The Barrooms* (MCA);
Merle Haggard's Greatest Hits (MCA); *Rainbow
Stew (Live At Anaheim Stadium)* (MCA); *More Of
The Best* (Rhino); VA—*Legends Of Country Guitar,
Vol. 1* (Rhino)

I Told You So (1988) Randy Travis: *Greatest Hits,

Vol. 1 (Warner Bros.); VA—*Contemporary Country:
The Late '80s* (Time Life); *Always & Forever*
(Warner Bros.)

I Walk Alone (1968) Marty Robbins: *Essential
Marty Robbins, 1951-1982* (Columbia); *Marty
Robbins' All-Time Greatest Hits* (Columbia)

I Walk The Line (1956) Johnny Cash: VA—
Country USA 1956 (Time Life); *Johnny Cash's
Greatest Hits* (Columbia); VA—*Legends* (Dunhill);
VA—*Sun Story* (Rhino); *Sun Years* (Rhino); *Johnny
Cash At Folsom Prison & San Quentin* (Columbia);
The Essential Johnny Cash (Columbia); *The Best
Of Johnny Cash* (Capitol/Curb); VA—*Sun's
Greatest Hits* (RCA); VA—*Classic Country Music*
(Smithsonian)

I Wanna Dance With You (1988) Eddie Rabbitt:
Greatest Country Hits (Capitol/Curb)

I Wanna Live (1968) Glen Campbell

I Wanna Play House With You (1951) Eddy
Arnold: VA—*Country USA 1951* (Time Life)

I Want To Be With You Always (1951) Lefty
Frizzell: VA—*Country USA 1951* (Time Life); *The
Best Of Lefty Frizzell* (Rhino); *American Originals*
(Columbia)

I Want To Go With You (1966) Eddy Arnold: *Last
Of The Love Song Singers: Then & Now* (RCA); VA—
Billboard Top Country Hits—1966 (Rhino); *The
Best Of Eddy Arnold* (RCA)

I Want You, I Need You, I Love You (1956)
Elvis Presley: *Country USA 1956* (Time Life);
Worldwide 50 Gold Award Hits, Vols. 1 & 2 (RCA);
Top Ten Hits (RCA); *Number One Hits* (RCA); *Elvis
Golden Records, Vol. 1* (RCA); *The King Of Rock &
Roll: The Complete 50s Masters* (RCA)

I Was Country When Country Wasn't Cool
(1981) Barbara Mandrell: VA—*Contemporary
Country: The Early '80s—Pure Gold* (Time Life);
Greatest Country Hits (Capitol/Curb); *Greatest
Hits* (MCA)

I Will Always Love You (1974 & 1982) Dolly
Parton: *The Best There Is* (RCA); VA—
Contemporary Country: The Early '80s (Time Life);
Greatest Hits (RCA); *The Best Little Whorehouse
In Texas* (MCA); *Collector's Series* (RCA); *The Best
Of Dolly Parton* (RCA)

I Will Be There (1987) Dan Seals: *The Best Of
Dan Seals* (Liberty)

I Wonder Do You Think Of Me (1989) Keith
Whitley: *Greatest Hits* (RCA); VA—*Contemporary
Country: The Late '80s* (Time Life)

I Wonder If They Ever Think Of Me (1973)
Merle Haggard: *Very Best Of Merle Haggard*
(Capitol); *Capitol Collector's Series* (Capitol);
Country USA 1972 (Time Life)

I Won't Come In While He's There (1967) Jim
Reeves

I Won't Mention It Again (1971) Ray Price: VA—
Country USA 1971 (Time Life); *Greatest Hits,
Vols. 1-3* (Step One); VA—*Contemporary Country:
The Early '70s—Pure Gold* (Time Life)

**I Won't Need You Anymore (Always And
Forever)** (1987) Randy Travis: *Always and
Forever* (Warner Bros.); *Greatest Hits, Vol. 2*
(Warner Bros.)

I Won't Take Less Than Your Love (1988)
Tanya Tucker: *Greatest Hits* (Liberty); *Love Me
Like You Used To* (Liberty)

I Wouldn't Change You If I Could (1983) Ricky
Skaggs: *Highways & Heartaches* (Epic)

I Wouldn't Have Missed It For The World
(1982) Ronnie Milsap: *Greatest Hits, Vol. 2* (RCA)

I Wouldn't Want To Live If You Didn't Love Me (1974) Don Williams: *Greatest Hits* (MCA)

(I'd Be) A Legend In My Time (1975) Ronnie Milsap: *Greatest Hits* (RCA)

I'd Love To Lay You Down (1980) Conway Twitty: *Number Ones* (MCA); VA—*Contemporary Country: The Early '80s—Pure Gold* (Time Life)

I'd Love You All Over Again (1991) Alan Jackson: *Here In The Real World* (Arista)

I'd Rather Love You (1971) Charley Pride

If Hollywood Don't Need You (1983) Don Williams: *Best Of Don Williams, Vol. 3* (MCA); *Greatest Country Hits* (Capitol/Curb)

If I Didn't Have You (1992) Randy Travis: *Greatest Hits, Vol. 1* (Warner Bros.)

If I Had You (1989) Alabama: *Southern Star* (RCA)

If I Know Me (1991) George Strait: *Chill Of An Early Fall* (MCA)

If I Said You Have A Beautiful Body Would You Hold It Against Me (1979) The Bellamy Brothers: *Greatest Hits* (MCA); VA—*Contemporary Country: The Late '70s* (Time Life)

If It Don't Come Easy (1988) Tanya Tucker: *Love Me Like You Used To* (Liberty); *Greatest Hits* (Liberty)

(If Loving You Is Wrong) I Don't Want To Be Right (1979) Barbara Mandrell: *Greatest Hits* (MCA)

If The Devil Danced (In Empty Pockets) (1991) Joe Diffie: *A Thousand Winding Roads* (Epic)

If Tomorrow Never Comes (1989) Garth Brooks: *Garth Brooks* (Capitol)

If We Make It Through December (1973) Merle Haggard: *More Of The Best* (Rhino); VA—*Contemporary Country: The Mid-'70s* (Time Life); *Very Best Of Merle Haggard* (Capitol)

If You Ain't Lovin' (You Ain't Livin') (1988) George Strait: *If You Ain't Lovin' (You Ain't Livin')* (MCA); *Ten Strait Hits* (MCA)

If You Change Your Mind (1988) Rosanne Cash: *King's Record Shop* (Columbia); VA—*Contemporary Country: The Late '80s* (Time Life)

If You Ever Change Your Mind (1980) Crystal Gayle: *Greatest Hits* (Capitol); *These Days* (Liberty)

If You Leave Me Tonight I'll Cry (1972) Jerry Wallace

If You're Gonna Play In Texas (1984) Alabama: VA—*Contemporary Country: The Mid-'80s—Pure Gold* (Time Life); *Roll On* (RCA); *Alabama 'Live'* (RCA)

If You've Got The Money I've Got The Time (1950) Lefty Frizzell: *American Originals* (Columbia); VA—*Country USA 1950* (Time Life); *The Best Of Lefty Frizzell* (Rhino); VA—*Columbia Country Classics, Vol. 2: Honky Tonk Heroes* (Columbia)

If You've Got The Money I've Got The Time (1976) Willie Nelson: VA—*Contemporary Country: The Mid-'70s—Pure Gold* (Time Life); *Greatest Hits & Some That Will Be* (Columbia); *Willie & Family Live* (Columbia); *Sound In Your Mind* (Columbia)

I'll Always Come Back (1988) K. T. Oslin: VA—*Contemporary Country: The Late '80s* (Time Life); *80's Ladies* (RCA)

I'll Be Coming Back For More (1980) T. G. Sheppard: *All-Time Greatest Hits* (Warner Bros.)

I'll Be Leaving Alone (1977) Charley Pride

I'll Be True To You (1978) The Oak Ridge Boys: *Room Service* (MCA); *Greatest Hits* (MCA); *Y'All Come Back Saloon* (MCA)

I'll Get Over You (1976) Crystal Gayle: *Classic Crystal* (EMI)

I'll Go On Alone (1953) Marty Robbins: VA—*Country USA 1953* (Time Life); *Essential Marty Robbins* (Columbia); *American Originals* (Columbia)

I'll Hold You In My Heart (Till I Can Hold You In My Arms) (1947) Eddy Arnold: *Pure Gold* (RCA); *The Best Of Eddy Arnold* (RCA)

I'll Leave This World Loving You (1988) Ricky Van Shelton: *Greatest Hits Plus* (Columbia); *Loving Proof* (Columbia)

I'll Never Find Another You (1967) Sonny James: VA—*Billboard Top Country Hits—1967* (Rhino); *Greatest Hits* (Capitol/Curb)

I'll Never Get Out Of This World Alive (1953) Hank Williams: *The Original Singles Collection . . . Plus* (PolyGram); *Let's Turn Back The Years (July 1951-June 1952)* (Polydor); *40 Greatest Hits* (Polydor); VA—*Country USA 1952* (Time Life)

I'll Never Stop Loving You (1985) Gary Morris: VA—*Contemporary Country: The Mid-'80s—Pure Gold* (Time Life); *Hits* (Warner Bros.)

I'll Sail My Ship Alone (1950) Moon Mullican: *Sings His All-Time Greatest Hits* (King)

I'll Still Be Loving You (1987) Restless Heart: *Wheels* (RCA); *The Best Of Restless Heart* (RCA)

I'll Think Of Something (1992) Mark Chesnutt: *Longnecks & Short Stories* (MCA)

I'm A Ramblin' Man (1974) Waylon Jennings: *Greatest Hits* (RCA)

(I'm A) Stand By My Woman Man (1976) Ronnie Milsap: VA—*Contemporary Country: The Mid-'70s—Pure Gold* (Time Life); *Greatest Hits* (RCA)

I'm For Love (1985) Hank Williams Jr.: *Hank 'Live'* (Warner/Curb); *Five-O* (Warner Bros.); *Greatest Hits III* (Warner/Curb)

I'm Gonna Get You (1988) Eddy Raven: *The Best Of Eddy Raven* (RCA); *Greatest Country Hits* (Capitol/Curb)

I'm Gonna Hire A Wino To Decorate Our Home (1982) David Frizzell: VA—*Contemporary Country: The Early '80s—Pure Gold* (Time Life)

I'm In A Hurry (1992) Alabama: *American Pride* (RCA)

I'm Just A Country Boy (1977) Don Williams: *Best Of Don Williams* (MCA); VA—*Contemporary Country: The Late '70s—Hot Hits* (Time Life)

I'm Just Me (1971) Charley Pride: *Country USA 1971* (Time Life)

I'm Losing My Mind Over You (1945) Al Dexter

I'm Moving On (1950) Hank Snow: *I'm Movin' On & Other Great Country Hits* (RCA); VA—*Country USA 1950* (Time Life); VA—*Classic Country Music* (Smithsonian)

I'm No Stranger To The Rain (1989) Keith Whitley: *Don't Close Your Eyes* (RCA); *Greatest Hits* (RCA)

I'm Not Lisa (1975) Jessi Colter: VA—*Contemporary Country: The Mid-'70s* (Time Life)

I'm Only In It For The Love (1983) John Conlee: *Best Of John Conlee* (Curb); *John Conlee's Greatest Hits, Vol. 2* (MCA)

(I'm So) Afraid Of Losing You Again (1969) Charley Pride

I'm Sorry (1975) John Denver: *John Denver's Greatest Hits, Vol. 2* (RCA)

I'm Still Crazy (1989) Vern Gosdin: *Alone* (Columbia); *Greatest Hits, Vol. 1* (Columbia)

I'm Throwing Rice (At The Girl I Love) (1949) Eddy Arnold

I'm Wastin' My Tears On You (1944) Tex Ritter: *Capitol Collector's Series* (Capitol)

In A Different Light (1991) Doug Stone: *Doug Stone* (Epic)

In A Letter To You (1989) Eddy Raven: *Temporary Sanity* (Liberty); *The Best Of Eddy Raven* (Liberty)

In Love (1986) Ronnie Milsap: *Lost In The Fifties Tonight* (RCA)

In My Eyes (1984) John Conlee: VA—*Contemporary Country: The Mid-'80s—Hot Hits* (Time Life); *Best Of John Conlee* (Curb); *John Conlee's Greatest Hits, Vol. 2* (MCA)

In The Jailhouse Now (1955) Webb Pierce: VA—*Country USA 1955* (Time Life)

In This Life (1992) Collin Raye: *In This Life* (Epic)

Inside (1983) Ronnie Milsap: *Greatest Hits, Vol. 2* (RCA); *Inside Ronnie Milsap* (RCA)

Is Anybody Goin' To San Antone (1970) Charley Pride: VA—*Classic Country Music* (Smithsonian); VA—*Contemporary Country: The Early '70s—Pure Gold* (Time Life); VA—*Country USA 1970* (Time Life)

Is It Really Over (1965) Jim Reeves: VA—*Country USA 1965* (Time Life); *Welcome To My World: The Essential Jim Reeves* (RCA)

Is It Still Over (1989) Randy Travis: *Old 8x10* (Warner Bros.); *Greatest Hits, Vol. 2* (Warner Bros.)

Is It Wrong (For Loving You) (1974) Sonny James

Is There Life Out There Reba McEntire: *For My Broken Heart* (MCA)

Islands In The Stream (1983) Kenny Rogers & Dolly Parton: *Kenny Rogers Eyes That See In The Dark* (RCA); *Kenny Rogers Greatest Hits* (RCA); VA—*Contemporary Country: The Early '80s* (Time Life)

It Ain't Cool To Be Crazy About You (1986) George Strait: *No. 7* (MCA); *George Strait Greatest Hits, Vol. 2* (MCA)

It Ain't Easy Bein' Easy (1982) Janie Frickie: *17 Greatest Hits* (Columbia); *The Very Best Of Janie Frickie* (Columbia)

It Ain't Nothin' (1990) Keith Whitley: *Greatest Hits* (RCA)

It Couldn't Have Been Any Better (1977) Johnny Duncan: VA—*Contemporary Country: The Late '70s—Hot Hits* (Time Life)

It Must Be Love (1979) Don Williams: *Best Of Don Williams, Vol. 3* (MCA); VA—*Contemporary Country: The Late '70s—Pure Gold* (Time Life)

It Only Hurts For A Little While (1978) Margo Smith

It Takes A Little Rain (To Make Love Grow) (1987) The Oak Ridge Boys: *Greatest Hits 3* (MCA) *The Oak Ridge Boys Collection* (MCA); *Where The Fast Lane Ends* (MCA)

It Was Almost Like A Song (1977) Ronnie Milsap: VA—*Contemporary Country: The Late '70s* (Time Life); *Greatest Hits* (RCA); *It Was Almost Like A Song* (RCA)

It Wasn't God Who Made Honky Tonk Angels (1952) Kitty Wells: VA—*Classic Country Music* (Smithsonian); VA—*Country USA 1952* (Time Life); *Country Music Hall Of Fame* (MCA); *Greatest Hits, Vol. 1* (Step One)

It'll Be Me (1986) Exile: *Hang On To Your Heart* (Epic)

It's A Sin (1947) Eddy Arnold

It's All In The Movies (1975) Merle Haggard: *More Of The Best* (Rhino); *Very Best Of Merle Haggard* (Capitol)

It's All Wrong, But It's All Right (1978) Dolly Parton: VA—*Contemporary Country: The Late '70s—Pure Gold* (Time Life); *Greatest Hits* (RCA)

It's Been So Long (1953) Webb Pierce: VA—*Country USA 1953* (Time Life)

It's Been So Long, Darling (1945) Ernest Tubb: *Country Music Hall Of Fame* (MCA)

It's Four In The Morning (1972) Faron Young: *Country Spotlight* (Dominion); *Greatest Hits, Vols. 1-3* (Step One); VA—*Contemporary Country: The Early '70s—Pure Gold* (Time Life)

It's Gonna Take A Little Bit Longer (1972) Charley Pride: VA—*Country USA 1972* (Time Life)

It's Just A Matter Of Time (1970) Sonny James: *Greatest Hits* (Capitol/Curb)

It's Just A Matter Of Time (1989) Randy Travis: *Greatest Hits, Vol. 2* (Warner Bros.); *No Holdin' Back* (Warner Bros.)

It's Like We Never Said Goodbye (1980) Crystal Gayle: *Miss The Mississippi* (Liberty); *Greatest Hits* (Capitol)

It's Not Love (But It's Not Bad) (1972) Merle Haggard: *Very Best Of Merle Haggard* (Capitol); *More Of The Best* (Rhino); VA—*Country USA 1972* (Time Life); VA—*Contemporary Country: The Early '70s—Pure Gold* (Time Life)

It's Such A Pretty World Today (1967) Wynn Stewart: VA—*Country USA 1967* (Time Life); VA—*Billboard Top Country Hits—1967* (Rhino)

It's Such A Small World (1988) Rodney Crowell & Rosanne Cash: *Rodney Crowell Diamonds & Dirt* (Columbia)

It's The Little Things (1967) Sonny James: VA—*Country USA 1967* (Time Life)

It's Time To Pay The Fiddler (1975) Cal Smith

I've Already Loved You In My Mind (1977) Conway Twitty: *The Very Best Of Conway Twitty* (MCA); *Silver Anniversary Collection* (MCA); VA—*Contemporary Country: The Late '70s—Hot Hits* (Time Life)

I've Always Been Crazy (1978) Waylon Jennings: *Greatest Hits* (RCA); VA—*Contemporary Country: The Late '70s—Hot Hits* (Time Life)

I've Been Around Enough To Know (1984) John Schneider: *Greatest Hits* (MCA); *Too Good To Stop Now* (MCA)

I've Been Everywhere (1962) Hank Snow: VA—*Billboard Top Country Hits—1962* (Rhino); VA—*Country USA 1962* (Time Life)

I've Come To Expect It From You (1990) George Strait: *Livin' It Up* (MCA); *Ten Strait Hits* (MCA)

I've Cried My Last Tear For You (1990) Ricky Van Shelton: *RVS III* (Columbia); *Greatest Hits Plus* (Columbia)

I've Got A Tiger By The Tail (1965) Buck Owens: VA—*Billboard Top Country Hits—1965* (Rhino); *Live At Carnegie Hall* (CMF); *The Buck Owens Collection, 1959-1990* (Rhino); *All-Time Greatest, Vol. 1* (Capitol/Curb); VA—*Country USA 1965* (Time Life)

Jailhouse Rock (1957) Elvis Presley: *Number One Hits* (RCA); *Great Performances* (RCA); *Elvis Sings Leiber & Stoller* (RCA); *Worldwide 50 Gold Award Hits, Vols. 1 & 2* (RCA); *Collector's Gold* (RCA);

'*Heartbreak Hotel,*' '*Hound Dog*' & *Other Top Ten Hits* (RCA); *Rocker* (RCA); *Elvis' Golden Records, Vol. 1* (RCA); *Elvis—In Concert* (RCA); *Elvis—NBC-TV Special* (RCA); *Elvis' Golden Records, Vol. 2* (RCA); *The King Of Rock & Roll: The Complete 50s Masters* (RCA) *Top Ten Hits* (RCA); *Essential Elvis—The First Movies* (RCA)

Jambalaya (On The Bayou) (1952) Hank Williams: *Rare Demos* (CMF); VA—*Country USA 1952* (Time Life); *The Original Singles Collection...Plus* (PolyGram); *40 Greatest Hits* (Polydor); *Let's Turn Back The Years (July 1951-June 1952)* (Polydor)

Joe Knows How To Live (1988) Eddy Raven: VA—*Contemporary Country: The Late '80s* (Time Life); *The Best Of Eddy Raven* (RCA)

Johnny B. Goode (1969) Buck Owens: *The Buck Owens Collection, 1959-1990* (Rhino)

Jolene (1974) Dolly Parton: *The Best There Is* (RCA); *Collector's Series* (RCA); VA—*Contemporary Country: The Mid-'70s* (Time Life); *The Best Of Dolly Parton* (RCA)

Jose Cuervo (1983) Shelly West

Joshua (1971) Dolly Parton: VA—*Contemporary Country: The Early '70s* (Time Life); VA—*Country · USA 1971* (Time Life)

Jukebox In My Mind (1990) Alabama: *Pass It On Down* (RCA)

Jukebox With A Country Song (1992) Doug Stone: *I Thought It Was You* (Epic)

Just A Little Lovin' (Will Go A Long, Long Way) (1948) Eddy Arnold: *The Best Of Eddy Arnold* (RCA); *Last Of The Love Song Singers: Then & Now* (RCA); *Pure Gold* (RCA)

Just Another Love (1986) Tanya Tucker: *Greatest Country Hits* (Capitol/Curb); *Greatest Hits* (Liberty)

Just Another Woman In Love (1984) Anne Murray: *Anne Murray's Country Hits* (Liberty); *Greatest Hits, Vol. 2* (Liberty); *15 Of The Best* (Liberty); *A Little Good News* (Liberty)

Just Get Up And Close The Door (1975) Johnny Rodriguez: VA—*Contemporary Country: The Mid-'70s—Pure Gold* (Time Life)

Just Good Ol' Boys (1979) Moe Bandy & Joe Stampley: VA—*Contemporary Country: The Late '70s—Pure Gold* (Time Life)

Just In Case (1986) The Forester Sisters: *Greatest Hits* (Warner Bros.)

Just Married (1958) Marty Robbins: VA—*Country USA 1958* (Time Life); *Essential Marty Robbins, 1951-1982* (Columbia)

Just To Satisfy You (1982) Waylon & Willie

Kaw-Liga (1953) Hank Williams: *Let's Turn Back The Years (July 1951-June 1952)* (Polydor); *40 Greatest Hits* (Polydor); *The Original Singles Collection...Plus* (PolyGram); VA—*Country USA 1953* (Time Life)

Keep It Between the Lines (1991) Ricky Van Shelton: *Greatest Hits Plus* (Columbia); *Backroads* (Columbia)

Keep Me In Mind (1973) Lynn Anderson

Kentucky Gambler (1975) Merle Haggard: *18 Rare Classics* (Capitol/Curb)

Kentucky Waltz (1951) Eddy Arnold: VA—*Country USA 1951* (Time Life)

Kids Of The Baby Boom (1987) The Bellamy Brothers: VA—*Classic Country Music* (Smithsonian); *Country Rap* (MCA); *Greatest Hits, Vol. 3* (MCA)

Kids Say The Darndest Things (1973) Tammy

Wynette: *Tears Of Fire—The 25th Anniversary Collection* (Epic); *Biggest Hits* (Epic); *Anniversary: 20 Years Of Hits* (Epic)

Killin' Time (1989) (Epic) Clint Black: *Killin' Time* (RCA)

King Of The Road (1965) Roger Miller: *Golden Hits* (Smash); *King Of The Road* (Laserlight); *The Best Of Roger Miller, Vol. 2—King Of The Road* (Mercury); VA—*Country USA 1965* (Time Life); VA—*Classic Country Music* (Smithsonian)

Kiss An Angel Good Mornin' (1971) Charley Pride: VA—*Contemporary Country: The Early '70s* (Time Life); VA—*Country USA 1971* (Time Life)

Lady (1980) Kenny Rogers: *Twenty Greatest Hits* (EMI); *Kenny Rogers' Greatest Hits* (EMI); *20 Great Years* (Reprise); *Greatest Country Hits* (Capitol/Curb)

Lady Down On Love (1983) Alabama: *Alabama 'Live'* (RCA); *The Closer You Get* (RCA); *Greatest Hits, Vol. II* (RCA)

Lady Lay Down (1979) John Conlee: *Rose Colored Glasses* (MCA); *Greatest Hits* (MCA); VA—*Contemporary Country: The Late '70s—Hot Hits* (Time Life)

Last Cheater's Waltz (1979) T. G.Sheppard: *All-Time Greatest Hits* (Warner Bros.); VA—*Contemporary Country: The Late '70s—Pure Gold* (Time Life)

The Last One To Know (1987) Reba McEntire: *The Last One To Know* (MCA); VA—*Contemporary Country: The Late '80s—Pure Gold* (Time Life)

Laura (What's He Got That I Ain't Got) (1967) Leon Ashley

Lead Me On (1971) Conway Twitty & Loretta Lynn: VA—*Country USA 1971* (Time Life); VA—*Contemporary Country: The Early '70s* (Time Life); *The Very Best Of Loretta Lynn & Conway Twitty* (MCA)

Leap Of Faith (1991) Lionel Cartwright: *Chasin' The Sun* (MCA)

Leave Me Lonely (1987) Gary Morris: *Hits* (Warner Bros.); *Plain Brown Wrapper* (Warner Bros.)

Leaving Louisiana In The Broad Daylight (1980) The Oak Ridge Boys: *Greatest Hits* (MCA); *The Oak Ridge Boys Have Arrived* (MCA)

The Legend Of Bonnie & Clyde (1968) Merle Haggard

A Lesson In Leavin' (1980) Dottie West

Let Me Be The One (1953) Hank Locklin

Let Me Go, Lover (1955) Hank Snow: *I'm Movin' On & Other Great Country Hits* (RCA); VA—*Country USA 1954* (Time Life)

Let Me Tell You About Love (1989) The Judds: *The Judds Collection 1983-1990* (RCA); *River Of Time* (RCA); *Greatest Hits, Vol. II* (RCA)

Let My Love Be Your Pillow (1977) Ronnie Milsap: *Greatest Hits* (RCA)

Let Old Mother Nature Have Her Way (1951) Carl Smith: VA—*Country USA 1951* (Time Life); VA—*Columbia Country Classics, Vol. 2: Honky Tonk Heroes* (Columbia); *Essential Carl Smith, 1950-1956* (Columbia)

Let's Chase Each Other Around The Room (1984) Merle Haggard: *It's All In The Game* (Epic); VA—*Contemporary Country: The Mid-80s—Pure Gold* (Time Life)

Let's Fall To Pieces Together (1984) George Strait: *Right Or Wrong* (MCA); *Greatest Hits* (MCA)

Let's Stop Talkin' About It (1984) Janie Frickie: *17 Greatest Hits* (Columbia); *The Very Best Of*

Janie Frickie (Columbia)
Let's Take The Long Way Around The World
(1978) Ronnie Milsap: *Greatest Hits* (RCA)
Life Turned Her That Way (1988) Ricky Van
Shelton: *Greatest Hits Plus* (Columbia); VA—
*Columbia Country Classics, Vol. 5: A New
Tradition* (Columbia); *Wild-Eyed Dream*
(Columbia)
Life's Highway (1986) Steve Wariner: *Life's
Highway* (MCA); VA—*Contemporary Country: The
Mid-'80s—Hot Hits* (Time Life); *Greatest Hits*
(MCA)
Linda On My Mind (1975) Conway Twitty: *Silver
Anniversary Collection* (MCA); *The Very Best Of
Conway Twitty* (MCA); *Greatest Hits, Vol. 2* (MCA)
A Little Good News (1983) Anne Murray: *A Little
Good News* (Liberty); *Greatest Hits, Vol. 2*
(Liberty); *15 Of The Best* (Liberty); *Anne Murray's
Country Hits* (Liberty)
Little Rock (1986) Reba McEntire: *Whoever's In
New England* (MCA); *Greatest Hits* (MCA)
Little Things (1985) The Oak Ridge Boys: *Greatest
Hits 3* (MCA); *Step On Out* (MCA)
Live Fast, Love Hard, Die Young (1955) Faron
Young: VA—*Country USA 1955* (Time Life);
Greatest Hits, Vols. 1-3 (Step One); VA—*Hillbilly
Music...Thank God!, Vol. 1* (Capitol); *All-Time
Greatest Hits* (Capitol/Curb)
Living In The Promiseland (1986) Willie Nelson:
The Promiseland (Columbia)
Living Proof (1989) Ricky Van Shelton: *Loving
Proof* (Columbia); *Greatest Hits Plus* (Columbia);
VA—*Contemporary Country: The Late '80s—Pure
Gold* (Time Life)
Lizzie And The Rainman (1975) Tanya Tucker:
Tanya Tucker's Greatest Hits (MCA); *Tanya Tucker
Collection* (MCA)
Lonely Again (1967) Eddy Arnold: *Last Of The
Love Song Singers: Then & Now* (RCA)
Lonely Nights (1982) Mickey Gilley: *Biggest Hits*
(Epic); *Ten Years Of Hits* (Epic)
Lonesome 7-7203 (1963) Hawshaw   awkins:
VA—*Country USA 1963* (Time Life)
Long Gone Lonesome Blues (1950) Hank
Williams: *Long Gone Lonesome Blues (Aug. 1949-
Dec. 1950)* (Polydor); *40 Greatest Hits* (Polydor);
The Original Singles Collection...Plus (PolyGram)
**Long Hard Road (The Sharecropper's
Dream)** (1984) Nitty Gritty Dirt Band: *Live To
Five* (Capitol)
A Long Line Of Love (1987) Michael Martin
Murphey: VA—*Contemporary Country: The Late
'80s—Pure Gold* (Time Life)
Lookin' For Love (1980) Johnny Lee: *The Best Of
Johnny Lee* (Capitol/Curb); *Greatest Hits* (Full
Moon); VA—*Contemporary Country: The Early '80s*
(Time Life)
Loose Talk (1955) Carl Smith: *Essential Carl
Smith, 1950-1956* (Columbia); VA—*Country USA
1954* (Time Life); *The Best Of Carl Smith*
(Capitol/Curb)
Lord, I Hope This Day Is Good (1982) Don
Williams: *Best Of Don Williams, Vol. 3* (MCA);
Especially For You (MCA)
The Lord Knows I'm Drinking (1973) Cal
Smith
Lord, Mr. Ford (1973) Jerry Reed
(Lost Her Love) On Our Last Date (1972)
Conway Twitty: VA—*Country USA 1972* (Time
Life); *Greatest Hits, Vol. 2* (MCA); *Silver
Anniversary Collection* (MCA)

(Lost His Love) On Our Last Date (1983)
Emmylou Harris: *Profile 2: The Best Of Emmylou
Harris* (Warner Bros.)
**Lost In The Fifties Tonight (In The Still Of
The Night)** (1985) Ronnie Milsap: VA—
Contemporary Country: The Mid-'80s (Time Life);
Lost In The Fifties Tonight (RCA); *Greatest Hits,
Vol. 2* (RCA)
Louisiana Woman, Mississippi Man (1973)
Conway Twitty & Loretta Lynn: VA—*Contemporary
Country: The Mid-'70s* (Time Life); *The Very Best
Of Loretta Lynn & Conway Twitty* (MCA)
Love Don't Care (Whose Heart It Breaks)
(1985) Earl Thomas Conley: *Greatest Hits* (RCA)
Love In The First Degree (1981) Alabama: VA—
Contemporary Country: The Early '80s (Time Life);
Alabama 'Live' (RCA); *Greatest Hits* (RCA); *Feels
So Right* (RCA)
Love Is Alive (1985) The Judds: *The Judds
Greatest Hits* (RCA); *The Judds Collection 1983-
1990* (RCA); *Why Not Me* (RCA)
Love Is Like A Butterfly (1974) Dolly Parton:
Collector's Series (RCA); VA—*Contemporary
Country: The Mid-'70s—Pure Gold* (Time Life); *The
Best Of Dolly Parton* (RCA)
Love Is On A Roll (1983) Don Williams: *Greatest
Hits* (MCA); VA—*Contemporary Country: The Early
'80s—Hot Hits* (Time Life)
Love Is The Foundation (1973) Loretta Lynn:
VA—*Contemporary Country: The Mid-'70s—Pure
Gold* (Time Life); *Greatest Hits, Vol. 2* (MCA)
Love, Love, Love (1955) Webb Pierce: VA—
Country USA 1955 (Time Life)
Love, Me (1992) Collin Raye: *All I Can Be* (Epic)
Love Me Over Again (1980) Don Williams: *Best
Of Don Williams, Vol. 3* (MCA)
Love On Arrival (1990) Dan Seals: *Classics
Collection, Vol. 2* (Liberty); *Greatest Hits* (Liberty);
The Songwriter (Liberty); *On Arrival* (Liberty)
Love Or Something Like That (1978) Kenny
Rogers: *Twenty Greatest Hits* (EMI)
Love Out Loud (1989) Earl Thomas Conley:
Greatest Hits, Vol. II (RCA); *Heart Of It All* (RCA)
Love Put A Song In My Heart (1975) Johnny
Rodriguez
Love Song (1983) The Oak Ridge Boys: *Greatest
Hits, Vol. 2* (MCA); *American Made* (MCA); *The
Oak Ridge Boys Collection* (MCA)
Love Will Find Its Way To You (1988) Reba
McEntire: *The Last One To Know* (MCA)
Love Will Turn You Around (1982) Kenny
Rogers: *Greatest Country Hits* (Capitol/Curb);
Twenty Greatest Hits (EMI)
Love Without End, Amen (1990) George Strait:
Ten Strait Hits (MCA); *Livin' It Up* (MCA)
Love's Gonna Live Here (1963) Buck Owens: *The
Buck Owens Collection, 1959-1990* (Rhino); VA—
Country USA 1963 (Time Life); VA—*Billboard Top
Country Hits—1963* (Rhino); *Live At Carnegie Hall*
(CMF)
Love's Got A Hold On You (1992) Alan Jackson:
Don't Rock The Jukebox (Arista)
Lovesick Blues (1949) Hank Williams: *The
Original Singles Collection...Plus* (PolyGram); *40
Greatest Hits* (Polydor); *Lovesick Blues (Aug.
1947-Dec. 1948)* (Polydor); VA—*Classic Country
Music* (Smithsonian)
Lovin' Only Me (1989) Ricky Skaggs: *Kentucky
Thunder* (Epic)
Loving Blind (1991) Clint Black: *Put Yourself In
My Shoes* (RCA)

Loving Up A Storm (1980) Razzy Bailey

Lucille (1977) Kenny Rogers: *Kenny Rogers' Greatest Hits* (EMI); *20 Great Years* (Reprise); *Twenty Greatest Hits* (EMI)

Lucille (You Won't Do Your Daddy's Will) (1983) Waylon Jennings

Luckenbach, Texas (Back To The Basics Of Love) (1977) Waylon Jennings: *Greatest Hits* (RCA); *Ol' Waylon* (RCA); VA—*Contemporary Country: The Late '70s* (Time Life)

Lynda (1987) Steve Wariner: *It's A Crazy World* (MCA); *Greatest Hits* (MCA)

Made In Japan (1972) Buck Owens: *The Buck Owens Collection, 1959-1990* (Rhino); VA—*Country USA 1972* (Time Life); VA—*Contemporary Country: The Early '70s* (Time Life); *All-Time Greatest, Vol. 1* (Capitol/Curb)

Make My Life With You (1985) The Oak Ridge Boys: *Greatest Hits, Vol. 2* (MCA)

Make No Mistake, She's Mine (1987) Ronnie Milsap & Kenny Rogers: *Kenny Rogers Greatest Hits* (RCA); *Kenny Rogers I Prefer The Moonlight* (RCA); *Ronnie Milsap Heart and Soul* (RCA)

Make The World Go Away (1965) Eddy Arnold: VA—*Country USA 1965* (Time Life); VA—*Billboard Top Country Hits—1965* (Rhino); *Last Of The Love Song Singers: Then & Now* (RCA); *The Best Of Eddy Arnold* (RCA)

Makin' Up For Lost Time (The Dallas Lovers' Song) (1986) Crystal Gayle & Gary Morris: *What If We Fall In Love?* (Warner Bros.); *Gary Morris Greatest Hits, Vol. II* (Warner Bros.)

Mama He's Crazy (1984) The Judds: *The Judds Collection 1983-1990* (RCA); *The Judds Greatest Hits* (RCA); *Why Not Me* (RCA); *The Judds (Wynonna & Naomi)* (RCA); VA—*Contemporary Country: The Mid-'80s* (Time Life)

Mama Sang A Song (1962) Bill Anderson: *The Best Of Bill Anderson* (Capitol/Curb); VA—*Country USA 1962* (Time Life)

Mama Tried (1968) Merle Haggard: *Best Of The Best Of Merle Haggard* (Capitol); *More Of The Best* (Rhino); VA—*Country USA 1968* (Time Life); *Very Best Of Merle Haggard* (Capitol)

Mama's Never Seen Those Eyes (1986) The Forester Sisters: VA—*Contemporary Country: The Mid '80s* (Time Life)

Mammas, Don't Let Your Babies Grow Up To Be Cowboys (1978) Waylon Jennings & Willie Nelson: VA—*Classic Country Music* (Smithsonian); *Waylon Jennings Greatest Hits* (RCA); VA—*Contemporary Country: The Late '70s* (Time Life)

Marie Laveau (1974) Bobby Bare

May The Bird Of Paradise Fly Up Your Nose (1965) Little Jimmy Dickens: VA—*Columbia Country Classics, Vol. 3: Americana* (Columbia)

Maybe Your Baby's Got The Blues (1987) The Judds: *The Judds Collection 1983-1990* (RCA); *Greatest Hits, Vol. II* (RCA); *Heartland* (RCA)

Meet In The Middle (1991) Diamond Rio: *Diamond Rio* (Arista)

Meet Me In Montana (1985) Marie Osmond & Dan Seals: *Dan Seals Classics Collection, Vol. 1* (Liberty); *The Best Of Marie Osmond* (Curb); *The Best Of Dan Seals* (Liberty)

Mexican Joe (1953) Jim Reeves: *Welcome To My World: The Essential Jim Reeves* (RCA); VA—*Country USA 1953* (Time Life); *Four Walls (The Legend Begins)* (RCA); *Live At The Opry* (CMF)

Midnight (1953) Red Foley: *Country Music Hall Of Fame* (MCA); VA—*Country USA 1952* (Time Life)

Midnight Hauler (1981) Razzy Bailey

Mind Your Own Business (1986) Hank Williams Jr.: *Montana Cafe* (Warner/Curb); *Greatest Hits III* (Warner/Curb); VA—*Contemporary Country: The Mid-'80s* (Time Life)

Misery Loves Company (1962) Porter Wagoner: VA—*Country USA 1962* (Time Life)

M-I-S-S-I-S-S-I-P-P-I (1950) Red Foley: VA—*Country USA 1950* (Time Life); *Country Music Hall Of Fame* (MCA)

Moanin' The Blues (1950) Hank Williams: *40 Greatest Hits* (Polydor); *Long Gone Lonesome Blues (Aug. 1949-Dec. 1950)* (Polydor); *The Original Singles Collection...Plus* (PolyGram); VA—*Country USA 1950* (Time Life)

Modern Day Romance (1985) Nitty Gritty Dirt Band: VA—*Contemporary Country: The Mid-80s* (Time Life)

Moody Blue (1977) Elvis Presley: *Moody Blue* (RCA); VA—*Contemporary Country: The Late '70s* (Time Life)

The Moon Is Still Over Her Shoulder (1987) Michael Johnson: *That's That* (RCA); *The Best Of Michael Johnson* (RCA)

More And More (1954) Webb Pierce: VA—*Country USA 1954* (Time Life)

More To Me (1977) Charley Pride

Mornin' Ride (1987) Lee Greenwood: *Love Will Find Its Way To You* (MCA); *Greatest Hits, Vol. 2* (MCA)

Morning Desire (1986) Kenny Rogers: VA—*Contemporary Country: The Mid-'80s* (Time Life); *Greatest Hits* (RCA)

The Most Beautiful Girl (1973) Charlie Rich: *Behind Closed Doors* (Epic); VA—*Contemporary Country: The Mid-'70s* (Time Life); *Greatest Hits* (Epic); *American Originals* (Columbia); VA—*Columbia Country Classics, Vol. 4: The Nashville Sound* (Columbia)

Mountain Music (1982) Alabama: *Greatest Hits* (RCA); *Mountain Music* (RCA); VA—*Contemporary Country: The Early '80s—Hot Hits* (Time Life)

Mountain Of Love (1982) Charley Pride

Movin' On (1975) Merle Haggard: *Very Best Of Merle Haggard* (Capitol); *Capitol Collectors Series* (Capitol)

Mule Train (1949) Tennessee Ernie Ford: VA—*Country USA 1950* (Time Life); *Capitol Collectors Series* (Capitol); *16 Tons Of Boogie—The Best Of Tennessee Ernie Ford* (Rhino)

My Baby Thinks He's A Train (1981) Rosanne Cash: *Seven Year Ache* (Columbia); *Hits, 1979-89* (Columbia); VA—*Contemporary Country: The Early '80s—Hot Hits* (Time Life)

My Elusive Dreams (1967) David Houston & Tammy Wynette: *David Houston American Originals* (Columbia); *Tammy's Greatest Hits, Vol. 1* (Epic); VA—*Columbia Country Classics, Vol. 4: The Nashville Sound* (Columbia); VA—*Billboard Top Country Hits—1967* (Rhino); VA—*Country USA 1967* (Time Life); *Tammy Wynette Tears of Fire—The 25th Anniversary Collection* (Epic)

My Eyes Can Only See As Far As You (1976) Charley Pride

My Favorite Memory (1981) Merle Haggard: VA—*Contemporary Country: The Early '80s—Pure Gold* (Time Life); *His Epic Hits—First Eleven* (Epic); *Big City* (Epic)

My Hang-Up Is You (1972) Freddie Hart: VA—*Contemporary Country: The Early '70s—Pure Gold* (Time Life)

My Heart (1980) Ronnie Milsap: *Collector's Series* (RCA); VA—*Contemporary Country: The Early '80s—Pure Gold* (Time Life)

My Heart Skips A Beat (1964) Buck Owens: *Live At Carnegie Hall* (CMF); VA—*Billboard Top Country Hits—1964* (Rhino); VA—*Country USA 1964* (Time Life); *The Buck Owens Collection, 1959-1990* (Rhino)

My Heroes Have Always Been Cowboys (1980) Willie Nelson: *My Heroes Have Always Been Cowboys* (RCA); *Greatest Hits & Some That Will Be* (Columbia); VA—*Contemporary Country: The Early '80s—Pure Gold* (Time Life)

My Life (Throw It Away If I Want To) (1969) Bill Anderson: *Best Of Bill Anderson* (Capitol/Curb)

My Love (1970) Sonny James: *The Best Of Sonny James* (Capitol/Curb)

My Man (1972) Tammy Wynette: *Biggest Hits* (Epic); *Tears Of Fire—The 25th Anniversary Collection* (Epic)

My Next Broken Heart (1991) Brooks & Dunn: *Brand New Man* (Arista)

My Only Love (1985) The Statler Brothers: *The Statler's Greatest Hits* (Mercury); *Atlanta Blue* (Mercury)

My Shoes Keep Walking Back To You (1957) Ray Price: VA—*Country USA 1957* (Time Life); *Essential Ray Price, 1951-1962* (Columbia); *Greatest Hits, Vols. 1-3* (Step One); *Ray Price's Greatest Hits* (Columbia)

My Special Angel (1957) Bobby Helms: VA— *Country USA 1957* (Time Life)

My Woman My Woman, My Wife (1970) Marty Robbins: VA—*Country USA 1970* (Time Life); *The Essential Marty Robbins* (Columbia)

Natural High (1985) Merle Haggard: *It's All In The Game* (Epic); VA—*Contemporary Country: The Mid-'80s—Hot Hits* (Time Life)

Near You (1977) George Jones & Tammy Wynette: *Greatest Hits* (Epic); *Tammy Wynette Tears Of Fire—The 25th Anniversary Collection* (Epic); VA— *Contemporary Country: The Late '70s* (Time Life)

Need You (1967) Sonny James

Neon Moon (1992) Brooks & Dunn: *Brand New Man* (Arista)

Never Be You (1986) Rosanne Cash: VA— *Contemporary Country: The Mid-'80s* (Time Life); *Hits 1979-1989* (Columbia); *Rhythm & Romance* (Columbia)

Never Been So Loved (In All My Life) (1981) Charley Pride: *Greatest Hits* (RCA)

New Fool At An Old Game (1989) Reba McEntire: *Reba* (MCA)

New Jole Blonde (1947) Red Foley

New Looks From An Old Lover (1983) B. J. Thomas

New Spanish Two Step (1946) Bob Wills & His Texas Playboys: *The Essential Bob Wills* (Columbia)

Next In Line (1968) Conway Twitty: *Greatest Hits, Vol. 1* (MCA); VA—*Country USA 1968* (Time Life)

Next To You, Next To Me (1990) Shenandoah: *Greatest Hits* (Columbia); *Extra Mile* (Columbia)

Night Games (1983) Charley Pride: VA— *Contemporary Country: The Early '80s—Pure Gold* (Time Life)

9 To 5 (1980) Dolly Parton: VA—*Classic Country Music* (Smithsonian); *Greatest Hits* (RCA); *The Best There Is* (RCA); VA—*Contemporary Country: The Early '80s—Hot Hits* (Time Life)

No Charge (1974) Melba Montgomery

No Help Wanted (1953) The Carlisles: VA— *Country USA 1953* (Time Life)

No Matter How High (1990) The Oak Ridge Boys: *American Dreams* (MCA)

No One Else On Earth (1992) Wynonna: *Wynonna* (MCA/Curb)

Nobody (1982) Sylvia: *Greatest Hits* (RCA)

Nobody Falls Like A Fool (1985) Earl Thomas Conley: *Greatest Hits* (RCA)

Nobody In His Right Mind Would've Left Her (1986) George Strait: *No. 7* (MCA); *Greatest Hits, Vol. II* (MCA)

Nobody Likes Sad Songs (1979) Ronnie Milsap

Nobody Loves Me Like You Do (1984) Anne Murray with Dave Loggins: *Greatest Hits, Vol. II* (Liberty); *Anne Murray's Country Hits* (Liberty); VA— *Contemporary Country: The Mid-'80s* (Time Life)

Nobody's Home (1990) Clint Black: *Killin' Time* (RCA)

North To Alaska (1961) Johnny Horton: *Greatest Hits* (Columbia); *American Originals* (Columbia); VA—*Columbia Country Classics, Vol. 3: Americana* (Columbia); VA—*Country USA 1960* (Time Life); VA—*Billboard Top Country Hits—1961* (Rhino)

Nothing I Can Do About It Now (1989) Willie Nelson: *Horse Called Music* (Columbia)

Now And Forever (You And Me) (1986) Anne Murray: *Greatest Hits, Vol. II* (Liberty)

Ocean Front Property (1987) George Strait: *Greatest Hits, Vol. II* (MCA); *Ocean Front Property* (MCA); VA—*Contemporary Country: The Late '80s* (Time Life)

Oh, Baby Mine (I Get So Lonely) (1954) Johnnie & Jack

Oh, Lonesome Me (1958) Don Gibson: VA— *Country USA 1958* (Time Life); *18 Greatest Hits* (Capitol/Curb); *All-Time Greatest Hits* (RCA)

Okie From Muskogee (1969) Merle Haggard: VA—*Country USA 1969* (Time Life); *Capitol Collector's Series* (Capitol); *Very Best Of Merle Haggard* (Capitol); *Best Of The Best Of Merle Haggard* (Capitol)

Oklahoma Hills (1945) Jack Guthrie: VA— *Country USA 1972* (Time Life)

(Old Dogs, Children And) Watermelon Wine (1973) Tom T. Hall: VA—*Country USA 1972* (Time Life)

Old Flame (1981) Alabama: VA—*Classic Country Music* (Smithsonian); *Greatest Hits* (RCA); *Feels So Right* (RCA)

Old Flames Can't Hold A Candle To You (1980) Dolly Parton: *Greatest Hits* (RCA)

Old Man From The Mountain (1974) Merle Haggard: *Epic Collection (Recorded Live)* (Epic); *Capitol Collector's Series* (Capitol); *Very Best Of Merle Haggard* (Capitol)

Older Women (1981) Ronnie McDowell: *Older Women & Other Greatest Hits* (Epic); VA— *Contemporary Country: The Early '80s—Hot Hits* (Time Life)

On My Knees (1978) Charlie Rich with Janie Frickie: VA—*Contemporary Country: The Late '70s—Hot Hits* (Time Life); *Charlie Rich American Originals* (Columbia)

On Second Thought (1990) Eddie Rabbitt: *Ten Years Of Greatest Hits* (Liberty)

On The Other Hand (1986) Randy Travis: VA— *Contemporary Country: The Mid-'80s* (Time Life); *Greatest Hits, Vol. 1* (Warner Bros.); *Storms Of Life* (Warner Bros.)

On The Road Again (1980) Willie Nelson:
VA—Contemporary Country: The Early '80s
(Time Life); *Greatest Hits & Some That Will
Be* (Columbia); *Honeysuckle Rose* (Columbia)

Once A Day (1964) Connie Smith: *The Best
Of Connie Smith* (Dominion); *VA—Country
USA 1964* (Time Life); *VA—Billboard Top
Country Hits-1964* (Rhino)

Once In A Blue Moon (1986) Earl Thomas
Conley: *Greatest Hits* (RCA)

One By One (1954) Kitty Wells & Red Foley:
Kitty Wells Greatest Hits, Vol. 2 (Step One);
Red Foley Country Music Hall Of Fame
(MCA); *VA—Country USA 1954* (Time Life)

One Day At A Time (1980) Cristy Lane

One Friend (1988) Dan Seals: *The Songwriter*
(Liberty); *The Best Of Dan Seals* (Liberty)

**One Has My Name (The Other Has My
Heart)** (1948) Jimmy Wakely

One In A Million (1980) Johnny Lee:
Greatest Hits (Full Moon)

One Kiss Too Many (1949) Eddy Arnold

One Of A Kind Pair Of Fools (1983)
Barbara Mandrell: *Greatest Hits* (MCA);
Greatest Country Hits (Capitol/Curb)

One Piece At A Time (1976) Johnny Cash:
The Essential Johnny Cash (Columbia); *VA—
Contemporary Country: The Mid-'70s—Pure
Gold* (Time Life)

One Promise Too Late (1987) Reba
McEntire: *Greatest Hits* (MCA); *What Am I
Gonna Do About You* (MCA)

One's On The Way (1972) Loretta Lynn:
VA—Country USA 1972 (Time Life); *Country
Music Hall Of Fame* (MCA); *Loretta Lynn's
Greatest Hits, Vol. 2* (MCA)

Only One Love In My Life (1978) Ronnie
Milsap: *Collector's Series* (RCA); *VA—
Contemporary Country: The Late '70s—Pure
Gold* (Time Life)

Only One You (1982) T. G. Sheppard: *All-
Time Greatest Hits* (Warner Bros.)

Only The Lonely (1969) Sonny James:
Capitol Collector's Series (Capitol)

Only You (Can Break My Heart) (1965)
Buck Owens: *The Buck Owens Collection,
1959-1990* (Rhino); *Live At Carnegie Hall*
(CMF)

Open Up Your Heart (1966) Buck Owens:
VA—Country USA 1966 (Time Life); *The
Buck Owens Collection, 1959-1990* (Rhino)

Our Love Is On The Faultline (1983)
Crystal Gayle: *The Best Of Crystal Gayle*
(Warner Bros.)

Out Of My Head And Back In My Bed
(1978) Loretta Lynn: *VA—Contemporary
Country: The Late '70s—Hot Hits* (Time
Life); *Country Music Hall Of Fame* (MCA)

Pancho & Lefty (1983) Willie Nelson &
Merle Haggard: *VA—Contemporary Country:
The Early '80s—Pure Gold* (Time Life);
*Columbia Country Classics, Vol. 3:
Americana* (Columbia); *Half Nelson*
(Columbia); *Pancho & Lefty* (Epic)

Paper Roses (1973) Marie Osmond: *The Best
Of Marie Osmond* (Curb)

Paradise Tonight (1983) Charly McClain &
Mickey Gilley: *Charly McClain Biggest Hits*
(Epic)

Party Time (1981) T. G. Sheppard: *All-Time*

Greatest Hits (Warner Bros.); *VA—
Contemporary Country: The Early '80s—Hot
Hits* (Time Life)

Pistol Packin' Mama (1944) Al Dexter:
*VA—Columbia Country Classics, Vol. 1: The
Golden Age* (Columbia); *VA—Classic Country
Music* (Smithsonian)

A Place To Fall Apart (1985) Merle
Haggard with Janie Frickie: *It's All In The
Game* (Epic)

Play, Guitar Play (1977) Conway Twitty: *The
Very Best Of Conway Twitty* (MCA)

Please Don't Stop Loving Me (1974)
Porter Wagoner & Dolly Parton

**Please Don't Tell Me How The Story
Ends** (1974) Ronnie Milsap: *Greatest Hits*
(RCA)

Please Help Me, I'm Falling (1960) Hank
Locklin: *VA—Billboard Top Country Hits—
1960* (Rhino); *VA—Country USA 1960* (Time
Life)

The Pool Shark (1970) Dave Dudley

Pure Love (1974) Ronnie Milsap: *Greatest
Hits* (RCA); *Collector's Series* (RCA)

Put Your Dreams Away (1982) Mickey
Gilley: *Ten Years Of Hits* (Epic)

Radio Heart (1985) Charly McClain: *Biggest
Hits* (Epic)

Rainbow At Midnight (1947) Ernest Tubb

Rated "X" (1973) Loretta Lynn: *VA—Country
USA 1972* (Time Life)

Ready For The Times To Get Better
(1978) Crystal Gayle: *Classic Crystal* (EMI)

Real Love (1985) Kenny Rogers & Dolly
Parton: *The Best Of Dolly Parton, Vol. 3*
(RCA); *VA—Contemporary Country: The Mid-
'80s* (Time Life)

Red Neckin' Love Makin' Night (1982)
Conway Twitty

Redneck Girl (1982) The Bellamy Brothers:
Greatest Hits (MCA)

Rest Your Love On Me (1981) Conway
Twitty: *Number Ones* (MCA)

Rhinestone Cowboy (1975) Glen Campbell:
The Best Of Glen Campbell (Liberty); *Classics
Collection* (Liberty); *All-Time Country
Classics, Vol. 2* (Liberty); *VA—Contemporary
Country: The Mid-'70s* (Time Life)

Rhumba Boogie (1951) Hank Snow: *I'm
Movin' On & Other Great Country Hits*
(RCA); *VA—Country USA 1951* (Time Life)

Ribbon Of Darkness (1965) Marty Robbins:
VA—Country USA 1965 (Time Life); *Marty
Robbins' All-Time Greatest Hits* (Columbia);
Biggest Hits (Columbia); *Essential Marty
Robbins, 1951-1982* (Columbia)

Ridin' My Thumb To Mexico (1973)
Johnny Rodriguez: *VA—Contemporary
Country: The Early '70s—Pure Gold* (Time
Life)

Right From The Start (1987) Earl Thomas
Conley

Right Or Wrong (1984) George Strait: *Right
Or Wrong* (MCA); *Greatest Hits* (MCA)

Ring Of Fire (1963) Johnny Cash: *VA—
Country USA 1963* (Time Life); *The Essential
Johnny Cash* (Columbia); *The Best Of Johnny
Cash* (Capitol/Curb); *VA—Billboard Top
Country Hits—1963* (Rhino); *VA—Columbia
Country Classics, Vol. 4: The Nashville Sound*
(Columbia); *Johnny Cash's Greatest Hits*

(Columbia); *Columbia Records 1958-1986*
(Columbia); *Classic Cash* (Mercury)
The River (1992) Garth Brooks: *Ropin' The Wind*
(Liberty)
Rockin' With The Rhythm Of The Rain (1986)
The Judds: *Rockin' With The Rhythm* (RCA); *The
Judds Greatest Hits* (RCA); *The Judds Collection
1983-1990* (RCA)
Rockin' Years (1991) Dolly Parton & Ricky Van
Shelton: *Dolly Parton Eagle When She Flies*
(Columbia); *Ricky Van Shelton Greatest Hits Plus*
(Columbia); *Ricky Van Shelton Backroads*
(Columbia)
Rocky (1975) Dickey Lee
Roll On (Eighteen Wheeler) (1984) Alabama:
Greatest Hits, Vol. II (RCA); *Roll On* (RCA); VA—
Contemporary Country: The Mid-'80s (Time Life)
Roll On Big Mama (1975) Joe Stampley
Rollin' With The Flow (1977) Charlie Rich:
Contemporary Country: The Late '70s—Pure Gold
(Time Life); *American Originals* (Columbia)
Room Full Of Roses (1974) Mickey Gilley:
Gilley's Greatest Hits, Vol. 1 (Epic); *Ten Years Of
Hits* (Epic)
The Roots Of My Raising (1976) Merle Haggard:
Very Best Of Merle Haggard (Capitol); *Capitol
Collector's Series* (Capitol)
Rosalita (1944) Al Dexter
The Rose (1983) Conway Twitty: *No. 1's: The
Warner Bros. Years* (Warner Bros.)
Rose Garden (1970) Lynn Anderson: VA—
Contemporary Country: The Early '70s (Time Life);
VA—*Country USA 1970* (Time Life); VA—
*Columbia Country Classics, Vol. 4: The Nashville
Sound* (Columbia)
Rose In Paradise (1987) Waylon Jennings: *New
Classic Waylon* (MCA)
Rub-A-Dub-Dub (1953) Hank Thompson: VA—
Country USA 1953 (Time Life); *Capitol Collector's
Series* (Capitol); *All-Time Greatest Hits*
(Capitol/Curb)
Rub It In (1974) Billy "Crash" Craddock
Ruby Ann (1963) Marty Robbins: *American
Originals* (Columbia); *Essential Marty Robbins,
1951-1982* (Columbia); VA—*Billboard Top Country
Hits—1963* (Rhino); VA—*Country USA 1963*
(Time Life)
Ruby, Baby (1975) Billy "Crash" Craddock
Rudolph, The Red-Nosed Reindeer (1950)
Gene Autry
Run, Woman, Run (1970) Tammy Wynette: VA—
Country USA 1970 (Time Life); *Biggest Hits*
(Epic); *Anniversary: 20 Years Of Hits* (Epic)
Runaway Train (1988) Rosanne Cash: *King's
Record Shop* (Columbia)
Running Bear (1969) Sonny James
Saginaw, Michigan (1964) Lefty Frizzell: *Best Of
Lefty Frizzell* (Rhino); VA—*Columbia Country
Classics, Vol. 3: Americana* (Columbia); VA—
Billboard Top Country Hits—1964 (Rhino); VA—
Country USA 1964 (Time Life); *American
Originals* (Columbia)
Sam's Place (1967) Buck Owens: VA—*Billboard
Top Country Hits—1967* (Rhino); *The Buck Owens
Collection, 1959-1990* (Rhino); VA—*Country USA
1967* (Time Life)
The Same Old Me (1959) Ray Price: *Ray Price's
Greatest Hits* (Columbia); VA—*Country USA 1959*
(Time Life); *Essential Ray Price, 1951-1962*
(Columbia)

San Antonio Stroll (1975) Tanya Tucker: *Tanya
Tucker Collection* (MCA); *Tanya Tucker's Greatest
Hits* (MCA); VA—*Contemporary Country: The Mid-
'70s—Pure Gold* (Time Life); *Greatest Hits Encore*
(Liberty)
Satin Sheets (1973) Jeanne Pruett: VA—
Contemporary Country: The Mid-'70s (Time Life)
A Satisfied Mind (1955) Porter Wagoner: VA—
Country USA 1955 (Time Life)
Say It Again (1976) Don Williams: *Best Of Don
Williams, Vol. 2* (MCA)
Say You'll Stay Until Tomorrow (1977) Tom
Jones
Secret Love (1975) Freddy Fender: *Freddy Fender
Collection* (Reprise)
Set 'Em Up Joe (1988) Vern Gosdin: VA—
Contemporary Country: The Late '80s (Time Life);
Chiseled In Stone (Columbia); *Greatest Hits, Vol. 1*
(Columbia)
Seven Spanish Angels (1985) Ray Charles with
Willie Nelson: *Ray Charles Seven Spanish Angels &
Other Hits* (Columbia); *Ray Charles Friendship*
(Columbia); *Willie Nelson Half Nelson* (Columbia)
Seven Year Ache (1981) Rosanne Cash: *Hits
1979-1989* (Columbia); *Seven Year Ache*
(Columbia); VA—*Contemporary Country: The Early
'80s* (Time Life); VA—*Columbia Country Classics,
Vol. 5: A New Tradition* (Columbia)
Shadows In The Moonlight (1979) Anne Murray:
Greatest Hits (Liberty); *15 Of The Best* (Liberty)
Shame On You (1945) Lawrence Welk with Red
Foley
Shame On You (1945) Spade Cooley: VA—
Columbia Country Classics, Vol. 1: The Golden Age
(Columbia)
Shameless (1991) Garth Brooks: *Ropin' The Wind*
(Liberty)
She And I (1986) Alabama: *Greatest Hits* (RCA)
She Believes In Me (1979) Kenny Rogers: *20
Great Years* (Reprise); *Twenty Greatest Hits*
(EMI); *Kenny Rogers' Greatest Hits* (EMI); *The
Gambler* (EMI); *Greatest Country Hits*
(Capitol/Curb)
She Called Me Baby (1974) Charlie Rich
**She Can Put Her Shoes Under My Bed
(Anytime)** (1978) Johnny Duncan: VA—
Contemporary Country: The Late '70s—Pure Gold
(Time Life)
She Got The Gold Mine (I Got The Shaft)
(1982) Jerry Reed
She Is His Only Need (1992) Wynonna: *Wynonna*
(MCA/Curb)
She Keeps The Home Fires Burning (1985)
Ronnie Milsap: VA—*Contemporary Country: The
Mid-'80s—Pure Gold* (Time Life)
She Left Love All Over Me (1982) Razzy Bailey:
VA—*Contemporary Country: The Early '80s—Hot
Hits* (Time Life)
**She Needs Someone To Hold Her (When She
Cries)** (1973) Conway Twitty: *Greatest Hits, Vol.
2* (MCA)
She Thinks I Still Care (1962) George Jones:
VA—*Billboard Top Country Hits—1962* (Rhino);
The Best Of George Jones (1955-1967) (Rhino);
VA—*Country USA 1962* (Time Life); *All-Time
Greatest Hits, Vol. 1* (Epic)
She's A Miracle (1985) Exile: *Greatest Hits* (Epic)
She's Actin' Single (I'm Drinkin' Doubles)
(1975) Gary Stewart: *Gary's Greatest* (Hightone);
VA—*Contemporary Country: The Mid-'70s* (Time
Life); *Out Of Hand* (Hightone)

She's Crazy For Leavin' (1989) Rodney Crowell: *Diamonds & Dirt* (Columbia)

She's Got The Rhythm (And I Got The Blues) (1992) Alan Jackson: *A Lot About Livin' (And A Little 'Bout Love)* (Arista)

She's Got To Be A Saint (1972) Ray Price: *Greatest Hits, Vol. 4 (By Request)* (Step One)

She's Got You (1962) Patsy Cline: *The Patsy Cline Collection* (MCA); *Live At The Opry* (MCA); *Sweet Dreams* (MCA); VA—*Country USA 1962* (Time Life); *The Patsy Cline Story* (MCA); *Sentimentally Yours* (MCA); *Greatest Hits* (MCA); VA—*Billboard Top Country Hits—1962* (Rhino)

She's Got You (1977) Loretta Lynn: *I Remember Patsy* (MCA); VA—*Contemporary Country: The Late '70s—Pure Gold* (Time Life)

She's In Love With The Boy (1991) Trisha Yearwood: *Trisha Yearwood* (MCA)

She's Just An Old Love Turned Memory (1977) Charley Pride: *Greatest Hits* (RCA)

She's Pulling Me Back Again (1977) Mickey Gilley: *Ten Years Of Hits* (Epic)

She's Too Good To Be True (1972) Charley Pride

She's Too Good To Be True (1987) Exile: *Hang On To Your Heart* (Epic)

Shine, Shine, Shine (1987) Eddy Raven: *Greatest Country Hits* (Capitol/Curb); *Right Hand Man* (RCA); *The Best Of Eddy Raven* (RCA)

The Shot Gun Boogie (1951) Tennessee Ernie Ford: *Capitol Collector's Series* (Capitol); *16 Tons Of Boogie* (Rhino)

A Shoulder To Cry On (1973) Charley Pride

Show Her (1984) Ronnie Milsap: *Greatest Hits, Vol. 2* (RCA); *Collector's Series* (RCA); *Keyed Up* (RCA)

Silver Dew On The Blue Grass Tonight (1945) Bob Wills & His Texas Playboys

Since I Met You, Baby (1969) Sonny James: *Greatest Hits* (Capitol/Curb); VA—*Country USA 1969* (Time Life)

Sing Me Back Home (1968) Merle Haggard: *Rainbow Stew (Live At Anaheim Stadium)* (MCA); *Capitol Collectors Series* (Capitol); VA—*Country USA 1967* (Time Life)

Singing My Song (1969) Tammy Wynette: *Tears Of Fire—The 25th Anniversary Collection* (Epic); *Tammy's Greatest Hits, Vol. 1* (Epic); *Anniversary: 20 Years Of Hits* (Epic); VA—*Country USA 1969* (Time Life)

Singing The Blues (1956) Marty Robbins: *American Originals* (Columbia); VA—*Columbia Country Classics, Vol. 4: The Nashville Sound* (Columbia); *The Essential Marty Robbins, 1951-1982* (Columbia); VA—*Country USA 1956* (Time Life)

Sioux City Sue (1945) Dick Thomas

Sixteen Tons (1955) Tennessee Ernie Ford: VA—*Classic Country Music* (Smithsonian); *16 Tons Of Boogie—The Best Of Tennessee Ernie Ford* (Rhino); VA—*Country USA 1955* (Time Life); *Capitol Collector's Series* (Capitol)

Skip A Rope (1968) Henson Cargill: VA—*Country USA 1968* (Time Life)

Sleeping Single In A Double Bed (1978) Barbara Mandrell: *The Best Of Barbara Mandrell* (MCA): VA—*Contemporary Country: The Late '70s* (Time Life)

Slippin' Around (1949) Ernest Tubb: *Live 1965* (Rhino)

Slipping Around (1949) Margaret Whiting & Jimmy Wakely

Slow Burn (1984) T. G. Sheppard: *All Time Greatest Hits* (Warner Bros.)

Slow Hand (1982) Conway Twitty: *No. 1's: The Warner Bros. Years* (Warner Bros.); VA—*Contemporary Country: The Early '80s* (Time Life); *Silver Anniversary Collection* (MCA)

Slow Poke (1951) Pee Wee King: VA—*Country USA 1951* (Time Life)

Slowly (1954) Webb Pierce: VA—*Legends Of Country Guitar, Vol. 1* (Rhino); VA—*Classic Country Music* (Smithsonian); VA—*Country USA 1954* (Time Life)

Small Town Girl (1987) Steve Wariner: *It's A Crazy World* (MCA); *Greatest Hits* (MCA)

Smoke On The Water (1944) Red Foley

Smoke On The Water (1945) Bob Wills & His Texas Playboys

Smoke! Smoke! Smoke! (That Cigarette) (1947) Tex Williams

Smoky Mountain Rain (1980) Ronnie Milsap: *Greatest Hits* (RCA)

Snap Your Fingers (1987) Ronnie Milsap: *Heart & Soul* (RCA); *Greatest Hits, Vol. 3* (RCA)

So Long, Pal (1944) Al Dexter

So Round, So Firm, So Fully Packed (1947) Merle Travis: *The Best of Merle Travis* (Rhino)

Soldier's Last Letter (1944) Ernest Tubb: *Country Music Hall Of Fame* (MCA); *Live 1965* (Rhino)

Some Broken Hearts Never Mend (1977) Don Williams: *Best Of Don Williams, Vol. 2* (MCA); *Greatest Country Hits* (Capitol/Curb)

Some Fools Never Learn (1985) Steve Wariner: *Greatest Hits* (MCA); *One Good Night Deserves Another* (MCA)

Some Girls Do (1992) Sawyer Brown: *Dirt Road* (Liberty)

Somebody Lied (1987) Ricky Van Shelton: *Greatest Hits Plus* (Columbia); VA—*Contemporary Country: The Late '80s* (Time Life); *Wild-Eyed Dream* (Columbia)

Somebody Like Me (1966) Eddy Arnold

Somebody Should Leave (1985) Reba McEntire: *My Kind Of Country* (MCA); VA—*Contemporary Country: The Mid-'80s—Hot Hits* (Time Life); *Greatest Hits* (MCA)

Somebody Somewhere (Don't Know What He's Missin' Tonight) (1976) Loretta Lynn

Somebody's Gonna Love You (1983) Lee Greenwood: *Somebody's Gonna Love You* (MCA); *Greatest Hits* (MCA)

Somebody's Needin' Somebody (1984) Conway Twitty: *No. 1's: The Warner Bros. Years* (Warner Bros.)

Someday (1991) Alan Jackson: *Don't Rock The Jukebox* (Arista)

Someday When Things Are Good (1984) Merle Haggard: *His Epic Hits—First Eleven* (Epic)

Someone Could Lose A Heart Tonight (1982) Eddie Rabbitt: *Step By Step* (Liberty)

Someone Loves You Honey (1978) Charley Pride: VA—*Contemporary Country: The Late '70s—Hot Hits* (Time Life); *Greatest Hits* (RCA)

Sometimes (1976) Bill Anderson & Mary Lou Turner

Somewhere Between Right And Wrong (1982) Earl Thomas Conley: VA—*Contemporary Country: The Early '80s* (Time Life); *Greatest Hits (RCA)*

Teddy Bear (1976) Red Sovine: *Teddy Bear* (Hollywood)

Teddy Bear Song (1973) Barbara Fairchild

Tell Me A Lie (1983) Janie Frickie: *17 Greatest Hits* (Columbia); *The Very Best Of Janie Frickie* (Columbia)

A Tender Lie (1988) Restless Heart: *The Best of Restless Heart* (RCA); *Big Dreams In A Small Town* (RCA)

Tender Years (1961) George Jones: *All-Time Greatest Hits, Vol. 1* (Epic); VA—*Billboard Top Country Hits—1961* (Rhino); *The Best Of George Jones (1955-1967)* (Rhino); VA—*Country USA 1961* (Time Life)

Tennessee Bird Walk (1970) Jack Blanchard & Misty Morgan

Tennessee Flat Top Box (1988) Rosanne Cash: *King's Record Shop* (Columbia); *Hits 1979-1989* (Columbia)

Tennessee Homesick Blues (1984) Dolly Parton: VA—*Contemporary Country: The Mid-'80s—Pure Gold* (Time Life); *The Best Of Dolly Parton, Vol. 3* (RCA)

Tennessee River (1980) Alabama: *Alabama 'Live'* (RCA); *Greatest Hits* (RCA); *My Home's In Alabama* (RCA)

Tennessee Saturday Night (1949) Red Foley: *Country Music Hall Of Fame* (MCA)

Texarkana Baby (1948) Eddy Arnold

Texas Women (1981) Hank Williams, Jr.: *Greatest Hits* (Warner Bros.); *Rowdy* (Warner/Curb); *The Bocephus Box* (Curb/Capricorn)

Thank God For The Radio (1984) The Kendalls: VA—*Contemporary Country: The Mid-'80s—Hot Hits* (Time Life); *20 Favorites* (Epic)

Thank God I'm A Country Boy (1975) John Denver: *Back Home Again* (RCA); *Evening With John Denver* (RCA); *John Denver's Greatest Hits, Vol. 2* (RCA)

That Do Make It Nice (1955) Eddy Arnold

That Heart Belongs To Me (1952) Webb Pierce: VA—*Country USA 1952* (Time Life)

That Rock Won't Roll (1986) Restless Heart: *Wheels* (RCA); *The Best Of Restless Heart* (RCA)

That Was A Close One (1987) Earl Thomas Conley: *Greatest Hits, Vol. III* (RCA)

That Was Yesterday (1977) Donna Fargo

That's All That Matters (1980) Mickey Gilley: *Biggest Hits* (Epic); *Ten Years Of Hits* (Epic)

That's My Pa (1962) Sheb Wooley

That's The Thing About Love (1984) Don Williams: *Greatest Hits* (MCA); VA—*Contemporary Country: The Mid-'80s—Hot Hits* (Time Life)

That's The Way Love Goes (1974) Johnny Rodriguez

That's The Way Love Goes (1984) Merle Haggard: *His Epic Hits—First Eleven* (Epic); VA—*Contemporary Country: The Mid-'80s—Hot Hits* (Time Life)

That's Why I Love You Like I Do (1972) Sonny James: *Greatest Hits* (Curb)

Theme From The Dukes Of Hazzard (Good Ol' Boys) (1980) Waylon Jennings: *Greatest Hits, Vol. 2* (RCA); VA—*Contemporary Country: The Early '80s—Hot Hits* (Time Life)

Then Who Am I (1975) Charley Pride

Then You Can Tell Me Goodbye (1968) Eddy Arnold: *Last Of The Love Song Singers: Then & Now* (RCA)

There Ain't Nothin' Wrong With The Radio

(1992) Aaron Tippin: *Read Between The Lines* (RCA)

There Goes My Everything (1966) Jack Greene: VA—*Billboard Top Country Hits—1966* (Rhino)

There Must Be More To Love Than This (1970) Jerry Lee Lewis: VA—*Country USA 1970* (Time Life)

There Stands The Glass (1953) Webb Pierce: VA—*Country USA 1953* (Time Life)

There Won't Be Anymore (1974) Charlie Rich

There You Go (1957) Johnny Cash: *Sun Years* (Rhino)

(There's A) Fire In The Night (1985) Alabama: *Roll On* (RCA); VA—*Contemporary Country: The Mid-'80s—Hot Hits* (Time Life)

There's A Honky Tonk Angel (Who'll Take Me Back In) (1974) Conway Twitty: *The Very Best Of Conway Twitty* (MCA)

There's A New Moon Over My Shoulder (1945) Jimmie Davis: *Country Music Hall Of Fame* (MCA)

There's Been A Change In Me (1951) Eddy Arnold: VA—*Country USA 1951* (Time Life)

(There's) No Gettin' Over Me (1981) Ronnie Milsap: *Greatest Hits, Vol. 2* (RCA)

There's No Stopping Your Heart (1986) Marie Osmond: *The Best Of Marie Osmond* (Curb)

There's No Way (1985) Alabama: *Alabama 'Live'* (RCA)

They Took The Stars Out Of Heaven (1944) Floyd Tillman: *Country Music Hall Of Fame* (MCA)

Things Aren't Funny Anymore (1974) Merle Haggard: *Epic Collection (Recorded Live)* (Epic); *Very Best Of Merle Haggard* (Capitol); *Capitol Collector's Series* (Capitol)

Think About Love (1986) Dolly Parton: *The Best There Is* (RCA); *The Best Of Dolly Parton, Vol. 3* (RCA)

Think Of Me (1966) Buck Owens: VA—*Country USA 1966* (Time Life); *The Buck Owens Collection, 1959-1990* (Rhino); *All-Time Greatest, Vol. 1* (Capitol/Curb)

Thinkin' Of A Rendezvous (1976) Johnny Duncan

This Crazy Love (1987) The Oak Ridge Boys: *Where The Fast Lane Ends* (MCA); *Greatest Hits 3* (MCA); VA—*Contemporary Country: The Late '80s—Pure Gold* (Time Life)

This Is It (1965) Jim Reeves: VA—*Country USA 1965* (Time Life); VA—*Billboard Top Country Hits—1965* (Rhino)

This Time (1974) Waylon Jennings

This Time I've Hurt Her More Than She Loves Me (1976) Conway Twitty

The Three Bells (1959) The Browns: VA—*Country USA 1959* (Time Life)

Three Time Loser (1987) Dan Seals: *The Best Of Dan Seals* (Liberty); *Early Dan Seals* (Liberty); *The Songwriter* (Liberty)

The Thunder Rolls (1991) Garth Brooks: *No Fences* (Liberty)

Tight Fittin' Jeans (1981) Conway Twitty: *Silver Anniversary Collection* (MCA)

'Til I Can Make It On My Own (1976) Tammy Wynette: *Anniversary: 20 Years Of Hits* (Epic); *Tears Of Fire—The 25th Anniversary Collection* (Epic); VA—*Contemporary Country: The Mid-'70s—Pure Gold* (Time Life)

'Til I Get It Right (1973) Tammy Wynette: *Biggest Hits* (Epic); *Tears Of Fire—The 25th Anniversary*

Collection (Epic); *Anniversary : 20 Years Of Hits*
(Epic); VA—*Contemporary Country: The Early
'70s—Pure Gold* (Time Life)

Till I Gain Control Again (1983) Crystal Gayle:
The Best Of Crystal Gayle (Warner Bros.)

Till The Rivers All Run Dry (1976) Don
Williams: *Best Of Don Williams, Vol. 2* (MCA);
VA—*Contemporary Country: The Mid-'70s* (Time
Life)

'Till You're Gone (1982) Barbara Mandrell

Timber, I'm Falling In Love (1989) Patty
Loveless: *Honky Tonk Angel* (MCA); VA—
Contemporary Country: The Late '80s (Time Life)

To All The Girls I've Loved Before (1984)
Julio Iglesias & Willie Nelson: *Half Nelson*
(Columbia)

To Know Him Is To Love Him (1987) Dolly
Parton, Linda Ronstadt, Emmylou Harris: *Trio*
(Warner Bros.)

To Make Love Sweeter For You (1969) Jerry
Lee Lewis

To See My Angel Cry (1969) Conway Twitty:
Silver Anniversary Collection (MCA)

Together Again (1964) Buck Owens: VA—
Billboard Top Country Hits—1964 (Rhino); *The
Buck Owens Collection, 1959-1990* (Rhino); *All-
Time Greatest, Vol. 1* (Capitol/Curb); VA—*Country
USA 1964* (Time Life); *Live At Carnegie Hall*
(CMF)

Together Again (1976) Emmylou Harris: VA—
Contemporary Country: The Mid-'70s (Time Life);
Profile (Best Of Emmylou Harris) (Warner Bros.);
Elite Hotel (Reprise)

Tomb Of The Unknown Love (1986) Kenny
Rogers

Tonight Carmen (1967) Marty Robbins: *Marty
Robbins' All-Time Greatest Hits* (Columbia); VA—
Country USA 1967 (Time Life); *American
Originals* (Columbia); *Essential Marty Robbins,
1951-1982* (Columbia)

Too Gone Too Long (1988) Randy Travis: *Always
& Forever* (Warner Bros.); *Greatest Hits, Vol. 1*
(Warner Bros.)

Too Late To Worry, Too Blue To Cry (1944) Al
Dexter

Too Many Lovers (1981) Crystal Gayle: *These
Days* (Liberty); *Greatest Hits* (Capitol)

Too Much Is Not Enough (1986) The Bellamy
Brothers: *Greatest Hits, Vol. 2* (MCA)

Too Much On My Heart (1985) The Statler
Brothers: *Partners In Rhyme* (Mercury); VA—
Contemporary Country: The Mid-'80s (Time Life)

Touch A Hand, Make A Friend (1985) The Oak
Ridge Boys: *Greatest Hits 3* (MCA); VA—
Contemporary Country: The Mid-'80s—Hot Hits
(Time Life); *Step On Out* (MCA)

Touch Me When We're Dancing (1986)
Alabama: *The Touch* (RCA)

Touch The Hand (1975) Conway Twitty: *Number
Ones* (MCA)

Trip To Heaven (1973) Freddie Hart

Trouble In Paradise (1974) Loretta Lynn

True Love Ways (1980) Mickey Gilley: *Biggest
Hits* (Epic); *Ten Years Of Hits* (Epic)

Tryin' To Beat The Morning Home (1975) T. G.
Sheppard

Trying To Love Two Women (1980) *Oak Ridge
Boys: Together* (MCA); *Greatest Hits* (MCA)

Tulsa Time (1979) Don Williams: *Best Of Don
Williams, Vol. 2* (MCA); VA—*Contemporary

Country: The Late '70s (Time Life)

Turn It Loose (1988) The Judds: *Heartland*
(RCA); *The Judds Collection 1983-1990* (RCA);
Greatest Hits, Vol. II (RCA)

(Turn Out The Light And) Love Me Tonight
(1975) Don Williams: *Best Of Don Williams, Vol. 2*
(MCA); VA—*Contemporary Country: The Mid-'70s—
Pure Gold* (Time Life)

Turn The World Around (1967) Eddy Arnold:
Last Of The Love Song Singers: Then & Now (RCA)

Turning Away (1984) Crystal Gayle: *The Best Of
Crystal Gayle* (Warner Bros.)

Twinkle, Twinkle Lucky Star (1988) Merle
Haggard: *Chill Factor* (Epic); VA—*Contemporary
Country: The Late '80s* (Time Life)

Two Dozen Roses (1989) Shenandoah: *The Road
Not Taken* (Columbia); *Greatest Hits* (Columbia)

Two More Bottles Of Wine (1978) Emmylou
Harris: *Quarter Moon In A Ten Cent Town* (Warner
Bros.); *Profile (Best Of Emmylou Harris)* (Warner
Bros.); VA—*Contemporary Country: The Late '70s*
(Time Life)

Two Of A Kind, Workin' On A Full House
(1991) Garth Brooks: *No Fences* (Liberty)

Unanswered Prayers (1991) Garth Brooks: *No
Fences* (Liberty)

Uncle Pen (1984) Ricky Skaggs: *Don't Cheat In
Our Hometown* (Epic); *Live In London* (Epic); VA—
*Columbia Country Classics, Vol. 5: A New
Tradition* (Columbia); VA—*Contemporary Country:
The Mid-'80s—Hot Hits* (Time Life)

Understand Your Man (1964) Johnny Cash:
Johnny Cash's Greatest Hits (Columbia); VA—
Country USA 1964 (Time Life); *The Essential
Johnny Cash* (Columbia); VA—*Billboard Top
Country Hits—1964* (Rhino)

Until I Met You (1986) Judy Rodman

Until My Dreams Come True (1969) Jack
Greene

A Very Special Love Song (1974) Charlie Rich:
VA—*Contemporary Country: The Mid-'70s—Pure
Gold* (Time Life)

Waitin' In Your Welfare Line (1966) Buck
Owens: *The Buck Owens Collection, 1959-1990*
(Rhino); *Live At Carnegie Hall* (CMF); VA—
Billboard Top Country Hits—1966 (Rhino); VA—
Country USA 1966 (Time Life)

Wake Up, Irene (1954) Hank Thompson: VA—
Country USA 1953 (Time Life); *Capitol Collector's
Series* (Capitol); *All-Time Greatest Hits*
(Capitol/Curb)

Wake Up Little Susie (1957) The Everly Brothers:
The Very Best Of The Everly Brothers (Warner
Bros.); *The Reunion Concert* (Mercury); *Cadence
Classics—Their 20 Greatest Hits* (Rhino); *Everly
Brothers* (Rhino); *All-Time Greatest Hits*
(Capitol/Curb)

Walk On By (1961) Leroy Van Dyke: VA—*Country
USA 1961* (Time Life); VA—*Billboard Top Country
Hits—1961* (Rhino)

Walk On Faith (1991) Mike Reid: *Turning For
Home* (Columbia)

Walk Through This World With Me (1967)
George Jones: *First Time Live* (Epic); *All-Time
Greatest Hits, Vol. 1* (Epic); VA—*Billboard Top
Country Hits—1967* (Rhino); VA—*Country USA
1967* (Time Life); *The Best Of George Jones (1955-
1967)* (Rhino)

Walkin' Away (1990) Clint Black: *Killin' Time* (RCA)

The Wanderer (1988) Eddie Rabbitt: *Greatest
Country Hits* (Capitol/Curb); VA—*Contemporary

Country: The Late '80s (Time Life)

War Is Hell (On The Homefront Too) (1982) T. G. Sheppard: *All-Time Greatest Hits* (Warner Bros.)

Wasted Days And Wasted Nights (1975) Freddy Fender: *Freddy Fender Collection* (Reprise); VA— *Contemporary Country: The Mid-'70s—Pure Gold* (Time Life)

Waterloo (1959) Stonewall Jackson: *American Originals* (Columbia); VA—*Country USA 1959* (Time Life); VA—*Billboard Top Country Hits— 1959* (Rhino); VA—*Columbia Country Classics, Vol. 3: Americana* (Columbia)

Way Down (1977) Elvis Presley: VA—*Contemporary Country: The Late '70s—Hot Hits* (Time Life); *Elvis' Golden Records, Vol. 5* (RCA); *Moody Blue* (RCA)

The Way We Make A Broken Heart (1987) Rosanne Cash: VA—*Contemporary Country: The Late '80s—Pure Gold* (Time Life); *King's Record Shop* (Columbia); *Hits 1979-1989* (Columbia)

The Ways To Love A Man (1969) Tammy Wynette: *Tears Of Fire—The 25th Anniversary Collection* (Epic); VA—*Country USA 1969* (Time Life)

We Believe In Happy Endings (1988) Earl Thomas Conley with Emmylou Harris: VA— *Contemporary Country: The Late '80s* (Time Life); *Emmylou Harris Duets* (Reprise); *Earl Thomas Conley Heart Of It All* (RCA)

A Week In A Country Jail (1970) Tom T. Hall: VA—*Country USA 1970* (Time Life)

The Weekend (1987) Steve Wariner: *Greatest Hits* (MCA); *It's A Crazy World* (MCA)

We're Gonna Hold On (1973) George Jones & Tammy Wynette: *Greatest Hits* (Epic); *Tammy Wynette Anniversary: 20 Years Of Hits* (Epic); *Tammy Wynette Tears Of Fire—The 25th Anniversary Collection* (Epic)

We've Got Tonight (1983) Kenny Rogers & Sheena Easton

What A Difference You've Made In My Life (1978) Ronnie Milsap: *It Was Almost Like A Song* (RCA); *Collector's Series* (RCA); *Greatest Hits* (RCA)

What A Man, My Man Is (1974) Lynn Anderson

What Am I Gonna Do About You (1987) Reba McEntire: *What Am I Gonna Do About You* (MCA); *Greatest Hits* (MCA); VA—*Contemporary Country: The Late '80s* (Time Life)

What Are We Doin' In Love (1981) Kenny Rogers & Dottie West

What Goes On When The Sun Goes Down (1976) Ronnie Milsap

What I'd Say (1989) Earl Thomas Conley: *Heart Of It All* (RCA); *Greatest Hits, Vol. II* (RCA)

What Is Life Without Love? (1947) Eddy Arnold

What She Is (Is A Woman In Love) (1988) Earl Thomas Conley: *Heart Of It All* (RCA)

What She's Doing Now (1992) Garth Brooks: *Ropin' The Wind* (Liberty)

What's A Memory Like You (Doing In A Love Like This) (1986) John Schneider: VA— *Contemporary Country: The Mid-'80s—Hot Hits* (Time Life); *Greatest Hits* (MCA); *Memory Like You* (MCA)

What's Forever For (1982) Michael Martin Murphey: *The Best Of Michael Martin Murphey* (EMI)

What's Going On In Your World (1989) George Strait: *Beyond The Blue Neon* (MCA); *Ten Strait Hits* (MCA)

What's He Doing In My World (1965) Eddy Arnold: VA—*Country USA 1965* (Time Life); *The Best Of Eddy Arnold* (RCA); *Last Of The Love Song Singers: Then & Now* (RCA)

What's Your Mama's Name (1973) Tanya Tucker: *Tanya Tucker's Greatest Hits* (Columbia); *Greatest Hits Encore* (Liberty); *Live* (MCA); *Contemporary Country: The Early '70—Pure Gold* (Time Life)

Whatever Happened To Old Fashioned Love (1983) B. J. Thomas

Wheels (1988) *Restless Heart: Wheels* (RCA); *The Best Of Restless Heart* (RCA)

When I'm Away From You (1983) The Bellamy Brothers: *Greatest Hits, Vol. 2* (MCA)

When It's Springtime In Alaska (It's Forty Below) (1959) Johnny Horton: VA—*Country USA 1959* (Time Life); *American Originals* (Columbia); *Johnny Horton's Greatest Hits* (Columbia)

When The Snow Is On The Roses (1972) Sonny James

When We Make Love (1984) Alabama: *Roll On* (RCA); *Alabama 'Live'* (RCA)

When Will I Be Loved (1975) Linda Ronstadt: *Heart Like A Wheel* (Capitol); *Greatest Hits* (Asylum)

When You Say Nothing At All (1988) Keith Whitley: *Don't Close Your Eyes* (RCA); *Greatest Hits* (RCA)

When You're Hot, You're Hot (1971) Jerry Reed: *The Best Of Jerry Reed* (RCA); VA—*Country USA 1971* (Time Life); VA—*Contemporary Country: The Early '70s* (Time Life)

Where Are You Now (1991) Clint Black: *Put Yourself In My Shoes* (RCA)

Where Did I Go Wrong (1989) Steve Wariner: *Greatest Hits, Vol. 2* (MCA); *I Got Dreams* (MCA)

Where Do I Put Her Memory (1979) Charley Pride: *Greatest Hits* (RCA); VA—*Contemporary Country: The Late '70s—Hot Hits* (Time Life)

Where Do The Nights Go (1988) Ronnie Milsap: *Heart & Soul* (RCA); *Greatest Hits, Vol. 3* (RCA)

Where Does The Good Times Go (1967) Buck Owens: *The Buck Owens Collection, 1959-1990* (Rhino)

White Cross On Okinawa (1946) Bob Wills & His Texas Playboys

The White Knight (1976) Cledus Maggard

White Lightning (1959) George Jones: *Super Hits* (Epic); *All-Time Greatest Hits, Vol. 1* (Epic); VA— *Billboard Top Country Hits—1959* (Rhino); *The Best Of George Jones (1955-1967)* (Rhino); VA— *Country USA 1959* (Time Life)

A White Sport Coat (And A Pink Carnation) (1957) Marty Robbins: VA—*Country USA 1957* (Time Life); *Essential Marty Robbins, 1951-1982* (Columbia)

Who's Cheatin' Who (1981) Charly McClain

Who's Gonna Mow Your Grass (1969) Buck Owens: *The Buck Owens Collection, 1959-1990* (Rhino); *All-Time Greatest, Vol. 1* (Capitol)

Who's Lonely Now (1990) Highway 101: *Paint The Town* (Warner Bros.); *Greatest Hits* (Warner Bros.)

Whoever's In New England (1986) Reba McEntire: *Greatest Hits* (MCA); *Whoever's In New England* (MCA); VA—*Contemporary Country: The Mid-'80s—Pure Gold* (Time Life)

Whole Lot Of Shakin' Going On (1957) Jerry Lee Lewis: *Jerry Lee Lewis* (Rhino); *Original Sun Greatest Hits* (Rhino)

Why Baby Why (1956) Red Sovine & Webb Pierce:

VA—*Country USA 1956* (Time Life)

Why Baby Why (1983) Charley Pride

Why Does It Have 1   e (Wrong Or Right)
(1987) Restless Heart   *.he Best Of Restless Heart*
(RCA); *Wheels* (RCA)

Why Don't You Haul off And Love Me (1949)
Wayne Raney

Why Don't You Love Me (1950) Hank Williams:
Long Gone Lonesome Blues (Aug. 1949-Dec. 1950)
(Polydor); *40 Greatest Hits* (Polydor); *The Original
Singles Collection...Plus* (PolyGram); VA—*Country
USA 1950* (Time Life)

Why Don't You Spend The Night (1980) Ronnie
Milsap

Why Have You Left The One You Left Me For
(1979) Crystal Gayle: VA—*Contemporary Country:
The Late '70s—Pure Gold* (Time Life); *Classic
Crystal* (EMI); *All-Time Greatest Hits*
(Capitol/Curb)

Why Lady Why (1980) Alabama: *Greatest Hits*
(RCA); *My Home's in Alabama* (RCA)

Why Me (1973) Kris Kristofferson: VA—*Classic
Country Music* (Smithsonian); *Contemporary
Country: The Early '70s* (Time Life); *Kris
Kristofferson Singer/Songwriter* (Columbia)

Why Not Me (1984) The Judds: VA—*Contemporary
Country: The Mid-'80s Hot Hits* (Time Life); *The
Judds Greatest Hits* (RCA); *Why Not Me* (RCA);
The Judds Collection 1983-1990 (RCA)

Why'd You Come In Here Lookin' Like That
(1989) Dolly Parton: *White Limozeen* (Columbia)

Wichita Lineman (1968) Glen Campbell: *Classics
Collection* (Liberty); VA—*Country USA 1968* (Time
Life); *The Best Of Glen Campbell* (Liberty)

Wild And Blue (1982) John Anderson: VA—
Contemporary Country: The Early '80s (Time Life);
Greatest Hits (Warner Bros.)

The Wild Side Of Life (1952) Hank Thompson:
VA—*Classic Country Music* (Smithsonian); *Capitol
Collector's Series* (Capitol); VA—*Country USA 1952*
(Time Life); *All-Time Greatest Hits* (Capitol/Curb)

Window Up Above (1975) Mickey Gilley: *Gilley's
Greatest Hits, Vol. 1* (Epic); *Ten Years Of Hits*
(Epic)

Wine, Women And Song (1946) Al Dexter

Wings Of A Dove (1960) Ferlin Husky: *Capitol
Collectors Series* (Capitol), VA—*Country USA 1960*
(Time Life); *Greatest Hits* (Capitol/Curb); VA—
Billboard Top Country Hits—1960 (Rhino)

With One Exception (1967) David Houston:
American Originals (Columbia)

With Tears In My Eyes (1945) Wesley Tuttle

Woke Up In Love (1984) Exile: *Greatest Hits*
(Epic); *Exile* (Epic)

Wolverton Mountain (1962) Claude King: VA—
Columbia Country Classics, Vol. 3: Americana
(Columbia); VA—*Billboard Top Country Hits—
1962* (Rhino); VA—*Country USA 1962* (Time Life);
American Originals (Columbia)

A Woman In Love (1989) Ronnie Milsap: *Stranger
Things Have Happened* (RCA); *Greatest Hits, Vol.
3* (RCA)

**Woman Of The World (Leave My World
Alone)** (1969) Loretta Lynn: VA—*Country USA
1969* (Time Life)

Woman (Sensuous Woman) (1972) Don Gibson:
VA—*Country USA 1972* (Time Life); *18 Greatest
Hits* (Capitol/Curb); VA—*Contemporary Country:
The Early '70s* (Time Life)

Wonder Could I Live There Anymore (1970)
Charley Pride: VA—*Country USA 1970* (Time Life)

Wondering (1952) Webb Pierce: VA—*Country USA
1952* (Time Life)

Workin' Man Blues (1969) Merle Haggard: *Epic
Collection (Recorded Live)* (Epic); *Very Best Of
Merle Haggard* (Capitol); *The Best Of Country
Blues* (Capitol/Curb); *Best Of The Best Of Merle
Haggard* (Capitol); VA—*Country USA 1969* (Time
Life); *Capitol Collector's Series* (Capitol)

World Of Make Believe (1974) Bill Anderson

A World Of Our Own (1968) Sonny James

Would You Lay With Me (In A Field Of Stone)
(1974) Tanya Tucker: *Live* (MCA); VA—*Columbia
Country Classics, Vol. 4: The Nashville Sound*
(Columbia); *Greatest Hits Encore* (Liberty); *Tanya
Tucker's Greatest Hits* (Columbia); VA—
Contemporary Country: The Mid-'70s (Time Life)

Would You Take Another Chance On Me
(1972) Jerry Lee Lewis: VA—*Country USA 1971*
(Time Life); *Contemporary Country: The Early '70s*
(Time Life)

**The Wurlitzer Prize (I Don't Want To Get
Over You)** (1977) Waylon Jennings

The Year That Clayton Delaney Died (1971)
Tom T. Hall: *Tom T. Hall's Greatest Hits*
(Mercury); VA—*Country USA 1971* (Time Life);
VA—*Contemporary Country: The Early '70s* (Time
Life)

Years (1980) Barbara Mandrell: *Greatest Hits*
(MCA); *Greatest Country Hits* (Capitol/Curb)

The Yellow Rose (Of Texas) (1984) Johnny Lee
with Lane Brody

Yellow Roses (1989) Dolly Parton: *White Limozeen*
(Columbia)

Yes, Mr. Peters (1965) Roy Drusky & Priscilla
Mitchell

Yesterday's Wine (1982) George Jones & Merle
Haggard: *Walking The Line* (Epic); *A Taste Of
Yesterday's Wine* (Epic)

You Again (1987) The Forester Sisters: VA—
Contemporary Country: The Late '80s—Pure Gold
(Time Life); *You Again* (Warner Bros.); *Greatest
Hits* (Warner Bros.)

You Always Come Back (To Hurting Me)
(1973) Johnny Rodriguez

You And I (1982) Eddie Rabbitt & Crystal Gayle

You And Me (1976) Tammy Wynette: *Anniversary:
20 Years Of Hits* (Epic); *Tears Of Fire—The 25th
Anniversary Collection* (Epic)

You Are My Treasure (1968) Jack Greene

You Can Dream Of Me (1986) Steve Wariner:
Greatest Hits (MCA); *Life's Highway* (MCA)

**You Can't Be A Beacon (If Your Light Don't
Shine)** (1974) Donna Fargo

You Can't Run From Love (1983) Eddie Rabbitt:
Radio Romance (Liberty)

You Could've Heard A Heart Break (1984)
Johnny Lee

You Decorated My Life (1979) Kenny Rogers: *20
Great Years* (Reprise); *Kenny Rogers' Greatest
Hits* (EMI); *Twenty Greatest Hits* (EMI)

You Don't Know Me (1981) Mickey Gilley: *Ten
Years Of Hits* (Epic); *Biggest Hits* (Epic)

You Don't Love Me Anymore (1978) Eddie
Rabbitt: *Greatest Country Hits* (Capitol/Curb);

You Know Me Better Than That (1991) George
Strait: *Chill Of An Early Fall* (MCA)

You Lie (1990) Reba McEntire: *Rumor Has It*
(MCA)

You Look So Good In Love (1984) George
Strait: *Greatest Hits* (MCA); *Right Or Wrong* (MCA)

You Make Me Want To Make You Mine (1985)
Juice Newton: *Old Flame* (RCA)

You Mean The World To Me (1967) David
Houston: VA—*Billboard Top Country Hits—1967*
(Rhino)

**You Never Miss A Real Good Thing (Till He
Says Goodbye)** (1977) Crystal Gayle: *Crystal*
(EMI); *Classic Crystal* (EMI); *All-Time Greatest
Hits* (Capitol/Curb)

You Really Had Me Going (1990) Holly Dunn:
Milestones—Greatest Hits (Warner Bros.); *Heart
Full Of Love* (Warner Bros.)

You Still Move Me (1987) Dan Seals: *The Best Of
Dan Seals* (Liberty); *Early Dan Seals* (Liberty)

You Take Me For Granted (1983) Merle
Haggard: *His Epic Hits—First Eleven* (Epic); *Going
Where The Lonely Go* (Epic)

You Two-Timed Me One Time Too Often
(1945) Tex Ritter: *Capitol Collector's Series*
(Capitol)

You Were Always There (1973) Donna Fargo

You Will Have To Pay (1946) Tex Ritter: *Capitol
Collector's Series* (Capitol)

You Win Again (1980) Charley Pride: VA—
Contemporary Country: The Early '80s—Hot Hits
(Time Life)

You'll Lose A Good Thing (1976) Freddy Fender:
Freddy Fender Collection (Reprise)

You're Gettin' To Me Again (1984) Jim Glaser

You're Gonna Ruin My Bad Reputation
(1983) Ronnie McDowell: *Older Women & Other
Greatest Hits* (Epic); VA—*Contemporary Country:
The Early '80s* (Time Life)

You're My Best Friend (1975) Don Williams:
Best Of Don Williams, Vol. 2 (MCA); VA—
Contemporary Country: The Mid-'70s (Time Life)

You're My Jamaica (1979) Charley Pride:
Greatest Hits (RCA)

You're My Man (1971) Lynn Anderson

You're So Good When You're Bad (1982)
Charley Pride

You're Still New To Me (1986) Marie Osmond
with Paul Davis: *The Best Of Marie Osmond* (Curb)

**You're The Best Break This Old Heart Ever
Had** (1982) Ed Bruce

**You're The Best Thing That Ever Happened
To Me** (1973) Ray Price: *Greatest Hits, Vols. 1-3*
(Step One)

**You're The First Time I've Thought About
Leaving** (1983) Reba McEntire: *The Best Of Reba
McEntire* (Mercury); *Unlimited* (Mercury); VA—
Contemporary Country: The Early '80s (Time Life)

You're The Last Thing I Needed Tonight
(1986) John Schneider: *Greatest Hits* (MCA); VA—
Contemporary Country: The Mid-'80s—Pure Gold
(Time Life); *Memory Like You* (MCA)

You're The Only One (1979) Dolly Parton

You're The Only World I Know (1965) Sonny
James: *Greatest Hits* (Capitol/Curb); VA—*Country
USA 1964* (Time Life)

You're The Reason God Made Oklahoma
(1981) David Frizzell & Shelly West: VA—
Contemporary Country: The Early '80s (Time Life)

You've Got The Touch (1987) Alabama: *The
Touch* (RCA)

You've Never Been This Far Before (1973)
Conway Twitty: *Greatest Hits* (Capitol/Curb);
Greatest Hits, Vol. 2 (MCA); *Silver Anniversary
Collection* (MCA); *The Very Best Of Conway Twitty*
(MCA)

Young Love (1957) Sonny James: *Greatest Hits*
(Capitol/Curb); *Capitol Collector's Series* (Capitol);
VA—*Classic Country Music* (Smithsonian); VA—
Country USA 1957 (Time Life)

Young Love (1989) The Judds: *River Of Time*
(RCA); *Greatest Hits, Vol. II* (RCA); *The Judds
Collection 1983-1990* (RCA)

Your Cheatin' Heart (1953) Hank Williams: *Rare
Demos* (CMF); *Classic Country Music*
(Smithsonian); VA—*Country USA 1953* (Time
Life); *The Original Singles Collection...Plus*
(PolyGram); *40 Greatest Hits* (Polydor); *I Won't Be
Home No More (June 1952-Sept. 1952)* (Polydor)

Your Heart's Not In It (1984) Janie Frickie: *17
Greatest Hits* (Columbia); *The Very Best Of Janie
Frickie* (Columbia)

Your Love's On The Line (1983) Earl Thomas
Conley: *Greatest Hits* (RCA)

Your Tender Loving Care (1967) Buck Owens:
The Buck Owens Collection, 1959-1990 (Rhino)